Taking Sides: Clashing Views
on Educational Issues,
18/e Expanded

Glenn L. Koonce

D0583836

http://create.mheducation.com

ISBN-10: 125934133X   ISBN-13: 9781259341335

Contents

Preface

There is much debate in education because there are as many opinions as there are issues. With education topics changing so fast who is right and who is wrong leads to followers on both sides armed with theory, knowledge, and their own practice for face to face deliberations. In today's society that would include blog to blog. Time-honored stances as well as new revelations are being challenged. The controversies are good for the field as improvements are made resulting from airing the many sides to an issue. These clashing issues in education inform our views in the political as well as the economic arenas. New ways of learning fuels decisions made at the school level as well as policy made in state and federal departments of education. All educators are affected by the outcomes driven in the debate on hot topics or age-old disagreements. It is why this book is needed. Whether you agree or disagree with an issue is not as important as the discovery of why you may feel one way or the other. Willingness to debate both strengths and weaknesses adds to the scholarly inquiry that results in improvements to the field of education.

This book presents opposing or sharply varying viewpoints on educational issues of current concern. Unit 1 offers consideration of five basic theoretical issues that have been discussed by scholars and practitioners in past decades and are still debated today: the purpose of education, curriculum content and its imposition upon the young, the motivational atmosphere of schools, the philosophical underpinning of the process of education, and the conception of public education. Unit 2 features five issues that are fundamental to understanding the present circumstances that shape American education: democratic classrooms for citizenship preparation, legitimization of school vouchers, federal initiatives in school improvement, improving schools for children of poverty, and the role of local school boards. Unit 3 examines more specific issues currently being discussed: undocumented immigrants, universal preschool, privatization, inclusive classrooms, single-sex instruction, zero-tolerance policies, computer usage, merit pay for teachers, teachers, unions, time allocation, and twenty-first century skills development.

Every effort has been made to select views from a wide range of thinkers—philosophers, psychologists, sociologists, professional educators, political leaders, historians, researchers, and gadflies. By combining the material in this volume with the informational background provided by a good introductory textbook, students should be prepared to address the problems confronting schools today. My hope is that students will find challenges in the material presented here—provocations that will inspire them to better understand the roots of educational controversy, to attain a greater awareness of possible alternatives in dealing with the various issues, and to stretch their personal powers of creative thinking in the search for more promising resolutions of the problems.

Changes to this edition This 18th edition offers *enhanced pedagogy!* New to this edition: Topic Guide; Expanded Introduction; Learning Outcomes; plus a new section titled Exploring the Issue featuring Critical Thinking and Reflection questions, Is There Common Ground?, Additional Resources, and Internet References relevant to each issue.

A word to the instructor An *Instructor's Resource Guide with Test Questions* (multiple choice and essay) is available through the publisher for the instructor using Taking Sides in the classroom. A general guidebook, called *Using Taking Sides in the Classroom*, which discusses methods and techniques for integrating the pro/con approach into any classroom setting, is also available. An online version of *Using Taking Sides in the Classroom* and a correspondence service for Taking Sides adopters can be found at the book's website.

Acknowledgments I am thankful for the kind and efficient assistance given to me by Jill Meloy and the other members of the editorial staff at McGraw-Hill Contemporary Learning Series, the work of James Wm. Noll (author of previous editions), and appreciation to my wife, Suzanne, for love, support, and assistance in completing this edition.

Glenn L. Koonce
Regent University

Editor of This Volume

GLENN L. KOONCE came to Regent University in 2003 with a proven record of leadership, having served for 30 years in leadership positions in the public schools and as a highly trained and highly decorated combat Squad & Platoon Leader with the First Air Calvary Division in Vietnam and Cambodia during 1970–71. He taught health and physical education at the elementary, junior high, and high school levels and coached football, basketball, wrestling, soccer, track, tennis, gymnastics, and weight training. He has held the positions of assistant principal at an alternative school and high school; principal at the elementary, junior and middle school, and high school levels; director in the central office; concluding his public school career as an Assistant Superintendent for Instructional Services and Personnel. He has been a visiting scholar at two universities, an adjunct professor at four universities, and directed a principal's center at one. He has been recognized as Principal of the Year for the State of Virginia, President of the Virginia Association of Secondary

School Principals, Boss of the Year several times in the public schools, and Education Professor of the Year for Regent University School of Education. He has been the recipient of numerous other awards and recognitions; member and officer of many professional/community associations and organizations; graduate of a large number of professional educational leadership training programs; member/leader on three Virginia Governor's, one Attorney General's, and one Secretary of Public Education tasks forces; numerous Virginia Department of Education programs and activities; professional associations (at all levels); scorer for the Educational Testing Services' School Leaders Licensure Assessment (SLLA) and School Superintendents Assessment (SSA); and other state agency, university; national, state, regional and local activities on a vast array of topics. He has been the President of the Virginia Education Research Association; Chairman of the Virginia Education Coalition; and President of the Virginia Professors of Educational Leadership. He is a Board Certified Auditor for the Virginia Department of Education and Lead Auditor for the Council for the Accreditation of Educator Preparation (CAEP). Research activities, consulting, publications, numerous presentations, etc. from the local level to international levels, and serving on the editorial review board and the state affiliate chair for the National Council of Professors of Educational Administration (NCPEA) and other professional publications round out his extensive experiences. His personal interests include spiritual, family, community, and wellness activities of all kinds. He loves music, travel, and adventure, in no particular order. He is married and has four children and six grandchildren.

Academic Advisory Board Members

Members of the Academic Advisory Board are instrumental in the final selection of articles for Takings Sides books and ExpressBooks. Their review of the articles for content, level, and appropriateness provides critical direction to the editor(s) and staff. We think that you will find their careful consideration reflected in this book.

Joseph Akpan
Mount Vernon Nazarene University

Brenda Alward
Macomb Community College

Daniel Anderson
Cincinnati State Tech
M. Graeme Armstrong
Upper Iowa University

Fred Bartelheim
University of Northern Colorado

Felicia Blacher-Wilson
Southeastern Louisiana University

Charles Blackledge
Bishop State Community College

Robert Blake
Towson University

Sally Blake
University of Memphis

Brenda Light Bredemeier
University of Missouri, St. Louis

Elizabeth Y. Brinkerhoff
University of Massachusetts, Amherst

Kathleen Briseno
College of DuPage

James C. Brown
Southern University, Shreveport

Mary Ellen Burke
National Louis University

Darilyn Butler
Queens University of Charlotte

James Calder
Middle Tennessee State University

Noble Corey
Indiana State University

David Cox
Arkansas State University

Patricia Cruzeiro
University of Nebraska, Kearney

Kimberly Dadisman
University of North Carolina, Chapel Hill

Ann V. Dean
SUNY New Paltz

Brian Dotts
The University of Georgia

Celina Echols
Southeastern Louisiana University

Dionne H. Edison
University of West Alabama

William Edwards
Missouri Southern State University

Deborah Ellermeyer
Clarion University of Pennsylvania

Joanne Ellsworth
Eastern Arizona College

R.L. Erion
South Dakota State University

Cheryl Fields-Smith
University of Georgia

Paul G. Fitchett
University of North Carolina, Charlotte

Betty Jane Fratzke
Indiana Wesleyan University

Shelly Furuness
Butler University

George Georgiou
Towson University

Gina Giuliano
University at Albany, SUNY

Francis Godwyll
Ohio University

Vella Goebel
University of Southern Indiana

Denise Greene
Roanoke College

Charles Grindstaff
Concord University

Jason Helfer
Knox College

Michael Hohn
Portland Community College

Jennifer Holleran
Community College of Allegheny County

Charles Jackson
Augusta State University

Mary Alice Jennings
Mississippi Valley State University

Leslie Jones
Nicholls State University

Tanya Judd Pucella
Marietta College

Steven Kaatz
Bethel University

Linda Karges-Bone
Charleston Southern University

Alan Karns
Wilkes University / Edinboro University

Harvey Karron
Stony Brook University

Amy Kavanaugh
Ferris State University

Susan Kelewae
Kent State University

Richard Kennedy
North Carolina Wesleyan College

Mary G. Klinger
SUNY Empire State College

Glenn L. Koonce
Regent University

Ellie Kunkel
Peru State College

Patricia Lanzon
Henry Ford Community College

Aaron J. Lawler
Benedictine University

Sandra L. Leslie
Shorter College

Ronald E. Lewis
Grand Canyon University

Lawanna M. Lewis
Grand Canyon University

Dennis A. Lichty
Wayne State College

Lennie Little
Jackson State University

Harold London
DePaul University

Christopher Lucas
University of Arkansas

Xavier McClung
Valdosta State University

Carmen McCrink
Barry University

John W. McNeeley
Daytona State College

Joanne Milke
Mitchell College

Greg Morris
Grand Rapids Community College

Thalia Mulvihill
Ball State University

Paul Nelson
Pacific Lutheran University

Susan J. Nix
West Texas A&M University

Introduction

Ways of Thinking about Educational Issues

Society needs a forum where philosophers, politicians, legislators, policymakers, practitioners, parents, and the community can freely deliberate educational issues. History has often chronicled these issues as problems to be fixed rather than issues to be debated. Problems were often resolved without dispute by strong willed leaders. Others chose to dispute first and fix later. The term *problem* seems to be disappearing from the conversations about schooling. Rather than to admit to perceiving problems, writers and speakers now frame their positions in terms of issues. Issues better lend themselves to taking sides often with clashing viewpoints.

If educators never take a stand then issues are in constant flux and ever wavering on the brink of discourse. There has been a perpetual and unresolved dialogue regarding the definition of education and what is expected of educators. There should be a relationship between schooling and society, and the distribution of decision-making powers. Options are formulated by deliberating pros and cons of an issue. Individuals can be very persuasive and should be provided the opportunity to do so.

The twenty-first century education system looks different today because the needs of students and the society they are growing up in are different. Many times the needs of students become a part of the issues that are debated, such as: democratic classrooms, free speech, preschool, inclusive classrooms, virtual schooling, zero-tolerance, and twenty-first century skills. Changes are necessary to help our youth reach their full potential and be college and career ready after 12 years of education. For change to occur, education issues must be clearly identified and deliberated by both educators and other members of society.

Ways of thinking about educational issues include a review of historical perspectives, examining viewpoints, philosophical considerations, and power and control. Three area of focus for debating are basic theoretical issues, current fundamental issues, and current specific issues.

Historical Perspectives

In recent decades the growing influence of thinking drawn from the humanities and the behavioral and social sciences has brought about the development of interpretive, normative, and critical perspectives, which have sharpened the focus on educational concerns. These perspectives have allowed scholars and researchers to closely examine the contextual variables, value orientations, and philosophical and political assumptions that shape both the status quo and reform efforts.

The study of education involves the application of many perspectives to the analysis of "what is and how it got that way" and "what can be and how we can get there." Central to such study are the prevailing philosophical assumptions, theories, and visions that find their way into real-life educational situations. The application situation, with its attendant political pressures, sociocultural differences, community expectations, parental influence, and professional problems, provides a testing ground for contending theories and ideals.

This "testing ground" image applies only insofar as the status quo is malleable enough to allow the examination and trial of alternative views. Historically, institutionalized education has been characteristically rigid. As a testing ground of ideas, it has often lacked an orientation encouraging innovation and futuristic thinking. Its political grounding has usually been conservative.

As social psychologist Allen Wheelis points out in *The Quest for Identity* (1958), social institutions by definition tend toward solidification and protectionism. His depiction of the dialectical development of civilizations centers on the tension between the security and authoritarianism of "institutional processes" and the dynamism and change-orientation of "instrumental processes."

The field of education seems to graphically illustrate this observation. Educational practices are primarily tradition bound. The twentieth-century reform movement, spurred by the ideas of John Dewey, A. S. Neill, and a host of critics who campaigned for change in the 1960s, challenged the structural rigidity of schooling. In more recent decades, reformers have either attempted to restore uniformity in the curriculum and in assessment of results or campaigned for the support of alternatives to the public school monopoly. The latter group comes from both the right and the left of the political spectrum.

We are left with the abiding questions: What is an "educated" person? What should be the primary purpose of organized education? Who should control the decisions influencing the educational process? Should the schools follow society or lead it toward change? Should schooling be compulsory?

Long-standing forces have molded a wide variety of responses to these fundamental questions. The religious impetus, nationalistic fervor, philosophical ideas, the march of science and technology, varied interpretations of "societal needs," and the desire to use the schools as a means for social reform have been historically influential. In recent times other factors have emerged to contribute to the complexity of the search for answers—social class differences, demographic shifts, increasing bureaucratization, the growth of the textbook industry, the changing financial base for schooling, teacher unionization, and strengthening of parental and community pressure groups.

The struggle to find the most appropriate answers to these questions now involves, as in the past, an interplay of societal aims, educational purposes, and individual intentions. Moral development, the quest for wisdom, citizenship training, socioeconomic improvement, mental discipline, the rational control of life, job preparation, liberation of the individual, freedom of inquiry—these and many others continue to be topics of discourse on education.

A detailed historical perspective on these questions and topics may be gained by reading the interpretations of noted scholars in the field. R. Freeman Butts has written a brief but effective summary portrayal in "Search for Freedom—The Story of American Education," *NEA Journal* (March 1960). A partial listing of other sources includes R. Freeman Butts and Lawrence Cremin, *A History of Education in American Culture;* S. E. Frost, Jr., *Historical and Philosophical Foundations of Western Education;* Harry Good and Edwin Teller, *A History of Education;* Adolphe Meyer, *An Educational History of the American People;* Robert L. Church and Michael W. Sedlak, *Education in the United States: An Interpretive History;* Merle Curti, *The Social Ideas of American Educators;* Henry J. Perkinson, *The Imperfect Panacea: American Faith in Education, 1865–1965;* Clarence Karier, *Man, Society, and Education;* V. T. Thayer, *Formative Ideas in American Education;* H. Warren Button and Eugene F. Provenzo, Jr., *History of Education and Culture in America;* David Tyack and Elisabeth Hansot, *Managers of Virtue: Public School Leadership in America, 1820–1980;* Joel Spring, *The American School, 1642–1990;* S. Alexander Rippa, *Education in a Free Society: An American History;* John D. Pulliam, *History of Education in America;* Edward Stevens and George H. Wood, *Justice, Ideology, and Education;* and Walter Feinberg and Jonas F. Soltis, *School and Society.*

These and other historical accounts of the development of schooling demonstrate the continuing need to address educational questions in terms of cultural and social dynamics. A careful analysis of contemporary education demands attention not only to the historical interpretation of developmental influences but also to the philosophical forces that define formal education and the social and cultural factors that form the basis of informal education.

Examining Viewpoints

In his book *A New Public Education* (1976), Seymour Itzkoff examines the interplay between informal and formal education, concluding that economic and technological expansion have pulled people away from the informal culture by placing a premium on success in formal education. This has brought about a reactive search for less artificial educational contexts within the informal cultural community, which recognizes the impact of individual personality in shaping educational experiences.

This search for a reconstructed philosophical base for education has produced a barrage of critical commentary. Those who seek radical change in education characterize the present schools as mindless, manipulative, factory-like, bureaucratic institutions that offer little sense of community, pay scant attention to personal meaning, fail to achieve curricular integration, and maintain a psychological atmosphere of competitiveness, tension, fear, and alienation. Others deplore the ideological movement away from the formal organization of education, fearing an abandonment of standards, a dilution of the curriculum, an erosion of intellectual and behavioral discipline, and a decline in adult and institutional authority.

Students of education (whether prospective teachers, practicing professionals, or interested laypeople) must examine closely the assumptions and values underlying alternative positions in order to clarify their own viewpoints. This tri-level task may best be organized around the basic themes of purpose, power, and reform. These themes offer access to the theoretical grounding of actions in the field of education, to the political grounding of such actions, and to the future orientation of action decisions.

A general model for the examination of positions on educational issues includes the following dimensions: identification of the viewpoint, recognition of the stated or implied assumptions underlying the viewpoint, analysis of the validity of the supporting argument, and evaluation of the conclusions and action-suggestions of the originator of the position. The stated or implied assumptions may be derived from a philosophical or religious orientation, from scientific theory, from social or personal values, or from accumulated experience. Acceptance by the reader of an author's assumptions opens the way for a receptive attitude regarding the specific viewpoint expressed and its implications for action. The argument offered in justification of the viewpoint may be based on logic, common experience, controlled experiments, information and data, legal precedents, emotional appeals, and a host of other persuasive devices.

Holding the basic model in mind, readers of the positions presented in this volume (or anywhere else, for that matter) can examine the constituent elements of arguments—basic assumptions, viewpoint statements, supporting evidence, conclusions, and suggestions for action. The careful reader will accept or reject the individual elements of the total position. One might see reasonableness in a viewpoint and its justification but be unable to accept the assumptions on which it is based. Or one might accept the flow of argument from assumptions to viewpoint to evidence but find illogic or impracticality in the stated conclusions and suggestions for action. In any event, the reader's personal view is tested and honed through the process of analyzing the views of others.

Philosophical Considerations

Historically, organized education has been initiated and instituted to serve many purposes—spiritual salvation, political socialization, moral uplift, societal stability, social mobility, mental discipline, vocational efficiency, and social reform, among others. The various purposes have usually reflected the dominant philosophical conception of human nature and the prevailing assumptions about the relationship between the individual and society. At any given time, competing conceptions may vie for dominance—social conceptions, economic conceptions, conceptions that emphasize spirituality, or conceptions that stress the uniqueness and dignity of the individual, for example.

These considerations of human nature and individual—society relationships are grounded in philosophical assumptions, and these assumptions find their way to such practical domains as schooling. In Western civilization there has been an identifiable (but far from consistent and clear-cut) historical trend in the basic assumptions about reality, knowledge, values, and the human condition. This trend, made manifest in the philosophical positions of idealism, realism, pragmatism, and existentialism, has involved a shift in emphasis from the spiritual world to nature to human behavior to the social individual to the free individual, and from eternal ideas to fixed natural laws to social interaction to the inner person.

The idealist tradition, which dominated much of philosophical and educational thought until the eighteenth and nineteenth centuries, separates the changing, imperfect, material world and the permanent, perfect, spiritual or mental world. As Plato saw it, for example, human beings and all other physical entities are particular manifestations of an ideal reality that in material existence humans can never fully know. The purpose of education is to bring us closer to the absolute ideals, pure forms, and universal standards that exist spiritually, by awakening and strengthening our rational powers. For Plato, a curriculum based on mathematics, logic, and music would serve this purpose, especially in the training of leaders whose rationality must exert control over emotionality and basic instincts.

Against this tradition, which shaped the liberal arts curriculum in schools for centuries, the realism of Aristotle, with its finding of the "forms" of things *within* the material world, brought an emphasis on scientific investigation and on environmental factors in the development of human potential. This fundamental view has influenced two philosophical movements in education: naturalism, based on following or gently assisting nature (as in the approaches of John Amos Comenius, Jean-Jacques Rousseau, and Johann Heinrich Pestalozzi), and scientific realism, based on uncovering the natural laws of human behavior and shaping the educational environment to maximize their effectiveness (as in the approaches of John Locke, Johann Friedrich Herbart, and Edward Thorndike).

In the twentieth century, two philosophical forces (pragmatism and existentialism) have challenged these traditions. Each has moved primary attention away from fixed spiritual or natural influences and toward the individual as shaper of knowledge and values. The pragmatic position, articulated in America by Charles Sanders Peirce, William James, and John Dewey, turns from metaphysical abstractions toward concrete results of action. In a world of change and relativity, human beings must forge their own truths and values as they interact with their environments and each other. The European-based philosophy of existentialism, emerging from such thinkers as Gabriel Marcel, Martin Buber, Martin Heidegger, and Jean-Paul Sartre, has more recently influenced education here. Existentialism places the burdens of freedom, choice, and responsibility squarely on the individual, viewing the current encroachment of external forces and the tendency of people to "escape from freedom" as a serious diminishment of our human possibilities.

These many theoretical slants contend for recognition and acceptance as we continue the search for broad purposes in education and as we attempt to create curricula, methodologies, and learning environments that fulfill our stated purposes. This is carried out, of course, in the real world of the public schools in which social, political, and economic forces often predominate.

Power and Control

Plato, in the fourth century B.C., found existing education manipulative and confining and, in the *Republic,* described a meritocratic approach designed to nurture intellectual powers so as to form and sustain a rational society. Reform-oriented as Plato's suggestions were, he nevertheless insisted on certain restrictions and controls so that his particular version of the ideal could be met.

The ways and means of education have been fertile grounds for power struggles throughout history. Many educational efforts have been initiated by religious bodies, often creating a conflict situation when secular authorities have moved into the field. Schools have usually been seen as repositories of culture and social values and, as such, have been overseen by the more conservative forces in society. To others, bent on social reform, the schools have been treated as a spawning ground for change. Given these basic political forces, conflict is inevitable.

When one speaks of the control of education, the range of influence is indeed wide. Political influences, governmental actions, court decisions, professional militancy, parental power, and student assertion all contribute to the phenomenon of control. And the domain of control is equally broad—school finances, curriculum, instructional means and objectives, teacher certification, accountability, student discipline, censorship of school materials, determination of access and opportunity, and determination of inclusion and exclusion.

The general topic of power and control leads to a multitude of questions: Who should make policy decisions? Must the schools be puppets of the government? Can the schools function in the vanguard of social change? Can cultural indoctrination be avoided? Can the schools lead the way to full social integration? Can the effects of social class be eradicated? Can and should the schools teach values? Dealing with such questions is complicated by the increasing power of the federal government in educational matters. Congressional legislation has broadened substantially from the early land grants and aid to agricultural and vocational programs to more recent laws covering aid to federally impacted areas, school construction aid, student loans and fellowships, support for several academic areas of the curriculum, work-study programs, compensatory education, employment opportunities for youth, adult education, aid to libraries, teacher preparation, educational research, career education, education of the handicapped, and equal opportunity for females. This proliferation of areas of influence has caused the federal administrative bureaucracy to blossom from its meager beginnings in 1867 into a cabinet-level Department of Education in 1979.

State legislatures and state departments of education have also grown in power, handling greater percentages of school appropriations and controlling basic curricular decisions, attendance laws, accreditation, research, and so on. Local school boards, once the sole authorities in policy making, now share the role with higher governmental echelons as the financial support sources shift away from the local scene. Simultaneously, strengthened teacher organizations and increasingly vocal pressure groups at the local, state, and national levels have forced a widening of the base for policy decisions.

Some Concluding Remarks

The schools often seem to be either facing backward or completely absorbed in the tribulations of the present, lacking a vision of possible futures that might guide current decisions. The present is inescapable, obviously, and certainly the historical and philosophical underpinnings of the present situation must be understood, but true improvement often requires a break with conventionality—a surge toward a desired future.

The radical reform critique of government-sponsored compulsory schooling has depicted organized education as a form of cultural or political imprisonment that traps young people in an artificial and mainly irrelevant environment and rewards conformity and docility while inhibiting curiosity and creativity. Constructive reform ideas that have come from this critique include the creation of open classrooms, the de-emphasis of external motivators, the diversification of educational experience, and the building of a true sense of community within the instructional environment.

Starting with Francis Wayland Parker's schools in Quincy, Massachusetts, and John Dewey's laboratory school at the University of Chicago around the turn of the twentieth century, the campaign to make schools into more productive and humane places has been relentless. The duplication of A. S. Neill's Summerhill model in the free school movement in the 1960s, the open classroom/open space experiments, the several curricular variations, and the emergence of schools without walls, charter schools, privatization of management, escalating federal involvement, and home schooling across the country testify to the desire to reform the present system or to build alternatives to it.

The progressive education movement, the development of "life adjustment" goals and curricula, and the "whole person" theories of educational psychology moved the schools toward an expanded concept of schooling that embraced new subject matters and new approaches to discipline during the first half of the twentieth century. Since the 1950s, however, pressure for a return to a narrower concept of schooling as intellectual training has sparked new waves of debate. Schools in the twenty-first century wrestle with more federal involvement that now is in hot debate on the reauthorization of the No Child Left Behind (NCLB) act and the Common Core State Standard (CCSS). Out of this situation have come attempts by educators and academicians to design new curricular approaches in the basic subject matter areas, efforts by private foundations to stimulate organizational innovations and to improve the training of teachers, and federal government support of educational technology. Yet criticism of the schools abounds. The schools, according to many who use their services, remain too factory-like, too age-segregated, and too custodial. Alternative paths are still sought—paths that would allow action-learning, work-study, and a diversity of ways to achieve success.

H. G. Wells has told us that human history becomes more and more a race between education and catastrophe. What is needed in order to win this race is the generation of new ideas regarding cultural change, human relationships, ethical norms, the uses of technology, and the quality of life. These new ideas, of course, may be old ideas newly applied. One could do worse, in thinking through the problem of improving the quality of education, than to turn to the third-century philosopher Plotinus, who called for an education directed to "the outer, the inner, and the whole." For Plotinus, "the outer" represented the public person, or the socioeconomic dimension of the total human being; "the inner" reflected the subjective dimension, the uniquely experiencing individual, or the "I"; and "the whole" signified the universe of meaning and relatedness, or the realm of human, natural, and spiritual connectedness. It would seem that education must address all of these dimensions if it is to truly help people in the lifelong struggle to shape a meaningful existence. If educational experiences can be improved in these directions, the end result might be people who are not just filling space, filling time, or filling a social role, but who are capable of saying something worthwhile with their lives.

The argument presented sets the stage for debate about educational issues that often result in clashing views. Healthy discourse will assure change comes to the field of education that results in higher student achievement and more democratic actions to improve the American education system.

Glenn L. Koonce
Regent University

Unit 1

UNIT

Basic Theoretical Issues

*W*hat is the basic purpose of education? How should the curriculum be organized and how much control should students have over their own development? What is the best way to teach and motivate students to learn? What philosophy of education should guide the process of education? These questions have been discussed throughout the history of American education and continue to be debated today.

Selected, Edited, and with Issue Framing Material by:
Glenn L. Koonce, *Regent University*

ISSUE

Should Schooling Be Based on Social Experiences?

YES: John Dewey, from *Experience and Education* (Macmillan, 1938)

NO: Roger Scruton, from "Schools and Schooling," *The American Spectator* (June 2006)

Learning Outcomes
After reading this issue, you will be able to:
• Differentiate old practices and traditions of education from the new.
• Gain an understanding of democracy (freedom) in education.
• Contrast the difference between subject matter and pedagogy.
• Explore why the term *organization* may not be good to use with the term traditional.
• Compare the one room school-house of yesteryear with today's state run system.

ISSUE SUMMARY

YES: Philosopher John Dewey suggests a reconsideration of traditional approaches to schooling, giving fuller attention to the social development of the learner and the quality of his or her total experience.

NO: British philosopher Roger Scruton expresses the traditionalist view that Dewey's progressive education, with its emphasis on "child-centeredness" and "relevance," has had a disastrous effect on quality education.

Throughout history, organized education has served many purposes—the transmission of tradition, knowledge, and skills; the acculturation and socialization of the young; the building and preserving of political–economic systems; the provision of opportunity for social mobility; the enhancement of the quality of life; and the cultivation of individual potential, among others. At any given time, schools pursue a number of such goals, but the elucidation of a primary or overriding goal, which gives focus to all others, has been a source of continuous contention.

Schooling in America has been extended in the last 100 years to vast numbers of young people, and during this time the argument over aims has gained momentum. At the turn of the century, John Dewey was raising serious questions about the efficacy of the prevailing approach to schooling. He believed that schooling was often arid, pedantic, and detached from the real lives of children and youths. In establishing his laboratory school at the University of Chicago, Dewey hoped to demonstrate that experiences provided by schools could be meaningful extensions of the normal social activities of learners, having as their primary aim the full experiential growth of the individual.

To accomplish this, Dewey sought to bring the learner into an active and intimate relationship with the subject matter. The problem-solving, or inquiry, approach that he and his colleagues at Columbia University in New York City devised became the cornerstone of the "new education"—the progressive education movement.

In 1938 Dewey himself (as expressed in the YES selection) sounded a note of caution to progressive educators who may have abandoned too completely the traditional disciplines in their attempt to link schooling with the needs and interests of the learners. Having spawned an educational revolution, Dewey, in his later years, emerges as more of a compromiser.

In that same year, William C. Bagley, in "An Essentialists' Platform for the Advancement of American Education," harshly criticized what he felt were anti-intellectual excesses promulgated by progressivism. In the 1950s and 1960s this theme was elaborated on by other academics, among them Robert M. Hutchins, Hyman Rickover, Arthur Bestor, and Max Rafferty, who demanded a return to intellectual discipline, higher standards, and moral guidance.

Hutchins' critique of Dewey's pragmatic philosophy was perhaps the best reasoned. He felt that the emphasis on immediate needs and desires of students and the focus on change and relativism detracted from the development of the intellectual skills needed for the realization of human potential.

A renewal of scholarly interest in the philosophical and educational ideas of both Dewey and Hutchins has resulted in a number of books, among which are *Hutchins' University: A Memoir of the University of Chicago* by William H. O'Neill (1991); *Robert M. Hutchins: Portrait of an Educator* by Mary Ann Dzuback (1991); *John Dewey and American Democracy* by Robert B. Westbrook (1991); *The End of Epistemology: Dewey and His Allies on the Spectator Theory of Knowledge* by Christopher B. Kulp (1992); and *The Promise of Pragmatism* by John Patrick Diggins (1994). Their continuing influence is charted by Rene Vincente Arcilla in "Metaphysics in Education After Hutchins and Dewey," *Teachers College Record* (Winter 1991).

More recent articles on the legacies of Dewey's progressivism and the traditionalism of Hutchins include "Why Traditional Education Is More Progressive," by E. D. Hirsch, Jr., *The American Enterprise* (March 1997); and "The Plight of Children Is Our Plight," by William H. Schubert, *Educational Horizons* (Winter 1998).

In the YES selection, Dewey charts what he considers a necessary shift from the abstractness and isolation of traditional schooling to the concreteness and vitality of the newer concept. In the NO selection, Scruton reviews his personal schooling experience, which he judges to be far superior to the antiacademic approaches inspired by Dewey and his followers.

YES ↵ John Dewey

Experience and Education

Mankind likes to think in terms of extreme opposites. It is given to formulating its beliefs in terms of *Either-Ors*, between which it recognizes no intermediate possibilities. When forced to recognize that the extremes cannot be acted upon, it is still inclined to hold that they are all right in theory but that when it comes to practical matters circumstances compel us to compromise. Educational philosophy is no exception. The history of educational theory is marked by opposition between the idea that education is development from within and that it is formation from without; that it is based upon natural endowments and that education is a process of overcoming natural inclination and substituting in its place habits acquired under external pressure.

At present, the opposition, so far as practical affairs of the school are concerned, tends to take the form of contrast between traditional and progressive education. If the underlying ideas of the former are formulated broadly, without the qualifications required for accurate statement, they are found to be about as follows: The subject-matter of education consists of bodies of information and of skills that have been worked out in the past; therefore, the chief business of the school is to transmit them to the new generation. In the past, there have also been developed standards and rules of conduct; moral training consists of forming habits of action in conformity with these rules and standards. Finally, the general pattern of school organization (by which I mean the relations of pupils to one another and to the teachers) constitutes the school as a kind of institution sharply marked off from other social institutions. Call up in imagination the ordinary schoolroom, its time schedules, schemes of classification, of examination and promotion, of rules of order, and I think you will grasp what is meant by "pattern of organization." If then you contrast this scene with what goes on in the family, for example, you will appreciate what is meant by the school being a kind of institution sharply marked off from any other form of social organization.

The three characteristics just mentioned fix the aims and methods of instruction and discipline. The main purpose or objective is to prepare the young for future responsibilities and for success in life, by means of acquisition of the organized bodies of information and prepared forms of skill which comprehend the material of instruction. Since the subject-matter as well as standards of proper conduct are handed down from the past, the attitude of pupils must, upon the whole, be one of docility, receptivity, and obedience. Books, especially textbooks, are the chief representatives of the lore and wisdom of the past, while teachers are the organs through which pupils are brought into effective connection with the material. Teachers are the agents through which knowledge and skills are communicated and rules of conduct enforced.

I have not made this brief summary for the purpose of criticizing the underlying philosophy. The rise of what is called new education and progressive schools is of itself a product of discontent with traditional education. In effect it is a criticism of the latter. When the implied criticism is made explicit it reads somewhat as follows: The traditional scheme is, in essence, one of imposition from above and from outside. It imposes adult standards, subject-matter, and methods upon those who are only growing slowly toward maturity. The gap is so great that the required subject-matter, the methods of learning and of behaving are foreign to the existing capacities of the young. They are beyond the reach of the experience the young learners already possess. Consequently, they must be imposed; even though good teachers will use devices of art to cover up the imposition so as to relieve it of obviously brutal features.

But the gulf between the mature or adult products and the experience and abilities of the young is so wide that the very situation forbids much active participation by pupils in the development of what is taught. Theirs is to do—and learn, as it was the part of the six hundred to do and die. Learning here means acquisition of what already is incorporated in books and in the heads of the elders. Moreover, that which is taught is thought of as essentially static. It is taught as a finished product, with little regard either to the ways in which it was originally built up or to changes that will surely occur in the future. It is to a large extent the cultural product of societies that assumed the future would be much like the past, and yet it is used as educational food in a society where change is the rule, not the exception.

If one attempts to formulate the philosophy of education implicit in the practices of the new education, we may, I think, discover certain common principles amid the variety of progressive schools now existing. To imposition from above is opposed expression and cultivation of individuality; to external discipline is opposed free activity; to learning from texts and teachers, learning through experience; to acquisition of isolated skills and techniques by drill, is opposed acquisition of them as means of attaining ends which make direct vital appeal; to preparation for a more or less remote future is opposed making the most of the opportunities of present life; to static aims and materials is opposed acquaintance with a changing world.

Now, all principles by themselves are abstract. They become concrete only in the consequences which result from their application. Just because the principles set forth are so fundamental and far-reaching, everything depends upon the interpretation given them as they are put into practice in the school and the home. It is at this point that the reference made earlier to *Either-Or* philosophies becomes peculiarly pertinent. The general philosophy of the new education may be sound, and yet the difference in abstract principles will not decide the way in which the moral and intellectual preference involved shall be worked out in practice. There is always the danger in a new movement that in rejecting the aims and methods of that which it would supplant, it may develop its principles negatively rather than positively and constructively. Then it takes its cue in practice from that which is rejected instead of from the constructive development its own philosophy.

I take it that the fundamental unity of the newer philosophy is found in the idea that there is an intimate and necessary relation between the processes of actual experience and education. If this be true, then a positive and constructive development of its own basic idea depends upon having a correct idea of experience. Take, for example, the question of organized subject-matter. . . . The problem for progressive education is: What is the place and meaning of subject-matter and of organization *within* experience? How does subject-matter function? Is there anything inherent in experience which tends towards progressive organization of its contents? What results follow when the materials of experience are not progressively organized? A philosophy which proceeds on the basis of rejection, of sheer opposition, will neglect these questions. It will tend to suppose that because the old education was based on ready-made organization, therefore it suffices to reject the principle of organization *in toto*, instead of striving to discover what it means and how it is to be attained on the basis of experience. We might go through all the points of difference between the new and the old education and reach similar conclusions. When external control is rejected, the problem becomes that of finding the factors of control that are inherent within experience. When external authority is rejected, it does not follow that all authority should be rejected, but rather that there is need to search for a more effective source of authority. Because the older education imposed the knowledge, methods, and the rules of conduct of the mature person upon the young, it does not follow, except upon the basis of the extreme *Either-Or* philosophy, that the knowledge and skill of the mature person has no directive value for the experience of the immature. On the contrary, basing education upon personal experience may mean more multiplied and more intimate contacts between the mature and the immature than ever existed in the traditional school, and

consequently more, rather than less, guidance by others. The problem, then, is: how these contacts can be established without violating the principle of learning through personal experience. The solution of this problem requires a well thought-out philosophy of the social factors that operate in the constitution of individual experience.

What is indicated in the foregoing remarks is that the general principles of the new education do not of themselves solve any of the problems of the actual or practical conduct and management of progressive schools. Rather, they set new problems which have to be worked out on the basis of a new philosophy of experience. The problems are not even recognized, to say nothing of being solved, when it is assumed that it suffices to reject the ideas and practices of the old education and then go to the opposite extreme. Yet I am sure that you will appreciate what is meant when I say that many of the newer schools tend to make little or nothing of organized subject-matter of study; to proceed as if any form of direction and guidance by adults were an invasion of individual freedom, and as if the idea that education should be concerned with the present and future meant that acquaintance with the past has little or no role to play in education. Without pressing these defects to the point of exaggeration, they at least illustrate what is meant by a theory and practice of education which proceeds negatively or by reaction against what has been current in education rather than by a positive and constructive development of purposes, methods, and subject-matter on the foundation of a theory of experience and its educational potentialities.

It is not too much to say that an educational philosophy which professes to be based on the idea of freedom may become as dogmatic as ever was the traditional education which is reacted against. For any theory and set of practices is dogmatic which is not based upon critical examination of its own underlying principles. Let us say that the new education emphasizes the freedom of the learner. Very well. A problem is now set. What does freedom mean and what are the conditions under which it is capable of realization? Let us say that the kind of external imposition which was so common in the traditional school limited rather than promoted the intellectual and moral development of the young. Again, very well. Recognition of this serious defect sets a problem. Just what is the role of the teacher and of books in promoting the educational development of the immature? Admit that traditional education employed as the subject-matter for study facts and ideas so bound up with the past as to give little help in dealing with the issues of the present and future. Very well. Now we have the problem of discovering the connection which actually exists *within* experience between the achievements of the past and the issues of the present. We have the problem of ascertaining how acquaintance with the past may be translated into a potent instrumentality for dealing effectively with the future. We may reject knowledge of the past as the *end* of education and thereby only emphasize its importance as a *means*. When we do that we have a problem that is new in the story of education: How shall the young become acquainted with the past in such a way that the acquaintance is a potent agent in appreciation of the living present? . . .

In short, the point I am making is that rejection of the philosophy and practice of traditional education sets a new type of difficult educational problem for those who believe in the new type of education. We shall operate blindly and in confusion until we recognize this fact; until we thoroughly appreciate that departure from the old solves no problems. What is said in the following pages is, accordingly, intended to indicate some of the main problems with which the newer education is confronted and to suggest the main lines along which their solution is to be sought. I assume that amid all uncertainties there is one permanent frame of reference: namely, the organic connection between education and personal experience; or, that the new philosophy of education is committed to some kind of empirical and experimental philosophy. But experience and experiment are not self-explanatory ideas. Rather, their meaning is part of the problem to be explored. To know the meaning of empiricism we need to understand what experience is.

The belief that all genuine education comes about through experience does not mean that all experiences are genuinely or equally educative. Experience and education cannot be directly equated to each other. For some experiences are miseducative. Any experience is miseducative that has the effect of arresting or distorting the growth of further experience. An experience may be such as to engender callousness; it may produce lack of sensitivity and of responsiveness. Then the possibilities of having richer experience in the future are restricted. Again, a given experience may increase a person's automatic skill in a particular direction and yet tend to land him in a groove or rut; the effect again is to narrow the field of further experience. An experience may be immediately enjoyable and yet promote the formation of a slack and careless attitude; this attitude then operates to modify the quality of subsequent experiences so as to prevent a person from getting out of them what they have to give. Again, experiences may be so disconnected from one another that, while each is agreeable or even exciting in itself, they are not linked cumulatively to one another. Energy is then dissipated and a person becomes scatterbrained. Each experience may be lively, vivid, and "interesting," and yet their disconnectedness may artificially generate dispersive, disintegrated, centrifugal habits. The consequence of formation of such habits is inability to control future experiences. They are then taken, either by way of enjoyment or of discontent and revolt, just as they come. Under such circumstances, it is idle to talk of self-control.

Traditional education offers a plethora of examples of experiences of the kinds just mentioned. It is a great mistake to suppose, even tacitly, that the traditional schoolroom was not a place in which pupils had experiences. Yet this is tacitly assumed when progressive education as a plan of learning by experience is placed in sharp opposition to the old. The proper line of attack is that the experiences which were had, by pupils and teachers alike, were largely of a wrong kind. How many students, for example, were rendered callous to ideas, and how many lost the impetus to learn because of the way in which learning was experienced by them? How many acquired special skills by means of automatic drill so that their power of judgment and capacity to act intelligently in new situations was limited? How many came to associate the learning process with ennui and boredom? How many found what they did learn so foreign to the situations of life outside the school as to give them no power of control over the latter? How many came to associate books with dull drudgery, so that they were "conditioned" to all but flashy reading matter?

If I ask these questions, it is not for the sake of wholesale condemnation of the old education. It is for quite another purpose. It is to emphasize the fact, first, that young people in traditional schools do have experiences; and, secondly, that the trouble is not the absence of experiences, but their defective and wrong character—wrong and defective from the standpoint of connection with further experience. The positive side of this point is even more important in connection with progressive education. It is not enough to insist upon the necessity of experience, nor even of activity in experience. Everything depends upon the *quality* of the experience which is had. The quality of an experience has two aspects. There is an immediate aspect of agreeableness or disagreeableness, and there is its influence upon later experiences. The first is obvious and easy to judge. The *effect* of an experience is not borne on its face. It sets a problem to the educator. It is his business to arrange for the kind of experiences which, while they do not repel the student, but rather engage his activities are, nevertheless, more than immediately enjoyable since they promote having desirable future experiences. Just as no man lives or dies to himself, so no experience lives or dies to itself. Wholly independent of desire or intent, every experience lives on in further experiences. Hence the central problem of an education based upon experience is to select the kind of present experiences that live fruitfully and creatively in subsequent experiences.

. . . Here I wish simply to emphasize the importance of this principle [of the continuity of experience] for the philosophy of educative experience. A philosophy of education, like my theory, has to be stated in words, in symbols. But so far as it is more than verbal it is a plan for conducting education. Like any plan, it must be framed with reference to what is to be done and how it is to be done. The more definitely and sincerely it is held that education is a development within, by, and for experience, the more important it is that there shall be clear conceptions of what experience is. Unless experience is so conceived that the result is a plan for deciding upon subject-matter, upon methods of instruction and discipline, and upon material equipment and social organization of the school, it is wholly in the air. It is reduced to a form of words which may be emotionally stirring but for which any other set of words might equally well be substituted unless they indicate operations to be initiated and executed. Just because traditional education was a matter of routine in which the plans and programs were handed down from the past, it does not follow that progressive education is a matter of planless improvisation.

The traditional school could get along without any consistently developed philosophy of education. About all it required in that line was a set of abstract words like culture, discipline, our great cultural heritage, etc., actual guidance being derived not from them but from custom and established routines. Just because progressive schools cannot rely upon established traditions and institutional habits, they must either proceed more or less haphazardly or be directed by ideas which, when they are made articulate and coherent, form a philosophy of education. Revolt against the kind of organization characteristic of the traditional school constitutes a demand for a kind of organization based upon ideas. I think that only slight acquaintance with the history of education is needed to prove that educational reformers and innovators alone have felt the need for a philosophy of education. Those who adhered to the established system needed merely a few fine-sounding words to justify existing practices. The real work was done by habits which were so fixed as to be institutional. The lesson for progressive education is that it requires in an urgent degree, a degree more pressing than was incumbent upon former innovators, a philosophy of education based upon a philosophy of experience.

I remarked incidentally that the philosophy in question is, to paraphrase the saying of Lincoln about democracy, one of education of, by, and for experience. No one of these words, *of, by,* or *for,* names anything which is self-evident. Each of them is a challenge to discover and put into operation a principle of order and organization which follows from understanding what education experience signifies.

It is, accordingly, a much more difficult task to work out the kinds of materials, of methods, and of social relationships that are appropriate to the new education than is the case with traditional education. I think many of the difficulties experienced in the conduct of progressive schools and many of the criticisms leveled against them arise from this source. The difficulties are aggravated and the criticisms are increased when it is supposed that the new education is somehow easier than the old. This belief is, I imagine, more or less current. Perhaps it illustrates again the *Either-Or* philosophy, springing from the idea that about all which is required is not to do what is done in traditional schools.

I admit gladly that the new education is *simpler* in principle than the old. It is in harmony with principles of growth, while there is very much which is artificial in the old selection and arrangement of subjects and methods,

and artificiality always leads to unnecessary complexity. But the easy and the simple are not identical. To discover what is really simple and to act upon the discovery is an exceedingly difficult task. After the artificial and complex is once institutionally established and ingrained in custom and routine, it is easier to walk in the paths that have been beaten than it is, after taking a new point of view, to work out what is practically involved in the new point of view. The old Ptolemaic astronomical system was more complicated with its cycles and epicycles than the Copernican system. But until organization of actual astronomical phenomena on the ground of the latter principle had been effected the easiest course was to follow the line of least resistance provided by the old intellectual habit. So we come back to the idea that a coherent *theory* of experience, affording positive direction to selection and organization of appropriate educational methods and materials, is required by the attempt to give new direction to the work of the schools. The process is a slow and arduous one. It is a matter of growth, and there are many obstacles which tend to obstruct growth and to deflect it into wrong lines.

. . . [W]e must escape from the tendency to think of organization in terms of the *kind* of organization, whether of content (or subject-matter), or of methods and social relations, that mark traditional education. I think that a good deal of the current opposition to the idea of organization is due to the fact that it is so hard to get away from the picture of the studies of the old school. The moment "organization" is mentioned imagination goes almost automatically to the kind of organization that is familiar, and in revolting against that we are led to shrink from the very idea of any organization. On the other hand, educational reactionaries, who are now gathering force, use the absence of adequate intellectual and moral organization in the newer type of school as proof not only of the need of organization, but to identify any and every kind of organization with that instituted before the rise of experimental science. Failure to develop a conception of organization upon the empirical and experimental basis gives reactionaries a too easy victory. But the fact that the empirical sciences now offer the best type of intellectual organization which can be found in any field shows that there is no reason why we, who call ourselves empiricists, should be "pushovers" in the matter of order and organization.

JOHN DEWEY (1859–1952) was a leading American philosopher who taught at the University of Michigan, the University of Chicago (where he founded a laboratory school to test his ideas), and Columbia University (where he spawned the progressive education movement). His most famous book is *Democracy and Education* (1916).

Roger Scruton

→ **NO**

Schools and Schooling

The school where I was educated from my 11th to my 17th year was an English "grammar" school—one of those old Tudor foundations that had become incorporated into the state educational system but which still retained, in those post-war decades, the ethos of public service. The teachers were graduates of the old universities; some had returned from active service in the colonies; one or two had held fellowships in Oxbridge colleges; almost all had wished to pursue an academic career, reluctantly accepting the role of schoolmaster as an honorable second-best.

Those teachers were distinguished from their successors by two all-important characteristics. First, they knew nothing about "education." The idea that there was such a subject—that there could be experts in education, theories of education, and recipes for putting those theories into practice—such an idea had never crossed their minds. A "professor of education" would have been, in their eyes, a creature as risible as a professor of television, of hairdressing, or of underwater basketball.

Secondly, although they knew nothing about education, they knew an awful lot about something else: namely, the subject they had been appointed to teach. Our physics master had worked with Rutherford on the splitting of the atom; our chemistry master had published a textbook on hydrocarbons; and the music master was an amateur composer, friend of our local celebrity, the symphonist Edmund Rubbra. Sixth-form English was taught by a pupil of F.R. Leavis, and the school library contained all of English literature, organized according to the system of T.S. Eliot, who had taught in the school in his Prufrock days. Our Latin master, whose infectious love of Virgil made many converts among the boys, also wrote poetry in Latin and English, and was something of an expert on both Catullus and Yeats.

Sure, it was an exceptional school. But the principles on which it was run were not exceptional at all. Each school, whether in the private or the public sector, recruited teachers with knowledge, on the quite reasonable assumption that knowledge was its business. Of course, the school would do its best to ascertain that its recruits were competent in the classroom. But it would act on the assumption that, failing some accident like vampire teeth or a crippling stutter, knowledge would tend to pass of its own accord from the one who displayed it to the one who saw it on display. And that assumption was, by and large, correct.

That public-sector schools are not like that today, either in Europe or in America, goes without saying. But it is worth asking why. Every place has its own sorry story to tell, but in each country we can trace the decline to a few common factors. The most important has been the rise of "education" as an academic subject. The question what to teach the young occupies many pages of Plato, Aristotle, Cicero, and Quintilian. But the idea that you could be an expert in education, while knowing next to nothing about anything else, is a peculiarly modern fallacy, and one whose appeal rests entirely on its subversive effect. The graduate in education, competing with the pupil of Lord Rutherford for a job teaching physics, can say: sure *he* knows some physics; but *I* know how to *teach* it. The idea of education as a field of expertise thereby gives the ignorant an insuperable advantage over the learned, whom they out-number in any case by ten to one.

But that is not all there is to it. Education, as an academic discipline, was itself shaped by subversives. It takes its inspiration from Rousseau, whose novel *Emile* outlines a new form of teaching, in which knowledge is not authoritatively displayed but gently *elicited,* in a mind already poised on the brink of it. Admirers of this preposterous book somehow fail to notice that education, as Rousseau conceives it, requires day-by-day one-to-one coaching from an expensive private tutor, whose devotion to the cause of knowledge has left him no time whatsoever to acquire it.

The other great influence on schools of education has been John Dewey, a figure with an equally preposterous and equally *a priori* approach. For Dewey education should be purged of all residues of authority, so as to proceed through the child's self-expression. People had made the mistake, he thought, of focusing on the teacher, when the true object of education is the child. Child-centered education proceeds by awakening, eliciting, encouraging: the child should be exploring the world, and the teacher must therefore present him with things that are relevant to his interests and stimulating to a mind like his.

Thus there entered into schooling the two ideas that have destroyed it: child-centered education, and relevance. Add them to the campaigning zeal of the egalitarians, who have always hated learning since real learning discriminates, and the result is a deadly weapon in the battle against knowledge. In Britain this battle took on a new form in the 1960s. My schoolmasters had never encountered "education," since the only qualification required of them was knowledge. Those who attended teacher-training colleges, however, who were by and large those who had failed to get to university, had encountered virtually nothing *except* "education." Competing for jobs with learned graduates they made it transparently obvious that they had nothing to offer save fashionable nonsense. The socialist government of Harold Wilson therefore devised a cunning strategy designed to give "education" an insuperable advantage over knowledge. A "post-graduate certificate of education" was invented, to provide a compulsory hurdle in the path of all who had made the mistake of learning something. Henceforth graduates with genuine competence in a subject could no longer teach in the public sector, unless they had undergone another year of study—which was not a year of study at all, but a period of mind-numbing indoctrination in official nonsense. The best of them shrugged their shoulders and went to work in the city.

Since then good teachers have been gradually driven from the system, often accused of "insensitivity" towards the needs of children, and castigated for the irrelevance of what they presume to know. Examinations have been reshaped to endorse the new "relevant" curriculum, and when it is pointed out that 30 percent of British children now leave school unable to read or write, the educationists cheerfully point to the "irrelevance" of reading and writing in the "information culture." And it is true that information, as currently conceived, is the enemy of knowledge—a mass of unsorted facts and factoids, pouring from the screen with the incoherence of a madman's monologue.

Not that the situation is better in France, Germany, or America. Everywhere we encounter the triumph of "education" over knowledge. And the mark of this triumph is the unchallenged belief that, if knowledge is to be permitted in school, it is in order to benefit the child. My teachers had the opposite belief. For them, if children are permitted in school it is in order to benefit knowledge. Children have their lives ahead of them; they can carry knowledge into the future and keep it from decay—they might even add to it. It is therefore right to allow them into the classroom, so long as nothing "relevant" occurs there, the mark of true knowledge being its total irrelevance to the world of a child. My teachers valued knowledge for its pristine uselessness. Like harmony and counterpoint, like Latin and poetry, like

the laws of quantum mechanics or the theory of transfinite cardinals, knowledge, for them, was its own justification, and never needed to stoop to a use. Any other way of treating it, my teachers thought, would lead to its disappearance. And they were right, since it did.

All attempts by the state to rectify the disaster are doomed, since they will be administered by the educationists. That is why Americans are right to turn to the home schooling movement, the first ray of hope for education since the state got its hands on it. When a mother sits down to teach her child, she is instinctively aware that her role is not to flatter ignorance but to pass on knowledge. She doesn't ask about the relevance or use of what she is teaching. To a child few beliefs are more useful than that the earth is flat, that all children are victims, that mine and thine are indistinguishable, or that $2 + 2 = 5$; few things are more relevant than pop stars, sitcoms, and advertising jingles. None of those appear on the home schooling curriculum since it is devoted, by its very nature, to passing on the knowledge that the parent values, whether or not the child perceives its relevance. My hope is that, as more and more parents take up the challenge, they will gradually learn to pool their resources, to divide the labor, to share their expertise, and to produce that precious thing which has all but disappeared from the world of ordinary people—the school.

Just down the road from us in rural Virginia is an old deserted cabin with a classroom, a tiny kitchen, and a toilet. From the windows you see the Blue Ridge Mountains, surmounted by Old Rag, and in the foreground a horse or two. The classroom has a blackboard, a bookshelf, and a few battered desks. No educationist has ever set foot in it, and no bureaucrat knows of its existence. All that it needs is a child or two, an adult or two, and the thing that they spontaneously generate when brought together, which is the pursuit of knowledge. It is from such costless resources that civilizations begin.

Roger Scruton is a British philosopher who has taught at Boston University, the Institute for the Psychological Sciences, and Princeton University. He is author of *Culture Counts* (2007).

EXPLORING THE ISSUE

Should Schooling Be Based on Social Experiences?

Critical Thinking and Reflection

1. What is the basic purpose of education?
2. Why has John Dewey been such an influence on American education?
3. Can the "either/or" polarities of this basic argument be overcome?
4. Is the articulation of overarching general aims essential to the charting of a worthwhile educational experience?
5. How can the classroom teacher relate to general philosophical aims?

Is There Common Ground?

Intellectual training versus social-emotional-mental growth—the argument between Dewey and Hutchins—reflects a historical debate that flows from the ideas of Plato and Aristotle and that continues today. Psychologists, sociologists, curriculum and instruction specialists, and popular critics have joined philosophers in commenting on this central concern.

Followers of Dewey contend that training the mental powers cannot be isolated from other factors of development and, indeed, can be enhanced by attention to the concrete social situations in which learning occurs. Critics of Dewey worry that the expansion of effort into the social and emotional realm only detracts from the intellectual mission that is schooling's unique province.

Was the progressive education movement ruinous, or did it lay the foundation for the education of the future? A reasonably even-handed appraisal can be found in Lawrence Cremin's *The Transformation of the School* (1961). The free school movement of the 1960s, at least partly derived from progressivism, is analyzed in Allen Graubard's *Free the Children* (1973) and Jonathan Kozol's *Free Schools* (1972). Diane Ravitch's *Troubled Crusade* (1983) and Mary Eberstadt's "The Schools They Deserve," *Policy Review* (October/November 1999) offer effective critiques of progressivism.

Among the best general explorations of philosophical alternatives are Gerald L. Gutek's *Philosophical and Ideological Perspectives on Education* (1988); Edward J. Power's *Philosophy of Education: Studies in Philosophies, Schooling, and Educational Policies* (1990); and *Philosophical Foundations of Education* by Howard Ozmon and Samuel Craver (1990).

Also worth perusing are Philip W. Jackson's "Dewey's Experience and Education Revisited," *The Educational Forum* (Summer 1996); Jerome Bruner's 1996 book *The Culture of Education* (particularly chapter 3, "The Complexity of Educational Aims"); Christine McCarthy's "Dewey's Ethics: Philosophy or Science?" *Education Theory* (Summer 1999); Debra J. Anderson and Robert L. Major, "Dewey, Democracy, and Citizenship," *The Clearing House* (November/December 2001).

Create Central

www.mhhe.com/createcentral

Additional Resources

David B. Ackerman, "Taproots for a New Century: Tapping the Best of Traditional and Progressive Education," *Phi Delta Kappan* (January 2003). Retrieved from: http://www.kappanmagazine.org/content/84/5/344.abstract

William Hayes, "The Future of Progressive Education," *Educational Horizons* (Spring 2008). Retrieved from: http://files.eric.ed.gov/fulltext/EJ798520.pdf

Stanley Pogrow, "The Bermuda Triangle of American Education: Pure Traditionalism, Pure Progressivism, and Good Intentions," *Phi Delta Kappan* (October 2006)

Diana Schaub, "Can Liberal Education Survive Liberal Democracy?" *The Public Interest* (Spring 2002)

Julie Webber, "Why Can't We Be Deweyan Citizens?" *Educational Theory* (vol. 51, no. 2, Spring 2001)

Internet References. . .

InTASC Model Core Teaching Standards: A Resource for State Dialogue, April 2011

www.ccsso.org/documents/2011/intasc_model_core_teaching_standards_2011.pdf

John Dewey: the Father of Progressive Education

www.renewamerica.com/columns/weaver/040308

How Progressive Education Gets It Wrong

www.hoover.org/publications/hoover-digest/article/6408

Support the Social Development and Participation of Young People

http://education.qld.gov.au/staff/development/standards/teachers/social.html

Traditional Education or Partnership Education: Which Educational Approach Might Best Prepare Students for the Future?

www.cnvc.org/sites/cnvc.org/files/NVC_Research_Files/NVC%20in%20Schools/TRADITIONAL_EDUCATION_OR_PARTNERSHIP_EDUCATION_S_Jones.pdf

Selected, Edited, and with Issue Framing Material by:
Glenn L. Koonce, *Regent University*

ISSUE

Should the Curriculum Be Standardized for All?

YES: **Mortimer J. Adler**, from "The Paideia Proposal: Rediscovering the Essence of Education," *American School Board Journal* (July 1982)

NO: **John Holt**, from *Escape from Childhood* (E. P. Dutton, 1974)

Learning Outcomes
After reading this issue, you will be able to:
• Compare and contrast reasons why public schools need a uniform curriculum for all students.
• Evaluate how a standardized curriculum may be adversarial to the human rights of students.
• Understand The Paideia Curriculum and expand on the justification to implement it in public schools.
• Define the concept "the barbarism of speculation."
• Critique how the quality of life depends on the quality of schooling.

ISSUE SUMMARY

YES: Philosopher Mortimer J. Adler contends that democracy is best served by a public school system that establishes uniform curricular objectives for all students.

NO: Educator John Holt argues that an imposed curriculum damages the individual and usurps a basic human right to select one's own path of development.

Controversy over the content of education has been particularly keen since the 1950s. The pendulum has swung from learner-centered progressive education to an emphasis on structured intellectual discipline to calls for radical reform in the direction of "openness" to the recent rally to go "back to basics."

The conservative viewpoint, articulated by such writers as Robert M. Hutchins, Clifton Fadiman, Jacques Barzun, Arthur Bestor, and Mortimer J. Adler, arises from concerns about the drift toward informalism and the decline in academic achievement in recent decades. Taking philosophical cues from Plato's contention that certain subject matters have universal qualities that prompt mental and characterological development, the "basics" advocates argue against incidental learning, student choice, and diminution of structure and standards. Barzun summarizes the viewpoint succinctly: "Nonsense is at the heart of those proposals that would replace definable subject matters with vague activities copied from 'life' or with courses organized around 'problems' or 'attitudes.'"

The reform viewpoint, represented by John Holt, Paul Goodman, Ivan Illich, Charles Silberman, Edgar Friedenberg, and others, portrays the typical traditional school as a mindless, indifferent, social institution dedicated to producing fear, docility, and conformity. In such an atmosphere, the viewpoint holds, learners either become alienated from the established curriculum or learn to play the school "game" and thus achieve a hollow success. Taking cues from the ideas of John Dewey and A. S. Neill, the "radical reformers" have given rise to a flurry of alternatives to regular schooling during recent decades. Among these are free schools, which follow the Summerhill model; urban storefront schools, which attempt to develop a true sense of "community"; "schools without walls," which follow the Philadelphia Parkway Program model; "commonwealth" schools, in which students, parents, and teachers share responsibility; and various "humanistic education" projects within regular school systems, which emphasize students' self-concept development and choice-making ability.

The utilitarian tradition that has descended from Benjamin Franklin, Horace Mann, and Herbert Spencer, Dewey's theory of active experiencing, and Neill's insistence on free and natural development support the reform position. The ideology rejects the factory model of schooling with its rigidly set curriculum, its neglect of individual differences, its social engineering function, and its pervasive formalism. "Basics" advocates, on the other hand, express deep concern over the erosion of authority and the watering down of demands upon students that result from the reform ideology.

Arguments for a more standardized curriculum have been embodied most recently in Theodore R. Sizer's Coalition of Essential Schools and the Core Knowledge Schools of E. D. Hirsch, Jr., whose 1996 book *The Schools We Need and Why We Don't Have Them* summarizes the basic points of this view. An interview with Hirsch by Mark F. Goldberg titled "Doing What Works" appeared in the September 1997 issue of *Phi Delta Kappan*. A thorough critique of Hirsch's position is presented by Kristen L. Buras in "Questioning Core Assumptions," *Harvard Educational Review* (Spring 1999). In 1998 Terry Roberts and the staff of the National Paideia Center at the University of North Carolina released *The Power of Paideia Schools: Defining Lives Through Learning.*

A broad spectrum of ideas on the curriculum may be found in John I. Goodlad's *A Place Called School* (1984), Maxine Green's *The Dialectic of Freedom* (1987), Theodore R. Sizer's *Horace trilogy*, and Ernest L. Boyer's *The Basic School* (1995). Some provocative ideas on this and related issues may be found in "The Goals of Education" by Richard Rothstein and Rebecca Jacobsen in *Phi Delta Kappan* (December 2006).

In the following selections, Mortimer J. Adler outlines his "Paideia Proposal," which calls for a uniform and unified curriculum and methodological approach—a common schooling for the development of a truly democratic society. In opposition, John Holt goes beyond his earlier concerns about the oppressiveness of the school curriculum to propose complete freedom for the learner to determine all aspects of his or her educational development.

YES ↵

Mortimer J. Adler

The Paideia Proposal: Rediscovering the Essence of Education

In the first 80 years of this century, we have met the obligation imposed on us by the principle of equal educational opportunity, but only in a quantitative sense. Now as we approach the end of the century, we must achieve equality in qualitative terms.

This means a completely on-track system of schooling. It means, at the basic level, giving all the young the same kind of schooling, whether or not they are college bound.

We are aware that children, although equal in their common humanity and fundamental human rights, are unequal as individuals, differing in their capacity to learn. In addition, the homes and environments from which they come to school are unequal—either predisposing the child for schooling or doing the opposite.

Consequently, the Paideia Proposal, faithful to the principle of equal educational opportunity, includes the suggestion that inequalities due to environmental factors must be overcome by some form of preschool preparation at least one year for all and two or even three for some. We know that to make such preschool tutelage compulsory at the public expense would be tantamount to increasing the duration of compulsory schooling from 12 years to 13, 14, or 15 years. Nevertheless, we think that this preschool adjunct to the 12 years of compulsory basic schooling is so important that some way must be found to make it available for all and to see that all use it to advantage.

The Essentials of Basic Schooling

The objectives of basic schooling should be the same for the whole school population. In our current two-track or multitrack system, the learning objectives are not the same for all. And even when the objectives aimed at those on the upper track are correct, the course of study now provided does not adequately realize these correct objectives. On all tracks in our current system, we fail to cultivate proficiency in the common tasks of learning, and we especially fail to develop sufficiently the indispensable skills of learning.

The uniform objectives of basic schooling should be threefold. They should correspond to three aspects of the common future to which all the children are destined: (1) Our society provides all children ample opportunity for personal development. Given such opportunity, each individual is under a moral obligation to make the most of himself and his life. Basic schooling must facilitate this accomplishment. (2) All the children will become, when of age, full-fledged citizens with suffrage and other political responsibilities. Basic schooling must do everything it can to make them good citizens, able to perform the duties of citizenship with all the trained intelligence that each is able to achieve. (3) When they are grown, all (or certainly most) of the children will engage in some form of work to earn a living. Basic schooling must prepare them for earning a living, but not by training them for this or that specific job while they are still in school.

To achieve these three objectives, the character of basic schooling must be general and liberal. It should have a single, required, 12-year course of study for all, with no electives except one—an elective choice with regard to a second language, to be selected from such modern languages as French, German, Italian, Spanish, Russian, and Chinese. The elimination of all electives, with this one exception, excludes what *should* be excluded—all forms of specialization, including particularized job training.

In its final form, the Paideia Proposal will detail this required course of study, but I will summarize the curriculum here in its bare outline. It consists of three main columns of teaching and learning, running through the 12 years and progressing, of course, from the simple to the more complex, from the less difficult to the more difficult, as the students grow older. Understand: The three columns (see Table 1) represent three distinct modes of teaching and learning. They do not represent a series of courses. A specific course or class may employ more than one mode of teaching and learning, but all three modes are essential to the overall course of study.

The first column is devoted to acquiring knowledge in three subject areas: (A) language, literature, and the fine arts; (B) mathematics and natural science; (C) history, geography, and social studies.

The second column is devoted to developing the intellectual skills of learning. These include all the language skills necessary for thought and communication—the skills of reading, writing, speaking, listening. They also include mathematical and scientific skills; the skills of observing, measuring, estimating, and calculating; and skills in the use of the computer and of other scientific instruments. Together, these skills make it possible to think clearly and critically. They once were called the

Table 1

The Paideia Curriculum

	Column One	Column Two	Column Three
Goals	Acquisition of Organized Knowledge	Development of Intellectual Skills and Skills of Learning	Improved Understanding of Ideas and Values
	by means of	*by means of*	*by means of*
Means	Didactic Instruction, Lecturing, and Textbooks	Coaching, Exercises, Supervised Practice	Maieutic or Socratic Questioning and Active Participation
	in these three subject areas	*in these operations*	*in these activities*
Subject Areas, Operations, and Activities	Language, Literature, and Fine Arts; Mathematics and Natural Science; History, Geography, and Social Studies	Reading, Writing, Speaking, Listening, Calculating, Problem Solving, Observing, Measuring, Estimating, Exercising Critical Judgment	Discussion of Books (Not Textbooks) and Other Works of Art; Involvement in Music, Drama, and Visual Arts

The three columns do not correspond to separate courses, nor is one kind of teaching and learning necessarily confined to any one class.

liberal arts—the intellectual skills indispensable to being competent as a learner.

The third column is devoted to enlarging the understanding of ideas and values. The materials of the third column are books (*not* textbooks), and other products of human artistry. These materials include books of every variety—historical, scientific, and philosophical as well as poems, stories, and essays—and also individual pieces of music, visual art, dramatic productions, dance productions, film or television productions. Music and works of visual art can be used in seminars in which ideas are discussed; but as with poetry and fiction, they also are to be experienced aesthetically, to be enjoyed and admired for their excellence. In this connection, exercises in the composition of poetry, music, and visual works and in the production of dramatic works should be used to develop the appreciation of excellence.

The three columns represent three different kinds of learning on the part of the student and three different kinds of instruction on the part of teachers.

In the first column, the students are engaged in acquiring information and organized knowledge about nature, man, and human society. The method of instruction here, using textbooks and manuals, is didactic. The teacher lectures, invites responses from the students, monitors the acquisition of knowledge, and tests that acquisition in various ways.

In the second column, the students are engaged in developing habits of performance, which is all that is involved in the development of an art or skill. Art, skill, or technique is nothing more than a cultivated, habitual ability to do a certain kind of thing well, whether that is swimming and dancing, or reading and writing. Here, students are acquiring linguistic, mathematical, scientific, and historical *know-how* in contrast to what they acquire in the first column, which is *know-that* with respect to language, literature, and the fine arts, mathematics and science, history, geography, and social studies. Here, the

method of instruction cannot be didactic or monitorial; it cannot be dependent on textbooks. It must be coaching, the same kind used in the gym to develop bodily skills; only here it is used by a different kind of coach in the classroom to develop intellectual skills.

In the third column, students are engaged in a process of enlightenment, the process whereby they develop their understanding of the basic and controlling ideas in all fields of subject matter and come to appreciate better all the human values embodied in works of art. Here, students move progressively from understanding less to understanding more—understanding better what they already know and appreciating more what they already have experienced. Here, the method of instruction cannot be either didactic or coaching. It must be the Socratic, or maieutic, method of questioning and discussing. It should not occur in any ordinary classroom with the students sitting in rows and the teacher in front of the class, but in a seminar room, with the students sitting around a table and the teacher sitting with them as an equal, even though a little older and wiser.

Of these three main elements in the required curriculum, the third column is completely innovative. Nothing like this is done in our schools, and because it is completely absent from the ordinary curriculum of basic schooling, the students never have the experience of having their minds addressed in a challenging way or of being asked to think about the important ideas, to express their thoughts, to defend their opinions in a reasonable fashion.

The only thing that is innovative about the second column is the insistence that the method of instruction here must be coaching carried on either with one student at a time or with very small groups of students. Nothing else can be effective in the development of a skill, be it bodily or intellectual. The absence of such individualized coaching in our schools explains why most of the students cannot read well, write well, speak well, listen well, or perform well any of the other basic intellectual operations.

The three columns are closely interconnected and integrated, but the middle column—the one concerned with linguistic, mathematical, and scientific skills—is central. It both supports and is supported by the other two columns. All the intellectual skills with which it is concerned must be exercised in the study of the three basic subject-matters and in acquiring knowledge about them, and these intellectual skills must be exercised in the seminars devoted to the discussion of books and other things.

In addition to the three main columns in the curriculum, ascending through the 12 years of basic schooling, there are three adjuncts: One is 12 years of physical training, accompanied by instruction in bodily care and hygiene. The second, running through something less than 12 years, is the development of basic manual skills, such as cooking, sewing, carpentry, and the operation of all kinds of machines. The third, reserved for the last year or two, is an introduction to the whole world of work—the range of occupations in which human beings earn their livings. This is not particularized job training. It is the very opposite. It aims at a broad understanding of what is involved in working for a living and of the various ways in which that can be done. If, at the end of 12 years, students wish training for specific jobs, they should get that in two-year community or junior colleges, or on the job itself, or in technical institutes of one sort or another.

Everything that has not been specifically mentioned as occupying the time of the school day should be reserved for after-hours and have the status of extracurricular activities.

Please, note: The required course of study just described is as important for what it *displaces* as for what it introduces. It displaces a multitude of elective courses, especially those offered in our secondary schools, most of which make little or no contribution to general, liberal education. It eliminates all narrowly specialized job training, which now abounds in our schools. It throws out of the curriculum and into the category of optional extracurricular activities a variety of things that have little or no educational value.

If it did not call for all these displacements, there would not be enough time in the school day or year to accomplish everything that is essential to the general, liberal learning that must be the content of basic schooling.

The Quintessential Element

So far, I have set forth the bare essentials of the Paideia Proposal with regard to basic schooling. I have not yet mentioned the quintessential element—the *sine qua non*—without which nothing else can possibly come to fruition, no matter how sound it might be in principle. The heart of the matter is the quality of learning and the quality of teaching that occupies the school day, not to mention the quality of the homework after school.

First, the learning must be active. It must use the whole mind, not just the memory. It must be learning by

discovery, in which the student, never the teacher, is the primary agent. Learning by discovery, which is the only genuine learning, may be either unaided or aided. It is unaided only for geniuses. For most students, discovery must be aided.

Here is where teachers come in—as aids in the process of learning by discovery not as knowers who attempt to put the knowledge they have into the minds of their students. The quality of the teaching, in short, depends crucially upon how the teacher conceives his role in the process of learning, and that must be as an aid to the student's process of discovery.

I am prepared for the questions that must be agitating you by now: How and where will we get the teachers who can perform as teachers should? How will we be able to staff the program with teachers so trained that they will be competent to provide the quality of instruction required for the quality of learning desired?

The first part of our answer to these questions is negative: We *cannot* get the teachers we need for the Paideia program from schools of education as *they are now constituted*. As teachers are now trained for teaching, they simply will not do. The ideal—an impracticable ideal—would be to ask for teachers who are, themselves, truly educated human beings. But truly educated human beings are too rare. Even if we could draft all who are now alive, there still would be far too few to staff our schools.

Well, then, what can we look for? Look for teachers who are actively engaged in the process of *becoming* educated human beings, who are themselves deeply motivated to develop their own minds. Assuming this is not too much to ask for the present, how should teachers be schooled and trained in the future? First, they should have the same kind of basic schooling that is recommended in the Paideia Proposal. Second, they should have additional schooling, at the college and even the university level, in which the same kind of general, liberal learning is carried on at advanced levels—more deeply, broadly, and intensively than it can be done in the first 12 years of schooling. Third, they must be given something analogous to the clinical experience in the training of physicians. They must engage in practice-teaching under supervision, which is another way of saying that they must be *coached* in the arts of teaching, not just given didactic instruction in educational psychology and in pedagogy. Finally, and most important of all, they must learn how to teach well by being exposed to the performances of those who are masters of the arts involved in teaching.

It is by watching a good teacher at work that they will be able to perceive what is involved in the process of assisting others to learn by discovery. Perceiving it, they must then try to emulate what they observe, and through this process, they slowly will become good teachers themselves.

The Paideia Proposal recognizes the need for three different kinds of institutions at the collegiate level: The two-year community or junior college should offer a wide choice of electives that give students some training in one or another specialized field, mainly those fields of study that have something to do with earning a living. The four-year college also should offer a wide variety of electives, to be chosen by students who aim at the various professional or technical occupations that require advanced study. Those elective majors chosen by students should be accompanied, for all students, by one required minor, in which the kind of general and liberal learning that was begun at the level of basic schooling is continued at a higher level in the four years of college. And we should have still a third type of collegiate institution—a four-year college in which general, liberal learning at a higher level constitutes a required course of study that is to be taken by all students. *It is this third type of college, by the way, that should be attended by all who plan to become teachers in our basic schools.*

At the university level, there should be a continuation of general, liberal learning at a still higher level to accompany intensive specialization in this or that field of science or scholarship, this or that learned profession. Our insistence on the continuation of general, liberal learning at all the higher levels of schooling stems from our concern with the worst cultural disease that is rampant in our society—*the barbarism of specialization.*

There is no question that our technologically advanced industrial society needs specialists of all sorts. There is no question that the advancement of knowledge in all fields of science and scholarship, and in all the learned professions, needs intense specialization. But for the sake of preserving and enhancing our cultural traditions, as well as for the health of science and scholarship, we need specialists who also are generalists—generally cultivated human beings, not just good plumbers. We need truly educated human beings who can perform their special tasks better precisely because they have general cultivation as well as intensely specialized training.

Changes indeed are needed in higher education, but those improvements cannot reasonably be expected unless improvement in basic schooling makes that possible.

The Future of Our Free Institutions

I already have declared as emphatically as I know how that the quality of human life in our society depends on the quality of the schooling we give our young people, both basic and advanced. But a marked elevation in the quality of human life is not the only reason improving the quality of schooling is so necessary—not the only reason we must move heaven and earth to stop the deterioration of our schools and turn them in the opposite direction. The other reason is to safeguard the future of our free institutions.

They cannot prosper, they may not even survive, unless we do something to rescue our schools from their current deplorable deterioration. Democracy, in the full sense of that term, came into existence only in this century and only in a few countries on earth, among which the United States is an outstanding example. But democracy came into existence in this century, only in its initial conditions, all of which hold out promises for the future that remain to be fulfilled. Unless we do something about improving the quality of basic schooling for all and the quality of advanced schooling for some, there is little chance that those promises ever will be fulfilled. And if they are not, our free institutions are doomed to decay and wither away.

We face many insistently urgent problems. Our prosperity and even our survival depend on the solution of those problems—the threat of nuclear war, the exhaustion of essential resources and of supplies of energy, the pollution or spoilage of the environment, the spiraling of inflation accompanied by the spread of unemployment.

To solve these problems, we need resourceful and innovative leadership. For that to arise and be effective, an educated populace is needed. Trained intelligence—not only on the part of leaders, but also on the part of followers—holds the key to the solution of the problems our society faces. Achieving peace, prosperity, and plenty could put us on the threshold of an early paradise. But a much better educational system than now exists also is needed, for that alone can carry us across the threshold. Without it, a poorly schooled population will not be able to put to good use the opportunities afforded by the achievement of the general welfare. Those who are not schooled to enjoy society can only despoil its institutions and corrupt themselves.

MORTIMER J. ADLER (1902–2001) taught philosophy at the University of Chicago, served on the board of the *Encyclopedia Britannica,* founded the Aspen Institute, and coedited *The Great Books of the Western World.*

John Holt

 NO

Escape from Childhood

Young people should have the right to control and direct their own learning, that is, to decide what they want to learn, and when, where, how, how much, how fast, and with what help they want to learn it. To be still more specific, I want them to have the right to decide if, when, how much, and by whom they want to be *taught* and the right to decide whether they want to learn in a school and if so which one and for how much of the time.

No human right, except the right to life itself, is more fundamental than this. A person's freedom of learning is part of his freedom of thought, even more basic than his freedom of speech. If we take from someone his right to decide what he will be curious about, we destroy his freedom of thought. We say, in effect, you must think not about what interests and concerns you, but about what interests and concerns *us*.

We might call this the right of curiosity, the right to ask whatever questions are most important to us. As adults, we assume that we have the right to decide what does or does not interest us, what we will look into and what we will leave alone. We take this right for granted, cannot imagine that it might be taken away from us. Indeed, as far as I know, it has never been written into any body of law. Even the writers of our Constitution did not mention it. They thought it was enough to guarantee citizens the freedom of speech and the freedom to spread their ideas as widely as they wished and could. It did not occur to them that even the most tyrannical government would try to control people's minds, what they thought and knew. That idea was to come later, under the benevolent guise of compulsory universal education.

This right to each of us to control our own learning is now in danger. When we put into our laws the highly authoritarian notion that someone should and could decide what all young people were to learn and, beyond that, could do whatever might seem necessary (which now includes dosing them with drugs) to compel them to learn it, we took a long step down a very steep and dangerous path. The requirement that a child go to school, for about six hours a day, 180 days a year, for about ten years, whether or not he learns anything there, whether or not he already knows it or could learn it faster or better somewhere else, is such gross violation of civil liberties that few adults would stand for it. But the child who resists is treated as a criminal. With this requirement we created an industry, an army of people whose whole work was to tell young people what they had to learn and to try to make them learn it. Some of these people, wanting to exercise even more power over others, to be even more "helpful," or simply because the industry is not growing fast enough to hold all the people who want to get into it, are now beginning to say, "If it is good for children for us to decide what they shall learn and to make them learn it, why wouldn't it be good for everyone? If compulsory education is a good thing, how can there be too much of it? Why should we allow anyone, of any age, to decide that he has had enough of it? Why should we allow older people, any more than young, not to know what we know when their ignorance may have bad consequences for all of us? Why should we not *make* them know what they *ought* to know?"

They are beginning to talk, as one man did on a nationwide TV show, about "womb-to-tomb" schooling. If hours of homework every night are good for the young, why wouldn't they be good for us all—they would keep us away from the TV set and other frivolous pursuits. Some group of experts, somewhere, would be glad to decide what we all ought to know and then every so often check up on us to make sure we knew it—with, of course, appropriate penalties if we did not.

I am very serious in saying that I think this is coming unless we prepare against it and take steps to prevent it. The right I ask for the young is a right that I want to preserve for the rest of us, the right *to decide what goes into our minds*. This is much more than the right to decide whether or when or how much to go to school or what school you want to go to. That right is important, but it is only part of a much larger and more fundamental right, which I might call the right to Learn, as opposed to being Educated, *i.e.*, made to learn what someone else thinks would be good for you. It is not just compulsory schooling but compulsory Education that I oppose and want to do away with.

That children might have the control of their own learning, including the right to decide if, when, how much, and where they wanted to go to school, frightens and angers many people. They ask me, "Are you saying that if the parents wanted the child to go to school, and the child didn't want to go, that he wouldn't have to go? Are you saying that if the parents wanted the child to go to one school, and the child wanted to go to another, that the child would have the right to decide?" Yes, that is what I say. Some people ask, "If school wasn't compulsory, wouldn't many parents take their children out of school to exploit their labors in one way or another?" Such questions are often both snobbish and hypocritical. The questioner assumes and implies (though rarely says) that these bad parents are people poorer and less schooled than he. Also, though he appears to be defending the right of children to go to school, what he really is defending is the right of the state to compel them to go whether they want to or not. What he wants, in short, is that children should be in school, not that they should have any choice about going.

But saying that children should have the right to choose to go or not to go to school does not mean that the ideas and wishes of the parents would have no weight. Unless he is estranged from his parents and rebelling against them, a child cares very much about what they think and want. Most of the time, he doesn't want to anger or worry or disappoint them. Right now, in families where the parents feel that they have some choice about their children's schooling, there is much bargaining about schools. Such parents, when their children are little, often ask them whether they want to go to nursery school or kindergarten. Or they may take them to school for a while to try it out. Or, if they have a choice of schools, they may take them to several to see which they think they will like the best. Later, they care whether the child likes his school. If he does not, they try to do something about it, get him out of it, find a school he will like.

I know some parents who for years had a running bargain with their children. "If on a given day you just can't stand the thought of school, you don't feel well, you are afraid of something that may happen, you have something of your own that you very much want to do—well, you can stay home." Needless to say, the schools, with their supporting experts, fight it with all their might— Don't Give in to Your Child, Make Him Go to School, He's Got to Learn. Some parents, when their own plans make it possible for them to take an interesting trip, take their children with them. They don't ask the schools' permission, they just go. If the child doesn't want to make the trip and would rather stay in school, they work out a way for him to do that. Some parents, when their child is frightened, unhappy, and suffering in school, as many children are, just take him out. Hal Bennett, in his excellent book *No More Public School,* talks about ways to do this.

A friend of mine told me that when her boy was in third grade, he had a bad teacher, bullying, contemptuous, sarcastic, cruel. Many of the class switched to another section, but this eight-year-old, being tough, defiant, and stubborn, hung on. One day—his parents did not learn this until about two years later—having had enough of the teacher's meanness, he just got up from his desk and without saying a word, walked out of the room and went home. But for all his toughness and resiliency of spirit, the experience was hard on him. He grew more timid and quarrelsome, less outgoing and confident. He lost his ordinary good humor. Even his handwriting began to go to pieces—it was much worse in the spring of the school year

than in the previous fall. One spring day he sat at breakfast, eating his cereal. After a while he stopped eating and sat silently thinking about the day ahead. His eyes filled up with tears, and two big ones slowly rolled down his cheeks. His mother, who ordinarily stays out of the school life of her children, saw this and knew what it was about. "Listen," she said to him, "we don't have to go on with this. If you've had enough of that teacher, if she's making school so bad for you that you don't want to go any more, I'll be perfectly happy just to pull you right out. We can manage it. Just say the word." He was horrified and indignant. "No!" he said, "I couldn't do that." "Okay," she said, "whatever you want is fine. Just let me know." And so they left it. He had decided that he was going to tough it out, and he did. But I am sure knowing that he had the support of his mother and the chance to give it up if it got too much for him gave him the strength he needed to go on.

To say that children should have the right to control and direct their own learning, to go to school or not as they choose, does not mean that the law would forbid the parents to express an opinion or wish or strong desire on the matter. It only means that if their natural authority is not strong enough the parents can't call in the cops to make the child do what they are not able to persuade him to do. And the law may say that there is no limit to the amount of pressure or coercion the parents can apply to the child to deny him a choice that he has a legal right to make.

When I urge that children should control their learning, there is one argument that people bring up so often that I feel I must anticipate and meet it here. It says that schools are a place where children can for a while be protected against the bad influences of the world outside, particularly from its greed, dishonesty, and commercialism. It says that in school children may have a glimpse of a higher way of life, of people acting from other and better motives than greed and fear. People say, "We know that society is bad enough as it is and that if children go out into the larger world as soon as they wanted, they would be tempted and corrupted just that much sooner."

They seem to believe that schools are better, more honorable places than the world outside—what a friend of mine at Harvard once called "museums of virtue." Or that people in school, both children and adults, act from higher and better motives than people outside. In this they are mistaken. There are, of course, some good schools. But on the whole, far from being the opposite of, or an antidote to, the world outside, with all its envy, fear, greed, and obsessive competitiveness, the schools are very much like it. If anything, they are worse, a terrible, abstract, simplified caricature of it. In the world outside the school, some work, at least, is done honestly and well, for its own sake, not just to get ahead of others; people are not everywhere and always being set in competition against each other; people are not (or not yet) in every minute of their lives subject to the arbitrary, irrevocable orders and judgement of others. But in most schools, a student is every minute doing what others tell him, subject to their judgement, in situations in which he can only win at the expense of other students.

This is a harsh judgement. Let me say again, as I have before, that schools are worse than most of the people in them and that many of these people do many harmful things they would rather not do, and a great many other harmful things that they do not even see as harmful. The whole of school is much worse than the sum of its parts. There are very few people in the U.S. today (or perhaps anywhere, any time) in *any* occupation, who could be trusted with the kind of power that schools give most teachers over their students. Schools seem to me among the most anti-democratic, most authoritarian, most destructive, and most dangerous institutions of modern society. No other institution does more harm or more lasting harm to more people or destroys so much of their curiosity, independence, trust, dignity, and sense of identity and worth. Even quite kindly schools are inhibited and corrupted by the knowledge of children and teachers alike that they are *performing* for the judgement and approval of others—the children for the teachers; the teachers for the parents, supervisors, school board, or the state. No one is ever free from feeling that he is being judged all the time, or soon may be. Even after the best class experiences teachers must ask themselves, "Were we right to do that? Can we prove we were right? Will it get us in trouble?"

What corrupts the school, and makes it so much worse than most of the people in it, or than they would like it to be, is its power—just as their powerlessness corrupts the students. The school is corrupted by the endless anxious demand of the parents to know how their child is doing—meaning is he ahead of the other kids—and their demand that he be kept ahead. Schools do not protect children from the badness of the world outside. They are at least as bad as the world outside, and the harm they do to the children in their power creates much of the badness of the world outside. The sickness of the modern world is in many ways a school-induced sickness. It is in school that most people learn to expect and accept that some expert can always place them in some sort of rank or hierarchy. It is in school that we meet, become used to, and learn to believe in the totally controlled society. We do not learn much science, but we learn to worship "scientists" and to believe that anything we might conceivably need or want can only come, and someday will come, from them. The school is the closest we have yet been able to come to Huxley's *Brave New World*, with its alphas and betas, deltas and epsilons—and now it even has its soma. Everyone, including children, should have the right to say "No!" to it.

JOHN HOLT (1923–1985) was an educator and a critic of public schooling who authored several influential books on education and promoted homeschooling.

EXPLORING THE ISSUE

Should the Curriculum Be Standardized for All?

Critical Thinking and Reflection

1. Is the Paideia Curriculum a feasible choice for public schools? If so, how would it be implemented for all students?
2. Do John Holt's educational views address the question of standardized curriculum?
3. How would a teacher or principal fully address the question of public educational systems need for or against a standardized curriculum?
4. Should young people have the right to choose and direct their own learning and are they really knowledgeable enough to be making those choices?
5. What is the nexus between standardized curriculum and the Common Core State Standards?

Is There Common Ground?

The free/open school movement values small, personalized educational settings in which students engage in activities that have personal meaning. One of the movement's ideological assumptions, emanating from the philosophy of Jean-Jacques Rousseau, is that given a reasonably unrestrictive atmosphere, the learner will pursue avenues of creative and intellectual self-development. This confidence in self-motivation is the cornerstone of Holt's advocacy of freedom for the learner, a position he elaborates upon in his books *Instead of Education* (1988) and *Teach Your Own* (1982). The argument has gained some potency with recent developments in home-based computer-assisted instruction.

Adler's proposal for a unified curricular and methodological approach, released in 1982 by the Institute for Philosophical Research, was fashioned by a group of distinguished scholars and practitioners and has its roots in such earlier works as Arthur Bestor's *Educational Wastelands* (1953), Mortimer Smith's *The Diminished Mind* (1954), and Paul Copperman's *The Literacy Hoax* (1978). The proposal has been widely discussed since its release, and it has been implemented in a number of school systems. See, for example, "Launching Paideia in Chattanooga," by Cynthia M. Gettys and Anne Wheelock, *Educational Leadership* (September 1994) and Terry Roberts and Audrey Trainor, "Performing for Yourself and Others: The Paideia Coached Project," *Phi Delta Kappan* (March 2004).

Holt's plea for freedom from an imposed curriculum has a champion in John Taylor Gatto, New York City and New York State Teacher of the Year. Gatto has produced two provocative books, *Dumbing Us Down: The Hidden Curriculum of Compulsory Schooling* (1992) and *Confederacy of Dunces: The Tyranny of Compulsory Schooling* (1992). Two other works that build upon Holt's basic views are Lewis J. Perelman's *School's Out: The New Technology and the End of Education* (1992) and George Leonard's "Notes: The End of School," *The Atlantic Monthly* (May 1992).

Create Central

www.mhhe.com/createcentral

Additional Resources

John Berlau, "What Happened to the Great Ideas?" *Insight on the News* (August 27, 2001)

Elliott W. Eisner, "The Kind of Schools We Need," *Phi Delta Kappan* (April 2002)

Alfie Kohn, "One-Size-Fits-All Education Doesn't Work," *The Boston Globe* (June 10, 2001)

Susan Ohanian, *Caught in the Middle: Nonstandard Kids and a Killing Curriculum* (2001)

Terry Roberts and Laura Billings, "Thinking Is Literacy, Literacy Thinking," *Educational Leadership* (February 2008)

Internet References . . .

Differentiate, Don't Standardize

www.edweek.org/ew
/articles/2010/01/14/17noddings-comm.h29.html

On Creating Robots: Standardized Curriculum

http://dreamsofeducation.wordpress.com/2010/04/15
/on-creating-robots-standardized-curriculum/

One Standard Fits All

www.usnews.com/education/articles/2007/11/02
/national-standards

Narratives on Culturally Relevant Pedagogy: Personal Responses to the Standardized Curriculum

http://cie.asu.edu/volume8/number22/

Should the Curriculum be Standardized for All?

http://ewhughes.wordpress.com/2010/02/13
/should-the-curriculum-be-standardized-for-all/

Selected, Edited, and with Issue Framing Material by:
Glenn L. Koonce, *Regent University*

ISSUE

Should Behaviorism Shape Educational Practices?

YES: **Carson M. Bennett**, from "A Skinnerian View of Human Freedom," *The Humanist* (July/August 1990)

NO: **Laura Zucca-Scott**, from "Know Thyself: The Importance of Humanism in Education," *International Education* (2010)

Learning Outcomes

After reading this issue, you will be able to:

- Explore the enormous strides that have been and are being made in modern psychological science and many other forces in modern life as well, that view man is not free, that he is controlled with no significant meaning, purpose, choice, or commitment.
- Appraise that self-understanding and responsible choice make a sharp and measurable difference in the behavior of an individual.
- Distinguish the different elements of behaviorism and humanism as they relate to educational practices.
- Determine the most productive theory behaviorism or humanism, for the future of education.
- Compare and contrast that different types of teaching make very different assumptions about what learning is.

ISSUE SUMMARY

YES: Professor of educational psychology Carson M. Bennett presents the case for adopting the radical behaviorism of B. F. Skinner to improve the power and efficiency of the process of learning.

NO: Laura Zucca-Scott, Professor of Education at Blackburn College, stresses the importance of humanism in today's educational practices.

Intimately enmeshed with considerations of aims, purposes, and determination of curricular elements are the psychological base that affects the total setting in which learning takes place and the basic means of motivating learners. Historically, the atmosphere of schooling has often been characterized by harsh discipline, regimentation, and restriction. The prison metaphor often used by critics in describing school conditions rings true all too often.

Although calls to make schools pleasant have been sounded frequently, they have seldomly been heeded. Roman rhetorician Marcus Fabius Quintilian (ca. AD 35–100) advocated a constructive and enjoyable learning atmosphere. John Amos Comenius in the seventeenth century suggested a gardening metaphor in which learners were given kindly nurturance. Johann Heinrich Pestalozzi established a model school in the nineteenth century that replaced authoritarianism with love and respect.

Yet school, as an institution, retains the stigma of authoritarian control—attendance is compelled, social and psychological punishment is meted out, and the decision-making freedom of students is limited and often curtailed. These practices lead to rather obvious conclusions: the prevailing belief is either that young people are naturally evil and wild, therefore, must be tamed in a restricting environment, or that schooling as such is so unpalatable that people must be forced and cajoled to reap its benefits—or both.

Certainly, philosopher John Dewey (1895–1952) was concerned about this circumstance, citing at one time the superintendent of his native Burlington, Vermont, school district as admitting that the schools were a source of "grief and mortification" and were "unworthy of patronage." Dewey rejected both the need for "taming" and the defeatist attitude that the school environment must remain unappealing. He hoped to create a motivational atmosphere that would engage learners in real problem-solving activities, thereby sustaining curiosity, creativity, and attachment. The rewards were to flow from the sense of accomplishment and freedom, which was to be achieved through the disciplined actions necessary to solve the problem at hand.

More recent treatment of the allied issues of freedom, control, and motivation has come from the two major camps in the field of educational psychology: the behaviorists (rooted in the early twentieth-century theories of Ivan Pavlov, Edward L. Thorndike, and John B. Watson) and the humanists (emanating from the Gestalt and field theory psychologies developed in Europe and America earlier in the twentieth century).

B. F. Skinner has been the dominant force in translating behaviorism into recommendations for school practices. He and his disciples, often referred to as "neobehaviorists," have contributed to widely used innovations such as behavioral objectives in instruction and testing, competency-based education, mastery learning, assertive discipline, and outcome-based education. The humanistic viewpoint has been championed by Carl R. Rogers, Abraham Maslow, Fritz Perls, Rollo May, and Erich Fromm, most of whom ground their psychological theories in the philosophical assumptions of existentialism and phenomenology.

Skinner believes that "inner" states are merely convenient myths and that motives and behaviors are shaped by environmental factors. These shaping forces, however, need not be negative, nor must they operate in an uncontrolled manner. Our present understanding of human behavior allows us the freedom to shape the environmental forces, which in turn shape us. With this power, Skinner contends, we can replace aversive controls in schooling with positive reinforcements that heighten the students' motivation level and make learning more efficient.

Recent manifestations of the continuing interest in Skinner's behaviorism and the humanistic psychology of Rogers include Virginia Richardson's "From Behaviorism to Constructivism in Teacher Education," *Teacher Education and Special Education* (Summer 1996) and Tobin Hart's "From Category to Contact: Epistemology and the Enlivening," "Deadening of Spirit in Education," *Journal of Humanistic Education and Development* (September 1997), and "Learning in Education" by Stanton Wortham, *University of Pennsylvania Scholarly Commons* (2003).

In the YES selection, Carson M. Bennett renews Skinner's call for greater attention to the external forces that shape all behavior. In the NO selection, Laura Zucca-Scott states that only through a humanistic approach can educational choices be feasible when goals and benchmarks arc part of a flexible system in which variations and individual differences are to be expected and encouraged.

YES ⬅

Carson M. Bennett

A Skinnerian View of Human Freedom

Without question, human freedom must be preserved and extended. The question is: what is the nature of this freedom? In his highly controversial (and misunderstood) book, *Beyond Freedom and Dignity,* B.F. Skinner criticized the traditional view of freedom as the ability to make choices which are not controlled by highly aversive stimuli. In his view, the "literature of freedom" has not dealt effectively with techniques that "do not breed escape or revolt but nevertheless have aversive consequences." These "positive" control techniques have traditionally been overlooked because they are less conspicuous. Skinner's discussion of government control provides a good example. We are keenly aware of negative government controls; as Skinner observes, the state "is frequently defined in terms of its power to punish." However, when a positive control technique is used by the state—such as paying farmers to reduce production—it is viewed as an *invitation,* not a *compulsion.* Positive controls are difficult to resist because they frequently masquerade as something else—for example, benefits. But they influence behavior just as effectively (sometimes much more so) as compulsory, negative controls.

Skinner also points out that freedom has mistakenly been defined "in terms of states of mind or feelings." This directs our attention away from the *actions* necessary to counteract subtle positive controls on our behavior. In the behavioral view, freedom is maintained or lost as the result of environmental changes which enlarge or limit the arena of possible actions, not as a result of changes in the hearts and minds of humans.

The traditional view of human freedom is grounded in custom and in the experience of choice. The powerful awareness of our thoughts and feelings at the moment of choice leads us to assume that those thoughts and feelings—rather than environmental influences—are the generators of our actions. Many of these experiences are highly rewarding and give us a feeling of mastery, an integral part of the experience of freedom. Our language is replete with words that describe the mental and emotional states which we are taught to believe generate our actions. Religions which posit a soul as an internal governing agent support this interpretation; psychology substitutes the "ego" or the "self" for the soul. But what we really experience as freedom is the opportunity and ability to behave in ways that produce rewards and avoid punishments, *not* the absence of environmental controls on our behavior.

The traditional view of freedom is hard to defend on logical and empirical grounds. It also decreases our ability to respond effectively to serious social problems because it causes us to look in the wrong place for the causes of behavior—at psychological factors rather than at observable and measurable environmental and genetic influences. This has prevented the development of a science of behavior providing the basis for a set of effective personal and social changes. We have also confused the issue of responsibility by crediting or blaming individuals for behaviors which are the result of past and present environmental influences. The radical behavioral viewpoint developed by B.F. Skinner presents a different view of the control of behavior. It is an effective framework for personal and social change and is compatible with the protection of individual freedoms.

In Skinner's radical behavioral view of freedom, *all* behavior is determined by the interaction of past and present environmental influences. As philosopher Brand Blanshard observes in his essay "The Case for Determinism," we cannot "choose our choice" even though we can choose one *behavior* over another. *Choices* are determined by the interaction of environmental and genetic influences. When we choose a specific behavior over a number of possible alternatives, it is likely that the chosen behavior has been rewarded more often in the past than any of the alternatives. In "avoidance" situations, the chosen behavior has most likely resulted in negative consequences less often than any of the available alternatives.

For example, picture a man walking through a supposedly empty cemetery at midnight. A prankster hiding behind a large headstone lets out an unexpected and unnerving moan. The man bursts into a run, and does not stop until he has sprinted out of the cemetery. An *ABC* behavioral analysis of this situation provides an interesting contrast with an analysis based on the traditional view of human freedom. *A* is the *Antecedent event:* the unexpected and unnerving groan in a supposedly empty cemetery. *B* is the *Behavior:* the man runs away. *C* is the *Consequence:* the man has escaped from a frightening situation. In this *ABC* analysis, thoughts and feelings *accompany* rather than *generate* behavior. They are as much shaped by the environment as the observable behavior is. In reality, the man does not run from the cemetery because he is scared; properly understood, the groan triggers his behavior—the action to avoid an aversive situation by running. (In our terms, escaping the aversive situation is the "reward.") The feelings of panicked fright result from the same environmental influence—the groan—as did the observable behavior (his hasty departure from the cemetery). An important advantage of looking in the environment for the causes of behavior is that unprofitable circular reasoning is avoided. (Why did the man run? Because he was scared. How do we know he was scared? Because he ran.) Of course, internal neurological and psychological factors influence behavior as well and should be taken into account when they are able to be observed and measured.

We feel free in situations in which our behavior is controlled by positive events (rewards) because this gives us a feeling of mastery. We are not as likely to feel free when our behavior is controlled by aversive stimuli. For example, we feel free when we are on vacation, engaging in highly rewarding activities. We may not feel free when meeting an unpleasant responsibility at work which we regard as an imposition. Our behavior, however, is *equally* under environmental control whether that control is positive or negative. This constant environmental control raises an important question, namely how can behavior be controlled in ethical ways? Control is ethical if it is agreed to by the individual or his or her parent or guardian *and* if it is in the best interest of the individual, *not* just in the interest or convenience of the controlling individual or institution. All relationships involve control and counter-control. "Powerless" groups such as children, the poor, the elderly, minority groups, and mental patients need to be helped to achieve more counter-control.

Why has the traditional view of human freedom persisted? There are many reasons. Most of the words we use in thinking describe the traditional view. The behavioral view seems both to threaten freedom and to contradict common sense. We appear to feel and think first and act second.

A number of factors contribute to this misunderstanding of freedom. It is rewarding to believe that our behavior can be free of any control except our thoughts and feelings. We think we are, as A.E. Henley's poem *Invictus* has it, the masters of our fate and captains of our soul. This is heady stuff! Moreover, when we make a choice, our attention is often directed toward the immediate (short-term) consequences of the act, not toward the past where the choice was shaped or the long-term consequences. For example, when a person buys an expensive sports car that is much more lavish than they really need or can afford, they are usually thinking about the immediate pleasures of owning such a fancy car, not reflecting on the past where their self-indulgent behavior was shaped or the long-term demands of making hefty car payments.

Finally, environmental influences are usually complex and subtle and thus difficult to detect. When we act, we are strongly aware of our thoughts and feelings and thus attribute our behavior to these things.

Skinner's radical behavioral view of freedom has frequently been misinterpreted. It is often confused with John Watson's earlier version of behaviorism, in which the role of consciousness was neglected, genetic influences were minimized, and learning occurred through Pavlovian conditioning. It is also often misunderstood as being inimical to freedom. Many people wonder if Skinner's approach would make a hash of the concept of personal responsibility. It would not. Society could continue to assign personal responsibility when needed. A distinction needs to be made between *personal* and *legal* responsibility. Individuals should be held responsible for illegal activities and accept the consequences. However, the assignment of *legal* responsibility should be tempered by a recognition of the need to help individuals change their environment. Responsibility—defined as the ability to and habit of considering the short- and long-term consequences of one's actions for oneself and others—should be taught both at home and at school.

What kind of social and personal gains would result if we adopted the radical behavioral viewpoint? For one thing, by looking for the determinants of behavior in the environment—where they are amenable to observation and change—we can control behavior more effectively. It seems clear, in retrospect, that many effective programs for social change have unknowingly used a radical behavioral approach. For example, attempts to reduce discriminatory behavior against minority groups by changing people's attitudes have been largely unsuccessful. Significant change occurred with the passage of civil rights legislation on education, housing, and employment. These provided a legislative and judicial system of rewards and punishments with which to control discriminatory behavior. This allowed individuals who *behaved* in nondiscriminatory ways to develop matching attitudes over time. For example, prejudiced students in desegregated schools frequently develop friendships with blacks. As behavior changes, so do the attitudes which *accompany* it.

Efforts to address the substantial underachievement of children in the lower socioeconomic class have been hampered by our tendency to look for the causes of underachievement in some personality defect of the children or their parents. In contrast, successful early childhood compensatory programs such as Head Start focused on specific environmental changes for children (for example, in learning materials and teaching methods), as well as on training parents how to change their home environment to increase achievement.

Many problems of the elderly could be addressed by designing environments which would compensate for their declining physical or intellectual resources. For example, approaches to adult education could be designed to compensate for the decline in old age of the ability to remember recently learned material.

By adopting the radical behavioral viewpoint, we would also avoid the pitfalls attendant upon our unwarranted and unproductive assignments of blame or credit. According to Skinner, "Any evidence that a person's behavior may be attributed to external circumstances seems to threaten his dignity or worth." He notes that the amount of credit a person receives is inversely related to the conspicuousness of the controlling factors. A speaker who is skilled in using a teleprompter may be given credit for extemporizing rather than reading well.

In *What Is B.F. Skinner Really Saying?*, behaviorist Robert D. Nye argues that even if we assume that "individuals are responsible for their behaviors" and thus "assigning blame for objectionable actions is justified, it doesn't consistently work well and it causes ill feelings." He suggests that when someone does something wrong, we should look at what is wrong with the environment, not what is wrong with the person.

The pitfalls of assigning unwarranted blame or credit have been addressed by writers as disparate as George Will and Nicholas von Hoffman. Will, in arguing for taxes as "a social obligation of the honorable," states, "Generally, people prosper, and pay more taxes, because of reasons for which they cannot claim responsibility." Von Hoffman characterizes "will power" as a "hard doctrine" because it leads to such "barbarously harsh" outcomes as sick people blaming themselves for their failure to get better.

Our society is fond of blaming the victim, such as the homeless or the welfare recipient. Society can help such victims by providing supportive environmental changes rather than by exhorting them to display more character or backbone. The assignment of exclusive personal credit or blame is both inappropriate and unproductive. This does not diminish the importance of frequently and consistently rewarding desirable behavior, but rewards should focus on the worth and skill of the *performance* to avoid the credit/blame pitfall.

Finally, by adopting the radical behavioral viewpoint, we would increase the effectiveness of behavioral controls by taking long-term consequences into consideration. Skinner has criticized our society for failing to teach its citizens to respond to the long-term as well as the short-term consequences of their actions. This limits our ability to respond adequately to many personal and social problems, such as poor health practices, environmental pollution, and the overconsumption of nonrenewable energy resources. On a personal level, overeating provides a good example of the failure to consider long-term consequences. The attractions of overeating—the pleasures of taste and the feelings of satiety and relaxation that accompany digestion—are short-term and immediately apparent; the negative consequences—increased potential for high blood pressure and heart attacks, decreased mobility, social and personal disapproval stemming from a less desirable appearance, and so on—are long-term and frequently ignored. There are also examples where the short-term consequences are negative and the long-term consequences are positive. A student will reluctantly forego the pleasures of an active social life and attend to the short-term unpleasant requirements of study in order to achieve the long-term

benefits of better grades, a more rewarding education, and a better start on his or her career.

Consider as well the impact of this view on the intimate relationships we have with our close friends and lovers. At the beginning of a romance, we shower the other person with strong rewards for almost every action. Subsequently, we reward less and less often. The other person frequently interprets this as rejection and responds negatively. The honeymoon is over! It should have been recognized from the start that one person cannot provide all the necessary social rewards for another and that individuals will want to maintain more than one relationship. Some people are offended by the notion that friendship can be reduced to the mutual exchange of positive rewards. Many readers reacted negatively to the comment made by behavioral engineer T.E. Frazier in *Walden Two*, Skinner's description of a behavioral utopia: "What is love except another name for the use of positive reinforcement?" But, as Nye has pointed out, relationships can be explained in large part in this manner.

Implementation of the radical behavioral viewpoint could increase our personal and social power and deepen our experience of freedom. It is difficult for many individuals to accept that behavioral determinism and human freedom are not contradictory or mutually exclusive concepts. But, as Nye observes (and as Skinner himself has suggested), Skinner's assumptions do not change what actually exists: "Either we live in a wholly determined system or we do not." If we do, we are still capable of believing that we are free and that our behavior is meaningful. However, we are also capable of changing our environments to improve our behavior and increase our feeling of freedom. Consider the experience of the English scientist Sir Francis Galton, who kept track for some time of the occasions when he felt a sense of personal freedom while making important choices. Shortly afterward, he would look back on each episode to try to find constraints on his behavior which he had not noted at the time. Brand Blanshard reports in "The Case for Determinism" that Galton "found it so easy to bring such constraining factors to light that he surrendered to the determinist view."

Unfortunately, we continue to interpret behavior in terms of internal psychological causation and to be ineffective in personal and social change. As Nye has pointed out, newspaper and magazine editorials and articles are still full of comments such as "the darkness in man's soul that corrupts his best intentions," "the destructive tendencies hidden deep within the human psyche," "the failing American character that is bringing us to the edge of national disaster," "the lack of morality and will power among our citizens," and so on. Analyzing and changing our environments so that positive controls can be maximized and punitive and aversive controls minimized is hard, time-consuming work. It is quicker and easier to blame our behavioral problems on such ineffable or intangible factors as "moral deficiency" and "the darkness in man's soul." Indeed, most people—psychologists, priests, and the general public alike—continue to believe in some inner spark which guides our destiny, whether it is called the "ego," and "soul," or the "self."

Let us celebrate and preserve our freedom! But let us do so by analyzing and changing our environments to produce the kinds of behavior and the kind of society we want, instead of continuing to substitute empty rhetoric about "internal failings" for action.

Carson M. Bennett (1924–2010) was a Professor of Educational Psychology at Ball State University in Muncie, Indiana.

Laura Zucca-Scott   ➡ **NO**

Know Thyself: The Importance of Humanism in Education

Introduction

A Nation at Risk, No Child Left Behind, and Race to the Top have become familiar terminology in the United States' education field. Students in this country seem to struggle academically in many different ways. All these initiatives have the declared intent to "fix" whatever is wrong with education. Unfortunately, the issues in this field are hard to define and often become the center of heated debates and controversial proposals. Furthermore, deciding which educational practices are best suited to promote stronger academic performances is not easy. There are many approaches to education and infinite nuances within each approach. It appears that a common, general approach to support failing schools is to provide detailed, step-by-step, prescriptive instruction. Nevertheless, I contend that only a learner-centered, humanistic approach can provide an ideal learning environment for each and every student.

Views on Learning and Teaching

A basic assumption derived from the current literature and data is that students do not learn what they need to learn in school. Based on the statistics, illiteracy and high school dropout rates in the United States are alarming (Institute of Education Sciences, 2010; National Assessment of Literacy, 2010). Thus, there is a perceived need for instruction that is carefully planned with a very systematic structure and scripted lessons to ensure quality control. However, this approach, after almost a decade of No Child Left Behind (NCLB), has not produced the desired results. In fact, some data seem to suggest that such an approach may be counterproductive (Meier & Wood, 2004). By trying to simplify education and engineer it into a highly structured, mistake-proof endeavor, learners, as well as teachers, are denied their uniqueness and their own complexity as human beings.

Palmer (1997) maintains that teaching has three facets that cannot be overlooked. Of these three, the most relevant is that students are defined and shaped by their own complexity (p. 1). Of course, the complexity of the subject matter and the complexity of the teachers and mentors only add further richness to the overall picture. In Palmer's words, good teachers, the "weavers," do not follow the same instructional approaches (1997); on the contrary,

they often vary significantly in everything that defines their teaching methods. More specifically, "the methods used by these weavers vary widely: lectures, Socratic dialogues, laboratory experiments, collaborative problem-solving, creative chaos" (p. 3); all of the good teachers, however, share a common trait: they display a "capacity for connectedness" (Palmer, 1997).

Drawing upon my personal experiences as a student in the Italian school system, I remember experiencing this connectedness firsthand when my high school Latin teacher spent an extensive amount of time during his breaks to discuss Hemingway's prose with me. Although as a high school first-year student, I had not been exposed to much literary criticism, there I was engaged in academic dialogue with an adult about a subject that had nothing to do with the day's topic or the school curriculum. I have since forgotten many of my high school lessons, but I will never forget those conversations. Later on, as a teacher, I realized that I could truly teach the students only when I was able to relate to them as people. According to Palmer (1997), this is a form of teaching that transcends technique and comes from the heart, "meaning 'heart' in its ancient sense, the place where intellect and emotion and spirit will converge in the human self" (p. 3). In order for this teaching to be possible, teachers need to be able to make educational choices.

Educational Choices and Curricula

Educational choices are feasible when goals and benchmarks are part of a flexible system in which variations and individual differences are to be expected and encouraged. Kozol (2005, December) describes school curricula that emphasize scripted instruction and procedures where spontaneous student teacher interactions are absent. Furthermore, Kozol (2005) denounces vehemently the many systemic injustices children face in education. In his view, education, particularly for the poor and minority students, has become an indoctrination of lower-level abilities and skills, which, in the best-case scenario, will "prepare" students for low-paying, menial jobs. This indoctrination offers no room for individualized instruction, and often relegates the curricula to a list of benchmarks.

These curricula are very different from those of the Italian elementary school system, which utilizes the

Zucca-Scott, Laura (2010). Know Thyself: The Importance of Humanism in Education. *International Education*, vol. 40, no. 1. Retrieved from: http://trace.tennessee.edu/internationaleducation/vol40/iss1/4

"Programmi della Scuola Elementare document." This 1985 document is still current, and it is regarded as a conceptual framework in which benchmarks are only a reference point for educators. The main frame of reference could be regarded as a humanistic approach to teaching and learning. In particular, creativity is viewed as one of the pivotal elements for the development of young learners (Educazione e Scuola, 2009). For instance, the acquisition of reading and writing skills at a basic level is considered as a benchmark for the end of first grade, with the stipulation that these skills may develop throughout second grade. It must be noted that the Italian system does not include a kindergarten level; thus, first grade is the first step into formal, compulsory education. In this perspective, the guidelines delineated into the official elementary school curriculum are considered as an ongoing working document for educators, who will adapt their instruction to the individual needs of their students in light of the spirit of the document more so than any prescriptive model (Educazione e Scuola, 2009). The Italian Elementary School system has often been regarded as a successful model in the European Community despite the numerous, chronic structural and financial challenges the whole educational world faces. In fact, Italian elementary school students ranked first in Europe and fifth in the world in language arts (Società Italiana di Statistica, 2010). I suspect that these students' performances are not a coincidence, but that instead there is a direct correlation to the humanistic approach to education so deeply rooted in the Italian school system. For students to become successful, engaged learners, attention to their individuality and flexibility of curriculum design need to be the main focus.

Teachers As Key Players

Teachers become key participants in the learning process. As Palmer explains, teachers need to resume their traditional roles as mentors (1997). According to Ayers (2009), "Education in a democracy is geared toward and powered by a particularly precious and fragile ideal" (p. 31). This ideal is founded on the belief that every person possesses an "infinite and incalculable value" (Ayers, 2009). Based on this premise, the role of the educator becomes much more complex than that of simple transmitter of information.

I personally find troubling the perspectives on education implying that, given the right training, most educators should be able to deliver the same type of content in analogous fashion. By denying the uniqueness of the learners, as well as of the educators, we are utterly denying the values of civilizations that have deeply believed in the transforming power of knowledge as an internal process of growth and self-discovery, the "know thyself" of the Socratic tradition. We are also denying the power of education as an agent of change (Hohr, 2002; Plaut, 2010). As Ayers (2009) so eloquently explains, the pedagogy of

questioning is part of a concerted effort to liberate and humanize education (p. 32). Furthermore, Ayers (2009) advocates for the end of standardized testing that makes young individuals and their communities losers or winners based on questionable pseudo-scientific criteria. Standardization appears indeed to be a problematic aspect of educational practices.

The Standardization Quandary

Standardized tests are ubiquitous across the United States. Although their goal may appear to be the attainment of students' success and equal opportunities, the reality students and educators face is rather different. The term "high stakes testing" has become a buzzword in education. As Barrier-Ferreira (2007) explains:

> Because the stakes have reached disproportionate levels, educators are often forced to abandon all things unrelated to the test and consequently lose sight of what is important: the whole child, who is not simply composed of intellect but is emotional and spiritual as well. (p. 139)

Although Barrier-Ferreira (2008) appears to believe that standardized testing "will ensure that we do not lose focus of academic excellence (p. 140)," Dodge (2009) does not seem to share the same belief: "Generally, the question of whether standardized tests measure what matters is troublesome" (p. 12). Furthermore, the instruments used for standardized testing, on many occasions, have been plagued by serious validity and reliability issues. Thus, the measurements convey flawed information (Dodge, 2009, p. 9).

As Dodge (2009) makes his concluding remarks on the role of assessment in education, he maintains:

> What we have here is a failure to communicate. Those who believe that children need space and time and freedom to make mistakes, to exercise their imagination as well as their bodies, to grow in fits and starts and on their own timetables, and to be understood as the complex organisms they are, seem to be at odds with those who believe in packaging promoting, distributing, codifying and simplifying school assessments. (p. 13)

Another troubling aspect of standardized testing is the strong correlation between socio-economic status and standardized tests results; students from low socio-economic status score consistently lower on standardized tests. The measuring instrument does nothing to address or even highlight the rooted inequities that so greatly affect students' performances, including scarcity of financial and human resources (Dodge, 2009, pp. 10–11). On the contrary, students may be penalized in their education because of their backgrounds while they also suffer from societal inequalities. The value that the U.S. educational system places on standardized testing more and more looks like an elusive chimera.

Conversely, the Italian school system does not traditionally rely on standardized testing; although there are state exams, these are not, typically, fill-in-the-blank style tests. Students are required to write lengthy essays and demonstrate their critical thinking skills from an early age. Although Italy is moving toward standardization of education, there is vehement resistance to this approach, based on the humanistic tradition that is deeply rooted in the country. There is a widespread awareness that by standardizing responses, the uniqueness of the learning experience for each individual is denied. Also, a wrong-versus-right type of answer is often regarded as a refutation of the essential, and yet complex, facets of knowledge (Caianiello, 2010; Leggere, Scrivere e Far di Conto, 2010; Lupia, 2010; Pisa-Scuola Pubblica, 2010). Ultimately, deciding the type of assessments we want to see in our schools has deep implications for our educational systems and our societies as a whole.

A Call to Action: Looking Back, Looking Forward

It would be very tempting to blame others for the many difficulties educational systems encounter. Although societal issues should not be ignored and systemic injustices should be addressed as part of the plan for a democratic education, teachers at all levels should be encouraged to assume the role of leaders in their communities as they develop their mentorship roles. Parents and administrators should not fear teachers who challenge children to go beyond their limitations by exploring and questioning their world. On the other hand, teachers who are choosing the safe route and relying on the reassuring comfort of prescribed programs should seriously reconsider their roles and their motifs for teaching (Kozol, 2005; Ravitch, 2010). Plaut (2010) maintains that "our youth are truly free only when they are fully literate" (p. 1). In her definition, true literacy is empowering as it helps individuals become critical thinkers and involved citizens.

Educational quality is strongly intertwined with creating opportunities for all students to be themselves. Schools need to help students find out who they are and what their talents are as individuals. All students have talents; they just do not always have the opportunity to express those talents. When I was a green elementary school teacher in Italy, a young fourth grader started dancing during recess. This child was a very unengaged student most of the time, yet, all of a sudden, he showed an impressive level of skill and intensity. Once his talent became known to me, we established a new, deeper rapport that ultimately led to a stronger overall performance on his part. I have witnessed this miracle repeating itself many times. Every time a student ceases to be an unknown entity, develops as a person, and is recognized as such, that student suddenly becomes invested in his or her learning and begins to truly learn. If we deny that students have talents, or if we simply ignore their potential, we are not seeing the students for who they are or who they could be. Without connections, human beings feel alienated and rejected. Yet in many learning environments, we are often telling students they need to forget who they are and what they like because there is work to be done. And so what could be exciting becomes, instead, the epitome of boredom. Then we try to entertain students in order to make learning fun again. We throw candies to our students when they get the answers "right," or we promise them all kinds of rewards. And we forget that learning would have been fun to begin with if we had not stripped it of its original interest through the sheer excitement of discovery. When I decided to become a teacher, it was not without trepidation. I made an intentional decision that I would pledge all my energies and abilities to ensure that every human being, young or old, rich or poor, would have a chance to discover the inner richness of knowledge. This richness is connected with understanding the essence of the adventure of being human with all the possibilities and flaws, with all the heartbreaks and joys.

Conclusions and Recommendations

It is imperative we recognize that education is made by individuals for individuals, who bring with them unique gifts and inclinations (Palmer, 1997). However, this realization alone is not enough if we want to see the future generations flourish and thrive in creative, stimulating learning environments. We need to ensure that students feel supported in developing their talents and individualities by designing curricula that allow flexibility and freedom of intellectual exploration. Although benchmarks and goals are useful indicators of performance, they should not be envisioned as rigid parameters by which we must wholly abide. Furthermore, we should dedicate intensive efforts in recruiting teachers who are truly experts in their fields and who are excited about engaging in academic discourse with their students and colleagues. As Palmer (1997) states, teachers are successful if and when they are invested in their disciplines and excited by teaching and learning in a dynamic, holistic fashion. The humanistic approach relies on the teachers' ability to truly reinvigorate the "know thyself" motto even if it means that we need to rethink schooling as a whole.

References

Ayers, W. (2009). Teaching in and for democracy. *Kappa Delta Pi Record, 46*(1), 30–33.

Barrier-Ferreira, J. (2008). Producing commodities or educating children? Nurturing the personal growth of students in the face of standardized testing. *Clearing House: A Journal of Educa-*

tional Strategies, Issues and Ideas, 81(3), 138–140. Retrieved from ERIC database.

Caianiello, V. (2010). Tradizione e innovazione a scuola. Retrieved from http://www.emsf.rai.it/grillo /trasmissioni.asp?d=771.

Dodge, A. (2009). Heuristics and NCLB standardized tests: A convenient lie. International Journal of Progressive Education. Retrieved from ERIC database.

Educazione e Scuola (2009). I programmi della scuola elementare. Retrieved from http://www.edscuola.it /archivio/norme/programmi/elementare.html.

Hohr, H. (2002). Does beauty matter in education? Friedrich Schiller's neo-humanistic approach. *Journal of Curriculum Studies,* 34(1), 59–75.

Institute of Education Sciences: National Center for Education Statistics (2010). Fast Facts. Retrieved from http://nces.ed.gov/fastfacts/display.asp?id=16.

Kozol, J. (2005). *The shame of the nation: The restoration of apartheid schooling in America.* New York: Crown Publishers.

Kozol, J. (2005, December). School, resegregation and the pedagogy of poverty. *Phi Delta Kappan,* 87(4), 264–275.

Leggere, Scrivere e Far di Conto (2010). Retrieved from http://www.lastoriasiamonoi.rai.it/puntata. aspx?id=270.

Lupia, M.R. (2010). Una scuola sempre piu' attenta alle esigenze degli studenti ed ai processi formativi. Retrieved ay 31, 2010 from &sub_ id=126&ad_id=625 http://www.aspei.it/portale/adDetail .asp?cat_id=34&sub_id=126&ad_id=625.

Meier, D., & Wood, G. (Eds.). (2004). *Many children left behind: How the No Child Left Behind Act is damaging our children and our schools.* Boston: Beacon Press.

National Assessment of Literacy (2010) Retrieved from http://nces.ed.gov/naal/.

Palmer, P.J. (1997). The heart of a teacher: Identity and integrity in teaching. Retrieved from http://www .newhorizons.org/strategies/character/palmer.htm.

Pisa-Scuola Pubblica (2010). Retrieved from http:// www.infoaut.org/articolo/pisa-scuola-pubblicanon- assecondiamo-il-disastro.

Plaut, S. (Ed.). (2010). *The right to literacy in secondary schools: Creating a culture of thinking.* New York: Teachers College Press.

Ravitch, D. (2010). *The death and life of the great American school system.* New York: Basic Books.

Societa' Italiana di Statistica. *Il falso e il vero verde: La scuola italiana funziona.* Retrieved from http://www .sis-statistica.it/magazine/spip.php?articleI26.

Laura Zucca-Scott is a Professor at Blackburn College located in the Greater St. Louis area.

EXPLORING THE ISSUE

Should Behaviorism Shape Educational Practices?

Critical Thinking and Reflection

1. Have behaviorist practices been harder to overcome than behaviorist theory?
2. Discuss the humanistic view of teaching that transcends technique and comes from the heart?
3. What other theories of learning are there besides behaviorism and humanism?
4. What is the definition of education and how more complex accounts of learning and human nature are needed to guide education practice?
5. Is behaviorism more difficult to understand than humanism, why or why not?

Is There Common Ground?

The freedom–determinism or freedom–control argument has raged in philosophical, political, and psychological circles down through the ages. Is freedom of choice and action a central, perhaps the central, characteristic of being human? Or is freedom only an illusion, a refusal to acknowledge the external shaping of all human actions?

Moving the debate into the field of education, John Dewey depicted a developmental freedom that is acquired through improving one's ability to cope with problems. A. S. Neill (*Summerhill: A Radical Approach to Child Rearing,* 1984), who advanced the ideas of early-twentieth century progressive educators and the establishment of free schools, sees a more natural inborn freedom in human beings, which must be protected and allowed to flourish. Skinner refuses to recognize this "inner autonomous man," but sees freedom resulting from the scientific reshaping of the environment that influences us.

Just as Skinner has struggled to remove the stigma from the word control, arguing that it is the true gateway to freedom, John Holt, in *Freedom and Beyond* (1972), contends that freedom and free activities are not "unstructured." Indeed, the structure of an open classroom is vastly more complicated than the structure of a traditional classroom.

If both of these views have validity, then we are in a position, as Dewey counseled, to go beyond either/or polemics on these matters and build a more constructive educational atmosphere. Jerome S. Bruner has consistently suggested ways in which free inquiry and subject matter structure can be effectively blended. Arthur W. Combs, in a report titled, Humanistic Education: Objectives and Assessment (1978), helped to bridge the ideological gap between humanists and behaviorists by demonstrating that subjective outcomes can be assessed by direct or modified behavioral techniques. In addition, much can be learned about the ideological gap from international experiences and the classical tradition of both behaviorism and humanism.

Create Central

www.mhhe.com/createcentral

Additional Resources

J. Dewey, *Democracy and Education: An Introduction to the Philosophy of Education* (Simon & Schuster, 1997)

M. Loomis, *Building Teachers: A Constructivist Approach to Introducing Education*, 2nd ed. (Cengage Learning, 2014)

N. Noddings, *Philosophy of Education*, 3rd ed. (Perseus, 2011)

B. F. Skinner, B. F., *Science and Human Behavior* (The Macmillan Company, 1953)

S. Wortham, *Learning in Education* (Graduate School of Education Publications, 2003)

Internet References. . .

Constructivism as a Paradigm for Teaching and Learning

www.thirteen.org/edonline/concept2class/
constructivism/

Humanism as an Instructional Paradigm

www-distance.syr.edu/romira1.html

Should Behaviorism Shape Educational Practices (Prezi)

http://prezi.com/ue9fxctogutp/should-behaviorism-
shape-educational-practices/

Should Behaviorism Shape Educational Practices (U-Tube)

www.youtube.com/watch?v=ffweG557wm0

Should the Teacher Be the Controller?

www.google.com/url?sa=t&rct=j&q=&esrc=s&frm=
1&source=web&cd=6&cad=rja&ved=0CFoQFjAF&url
=http%3A%2F%2Frachieg1.tripod.com%2Fsitebuilder
content%2Fsitebuilderfiles%2Fphilosophypresentat
ion.ppt&ei=CXFxUqKtCcTgyQGz7lCAAw&usg=AFQj
CNEb36SZkQWhoJr5_v2eyXChhKQ7lw&sig2=lpdV5_
Bsa_M_VibhXnZHBw

Selected, Edited, and with Issue Framing Material by:
Glenn L. Koonce, *Regent University*

ISSUE

Is Constructivism the Best Philosophy of Education?

YES: **David Elkind**, from "The Problem with Constructivism," *The Educational Forum* (Summer 2004)

NO: **Jamin Carson**, from "Objectivism and Education: A Response to David Elkind's 'The Problem with Constructivism'," *The Educational Forum* (Spring 2005)

Learning Outcomes

After reading this issue, you will be able to:

- Compare and contrast constructivism and objectivism sphilosophies of education.
- Translate constructivism in education into a practical pedagogy.
- Explore how behaviorism views prior knowledge informing new, consequently making the new knowledge meaningful.
- Identify current practices in the classroom as constructivism, behaviorism or different philosophical orientation altogether.
- Analyze problems with a constructivism mindset.

ISSUE SUMMARY

YES: Child Development Professor David Elkind contends that the philosophical positions found in constructivism, though often difficult to apply, are necessary elements in a meaningful reform of educational practices.

NO: Jamin Carson, an Assistant Professor of Education and former high school teacher, offers a close critique of constructivism and argues that the philosophy of objectivism is a more realistic and usable basis for the process of education.

For years the term constructivism appeared only in journals read primarily by philosophers, epistemologists, and psychologists. Nowadays, constructivism regularly appears in the teacher's manuals of textbook series, state education department curriculum frameworks, education reform literature, and education journals. Constructivism now has a face and a name in education. So say educators Martin G. Brooks and Jacqueline Grennon Brooks in "The Courage to Be Constructivist," *Educational Leadership* (November 1999). According to them, the heart of the constructivist approach to education is that learners control their learning. This being the case, the philosophical orientation provided by John Dewey, John Holt, and Carl R. Rogers would seem to feed into the development of David Elkind's ideas on this educational theory. The contrary positions taken by Hutchins, Adler, and Skinner would seem to contribute to the objectivist philosophy espoused by Jamin Carson.

Constructivism, which is additionally influenced by the theories of Jean Piaget, Lev Vygotsky, and Jerome Bruner, is an approach to learning in which students construct new understandings through active engagement with their past and present experiences. Constructivists contend that traditional instructional models emphasize knowledge transmission without producing deeper levels of understanding and internalization.

Objectivists and other critics of constructivism say that this approach to learning is imprecise, overly permissive, and lacking in rigor. This argument is quite well-illustrated in a *Phi Delta Kappan* exchange between Lawrence A. Baines and Gregory Stanley on one hand and Lynn Chrenka on the other (Baines and Stanley, "We Want to See the Teacher: Constructivism and the Rage Against Expertise," in the December 2000 issue and Chrenka, "Misconstructing Constructivism," in the May 2001 issue). Baines and Stanley condemn the constructivists' adamant stand against direct instruction by lecturing and the sin of memorization. Chrenka replies that expertise is central in a constructivist classroom in which the teacher must develop "scaffolding strategies" needed for the learners to begin to construct their own meanings.

David N. Perkins of the Harvard Graduate School of Education, in "The Many Faces of Constructivism," *Educational Leadership* (November 1999), describes a tension between ideological constructivism and pragmatic constructionism, the former being seen as a rather rigid cure-all for traditional school ills and the latter as a flexible, circumstance-driven means of school improvement. While the constructivists' goal of producing active, collaborative, creative learners is certainly an antidote to the often prevalent emphasis on knowledge absorption by passive learners, the techniques for moving toward that goal are often difficult to implement and most always require more time than traditional methods.

These "theory-into-practice" difficulties have been elaborated upon by Mark Windschitl in "The Challenges of Sustaining a Constructivist Classroom Culture," *Phi Delta Kappan* (June 1999), and by Peter W. Airasian and Mary E. Walsh in "Constructivist Cautions," *Phi Delta Kappan* (February 1997). Windschitl sees constructivism as a culture, not a mere collection of practices, so its effectiveness as a guiding philosophy is realized only through major changes in curriculum, scheduling, and assessment. Airasian and Walsh insist that the "catch phrases" that flow from theorists to teachers are inadequate for dealing with implementation complexities.

These and similar concerns are addressed in the first of the following articles, in which constructivism advocate David Elkind examines three major barriers—societal, curricular, and pedagogical—that must be removed if the philosophy is to flourish in school settings. In the second article, Jamin Carson, an objectivist, attacks not only the practical aspects of constructivism's implementation but the very basic principles on which it is based.

YES ↩

David Elkind

The Problem with Constructivism

Constructivism, in all of its various incarnations, is now a major educational philosophy and pedagogy. What the various interpretations of constructivism have in common is the proposition that the child is an active participant in constructing reality and not just a passive recorder of it. Constructivism thus echoes the philosophy implicit in Rousseau's *Emile* (1962) in which he argued that children have their own ways of knowing and that these have to be valued and respected. It also reflects the Kantian (Kant 2002) resolution of the nature/nurture controversy. Kant argued that the mind provides the categories of knowing, while experience provides the content. Piaget (1950) created the contemporary version of constructivism by demonstrating that the categories of knowing, no less than the contents of knowledge, are constructed in the course of development. Vygotsky (1978) added the importance of social context to the constructivist epistemology—a theory of knowledge and knowledge acquisition.

Constructivism in education has been approached at many different levels and from a variety of perspectives (e.g., Larochelle, Bednarz, and Garrison 1998). In this essay, I will limit the discussion to those writers who have attempted to translate constructivism into a practical pedagogy (e.g., Brooks and Brooks 1993; Fosnot 1996; Gagnon and Collay 2001; Lambert et al. 1997). Though many different models have been created and put to test, none have been satisfactorily implemented. The failure of the constructivist reform movement is yet another in the long list of ill-fated educational reform movements (Gibboney 1994).

The inability to implement constructivist reforms is particularly instructive with regard to the failures of educational reforms in general. Constructivist reforms start from an epistemology. This sets constructivism apart from those educational reforms inspired by political events (such as the curriculum reform movement spurred by the Russian launching of the Sputnik) or by social events (such as the school reforms initiated by the Civil Rights Movement) or by a political agenda (e.g., *A Nation at Risk* [National Commission on Excellence in Education 1983]; the No Child Left Behind initiative). That is to say, the constructivist movement is generated by genuine pedagogical concerns and motivations.

The lack of success in implementing this widely accepted educational epistemology into the schools can be attributed to what might be called *failures of readiness*.

Consider three types of readiness: teacher readiness, curricular readiness, and societal readiness. Teacher readiness requires teachers who are child development specialists with curricular and instructional expertise. Curriculum readiness requires courses of study that have been researched as to what, when, and how the subject matter should be taught. Societal readiness requires a nation that is willing—indeed eager—to accept educational change. For a reform movement to succeed, all three forms of readiness must be in alignment.

Teacher Readiness

Those who have tried to implement a constructivist pedagogy often argue that their efforts are blocked by unsupportive teachers. They claim that some teachers are wedded to an objectivist view that knowledge has an independent existence and needs only to be transmitted. Others have difficulty understanding how to integrate the learner's intuitive conceptions into the learning process. Still others are good at getting children actively involved in projects but are not able to translate them effectively into learning objectives. These problems are aggravated by an increasingly test-driven curriculum with little opportunity for creativity and innovation.

The problem, however, is not primarily with teachers but with teacher training. In the United States, many universities and colleges have done away with the undergraduate major in education. In Massachusetts, for example, a student with a bachelor's degree in any field can get a provisional certification after a year of supervised internship. After five years and the attainment of a master's degree, the candidate is eligible for permanent certification.

The demise of the undergraduate major in education can be attributed to a number of different factors that were enunciated in *Tomorrow's Schools of Education* (Holmes Group 1995) written by the deans of 80 of some of the nation's most prestigious schools of education. The report (1995, 45–46) targeted the education faculty who "ignore public schools to concentrate on theoretical research or to work with graduate students who do not intend careers as classroom teachers." In effect, the education faculty has failed to provide the kind of research that would be useful to teachers. As the report (1995, 45–46) argued, "Traditional forms of academic scholarship have a place in professional schools, but such institutions are obliged as well to learn from practice and to concern themselves with questions

From *The Educational Forum*, vol. 68, Summer 2004, pp. 306–312. Copyright © 2004 by Kappa Delta Pi. Reprinted by permission.

of applying knowledge." These observations are supported by the facts. Few teachers read the educational research journals, and few educational researchers read the journals directed at teachers such as *Educational Leadership* and *Young Children*. This also is true for researchers in the field of child development. Much of the research on children's cognitive, social, and emotional development is directly relevant to teaching. Yet, the educational implications of these studies are rarely, if ever, discussed in the literature.

The end result is that much of teaching as a profession has to be learned in the field. While this is true for all professions to a certain extent, it is particularly true of education. Indeed, one could make the case that teaching is, as yet, more art than profession. Professional training implies a body of knowledge and skills that are unique and that can be acquired only through a prescribed course of study. It is not clear that such a body of knowledge and skills exists for education. In fact, each educational reform movement challenges the practices currently in play. Perhaps it is because there is no agreed upon body of knowledge and skills that reform in education is so frequent and so unsuccessful. To be sure, all professions have disagreements but they all share some fundamental common ground, whether it is anatomy in medicine or legal precedence in the field of law. There is, however, no such common base in education.

Teaching will become a true profession only when we have a genuine science of education. Such a science will have to be multidisciplinary and include workers from traditional educational psychology, developmental psychology, sociology, and various subject matter disciplines. Researchers would investigate individual and group differences in learning styles in relation to the acquisition of the various tool subjects (i.e., reading, writing, arithmetic, science, and social studies) at different age levels. Teacher training would provide not only a solid grounding in child development but also would require domain specific knowledge as it applies to young people at different age levels. Teachers also would be knowledgeable about research and would have access to journals that serve both teachers and investigators.

The failure to treat education as a profession has a long history but was made patent by Flexner's (1910) report *Medical Education in the United States and Canada*. That report was critical of medical education in the United States and suggested that training in medicine should be a graduate program with an undergraduate major. It also argued for the establishment of teaching hospitals as a means of practical training under supervision. Though the report was mandated by the Carnegie Foundation for the Advancement of Teaching, no comparable critique and suggestions were made for teachers and teacher training. The only innovation taken from this report was the founding of lab schools which would serve the same function as teaching hospitals at various universities. These schools, however, were more often used for research than for training. Today, only a few lab schools remain in operation.

Before any serious, effective reform in education can be introduced, we must first reinvent teacher training. At the very least, teachers should be trained as child development specialists. But teachers need much more. Particularly today, with the technological revolution in our schools, teacher training should be a graduate program. Even with that, teaching will not become a true profession unless and until we have a true science of education (Elkind 1999).

Curricular Readiness

A constructivist approach to education presupposes a thorough understanding of the curriculum to be taught. Piaget understood this very well. Much of his research was aimed at shedding light on what might be called the *logical substructure* of the discipline. That is to say, to match the subject matter to the child's level of developing mental abilities, you have to understand the logical demands it makes upon the child's reasoning powers. In his research with Inhelder (1964), Piaget demonstrated that for a child to engage in the addition and multiplication of classes, relations, and numbers, children first need to attain concrete operations. Similarly, Inhelder and Piaget (1958) showed that true experimental thinking and dealing with multiple variables require the formal mental operations not attained until adolescence. Task analysis of this sort is required in all curricular domains. Only when we successfully match children's ability levels with the demands of the task can we expect them to reconstruct the knowledge we would like them to acquire.

In addition to knowing the logical substructure of the task, we also need research regarding the timing of the introduction of various subject matters. For example, the planets often are taught at second grade. We know that children of seven or eight do not yet have a firm grasp of celestial space and time. Does teaching the planets at grade two give the child an advantage when studying astronomy at the college level? Similar questions might be asked about introducing the explorers as a social study topic in the early elementary grades. I am not arguing against the teaching of such material; I am contending that we need to know whether this is time well spent. We have little or no research on these issues.

Another type of curriculum information has to do with the sequence of topics within any particular course of study. In elementary math, is it more effective to teach coins before or after we teach units of distance and weight? Some sequences of concepts are more effective for learning than others. In most cases, we don't have data upon which to make that kind of decision. In most public school textbooks, the order of topical instruction is determined more by tradition, or by the competition, than by research. We find this practice even at the college level. Most introductory courses begin with a chapter on the history of the discipline. Yet many students might become more engaged in the subject if the first topic was one to which they could immediately relate. Again, we have little or no research on such matters. This is true for teaching in an integrated or linear curriculum format.

The argument that there is little connection between academic research and practical applications has many exceptions. Nonetheless, as long as these remain exceptions rather than the rule, we will not move toward a true science of education.

Societal Readiness

If the majority of teachers are not ready to adopt a constructivist pedagogy, neither are educational policy makers and the larger society. To be successfully implemented, any reform pedagogy must reflect a broad and energized social consensus. John Dewey was able to get broad backing for his Progressive Education Reform thanks to World War I and the negative reaction to all things European. Up until the First World War, our educational system followed the European classical model. It was based on the doctrine of formal discipline whereby training in Greek and Latin, as well as the classics, rigorously trained the mind. In contrast, Dewey (1899) offered a uniquely American functional pedagogy. He wanted to prepare students for the demands and occupations of everyday life. There was general consensus that this was the way to go.

The launching of the Russian Sputnik in 1957 was another event that energized the nation to demand curriculum reform. Russia, it seemed, had outstripped us scientifically, and this reflected badly on our math and science education. The National Science Foundation embarked on a program of science and math curriculum reform. To this end, the foundation recruited leading figures in the fields of science and math to construct new, up-to-date curricula in these fields. These scholars knew their discipline but, for the most part, they did not know children. The new curricula, which included variable-base arithmetic and teaching the principles of the discipline, were inappropriate for children. When these curricula failed, a new consensus emerged to advocate the need to go "back to basics." The resulting teacher-made curricula dominated education prior to the entrance of the academicians. While "back to basics" was touted as a "get tough" movement, it was actually a "get easier" movement because it reintroduced more age-appropriate material.

Many of the educational reforms of any category have not had much success since that time. Though *A Nation at Risk* (NCEE 1983) created a number of reforms, the report itself did not energize the nation, and there was not sufficient motivation to bring about real change. In large part, I believe that this was because there was no national consciousness of a felt need for change. The current educational movement, No Child Left Behind, was introduced for political rather than pedagogical reasons. This legislation was avowedly for the purpose of improving student achievement and changing the culture of American schools. These aims are to be achieved by requiring the states to test all children every year from grades three through eight. Schools that do not meet statewide or national standards may be closed or parents given an opportunity to send their children to other schools.

This is an ill-conceived program based on a business model that regards education as akin to a factory turning out products. Obviously, children are not containers to be filled up to a certain amount at each grade level. The program forces schools to focus on tests to the exclusion of what is really important in the educational process. Testing is expensive and depletes already scarce educational resources. Students are being coached to do well on the tests without regard to their true knowledge and understanding. The policy is corrupt in that it encourages schools to cheat. The negative results of this policy already are being felt. A number of states are choosing to opt out of the program. The No Child Left Behind legislation is a good example of bad policy promoted for political gain that is not in the best interests of children.

Other than a national crisis, there is another way for social consensus to bring about educational reform. In Kuhn's (1996) innovative book on scientific revolutions, he made the point that such revolutions do not come about by the gradual accretion of knowledge. Rather they come about as a result of conflicts between opposing points of view with one eventually winning out over the other. Evolution, for example, is still fighting a rearguard action against those who believe in the biblical account of the origin of man. In education, the long-running battle between nature and nurture (read development and learning) is not likely to be resolved soon by a higher order synthesis.

An alternative view was offered by Galison (1997), who argued that the history of science is one of tools rather than ideas. He used the history of particle physics as an example. The tools of particle physics are optical-like cloud chambers and electronic-like photographic emulsions that display particle interactions by way of images. One could make equal claims for the history of biology and astronomy. As both Kuhn and Galison acknowledged, scientific progress can come about by conflict or the introduction of new technologies.

Education seems likely to be changed by new tools rather than conflicting ideas. Computers are changing education's successive phases. In the first phase, computers simply replaced typewriters and calculators. In the second phase, computers began to change the ways in which we teach. The widespread use of e-mail, Blackboard, PowerPoint, and simulations are examples. And there is an active and growing field of computer education with its own journals and conferences (e.g., Advancement of Computer Education and Association for the Advancement of Computing in Education). The third phase already has begun, and we are now seeing changes in math and science curricula as a direct result of the availability of technology. Education is one of the last social institutions to be changed by technology, but its time has come.

Conclusion

In this paper, I have used the failure of the constructivist reform movement to illustrate what I believe is necessary for any true educational innovation to succeed. There must be teacher, curricular, and societal readiness for any educational innovation to be accepted and put into practice. In the past, reforms were generated by one or the other form of readiness, but without the support of the others. I believe that technology will change this. It is my sense that it will move us toward making teaching a true profession, the establishment of a multidisciplinary science of education, and a society ready and eager to embrace a technologically based education.

Education is, however, more than technology. It is, at its heart, people dealing with people. That is why any successful educational reform must build upon a human philosophy that makes clear its aims and objectives. Technology without a philosophy of education is mechanical, and a philosophy without an appropriate technology will be ineffective. Technology is forcing educational reform, but we need to harness it to the best philosophy of education we have available. I believe this to be constructivism. The current failure to implement constructivism is not because of its merits but because of a lack of readiness for it. We need to make every effort to ensure that the technological revolution in education creates the kinds of teachers, curricula, and social climate that will make constructivism a reality in our classrooms.

References

Brooks, J. G., and M. G. Brooks. 1993. *In search of understanding: The case for constructivist classrooms*. Alexandria, Va.: Association for Supervision and Curriculum Development.

Dewey, J. 1899. *The school and society*. Chicago: University of Chicago Press.

Elkind, D. 1999. Educational research and the science of education. *Educational Psychology* 11(3): 171–87.

Flexner, A. 1910. *Medical education in the United States and Canada*. New York: Carnegie Foundation for the Advancement of Teaching.

Fosnot, C. T. 1996. *Constructivism: Theory, perspectives, and practice*. New York: Teachers College Press.

Gagnon, G. W. J., and M. Collay. 2001. *Designing for learning: Six elements in constructivist classrooms*. Thousand Oaks, Calif.: Corwin Press.

Galison, P. L. 1997. *Image and logic: A material culture of microphysics*. Chicago: University of Chicago Press.

Gibboney, R. A. 1994. *The stone trumpet: A story of practical school reform*. Albany, N.Y.: State University of New York Press.

Holmes Group. 1995. *Tomorrow's schools of education*. Ann Arbor: University of Michigan.

Inhelder, B., and J. Piaget. 1958. *The growth of logical thinking from childhood to adolescence: An essay on the construction of formal operational structures*, trans. A. Parsons and S. Milgram. New York: Basic Books.

Inhelder, B., and J. Piaget. 1964. *The early growth of logic in the child, classification and seriation*, trans. E. A. Lunzer and D. Papert. New York: Harper and Row.

Kant, I. 2002. *Immanuel Kant: Theoretical philosophy after 1781*, trans. G. Hatfield and M. Friedman. New York: Cambridge University Press.

Kuhn, T. S. 1996. *The structure of scientific revolutions*, 3rd ed. Chicago: University of Chicago Press.

Lambert, L., M. Collay, M. Dietz, K. Kent, and A. E. Richert. 1997. *Who will save our schools? Teachers as constructivist leaders*. Thousand Oaks, Calif.: Corwin Press.

Larochelle, M., N. Bednarz, and J. Garrison. 1998. *Constructivism and education*. Cambridge, England: Cambridge University Press.

National Commission on Excellence in Education. 1983. *A nation at risk: The imperative for educational reform*. Washington, D.C.: U.S. Government Printing Office.

Piaget, J. 1950. *The psychology of intelligence*, trans. M. Piercy and D. E. Berlyne. London: Routledge and Paul.

Rousseau, J. J. 1962. *Emile*, trans. W. Boyd. New York: Teachers College Press.

Vygotsky, L. S. 1978. *Mind in society: The development of higher psychological processes*, ed. M. Cole. Cambridge, Mass.: Harvard University Press.

DAVID ELKIND is Professor of Child Development at Tufts University where he conducts research in the cognitive, perceptual, and social growth of children based on the theories of Jean Piaget.

Jamin Carson

 **NO**

Objectivism and Education: A Response to David Elkind's 'The Problem with Constructivism'

In "The Problem with Constructivism," David Elkind (2004) made several claims about why constructivism has not been implemented in schools. He argued that constructivism will be implemented only when we have *teacher*, *curricular*, and *societal readiness*; that teaching needs to become a science before it can be a true profession; and that constructivism is the only philosophy that will reform education. In this essay, I present counterarguments for each of these claims.

Constructivism is the theory that students learn by individually or socially transforming information (Slavin 1997). This theory necessarily entails certain metaphysical and epistemological assumptions. To accept constructivism, one must believe that:

- reality is dependent upon the perceiver, and thus constructed;
- reason or logic is not the only means of understanding reality, but one of many; and
- knowledge or truth is subjective and relative to the individual or community.

One philosophy of education that challenges this theory is objectivism, which asserts that students must be engaged actively in the subject matter to learn. This theory does not advocate, however, that students "transform" or "construct" reality, reason, knowledge, or truth. Objectivism holds that one reality exists independent of anyone perceiving it, humankind is capable of knowing this reality only by the faculty of reason, and objective knowledge and truth is possible (Peikoff 1993). I argue against Elkind's claims primarily from an objectivist viewpoint.

Failures of Readiness

Elkind's main thesis was that constructivism has not been implemented in schools because of failures of teacher, curricular, and societal readiness. Teacher readiness requires that a teacher be educated in a science of education such as child development. Curricular readiness involves knowing exactly when and how students are developmentally ready to learn specific information. Societal readiness is when society is eager for educational reform or change.

Elkind did not explain the causal relationship between these states of readiness and the implementation of constructivism. He only implied that a causal relationship exists. There is no reason to believe that a relationship exists or that any state of readiness would lead to a specific philosophy of education. A teacher must accept the metaphysical and epistemological assumptions of a pedagogic practice before he or she can implement it.

Elkind's definitions of readiness also were problematic. When defining teacher readiness as having good teacher "training"—which comes only from scientific knowledge (e.g., child development)—he stated (2004, 308), "Teaching will become a true profession only when we have a genuine science of education." Though education is not a true science, teachers generally are taught one unique body of knowledge. Most college and university teacher preparation programs, alternative certification programs, and professional development seminars teach the same information, and a great deal of it is constructivist in nature or a variant of it.

Elkind's definition of curricular readiness also has problems. He (2004, 307–08) defined curricular readiness as knowledge of "what, when, and how the subject matter should be taught" and then claimed that "only when we successfully match children's ability levels with the demands of the task can we expect them to reconstruct the knowledge we would like them to acquire." The phrase "we would like them to acquire" contradicts constructivist metaphysics and epistemology. If constructivism assumes that students construct their own knowledge, then how can a constructivist teacher choose the knowledge they would like students to acquire? The phrase "we would like them to acquire" presupposes an objective philosophy which holds that given a specific context, some knowledge is objectively superior to other knowledge. For a constructivist, this is a contradiction, if one views reality, reason, knowledge, and truth as subjective and relative to the perceiver, then what is the basis for arguing for any knowledge at all, let alone one over another? Any curricular choice, according to constructivist philosophy, should be as valid as any other. When constructivists make absolute claims about what, when, and how something should be taught, they are either objectivists or making arbitrary claims.

From *The Educational Forum*, vol. 69, Spring 2005, pp. 232–238. Copyright © 2005 by Kappa Delta Pi. Reprinted by permission.

Finally, there are problems with societal readiness. Elkind (2004, 310) suggested that "to be successfully implemented, any reform pedagogy must reflect a broad and energized social consensus," which the United States currently does not have. Yet, a broad and energized social consensus in the United States does exist. The concensus is that public education has not adequately educated its students, particularly those of lower socioeconomic status. This societal readiness has paved the way for programs like No Child Left Behind. Progressive reform pedagogies like constructivism are usually prescribed by administrators to improve education or raise test scores. Despite the social consensus that education needs reform pedagogy and constructivism has been one of those pedagogies, education still has not closed the gap between rich and poor—assuming that is education's aim in the first place.

Science of Education

Most teachers receive the same education, but not all teachers readily accept what they are taught, whether it be constructivism or some other philosophy of education. Unlike medical practitioners, for example, educators disagree about nearly all issues within their field. Medical practitioners simply observe whether or not the treatment cured the patient. They may disagree about why or how a treatment worked, but at least they have objective and verifiable evidence of whether or not the treatment worked. Education, on the other hand, possesses many more points of disagreement. How do people learn? What should people learn? How do we measure learning? The complexity of these questions results in virtually no consensus about what works among all educators. Though education draws from a unique body of knowledge to prepare its teachers, it is not scientific and probably never will be because there is so much disagreement about the definition of education.

Assuming that Elkind is correct in believing that education must become a science, his argument is still flawed. It is contradictory for a constructivist to advocate a science of education. The philosophical foundation of constructivism rejects an objectively knowable reality. The philosophical foundation of science claims that one reality is objectively knowable through the senses and reason. Science, therefore, undermines constructivism rather than serves as a prerequisite to it.

If Elkind used Kuhn's (1996) definition of science—reality is observed by a perceiver who sees it through the lens of socially constructed paradigms that are periodically overthrown by new paradigms that are incommensurate with past paradigms—then any science of education still has no claim of truth over any other method of inquiry within education. Claims like "teaching will become a true profession only when we have a genuine science of education" are equivalent to saying that teaching will be a profession only when it becomes an art. If we construct our own reality, what is the difference?

If Elkind believes that most of what educators consider science comes from constructivists like Rousseau, Kant, Piaget, and Vygotsky, his argument is flawed. It is circular logic for a constructivist to claim that a science of education is needed and then to select only constructivists as the founders of that science. Though some beliefs are obtained in experiments, most are not—especially philosophical views about *literally* constructing reality, which are not testable or falsifiable and thus should not be accepted as scientific.

Philosophy of Education

Elkind seems to have overlooked the role of the educator's metaphysical and epistemological assumptions in accepting constructivism or any philosophy of education. He admitted that educators who "are wedded to an objectivist view that knowledge has an independent existence" have resisted constructivism, but he quickly dismissed this cause in favor of teacher readiness. Ironically, teacher readiness is more likely the cause of resistance to constructivism. For an educator to implement a pedagogical practice, he or she must consciously or unconsciously accept its metaphysical and epistemological assumptions. Constructivists possess certain metaphysical and epistemological assumptions that lead to constructivist practices, while objectivists possess other metaphysical and epistemological assumptions that lead to objectivist practices. Elkind overlooked the possibility that not everyone holds the same assumptions about reality, reason, knowledge, and truth that lead to constructivist practices. Some have other worldviews and, therefore, reject constructivism as a theory of learning because it contradicts their philosophical assumptions.

Elkind said that constructivism is the "best philosophy of education we have available," and that it has been "widely accepted." This is true only at the university level, where the majority of professors possess the metaphysical and epistemological assumptions that lead to constructivism. It is not true at other levels of education, where one is likely to encounter different metaphysical and epistemological assumptions that lead to other pedagogical practices.

Constructivism is not the best philosophy of education. Objectivism is more reasonable from a theoretical and practical perspective than constructivism. Objectivism holds that there is one reality independent of anyone perceiving it. This means that regardless of whether or not someone perceives something, it still exists. For example, I can leave the room with a table in it and be convinced that the table still exists. Most people probably would agree with this statement. Constructivism, on the other hand, holds that reality is dependent upon the perceiver. This means that something exists only if someone perceives it. From a constructivist perspective, if I leave a room with a table in it, the table ceases to exist. Most people would disagree with such a statement or at least have difficulty accepting it.

Objectivism also holds that humankind takes in data through the senses and uses reason to obtain knowledge. Constructivism does not deny the efficacy of reason completely, but does consider it as only one of many ways of knowing. This belief is another theory that does not stand up in practice. The theory of multiple intelligences, for example, proposes at least ten "intelligences" or ways of knowing: verbal, logical, musical, physical, spatial, inter- and intra-personal, natural, existential, and spiritual. When analyzed or reduced to their epistemological foundation, these intelligences seem more like specialized bodies of acquired knowledge than actual processors of information. Reason exists in all of them, which suggests that each is the *primary* way of knowing.

Objectivism also holds that we have objective knowledge and truth. A person observes reality via his or her senses, forms concepts through the use of noncontradictory (i.e., Aristotelian) logic, and thus acquires knowledge and truth. Constructivism posits that only subjective knowledge and relative truth are possible. If knowledge is subjective or relative to an individual or a group, then *any* knowledge could be true. Sacrificing virgins to appease the gods or believing that the universe revolves around the earth would count as knowledge and truth. Notable constructivists (Lawson 1989; Noddings 1998; Rorty 2003) have raised these criticisms about constructivist metaphysics and epistemology and have admitted that they have no answer to them.

Constructivism in Practice

Practically, objectivism is more reasonable than constructivism. As a high school English teacher, I implemented constructivism in my classes by allowing the students to construct what an English class is—choosing its purpose, curriculum, and instruction. Most of the students did not understand how they could "construct" an English class. They expected me to define the English class for them—a very reasonable assumption considering how young they were and how limited their experience. After a fair amount of prompting, a few bold students thought English should be spelling and grammar. Some might argue that the students' answer proves only that they had been prevented from constructing previous curriculums, and thus had not learned to think for themselves or to question the curriculum. I concede that the students' previous conception of what constitutes schooling was part of their inability to construct the course. However, perhaps children naturally look to adults to share with them their learned and acquired knowledge. They expect teachers to pass on to them a body of knowledge, imperfect though it may be, that they can update according to their discoveries. Many practicing constructivists refuse to do this, believing instead that a child's knowledge is equal to that of an adult's and a student is no less an authority on a subject than a teacher. This assumption is untrue and dangerous. It assumes that children are better off entering a world

with no knowledge and creating their own rather than entering a world full of knowledge, learning it, and then updating it if it does not stand the test of their scrutiny.

The students in my English class could not be pure constructivists in the context of day-to-day assignments either. For example, when we read *Romeo and Juliet* by William Shakespeare, the reality of the story presented obstacles. If the students would have said that the story was about an aging salesman who imagines he is a success when he is not, a constructivist teacher would have to accept their response—right or wrong—because reality is constructed. For an objectivist English teacher, however, every claim must be supported by textual evidence and logic—by reality. *Romeo and Juliet*, therefore, must be about what the text supports and what logic dictates, not about the subjective feelings of the reader, which may not be in accordance with reality. Constructivist English teachers who tell students that there are no right-or-wrong answers or that their interpretation is as correct as anyone else's only encourage students to be careless and uncritical readers, writers, and thinkers.

I shifted to giving students a choice supported by evidence and logic because of the flaws in the practical application of constructivism. Students could choose the purpose, curriculum, and assignments of the course, but ultimately their choices had to conform to reality, not to their subjective whims. In other words, their choices had to have a compelling connection to their literacy development.

Conclusion

Constructivists must ask themselves whether they want to cling to the literal interpretation of constructivism that sees reality as constructed or simply believe that students learn best when they are actively engaged in the learning process. The two definitions are not the same metaphysically or epistemologically. The former entails an untenable theory and practice and should be modified or rejected.

Noddings (1998, 117–18) addressed the distinction between moderate and radical constructivism in this way:

> [I]f radical constructivists are just saying that our perception and cognition are theory-laden, that all knowledge is mediated by our cognitive structures and theories, then they have lots of company among contemporary theorists. However, if they are saying that there is no mind-independent reality, then they seem to be arguing a line long ago rejected.

Though Noddings seemed to advocate a moderate constructivist view that denies a mind-dependent reality, I maintain that constructivists cannot be moderates. All constructivists necessarily must believe that reality is dependent upon the perceiver. It is logically impossible to believe that a person's perception and cognitive structures are theory-laden, while simultaneously believing that reality is independent of the perceiver. If reality is perceived by a theory-laden perceiver, then the reality is theory-laden too. The moment that one becomes theory-laden, one is prevented from knowing an objective reality.

Objectivists believe humans are not theory-laden in the pejorative sense of that word. Objectivists do not consider prior knowledge or cognitive structures as a subjective lens through which one views reality. Rather, one possesses prior knowledge that informs new knowledge and, consequently, makes the new knowledge meaningful. If the prior knowledge or cognitive structure is incorrect, eventually the new correct knowledge will conflict with it and a person will be forced to update his or her old knowledge. If constructivists believe in an independent reality, then they not only must believe in it, but also must possess an objective method of perceiving it and, therefore, have objective knowledge and truth. There is no middle ground.

References

Elkind, D. 2004. The problem with constructivism. *The Educational Forum* 68(4): 306–12.

Kuhn, T. S. 1996. *The structure of scientific revolutions*, 3rd ed. Chicago: The University of Chicago Press.

Lawson, H. 1989. Stories about stories. In *Dismantling truth: Reality in the post-modern world*, ed. H. Lawson and L. Appignanesi, xi–xxviii. London: Weidenfeld and Nicolson.

Noddings, N. 1998. *Philosophy of education*. Boulder, CO: Westview Press.

Piekoff, L. 1993. *Objectivism: The philosophy of Ayn Rand*. New York: Penguin Books.

Rorty, R. 2003. Dismantling truth: Solidarity versus objectivity. In *The theory of knowledge: Classical and contemporary readings*, 3rd ed., ed. L. P. Pojman, 324–30. Belmont, CA: Wadsworth/Thomson Learning.

Slavin, R. E. 1997. *Educational psychology: Theory and practice*, 5th ed. Boston: Allyn & Bacon.

Jamin Carson is Assistant Professor at East Carolina University. His research interest is in the philosophical foundations of education.

EXPLORING THE ISSUE

Is Constructivism the Best Philosophy of Education?

Critical Thinking and Reflection

1. How would multiple intelligences theory fit into constructivism or behaviorism viewpoints?
2. Is constructivism not the best philosophy of education, why or why not?
3. How is the "science" of education linked to constructivist thought and action?
4. Why does Carson take a behaviorist viewpoint to attack constructionism?
5. How many philosophies of education are there?

Is There Common Ground?

So it can be seen that present-day constructivists like David Elkind draw a lot of inspiration from Dewey's portrayal of the active, probing learner immersed in social experience, Holt's learners who steer their own personal development unfettered by imposed curricula, and Rogers' self-exploring students whose subjective knowledge takes precedence. In contrast, objectivists like Carson most likely find comfort in Scruton's timeless rationality, Adler's concept of a single best curriculum for all, and Skinner's use of scientific principles and quantitative methods to create effective learners.

Elkind responded to Carson's critique in the Summer 2005 issue of *The Educational Forum*, primarily refuting the accusation that constructivists deny that a physical world exists outside our sensory experiences. He states that "it is not that an external reality does not exist, only that we have to reconstruct it to know it . . . it is because humans share a common sensory apparatus that we can agree upon an external reality existing outside our experience." Our senses can be mistaken but "objective" reasoning is fallible as well, he concludes.

In the past decade, the philosophy of constructivism has been widely treated by those who praise it and those who deplore it. A sampling of sources includes Jacqueline Grennon Brooks and Martin G. Brooks, *In Search of Understanding: The Case for Constructivist Classrooms* (1993); Susan Ohanian, *One Size Fits Few* (1999); Karen R. Harris and Steve S. Graham, "Memo to Constructivists: Skills Count, Too," *Educational Leadership* (February 1996); Tony Wagner, "Change as Collaborative Inquiry: A 'Constructivist' Methodology for Reinventing Schools," *Phi Delta Kappan* (March 1998); Heinrich Mintrop, "Educating Students to Teach in a Constructivist Way—Can It All Be Done?" *Teachers College Record* (April 2001); and Rhoda Cummings and Steve Harlow, "The Constructivist Roots of Moral Education," *The Educational Forum* (Summer 2000).

Additional commentary may be found in Michael Glassman, "Running in Circles: Chasing Dewey," *Educational Theory* (August 2004); Donald G. Hackmann, "Constructivism and Block Scheduling: Making the Connection," *Phi Delta Kappan* (May 2004); Ian Moll, "Towards a Constructivist Montessori Education," *Perspectives in Education* (June 2004); and David Chicoine, "Ignoring the Obvious: A Constructivist Critique of a Traditional Teacher Education Program," *Educational Studies* (December 2004).

The discussion launched by Elkind and Carson has been continued in the Spring 2006, Fall 2006, and Summer 2007 issues of *The Educational Forum*. See especially the Henry Pegues's article, "Of Paradigm Wars: Constructivism, Objectivism, and Postmodern Stratagems," in the Summer 2007 issue.

Create Central

www.mhhe.com/createcentral

Additional Resources

D. Elkind, "The Problem With Constructivism," *The Educational Forum* (vol. 68, no. 4, pp. 306–312, 2004)

T. S. Kuhn, *The Structure of Scientific Revolutions*, 3rd ed. (University of Chicago Press, 1996)

H. Lawson, "Stories About Stories," in H. Lawson and L. Appignanesi, eds., *Dismantling Truth: Reality in the Post-Modern World*, pp. xi–xxviii (Weidenfeld and Nicolson, 1989)

N. Noddings, *Philosophy of Education* (Westview Press, 1998)

L. Piekoff, *Objectivism: The Philosophy of Ayn Rand* (Penguin Books, 1993)

R. Rorty, "Dismantling Truth: Solidarity Versus Objectivity," in L. P. Pojman, ed., *The Theory of Knowledge: Classical and Contemporary Readings* (3rd ed., pp. 324–330) (Thomson Learning, 2003)

R. E. Slavin, *Educational Psychology: Theory and Practice* (5th ed.) (Allyn & Bacon, 1997)

Internet References . . .

Constructivism in Education: An Overview of Contributions to the Literature and to the JPACTe Annotated Bibliography

www.jpacte.org/uploads/9/0/0/6/9006355/
2007-1-richardson.pdf

Constructivist Learning Theory

www.exploratorium.edu/ifi/resources
/constructivistlearning.html

Constructivism PowerPoint

www.google.com/url?sa=t&rct=j&q=&esrc=s&frm=1&
source=web&cd=21&ved=0CCsQFjAAOBQ&url=http
%3A%2F%2Fwww.mrgibbs.com%2Ftu%2Fppts%
2FConstructivism.ppt&ei=qBV0UuSsN6mCygGjs4Hg
Bg&usg=AFQjCNGaADK0GpBlyrAriRHpBhLzoij4iw&
sig2=Q68dACbflb2wM8f-mrxzeA

Teaching with the Constructivist Learning Theory

www.ndt-ed.org/TeachingResources/
ClassroomTips/Constructivist%20_Learning.htm

Vygotsky's Pphilosophy: Constructivism and its Criticisms Examined

http://files.eric.ed.gov/fulltext/EJ854992.pdf

Selected, Edited, and with Issue Framing Material by:
Glenn L. Koonce, *Regent University*

ISSUE

Should "Public Schooling" Be Redefined?

YES: Frederick M. Hess, from "What Is a 'Public School?' Principles for a New Century," *Phi Delta Kappan* (February 2004)

NO: Linda Nathan, Joe Nathan, Ray Bacchetti, and Evans Clinchy, from "A Response to Frederick Hess," *Phi Delta Kappan* (February 2004)

Learning Outcomes

After reading this issue, you will be able to:

- Contrast varying meanings for the term "public schooling."
- Define who should be permitted to provide public schooling.
- Compare and contrast politicizing verses.
- Analyze the four responses to Hess's view of a public school.
- Identify how new technologies complicate the definition of public schooling.

ISSUE SUMMARY

YES: Frederick M. Hess, a resident scholar at the American Enterprise Institute, advocates a broadening of the definition of "public schooling" in light of recent developments such as vouchers, charter schools, and home schooling.

NO: Linda Nathan, Joe Nathan, Ray Bacchetti, and Evans Clinchy express a variety of concerns about the conceptual expansion that Hess proposes.

The original public school crusade, led by Massachusetts education official Horace Mann (1796–1859) and other activists, built on the growing sentiment among citizens, politicians, and business leaders that public schools were needed to deal with the increase in immigration, urbanization, and industrialism, as well as to bind together the American population and to prepare everyone for participatory democracy. For the most part, the right of the government to compel school attendance, dating from Massachusetts legislation in 1852, went unchallenged, although Catholics formed their own private school system in reaction to the predominant Protestantism of public schools in certain areas. In the 1920s there were efforts to eliminate all alternatives to government-run public schools to ensure attendance compliance and curricular standardization. Such an effort in Oregon was challenged in court, and the U.S. Supreme Court ultimately ruled, in *Pierce v. Society of Sisters* (1925), that such legislation unreasonably interferes with parental rights. While this ruling preserved the private school

option, it did not alter the governmental prerogative to compel school attendance.

This governmental authority met with sharp criticism from liberal writers in the 1950s and beyond, in works such as Paul Goodman's *Compulsory Mis-education* (1964), Ivan Illich's *Deschooling Society* (1971), John Holt's *Instead of Education* (1976), and John Taylor Gatto's *Dumbing Us Down: The Hidden Curriculum of Compulsory Schooling* (1992). Gatto condemned the public school system for its emphasis on obedience and subordination rather than the unleashing of the intellectual and creative powers of the individual. Since the 1980s, a parallel attack has come from conservatives, such as William J. Bennett, E. D. Hirsch, Jr., Chester E. Finn, Jr., Charles J. Sykes, Grover Norquist, and Cal Thomas, and conservative groups, such as Parents for School Choice, the Cato Institute, and the Alliance for Separation of School and State. Building on the findings of the 1983 *A Nation at Risk* report, a significant segment of the American population continues to express disdain for the public education "establishment" (the U.S. Department of Education, the National Education Association, and teacher-training institutions) for its inability or unwillingness to improve public school performance. Their basic contention is that only choice-driven competition will bring about lasting improvement. William J. Bennett, in "A Nation Still at Risk," *Policy Review* (July/August 1998), has stated that although choices are spreading, charter schools are proliferating, privately managed public schools have long waiting lists, and home-schooling is expanding, "the elephant still has most of the power." He concludes that "we must never again assume that the education system will respond to good advice. It will change only when power relationships change, particularly when all parents gain the power to decide where their children go to school."

Educator-reformer Deborah Meier, in "The Road to Trust," *American School Board Journal* (September 2003), argues that we must make public education feel like a public enterprise again. Hers is a call for the rebuilding of trust between public schools and the communities they directly serve. "Our school boards need to turn their eyes to their constituencies—not just to following the dictates of state and federal government micromanagers."

In the following articles, Frederick M. Hess makes the case that the time has come for a reconception of "public schooling" while four prominent educators challenge what they perceive to be an unproductive assault on public schooling.

YES ⤶

Frederick M. Hess

What Is a 'Public School'? Principles for a New Century

The phrase "public schooling" has become more a rhetorical device than a useful guide to policy. As our world evolves, so too must our conception of what "public" means. James Coleman eloquently made this point more than two decades ago, implying a responsibility to periodically reappraise our assumptions as to what constitutes "public schooling."[1] In a world where charter schooling, distance education, tuition tax credits, and other recent developments no longer fit neatly into our conventional mental boxes, it is clearly time for such an effort. Nonetheless, rather than receiving the requisite consideration, "public schooling" has served as a flag around which critics of these various reforms can rally. It is because the phrase resonates so powerfully that critics of proposals like charter schooling, voucher programs, and rethinking teacher licensure have at times abandoned substantive debate in order to attack such measures as "anti-public schooling."[2]

Those of us committed to the promise of public education are obliged to see that the ideal does not become a tool of vested interests. The perception that public schooling has strayed from its purpose and been captured by self-interested parties has fueled lacerating critiques in recent years. Such critics as Andrew Coulson and Douglas Dewey find a growing audience when they suggest that the ideal of public schooling itself is nothing more than a call to publicly subsidize the private agendas of bureaucrats, education school professors, union officials, and leftist activists.[3] While I believe such attacks are misguided, answering them effectively demands that we discern what it is that makes schooling public and accept diverse arrangements that are consistent with those tenets. Otherwise, growing numbers of reformers may come to regard public schooling as a politicized obstacle rather than a shared ideal.

While I do not aim to provide a precise answer as to what public schooling should mean in the early 21st century, I will argue that public schools are broadly defined by their commitment to preparing students to be productive members of a social order, aware of their societal responsibilities, and respectful of constitutional strictures; that such schools cannot deny access to students for reasons unrelated to their educational focus; and that the system of public schools available in any community must provide an appropriate placement for each student. In short,

I suggest that it is appropriate to adopt a much more expansive notion of public schooling than the one the education community holds today.

What Isn't Public?

Traditionally, "public schools" are deemed to be those directly accountable to elected officials or funded by tax dollars.[4] As a practical matter, such definitions are not very useful, largely because there are conventional "public" schools that do not fit within these definitions, while there are "private" providers that do.

We generally regard as "public schools" those in which policy making and oversight are the responsibility of governmental bodies, such as a local school board. Nongovernmental providers of educational services, such as independent schools or educational management organizations (EMOs), are labeled "nonpublic." The distinction is whether a formal political body is in charge, since these officials are accountable by election or appointment to the larger voting "public."

There are two particular problems here. First, how "hands on" must the government be for us to regard a service as publicly provided? The National Aeronautics and Space Administration, the Environmental Protection Agency, the U.S. Department of Education, and most other state, federal, and local government agencies contract with for-profit firms for support, to provide services, and to evaluate service delivery. Yet we tend to regard the services as "public" because they were initiated in response to a public directive and are monitored by public officials. It is not clear when government-directed activity ceases to be public. For instance, if a for-profit company manages a district school, is the school less public than it was when it purchased its texts from a for-profit textbook publisher and its professional development from a private consultant?

A second approach to defining "public" focuses on inputs. By this metric, any activity that involves government funds is public because it involves the expenditure of tax dollars. However, this distinction is more nebulous than we sometimes suppose. For instance, schools in the Milwaukee voucher program receive Wisconsin tax dollars. Does this mean that voucher schools ought to be regarded as de facto public schools? Similarly, Wisconsin dairy farmers receive federal subsidies. Does this make their farms public enterprises?

A particular complication is that many traditional public schools charge families money. For instance, during 2002–03, the families of more than 2,300 Indiana students were paying tuition of as much as $6,000 to enroll their children in a public school in another district. Public schools routinely charge fees to families that participate in interdistrict public choice plans, and they frequently charge families fees if a child participates in extracurricular activities. Would proponents of a revenue-based definition suggest that such practices mean that these schools are no longer "public"?

A third approach, famously advanced by John Dewey, the esteemed champion of "public" education, recognizes that private institutions may serve public ends and that public institutions may fail to do so.[5] Such a recognition suggests that public schools are those that serve public ends, regardless of the monitoring arrangements or revenue sources. This approach is ultimately problematic, however, because we do *not* have clear agreement on appropriate public purposes. I'll have more to say on this point shortly.

What Is Public Schooling?

Previously, I have posed five questions to guide our efforts to bring more precision to our understanding of "public schooling."[6] Here, I offer these questions as a way to sketch principles that may help shape a contemporary conception of "public schooling."

What are the purposes of public schooling? Schooling entails both public and private purposes, though we often fail to note the degree to which the private benefits may serve the public interest. In particular, academic learning serves the individual and also the needs of the state. Successful democratic communities require a high level of literacy and numeracy and are anchored by the knowledge and the good sense of the population. Citizens who lack these skills are less likely to contribute effectively to the well-being of their communities and more likely to be a drain on public resources. Therefore, in a real sense, any school that helps children master reading, writing, mathematics, and other essential content is already advancing some significant public purposes.[7] It is troubling that prominent educational thinkers, including Frank Smith, Susan Ohanian, Deborah Meier, and Alfie Kohn, have rejected this fundamental premise and encouraged "public schools" to promote preferred social values even at the expense of basic academic mastery.[8]

More fundamentally, there are two distinct ways to comprehend the larger public purposes of education. One suggests that schools serve a public interest that transcends the needs of individuals. This line of thought, understood by Rousseau as the "general will," can be traced to Plato's conviction that nations need a far-sighted leader to determine their true interests, despite the shortsighted

preferences of the mob. A second way of thinking about the public purposes of education accepts the classically "liberal" understanding of the public interest as the sum of the interests of individual citizens and rejects the idea of a transcendent general will. This pragmatic stance helped shape American public institutions that protect citizens from tyrannical majorities and overreaching public officials.

While neither perspective is necessarily "correct," our government of limited powers and separate branches leans heavily toward the more modest dictates of liberalism. Despite our tendency to suffuse education with the sweeping rhetoric of a disembodied national interest, our freedoms are secured by a system designed to resist such imperial visions.

The "public" components of schooling include the responsibility for teaching the principles, habits, and obligations of citizenship. While schools of education typically interpret this to mean that educators should preach "tolerance" or affirm "diversity," a firmer foundation for citizenship education would focus on respect for law, process, and individual rights. The problem with phrases like "tolerance" and "diversity" is that they are umbrella terms with multiple interpretations. When we try to define them more precisely—in policy or practice—it becomes clear that we must privilege some values at the expense of others. For instance, one can plausibly argue that tolerant citizens should respectfully hear out a radical Muslim calling for jihad against the U.S. or that tolerance extends only to legalistic protection and leaves one free to express social opprobrium. If educators promote the former, as their professional community generally advises, they have adopted a particular normative view that is at odds with that held by a large segment of the public.

Promoting any one particular conception of tolerance does not make schools more "public." In a liberal society, uniformly teaching students to accept teen pregnancy or homosexuality as normal and morally unobjectionable represents a jarring absolutism amidst profound moral disagreement.

Nonetheless, many traditional "public" schools (such as members of the Coalition of Essential Schools) today explicitly promote a particular world view and endorse a particular social ethos. In advancing "meaningful questions," for instance, faculty members at these schools often promote partisan attitudes toward American foreign policy, the propriety of affirmative action, or the morality of redistributive social policies. Faculty members in these schools can protest that they have no agenda other than cultivating critical inquiry, but observation of classrooms or perusal of curricular materials makes clear that most of these schools are not neutral on the larger substantive questions. This poses an ethical problem in a pluralist society where the parents of many students may reject the public educators' beliefs and where the educators have never been clearly empowered to stamp out "improper" thoughts.

Public schools should teach children the essential skills and knowledge that make for productive citizens, teach them to respect our constitutional order, and instruct them in the framework of rights and obligations that secure our democracy and protect our liberty. Any school that does so should be regarded as serving public purposes.

How should we apportion responsibility between families and public schools? The notion that schools can or should serve as a "corrective" against the family was first promulgated in the early 19th century by reformers who viewed the influx of immigrants as a threat to democratic processes and American norms. In the years since, encouraged by such thinkers as George Counts, Paulo Freire, Michael Apple, Peter McLaren, and Amy Gutmann, educational thinkers have unapologetically called for schooling to free students from the yoke of their family's provincial understandings.

The problem is that this conception of the "public interest" rests uneasily alongside America's pluralist traditions. American political thought, dating back to Madison's pragmatic embrace of "faction," has presumed that our various prejudices and biases can constructively counter one another, so long as the larger constitutional order and its attendant protections check our worst impulses.

The notion that schools are more "public" when they work harder to stamp out familial views and impress children with socially approved beliefs is one that ought to give pause to any civil libertarian or pluralist. Such schools are more attuned to the public purposes of a totalitarian regime than those of a democratic one. While a democratic nation can reasonably settle upon a range of state/family relationships, there is no reason to imagine that a regime that more heavily privileges the state is more "public." The relative "publicness" of education is not enhanced by having schools intrude more forcefully into the familial sphere.

Who should be permitted to provide public schooling? Given publicly determined purposes, it is not clear that public schooling needs to impose restrictions on who may provide services. There is no reason why for-profit or religious providers, in particular, ought to be regarded as suspect.

While traditional public schools have always dealt with for-profit providers of textbooks, teaching supplies, professional development, and so on, profit-seeking ventures have recently emerged as increasingly significant players in reform efforts. For instance, the for-profit, publicly held company Edison Schools is today managing scores of traditional district schools across the nation. Yet these are still regarded as "public" schools. In fact, Edison is managing the summer school programs, including curricula and personnel, for more than 70 public school *districts.* Yet those communities continue to regard summer school as public schooling.

Such arrangements seem to run afoul of our conventional use of the term "public," but the conflict is readily resolved when we recognize that all public agencies, including public hospitals and public transit systems, routinely harness the services of for-profit firms. Just as a public university is not thought to lose its public status merely because portions of it enter into for-profit ventures with regard to patents or athletics, so the entry of for-profit providers into a K–12 public school does not necessarily change the institution's fundamental nature. What matters in public higher education is whether the for-profit unit is controlled and overseen by those entrusted with the university's larger public mission. What matters in public schooling is whether profit seekers are hired to serve public ends and are monitored by public officials.

The status of religious providers has raised great concern among such groups as People for the American Way and the Center on Education Policy. However, the nation's early efforts to provide public education relied heavily upon local church officials to manage public funds, to provide a school facility, and to arrange the logistics of local schooling. It was not until the anti-Catholic fervor of the mid- and late-19th century that states distanced themselves from religious schooling. It was not until the mid-20th century that advocacy groups such as the American Civil Liberties Union pushed the remnants of religion out of state-run schools.

In recent decades, the U.S. Supreme Court has made clear that the push for a "wall of separation" had overreached and run afoul of First Amendment language protecting the "free exercise" of religion. Moreover, contemporary America has continued to evolve since the anti-Catholic zeal of the 19th century and the anti-religious intellectualism of the mid-20th century. Those conflicts were of a particular time and place. Today, church officials have less local sway and lack the unquestioned authority they once held, while they are more integrated into secular society. Just as some onetime opponents of single-sex schools can now, because of changes in the larger social order, imagine such schools serving the public interest, so too we should not reflexively shrink from viewing religious schools in a similar light. In most industrial democracies, including such nations as Canada, France, and the Netherlands, religious schools operate as part of the public system and are funded and regulated accordingly.

What obligations should public schools have to ensure opportunity for all students? We have never imagined that providing opportunity to all students means treating all students identically. The existence of magnet schools, special education, gifted classes, and exam schools makes it clear that we deem it appropriate for schools to select some children and exclude others in order to provide desirable academic environments. Our traditional school districts have never sought to ensure that every school or classroom should serve a random cross-section of children, only that systems as a whole should appropriately serve all children.

Given the tension between families who want their child schooled in an optimal environment and public officials who must construct systems that address competing needs, the principle that individual schools can exclude children but that systems cannot is both sensible and morally sound. That said, this principle does mean that some children will not attend school with the peers their parents might prefer.

The dilemma this presents is that no solitary good school can serve all the children who might wish to attend and that randomly admitting students may impede a school's effectiveness. Demanding that a science magnet school accept students with minimal science accomplishments or that any traditional school accept a habitually violent student threatens the ability of each school to accomplish its basic purposes. This is clearly not in the public interest. The same is true when a constructivist school is required to admit students from families who staunchly prefer back-to-basics instruction and will agitate for the curricula and pedagogy they prefer. In such cases, allowing schools to selectively admit students is consistent with the public interest—so long as the process furthers a legitimate educational purpose and the student has access to an appropriate alternative setting. Such publicly acceptable exclusion must be pursued for some reasonable educational purpose, and this creates a gray area that must be monitored. However, the need to patrol this area does not require that the practice be preemptively prohibited.

Moreover, self-selected or homogeneous communities are not necessarily less public than others. For instance, no one suggests that the University of Wyoming is less public than the University of Texas, though it is less geographically and ethnically representative of the nation. It has never been suggested that elections in San Francisco or Gopher Springs, West Virginia, would be more public if the communities included more residents who had not chosen to live there or whose views better reflected national norms. Nor has it been suggested that selective public institutions, such as the University of Michigan, are less public than are community colleges, even though they are selective about whom they admit. Moreover, there is always greater homogeneity in self-selected communities, such as magnet schools, as they attract educators and families who share certain views. None of this has been thought to undermine their essential "publicness."

Even champions of "public education," such as Deborah Meier and Ted Sizer, argue that this shared sense of commitment helps cultivate a participatory and democratic ethos in self-selected schools. In other words, heightened familial involvement tends to make self-selected schools more participatory and democratic. Kneeling before the false gods of heterogeneity or nonselectivity undermines our ability to forge participatory or effective schools without making schools commensurately more "public."

Nowhere, after all, does the availability of a "public service" imply that we get to choose our fellow users. In every field—whether public medicine, public transportation, or public higher education—the term "public" implies our right to a service, not our right to have buses

serve a particular route or to have a university cohort configured to our preferences. Even though such considerations influence the quality of the service, the need for public providers to juggle the requirements of all the individuals they must serve necessarily means that each member of the public cannot necessarily receive the service in the manner he or she would ultimately prefer. "Public schooling" implies an obligation to ensure that all students are appropriately served, not that every school is open to all comers.

What parts of public schooling are public? Debates about publicness focus on the classroom teaching and learning that is central to all schools. Maintenance, accounting, payroll, and food services are quite removed from the public purposes of education discussed above. Even though these peripheral services may take place in the same facility as teaching and learning, their execution does not meaningfully affect the "publicness" of schooling. Rather, we understand that it is sufficient to have ancillary services provided in a manner that is consistent with the wishes of a public education provider. For example, federal courts and state legislatures are indisputably public institutions, yet they frequently procure supplies, services, and personnel from privately run, for-profit enterprises. We properly regard these institutions as public because of their core purposes, not because of the manner in which they arrange their logistics.

Today's 'Public' Schools Often Aren't

Given the haphazard notion of public schooling that predominates today, it comes as little surprise that we offer contemporary educators little guidance in serving the public interest. This poses obvious problems, given that employment as an educator doesn't necessarily grant enhanced moral wisdom or personal virtue. If schools are to serve as places where educators advance purposes and cultivate virtues that they happen to prefer, it is not clear in what sense schools are serving "public purposes."

Blindly hoping that educators have internalized shared public purposes, we empower individuals to proselytize under the banner of "public schooling." This state of affairs has long been endorsed by influential educational theorists like George Counts, Paulo Freire, Henry Giroux, and Nel Noddings, who argue that teachers have a charge to use their classrooms to promote personal visions of social change, regardless of the broader public's beliefs. For these thinkers, "public schooling" ironically implies a community obligation to support schools for the private purposes of educators. The problem is that public institutions are not personal playthings. Just as it is unethical for a judge to disregard the law and instead rule on the basis of personal whimsy, so it is inappropriate for public school teachers to use their office to impose personal views upon a captive audience.

One appropriate public response is to specify public purposes and to demand that teachers reflect them, though we are reasonably cautious about adopting such an intrusive course. To the extent that explicit direction is absent, however, educators are left to their own devices. In such a case, our liberal tradition would recommend that we not subject children to the views of educators at an assigned school but allow families to avail themselves of a range of schools with diverse perspectives, so long as each teaches respect for our democratic and liberal tradition.

Conclusion

Today, our system of "public schooling" does little to ensure that our schools serve public purposes, while permitting some educators to use a publicly provided forum to promote their personal beliefs. Meanwhile, hiding behind the phrase's hallowed skirts are partisans who furiously attack any innovation that threatens their interests or beliefs.

There are many ways to provide legitimate public education. A restrictive state might tightly regulate school assignment, operations, and content, while another state might impose little regulation. However, there is no reason to regard the schools in the one state as more "public" than those in the other. The "publicness" of a school does not depend on class size, the use of certified teachers, rules governing employee termination, or the rest of the procedural apparatus that ensnares traditional district schools. The fact that public officials have the right to require public schools to comply with certain standards does not mean that schools subjected to more intrusive standards are somehow more public. The inclusion of religious schools in European systems, for instance, has been accompanied by intensive regulation of curricula and policy. Regulation on that order is not desirable, nor is it necessary for schools to operate as part of a public system; it is merely an operational choice made by officials in these relatively bureaucratic nations.

As opportunities to deliver, structure, and practice education evolve, it is periodically necessary to revisit assumptions about what constitutes public schooling. The ideology and institutional self-interest that infuse the dominant current conception have fueled withering attacks on the very legitimacy of public schooling itself. Failure to address this impoverished status quo will increasingly offer critics cause to challenge the purpose and justification of public education. Maintaining and strengthening our commitment to public schooling requires that we rededicate ourselves to essential principles of opportunity, liberal democracy, and public benefit, while freeing ourselves from political demands and historic happenstance.

In an age when social and technological change have made possible new approaches to teaching and learning, pinched renderings of "public schooling" have grown untenable and counterproductive. They stifle creative efforts, confuse debates, and divert attention from more useful questions. A more expansive conception is truer to our traditions, more likely to foster shared values, and better suited to the challenges of the new century.

Notes

1. James Coleman, "Public Schools, Private Schools, and the Public Interest," *Public Interest,* Summer 1981, pp. 19–30. See also idem, "Quality and Equality in American Education," *Phi Delta Kappan,* November 1981, pp. 159–64.
2. For the best empirical examination of the scope and nature of the "public school ideology," see Terry Moe, *Schools, Vouchers, and the American Public* (Washington, D.C.: Brookings, 2001).
3. See Andrew Coulson, *Market Education: The Unknown History* (New Brunswick, N.J.: Transaction Publishers, 1999); and Douglas Dewey, "An Echo, Not a Choice: School Vouchers Repeat the Error of Public Education," *Policy Review,* November/December 1996. . . .
4. See Frederick M. Hess, "Making Sense of the 'Public' in Public Education," unpublished paper, Progressive Policy Institute, Washington, D.C., 2002.
5. John Dewey, *The Public and Its Problems* (1927; reprint, Athens: Ohio University Press, 1954).
6. See Frederick M. Hess, "What Is 'Public' About Public Education?," *Education Week,* 8 January 2003, p. 56.
7. An extended discussion of this point can be found in Paul T. Hill, "What Is Public About Public Education?," in Terry Moe, ed., *A Primer on America's Schools* (Stanford, Calif.: Hoover Institution, 2001), pp. 285–316.
8. Frank Smith, "Overselling Literacy," *Phi Delta Kappan,* January 1989, pp. 353–59; Alfie Kohn, *No Contest: The Case Against Competition* (Boston: Houghton Mifflin, 1986); Susan Ohanian, "Capitalism, Calculus, and Conscience," *Phi Delta Kappan,* June 2003, pp. 736–47; and Deborah Meier, "Educating a Democracy," in idem, ed., *Will Standards Save Public Education?* (Boston: Beacon Press, 2000).

FREDERICK M. HESS is a Resident Scholar at the American Enterprise Institute in Washington, DC, and author of *Common Sense School Reform.*

Linda Nathan et al.

 **NO**

A Response to Frederick Hess

Linda Nathan, The Larger Purpose of Public Schools

At times I want to cheer for Frederick Hess's words in "What Is a 'Public School'? Principles for a New Century." How true it is that many reformers "regard public schooling as a politicized obstacle rather than a shared ideal." How true that "those of us committed to the promise of public education are obliged to see that the idea does not become a tool of vested interests."

Yet there is also something chilling about his article that stops the cheer in my throat. His use of innuendo in place of evidence, his sloppy logic, and his attacks on some of the most effective public school reformers—painting them as the enemy—suggest that his real agenda is not strengthening public education but privatizing it through vouchers and for-profit takeover schemes.

Hess's labored analysis obscures a simple fact: public schools have a larger and more democratic purpose than private and parochial schools (although this is not to say that these schools contribute nothing to public life). Public school systems are open to everyone regardless of disability, wealth, status, race, or religion. Private and parochial schools are not. While some are more open than others, they can have entrance exams and can explicitly exclude students with disabilities or those who otherwise don't fit a preferred profile. And of course they can also exclude those who can't pay. They can expel students who cause trouble, at their sole discretion, without recourse.

Hess himself acknowledges this core principle of universal access, conceding that public schooling "implies an obligation to ensure that all students are appropriately served." But he seems indifferent to the inequities inherent in his "more expansive" notion of what makes a school public.

Hess makes a false analogy when he equates schools that buy textbooks from for-profit companies with schools that are managed by for-profit firms. Basic educational decisions should be made by citizens of the local school community—not by distant shareholders looking only at a corporate balance sheet. (It's ironic that Hess picks as his exemplar Edison Schools, Inc., which sold off the textbooks, computers, lab supplies, and musical instruments of the Philadelphia public schools it had been hired to manage just days before school was to open in 2002 in order to pay down the company's mounting debt.)

Hess objects to teaching "tolerance" and affirming "diversity" because, he says, these words are open to multiple interpretations. Then he states that "public schools should teach children the essential skills and knowledge that make for productive citizens" and "teach them to respect our constitutional order," as if these were absolute truths *not* open to interpretation. The example of tolerance he cites, wherein a radical Muslim is calling for jihad, slyly exploits a hot-button issue to imply that the "professional community" of educators condones terrorism. Similarly, he smears the notion of defending tolerance as "uniformly teaching students to accept teen pregnancy as normal" and implies that liberals equate these activities with their definition of "public schooling." Nonsense.

His attack on Deborah Meier, Alfie Kohn, and others is equally baseless. It's the classic straw man fallacy: he attributes a position to them—that they oppose the teaching of basic academic mastery in favor of promoting "preferred social values"—that they have in fact never espoused. Meier's argument, with which Hess is surely familiar, is that such a tradeoff is unnecessary and that strong academic habits and mastery of literacy are essential and are furthered by an intellectually open and challenging spirit of inquiry.

The Coalition of Essential Schools, another of Hess's targets, gets similar treatment. Without offering a single example or other evidence of any kind, he asserts that faculty members at Coalition schools routinely promote partisan political views and are determined to "stamp out 'improper' thoughts." Of course, he's right that some teachers and schools—including many private and religious schools—do have a "party line," whether they're conscious of it or not. But he wants to have it both ways.

While he attacks Coalition teachers for promoting values he dislikes, he argues at the same time that there should be choice in education so that parents can select schools that reflect their values.

Hess's argument with regard to the personal views and political leanings of educators is simply a red herring. The underlying issue is his fear that his own preferred values are being "stamped out." He uses that phrase again in making the absurd claim that the goal of liberal educators is to subvert the influence of families on their children. If he were serious about the rights of parents, Hess would be attacking the idea of a federalized education system—with or without vouchers—in which the *state* defines which values, priorities, intellectual habits, and performance standards will dominate and in which schools must accept intrusive guidelines to receive a stamp of approval and public funding. It seems to me that his scorn should fall not on Deborah Meier and Ted Sizer but on George W. Bush and the other proponents of top-down standardization.

Hess wants teachers to promote respect for the law—unless the laws in question are those that guarantee equal rights to people regardless of sexual orientation. When I began teaching in the late 1970s, it was dangerous for a teacher to be homosexual, not because of students' or parents' reactions but because of administrative reprisals. And it was dangerous in those days to talk about the threat of nuclear war or to suggest that the U.S.-sponsored war in El Salvador was unjust or even to imply that there was another view of these issues than the government's. My colleagues daily taught their students that might was

right and homosexuality was a sin. I had my tires slashed by colleagues who felt that desegregation had ruined the Boston Public Schools. That we have created schools in which more open dialogue is possible indeed represents progress.

In calling for more innovation and choice in public education, Hess is absolutely right. In diversity, after all, there is strength. The U.S. has tried many experiments in public schooling over the past two centuries. We are in the midst of yet another experiment with our charter schools. In many ways, this kind of exploration is healthy. It allows us to look at different models and seek out best practices. Yet the charter school experiment has largely ignored issues of equity. In Boston and many other districts, charter schools often make no provision for accepting students who require special educational services or facilities, while traditional public schools are required to do so. This is one reason that some see charter schools as less "public" than other public schools. The same inequities exist in many parochial schools.

We need schools that help young people and adults learn and practice the skills necessary to be participants in a vibrant democracy. Such schools will be messy places that must balance the public interest with America's pluralist tradition. In their classrooms everyone learns to ask probing questions, to use evidence well, to make legitimate arguments, and to recognize fallacies and lies. I invite Frederick Hess to come to the Boston Arts Academy, where we will be happy to give him the opportunity to practice these skills with our students.

Joe Nathan, Some Questions for Advocates of Public Education

Three very specific questions for advocates of public education came to my mind as I read Frederick Hess's argument that we need to "reappraise our assumptions as to what constitutes 'public schooling.'" Let me pose them to *Kappan* readers, who no doubt are advocates for public education.

What is public about a suburban district in which the price of admission to the local public schools is the ability to purchase a home for more than one million dollars (and to pay tax-deductible property taxes on that home)?

What is public about an inner-city school with an admissions test that screens out all students with mental disabilities and more than 95% of the students in the surrounding district and so proclaims that it serves only the "cream of the crop"?

What is public about preventing some inner-city students from attending a magnet school just a few blocks from their homes that receives $1,500 per pupil more than the neighborhood school they attend? At the same time,

in the name of integration, white students from wealthy suburbs are transported to this school—some via taxi.

These three questions form the basis for two larger questions that continue to trouble me even after being involved with public education for 33 years. I don't have definitive answers to these larger questions. But I share them with readers in the hope that they, too, will find them worth pondering. . . .

◦◦◦

. . . 1. *Since all public schools are not open to all kinds of students, what admissions standards should be acceptable for schools supported by public funds?* When my teachers in the Wichita public schools talked about public education, they stressed that a key difference between public and private schools was that public schools were open to all. Many of the authorities I read while I was at Carleton College, preparing to become a teacher, said the same thing.

This idea of "open to all" makes great sense to me. It seems like the right and just way to operate. Hess writes that he thinks it "appropriate" for some public schools to select some children and exclude others. I've disagreed with this position for more than 30 years. But lately, I'm not so sure.

When I began teaching I learned that many public schools were *not* open to all students. As I traveled the country, I learned that there were more than a thousand magnet schools and programs that have admissions tests. A study some years ago found that more than half of the nation's secondary magnet schools have admissions tests, as do about a quarter of the elementary magnets.[1]

Wisconsin Rep. Polly Williams, a Democrat and an African American state legislator, was enraged because most of the youngsters in her inner-city Milwaukee district were not able to get into exclusive magnet schools in the neighborhood, which brought in affluent, white, suburban students. Her frustration led her to fight successfully for the nation's first formal voucher plan.

Some opponents of vouchers insist that a level playing field isn't available when private schools can cherrypick their students. I agree. But many educators, including me, have the same frustration about elite magnet schools: they have an unfair advantage over neighborhood public schools that are open to all in that they can screen out students with whom they don't wish to work.

I also learned that the country's single biggest choice system is called the suburbs. Millions of youngsters attend schools in the suburbs, and these schools clearly are *not* open to all students. They are open only to those whose families can afford to live in suburban communities.

A few years ago, I visited a school district on the northern coast of Long Island. Administrators there told me that the least expensive home in the district sold for $1,000,000. None of the district's teachers could afford to live there.

Today, some people argue that there should be publicly funded schools that are open only to young women. Two such schools have opened—one in New York, the other in Chicago. Even though I was not fond of this type of school, I visited the New York City district school, Young Women's Leadership Academy. I was impressed. The young women reported that, without boys around, they felt much more comfortable raising their hands in class and much more comfortable doing well on tests.

Should public funds go to some schools of choice that are only open to women? Or only to men? Five years ago, I would have said emphatically not. Today, I don't know.

2. Shouldn't schools we describe as public accept and use some of the country's basic ideas to help improve education? Americans generally endorse a number of ideas:

- choice of religion, job, neighborhood, places to obtain services, and so on;

- the provision of opportunities to try new ideas and approaches;
- the shared belief that this is a country not just of rights, but of responsibilities; and
- the notions that our cherished freedoms are not unlimited.

However, for three decades I've watched major public education groups vigorously oppose school choice programs, including public school choice programs, that are built on these principles. For example, there was intense opposition from educators in 1970 to the creation of the St. Paul Open School.

These organized groups ignore the professional and pedagogical rationales for public school choice, expressed best by veteran educator Deborah Meier:

> Choice is an essential tool in the effort to create . . . good public education. . . . We'll have to allow those most involved (teachers, administrators, parents) to exercise greater on-site power to put their collective wisdom into practice. Once we do all this, however, school X and school Y are going to start doing things differently. . . . Creating a school different from what any of those who work in the system are familiar with, one that runs counter to the experiences of most families, is possible only if teachers, parents, and students have time to agree on changes and a choice on whether or not they want to go along with them.[2]

Colleagues involved in other efforts to create new options over the last three decades have had similar experiences. During his tenure as president of the American Federation of Teachers, Al Shanker described what happened to teachers who proposed schools-within-schools:

> Many schools-within-schools were or are treated like traitors or outlaws for daring to move out of the lockstep and do something different. Their initiators had to move Heaven and Earth to get school officials to authorize them, and if they managed that, often they could look forward to insecurity, obscurity, or outright hostility.[3]

Over the past decade, with help from the Gates, Blandin, and Annenberg Foundations, the Center for School Change at the University of Minnesota has tried to help educators create new schools-within-schools in a number of communities. Shanker's words have often proved to be very accurate. The most intense, vigorous critics of offering a different kind of school—whether in a single building or in a district—have often been other educators.

Many educators have argued over the past 30 years that public, district schools serving racial minorities and students from low-income families are doing the best job they can with existing funds. According to the most recent Phi Delta Kappa/Gallup poll, 80% of the public thinks the achievement gap between white children and minority children is mostly related to factors other than the quality of schooling.[4]

Perhaps in part because some educators have helped to convince the public that inner-city schools are mostly not responsible for the achievement gap, 58% of the nation and 62% of public school parents think it is possible to narrow the achievement gap *without* spending more money than is currently being spent on these students.[5] Unfortunately, many state legislators are opting not to raise taxes and not to give more to schools serving low-income, limited-English-speaking students.

Some of us vigorously disagree with these legislative actions and think that both more public school choice and more funding would help reduce the achievement gap. We have seen—and in some cases have worked in— schools that have served the public interest by helping all youngsters achieve their potential and have done much to close the gap between students of different races.

Despite encouragement from such strong public school supporters as former President Bill Clinton, former Secretary of Education Richard Riley, and the late Sen. Paul Wellstone (D-Minn.), efforts to create independent charter public schools still face huge opposition from state teacher, school board, and superintendent groups. The opposition uses the same arguments used in 1970 against the St. Paul Open School: new options take away our money.

But it isn't their money. Legislatures allocate money for the education of children, not for the preservation of a system. If 50 students move from a city to a suburb or from a suburb to a city, the dollars follow them. The money doesn't belong to "the system."

Thousands of parents and educators are voting with their feet. The number of states with a charter law has gone from one in 1991 to 40 in 2003. The number of charter schools has gone from one school in 1991 to more than 3,000 in 2003. Federal statistics show that low-income students and racial minorities are overrepresented in charter schools. While the evidence is mixed—and almost certainly will be so when charter and district schools are compared—some charters are clearly producing major achievement gains. Shouldn't we learn from and replicate their best practices?

Starting new schools is extremely difficult work. But whether it's a Pilot School in the Boston Public Schools or a New Visions option in New York City or a charter school in any of 40 states, the opportunity to try new approaches is as vital for education as it is for medicine, business, or technology.

Some Tentative Conclusions

So Frederick Hess wants to "discern what . . . makes schooling public and accept diverse arrangements that are consistent with those tenets." I'm not sure what

standards all publicly supported schools should meet. But after 33 years, I offer these as minimum requirements for schools that serve the public interest and are thus eligible to receive public funds. Public schools should:

- be open to all kinds of students and not use admissions tests;
- follow due process procedures with regard to students and educators;
- use state-approved, standardized, and other measures to help monitor student progress or lack thereof;
- have closing the achievement gap between white students and racial minority and low-income students as an explicit, measurable goal;[6] and
- be actively chosen by faculty, families, and students.

Thanks to Hess and to the *Kappan* for urging a timely reconsideration of the basic principles of public education. As social justice activist Leonard Fein states it:

The future is not something we discover around the next corner. It is something we shape, we create, we invent. To hold otherwise would be to view ourselves as an audience to history, and not its authors. History, and even our own lives, cannot always be turned and twisted to make them go exactly where we should like. But there is, for people of energy and purpose, more freedom of movement than most ever exercise.[7]

Notes

1. Lauri Steel and Roger Levine, *Educational Innovation in Multiracial Contexts: The Growth of Magnet Schools in American Education* (Palo Alto, Calif.: American Institutes for Research, 1994). This study was prepared for the U.S. Department of Education under Contract No. LC 90043001.
2. Deborah Meier, "Choice Can Save Public Education," *The Nation,* 4 March 1991.
3. Al Shanker, "Where We Stand: Convention Plots New Course—A Charter for Change," *New York Times* (paid advertisement), 10 July 1988, p. E-7.
4. Lowell C. Rose and Alec M. Gallup, "The 35th Annual Phi Delta Kappa/Gallup Poll of the Public's Attitudes Toward the Public Schools," *Phi Delta Kappan,* September 2003, p. 48.
5. Ibid.
6. Student progress should be monitored using various measures, not just standardized tests. If there is not major improvement in narrowing the achievement gap in most areas over a five-year period, the school should be "reconstituted."
7. Leonard Fein et al., *Reform Is a Verb: Notes on Reform and Reforming Jews* (New York: Union of American Hebrew Congregations, 1972), p. 152.

Ray Bacchetti, An Ongoing Conversation

We don't look at the big issues of the principles and purposes of public schools often or carefully enough. Sadly, the political and philosophical conversation seems increasingly polarized. In Venn diagram terms, the two circles—labeled right/left, basics/constructivist, academic/child-centered, etc.—reveal at best a vanishingly thin region of overlap. When the true believers on either side look in the mirror, they see Dumbledore. Over their shoulders and gaining, they see Voldemort.

Frederick Hess's beefy rhetoric stakes out a position that reflects a more conservative world view than my own. In essence, he argues that the purposes of public education will be better served if we narrow the number of principles that define its publicness and expand the number of ways those principles can be implemented. In that expanded universe, religious schools, vouchers, for-profit ventures, and other alternatives would be welcome.

The principles advertised in Hess's title are woven through his essay, making it difficult to distinguish his main point from his subsidiary concerns. Here is what I take to be the core of his definition of what makes a school public. In addition to teaching skills and content, public schools should:

- prepare students to be "productive members of the social order";
- enable students to "become aware of their societal responsibilities," including the "principles, habits, and obligations of citizenship"; and
- educate students to be "respectful of constitutional strictures," including laws, process, and individual rights.

In carrying out these functions, public school systems should also:

- not "deny access to students for reasons unrelated to [a school's] educational focus"; and
- "provide an appropriate placement for each student" in every community.

Asserting by implication that the meanings of his key terms are inherently obvious, Hess goes on to argue that the terms others might use to set forth other principles are not. For example, he observes that "diversity" and "tolerance" are "umbrella terms with multiple interpretations." Therefore, they lie outside his cluster of principles because, when we try to define them more precisely, "it becomes clear that we must privilege some values at the expense of others." If he believes that a similar privileging of certain values might color his own key terms, such as "obligations of citizenship," "productive members of the social order," "societal responsibilities," "individual rights," and the like, he gives no indication.

Hess seems to arrive at his position partly for affirmative reasons (e.g., an emphasis on academic learning) and partly because of a surprisingly bitter view of educators (some of whom he names, but most of whom he only characterizes). In his view, these educators:

- "explicitly promote a particular world view and endorse a particular social ethos";
- "promote partisan attitudes toward American foreign policy, the propriety of affirmative action, or the morality of redistributive social policies";
- teach students to "accept teen pregnancy or homosexuality as normal and morally unobjectionable";
- attempt to "stamp out familial views and impress children with socially approved beliefs"; and
- treat public institutions as their personal playthings.

To illustrate his more general points, Hess portrays the "meaningful questions" asked in the classrooms of the Coalition of Essential Schools as a herd of Trojan ponies surreptitiously unloading the teachers' agendas. It's not clear what "meaningful questions" might be in the classrooms he approves of, though readers might infer that they would be limited to the rational analysis of topics that arise from well-developed and authoritatively taught subject matter. There is nothing wrong with such questions, of course. But anyone who thinks that they—or the answers to them—would be value-free is likely to have slept through his or her undergraduate philosophy classes.

More to the point, however, a narrow and academic definition of such questions would exclude from the public school universe those who think students should also wrestle with forming habits of the heart as well as the mind, should learn to use critical inquiry to amend and expand values and understandings as well as to confirm them, and should go beyond "my country, right or wrong" to embrace the rest of Carl Schurz's famous phrase, "if right, to be kept right; and if wrong, to be set right."

I have spent a fair amount of time in schools of late, witnessing heroic efforts of underfinanced and overregulated teachers to enact both the academic preparation *and* the democracy-building ethos that our schools were meant to embody. If Hess is suggesting that generally left-leaning personal agendas have dominated public school instruction for a generation or more, then we should be able to see around us a widely shared value system that reflects those views. However, when I survey newspapers, polls, elections, and even school reform debates at national and local levels, I see instead an enormous variety of values and priorities. Some may find that diversity of views troubling. What troubles me is not that people disagree but that we seem increasingly incapable of working through our differences to embed public school policies and practices in a conception of the common good that can transcend political perspectives without disrespecting them.

The sort of public conversations about public education that would open minds to a critical look at new ideas would be, as I'm sure Hess would agree, tough to structure and to conduct. Where he and I are likely to disagree is on whether the topic of those conversations will ever be settled and, more important, whether it ever should be. Teaching skills and developing in each generation the social cohesion on which so much else depends will be easier (though never easy) to approach than will matters of values, educational philosophies, social goals, and civic priorities. Moreover, balancing the relative claims of the student, family, community, nation, and the wider world on how and what schools teach is a democratic journey, not a settled destination.

From the start, Hess acknowledges the powerful resonance of the concept of public education. What seems to make him impatient, even exasperated, is that the people who lead what he and some others pejoratively call "government-run schools" aren't listening to him. Not listening can be a stance or a reaction. Seeing it as a *stance,* I join him in his exasperation. The habit of "reflexively shrinking" from a consideration of alternatives hardens the democratic arteries. Seeing it as a *reaction,* I worry that world views (a term I prefer to "ideology") too often appear as righteous opposites, leaving all but the most robust listeners wondering what's the point.

Finding areas of overlap in our views under such conditions isn't easy. Developing the skills of measured and thoughtful dialogue needed to create such overlap is even harder. The challenge of doing so, however, demonstrates why a free nation needs public schools that are set up to make public decision making meaningful at the daily, close-to-home levels, as well as at higher levels. Such deliberative procedures force us to ask not only what we want our own children to learn but also what we want all children to learn. Children are, after all, collectively as well as individually the next generation, and the education we bequeath to them is communal as well as personal.

We need to talk and listen our way into more overlap in our political/philosophical Venn diagrams. Having that running conversation looms large in my definition of what makes the public schools public. Hess seems to argue that, through a few principles and a multitude of entities all claiming the mantle of public education, we can make the need for that conversation go away. I would argue instead that getting better at it should be our number-one priority.

Evans Clinchy, Reimagining Public Education

I heartily agree with Frederick Hess that we need to rethink and reimagine our antiquated American system of public education. But not for the reasons he sets forth.

I also agree with his broad definition of the purposes of public schooling: "that public schools are . . . defined by their commitment to preparing students to be productive members of the social order" (and therefore active citizens of a democratic society) who are able to think and use their minds well and are "aware of their societal responsibilities and respectful of constitutional strictures" (including an understanding of the Constitution and especially the Bill of Rights); "that such schools cannot deny access to students for reasons unrelated to their educational focus" (i.e., no racially, ethnically, or economically segregated schools); "and that the system of public schools available in any community must provide an appropriate placement for each student" (all students and their parents must be offered the kind of schooling they believe is most suitable). But I do not agree that we should seek to create the kind of reimagined system Hess appears to be proposing.

Questions of Definition, Control, and Funding

Throughout most of the history of the U.S., a public school has been defined as a school created, operated, and largely paid for by the citizens of each community through a locally elected board of education. While the Constitution leaves the basic authority for education in the hands of the individual states, and even though such locally controlled schools have, over the past century, received increased funding from both state and federal sources, this tradition of local control has managed to endure more or less intact—at least until the past 25 or so years.

The continued importance of this tradition was underscored in 1973 by the U.S. Supreme Court in its *Rodriguez* decision. The majority opinion put the matter this way:

> In an era that has witnessed a consistent trend toward centralization of the functions of government, local sharing of responsibility for public

education has survived. The merit of local control was recognized in both the majority and dissenting opinions in *Wright v. Council of the City of Emporia*. Mr. Justice Stewart stated there that "direct control over decisions vitally affecting the education of one's children is a need that is strongly felt in our society." The Chief Justice in his dissent agreed that local control is not only vital to continued public support of the schools, but it is of overriding importance from an educational standpoint as well.

The persistence of attachment to government at its lowest level where education is concerned reflects the depth of commitment of its supporters. In part local control means . . . the freedom to devote more money to the education of one's children. Equally important, however, is the opportunity it offers for participation in the decision-making process that determines how those local dollars will be spent. Each locality is free to tailor local programs to local needs. Pluralism also affords some opportunity for experimentation, innovation, and a healthy competition for educational excellence. An analogy to the Nation-State relationship in our federal system seems uniquely appropriate. Mr. Justice Brandeis identified as one of the peculiar strengths of our form of government each state's freedom to "serve as a laboratory; to try novel social and economic experiments." No area of social concern stands to profit more from a multiplicity of viewpoints and from a diversity of approaches than does public education.

Further, Justice William Brennan found in his dissent that "Here, there can be no doubt that education is inextricably linked to the right to participate in the electoral process and to the rights of free speech and association guaranteed by the First Amendment."[1]

During the past quarter century, however, the "consistent trend toward centralization of the functions of government" has run rampant in the field of public schooling. In the name of public school "reform," the states have usurped local control by imposing uniform, authoritarian, "high," "rigorous," one-size-fits-all academic standards and punitive high-stakes standardized testing on all students, all schools, and all school systems.

The federal education establishment, through its No Child Left Behind Act, has carried this intrusive, antidemocratic curricular control and standardized testing program to ludicrous extremes, requiring the testing of all students in grades 3 through 8 and insisting on annual progress in test scores with severe sanctions for schools that fail to show such progress. However, neither the federal government nor the states have provided the financial resources to pay for all this "reform" or to remedy the gross inequities that exist between those school systems that serve the wealthy and those that serve our poor and minority students and parents. I find these events distressing, but none of them appear to worry Hess very much.

If the powerful democratic tradition of local control is to be maintained and if we are to genuinely reimagine our public education system, we will need to do several things. First, we will have to abandon the authoritarian standards and high-stakes testing agenda that currently afflict our public schools and return to the citizens of our local communities the control over what is taught, how it will be taught, and who will teach it. State and federal interference should be limited to ensuring minimum competency in the basic skills of reading, writing, and mathematics.

Second, we will simultaneously need both state and federal governments to guarantee that all of the nation's public schools are fully and equitably funded and that the civil rights of all students and parents—but especially our poor and minority students and parents—are fully protected. Hess does not appear to recommend any of these policies.

The Threat of Vouchers and Privatization

We will also have to erect strong safeguards against the threat of vouchers and any further encroachment of the private corporate sector into the field of public schooling. Now that the Supreme Court has permitted the use of public funds to finance vouchers that can be used to pay tuition at nonpublic, including religious, schools, Hess appears to be saying that we should aim to create a system of public education similar to that of many European countries, where public funding is given directly to all nonpublic schools. Such a proposal would still violate both the First Amendment's separation of church and state and the democratic commitment to local public citizen control.

In addition, Hess proposes that we permit the private, for-profit sector to run both schools and school systems so long as those schools are monitored by some public body—despite the fact that the track record of Edison and other corporate EMOs (education management organizations) is educationally and economically dismal. Hess appears to believe that it is morally legitimate for private corporations to profit from the education of children, rather than being required to plow "profits" back into our chronically underfunded public schools. This thinking parallels the already-established view that it is somehow morally legitimate for corporate HMOs to make a profit out of caring for the sick, rather than being required to plow that money back into the health-care system. Neither of these policies is morally acceptable in any fair, just, and equitable system of democratic government.

A Truly Reimagined, Genuinely Democratic Public System of Diversity and Choice

Hess does raise an issue of fundamental importance when he points out that "there are many ways to provide legitimate public education." I assume that he means that there is no single kind of school—be it rigidly "traditional," wildly "progressive," or something in between—that could possibly serve the diverse educational beliefs of this nation's parents, the equally diverse professional philosophies of our public school educators, and most especially the enormously varied educational needs of our children and young people.

Strangely, however, Hess believes that many "prominent educational thinkers" (among others, he names Frank Smith, Susan Ohanian, Deborah Meier, and Alfie Kohn) have encouraged the public schools to promote "preferred social values" to the American public rather than advocating that all public schools limit themselves to teaching children "the essential skills and knowledge that make for productive citizens." He asserts that the "public schools should teach children . . . to respect our constitutional order and instruct them in the framework of rights and obligations that secure our democracy and protect our liberty." He argues this point as if this educational prescription were not itself an ideology—even if it is one that may be widely shared and one that in its main outlines is most certainly shared by his list of misguided thinkers.

Hess then goes on to advocate not just his own ideological prescription but the basic rule of what I would see as that truly reimagined public system we should be attempting to create. In order to encompass those diverse educational beliefs of parents and professional educators and to meet the varied educational needs of our children and young people, he says that we should "allow families to avail themselves of a range of schools with diverse perspectives, so long as each teaches respect for our democratic and liberal tradition." Thus we need that wide diversity of public schools—ranging from traditional to progressive—

from which parents, teachers, administrators, and older students can choose the type of schooling they believe will most benefit each child and young person. As Hess puts it, such strictly public school choice would create "heightened family involvement" and produce "a shared sense of commitment" that would tend to make such "self-selected schools more participatory and democratic."

It is, I believe, the job of our local public school systems, assisted and encouraged by state and federal governments, to provide that diversity of options. But the basic control of what goes on in all of our public schools must always remain solely in the public domain and solidly anchored in the will of the citizens of our local communities.

Note

1. *San Antonio Independent School District* v. *Rodriguez*, U.S. Supreme Court, 411 U.S. 1 (1973).

Linda Nathan is Headmaster of the Boston Arts Academy, a public high school for the visual and performing arts.

Joe Nathan is Director of the Center for School Change in the Hubert H. Humphrey Institute of Public Affairs at the University of Minnesota, Minneapolis.

Ray Bacchetti is former Vice President for Planning and Management at Stanford University and is a scholar at the Carnegie Foundation for the Advancement of Teaching.

Evans Clinchy is Senior Consultant at the Institute for Responsive Education at Northeastern University in Boston and Editor of *Transforming Public Education*.

EXPLORING THE ISSUE

Should "Public Schooling" Be Redefined?

Critical Thinking and Reflection

1. How many ways are there to provide legitimate public schooling?
2. Is the word "choice" a part of public schooling?
3. Are schools underfinanced and teachers overregulated?
4. Why is the Coalition of Essential Schools one of Hess's targets in his article?
5. Has public schooling strayed from its purpose and been captured by self-interested parties?

Is There Common Ground?

In the February 2004 issue of *Phi Delta Kappan*, Frederick M. Hess put forth a rejoinder to his four critics in an article titled "Debating Principles for Public Schooling in a New Century." He lists some significant points of agreement, including that it is necessary and useful to reconsider the essence of "public schooling" in an age marked by radical changes in how education is being provided. However, these critics, Hess contends, attack reforms as "anti-public education" for permitting the same practices that some "public schools" already engage in—for example, schools that are not open to all students when located in an affluent community. He feels that some critics allow the notion of public schooling to become a rhetorical banner for bolstering partisan positions and delegitimizing opposing ideas. Hess further states that "there is a real danger to the rhetorical strategy of branding objectionable reforms as de facto 'assaults on public schooling.' This device is fruitless and divisive. Perhaps more forebodingly, it excommunicates many who honor public education because they fail to endorse the 'right kind' of public schooling."

John C. Lundt, a professor of educational leadership, says that education is leaving the schoolhouse as technology increasingly makes it an anytime-anywhere activity. In a provocative article in the December 2004 issue of *The Futurist* titled "Learning for Ourselves: A New Paradigm for Education," Lundt concludes that the antiquated structure of today's school was designed to meet the needs of a world that no longer exists, that public schools will not change as long as they monopolize educational funding, and that growing numbers of parents find the activities and values of public schools inappropriate for their children. This basic concern about funding is echoed by reporter Joe Williams in his book *Cheating Our Kids: How Politics and Greed Ruin Education* (2005). Williams examines the impact of special-interest groups on local public school systems (specifically in New York and Milwaukee), finding that most "reform" money only expands already bloated district bureaucracies. He calls for a concerted effort by concerned parents to reclaim power.

Create Central

www.mhhe.com/createcentral

Additional Resources

Ross Hubbard, "Tinkering Change Vs. System Change," *Phi Delta Kappan* (June 2009)

Hannah Lobel, "Putting the Public Back in Public Education," *Utne* (January–February 2009)

Susan Ohanian, "Refrains of the School Critics," *The School Administrator* (August 2005)

James Schuls, "It is Time We Redefine Public Education," *Re-define Ed* (August 1, 2013)

Paul A. Zoch, *Doomed to Fail: The Built-in Defects of American Education* (2004)

Internet References . . .

Center for Education Reform

www.edreform.com

Inner City Education Foundation

www.icefla.org

National Alliance for Civic Education

www.civnet.net

Rethinking Schools

www.rethinkingschools.org

Turnaround for Children

http://turnaroundusa.org

Unit 2

UNIT

Current Fundamental Issues

*T*he issues discussed in this unit cover a number of fundamental social, cultural, and political problems currently under consideration by education experts, social scientists, and politicians, as well as by parents, teachers, and the media. Positions on these issues are expressed by Kristan A. Morrison, Gary K. Clabaugh, Chief Judge Honorable Theodore A. McKee, The Albert Shanker Institute, Jay P. Greene, Sandra Stotsky, Bill Evers, Greg Forster, Ze'ev Wurman, William H. Schmidt, Nathan A. Burroughs, Karin Chenoweth, Andy Smarick, Marc Tucker, and Diane Ravitch.

Selected, Edited, and with Issue Framing Material by:
Glenn L. Koonce, *Regent University*

ISSUE

Are Truly Democratic Classrooms Possible?

YES: Kristan A. Morrison, from "Democratic Classrooms: Promises and Challenges of Student Voice and Choice, Part One," *Educational Horizons* (Fall 2008)

NO: Gary K. Clabaugh, from "Second Thoughts about Democratic Classrooms," *Educational Horizons* (Fall 2008)

Learning Outcomes
After reading this issue, you will be able to: • Define and describe a democratic classroom.   • Analyze and describe internal and external factors that shape democratic classrooms.   • Explore how schools are a reflection of society.   • Identify the closest challenges to democratic education.   • Gain an understanding of the role of federal government in democratic education.

ISSUE SUMMARY

YES: Associate Professor of Education Kristan A. Morrison explores historical and theoretical bases for implementing democratic practices in schools that would make student experience more appealing and productive.

NO: Professor of Education Gary K. Clabaugh examines such factors as top-down management, compulsory attendance, business world influences, and federal mandates to declare Morrison's ideas to be "out of touch" with reality.

Certainly everyone would agree that one of the primary aims of education is to produce citizens capable of effectively participating in their society. The controversial aspect of this aim resides in determining the best way of carrying it out. In recent years educators and theorists have renewed a basic question that has been discussed for over a hundred years, namely "Is it possible to produce democratic citizens if the schooling the young are subjected to is clearly undemocratic?"

As Charles C. Haynes, in "Schools of Conscience," *Educational Leadership* (May 2009), states, "We need schools that actually practice what their civics classes are supposed to teach. . . . At a time when the United States faces unprecedented challenges at home and abroad, public schools must do far more to prepare young people to be engaged, ethical advocates of 'liberty and justice for all.'" Haynes contends that education's highest aim is to create moral and civic habits of the heart. This central purpose was articulated by the early leaders of American education. Thomas Jefferson made the principles of democratic government an essential element in the free public education

of the general citizenry. Horace Mann's common school was dedicated to producing people able to critically judge the political and social needs of the nation. Waves of European immigrants in the nineteenth century prompted a new emphasis on socialization strategies and the development of patriotism. As Joel Spring has pointed out in his book *Conflict of Interests*, "In a totalitarian society it is possible to teach a single interpretation of the laws and government in the public schools, but in a society such as that of the United States, which fosters a variety of political beliefs . . . , attempts to teach principles of government can result in major political battles."

In "Civic Education and Political Participation," *Phi Delta Kappan* (September 2003), William A. Galston declares that school-based civic education has been in decline over recent decades. He claims that every significant indicator of political engagement among the young has fallen. Community service programs in high schools are on the increase, but there is no evidence that such "mandatory volunteerism" leads to wider civic participation. He states that "the surge of patriotic sentiment among young people in the immediate wake of

September 11th has not yielded a comparable surge in engaged, active citizenship."

If the school atmosphere is by design, by tradition, or by habit undemocratic can truly democratic citizens emerge? Haynes states that "to prepare students to be ethical, engaged citizens we must give them . . . meaningful opportunities to practice freedom responsibly in a school culture that encourages shared decision-making. . . . In short we need schools that actually practice . . . freedom and democracy, not censorship and repression."

Similarly, Marion Brady, in "Cover the Material—Or Teach Students to Think?" *Educational Leadership* (February 2008), claims that students need to tackle issues straight out of the complex world in which they live. "A focus on real-world issues . . . enables students and teachers to experience the 'meatiness' of the direct study of reality. . . . It shows respect for students, who become more than mere candidates for the next higher grade. . . . It disregards the arbitrary, artificial boundaries of the academic disciplines."

In "Democracy and Education: Empowering Students to Make Sense of Their World," *Phi Delta Kappan* (January 2008), William H. Garrison contends that the best learning happens under a truly democratic system in which students assume the freedom and responsibility to make choices and direct their learning experiences. His ideas certainly reflect the basic philosophy of John Dewey and the sentiments of John Holt.

In the articles presented here, Kristan A. Morrison aligns herself with critical theorists in the field of education who feel that the public schools have been used by societal and political forces to curtail rather than release student freedom. Gary K. Clabaugh thinks that while some of Morrison's points are well taken she naively ignores the shaping power of numerous internal and external factors.

YES ↵

Kristan A. Morrison

Democratic Classrooms: Promises and Challenges of Student Voice and Choice

Abstract

If we ever hope to have schools that are engaging and that truly embody democracy, then the classes within them must provide opportunities for students to experience autonomy, freedom, and choice in what is studied, when, and how. This article explores both the historical and theoretical framework of democratic freedom-based education and the promises and challenges of implementing democratic practices in schools.

. . .

Introduction

Schools and society are reflections of one another. Certain values and beliefs are dominant in our society and inculcated in school. They include

- a competitive ethos and firm conviction that a meritocracy exists in our society
- a view that instrumental and extrinsic motivations are more important than intrinsic motivations
- an excessive valuing of academics
- a belief in the atomization and fragmentation of subjects of study, people, and nature
- the conviction that the characteristic of obedience (doing as one is told or believing as one is told) is of more value in our society than that of criticality
- the belief that one's worth can be defined by others (as good student or bad student)

Once students become adults, they perpetuate those same dominant values in both society and school.

This cycle is complicated, however, because beyond those dominant values, schools are "terrains of struggle" (Giroux 1988), places where contradictory values and ideals compete for prominence.

Critical educational theorists, who include John Dewey and more-contemporary authors such as Henry Giroux, Paulo Freire, Peter McLaren, bell hooks, David Purpel, and Maxine Greene, argue that certain moral, political, and intellectual ideals should take precedence over others in schools. They assert that our schools should emphasize commitment to a democratic system in which each citizen's autonomy and dignity are honored in an open, just, respectful, and pluralistic community, a community that values and encourages a critical approach in the intellectual search for truth and meaning in each individual's life (Purpel 1989).

The community these theorists seek is a delicately balanced synthesis between the individual (thesis) and a collection of individuals (antithesis). In other words, an individual's autonomy is delimited by others' rights to dignity, respect, safety, and the search for truth and meaning to everyone's lives; if person A decides to do something that somehow infringes on person B's rights, then person A is prohibited from taking that action and encouraged to find actions that can both express his or her autonomy and honor the rights of others.

Many of us know from experience that our society's schools often fall far short of fostering the development of people who value diversity, who are both autonomous yet cognizant of others' needs and rights, and who are open-minded yet equipped with critical-thinking skills to analyze contradictory ideas. Instead, many of our schools foster the development of very different sorts of individuals.

Does that indicate that the critical educational theorists are wrong? No, it just means that they and like-minded educators must struggle to actualize their ideals in schools. One way to do that, I would argue, is to institute more democratic and freedom-based practices within our educational system. This article explores the historical and theoretical framework of such practices, and then goes on to detail their promises and challenges.

Definitions and Historical/ Theoretical Framework

The term "democratic education" as used in this article is linked with and synonymous with the term "freedom-based education," for just as democracy as a political system is grounded in individual freedoms, democracy as an educational system is also grounded in freedoms. The linkage between the two terms is supported by the

Reprinted with permission of *Educational Horizons*, quarterly journal of Pi Lambda Theta Inc., International Honor Society and Professional Association in Education, P O Box 6626, Bloomington, IN 47401, Fall 2008, pp. 50–59.

self-descriptions of most freedom-based schools in the United States (e.g., "free schools," Sudbury Valley-modeled schools, "unschooling" families, etc.), which also identify themselves as sites of democratic education.

In democratic and freedom-based education, students are free to decide what they study, and how, and when they study it. This form of schooling has a number of historical antecedents, outlined by Bennis (2006). He argues that one genesis of this model of education is the form of learning found in most pre-industrial societies. In these societies (past and present), children are actively engaged in the life of a given society; they learn skills and knowledge by means of imitation, apprenticeship, modeling, and conversation rather than in any formal school setting. Freedom-based education is also rooted in the Western philosophical tradition of the ancient Greeks, in the Romantic thinkers (e.g., Rousseau and Froebel), in the libertarian-anarchist tradition, in the transcendentalist movement of nineteenth-century America, and in the twentieth-century free-school movement (e.g., Summerhill School, led by A. S. Neill, and the many U.S. free schools that cropped up during the countercultural revolution of the 1960s and 1970s) (pp. 23–32).

Democratic and freedom-based education is grounded in the premise that people are naturally curious and have an innate desire to learn and grow. If left unfettered, un-coerced, and un-manipulated (e.g., by conventional educational practices that often diminish those innate characteristics), people will pursue their interests vigorously and with gusto, and thus learn and make meaning on their own and in concert with others. Individuals honored and respected in this process become socialized to honor and respect the dignity and autonomy of others (Dennison 1969; Hern 1996; Holt 1972, 1989; Illich 1971; Llewellyn 1997; Mercogliano 1998; Neill and Lamb 1992).

Although most contemporary freedom-based education is found in the form of private schools or the home-schooling version, "unschooling" (Morrison 2007b), American public schools could shift more closely to this model by adopting more-democratic practices and organizational structures (Reitzug 2003). Thus, enacting democratic practices within conventional, more-authoritarian and -bureaucratic schools could serve as a steppingstone toward adopting the model of democratic and freedom-based education more fully.

Democratic education can take multiple forms, ranging from the micro level of within-class democracy to the more-ideal macro level of whole-school democracy, and within each level, a number of different democratic practices can be enacted. For example, at the micro level, a teacher can utilize discussion; offer students test and assignment choices that attend to their unique learning preferences; allow students "protest rights" (Shor 1996); practice contract grading (Shor 1996) or self-grading; allow students to call the teacher by first name; and ask students to co-construct the course (have a voice in course content, grading, rubric creation, etc.). At the macro, whole-school level, schools can allow students to construct their entire curricula. (See Morrison 2007a, which examines the Albany Free School, a school where pre-K through eighth-grade students choose what, how, and when they study subjects, or see Goddard College for university-level self-development of curricula.)

Promises of Democratic Education

Proponents of democratic and freedom-based education argue that with autonomy and choice, people experience a much-different, much-better form of education than that offered by the conventional, hierarchical, more-coercive education system present in most public schools.

First, they argue that a democratic education promises much more meaningful learning. If people have choice and freedom to study what interests them, then they become more deeply engaged in, and thus less alienated from, their learning. More engagement leads to better retention and better critical reflection and analysis. For example, Watson wrote in *Summerhill: For and Against* (1970) that "pupils given freedom to decide what they will do, when, and how develop increasing independence, stronger interests, and better quality of work" (p. 177).

Gatto, in *Dumbing Us Down: The Hidden Curriculum of Compulsory Schools* (1992), echoes that argument, stating that our conventional education system infantilizes students by constantly compelling them and that this compulsion "guarantees that they will do [work] poorly, with a bad will, or indifferently" (p. 93). Democratic education, conversely, has no infantilizing effect; instead, it places great trust in the students, and they, more often than not, rise to the challenge. In the process, students become more mature, self-disciplined, and intrinsically motivated, seeing the value of learning above and beyond its usefulness to getting a "good job" (Bhave 1996; Labaree 1997).

Proponents of democratic education further argue that people who are given freedom and choice will ultimately become better democratic citizens because they have learned how to negotiate with others, to name obstacles, and to know themselves (Bhave 1996; Dewey 1916; Gatto 1992; Goodman 1962; Holt 1972; Holzman 1997; Illich 1971; Morrison 2007a; Shor 1996). That ultimately benefits all of society by developing people who are open to change and to listening to others so that all consider themselves vital to society. As Shor argued in *When Students Have Power* (1996): "Power-sharing . . . creates the desire and imagination of change while also creating the experience and skills for it. The critical-democratic class, then, is a context for change that develops the desire and imagination to make change" (p. 176).

Challenges of Democratic Education

Democratic education is, in many ways, antithetical to conventional school practices in our society. Student voice and choice don't fit particularly well into a system characterized by bureaucracy and hierarchical structure (Reitzug 2003). There are three main areas of challenge to instituting democratic practices in classrooms and schools—students, teachers, and the institution as a whole.

Student Challenges

Students educated in conventional schools for the majority of their lives represent one of the biggest challenges to democratic education. Because soliciting student voice and choice in the classroom lies so far outside the educational norm in our society, democratic education practices may be met, initially, by considerable student resistance. Most students are accustomed to being told what to do and to acting passively in the classroom; they are viewed, and may view themselves, as safe-deposit boxes waiting for deposits of knowledge to fill them (Freire 1970). The hidden curriculum trains students to be quiet and docile, to be indifferent to and bored with course content (because they have no say in what it is), and to accept being told what they and their work are worth (Gatto 1992; Giroux 1978; Illich 1971; Vallance 2003).

It should come as no surprise that students who have experienced this training, especially those students who have succeeded in the "game" of schooling, might resist changed rules that ask them to go against all they have been taught. Students who come from conventional education into classrooms or schools employing democratic practices will often feel uncomfortable with or even fearful of jeopardizing the only pattern of life they know (Goodman 1964). They may become "Siberians" (Shor 1996) who gravitate to the periphery of the class, where they sit silent and disconnected from democratic processes. Asked to play a role in content construction (e.g., explain what they are generally interested in studying, or a particular topic), they may be at a loss, for many have never even considered what their own interests might be. Spontaneous initiative, curiosity, and trust in themselves, by and large, may have been drummed out of them; they may have learned to view education as purely instrumental—a means to an end rather than an end in itself (Bhave 1996; Holt 1972; Labaree 1997). Students thus may resent anyone trying to show them differently. This resentment will be connected to a lack of trust and the antagonistic teacher-student relationships that are the norm. Students have been trained to start out viewing most teachers as "the enemy"—people who infringe on their will and their freedoms. To be asked suddenly to change this view is more than many students can handle.

Besides student resistance to democratic education, another challenge that arises is students mistaking positive freedom for negative freedom. Maxine Greene, in *The Dialectic of Freedom* (1988), has defined negative freedom as freedom from constraints. That is the starting point for positive freedom, but positive freedom also encompasses the freedom to work in concert with others to overcome limits. Democratic education is not negative freedom

alone; it does not only mean freeing students to do whatever they want. As Dewey wrote in *Experience and Education* (1938): "For freedom from restriction, the negative side, is to be prized only as a means to a freedom which is power: power to frame purposes, to judge wisely; . . . power to select and order means to carry chosen ends into operation" (pp. 63–64). Because conventionally educated students have so little experience of any freedom in school, so little practice with democratic discussion or with assuming authority on their own, they will often mistake democratic, positive freedom practices for negative freedom only. Students may thus see the teacher who asks for democratic input as weak or unprepared, and they may attempt to evade, rather than make, their opportunities (e.g., push for lowered workloads, etc.) (Shor 1996).

Teacher Challenges

Students will not be the only ones who resist changes; teachers will balk as well. Very few teachers have experienced democratic education themselves, so to attempt to institute democratic practices in their classrooms represents a sizable leap into the unknown. Teachers may be fearful of this unknown, fearful that involving students' voices and choices in running a course will produce chaos and an overall lack of learning. Part of this fear stems from lack of trust in students. Teachers have become accustomed to viewing most students as lazy and uninterested, people who must be pushed, prodded, cajoled, and threatened into doing "what's best for them," and thus they fear that students will try to minimize challenges and take the easy way out (Goodman 1962; Gross 1973; Holt 1970, 1972; Rogers 1969; Sheffer 1996; Watson 1970). Another part of this fear of chaos and lack of learning lies in conventional ideas about what learning is. Many teachers, themselves schooled in conventional educational institutions, believe that their role is to fill students with curricular information. They might argue that students, who don't know what they don't know, cannot possibly exercise choice and freedom in curricular content to create real learning.

The idea that knowledge can be stuffed into the individual, as opposed to being constructed and mediated through the individual (Lamm 1972), has led to the conventional educational practices of mandated courses and pre-established syllabi. Teachers are used to coming, and in fact are expected by both students and their administrators to come, to the first class with content ready for delivery to interchangeable students. Teachers may feel that if they arrive without a pre-set syllabus and lesson plans, students and administrators will view them as weak, unprepared, or lacking in authority. The class's disrespect could lead to poor course and teacher evaluations as well as jeopardize their jobs. Besides losing control, teachers might also fear silence and an emptiness if they attempt democratic practices. They might also fear that some students will take over and silence others. Last, inviting student voice and choice might ill prepare students for the "real world," where they will have to learn to bow their wills to others and see their needs go unmet (Guterson 1996).

Conventionally schooled teachers who dare to implement democratic practices must grapple with all these fears. They must be willing to abandon plans and adjust to the process of dialogue; they must learn to listen more than talk, not apply one lesson plan to all sections of the same class, and surrender their authoritarian supports (Shor 1996). They must learn to trust students' innate curiosity, and if this curiosity has been crushed in the past, they must work to bring it back to life. Teachers must take to heart what Rogers wrote in *Freedom to Learn* (1969):

> If I distrust the human being, then I must cram him with information of my own choosing, lest he go his own mistaken way. But if I trust the capacity of the human individual for developing his own potentiality, then I can provide him with many opportunities and permit him to choose his own way and his own direction in his learning. (p. 114)

And teachers need to recognize that democratic educational practices may well lead students to reject the "real world" of hierarchical authority and to work for more true democracy in the larger economic, political, and social systems. Teachers who attempt more-democratic educational practices thus embrace education for the world that might be rather than for the world that is.

Institutional Challenges

The institutional structures of conventional education also represent significant stumbling blocks to enacting more-democratic practices. Unless the entire institution is itself fully democratic, teachers who attempt to bring democracy into heretofore undemocratic spaces will encounter challenges.

The "deep structures" of schools compose one such challenge: those "widely shared assumptions about what schools are for and how they should function" (Tye 1998, paragraph 5). One example of such deep structures is the conventional schools' view that knowledge exists outside and separate from human mediation and construction and that learning equals the transmission of this information from holders of this knowledge (teachers) to empty vessels (students).

This view of knowledge leads to conventional school practices: mandating that all students learn certain subjects; insisting that subjects be fragmented one from the other; and enforcing a certain progression of information that follows an external, discipline-specific logic (e.g., take algebra before geometry). Educational managers who hold this view of knowledge might argue, as mentioned in "Teacher Challenges," above, that students don't know what they don't know, so how could they possibly decide what should be included in a class? The managers also

might worry that students who have voice and choice on subject inclusion might choose not to learn what the institution considers vital information.

That concern, a valid one, can be dealt with by establishing institutional structures and practices that allow time to explore the ideas of negative and positive freedom described earlier. Students' resistance to learning certain ideas often stems from feelings of powerlessness rather than from willed ignorance; if educational institutions can set forth rational and personalized arguments for the worth of some topic (beyond stating in a course catalog that the subject will make one liberally educated), students will willingly include that topic in their studies. Certainly this process can become time-consuming, but that is intrinsic to learning democratic habits of mind.

The view of knowledge and learning described above also impacts assumptions about class sizes. If the subject knowledge is simply to be transmitted to students, a high teacher-student ratio is logically efficient. Institutional structures of large classes and mandated, pre-arranged content render attempts to institute democratic practices uncertain. How can a teacher truly get a large number of students' voices and choices heard? Can a teacher stray too far from the mandated content if the teachers around her are working to perpetuate the curricular status quo? Won't a democratic teacher in a required class have a more difficult time breaking through and connecting with the students who resent this limitation of their freedom of choice?

An additional institutional constraint is the conventional system of grading. I have written elsewhere (Morrison 2003a, 2003b) about how grades can deflect students from creating personal meaning and toward simply performing for sought-for ends (e.g., diploma, college acceptance, scholarships, praise, lack of punishment, etc.). This performance orientation complicates the teacher-student relationship: students come to feel less powerful vis-à-vis the teacher and thus act subserviently to earn good grades. Student subservience manifests itself in not questioning or challenging the teacher in any really meaningful way; in essence, students have learned that classroom success often requires that they check their democratic rights at the door. Grading has, perhaps unintentionally, rendered many students voiceless and dependent. (Admittedly, students participate in their own oppression in this regard, but that makes it no less a form of oppression.)

A last major institutional constraint on introducing democratic educational practices to conventional school settings is the use of space and time. The conventional school day is broken into a series of relatively short periods (forty-five to ninety minutes each); school plants are typically divorced from the wider community (separate, often closed, campuses); and there is an extremely high population density. Such use of space and time is inimical to democracy, in which decisions, discussions, and building trust take time (longer than a semester or academic year, or longer than a single class period); connections to and involvement in community activities and spaces are highly valued; and the ability and space necessary to move about freely, and group and regroup, are needed.

Conclusion

Critical educational theorists believe that democratic values—the search for truth and personal meaning, justice, equality, and respect for the thoughts and humanity of others—will rarely result from schools in which students never have an opportunity to practice democratic habits of mind. Thus, these theorists support including democratic practices in school wherever possible. Clearly, though, there are significant roadblocks to instituting such practices, especially the more deeply these practices infiltrate the organizational structures of schools.

Some might argue that our schools were never meant to create democratic citizens because our society is not now and never truly will be a democracy; the undemocratic characteristics of our conventional schools exist by design. Although such cynicism may be warranted, given what we know about how power is used and abused in our society, critical educational theorists would counter that it is our "ontological vocation" (Freire 1970) to struggle for seemingly far-off ideals. Although we might lack a true democracy now, one will never be attained unless people work for it both inside and outside our educational institutions.

References

Bennis, D. M. 2006. "De-Mystifying Freedom-based Education." Master's thesis, Vermont College of Union Institute & University.

Bhave, V. 1996. "The Intimate and the Ultimate." In *Deschooling Our Lives,* ed. M. Hern, 16–22. Gabriola Island, B.C.: New Society Publishers.

Dennison, G. 1969. *The Lives of Children: The Story of the First Street School.* New York: Random House.

Dewey, J. 1916. *Democracy and Education.* New York: Macmillan Company.

———. 1938. *Experience and Education.* New York: Collier Macmillan Publishers.

Freire, P. 1970. *The Pedagogy of the Oppressed.* New York: Herder and Herder.

Gatto, J. T. 1992. *Dumbing Us Down: The Hidden Curriculum of Compulsory Schooling.* Gabriola Island, B.C.: New Society Publishers.

Giroux, H. 1978. "Developing Educational Programs and Overcoming the Hidden Curriculum." *Clearing House* 52(4): 148–151.

———. 1988. *Teachers as Intellectuals: Toward a Critical Pedagogy of Learning.* Westport, Conn.: Bergin and Garvey.

Goodman, P. 1962. *The Community of Scholars.* New York: Vintage Books.

———. 1964. *Compulsory Miseducation.* New York: Vintage Books.

Greene, M. 1988. *The Dialectic of Freedom.* New York: Teachers College Press.

Gross, R. 1973. "After Deschooling, Free Learning." In *After Deschooling, What?* ed. I. Illich, 148–160. New York: Harper and Row.

Guterson, D. 1996. "Family Matters: Why Home Schooling Makes Sense." In *Deschooling Our Lives,* ed. M. Hern, 16–22.

Hern, M., ed. 1996. *Deschooling Our Lives.* Gabriola Island, B.C.: New Society Publishers.

Holt, J. 1970. In *Summerhill: For and Against,* ed. H. Hart. New York: Hart Publishing Co.

———. 1972. *Freedom and Beyond.* New York: E.P. Dutton and Co.

———. 1989. *Learning All the Time.* New York: Addison-Wesley Publishing.

Holzman, L. 1997. *Schools for Growth.* Mahwah, N.J.: Lawrence Erlbaum Associates.

Illich, I. 1971. *Deschooling Society.* New York: Harper and Row.

Labaree, David E 1997. *How to Succeed in School without Really Learning: The Credentials Race in American Education.* New Haven: Yale University Press.

Lamm, Z. 1972. "The Status of Knowledge in the Radical Concept of Education." In *Curriculum and the Cultural Revolution,* ed. D. Purpel and M. Belanger, 149–168. Berkeley, Calif.: McCutchan.

Llewellyn, G. 1997. *The Teenage Liberation Handbook: How to Quit School and Get a Real Life and Education.* Shaftsbury, Dorset, U.K.: Element Books Limited.

Mercogliano, C. 1998. *Making It Up as We Go Along: The Story of the Albany Free School.* Portsmouth, N.H.: Heinemann.

Morrison, K. 2003a. "Is Grading Doing What We Want It to Do?" *Paths of Learning* 15 (Winter): 20–23.

———. 2003b. "What Else Besides Grading? Looking for Alternatives in All the Right Places." *Paths of Learning* 16 (Spring): 22–28.

———. 2007a. *Free School Teaching: A Journey into Radical Progressive Education.* Albany, N.Y.: SUNY Press.

———. 2007b. "Unschooling: Homeschools Can Provide the Freedom to Learn." *Encounter: Education for Meaning and Social Justice* 20(2): 42–49.

Neill, A. S., and A. Lamb, eds. 1992. *Summerhill School: A New View of Childhood.* New York: St. Martin's Press.

Purpel, D. 1989. *The Moral and Spiritual Crisis in Education.* New York: Bergin and Garvey.

Reitzug, U. 2003. "Bureaucratic and Democratic Ways of Organizing Schools: Implications for Teachers, Principals, Students, Parents, and Community." In *The Institution of Education,* ed. H. S. Shapiro, S. Harden, and A. Pennell, 4th ed., 85–98. Boston: Pearson Custom Publishing.

Rogers, C. 1969. *Freedom to Learn.* Columbus, Ohio: Charles E. Merrill Publishing.

Sheffer, S. 1996. "Doing Something Very Different: Growing without Schooling." In *Deschooling Our Lives,* ed. M. Hern, 16–22.

Shor, Ira. 1996. *When Students Have Power: Negotiating Authority in a Critical Pedagogy.* Chicago: The University of Chicago Press.

Tye, B. B. 1998. "The Deep Structure of Schooling: What It Is and How It Works." *The Clearing House* 71(6): 332–335. Retrieved February 1, 2006, from Info Trac One File database.

Vallance, E. 2003. "Hiding the Hidden Curriculum." In *The Institution of Education,* ed. Shapiro, Harden, and Pennell, 85–98. (Originally published in 1974. *Curriculum Theory Network* 4[1], 5–21.)

Watson, G. 1970. In *Summerhill,* ed. H. Hart. New York: Hart Publishing.

. . . .

KRISTAN A. MORRISON is Associate Professor in the School of Teacher Education and Leadership at Radford University and author of *Free School Teaching: A Journey into Radical Progressive Education* (2007).

Gary K. Clabaugh

 **NO**

Second Thoughts about Democratic Classrooms

. . . Kristan A. Morrison's "Democratic Classrooms: Promises and Challenges of Student Voice and Choice" argues that students must experience autonomy, freedom, and choice if schools will ever be appealing and truly embody democracy. Those who found or find school tedious, oppressive, and uninteresting may be quick to agree, but how realistic is this proposal?

Cutting Costs with Mass Production

It has been well over one hundred years since America embarked on the ambitious venture of universal public schooling. The costs of this endeavor quickly became burdensome, and it was decided to model schools on factories and emphasize mass production and cost-effectiveness, rather than democracy or individuality.

For the most part, today's public schools still are factories. Management is top-down all the way. The federal government sets basic rules. State authorities implement the rules while adding many more. School boards make decisions based on federal and state rules plus fiscal and political realities. The superintendent executes the will of the board through his or her principals. They, in turn, tell teachers what to do and when to do it, and the teachers direct the youngsters in similar manner. Knowledge is fragmented and atomized. Children are compared to one another. Social and emotional development is neglected for more measurable outcomes. Economies of scale are sought at the expense of individuality. Teachers and students are managed.

Sometimes this industrial approach produces not only undemocratic, but peculiarly inefficient, results. One superintendent of the School District of Philadelphia, for example, boasted to the press that she could tell them what was happening in any classroom in the city at any given moment. What was actually happening was administratively induced chaos, because her standardized, teacher-proof curriculum was incapable of accommodating individual differences. Second-grade teachers were forbidden to use anything other than second-grade readers and the canned lesson of the day, even if some of the kids still couldn't read. Similarly, seventh-grade math teachers were forced to "teach" algebra to kids who couldn't even do fractions or long division.

In this kind of school system, autonomy, freedom, and choice are anathema. The focus is on standardization, teacher proofing, measured outcomes, and the prison shuffle.

Compulsory Freedom?

We should also consider that democratic, freedom-based schooling would be introduced into an institution in which attendance is compulsory. True, if one can afford an alternative, there is no requirement that kids attend public school. But in every state in the union school attendance of some kind, even if it is only home schooling, is required.

"Democratic Classrooms" indicates that democratic and freedom-based education is *grounded in the premise that people are naturally curious and have an innate desire to learn and grow. If left un-fettered, un-coerced and un-manipulated . . . people will pursue their interests vigorously and with gusto. . . .* Trouble is, when people are compelled to go to school they already are fettered, coerced, and manipulated. That's what we mean by compulsion. Wouldn't compulsory education have to be abolished before freedom-based education could be meaningfully initiated?

And why imagine that youngsters' natural curiosity will be directed at constructive things? One can imagine six-year-olds happily burning insects to death with sunlight and a magnifying glass, or sixteen-year-old inner-city gang members fulfilling their urgent desire to learn small-unit military tactics. Besides which, why assume that everyone is naturally curious? I've taught seventh-graders whose curiosity seemed decidedly undersized.

Of course kids of that age are terribly concerned about peer acceptance, and that places a profound limit on their freedom. Do advocates of freedom-based education adequately consider the tyranny of peers?

The Feds Weigh In

Remember too that there is a powerful new restriction on autonomy, freedom, choice, and democracy in schooling. Emphasizing measurable results, quality control, instrumental and extrinsic motivations, and atomization and

Reprinted with permission of *Educational Horizons*, quarterly journal of Pi Lambda Theta Inc., International Honor Society and Professional Association in Education, P O Box 6626, Bloomington, IN 47401, Fall 2008, pp. 20–25.

fragmentation of knowledge, No Child Left Behind represents the near-total triumph of factory-model schooling in contemporary America. The whole weight of the federal government welds the public school as factory in place as never before.

"Democratic Classrooms" offers the happy prospect of dismantling factory schools and refocusing on student voice and choice. But it's not as if the article advocates moving from A to B. Given the present environment, it advocates moving from A to Z. What are the chances?

"The Business of America Is Business"[1]

Another factor militating against the success of the "Democratic Classrooms" prescription is that most Americans spend far more time in the business world than they do where they have a voice and a choice.

What are the work world's characteristics? It's competitive; instrumental and extrinsic motivations dominate, tasks are atomized and fragmented, obedience is required, believing what one is told is valued over criticality, and a person's worth is defined by comparison to others. In short, work-world values are virtually identical to the present school values decried in "Democratic Classsrooms." Surely that is not an accident.

What would happen if business leaders suddenly found themselves confronted with employees who expected a voice and a choice? Would the CEO of General Electric or Macy's, for example, be grateful? And could our lawmakers sleep if the nation's corporate moguls were dissatisfied?

The claim here isn't that the business of America *should* be business. It is that the business of America *is* business, and this reality has to be taken into account in any prescription written for the public schools.

Freedom: A Modern Luxury?

The article comments: *In democratic and freedom-based education, students are free to decide what they study, and how, and when they study it.* The article links that to *the form of learning found in most pre-industrial societies* [in which] *the children are actively engaged in the lives of a given society; they learn skills and knowledge by means of imitation, apprenticeship, modeling and conversation rather than in any formal school setting.*

Pre-industrial education, though, was not all that free and spontaneous. In my youth, for example, I learned barbering by means of an apprenticeship that closely resembled the apprentice system of the pre-industrial guilds; I was most emphatically *not* free to decide what to learn, or how and when to learn it. The master barber decided.

Remember too that in the pre-industrial era most children grew up on farms. And while those youngsters did learn to farm by imitation, modeling, and conversation, they did *not* have the luxury of freely choosing what

they wanted to do and how and when they were going to do it. That's not farm life. If you are haying and it looks like rain, you have to work like hell to get the hay in the barn before it gets wet and spoils; otherwise the livestock starves that winter. Similarly, a kid might prefer not to spend hour after hour in the broiling sun picking potato bugs, but he or she still has to do it for the family to eat potatoes.

Perhaps freedom-based education is a luxury reserved for well-fixed modern kids whom harsh reality doesn't require to do tasks of immediate and urgent importance.

The True Secret of Education

John Locke, a philosopher who inspired the nation's founders, observes in *On Education*: "[I]f the mind be curb'd, and humbled too much in children; if their spirits be abas'd and broken much, by too strict an hand over them, they lose all their vigour and industry."

But Locke also cautions that

He that has not a mastery over his inclinations, he that knows not how to resist the importunity of present pleasure or pain, for the sake of what reason tells him is fit to be done, wants the true principle of virtue and industry, and is in danger never to be good for anything.

Locke, however, does not stop there. He immediately adds:

To avoid the danger that is on either hand, is the great art; and he that has found a way how to *keep up a child's spirit easy, active, and free, and yet at the same time to restrain him from many things he has a mind to, and to draw him to things that are uneasy to him* [emphasis added]; he, I say, that knows how to reconcile these seeming contradictions, has, in my opinion, got the true secret of education.[2]

The advocates of freedom-based education, then, may have avoided the first error Locke cautions against, only to stumble into the second. They seem to be overlooking the fact that some measure of mastery over one's inclinations is necessary to ever be good at anything. How can anyone learn to accomplish a truly skilled enterprise such as ballet, glass blowing, or engineering in a reasonable time if the initiate, not the expert, decides what to learn and when to learn it?

To be sure, present-day schooling hasn't got the balance right either. Here, in Locke's words, the mind is "curb'd and humbled too much" and the youngsters too frequently "lose all their vigour and industry." That is what "Democratic Classrooms" quite rightly condemns.

The Principle of Correspondence

Historically there has always been a close correspondence between any society's social structure, values, and norms and its schooling practices. In fact, a case can be made that such correspondence is a universal feature of schooling. And "Democratic Classrooms" gets it wrong when it says, "Schools and society are reflections of one another." No, the history of education demonstrates that schooling practices reflect the values and structures of the host society.

That is not to say that alternative schools of a freer, more-democratic nature can't exist in less-free societies. Various forms of them can be found in nations as different as Israel, Japan, New Zealand, Thailand, and the United States; A. S. Neill's Summerhill, perhaps the best-known, is located in Suffolk, England.[3] But these schools owe their uniqueness to the fact that they do not serve the broad masses at public expense. They have a self-selecting clientele and do not depend on public consensus or public funding.

Still, it's instructive to know that in 1999 Summerhill ran into difficulties with the U.K.'s educational bureaucracy. Despite the school's higher-than-national-average exam pass rates and extraordinary parental and pupil satisfaction, the U.K.'s education bureaucracy inspected the school and found it wanting. It called Summerhill's pupils "foul-mouthed" and accused them of "mistaking idleness for personal liberty." In effect, the report called for Summerhill's closure if the school failed to abandon the key freedoms it afforded its pupils.

Summerhill took the government to court and won the right to continue its practices. The school survived, and in 2007 another government inspection produced entirely different results. *The Guardian* quotes the new report as saying, "Pupils' personal development, including their spiritual, moral, social and cultural development, is outstanding." Students are "courteous, polite and considerate," make "good progress," and are "well-rounded, confident, and mature" when they leave.

Zoe Readhead, the head teacher and daughter of founder A. S. Neill, said: "The government has persistently refused to acknowledge the individual philosophy of the school, such as that children can learn just as well out of the classroom. We feel vindicated." She also added, "It is not the school that changed."[4] Her point, of course, was that it was the U.K. that had changed.[5]

Undemocratic Americans

"Democratic Classrooms" seems at least as out of step with American values in 2008 as Summerhill was to the U.K.'s in 1999. Certainly the values that "Democratic Classrooms" hopes to promote are anything but widespread. Only some Americans "truly value diversity" and are "truly autonomous yet cognizant of others' needs and rights." And only some Americans "are open-minded yet equipped with critical thinking skills to analyze contradictory ideas." Other Americans angrily deny marriage to gay couples; salivate whenever Rush Limbaugh and his ilk ring a bell; and don't have the vaguest understanding of either freedom or democracy. (They eagerly deny the former to anyone who's different and think of American democracy merely as majority rule.)

Individuals of this persuasion pack a political punch. And they will undoubtedly regard as un-American the values "Democratic Classrooms" prescribes for U.S. public schools. Its new freedoms for students would be understood as self-indulgence and an attack on traditional values such as hard work, discipline, and self-denial—none of which are they particularly keen on practicing themselves.

Remember too that day-to-day U.S. public school policy is set locally by some fifteen thousand elected school boards and, except for large urban districts, broadly representative of village values. So America's public schools have achieved their undemocratic condition in a decidedly democratic manner.

Conclusion

History suggests that public schools rarely, if ever, get out ahead of society. Indeed, they generally lag behind. That is why student voice and choice and all that goes with it will have to await a freer, more-democratic America. If and when that societal change happens, the public schools will follow. Until then, support will be lacking. That's not to say that what "Democratic Classrooms" champions is undesirable. But it may be unattainable, and it is certainly unlikely in the near or intermediate future.

Happily, reform need not be all or nothing. One can, with a little luck, quietly introduce more student voice and choice into one's own classroom. And we should all congratulate any teacher who can elevate the importance of intrinsic motivation; emphasize social and emotional development as well as academics; de-emphasize mere obedience; and get kids to define their own worth rather than let others do it for them. But it had better be done without fanfare and well out of sight of the philistines.

Notes

1. A statement made by Calvin Coolidge in the 1920s.
2. John Locke, "Some Thoughts Concerning Education" (sections 41–50), in *The Harvard Classics,* available at http://www.bartleby.com/37/1/5.html.
3. See Summerhill School's Web site: http://www.summerhillschool.co.uk/pages/index.html.
4. Jessica Shepherd, *Guardian* (Manchester), December 1, 2007, available at http://www.guardian.co.uk/uk/2007/dec/01/ofsted.schools.
5. Summerhill School, available at http://www.summerhillschool.co.uk/bbc-drama.html.

. . . .

GARY K. CLABAUGH is Professor of Education at La Salle University in Philadelphia and co-founder (with Edward G. Rozycki) of newfoundations.com, which explores reflective educational practice.

EXPLORING THE ISSUE

Are Truly Democratic Classrooms Possible?

Critical Thinking and Reflection

1. What values are sought or lost in designing democratic classrooms?
2. Does the federal government play a role in democratic classrooms?
3. How do societal values compare and contrast with school values?
4. How is diversity valued in a democratic classroom?
5. What are elements in our society that transfer to designing classrooms that are described as democratic?

Is There Common Ground?

E. D. Hirsch, Jr., the well-known core knowledge advocate, in his latest book *The Making of Americans: Democracy and Our Schools* (2009), is clearly at odds with the "truly democratic classrooms produce engaged citizens" ideology. As he has in his past works, Hirsch has no kind words for the followers of John Dewey whose progressive ideas, he claims, led to an abandonment of definite academic studies resulting in the diminishment of Americans' intellectual standing in the world. He sees hope in recent trends toward higher standards and the rise of Advanced Placement and International Baccalaureate programs in high schools. In a review of The Making of Americans, titled "I Pledge Allegiance to Core Knowledge" in *The Washington Post* (August 30, 2009), Jay Mathews states that Hirsch will settle for nothing less than "a coherent, content-based, multi-year curriculum right now to save our democracy from factionalism, inequality, and incompetence."

Another group of theorists settle in a middle-ground position between subject matter centeredness and an emphasis on student voice and choice. See, for example, "Disciplining the Mind" by Veronica Boix Mansilla and Howard Gardner in *Educational Leadership* (February 2008). They recommend the teaching of disciplinary thinking so as to prepare students to understand the real world in which they live and equip them for the future.

The following writers are supportive of Kristan A. Morrison's point of view: Dana L. Mitra, "Amplifying Student Voice," *Educational Leadership* (November 2008), who reviews research into student voice initiatives, including student involvement in reform and the professional development of teachers, and Eric B. Freedman, "Is Teaching for

Social Justice Undemocratic?" *Harvard Educational Review* (Winter 2007), who examines the "critical consciousness" approaches of Ira Shor and Paulo Freire, addressing the question "When is education democratic?"

Additional interesting sources are Thomas R. Guskey and Eric M. Anderman, "Students at Bat," *Educational Leadership* (November 2008); Deborah Meier, "Democracy at Risk," *Educational Leadership* (May 2009); Chris W. Gallagher, "Democratic Policy Making and the Arts of Engagement," *Phi Delta Kappan* (January 2008); and Stephen Macedo, "Crafting Good Citizens," *Education Next* (Spring 2004). Exploration of some of these articles will open doors to a number of important related issues.

Create Central

www.mhhe.com/createcentral

Additional Resources

James A. Banks, "Human Rights, Diversity, and Citizenship Education," *The Educational Forum* (April 2009)

Peter Levine, "The Civic Opportunity Gap," *Educational Leadership* (May 2009)

Richard Neumann, "American Democracy at Risk," *Phi Delta Kappan* (January 2008)

Joetta Sack-Min, "A Valued Democracy," *American School Board Journal* (January 2009)

Patrick J. Wolfe, "Civics Exam: Schools of Choice Boost Civic Values," *Education Next* (Summer 2007)

Internet References. . .

A Hidden Downside of Democratic Classrooms

www.educationrethink.com/2013/02/a-hidden-downside-of-democratic.html

Are Truly Democratic Classrooms Possible? Aa Prezi Ppresentation

http://prezi.com/0stlwjcb6k9y/are-truly-democratic-classrooms-possible-character-education-and-social-responsibility/

Democracy in Schools: Preached but not Practiced

http://voices.washingtonpost.com/answer-sheet/george-wood/democracy-in-schools-preached.html

Evidence of Democratic Principles in Our Schools

http://edweb.sdsu.edu/people/cmathison/truths/truths.html

Meaningful Practice: Democratic Classrooms

http://gordonbwest.com/critical-toolbox/democratic-classrooms/

Selected, Edited, and with Issue Framing Material by:
Glenn L. Koonce, *Regent University*

ISSUE

Do Public Schools Have Grounds to Punish Students for Their Off-Campus Online Speech?

YES: Theodore A. McKee, from *Layshock v. Hermitage School District*, United States Third Circuit Court of Appeals (June 13, 2011)

NO: Theodore A. McKee, from *J.S. v. Blue Mountain School District*, United States Third Circuit Court of Appeals (June 13, 2011)

Learning Outcomes

After reading this issue, you will be able to:

- Evaluate student First Amendment Rights and their impact on the *Layshock v. Hermitage School District* case.
- Evaluate student First Amendment Rights and their impact on the *J.S. v. Blue Mountain School District*.
- Appraise social media concerns of the public schools.
- Compare and contrast the 1975 *Tinker v. Des Moines* court case as it applies to today's student rights cases involving social media.
- Assess the impact of U.S. Supreme Court decision on school officials.

ISSUE SUMMARY

YES: In *Layshock v. Hermitage School District*, Third Circuit Court judges approved a local Pennsylvania school officials' 10-day suspension of a high school student who mocked his principal with a fake MySpace profile that he accessed off-campus.

NO: On the same day and in the same circuit court as *Layshock v Hermitage School District*, a different set of judges ruled in *J.S. v. Blue Mountain School District* that local Pennsylvania school officials overreacted and breached the First Amendment Rights of a junior high school student who ridiculed her principal online using MySpace with a computer that was accessed off-campus. Chief Judge Theodore McKee wrote the court's opinion for both cases. In 2012, the U.S. Supreme Court declined to hear either of these social media cases.

Conflicting decisions regarding student First Amendment Rights in social media disciplinary cases occurred on the same day and in the same court in February 2012. The Third Circuit Court of Appeals heard two cases, both out of Pennsylvania, involving fake MySpace profiles that students created to mock their principal. Although neither student created their profiles on school time, used school computers, or other school resources, they were punished by school authorities. Both students and their parents sued their respective school districts. When heard by the Third Circuit Court, a Pennsylvania school officials' suspension of a male high school student was upheld and a different ruling against a school official's suspension against a junior high school female. The official court briefs for each case

are included in this issue for review of the facts and rulings by the two different panels of judges. The uniqueness of these cases include: the similarities in the student's actions, action taken by school officials, and final oppositional rendering by the same court on the same day (Cain, 2012).

Prior to the 1970s, public schools were largely immune to Constitutional law handed down by the courts being "school friendly" and upheld almost all school officials' decisions if the court felt those actions were "reasonable." *In loco parentis* (corresponding to parental prerogatives) accompanied this status in many court cases making it unclear whether constitutional rights extended to non-adult students (Palistini & Palistini, 2012).

Clarity soon came and changed the way courts view student rights, especially freedom of speech and expression, with the 1969 landmark *Tinker v. Des Moines Independent Community School District* case. In this case, the U.S. Supreme Court ruled that students do not "shed their constitutional rights" at the school house door. Six years later another landmark U.S. Supreme Court case *Goss v. Lopez* (1975), held that students in public schools possess liberty and property interests in their education, thus are afforded due process before disciplinary action may be taken by school officials (Palistini & Palistini, 2012).

Even with these transforming U.S. Supreme Court decisions, further decisions sided more with schools when a student's actions were a significant disruption to the education process or a threat to safety (weapons, serious injury, or drugs). One example is *Morse v. Fredrick* (June 26, 2006), where the U.S. Supreme Court ruled against a high school student limiting student free speech rights. Joseph Frederick was an 18 year old senior in 2002 in Juneau, Alaska, who did not attend school on this particular day but did attend an off-campus school activity where he raised a banner with the words "Bong Hits 4 Jesus" written on it. Confiscated by the principal and suspended from school, the student sued. The principal cited her actions as being appropriate since the student's sign clearly made reference to drugs. Although the student was not physically on-campus, he certainly was in the midst of the off-campus activities even having some students help him unfurl and display the banner. "It was reasonable for (the principal) to conclude that the banner promoted illegal drug use, and that failing to act would send a powerful message to the students in her charge," Chief Justice John Roberts wrote for the court's 6-3 majority (Alexander & Alexander, 2009).

Recently, the tide has turned with the advent of social media and its disruptive or nondisruptive impact on the sacred education learning process. These are different times for schools and, for society, thus growing technology has challenged school authority in matters regarding student freedom of expression. Even the U.S. Supreme Court has refused to act denying cert in the *Layshock v. Hermitage School District* and *J.S. v. Blue Mountain School District* cases. It is apparent why school officials in the Third Circuit may be confused and are attempting to design school board policy to deal with the new social media threats to a peaceful learning environment for all. The statement is meant for teachers and other staff as well as student to student threats that include cyberbullying.

Although the Layshock and J.S. cases both involve students using social media to mock their principal, cyberbullying (particularly off-campus) by students on fellow students continues to be the primary social media issues schools are facing. Cyberbullying includes hurtful or embarrassing text or images from electronic devices that are intended to intimidate or cause emotional distress to another student. In some cases, such as with Megan Mieier

in 2009, the messages have been so intensely upsetting that the student commits suicide.

Other districts have acted differently in social media cases. For example in the Fourth Circuit Court of Appeals, a West Virginia High School student was punished by the school when she invited classmates to a questionable MySpace group (*Kowalsky v. Berkeley County Schools*, July 27, 2011). Kara Kowalsky sued against her five-day suspension from the principal for creating a web page suggesting another student had a sexually transmitted disease and invited classmates to comment. Her major defense was that she created the site on a home computer and at a time when she was not in school. The appeals court sided with the school and indicated the learning environment had been disrupted because Kowolsky created the site primarily for her classmates.

A growing trend of bullying and threatening behavior by students using social media on and off school grounds has resulted in changes and upgrades to school policy and regulations and more support from the courts. Student on student, student on staff, and staff on staff have all been problematic. It is anticipated that in the near future the U.S. Supreme Court will intervene with definitive answers as to whether inappropriate social media behavior is protected under free speech rights (Cain, 2012).

In the selections that follow, *Layshock v. Hermitage School District* indicates the court sided with the school district because the district convinced the court that a sufficient nexus existed between the student's vulgar and defamatory profile of his principal and the school. In *J.S. v. Blue Mountain School District*, the court reviewed the facts where the student's suspension did not pass constitutional muster for lewd, vulgar, and offensive profile of her principal that was created off-campus.

References

K. Alexander & M. Alexander, *Tinker v Des Moines Independent School District*, in *American Public School Law* (Wadsworth Cengage Learning, 2009)

R. Cain, Supreme Court Denies Cert in Student's Free Speech Rights Case. *Findlaw* (January 17, 2012). Retrieved from: http://blogs.findlaw.com/supreme_court/2012/01/supreme-court-denies-cert-in-student-free-speech-rights-cases.html

Kowalsky v. Berkley County Schools. United States Court of Appeals for the Fourth Circuit (2011). Retrieved from: www.ca4.uscourts.gov/Opinions/Published/101098.P.pdf

R. Palistini, & K. Palistini, *The Law and American Education: A Case Brief Approach* (Rowman & Littlefield, 2012)

YES ⤶

Theodore A. McKee

Layshock v. Hermitage School District

McKee, *Chief Judge.*

We are asked to determine if a school district can punish a student for expressive conduct that originated outside of the schoolhouse, did not disturb the school environment and was not related to any school sponsored event. We hold that, under these circumstances, the First Amendment prohibits the school from reaching beyond the schoolyard to impose what might otherwise be appropriate discipline.

It all began when Justin Layshock used his grandmother's computer to access a popular social networking internet web site where he created a fake internet "profile" of his Hickory High School Principal, Eric Trosch. His parents filed this action under 42 U.S.C. § 1983, after the School District punished Justin for that conduct. The suit alleges, *inter alia,* that the School District's punishment transcended Justin's First Amendment right of expression. The district court granted summary judgment in favor of Justin on his First Amendment claim. We originally affirmed the district court. *See Layshock v. Hermitage School Dist.,* 593 F.3d 249 (3d Cir. 2010). Thereafter, we entered an order vacating that opinion and granting rehearing en banc. For the reasons that follow, we once again affirm the district court's holding that the school district's response to Justin's conduct transcended the protection of free expression guaranteed by the First Amendment.

Factual Background

In December of 2005, Justin Layshock was a seventeen-year-old senior at Hickory High School, which is part of the Hermitage School District in Hermitage, Pennsylvania. Sometime between December 10th and 14th, 2005, while Justin was at his grandmother's house during non-school hours, he used her computer to create what he would later refer to as a "parody profile" of his Principal, Eric Trosch. The only school resource that was even arguably involved in creating the profile was a photograph of Trosch that Justin copied from the School District's website. Justin copied that picture with a simple "cut and paste" operation using the computer's internet browser and mouse. Justin created the profile on "MySpace."[1] MySpace is a popular social-networking website that "allows its members to create online 'profiles,' which are individual web pages on which members post photographs, videos, and information about their lives and interests." *Doe v. MySpace, Inc.,* 474 F.Supp. 2d 843, 845 (W.D. Tex. 2007).[2]

Justin created the profile by giving bogus answers to survey questions taken from various templates that were designed to assist in creating a profile. The survey included questions about favorite shoes, weaknesses, fears, one's idea of a "perfect pizza," bedtime, etc. All of Justin's answers were based on a theme of "big," because Trosch is apparently a large man. For example, Justin answered "tell me about yourself" questions as follows:

> Birthday: too drunk to remember
> Are you a health freak: big steroid freak
> In the past month have you smoked: big blunt[3]
> In the past month have you been on pills: big pills
> In the past month have you gone Skinny Dipping:
>   big lake, not big dick
> In the past month have you Stolen Anything: big keg
> Ever been drunk: big number of times
> Ever been called a Tease: big whore
> Ever been Beaten up: big fag
> Ever Shoplifted: big bag of kmart
> Number of Drugs I have taken: big

Under "Interests," Justin listed: "Transgender, Appreciators of Alcoholic Beverages." Justin also listed "Steroids International" as a club Trosch belonged to.

Justin afforded access to the profile to other students in the School District by listing them as "friends" on the MySpace website, thus allowing them to view the profile. Not surprisingly, word of the profile "spread like wildfire" and soon reached most, if not all, of Hickory High's student body.[4]

During mid-December 2005, three other students also posted unflattering profiles of Trosch on MySpace. Each of those profiles was more vulgar and more offensive than Justin's. Trosch first learned about one of the other profiles from his daughter, who was in eleventh grade. On Monday, December 12, 2005, Trosch told his Co-Principal, Chris Gill, and the District Superintendent, Karen Ionta, about this other profile and asked the Technology Director, Frank Gingras, to disable it. However, despite the administration's best efforts, students found ways to access the profiles. Trosch discovered Justin's profile on Thursday evening, December 15th, and a fourth profile on Sunday, December 18th.

Trosch believed all of the profiles were "degrading," "demeaning," "demoralizing," and "shocking." He was also concerned about his reputation and complained to the local police. Although he was not concerned for his safety, he was interested in pressing charges against those responsible for the bogus profiles, and he discussed whether the first profile he discovered might constitute harassment, defamation, or slander. However, no criminal charges were ever filed against Justin or any of the other student authors of profiles.

On December 15th, Justin used a computer in his Spanish classroom to access his MySpace profile of Trosch. He also showed it to other classmates, although he did not acknowledge his authorship. After viewing the profile, the students logged off of MySpace. Justin again attempted to access the profile from school on December 16th, purportedly to delete it. School district administrators were unaware of Justin's in-school attempts to access MySpace until their investigation the following week. Teacher Craig Antush glimpsed the profile in his computer lab class and told the students who were congregating around a computer and giggling to shut it down.

The School District administrators were not able to totally block students from visiting the MySpace web page at school because Gingras, the Technology Coordinator, was on vacation on December 16th. However, the school was able to control students' computer access by limiting the students' use of computers to computer labs or the library where internet access could be supervised. School officials continued to limit computer use from December 16th until December 21st, which was the last day of school before Christmas recess. Computer programming classes were also cancelled.

According to the district court, the School District's investigation revealed how many students had accessed MySpace before access to the site at school was disabled, but the school could not determine how many students actually accessed any of the Trosch profiles, or which Trosch profiles had been viewed while a student was on the MySpace website.

School District officials first learned that Justin might have created one of the Trosch profiles on December 21. On that day, Justin and his mother were summoned to a meeting with Superintendent Ionta and Co-Principal Gill. During that meeting, Justin admitted creating a profile, but no disciplinary action was then taken against him. After the meeting, without prompting from anyone, Justin went to Trosch's office and apologized for creating the profile.[5]

Justin's parents were understandably upset over Justin's behavior. They discussed the matter with him, expressed their extreme disappointment, "grounded" him, and prohibited him from using their home computer.

On January 3, 2006, the school district sent a letter to Justin and his parents giving them notice of an informal hearing that was to be held. The letter read, in pertinent part, as follows:

> Justin admitted prior to the informal hearing that he created a profile about Mr. Trosch.
>
> This infraction is a violation of the Hermitage School District Discipline Code: Disruption of the normal school process; Disrespect; Harassment

of a school administrator via computer/internet with remarks that have demeaning implications; Gross misbehavior; Obscene, vulgar and profane language; Computer Policy violations (use of school pictures without authorization).

The School District subsequently found Justin guilty of all of those charges.

In addition to a ten-day, out-of-school suspension, Justin's punishment consisted of (1) being placed in the Alternative Education Program (the "ACE" program) at the high school for the remainder of the 2005–2006 school year;[6] (2) being banned from all extracurricular activities, including Academic Games and foreign-language tutoring;[7] and (3) not being allowed to participate in his graduation ceremony.[8] The Layshocks were also informed that the School District was considering expelling Justin. Ironically, Justin, who created the least vulgar and offensive profile, and who was the only student to apologize for his behavior, was also the only student punished for the MySpace profiles.

District Court Proceedings

The Layshocks initiated this action on January 27, 2006, by filing a three count complaint pursuant to 42 U.S.C. § 1983 individually, and on Justin's behalf, against the Hermitage School District, Karen Ionta, Eric Trosch, and Chris Gill, in their official and individual capacities (hereinafter collectively referred to as the "School District" or "District"). The Layshocks also filed a motion for a temporary restraining order and/or preliminary injunction. Count I of the complaint alleged that the District's punishment of Justin violated his rights under the First Amendment. Count II alleged that the District's policies and rules were unconstitutionally vague and/or overbroad, both on their face and as applied to Justin. Count III alleged that the District's punishment of Justin interfered with, and continued to interfere with, their right as parents to determine how to best raise, nurture, discipline and educate their child in violation of their rights under the Due Process Clause of the Fourteenth Amendment.

The district court denied the request for a temporary restraining order, *Layshock v. Hermitage Sch. Dist.*, 412 F. Supp.2d 502, 508 (W.D. Pa. 2006), and the Layshocks withdrew their motion for a preliminary injunction pursuant to the district court's efforts at mediation.[9] On March 31, 2006, the district court denied the District's motion to dismiss the Layshocks' claims. The court ruled that the parents may assert a claim for a violation of their own due process right to "raise, nurture, discipline and educate their children" based on a school district's punishment of their child for speech the child uttered in the family home.

After discovery, both sides moved for summary judgment, and the court thereafter entered summary judgment in favor of Justin and against the School District only on the First Amendment claim.[10] The court concluded that a jury trial was necessary to determine compensatory damages and attorneys' fees. *See id.* at 607.

Thereafter, the district court denied the District's motion for entry of judgment pursuant to Fed.R.Civ.P. 54(b) or, in the alternative, for the issuance of a certificate of appealability pursuant to 28 U.S.C. § 1292(b).

The parties subsequently filed a joint motion in which they stipulated to damages and requested entry of final judgment while preserving all appellate issues pertaining to liability. The district court then entered a consent judgment, and the School District appealed the district court's grant of summary judgment in favor of Justin on his First Amendment claim.[11]

Summary Judgment

"Summary judgment is proper when the pleadings, depositions, answers to interrogatories, and admissions on file, together with the affidavits, if any, show that there is no genuine issue as to any material fact and that the moving party is entitled to judgment as a matter of law." *Bjorgung v. Whitetail Resort, LP,* 550 F.3d 263, 268 (3d Cir. 2008) (citation and internal quotation marks omitted). In ruling on a motion for summary judgment, the district court must view the facts in the light most favorable to the non-moving party. *Merkle v. Upper Dublin Sch. Dist.,* 211 F.3d 782, 788 (3d Cir. 2000). However, "the mere existence of *some* alleged factual dispute between the parties will not defeat an otherwise properly supported motion for summary judgment." *Anderson v. Liberty Lobby, Inc.,* 477 U.S. 242, 247-48 (1986). "As our review of a grant of summary judgment is plenary, we operate under the same legal standards as the District Court." *Bjorgung,* 550 F.3d at 268.

Discussion

The First Amendment's Application in Public Schools

In the landmark case of *Tinker v. Des Moines Indep. Cmty. Sch. Dist.,* 393 U.S. 503 (1969), a group of high school students decided to wear black arm bands to school to protest the war in Vietnam. When school officials learned of the planned protest, they preemptively prohibited students from wearing armbands. Several students who ignored the ban and wore armbands to school anyway were suspended. *Id.* at 504. Those students brought an action against the school through their parents under 42 U.S.C. § 1983, alleging that their First Amendment rights had been violated. The district court rejected that claim and upheld the constitutionality of the school officials' action, finding that it had been reasonable to preserve discipline. *Id.* 504–505. The district court's decision was affirmed without opinion by an equally divided court of appeals sitting *en banc. Id.* at 505.

The case was appealed to the Supreme Court, which held that student expression may not be suppressed unless school officials reasonably conclude that it will "materially and substantially disrupt the work and discipline of the school." *Id.* at 513. The Court concluded that the students were doing nothing more than engaging in political speech, and wearing armbands to express "their disapproval of the Vietnam hostilities and their advocacy of a truce, to make their views known, and, by their example, to influence others to adopt them." *Id.* at 514. The school district's only interest in banning the speech had been the "mere desire to avoid the discomfort and unpleasantness that always accompany an unpopular viewpoint" or "an urgent wish to avoid the controversy which might result from the expression." *Id.* at 509-10. The Court held that this interest was not enough to justify banning "a silent, passive expression of opinion, unaccompanied by any disorder or disturbance." *Id.* at 508. In one of its most famous passages, the Court explained:

> First Amendment rights, applied in light of the special characteristics of the school environment, are available to teachers and students. It can hardly be argued that either students or teachers shed their constitutional rights to freedom of speech or expression at the schoolhouse gate.

Id. at 506.

Thus, although the Court concluded that the First Amendment did reach inside the "schoolhouse gate," it also recognized that the unique nature of the school environment had to be part of any First Amendment inquiry. The Court explained that it "ha[d] repeatedly emphasized the need for affirming the comprehensive authority of the States and of school officials, consistent with fundamental constitutional safeguards, to prescribe and control conduct in the schools." *Id.* at 507.

The Court next addressed the scope of the First Amendment in the context of student speech in *Bethel School District No. 403 v. Fraser,* 478 U.S. 675 (1986). There, the Court upheld the school's suspension of a high school student for delivering a nominating speech at a school assembly using "an elaborate, graphic, and explicit sexual metaphor." *Id.* at 678. The Court explained:

> The schools, as instruments of the state, may determine that the essential lessons of civil, mature conduct cannot be conveyed in a school that tolerates lewd, indecent, or offensive speech and conduct such as that indulged in by [Fraser].[12]

Id. at 683. In reaching this conclusion, the Court distinguished its prior holding in *Cohen v. California,* 403 U.S. 15 (1971). There, the Court had struck down an adult's conviction for disorderly conduct that was based on his wearing a jacket, inside a court house, that had an obscenity about the draft printed on it. The *Fraser* Court explained:

> It does not follow . . . that simply because the use of an offensive form of expression may not be prohibited to adults making what the speaker

considers a political point, the same latitude must be permitted to children in public school. . . . [T]he First Amendment gives a high school student the classroom right to wear Tinker's armband, but not Cohen's jacket.

Id. at 682 (citation and internal quotation marks omitted). The Court concluded that the school could punish Fraser for his offensive nominating speech during a school assembly because the First Amendment does not prevent schools from encouraging the "fundamental values of 'habits and manners of civility,'" *id.* at 681, by "insisting that certain modes of expression are inappropriate and subject to sanctions." *Id.* at 683. Thus, "[t]he determination of what manner of speech in the classroom or in school assembly is inappropriate properly rests with the school board." *Id.*

Similarly, in *Hazelwood School District. v. Kuhlmeier,* 484 U.S. 260 (1988), the Court held that a principal's deletion of student articles on teen pregnancy from a school-sponsored newspaper did not violate the First Amendment. The Court distinguished *Tinker* by noting that because the school had not opened the newspaper up as a public forum, the school could "exercis[e] editorial control over the style and content of student speech in school-sponsored expressive activities so long as [its] actions are reasonably related to legitimate pedagogical concerns." *Id.* at 273. The Court explained:

> The question whether the First Amendment requires a school to tolerate particular student speech—the question that we addressed in *Tinker*—is different from the question whether the First Amendment requires a school affirmatively to promote particular student speech. The former question addresses educators' ability to silence a student's personal expression that happens to occur on the school premises. The latter question concerns educators' authority over school-sponsored . . . expressive activities that students, parents, and members of the public might reasonably perceive to bear the imprimatur of the school. . . . Educators are entitled to exercise greater control over this second form of student expression.

Id. at 270–71.

The extent to which First Amendment protections apply in the public school context was most recently addressed in *Morse v. Frederick,* 551 U.S. 393 (2007). There, "[a]t a school-sanctioned and school-supervised event, a high school principal [Morse] saw some of her students unfurl a large banner conveying a message she reasonably regarded as promoting illegal drug use." *Id.* at 396. The banner read: "BONG HiTS 4 JESUS." *Id.* at 397. "Consistent with established school policy prohibiting such messages at school events, [Morse] directed the students to take down the banner." *Id.* at 396. Frederick, one of the students who brought the banner to the event, refused to remove it, and Morse "confiscated the banner and later suspended [Frederick]." *Id.* Frederick sued Morse and the school district pursuant to 42 U.S.C. § 1983, alleging a violation of his First Amendment right of expression. The district court granted summary judgment to the school district and Morse, holding that they were entitled to qualified immunity and that they had not infringed Frederick's First Amendment rights. *Id.* at 399. The Court of Appeals for the Ninth Circuit reversed.

The Supreme Court granted certiorari to determine "whether Frederick had a First Amendment right to wield his banner, and, if so, whether that right was so clearly established that the principal may be held liable for damages." *Id.* at 400.[13] The Court "resolve[d] the first question against Frederick," and, therefore, did not have to reach the second. *Id.* The Court explained that its Fourth Amendment jurisprudence recognized that "deterring drug use by school children is an important—indeed, perhaps compelling interest." *Id.* at 407 (citation omitted). The "special characteristics of the school environment, and the governmental interest in stopping student drug abuse allow schools to restrict student expression that they reasonably regard as promoting such abuse." *Id.* at 408. Thus, "a principal may, consistent with the First Amendment, restrict student speech at a school event, when that speech is reasonably viewed as promoting illegal drug use." *Id.* at 402. The Court rejected Frederick's claim that since he was across the street from the school and not on school property, he was not inside *Tinker's* "schoolhouse gate," and school officials therefore had lost authority over him. The Court reasoned that the event where the banner was unfurled occurred during school hours, and it had been approved by the school's principal as a school event. *Id.* at 400. School events and field trips off school grounds were subject to the school's rules for student conduct. *Id.* at 400-01.

It is against this legal backdrop that we must determine whether the District's actions here violated Justin's First Amendment rights.

At the outset, it is important to note that the district court found that the District could not "establish[ ] a sufficient nexus between Justin's speech and a substantial disruption of the school environment[,]" *Layshock,* 496 F. Supp. 2d at 600, and the School District does not challenge that finding on appeal. Therefore, the School District is not arguing that it could properly punish Justin under the *Tinker* exception for student speech that causes a material and substantial disruption of the school environment. *See Tinker,* 393 U.S. at 513. Rather, the District's argument is twofold:

> [A] sufficient nexus exists between Justin's creation and distribution of the vulgar and defamatory profile of Principal Trosch and the School District to permit the School District to regulate this conduct. The "speech" initially began on-campus: Justin entered school property, the School District web site, and misappropriated a

picture of the Principal. The "speech" was aimed at the School District community and the Principal and was accessed on campus by Justin. It was reasonably foreseeable that the profile would come to the attention of the School District and the Principal.

District's Br. at 9.

Justin's "Entry" onto the District's Website

The School District's attempt to forge a nexus between the School and Justin's profile by relying upon his "entering" the District's website to "take" the District's photo of Trosch is unpersuasive at best. The argument equates Justin's act of signing onto a web site with the kind of trespass he would have committed had he broken into the principal's office or a teacher's desk; and we reject it. *See Thomas v. Board of Educ.*, 607 F.2d 1043 (2d Cir. 1979).

We find the reasoning in *Thomas v. Board of Educ.*, 607 F.3d 1043 (2d Cir. 1979), far more persuasive.[14] *Thomas* involved a group of students who were suspended for producing "a satirical publication addressed to the school community." *Id.* at 1045. The articles included such topics as masturbation and prostitution, as well as more standard fare such as "school lunches, cheerleaders, classmates, and teachers." *Id.* "Some of the initial preparation for publication occurred after school hours in the classroom" of a teacher whom the students consulted "for advice on isolated questions of grammar and content." *Id.* In addition, "an occasional article was composed or typed within the school building, always after classes," and the finished magazine was stored in a "classroom closet" with the classroom teacher's permission. *Id.*

However, the students were very careful to distribute the periodical only after school and off campus, and the vast majority of their work on the publication was done "in their homes, off campus and after school hours." *Id.* The school principal learned of the magazine when a teacher confiscated a copy from another student on campus, and "following consultation with the Board of Education," the principal imposed penalties that included a five-day suspension of the students involved.[15] *Id.* at 1046. The punishment was based on the students' publication of "an allegedly 'morally offensive, indecent, and obscene,' tabloid." *Id.* at 1050 n.12.

The students sued the school board and other school officials under 42 U.S.C. § 1983. They sought "injunctive and declaratory relief from alleged deprivations of their First and Fourteenth Amendment rights." *Id.* at 1046. The district court denied the students' request for injunctive relief based upon its conclusion that the publication "was potentially destructive of discipline in [the school], and therefore not protected by the First Amendment." *Id.* at 1047.

The Court of Appeals for the Second Circuit concluded that the students' conduct was not sufficiently related to the school to justify the school's exercise of authority. The court explained:

> [A]ll but an insignificant amount of relevant activity in this case was deliberately designed to take place beyond the schoolhouse gate. Indeed, the [students] diligently labored to ensure that [the magazine] was printed outside the school, and that no copies were sold on school grounds. That a few articles were transcribed on school typewriters, and that the finished product was secretly and unobtrusively stored in a teacher's closet do not alter the fact that [the magazine] was conceived, executed, and distributed outside the school. At best, therefore, any activity within the school itself was De minimis.

Id. at 1050.

The court reached that conclusion even though the students actually stored the offending publication inside a classroom and did some minimal amount of work on the periodical in school using school resources. Here, the relationship between Justin's conduct and the school is far more attenuated than in *Thomas*. We agree with the analysis in *Thomas*. Accordingly, because the School District concedes that Justin's profile did not cause disruption in the school, we do not think that the First Amendment can tolerate the School District stretching its authority into Justin's grandmother's home and reaching Justin while he is sitting at her computer after school in order to punish him for the expressive conduct that he engaged in there.

We realize, of course, that it is now well established that *Tinker*'s "schoolhouse gate" is not constructed solely of the bricks and mortar surrounding the school yard. Nevertheless, the concept of the "school yard" is not without boundaries and the reach of school authorities is not without limits. In *Morse*, the Court held that the First Amendment does not prevent a principal from "restrict[ing] student speech *at a* school *event*, when that speech is reasonably viewed as promoting illegal drug use." 551 U.S. at 403 (emphasis added). Nevertheless, with regard to expressive conduct that occurs outside of the school context, the Court, referring to its earlier decision in *Fraser*, was careful to note that "[h]ad Fraser delivered the same speech in a public forum outside the school context, it would have been protected." 551 U.S. at 404 (citations omitted).

It would be an unseemly and dangerous precedent to allow the state, in the guise of school authorities, to reach into a child's home and control his/her actions there to the same extent that it can control that child when he/she participates in school sponsored activities. Allowing the District to punish Justin for conduct he engaged in while at his grandmother's house using his grandmother's computer would create just such a precedent, and we therefore conclude that the district court correctly ruled that the District's response to Justin's expressive conduct violated the First Amendment guarantee of free expression.

The District Cannot Punish Justin Merely Because His Speech Reached Inside the School

As noted above, the School District also claims that Justin's speech can be treated as "on-campus" speech because it "was aimed at the School District community and the Principal and was accessed on campus by Justin [and] [i]t was reasonably foreseeable that the profile would come to the attention of the School District and the Principal."

The district court held that the School District's punishment of Justin was not appropriate under *Fraser* because "[t]here is no evidence that Justin engaged in any lewd or profane speech while in school." *Layshock*, 496 F. Supp.2d at 599–600. It also held that Justin's punishment was not appropriate under *Tinker* because the School District did "not establish[ ] a sufficient nexus between Justin's speech and a substantial disruption of the school environment." *Id.* at 600.

The School District does not dispute the district court's finding that its punishment of Justin was not appropriate under *Tinker*; it rests its argument on the Supreme Court's analysis in *Fraser*. In the School District's view, Justin's speech—his MySpace profile of Trosch—was unquestionably vulgar, lewd and offensive, and therefore not shielded by the First Amendment because it ended up inside the school community.[16] Similarly, the School District argues that under our decision in *Saxe, see* n.12, *supra*, there is no First Amendment protection for lewd, vulgar, indecent or plainly offensive speech in schools.[17]

The District rests this argument primarily on three cases which it claims allow it to respond to a student's vulgar speech when that speech is posted on the internet. The District cites *J.S. v. Bethlehem Area Sch. Dist.*, 807 A.2d 847 (Pa. 2002); *Wisniewski v. Bd. of Educ. of Weedsport Cent. Sch. Dist.*, 494 F.3d 34 (2d Cir. 2007); and *Doninger v. Niehoff*, 527 F.3d 41 (2d Cir. 2008). However, as we will explain, each of those cases involved off campus expressive conduct that resulted in a substantial disruption of the school, and the courts allowed the schools to respond to the substantial disruption that the student's out of school conduct caused.

In *J.S.*, an eighth grade student created a threatening website aimed at his algebra teacher that went so far as to explain "[w]hy Should She Die," and requested money "to help pay for the hitman." 807 A.2d at 851. The site frightened several students and parents and the algebra teacher was so badly frightened that she ended up having to take medical leave from her teaching responsibilities. As a result of her inability to return to teaching, "three substitute teachers were required to be utilized which disrupted the educational process of the students." *Id.* at 852. "In sum, the web site created disorder and significantly and adversely impacted the delivery of instruction." *Id.* at 869. The Supreme Court of Pennsylvania concluded that

the resulting disruption of instruction and the educational environment allowed the school to punish the student for his expressive conduct even though the student created the website from his home.[18]

Similarly, the school suspended the student in *Wisniewski*, for creating an image on the internet from his home computer that depicted a pistol firing a bullet at a teacher's head with dots representing splattered blood above the head. 494 F.3d at 36. The words: "Kill Mr. VanderMolen" were printed beneath the drawing. VanderMolen was the student's English teacher. The student created the image a couple of weeks after his class was instructed that threats would not be tolerated at the school, and would be treated as acts of violence. The court of appeals affirmed the district court's grant of summary judgment in favor of the school district in a suit alleging a violation of the First Amendment based on the school's suspension of the student for the out-of-school conduct. The court reasoned that "[t]he fact that [the student's] creation and transmission of the icon occurred away from school property [did] not necessarily insulate him from school discipline." 494 F.3d at 39. The court reasoned that "even if [the student's] transmission of an [image] depicting and calling for the killing of his teacher could be viewed as an expression of opinion within the meaning of *Tinker*," it was not protected by the First Amendment because "it cross[ed] the boundary of protected speech and pose[d] a reasonably foreseeable risk [of] materially and substantially disrupting the work and discipline of the school." *Id.* at 38-9 (internal quotation marks omitted).

Finally, in *Doninger*, a student, who was a class officer, posted a message on her publicly accessible web log or "blog" that resulted in school authorities not allowing her to participate in an election for class office.[19] *Id.* at 43. In her message, she complained about a school activity that was cancelled "due to douchebags in central office," and encouraged others to contact the central office to "piss [the district superintendent] off more." *Id.* at 45. When the principal learned of the student's posting, she prohibited her from running for senior class secretary "because [the student's] conduct had failed to display the civility and good citizenship expected of class officers." *Id.* at 46. The student and her parents then sought injunctive relief in the form of a court order allowing her to run for class office. The court of appeals affirmed the district court's denial of relief because the student's out of school expressive conduct "created a foreseeable risk of substantial disruption to the work and discipline of the school." *Id.* at 53.[20] "[The student] herself testified that . . . students were 'all riled up' and that a sit-in was threatened." *Id.* at 51. Accordingly, the court of appeals held that the student's mother "failed to show clearly that [the student's] First Amendment rights were violated when she was disqualified from running" for class office. *Id.* at 53.

However, for our purposes, it is particularly important to note that the court in *Doninger* was careful to explain that it "[had] no occasion to consider whether a different, more serious consequence than disqualification from student office would raise constitutional concerns." *Id.* at 53. Of course, Justin's consequences were more serious; he was suspended. Moreover, in citing *Doninger*, we do not suggest that we agree with that court's conclusion that the student's out of school expressive conduct was not protected by the First Amendment there. Rather, we cite *Doninger* only to respond to the School District's contention that that case supports its actions against Justin.

As noted earlier, the District's January 3, 2006, letter to the Layshocks advising them of Justin's suspension reads, in relevant part, that it was punishing Justin because "Justin admitted prior to the informal hearing that he created a profile about Mr. Trosch." Although the letter also mentions disruption, we have taken care to stress that the District does not now challenge the district court's finding that Justin's conduct did not result in any substantial disruption. Moreover, when pressed at oral argument, counsel for the School District conceded that the District was relying solely on the fact that Justin created the profile of Trosch, and not arguing that it created any substantial disruption in the school. However, as noted above, *Fraser* does not allow the School District to punish Justin for expressive conduct which occurred outside of the school context. *See Morse*, 551 U.S. at 404 ("Had Fraser delivered the same speech in a public forum outside the school context, it would have been protected.") (citations omitted). Moreover, we have found no authority that would support punishment for creating such a profile unless it results in foreseeable and substantial disruption of school.

We believe the cases relied upon by the School District stand for nothing more than the rather unremarkable proposition that schools may punish expressive conduct that occurs outside of school, as if it occurred inside the "schoolhouse gate," under certain very limited circumstances, none of which are present here.

As the court of appeals explained in *Thomas*: "[O]ur willingness to defer to the schoolmaster's expertise in administering school discipline rests, in large measure, upon the supposition that the arm of authority does not reach beyond the schoolhouse gate." 607 F.2d at 1045. We need not now define the precise parameters of when the arm of authority can reach beyond the schoolhouse gate because, as we noted earlier, the district court found that Justin's conduct did not disrupt the school, and the District does not appeal that finding. Thus, we need only hold that Justin's use of the District's web site does not constitute entering the school, and that the District is not empowered to punish his out of school expressive conduct under the circumstances here.

Based on those two conclusions, we will affirm the district court's grant of summary judgment to Justin Layshock on his First Amendment claim.[21]

Notes

1. MySpace is found at: http://www.myspace.com.
2. Social online networking sites allow members to use "their online profiles to become part of an online community of people with common interests. Once a member has created a profile, she can extend 'friend invitations' to other members and communicate with her friends over the MySpace.com platform via e-mail, instant messaging, or blogs." *Doe,* 474 F. Supp.2d at 846.
3. Justin explained that a "blunt" was a marijuana cigarette.
4. Justin later explained that he made the profile to be funny, and did not intend to hurt anyone. However, there was obviously nothing "funny" about the profile in the eyes of the school administration.
5. Trosch later testified that he found Justin's apology respectful and sincere. Justin followed up with a written letter of apology on January 4, 2006.
6. Students assigned to ACE meet in a segregated area of the high school for three hours each day. The program is typically reserved for students with behavior and attendance problems who are unable to function in a regular classroom.

   Prior to creating the Myspace profile, Justin was classified as a gifted student, was enrolled in advanced placement classes, and had won awards at interscholastic academic competitions. The record does not reveal how the School District determined that it was appropriate to place such a student in a program designed for students who could not function in a classroom.
7. Justin had been a French tutor to middle school students.
8. Justin did graduate in 2006 and went on to attend a university in New York City.
9. The Layshocks agreed to withdraw their motion for a preliminary injunction in exchange for the District's agreement to remove Justin from the ACE program, reinstate him to his regular classes, allow him to participate in Academic Games, and attend his graduation.
10. The district court ruled that Trosch was entitled to summary judgment on all counts because he was not involved in disciplining Justin. It also held that Ionta and Gill were entitled to summary judgment on Justin's First Amendment claim based on qualified immunity, and that all of the defendants were entitled to summary judgment on the vagueness/overbreadth challenge and the parents' substantive due process claim.
11. The Layshocks filed a cross-appeal (No. 07-4555) from the district court's grant of summary judgment in favor of the School District on their Fourteenth Amendment Due Process claim. In our opinion filed on February 4, 2010, we affirmed the district court's grant of summary judgment to the School District on that claim,

and the Layshocks did not seek rehearing en banc on that claim. Therefore, although we vacated the February 4, 2010, opinion and judgment as to the School District's appeal at No. 07-4464, and granted the School District's petition for rehearing en banc, we also, on April 9, 2010, ordered that "the opinion and judgment entered by this Court on February 4, 2010 stands with respect to the affirmance of the district court's grant of summary judgment to the [School District] on [the Layshocks'] Fourteenth Amendment Due Process claim."

12. In *Saxe v. State College Area School District,* 240 F.3d 200, 213 (3d Cir. 2001), we interpreted *Fraser* as establishing that "there is no First Amendment protection for 'lewd,' 'vulgar,' 'indecent,' and 'plainly offensive' speech in school."

13. The court of appeals had ruled that the principal was not entitled to qualified immunity.

14. *Thomas* was decided after *Tinker* but before *Fraser.*

15. The Principal and Superintendent of Schools had initially decided to take no action pending assessment of the publication's impact. However, they ultimately decided to act after being contacted by the President of the Board of Education. *Thomas,* 607 F.2d at 1045-46.

16. The District's argument in this regard is not crystal clear as its brief suggests that it can react to Justin's profile merely because it was lewd and vulgar. For example, the District summarizes one of its arguments as follows:

> The School District did not violate the First Amendment by punishing Justin for engaging in conduct which interfered with the School District's "highly appropriate function . . . to prohibit the use of vulgar and offensive terms in public discourse."

District's Br. at 10 (ellipsis in original).

> However, we reject out of hand any suggestion that schools can police students' out-of-school speech by patrolling "the public discourse." Accordingly, we will assume that the District is arguing that it can control lewd and vulgar speech as authorized under *Fraser.*

17. In *Saxe,* we did state: "Under *Fraser,* a school may categorically prohibit lewd, vulgar or profane language." 240 F.3d at 214. However, when read in context, it is clear that we were there referring only to speech inside *Tinker's* schoolhouse gate. Thus, we summarized the holding in *Fraser* as follows: "According to *Fraser,* . . . there is no First Amendment protection for 'lewd,' 'vulgar,' 'indecent,' and 'plainly offensive' speech *in school.*" *Id.* at 213 (emphasis added).

18. The district court believed that *J.S.* was "on point" but "respectfully reache[d] a slightly different balance between student expression and school authority." *Layshock,* 496 F. Supp. 2d at 602. However, we do not think *J.S.* is "on point" or the least bit helpful because there is no comparison between the impact of the conduct there and the impact of the conduct here.

19. "A blog (a contraction of the term 'web log') is a type of website, usually maintained by an individual with regular entries or commentary, descriptions of events, or other material such as graphics or video. . . . 'Blog' can also be used as a verb, *meaning to maintain or add content to a blog.*" (http://en.wikipedia.org/wiki/Blog) (last visited September 23, 2010).

20. The blog had resulted in numerous calls and emails to the principal, and the court of appeals noted that the blog also used inaccurate and misleading information to rally those who read it to contact the school principal.

21. The District argues in the alternative that it did not violate the First Amendment by punishing Justin because his speech was defamatory and not protected by the First Amendment. The Layshocks respond by arguing that Justin's profile is a parody that cannot constitute defamation. However, whether or not we accept the characterization of a "parody," the issue before us is limited to whether the District had the authority to punish Justin for expressive conduct outside of school that the District considered lewd and offensive.

THE UNITED STATES COURT OF APPEALS FOR THE THIRD CIRCUIT serves the areas of Pennsylvania, New Jersey, Delaware, and the Virgin Islands.

Theodore A. McKee   ➔ **NO**

J.S. v. Blue Mountain School District

J.S., a minor, by and through her parents, Terry Snyder and Steven Snyder, individually and on behalf of their daughter, appeal the District Court's grant of summary judgment in favor of the Blue Mountain School District ("the School District") and denial of their motion for summary judgment. This case arose when the School District suspended J.S. for creating, on a weekend and on her home computer, a MySpace profile (the "profile") making fun of her middle school principal, James McGonigle. The profile contained adult language and sexually explicit content. J.S. and her parents sued the School District under 42 U.S.C. § 1983 and state law, alleging that the suspension violated J.S.'s First Amendment free speech rights, that the School District's policies were unconstitutionally overbroad and vague, that the School District violated the Snyders' Fourteenth Amendment substantive due process rights to raise their child, and that the School District acted outside of its authority in punishing J.S. for out-of-school speech.

Because J.S. was suspended from school for speech that indisputably caused no substantial disruption in school and that could not reasonably have led school officials to forecast substantial disruption in school, the School District's actions violated J.S.'s First Amendment free speech rights. We will accordingly reverse and remand that aspect of the District Court's judgment. However, we will affirm the District Court's judgment that the School District's policies were not overbroad or void-for-vagueness, and that the School District did not violate the Snyders' Fourteenth Amendment substantive due process rights.

I

J.S. was an Honor Roll eighth grade student who had never been disciplined in school until December 2006 and February 2007, when she was twice disciplined for dress code violations by McGonigle. On Sunday, March 18, 2007, J.S. and her friend K.L., another eighth grade student at Blue Mountain Middle School, created a fake profile of McGonigle, which they posted on MySpace, a social networking website. The profile was created at J.S.'s home, on a computer belonging to J.S.'s parents.

The profile did not identify McGonigle by name, school, or location, though it did contain his official photograph from the School District's website. The profile was presented as a self-portrayal of a bisexual Alabama middle school principal named "M-Hoe." The profile contained crude content and vulgar language, ranging from nonsense and juvenile humor to profanity and shameful personal attacks aimed at the principal and his family. For instance, the profile lists M-Hoe's general interests as: "detention, being a tight ass, riding the fraintrain, spending time with my child (who looks like a gorilla), baseball, my golden pen, fucking in my office, hitting on students and their parents." Appendix ("App.") 38. In addition, the profile stated in the "About me" section:

> HELLO CHILDREN[.] yes. it's your oh so wonderful, hairy, expressionless, sex addict, fagass, put on this world with a small dick PRINCIPAL[.] I have come to myspace so i can pervert the minds of other principal's [sic] to be just like me. I know, I know, you're all thrilled[.] Another reason I came to myspace is because - I am keeping an eye on you students (who[m] I care for so much)[.] For those who want to be my friend, and aren't in my school[,] I love children, sex (any kind), dogs, long walks on the beach, tv, being a dick head, and last but not least my darling wife who looks like a man (who satisfies my needs) MY FRAINTRAIN. . . .

Id. Though disturbing, the record indicates that the profile was so outrageous that no one took its content seriously. J.S. testified that she intended the profile to be a joke between herself and her friends. At her deposition, she testified that she created the profile because she thought it was "comical" insofar as it was so "outrageous." App. 190.

Initially, the profile could be viewed in full by anyone who knew the URL (or address) or who otherwise found the profile by searching MySpace for a term it contained. The following day, however, J.S. made the profile "private" after several students approached her at school, generally to say that they thought the profile was funny. App. 194. By making the profile "private," J.S. limited access to the profile to people whom she and K.L. invited to be a MySpace "friend." J.S. and K.L. granted "friend" status to about twenty-two School District students.

The School District's computers block access to MySpace, so no Blue Mountain student was ever able to view the profile from of school. McGonigle first learned about the profile on Tuesday, March 20, 2007, from a student who was in his office to discuss an unrelated incident. McGonigle asked this student to attempt to find out who had created the profile. He also

From *United States Court of Appeals*, June 13, 2011.

attempted—unsuccessfully—to find the profile himself, even contacting MySpace directly.

At the end of the school day on Tuesday, the student who initially told McGonigle about the profile reported to him that it had been created by J.S. McGonigle asked this student to bring him a printout of the profile to school the next day, which she did. It is undisputed that the only printout of the profile that was ever brought to school was one brought at McGonigle's specific request.

On Wednesday, March 21, 2007, McGonigle showed the profile to Superintendent Joyce Romberger and the Director of Technology, Susan Schneider-Morgan. The three met for about fifteen minutes to discuss the profile. McGonigle also showed the profile to two guidance counselors, Michelle Guers and Debra Frain (McGonigle's wife). McGonigle contacted MySpace to attempt to discover what computer had been used to create the profile, but MySpace refused to release that information without a court order. The School District points to no evidence that anyone ever suspected the information in the profile to be true.

McGonigle ultimately decided that the creation of the profile was a Level Four Infraction under the Disciplinary Code of Blue Mountain Middle School, Student-Parent Handbook, App. 65–66, as a false accusation about a staff member of the school and a "copyright" violation of the computer use policy, for using McGonigle's photograph. At his deposition, however, McGonigle admitted that he believed the students "weren't accusing me. They were pretending they were me." App. 327.[1]

J.S. was absent from school on Wednesday, the day McGonigle obtained a copy of the profile. When she returned, on Thursday, March 22, 2007, McGonigle summoned J.S. and K.L. to his office to meet with him and Guidance Counselor Guers. J.S. initially denied creating the profile, but then admitted her role. McGonigle told J.S. and K.L. that he was upset and angry, and threatened the children and their families with legal action. App. 333–34. Following this meeting, J.S. and K.L. remained in McGonigle's office while he contacted their parents and waited for them to come to school.

McGonigle met with J.S. and her mother Terry Snyder and showed Mrs. Snyder the profile. He told the children's parents that J.S. and K.L. would receive ten days out-of-school suspension, which also prohibited attendance at school dances. McGonigle also threatened legal action. J.S. and her mother both apologized to McGonigle, and J.S. subsequently wrote a letter of apology to McGonigle and his wife.

McGonigle next contacted MySpace, provided the URL for the profile and requested its removal, which was done. McGonigle also contacted Superintendent Romberger to inform her of his decision regarding J.S. and K.L.'s punishment. Although Romberger could have overruled McGonigle's decision, she agreed with the punishment. On Friday, March 23, 2007, McGonigle sent J.S.'s parents a disciplinary notice, which stated that J.S.

had been suspended for ten days.[2] The following week, Romberger declined Mrs. Snyder's request to overrule the suspension.

On the same day McGonigle met with J.S. and her mother, he contacted the local police and asked about the possibility of pressing criminal charges against the students. The local police referred McGonigle to the state police, who informed him that he could press harassment charges, but that the charges would likely be dropped. McGonigle chose not to press charges. An officer did, however, complete a formal report and asked McGonigle whether he wanted the state police to call the students and their parents to the police station to let them know how serious the situation was. McGonigle asked the officer to do this, and on Friday, March 23, J.S. and K.L. and their mothers were summoned to the state police station to discuss the profile.

The School District asserted that the profile disrupted school in the following ways. There were general "rumblings" in the school regarding the profile. More specifically, on Tuesday, March 20, McGonigle was approached by two teachers who informed him that students were discussing the profile in class. App. 322. Randy Nunemacher, a Middle School math teacher, experienced a disruption in his class when six or seven students were talking and discussing the profile; Nunemacher had to tell the students to stop talking three times, and raised his voice on the third occasion. App. 368–73. The exchange lasted about five or six minutes. App. 371. Nunemacher also testified that he heard two students talking about the profile in his class on another day, but they stopped when he told them to get back to work. App. 373–74. Nunemacher admitted that the talking in class was not a unique incident and that he had to tell his students to stop talking about various topics about once a week. Another teacher, Angela Werner, testified that she was approached by a group of eighth grade girls at the end of her Skills for Adolescents course to report the profile. App. 415–16. Werner said this did not disrupt her class because the girls spoke with her during the portion of the class when students were permitted to work independently. App. 417–18.

The School District also alleged disruption to Counselor Frain's job activities. Frain canceled a small number of student counseling appointments to supervise student testing on the morning that McGonigle met with J.S., K.L., and their parents. Counselor Guers was originally scheduled to supervise the student testing, but was asked by McGonigle to sit in on the meetings, so Frain filled in for Guers. This substitution lasted about twenty-five to thirty minutes. There is no evidence that Frain was unable to reschedule the canceled student appointments, and the students who were to meet with her remained in their regular classes. App. 352–53.

On March 28, 2007, J.S. and her parents filed this action against the School District, Superintendent Romberger, and Principal McGonigle. By way of stipulation, on January 7, 2008, all claims against Romberger and

McGonigle were dismissed, and only the School District remained as a defendant. After discovery, both parties moved for summary judgment.

After analyzing the above facts, the District Court granted the School District's summary judgment motion on all claims, though specifically acknowledging that *Tinker v. Des Moines Independent Community School District,* 393 U.S. 503 (1969), does not govern this case because no "substantial and material disruption" occurred. App. 10–12 (refusing to rely on *Tinker*); App. 17 (concluding that "a substantial disruption so as to fall under *Tinker* did not occur"). Instead, the District Court drew a distinction between political speech at issue in *Tinker,* and "vulgar and offensive" speech at issue in a subsequent school speech case, *Bethel School District v. Fraser,* 478 U.S. 675 (1986). App. 11–12. The District Court also noted the Supreme Court's most recent school speech decision, *Morse v. Frederick,* 551 U.S. 393 (2007), where the Court allowed a school district to prohibit a banner promoting illegal drug use at a school-sponsored event.

Applying a variation of the *Fraser* and *Morse* standard, the District Court held that "as vulgar, lewd, and potentially illegal speech that had an effect on campus, we find that the school did not violate the plaintiff's rights in punishing her for it even though it arguably did not cause a substantial disruption of the school." App. 15–16. The Court asserted that the facts of this case established a connection between off-campus action and on-campus effect, and thus justified punishment, because: (1) the website was about the school's principal; (2) the intended audience was the student body; (3) a paper copy was brought into the school and the website was discussed in school; (4) the picture on the profile was appropriated from the School District's website; (5) J.S. created the profile out of anger at the principal for disciplining her for dress code violations in the past; (6) J.S. lied in school to the principal about creating the profile; (7) *"although a substantial disruption so as to fall under Tinker did not occur ... there was in fact some disruption during school hours"*; and (8) the profile was viewed at least by the principal at school. App. 17 (emphasis added).

The District Court then rejected several other district court decisions where the courts did not allow schools to punish speech that occurred off campus, including the decision in *Layshock v. Hermitage School District,* 496 F. Supp. 2d 587 (W.D. Pa. 2007), a case substantially similar to the one before us, and which is also being considered by this Court. See App. 18–20. In distinguishing these cases, the District Court made several qualitative judgments about the speech involved in each. See, e.g., App. 18 (asserting that the statements in *Flaherty v. Keystone Oaks School District,* 247 F. Supp. 2d 698 (W.D. Pa. 2003), were "rather innocuous compared to the offensive and vulgar statements made by J.S. in the present case"); App. 19 (contending that "[t]he speech in the instant case . . . is distinguishable" from the speech in *Killion v. Franklin Regional School District,* 136 F. Supp. 2d 446 (W.D. Pa. 2001), because

of, *inter alia,* "the level of vulgarity that was present" in the instant case); App. 20 (claiming that, as compared to *Layshock,* "the facts of our case include a much more vulgar and offensive profile").

Ultimately, the District Court held that although J.S.'s profile did not cause a "substantial and material" disruption under *Tinker,* the School District's punishment was constitutionally permissible because the profile was "vulgar and offensive" under *Fraser* and J.S.'s off-campus conduct had an "effect" at the school. In a footnote, the District Court also noted that "the protections provided under *Tinker* do not apply to speech that invades the rights of others." App. 16 n.4 (citing *Tinker,* 393 U.S. at 513).

Next, the District Court held that the School District's policies were not vague and overbroad. The District Court first approached the issue in a somewhat backwards manner: it concluded that because the punishment was appropriate under the First Amendment, the policies were not vague and overbroad even though they can be read to apply to off-campus conduct. App. 21. Alternatively, the District Court held that the policy language was "sufficiently narrow . . . to confine the policy to school grounds and school-related activities." *Id.* (quoting the Handbook, which provides that the "[m]aintenance of order applies during those times when students are under the direct control and supervision of school district officials," and noting that the computer use policy incorporates the limitations of the Handbook).

The District Court also held that the School District did not violate the Snyders' parental rights under the Fourteenth Amendment. The Court concluded that "the school did not err in disciplining J.S., and her actions were not merely personal home activities[,]" and that therefore the Snyders' parental rights were not violated. The Court did not address directly the plaintiffs' state law argument, but did note that Pennsylvania law allows school districts to "punish students [ ] 'during such times as they are under the supervision of the board of school directors and teachers, including the time necessarily spent in coming to and returning from school.'" App. 22 (quoting 24 Pa. Cons. Stat. § 5-510). J.S. and her parents filed a timely appeal from the District Court's entry of summary judgment in favor of the School District and from its decision to deny their motion for summary judgment.

II

The District Court had jurisdiction over the federal claims pursuant to 28 U.S.C. § 1331 and 28 U.S.C. § 1343(a)(3) and (4), and exercised supplemental jurisdiction over the state law claim under 28 U.S.C. § 1367. We exercise jurisdiction under 28 U.S.C. § 1291.

We review a District Court's disposition of a summary judgment motion *de novo. Pichler v. UNITE,* 542 F.3d 380, 385 (3d Cir. 2008) (citing *Marten v. Godwin,* 499 F.3d 290, 295 (3d Cir. 2007)). In conducting this review, we use the same standard as the District Court should have applied. *Farrell v. Planters Lifesavers Co.*, 206 F.3d 271, 278 (3d Cir. 2000). "The court shall grant summary judgment if the movant shows that there is no genuine dispute as to any material fact and the movant is entitled to judgment as a matter of law." Fed. R. Civ. P. 56(a) (setting forth the legal standard formerly found in Fed. R. Civ. P. 56(c)). All inferences must be viewed in the light most favorable to the nonmoving party, *Matsushita Elec. Indus. Co. v. Zenith Radio Corp.*, 475 U.S. 574, 587 (1986); *Farrell*, 206 F.3d at 278, and where, as was the case here, the District Court considers crossmotions for summary judgment "the court construes facts and draws inferences 'in favor of the party against whom the motion under consideration is made,'" *Pichler*, 542 F.3d at 386 (quoting *Samuelson v. LaPorte Cmty. Sch. Corp.*, 526 F.3d 1046, 1051 (7th Cir. 2008)).

"A disputed fact is 'material' if it would affect the outcome of the suit as determined by the substantive law." *Gray v. York Newspapers, Inc.*, 957 F.2d 1070, 1078 (3d Cir. 1992). Importantly, the nonmoving party cannot satisfy its requirement of establishing a genuine dispute of fact merely by pointing to unsupported allegations found in the pleadings. *Celotex Corp. v. Catrett*, 477 U.S. 317, 322-23 (1986). Instead, the party must raise more than "some metaphysical doubt," *Matsushita*, 475 U.S. at 586, and the court must determine that "a fair-minded jury could return a verdict for the [nonmoving party] on the evidence presented." *Anderson v. Liberty Lobby, Inc.*, 477 U.S. 242, 252 (1986); *see also Bouriez v. Carnegie Mellon Univ.*, 585 F.3d 765, 770-71 (3d Cir. 2009). It is impermissible for the court to intrude upon the duties of the fact-finder by weighing the evidence or making credibility determinations. *Pichler*, 542 F.3d at 386. Finally, when the nonmoving party is the plaintiff, he must produce sufficient evidence to establish every element that he will be required to prove at trial. *Celotex*, 477 U.S. at 322.

III

Although the precise issue before this Court is one of first impression, the Supreme Court and this Court have analyzed the extent to which school officials can regulate student speech in several thorough opinions that compel the conclusion that the School District violated J.S.'s First Amendment free speech rights when it suspended her for speech that caused no substantial disruption in school and that could not reasonably have led school officials to forecast substantial disruption in school.

A

We begin our analysis by recognizing the "comprehensive authority" of teachers and other public school officials. *Tinker*, 393 U.S. at 507. *See generally Veronia Sch. Dist. 47J v. Acton*, 515 U.S. 646, 655 (1995) (describing the public schools' power over public school children as both "custodial and tutelary"). Those officials involved in the educational process perform "important, delicate, and highly discretionary functions." *W. Va. State Bd. of Educ. v. Bar-*

nette, 319 U.S. 624, 637 (1943). As a result, federal courts generally exercise restraint when considering issues within the purview of public school officials. See *Bd. of Educ., Island Trees Union Free Sch. Dist. v. Pico*, 457 U.S. 853, 864 (1982) ("[F]ederal courts should not ordinarily 'intervene in the resolution of conflicts which arise in the daily operation of school systems.'" (quoting *Epperson v. Arkansas*, 393 U.S. 97, 104 (1968)); see also *Hazelwood Sch. Dist. v. Kuhlmeier*, 484 U.S. 260, 266 (1988) ("[T]he education of the Nation's youth is primarily the responsibility of parents, teachers, and state and local school officials, and not of federal judges.").

The authority of public school officials is not boundless, however. The First Amendment unquestionably protects the free speech rights of students in public school. *Morse*, 551 U.S. at 396 ("Our cases make clear that students do not 'shed their constitutional rights to freedom of speech or expression at the schoolhouse gate.'" (quoting *Tinker*, 393 U.S. at 506)). Indeed, "[t]he vigilant protection of constitutional freedoms is nowhere more vital than in the community of American schools." *Shelton v. Tucker*, 364 U.S. 479, 487 (1960). The exercise of First Amendment rights in school, however, has to be "applied in light of the special characteristics of the school environment," *Tinker*, 393 U.S. at 506, and thus the constitutional rights of students in public schools "are not automatically coextensive with the rights of adults in other settings," *Fraser*, 478 U.S. at 682. Since *Tinker*, courts have struggled to strike a balance between safeguarding students' First Amendment rights and protecting the authority of school administrators to maintain an appropriate learning environment.

The Supreme Court established a basic framework for assessing student free speech claims in *Tinker*, and we will assume, without deciding, that *Tinker* applies to J.S.'s speech in this case.[3] The Court in *Tinker* held that "to justify prohibition of a particular expression of opinion," school officials must demonstrate that "the forbidden conduct would *materially and substantially interfere* with the requirements of appropriate discipline in the operation of the school." *Tinker*, 393 U.S. at 509 (emphasis added) (quotation marks omitted). This burden cannot be met if school officials are driven by "a mere desire to avoid the discomfort and unpleasantness that always accompany an unpopular viewpoint." *Id.* Moreover, "*Tinker* requires a specific and significant fear of disruption, not just some remote apprehension of disturbance." *Saxe v. State Coll. Area Sch. Dist.*, 240 F.3d 200, 211 (3d Cir. 2001). Although *Tinker* dealt with political speech, the opinion has never been confined to such speech. See *id.* at 215–17 (holding that the school's anti-harassment policy was overbroad because it "appears to cover substantially more speech than could be prohibited under *Tinker's* substantial disruption test"); see also *Killion*, 136 F. Supp. 2d at 455–58 (holding that the school overstepped its constitutional bounds under Tinker when it suspended a student for making "lewd" comments about the school's athletic director in an e-mail the student wrote at home and circulated to the non-school e-mail accounts of several classmates).

As this Court has emphasized, with then-Judge Alito writing for the majority, *Tinker* sets the general rule for regulating school speech, and that rule is subject to several *narrow* exceptions. *Saxe*, 240 F.3d at 212 ("Since *Tinker*, the Supreme Court has carved out a number of narrow categories of speech that a school may restrict even without the threat of substantial disruption."). The first exception is set out in *Fraser*, which we interpreted to permit school officials to regulate "'lewd,' 'vulgar,' 'indecent,' and 'plainly offensive' speech *in school*." *Id.* at 213 (quoting *Fraser*, 478 U.S. at 683, 685) (emphasis added); see also *Sypniewski v. Warren Hills Reg'l Bd. of Educ.*, 307 F.3d 243, 253 (3d Cir. 2002) (quoting *Saxe's* narrow interpretation of the *Fraser* exception). The second exception to *Tinker* is articulated in *Hazelwood School District v. Kuhlmeier*, which allows school officials to "regulate school-sponsored speech (that is, speech that a reasonable observer would view as the school's own speech) on the basis of any legitimate pedagogical concern." *Saxe*, 240 F.3d at 214.

The Supreme Court recently articulated a third exception to *Tinker's* general rule in *Morse*. Although, prior to this case, we have not had an opportunity to analyze the scope of the *Morse* exception, the Supreme Court itself emphasized the narrow reach of its decision. In *Morse*, a school punished a student for unfurling, at a school-sponsored event, a large banner containing a message that could reasonably be interpreted as promoting illegal drug use. 551 U.S. at 396. The Court emphasized that *Morse* was a school speech case, because "[t]he event occurred during normal school hours," was sanctioned by the school "as an approved social event or class trip," was supervised by teachers and administrators from the school, and involved performances by the school band and cheerleaders. *Id.* at 400–01 (quotation marks omitted). The Court then held that "[t]he 'special characteristics of the school environment,' *Tinker*, 393 U.S.[ ] at 506 [ ], and the governmental interest in stopping student drug abuse . . . allow schools to restrict student expression that they reasonably regard as promoting illegal drug use." *Id.* at 408.

Notably, Justice Alito's concurrence in *Morse* further emphasizes the narrowness of the Court's holding, stressing that *Morse* "stand[s] at the far reaches of what the First Amendment permits." 551 U.S. at 425 (Alito, J., concurring). In fact, Justice Alito only joined the Court's opinion "on the understanding that the opinion does not hold that the special characteristics of the public schools necessarily justify any other speech restrictions" than those recognized by the Court in *Tinker*, *Fraser*, *Kuhlmeier*, and *Morse*. *Id.* at 422–23. Justice Alito also noted that the *Morse* decision "does not endorse the broad argument . . . that the First Amendment permits public school officials to censor any student speech that interferes with a school's 'educational mission.' This argument can easily be manipulated in dangerous ways, and I would reject it before such abuse occurs." *Id.* at 423 (citations omitted).

Moreover, Justice Alito engaged in a detailed discussion distinguishing the role of school authorities from the role of parents, and the school context from the "[o]utside of school" context. *Id.* at 424–25.

B

There is no dispute that J.S.'s speech did not cause a substantial disruption in the school. The School District's counsel conceded this point at oral argument and the District Court explicitly found that "a substantial disruption so as to fall under Tinker did not occur." App. at 17. Nonetheless, the School District now argues that it was justified in punishing J.S. under Tinker because of "facts which might reasonably have led school authorities to forecast substantial disruption of or material interference with school activities. . . . ." Tinker, 393 U.S. at 514. Although the burden is on school authorities to meet Tinker's requirements to abridge student First Amendment rights, the School District need not prove with absolute certainty that substantial disruption will occur. Doninger v. Niehoff, 527 F.3d 41, 51 (2d Cir. 2008) (holding that Tinker does not require "actual disruption to justify a restraint on student speech"); Lowery v. Euverard, 497 F.3d 584, 591–92 (6th Cir. 2007) ("Tinker does not require school officials to wait until the horse has left the barn before closing the door. . . . [It] does not require certainty, only that the forecast of substantial disruption be reasonable."); LaVine v. Blaine Sch. Dist., 257 F.3d 981, 989 (9th Cir. 2001) ("Tinker does not require school officials to wait until disruption actually occurs before they may act.").

The facts in this case do not support the conclusion that a forecast of substantial disruption was reasonable. In Tinker, the Supreme Court held that "our independent examination of the record fails to yield evidence that the school authorities had reason to anticipate that the wearing of the armbands [to protest the Vietnam War] would substantially interfere with the work of the school or impinge upon the rights of other students." 393 U.S. at 509. Given this holding, it is important to consider the record before the Supreme Court in Tinker and compare it to the facts of this case.

The relevant events in Tinker took place in December 1965, the year that over 200,000 U.S. troops were deployed to Vietnam as part of Operation Rolling Thunder. Justice Black dissented in Tinker, noting that "members of this Court, like all other citizens, know, without being told, that the disputes over the wisdom of the Vietnam war have disrupted and divided this country as few other issues [e]ver have." Id. at 524 (Black, J., dissenting). In fact, the Tinker majority itself noted the school authorities' concern about the effect of the protest on friends of a student who was killed in Vietnam. See id. at 509 n.3. Justice Black also emphasized the following portions of the record:

> the [ ] armbands caused comments, warnings by other students, the poking of fun at them, and a warning by an older football player that other,

nonprotesting students had better let them alone. There is also evidence that a teacher of mathematics had his lesson period practically 'wrecked' chiefly by disputes with [a protesting student] who wore her armband for her 'demonstration.'

Id. at 517 (Black, J., dissenting). Based on these facts, Justice Black disagreed with the *Tinker* majority's holding that the armbands did not cause a substantial disruption in school: "I think the record overwhelmingly shows that the armbands did exactly what the elected school officials and principals foresaw they would, that is, took the students' minds off their classwork and diverted them to thoughts about the highly emotional subject of the Vietnam war." *Id.* at 518; see also *id.* at 524 ("Of course students, like other people, cannot concentrate on lesser issues when black armbands are being ostentatiously displayed in their presence to call attention to the wounded and dead of the war, some of the wounded and the dead being their friends and neighbors.").

This was the record in *Tinker*, and yet the majority in that case held that "the record does not demonstrate *any facts* which might reasonably have led school authorities to forecast substantial disruption of or material interference with school activities," and thus that the school violated the students' First Amendment rights. *Id.* at 514 (emphasis added). Turning to our record, J.S. created the profile as a joke, and she took steps to make it "private" so that access was limited to her and her friends. Although the profile contained McGonigle's picture from the school's website, the profile did not identify him by name, school, or location. Moreover, the profile, though indisputably vulgar, was so juvenile and nonsensical that no reasonable person could take its content seriously, and the record clearly demonstrates that no one did.[4] Also, the School District's computers block access to MySpace, so no Blue Mountain student was ever able to view the profile from school.[5] And, the only printout of the profile that was ever brought to school was one that was brought at McGonigle's express request. Thus, beyond general rumblings, a few minutes of talking in class, and some officials rearranging their schedules to assist McGonigle in dealing with the profile, no disruptions occurred.[6]

In comparing our record to the record in *Tinker,* this Court cannot apply *Tinker's* holding to justify the School District's actions in this case. As the Supreme Court has admonished, an "undifferentiated fear or apprehension of disturbance is not enough to overcome the right to freedom of expression." *Tinker,* 393 U.S. at 508. If *Tinker's* black armbands—an ostentatious reminder of the highly emotional and controversial subject of the Vietnam war—could not "reasonably have led school authorities to forecast substantial disruption of or material interference with school activities," *id.* at 514, neither can J.S.'s profile, despite the unfortunate humiliation it caused for McGonigle.[7]

Courts must determine when an "undifferentiated fear or apprehension of disturbance" transforms into a reasonable forecast that a substantial disruption or material interference will occur. The School District cites several cases where courts held that a forecast of substantial and material disruption was reasonable. See, e.g., *Doninger,* 527 F.3d at 50–51 (holding that punishment was justified, under *Tinker,* where a student's derogatory blog about the school was "purposely designed by [the student] to come onto the campus," to "encourage others to contact the administration," and where the blog contained "at best misleading and at worst false information" that the school "need[ed] to correct" (quotation marks and alteration omitted)); *Lowery,* 497 F.3d at 596 (holding that punishment was justified, under *Tinker,* where students circulated a petition to fellow football players calling for the ouster of their football coach, causing the school to have to call a team meeting to ensure "team unity," and where not doing so "woul have been a grave disservice to the other players on the team"); *LaVine,* 257 F.3d at 984, 989–90 (holding that the school district did not violate a student's First Amendment rights when it expelled him on an emergency basis "to prevent [ ] potential violence on campus" after he showed a poem entitled "Last Words" to his English teacher, which was "filled with imagery of violent death and suicide" and could "be interpreted as a portent of future violence, of the shooting of [ ] fellow students").

The School District likens this case to the above cases by contending that the profile was accusatory and aroused suspicions among the school community about McGonigle's character because of the profile's references to his engaging in sexual misconduct. As explained above, however, this contention is simply not supported by the record. The profile was so outrageous that no one could have taken it seriously, and no one did. Thus, it was clearly not reasonably foreseeable that J.S.'s speech would create a substantial disruption or material interference in school, and this case is therefore distinguishable from the student speech at issue in *Doninger, Lowery,* and *LaVine.*

Moreover, unlike the students in *Doninger, Lowery,* and *LaVine,* J.S. did not even intend for the speech to reach the school—in fact, she took specific steps to make the profile "private" so that only her friends could access it. The fact that her friends happen to be Blue Mountain Middle School students is not surprising, and does not mean that J.S.'s speech targeted the school. Finally, any suggestion that, absent McGonigle's actions, a substantial disruption would have occurred, is directly undermined by the record. If anything, McGonigle's response to the profile exacerbated rather than contained the disruption in the school.[8]

The facts simply do not support the conclusion that the School District could have reasonably forecasted a substantial disruption of or material interference with the school as a result of J.S.'s profile. Under *Tinker,* therefore, the School District violated J.S.'s First Amendment free speech rights when it suspended her for creating the profile.[9]

C

Because Tinker does not justify the School District's suspension of J.S., the only way for the punishment to pass constitutional muster is if we accept the School District's argument—and the District Court's holding—that J.S.'s speech can be prohibited under the Fraser exception to Tinker.[10] The School District argues that although J.S.'s speech occurred off campus, it was justified in disciplining her because it was "lewd, vulgar, and offensive [and] had an effect on the school and the educational mission of the District." School District Br. 7. The School District's argument fails at the outset because Fraser does not apply to off-campus speech. Specifically in Morse, Chief Justice Roberts, writing for the majority, emphasized that "[h]ad Fraser delivered the same speech in a public forum outside the school context, it would have been protected." 551 U.S. at 405 (citing Cohen v. Cal., 403 U.S. 15 (1971)).[11] The Court's citation to the Cohen decision is noteworthy. The Supreme Court in Cohen held, in a non-school setting, that a state may not make a "single fourletter expletive a criminal offense." 403 U.S. at 26. Accordingly, Chief Justice Roberts's reliance on the Cohen decision reaffirms that a student's free speech rights outside the school context are coextensive with the rights of an adult.

Thus, under the Supreme Court's precedent, the Fraser exception to Tinker does not apply here. In other words, Fraser's "lewdness" standard cannot be extended to justify a school's punishment of J.S. for use of profane language outside the school, during non-school hours.[12]

The School District points out that "a hard copy or printout of the profile *actually* came into the school." School District Br. 22. However, the fact that McGonigle caused a copy of the profile to be brought to school does not transform J.S.'s off-campus speech into school speech. The flaws of a contrary rule can be illustrated by extrapolating from the facts of Fraser itself. As discussed above, the Supreme Court emphasized that Fraser's speech would have been protected had he delivered it outside the school. Presumably, this protection would not be lifted if a school official or Fraser's fellow classmate overheard the off-campus speech, recorded it, and played it to the school principal.[13] Similarly here, the fact that another student printed J.S.'s profile and brought it to school at the express request of McGonigle does not turn J.S.'s off-campus speech into on-campus speech.

Under these circumstances, to apply the Fraser standard to justify the School District's punishment of J.S.'s speech would be to adopt a rule that allows school officials to punish any speech by a student that takes place anywhere, at any time, as long as it is *about* the school or a school official, is brought to the attention of a school official, and is deemed "offensive" by the prevailing authority. Under this standard, two students can be punished for using a vulgar remark to speak about their teacher at a private party, if another student overhears the remark, reports it to the school authorities, and the school authorities find the remark "offensive." There is no principled way to distinguish this hypothetical from the facts of the instant case.

Accordingly, we conclude that the Fraser decision did not give the School District the authority to punish J.S. for her off-campus speech.

Neither the Supreme Court nor this Court has ever allowed schools to punish students for off-campus speech that is not schools ponsored or at a school-sponsored event and that caused no substantial disruption at school. We follow the logic and letter of these cases and reverse the District Court's grant of summary judgment in favor of the School District and denial of J.S.'s motion for summary judgment on her free speech claim. An opposite holding would significantly broaden school districts' authority over student speech and would vest school officials with dangerously overbroad censorship discretion. We will remand to the District Court to determine appropriate relief on this claim.

IV

We next turn to the argument of J.S.'s parents that the School District violated their Fourteenth Amendment due process right to raise their child in the manner that they saw fit. Specifically, they argue that, in disciplining J.S. for conduct that occurred in her parents' home during non-school hours, the School District interfered with their parental rights.

As the Supreme Court has noted, "it cannot now be doubted that the Due Process Clause of the Fourteenth Amendment protects the fundamental right of parents to make decisions concerning the care, custody, and control of their children." Troxel v. Granville, 530 U.S. 57, 66 (2000). This liberty interest, however, is not absolute, Anspach v. City of Phila., 503 F.3d 256, 261 (3d Cir. 2007), and "there may be circumstances in which school authorities, in order to maintain order and a proper educational atmosphere in the exercise of police power, may impose standards of conduct on students that differ from those approved by some parents," Gruenke v. Seip, 225 F.3d 290, 304 (3d Cir. 2000). Should the school policies conflict with the parents' liberty interest, the policies may only prevail if they are "tied to a compelling interest." Id. at 305.

A conflict with the parents' liberty interest will not be lightly found, and, indeed, only occurs when there is some "manipulative, coercive, or restraining conduct by the State." Anspach, 503 F.3d at 266. In other words, the parents' liberty interest will only be implicated if the state's action "deprived them of their right to make decisions concerning their child," and not when the action merely "complicated the making and implementation of those decisions." C.N. v. Ridgewood Bd. of Educ., 430 F.3d 159, 184 (3d Cir. 2005). On the other hand, however, the level of interference required to find a conflict between the school district's policy and the parents' liberty interest may vary depending on the significance of the subject at issue, and the threshold for finding a conflict will not be as high when the school district's actions "strike at the heart of parental decision making authority on matters of the greatest importance." *Id.*

In this case, J.S.'s parents allege that the School District interfered with their ability to determine what out-of-school behavior warranted discipline and what form that discipline took. This, however, is not an accurate description of the impact that the School District's actions had upon J.S.'s parents' ability to make decisions concerning their daughter's upbringing. The School District's actions in no way forced or prevented J.S.'s parents from reaching their own disciplinary decision, nor did its actions force her parents to approve or disapprove of her conduct. Further, there was no triggering of the parents' liberty interest due to the subject matter of the School District's involvement; a decision involving a child's use of social media on the internet is not a "matter[ ] of the greatest importance." Compare *C.N.*, 430 F.3d at 184-85 (determining that no due process violation occurred when a school, without first receiving permission from parents, distributed surveys to students that included questions about sexual activity and substance abuse), with *Gruenke*, 225 F.3d at 306-07 (finding a due process violation when a school coach did not inform a student's parents of their daughter's positive pregnancy test). Under these circumstances, we cannot find that J.S.'s parents' liberty interest was implicated, and will affirm the District Court's grant of summary judgment on their Fourteenth Amendment due process claim.

V

Finally, J.S. challenges the Blue Mountain Student-Parent Handbook ("Handbook") and the Acceptable Use of the Computers, Network, Internet, Electronic Communications System and Information Policy ("AUP") as unconstitutionally overbroad and vague. Relying largely on the testimony of McGonigle and Romberger, J.S. encourages this Court to strike down these School District policies.

"A regulation is unconstitutional on its face on overbreadth grounds where there is [ ]'a likelihood that the statute's very existence will inhibit free expression' by 'inhibiting the speech of third parties who are not before the Court.'" *Saxe*, 240 F.3d at 214 (quoting *Members of City Council v. Taxpayers for Vincent*, 466 U.S. 789, 799 (1984)). "[T]he overbreadth doctrine is not casually employed," *Sypniewski*, 307 F.3d at 258 (quoting *L.A. Police Dep't v. United Reporting Publ'g Corp.*, 528 U.S. 32, 39 (1999)), and before concluding that a law is unconstitutionally overbroad, the court must first determine that the regulation is not "susceptible to a reasonable limiting construction," *Saxe*, 240 F.3d at 215. Further, a law will only be struck down as overbroad if the overbreadth is "not only real but substantial in relation to the statute's plainly legitimate sweep." *Broadrick v. Oklahoma*, 413 U.S. 601, 615 (1973). In undertaking this analysis in the public school setting, however, it is important to recognize that the school district may permissibly

regulate a broader range of speech than could be regulated for the general public, giving school regulations a larger plainly legitimate sweep. *Sypniewski*, 307 F.3d at 259. Due to this consideration and concerns about the responsibilities with which public schools are tasked, we have adopted a "more hesitant application," *id.* at 259, of the overbreadth doctrine within public schools. Accordingly, "a school disciplinary policy will be struck down as overbroad only after consideration of the special needs of school discipline has been brought to bear together with the law's general hesitation to apply this 'strong medicine.'" *Id.* at 260.

J.S.'s argument that the School District's policies are overbroad in that they reach out-of-school speech fails on factual grounds, as the policies are explicitly limited to in-school speech. The Handbook states that the authority of the principals and teachers within the District is limited to "those times when students are under the direct control and supervision of school district officials." App. 58. In addition, the specific policy on computer usage in the Handbook states that "[s]tudents may not create, copy, receive, or use data, language or graphics which are obscene, threatening, abusive, or otherwise inappropriate at school or on sign out equipment at home." App. 61. The AUP is similarly limited in scope, and defines "computer" as

> any school district owned, leased or licensed or employee, student and guest owned personal hardware, software or other technology used on school district premises or at school district events, or connected to the school district network, containing school district programs or school district or student data . . . attached or connected to, installed in, or otherwise used in connection with a computer.

App. 40. We need not give these regulations a limiting construction, therefore, as the School District has already limited the reach of its policies.

What J.S. challenges here is not the policies themselves, but the interpretation of these policies that allows the School District to apply its regulations beyond the times when she was within the direct control and supervision of the School District, or beyond times when she was using a school computer. The misinterpretation of these policies by specific individuals, however, does not make the policies overbroad. Although the Handbook and AUP can be applied in a way that violates a student's constitutional rights, as happened in this case, the regulations themselves are not constitutionally infirm on the basis of being overbroad. For this reason, we will affirm the District Court's grant of summary judgment on this issue.

Our vagueness inquiry is grounded in the notice requirement of the Fourteenth Amendment's due process clause. *City of Chicago v. Morales*, 527 U.S. 41, 56 (1999). A statute will be considered void for vagueness if it does not allow a person of ordinary intelligence to determine what conduct it prohibits, or if it authorizes arbitrary enforcement. *Hill v. Colorado*, 530 U.S. 703, 732 (2000). This standard, however, is more relaxed in the school environment: "Given the school's need to be able to impose disciplinary sanctions for a wide range of unanticipated conduct disruptive of the educational process, the school disciplinary rules need not be as detailed as a criminal code which imposes criminal sanctions." *Fraser*, 478 U.S. at 686. This Court has declared that school disciplinary rules should be struck down "only when the vagueness is especially problematic," *Sypniewski*, 307 F.3d at 266, and has upheld a school disciplinary policy that required students to conform to "'an imprecise but comprehensible normative standard,'" id. (quoting *Coates v. City of Cincinnati*, 402 U.S. 61, 614 (1971)). Again, we will affirm the District Court's determination that the School District's policies were not facially unconstitutional. The policies clearly define when and where they apply. Further, the content of the regulations is not impermissibly vague. Although the AUP prohibits a broad range of uses of the School District's computers (including accessing or transmitting "material likely to be offensive or objectionable to recipients," App. 47), the addition of specific examples of impermissible usages draws this policy within the purview of Sypniewski, and articulates a comprehensible normative standard. For example, under the general prohibition against offensive material, the AUP specifically prohibits defamatory, sexually explicit, discriminatory, and violent material. App. 47–48. There can be no doubt that J.S. would have expected to have been punished under the Handbook and the AUP had she taken the same actions from a school computer or while on school grounds. In this sense, they establish a comprehensible normative standard that is appropriate for use in disciplining student misconduct. As with the discussion of over breadth above, J.S.'s argument seems to rely on specific individuals' misinterpretations of the policies, and not the invalidity of the policies themselves. It was the extension and application of these policies to speech undertaken from her personal computer at her parents' home to which she objects here. This punishment, however, was not allowed by the vagueness of the policies. Instead, it was implemented despite the fact that these policies quite clearly did not extend to the conduct at issue. As the policies are not unconstitutionally vague, much less vague in a manner that is "especially problematic," we will affirm the District Court's grant of summary judgment on this issue.

VI

For the foregoing reasons, the District Court's judgment will be affirmed in part, reversed in part and remanded.

Notes

1. In addition, Romberger testified as to her knowledge that it was actually K.L. and not J.S. who appropriated McGonigle's photograph from the School District's website. App. 305–06. Further, it was not until March 29, 2007 that the School District placed a warning on its website prohibiting the duplication of photographs or other content from the website. See App. 79, 180.

2. McGonigle testified that the other times he imposed a tenday suspension were when students brought to school a knife, razor, alcohol, and marijuana. App. 317.

3. The appellants argue that the First Amendment "limits school official['s'] ability to sanction student speech to the schoolhouse itself." Appellants' Br. 25. While this argument has some appeal, we need not address it to hold that the School District violated J.S.'s First Amendment free speech rights.

4. Indeed, although Superintendent Romberger had a duty to report allegations of inappropriate sexual contact or other misconduct by officials in the School District, she did not report McGonigle, because she believed the content of the profile was not true. App. 295–307. In fact, Romberger did not even question McGonigle as to whether any of the content was true. App. 307.

5. We agree with the appellants' argument that 24 Pa. Cons. Stat. § 5-510 also barred the School District from punishing J.S. for her off-campus speech. Section 5-510 limited the authority of the School District to:

> adopt[ing] and enforc[ing] such reasonable rules and regulations . . . regarding the conduct and deportment of all pupils attending the public schools in the district, *during such time as they are under the supervision of the board of school directors and teachers, including the time necessarily spent in coming to and returning from school.*

24 Pa. Cons. Stat. § 5-510 (emphasis added). The dissent notes that § 5-510 permits a school district to exercise "such control as is necessary to prevent infractions of discipline and interference with the educational process." *D.O.F. v. Lewisburg Area Sch. Dist. Bd. of Sch. Dirs.*, 868 A.2d 28, 36 (Pa. Commw. Ct. 2004). While that may be true, the Pennsylvania Commonwealth Court has interpreted this provision to prohibit a school district from punishing students for conduct occurring outside of school hours—even if such conduct occurs on school property. See *id.* at 35–36.

All of the integral events in this case occurred outside the school, during non-school hours. Accordingly, § 5-510 also barred the School District from punishing J.S.

6. McGonigle testified that after this lawsuit was filed, there was a general decline in student discipline and that he believed this litigation itself encouraged other students to misbehave because they thought they could simply file a lawsuit to alleviate any trouble. App. 350-51. McGonigle's testimony in this regard is irrelevant to the issues before this Court because these disruptions did

not arise out of the creation of the profile itself, but rather, were the direct result of the School District's response to the profile and the ensuing litigation. This testimony, therefore, is not relevant to determining the level of disruption that *the profile* caused in the school.

7. We recognize that vulgar and offensive speech such as that employed in this case—even made in jest—could damage the careers of teachers and administrators and we conclude only that the punitive action taken by the School District violated the First Amendment free speech rights of J.S.

   To the extent the dissent supports its arguments regarding material and substantial disruption by speculating about the possibility of discomfort by the recipients of the speech in this case, we cite then-Judge Alito's admonition in *Saxe* that "[t]he Supreme Court has held time and time again, both within and outside of the school context, that the mere fact that someone might take offense at the content of the speech is not sufficient justification for prohibiting it." 240 F.3d at 215; see also *Tinker*, 393 U.S. at 509 (holding school officials cannot prohibit student speech based upon the desire to avoid "discomfort and unpleasantness").

8. The dissent concludes that our decision creates a circuit split with the Court of Appeals for the Second Circuit, positing that that court has determined "that off-campus hostile and offensive student internet speech that is directed at school officials results in a substantial disruption of the classroom environment." Dissenting Op. 22. We disagree, largely because the dissent has overstated our sister circuit's law. Each case applying *Tinker* is decided on its own facts, see *Doninger*, 527 F.3d at 53 ("We decide only that based on the existing record, [the student's] post created a foreseeable risk of substantial disruption to the work and discipline of the school. . . ."), *Wisniewski v. Bd. of Educ. of Weedsport Cent. Sch. Dist.*, 494 F.3d 34, 40 (2d Cir. 2007) (deciding case "on this record"), so all "off-campus hostile and offensive student internet speech" will not necessarily create a material and substantial disruption at school nor will it reasonably lead school officials to forecast substantial disruption in school. Further, the facts of the cases cited by the dissent in support of its proposition that we have created a circuit split differ considerably from the facts presented in this case. See, e.g., *Doninger*, 527 F.3d at 50-51; *Wisniewski*, 494 F.3d at 35 (involving a student "sharing with friends via the Internet a small drawing crudely, but clearly, suggesting that a named teacher should be shot and killed"). Accordingly, we do not perceive any circuit split and will continue to decide each case on its individual facts.

9. The School District seizes upon language in *Tinker* that is arguably dicta, claiming that it was justified in abridging J.S.'s First Amendment rights because the profile defamed McGonigle. School District Br. 28-33. In *Tinker*, the Court discussed its concern with "the rights of other students to be let alone." 393 U.S. at 508. As a result, the Court appeared to indicate that school officials could stop conduct that would "impinge upon the rights of other students." *Id.* at 509. Later in the opinion, the Court reiterated the point, but referred simply to "invasion of the rights of others." *Id.* at 513. Although McGonigle is not a student, the School District claims J.S's speech is not immunized by the First Amendment because McGonigle's right to be free from defamation fits within this language in *Tinker*. We are not aware of any decisions analyzing whether this language applies to anyone other than "students," but we do note that our cases have employed both of these clauses. See, e.g., *Walker-Serrano*, 325 F.3d at 416-17; *Sypniewski*, 307 F.3d at 264, 265; *Saxe*, 240 F.3d at 214, 217. We further note there is a danger in accepting the School District's argument: if that portion of *Tinker* is broadly construed, an assertion of virtually any "rights" could transcend and eviscerate the protections of the First Amendment. See generally *Snyder v. Phelps*, 131 S. Ct. 1207 (2011) (noting that the First Amendment imposes limitations on the ability to recover in tort). In any event, we agree with J.S. that, as a matter of law, McGonigle could not succeed in his claim that the profile violated his right to be free from defamation. *See Hustler Magazine, Inc. v. Falwell*, 485 U.S. 46, 57 (1988) (holding that a libel claim cannot survive where no reasonable observer can understand the statements to be describing actual facts or events); *Wecht v. PG Publ'g Co.*, 510 A.2d 769, 774 (Pa. Super Ct. 1986) ("Even the most inattentive reader would not accept this article as a factual narrative. Considering the totality of the printed material . . . we find this publication incapable of defamatory meaning."); see also *Davis v. Monroe County Bd. of Educ.*, 526 U.S. 629, 652 (1999) (holding "simple acts of teasing and name-calling" are not actionable).

10. Indisputably, neither *Kuhlmeier* nor *Morse* governs this case.

11. Notably, in *Morse*, Chief Justice Roberts also cited Justice Brennan's concurrence in *Fraser*, which noted, "[i]f respondent had given the same speech outside of the school environment, he could not have been penalized simply because government officials considered his language to be inappropriate." *Fraser*, 478 U.S. at 688 (Brennan, J., concurring) (citing *Cohen*, 403 U.S. 15).

12. The School District notes that the courts in Doninger and Bethlehem Area School District suggested that Fraser applies to vulgar off-campus speech. See Doninger, 527 F.3d at 49 ("It is not clear . . . [whether] Fraser applies to off-campus speech."); Bethlehem Area Sch. Dist., 807 A.2d at 867 ("[W]e are not convinced that reliance solely on Tinker is appropriate."). Not

only are these cases not binding on this Court, but also both Doninger and Bethlehem Area School District ultimately relied on Tinker, not Fraser, in upholding school censorship. Thus, the courts' suggestion that the Fraser standard may apply to off-campus speech is dicta. Most importantly, that dicta is undermined directly by Chief Justice Roberts's statement in Morse: "Had Fraser delivered the same speech in a public forum outside the school context, it would have been protected." 551 U.S. at 405 (citing Cohen, 403 U.S. 15). The most logical reading of Chief Justice Roberts's statement prevents the application of Fraser to speech that takes place off-campus, during non-school hours, and that is in no way sponsored by the school.

13. Note that the question of whether a school has the authority to punish a student who brings vulgar speech into school is separate from whether the school can punish the source of that speech.

THE UNITED STATES COURT OF APPEALS FOR THE THIRD CIRCUIT serves the areas of Pennsylvania, New Jersey, Delaware, and the Virgin Islands.

EXPLORING THE ISSUE

Do Public Schools Have Grounds to Punish Students for Their Off-Campus Online Speech?

Critical Thinking and Reflection

1. How do the rulings in the *Layshock v. Hermitage* and *J.S. v. Blue Mountain School District court* cases apply only to the Third Circuit?
2. What types of activities should officials be focused on regarding social media issues in their schools?
3. What other U.S. Supreme Court cases impact the issues and outcomes in these two court cases?
4. Will there be more concerns in the future regarding schools and students' First Amendment rights?
5. What are the steps in a case being heard at the U.S. Supreme Court?

Is There Common Ground?

Layshock v. Hermitage School District and *J.S. v. Blue Mountain School District* have many similarities regarding student free speech. As well, there are differences. First, it is alarming to many that the language and graphics created by both students in these cases actually occur with youth attending our schools today and, second, that in some cases school officials are strapped from being able to effectively respond to inappropriateness of the behavior. It is also difficult to understand how some students in some localities are allowed First Amendment protection yet denied in others as the cases point out. The problem is magnified considering how different circuits in the country deal with social media behavior. How are these courts viewing "nexus" to the school, defining disruption to the education learning environment, and how is the Tinker v. DesMoine and Goss v. Lopez cases factored into the decisions?

For a nexus to occur, there must be a connection between the off-campus activity of students and the disruption to the learning environment in the school. Under *Tinker*, this would be termed a "disruption" to the learning environment.

The common ground for the time being is murky. One tactic is to identify all the social media cases occurring in schools in all Circuit Courts. Doing so could provide data for a very relevant study and provide a clearer picture across the nation of how our judicial system views the cases under the guise of students First Amendment Rights protection. Will the common ground be brought together in the U.S. Supreme Court to take on a case and make a ruling for the entire nation?

To conclude, student to staff or student to student inappropriate texting and imaging is a larger part of a problem with the complexities of dealing with a technological society. Teachers and other staff have been caught using district-owned digital technology for similar behaviors as students. "Sexting" among staff, to predatory behaviors directed from adults to minors have occurred. These publically owned devices can be monitored by the district information technology departments. Teachers are being fired and some criminally charged with incidents like the New York special education teacher discovered using a district-owned email account to arrange sexual encounters via the website Craigslist or the more recent incident of a Pennsylvania superintendent texting racial slurs about students and staff between exchanges with the school's athletic director (Harold, 2013). Professional development about appropriate use of public or private devises, network, and email is vitally important.

Reference

B. Harold, "PA Texting Scandal highlights Complexities for IT Leaders," *Education Week*, October 15 (2013), retrieved from: www2.edweek.org/ew/articles /2013/10/16/08whistleblower.h33.html?print=1

Create Central

www.mhhe.com/createcentral

Additional Resources

American Civil Liberties Union of Pennsylvania, *J.S. v. Blue Mountain School District* (2012), retrieved from: www.aclupa.org/our-work/legal/legaldocket/ jsvbluemountainschooldistr/

American Civil Liberties Union of Pennsylvania, *Layshock v. Hermitage School District* (2012), retrieved from: www.aclupa.org/our-work/legal/ legaldocket/layshock-v-hermitage-school-district/

N. Lind and E. Rankin, *First Amendment Rights: An Encyclopedia* (ABC-CLIO, LLC, 2013)

D. Shilling, *Lawyers Desk Book* (p. 28) (Wolters Kluwer Law and Business, 2013)

K. Williams, Public Schools vs. Myspace & (and) Facebook: The Newest Challenge to Student Speech Rights (2012), retrieved from: http://heinon-line.org/HOL/LandingPage?handle=hein.journals/ucinlr76&div=33&id=&page=

Internet References. . .

Layshock v. Hermitage School District Overview

Legal Clips: Federal court issues en banc decision in *Layshock v. Hermitage School district* violated First Amendment by disciplining student for off-campus online speech. The Source for Recent Developments in School Law.

http://legalclips.nsba.org/2011/06/15/federal-appellate
-court-issues-en-banc-decision-holding-pennsylvania-
school-districts-discipline-of-student-for-off-campus-
online-speech-violated-the-first-amendment/

J.S. v. Blue Mountain School District Overview

Legal Clips: Federal court issues en bancdecision in J.S. v. Blue Mountain Sch. Dist..: school district violated First Amendment by disciplining student for off-campus online speech. The Source for Recent Developments in School Law.

http://legalclips.nsba.org/2011/06/15/federal-appellate
-court-issued-en-banc-decision-that-students-off-
campus-online-speech-is-not-properly-subject-to-
regulation-by-pennsylvania-school-district/:

Third Circuit Sides with Students in Online Speech Fight Landmark Rulings Leave Some Questions Unanswered

www.splc.org/news/newsflash.asp?id=2238

Facts and Case Summary: Morse v. Frederick

www.uscourts.gov/educational-resources/get-
involved/constitution-activities/first-amendment/free-
speech-school-conduct/facts-case-summary.aspx

Supreme Court Will Not Hear Off-Campus Speech Cases

www.splc.org/news/newsflash.asp?id=2315

Selected, Edited, and with Issue Framing Material by:
Glenn L. Koonce, *Regent University*

ISSUE

Do American Schools Need a Common Curriculum?

YES: The Albert Shanker Institute, from "A Call for Common Content," *American Educator* (Spring 2011)

NO: Jay P. Greene, Sandra Stotsky, Bill Evers, Greg Forster, and Ze'ev Wurman, from "Closing the Door on Innovation," *Education Next* (May 9, 2011)

Learning Outcomes
After reading this issue, you will be able to:
• Give examples of how a common core curriculum guide will benefit all students regardless of their socioeconomic standing.
• Critique why a uniform core curriculum is key to systemic reform.
• Summarize the recommendations that will be necessary to raise achievement nationally and narrow the achievement gaps.
• List the reasons why the current proposed nationalized curriculum does not meet the criteria for a sound public policy.
• Evaluate the justification for a common core curriculum.

ISSUE SUMMARY

YES: The Albert Shanker Institute, an affiliate of the American Federation of Teachers, promotes a common curriculum to build a bridge from standards to achievement across the nation.

NO: A coalition of opponents, led by Jay P. Greene, Sandra Stotsky, Bill Evers, Greg Forster, and Ze'ev Wurman, offers a critical response to what they see as an effort to nationalize public education.

The motives for a national curriculum and a national examination system emanate from low-level confidence in our schools. "The proposal to develop a national curriculum is a 'natural' outgrowth of the public's feeling of desperation that our educational ship is sinking and that a national examination system is necessary to provide data that make it possible to interpret student performance." Such a statement could easily be made today, but, in fact, this appeared in a 1991 *Educational Leadership* article by curriculum expert Elliot W. Eisner. The controversy about a common curriculum in American schools has been brewing for a long time. In contrast with most European and Asian educational systems, the United States has historically resisted centralization, allowing states and localities to fashion the content of their programs. Since the 1950s the federal government, however, has played an increasingly significant role in specific areas of concern (inner-city schools, handicapped students, equal opportunity, etc.), and since the 1980s political leaders, backed by public opinion, have moved in the direction of further centralization.

The movement toward a common national curriculum gained momentum in 2011 because a diverse group of leaders in the field of education released clear delineations of their opposing views on the matter in the two documents presented in this issue, "A Call for Common Content" and "Closing the Door on Innovation." Mike Klonsky, in a *The Huffington Post* blog on April 8, 2011 titled "Common Core Curriculum—Who's on Board? Who's Not?" exclaims, "I haven't seen anything like this since the bipartisan coalition behind No Child Left Behind during the early days of the Bush era." He observes that the supporters of common content include liberal policy wonks and teacher union leaders together with corporate reformers and right-wing think tanks. Members of the opposing group, also diverse, share a fear that the core curriculum, a voluntary program originally initiated by governors and scheduled to be implemented in 2014, will lead to centralized control of education, creating a greater opportunity for special interests to distort policy. Education Secretary Arne Duncan has dismissed such concerns as "a conspiracy theory in search of a conspiracy" and AFT President Randi Weingarten has called such fears "ridiculous," according to *USA Today*'s Greg Toppo in "Common Core Standards Drive Wedge in Education Circles."

In a May 10, 2011 posting for Education Next titled "Common Core: Now It Gets Interesting," Frederick Hess, in a balanced analysis, states that if done right the Common Core effort could be "a terrific boon to assessment, accountability, research, tool-building, and instruction," but if it is done wrong "it may unravel what leading states have accomplished on standards, undercut charter schooling and autonomous district schools, stifle online learning, compromise school accountability, and fuel a more destructive replay of the '90s national standards fight." Standards developed by individual states prior to the Common Core effort often lacked necessary rigor and consistency. According to Robert Rothman in "A Common Core of Readiness," *Educational Leadership* (April 2012), the current unified approach more clearly reflects research on college and career readiness, with readiness being defined as the ability to succeed in entry-level, credit-bearing academic college courses and in workforce training programs that prepare students for careers that offer competitive, livable salaries and opportunities for advancement in a growing or sustainable industry.

An interesting point was made by educator Deborah Meier, in "Are National Standards the Right Move?" *Reimagining School* (April 2010), that "setting fixed standards for what students should learn means aiming either too low or too high—never on target for each individual learner. . . . Every time we try to fix goals for public schooling we end up in the same fix as the Constitutional originalists (who assume the U.S. Constitution has one immutable meaning); we sacrifice flexibility for immutability." Another important concern is expressed by Stephanie Hirsh, in "The Common Core Contradiction," *Education Week* (February 1, 2012), who states that "while we are promoting radical change in creating a coherent national framework for what students should know and the way they learn, we have not yet committed to offering teachers the deep learning they will need to transform the way they work." This concern is addressed in detail by Vicki Phillips and Carina Wong in "Teaching to the Common Core by Design, Not Accident," *Phi Delta Kappan* (April 2012).

The following selections present the so-called manifesto of the Albert Shanker Institute and the opposition's "counter-manifesto."

YES ↵

The Albert Shanker Institute

A Call for Common Content

We, the undersigned, representing viewpoints from across the political and educational spectrum, believe that whether children live in Mississippi or Minnesota, Berkeley or the Bronx, our expectations for their achievement should be equally high.

We therefore applaud the goals of the recently released Common Core State Standards, already adopted in most states, which articulate a much clearer vision of what students should learn and be able to do as they progress through school. For our nation, this represents a major advance toward declaring that "equal educational opportunity" is a top priority—not empty rhetoric.

We also caution that attaining the goals provided by these standards requires a clear road map in the form of rich, common curriculum content, along with resources to support successfully teaching all students to mastery. Shared curriculum in the core academic subjects would give shape and substance to the standards, and provide common ground for the creation of coherent, high-quality instructional supports—especially texts and other materials, assessments, and teacher training.

To accomplish this, our nation must finally answer questions it has avoided for generations: What is it, precisely, that we expect all educated citizens to have learned? What explicit knowledge, skills, and understanding of content will help define the day-to-day work of teaching and learning?

With U.S. education's long history of state administration and local control, the very idea of common curriculum guidance will strike many as overly controversial. The fear of centralization, institutional rigidity, and narrow-minded political orthodoxy is deeply ingrained in our political sensibility—beginning with our Constitution's implicit delegation of education's governance to the states.

But now, in an era when states are coming to recognize the national importance of a coherent education system, they are working together to find ways to raise expectations for all. They are showing a willingness to trade state-by-state invention and reinvention for a more shared implementation of successful practices together with the possibility of greater economies of scale—in effect, to create a new and more consistent system.

Common curriculum guidance does not represent a straitjacket or a narrowing of learning possibilities. States' use of the kinds of curriculum guidelines that we advocate in the core academic subjects would be purely voluntary, comprising only about 50 to 60 percent of what is to be taught—leaving room for state, regional, and local variations to reflect student contexts and state and local prerogatives.

The curriculum guides we seek would offer a practical road map for achieving the goals set by standards in the limited instructional time available to teachers. They would illuminate grade-level expectations for teaching and learning progressions for students. They would provide a coherent, substantive, sequential plan that clarifies the knowledge and skills that students are expected to learn in the core academic subjects. They would enable the creation of all kinds of matching resources—technology offerings, texts, and teacher-made materials, as well as field trips and other outside-of-school resources—which teachers could use, share, and adapt across state and district lines, confident that their students were being adequately prepared for each succeeding grade and for the academic demands of college and career.

While the work before us begins with the Common Core State Standards in English language arts and mathematics, we want to stress that a quality education should also include history, geography, the sciences, civics, the arts, foreign languages, technology, health, and physical education. Standards-setting and curriculum development must be done for these as well.

All teachers and students will ultimately profit from thoughtful curriculum guidance—based on the demands of the disciplines and an understanding of how children learn at various stages of their development. In a society much more diverse than that of our forebears, we expect that this work—deciding what knowledge and skills are most essential for our children to have, and how they can best be acquired—will be challenging. Yet educational quality and equity demand that our schools take on this important task.

Why Common, Rich Curriculum Content Is Key to Systemic Reform

At any age and in any field, what we already know enables us to understand, retain, and employ new knowledge. Knowledge accumulation begins from the earliest days of life. It builds through years of verbal and nonverbal interactions with parents, caregivers, and teachers, who model spoken language and help young children develop vocabulary, concepts, and theories about the world. As might be expected, children from more economically advantaged backgrounds typically have an early start in this process of knowledge acquisition—with a significant advantage in oral language skill and information mastery by the time they enter preschool.

These differences turn out to be crucial: high-quality research demonstrates that disparities in oral language and general knowledge at school entry explain most of the effect of socioeconomic status on elementary school performance.[1] It is not poverty in itself, but poverty's accompanying life conditions that help to explain performance gaps that begin at home and extend into secondary school and beyond.

Today, the information we need to minimize these performance gaps is in our hands, waiting to be used. Thanks to advances in cognitive science, we now understand that reading comprehension—so essential to almost all academic learning—depends in large part on knowledge.[2] In experiments, when students who are "poor" readers are asked to read about a topic they know well (such as baseball), they do much better on comprehension measures than "good" readers who know less about the subject.[3]

The systematic effort to establish common, knowledge-building content must therefore begin as early as possible. The younger we start, the greater the hope that we can boost achievement across all schools and classrooms, but especially among our most disadvantaged students.

Further, by articulating learning progressions linked to a grade-by-grade sequence for how learning should build over time, a defined curriculum will better enable each teacher to build on what students have already been taught. Students will also benefit, as they will be much less likely to find themselves either struggling to overcome gaps in their knowledge or bored by the repetition of what they have already learned.

Some will fear that this is a call for an antiquated vision of schooling, centered on the rote memorization of dry facts or the superficial coverage of hundreds of pieces of inert information. It is not. A crucial feature of the common core standards is that they seek to identify a lean set of concepts and ideas that are central to applying knowledge in each discipline. Dozens of studies have found that greater content knowledge enables better critical thinking, problem solving, reasoning, and analysis.[4] Thus, the goal of teaching students to "think critically" about any particular subject requires a curriculum that builds knowledge upon knowledge.

Others may fear that grade-level curriculum expectations will discourage teachers from attending to the needs of students who are achieving above or below grade level. Yet, when used by well-prepared teachers as a guide to the learning process, a curriculum sequence will allow teachers to see where each student is along a learning trajectory for the discipline, as well as where students are expected to go and how to help them get there.

Finally, some may fear that common curriculum guidance will neglect important cultural referents or ignore the diversity of student experiences. However, as national curriculum standards in several high-performing nations illustrate, a modern conception of curriculum in a diverse nation is explicitly mindful of how to attend to cultural connections, and how to leave room for local adaptations and resources that enable students to connect to the curriculum from their different vantage points.

In nations with core curriculum standards, such as Finland, Singapore, and South Korea, this systemic approach—coupled with equitable resources and strong teacher training—has resulted in both very high average achievement and a diminishing gap between high- and low-achieving students. These countries have demonstrated that a sequential curriculum in the core subjects from school entry through eighth or ninth grade prepares virtually all students for college or careers—whether in a set of required courses or in electives tailored to students' various interests and postsecondary goals. This kind of support is at least as necessary in the United States, where children tend to change homes and schools more frequently than in other industrialized nations[5]—and disadvantaged children, in particular, may change classrooms, schools, districts, and even states at alarmingly high rates.

Student Curriculum to Guide Staff Preparation, Development, and Evaluation

Currently, there are efforts under way to develop assessments aligned to the Common Core State Standards. But, as the past 30 years of the standards movement has shown, without attention to curriculum, standards are not specific enough to guide the development of valid measures of student progress. Simple logic suggests that it is impossible to assess student learning accurately when there has been no decision about what it is students are expected to learn. In order to create a rational system, we must begin with standards, then adopt curriculum and curriculum materials, and then develop assessments—*in that order.*

Countries that already enjoy the benefits of a knowledge-rich curriculum are able to design course-related assessments—tying classroom and system-wide evaluations to what students are actually being taught. Rather than waste time prepping for what might be on the test, students and teachers can be confident that mastering the course content will prepare them for what they will be asked to demonstrate and do.

With rich curriculum content, meaningful assessments, and quality teaching resources in place, we would finally be ready to dramatically improve teacher preparation, development, and evaluation. New teachers would enter classrooms having already studied and practiced teaching the curriculum they are to use. Their on-the-job professional development would be based on the curriculum, giving them common ground to work together, observe each other, and share and refine lessons. And, how much more meaningful and fair could teacher evaluation become once teaching is based on common learning expectations and a common professional understanding of what constitutes excellent instruction?[6]

If teacher preparation, on-the-job professional development, texts and other instructional materials, and assessments could all be tied to the curriculum, we would have a better foundation for identifying teachers' strengths and weaknesses, for helping them do better, and for telling those who can't improve to find new jobs.

Recommendations

In calling for the development of common curriculum content, we are well aware that this will require a sea change in the way that education in America is structured. We do not believe that it will be easy, but are convinced it is necessary to raise achievement nationally and narrow our disgraceful achievement gaps. Specifically, we call for the following:

1. *Developing one or more sets of curriculum guides that map out the core content students need to master the new Common Core State Standards.* States could collaborate with each other in the development of their curricula, each could develop its own, or each could adopt an exemplary curriculum developed by an independent organization. Regardless of its origins, each curriculum guide should be coherent and sequenced, and lead to roughly the same store of student knowledge and capabilities by grade 12. Each should approximate what students in other high-performing countries study at comparable ages. And, each should establish a content sequence for teaching that reflects the best of what is known about how students build knowledge upon knowledge, concept upon concept.
2. *Involving teachers, content experts, and cognitive scientists—not just curriculum designers by trade—in the development of such curriculum guides.* Of these, expert teachers tend to be the most overlooked. But they have special insights into the interaction between content knowledge and the ways students acquire it—including students' most common mistakes and misunderstandings, and the most effective methods to help overcome them.
3. *Writing the common core curriculum guides with care and restraint, such that—when taught at a reasonable pace, with reasonable depth—they would account for about 50 to 60 percent of a school's available academic time.* Such curricula should allow sufficient time to add important content desired by teachers, the local community, district, or state. For example, some states may want to add state

history; individual districts may want to use local resources to expand upon particular art or science topics; a particular teacher may want to incorporate his love of art into English classes; and a particular class of students may want to extend the planned unit on thermodynamics. Teachers will want to tailor instruction to the academic needs, interests, and experiences of students in their classrooms, and will need the curricular space to do so.

4. *Including sample lessons, examples of acceptable levels of student work, and assessments that help teachers focus instruction as well as measure student outcomes.* We do not, however, recommend that any specific pedagogical approach be adopted for broad-scale use. If the curriculum guide calls for the structure and movement of the solar system to be learned in the fourth grade, then supporting materials may offer ideas for how to teach it. But some teachers may choose to have students spend a week building scale models of the solar system; others may give an engaging lecture followed by a NOVA video; others may integrate the lessons with other concepts (such as the chemical properties of gasses and solids) or disciplines (such as drawing and writing about planetary characteristics).
5. *Establishing a nongovernmental quality control body, with a governance structure composed of professionals: teachers, content experts, cognitive scientists, curriculum designers, and assessment authorities.* This body could help judge the strengths and weaknesses of particular curricula, as well as the quality and relevance of the textbooks, trade books, software, classroom materials, and assessments developed to support their implementation. Such a body might also sponsor research on the effectiveness of various curricula and approaches in reaching the Common Core State Standards, and oversee periodic revisions (possibly every five years).
6. *Creating state teaching quality oversight bodies to work on linking student standards and curriculum guidance to teacher preparation and development, and to ensure that sufficient resources are allotted to these efforts.*
7. *Increasing federal investments in implementation support, in comparative international studies related to curriculum and instruction, and in evaluations aimed at finding the most effective curriculum sequences, curriculum materials, curricular designs, and instructional strategies.*

Endnotes

1. Rachel E. Durham, George Farkas, Carol Scheffner Hammer, J. Bruce Tomblin, and Hugh W. Catts, "Kindergarten Oral Language Skill: A Key Variable in the Intergenerational Transmission of Socioeconomic Status," *Research in Social Stratification and Mobility* 25, no. 4 (2007): 294–305;

David Grissmer, Kevin J. Grimm, Sophie M. Aiyer, William M. Murrah, and Joel S. Steele, "Fine Motor Skills and Early Comprehension of the World: Two New School Readiness Indicators," *Developmental Psychology* 46, no. 5 (2010): 1008–1017, http://128.143.21.143/temp/grissmer_motorskills.doc; and Betty Hart and Todd R. Risley, *Meaningful Differences in the Everyday Experience of Young American Children* (Baltimore: Brookes Publishing, 1995).

2. For a fuller explanation of why this is so, see E. D. Hirsch, Jr., *The Knowledge Deficit: Closing the Shocking Education Gap for American Children* (Boston: Houghton Mifflin, 2006).

3. Donna R. Recht and Lauren Leslie, "Effect of Prior Knowledge on Good and Poor Readers' Memory of Text," *Journal of Educational Psychology* 80, no. 1 (1988): 16–20.

4. Marilyn Jager Adams, "The Challenge of Advanced Texts: The Interdependence of Reading and Learning," in *Reading More, Reading Better: Are American Students Reading Enough of the Right Stuff?*, ed. Elfrieda H. Hiebert (New York: Guilford, 2009), www.childrenofthecode.org/library/MJA-ChallengeofAdvancedTexts.pdf.

5. General Accounting Office, *Elementary School Children: Many Change Schools Frequently, Harming Their Education* (Washington, DC: GAO, 1994); and Larry Long, "International Perspectives on the Residential Mobility of America's Children," *Journal of Marriage and the Family* 54, no. 4 (1992): 861–869.

6. For more on this, see David K. Cohen, "Teacher Quality: An American Educational Dilemma," in *Teacher Assessment and the Quest for Teacher Quality: A Handbook,* ed. Mary Kennedy (San Francisco: Jossey-Bass, 2010).

Signatories

A complete list of signatories is available online at www.aft.org/pdfs/americaneducator/spring2011/ASI.pdf. Titles and organizations appear for identification purposes only.

THE ALBERT SHANKER INSTITUTE is a nonprofit institute established in 1998. Its focus is to bring together influential leaders and thinkers from business, labor, government, and education from across the political spectrum. It sponsors research, promotes discussions, and seeks new and workable approaches to the issues that will shape the future of democracy, education, and unionism.

Jay P. Greene et al.

➔ **NO**

Closing the Door on Innovation

We, the undersigned, representing viewpoints from across the political and educational spectrum, oppose the call for a nationalized curriculum in the Albert Shanker Institute Manifesto "A Call for Common Content."[1] We also oppose the ongoing effort by the U.S. Department of Education to have two federally funded testing consortia develop national curriculum guidelines, national curriculum models, national instructional materials, and national assessments using Common Core's national standards as a basis for these efforts.[2]

We agree that our expectations should be high and similar for all children whether they live in Mississippi or Massachusetts, Tennessee or Texas. We also think that curricula should be designed before assessments are developed, not the other way around.

But we do not agree that a one-size-fits-all, centrally controlled curriculum for every K-12 subject makes sense for this country or for any other sizable country. Such an approach threatens to close the door on educational innovation, freezing in place an unacceptable status quo and hindering efforts to develop academically rigorous curricula, assessments, and standards that meet the challenges that lie ahead. Because we are deeply committed to improving this country's schools and increasing all students' academic achievement, we cannot support this effort to undermine control of public school curriculum and instruction at the local and state level—the historic locus for effective innovation and reform in education—and transfer control to an elephantine, inside-the-Beltway bureaucracy.

Moreover, transferring power to Washington, D.C., will only further subordinate educational decisions to political imperatives. All presidential administrations—present and future, Democratic and Republican—are subject to political pressure. Centralized control in the U.S. Department of Education would upset the system of checks and balances between different levels of government, creating greater opportunities for special interests to use their national political leverage to distort policy. Our decentralized fifty-state system provides some limitations on special-interest power, ensuring that other voices can be heard, that wrongheaded reforms don't harm children in every state, and that reforms that effectively serve children's needs can find space to grow and succeed.

The nationalized curriculum the Shanker Manifesto calls for, and whose development the U.S. Department of Education is already supporting, does not meet the criteria for sound public policy for the following reasons.

First, there is no constitutional or statutory basis for national standards, national assessments, or national curricula. The two testing consortia funded by the U.S. Department of Education have already expanded their activities beyond assessment, and are currently developing national curriculum guidelines, models, and frameworks in accordance with their proposals to the Department of Education (see the Appendix). Department of Education officials have so far not explained the constitutional basis for their procedures or forthcoming products. The U.S. Constitution seeks a healthy balance of power between states and the federal government, and wisely leaves the question of academic standards, curriculum, and instruction up to the states.[3] In fact, action by the U.S. Department of Education to create national standards and curricula is explicitly proscribed by federal law, reflecting the judgment of Congress and the public on this issue.[4]

Even if the development of national curriculum models, frameworks or guidelines were judged lawful, we do not believe Congress or the public supports having them developed by a self-selected group behind closed doors and with no public accountability. Whether curriculum developers are selected by the Shanker Institute or the U.S. Department of Education's testing consortia, they are working on a federally funded project to dramatically transform schools nationwide. They therefore ought to be transparent and accountable to Congress and the public.

Second, there is no consistent evidence that a national curriculum leads to high academic achievement. The Shanker Manifesto suggests that the only possible way to achieve high academic achievement is through a single national curriculum. Yet France and Denmark have centralized national curricula and do not show high average achievement on international tests or a diminishing gap between high- and low-achieving students. Meanwhile, Canada and Australia, both of which have many regional curricula, achieve better results than many affluent single-curriculum nations. The evidence on this question has been exhaustively addressed elsewhere.[5] It does not support the conclusion that national standards are necessary either for high achievement or for narrowing the achievement gap.

Greene, Jay P. et al. From *Education Next*, May 9, 2011. Copyright © 2011 by Education Next. Reprinted by permission of Hoover Institution, Stanford University.

Moreover, population mobility does not justify a national curriculum. Only inter-state mobility is relevant to the value of a national curriculum, and inter-state mobility in this country is low. The Census Bureau reports a total annual mobility rate of 12.5% in 2008–9,[6] but only 1.6% of the total rate consists of inter-state moves that a national curriculum may influence. Other data indicate that inter-state mobility among school-age children is even lower, at 0.3%.[7]

Third, the national standards on which the administration is planning to base a national curriculum are inadequate. If there are to be national academic-content standards, we do not agree that Common Core's standards are clear, adequate, or of sufficient quality to warrant being this country's national standards. Its definition of "college readiness" is below what is currently required to enter most four-year state colleges. Independent reviews have found its standards to be below those in the highest-performing countries and below those in states rated as having the best academic standards.[8]

Fourth, there is no body of evidence for a "best" design for curriculum sequences in any subject. The Shanker Manifesto assumes we can use "the best of what is known" about how to structure curriculum. Yet which curriculum would be best is exactly what we do not know, if in fact all high school students should follow one curriculum. Much more innovation and development, and research evaluating it, is needed to address this knowledge gap. This means we should be encouraging—not discouraging—multiple models. Furthermore, the Shanker Manifesto calls for national curricula to encompass English, mathematics, history, geography, the sciences, civics, the arts, foreign languages, technology, health, and physical education. We wonder what is not included in its sweeping concept of a national curriculum.

Fifth, there is no evidence to justify a single high school curriculum for all students. A single set of curriculum guidelines, models, or frameworks cannot be justified at the high school level, given the diversity of interests, talents and pedagogical needs among adolescents. American schools should not be constrained in the diversity of the curricula they offer to students. Other countries offer adolescents a choice of curricula; Finland, for example, offers all students leaving grade 9 the option of attending a three-year general studies high school or a three-year vocational high school, with about 50% of each age cohort enrolling in each type of high school. We worry that the "comprehensive" American high school may have outlived its usefulness, as a recent Harvard report implies.[9] A one-size-fits-all model not only assumes that we already know the one best curriculum for all students; it assumes that one best way for all students exists. We see no grounds for carving that assumption in stone.

Conclusion

The Shanker Manifesto does not make a convincing case for a national curriculum. It manifests serious shortcomings in its discussion of curricular alignment and coherence, the quality of Common Core's national standards, course sequence and design, academic content, student mobility, sensitivity to pluralism, constitutionality and legality, transparency and accountability, diverse pedagogical needs, and the absence of consensus on all these questions. For these reasons, we the undersigned oppose the Shanker Manifesto's call for a nationalized curriculum and the U.S. Department of Education's initiative to develop a national curriculum and national tests based on Common Core's standards.

Signatories

Initial signatories before May 6, 2011

John Agresto President, St. John's College, Santa Fe, 1989–2000, Member Board of Trustees & Past Provost, American University of Iraq, Author, *The Supreme Court & Constitutional Democracy.*

John E. Chubb Distinguished Visiting Fellow & Koret K-12 Education Task Force Member, Hoover Institution, Stanford University, Former Chief Academic Officer & Co-Founder, Edison Learning, Co-Author, *Politics, Markets, and America's Schools.*

Bill Evers Research Fellow & Koret K-12 Education Task Force Member, Hoover Institution, Stanford University, U.S. Assistant Secretary of Education for Policy, 2007–2009, Commissioner, California State Academic Standards Commission, 1996–98, 2010.

Greg Forster Senior Fellow, Foundation for Educational Choice.

Jay P. Greene 21st Century Chair & Head of the Department of Education Reform, University of Arkansas, Fellow in Education Policy, George W. Bush Institute.

Edwin Meese III Former Attorney General of the United States, Former Rector (chairman of governing board), George Mason University, Former Professor of Law, University of San Diego.

Grover Norquist President, Americans for Tax Reform, Member, Board of Directors, ParentalRights.org, Former Economist & Chief Speechwriter, U.S. Chamber of Commerce.

John Silber Dean, College of Arts & Sciences, University of Texas, 1967–70, President, Boston University, 1971–96, Chairman, Massachusetts State Board of Education, 1996–99.

Lisa Snell Director of Education & Child Welfare, Reason Foundation.

Joel Spring Professor, Department of Elementary & Early Childhood Education, Queens College & Graduate Center, City University of New York.

Sandra Stotsky 21st Century Chair in Teacher Quality, Department of Education Reform, University of Arkansas, Senior Associate Commissioner of Education, Commonwealth of Massachusetts, 1999–2003, Member, Validation Committee, Common Core Standards, 2009–10.

Ze'ev Wurman Senior Policy Adviser, U.S. Department of Education, 2007–2009, Commissioner, California State Academic Commission, 2010, Past Member, California State Mathematics Curriculum Framework and Criteria Committee.

A complete list of signatories is available online at www .k12innovation.com/Manifesto/_V2_Home.html

Appendix: Excerpts from the Assessment Consortia's Plans to Develop a National Curriculum

According to the proposal by the SMARTER Balanced Assessment Consortium in its application for a U.S. Department of Education grant in June 2010, it intends to:

- "interpret or translate [Common Core's] standards before they can be used effectively for assessment or instruction" [SMARTER Balanced Proposal page 34]
- "translate the standards into content/curricular frameworks, test maps, and item/performance event specifications to provide assessment specificity and to clarify the connections between instructional processes and assessment outcomes." [SMARTER Proposal, page 35]
- provide "a clear definition of the specific grade-level content skills and knowledge that the assessment is intended to measure." [SMARTER Balanced Proposal, page 48]
- "convene key stakeholders and content specialists to develop assessment frameworks that precisely lay out the content and cognitive demands that define college- and career-readiness for each grade level." [SMARTER Balanced Proposal, page 74]
- "develop cognitive models for the domains of ELA and mathematics that specify the content elements and relationships reflecting the sequence of learning that students would need to achieve college and career-readiness." [SMARTER Balanced Proposal, page 76]

Similarly, the Partnership for the Assessment of Readiness for College and Careers (PARCC) consortium proposed in its application to the U.S. Department of Education in June 2010 to:

- "unpack the standards to a finer grain size as necessary to determine which standards are best measured through the various components. . . . To do this, the Partnership will engage lead members of the CCSS writing teams . . . and the content teams from each state, assessment experts and teachers from Partnership states." [PARCC Proposal, page 174]
- "develop challenging performance tasks and innovative, computer-enhanced items . . . [that] will send a strong, clear signal to educators about the kinds of instruction and types of performances needed for students to demonstrate college and career readiness." [PARCC Proposal, page 7]
- "develop model curriculum frameworks that teachers can use to plan instruction and gain a deep understanding of the CCSS, and released items and tasks that teachers can use for ongoing formative assessment." [PARCC Proposal, page 57]

Endnotes

1. "A Call for Common Content," *American Educator* (published by American Federation of Teachers), vol. 35, no. 1 (Spring 2011), pp. 41–45.
2. For a description of the curriculum and instructional guidance to teachers the consortia are developing, which go beyond even what their application language indicated, see Catherine Gewertz, "Common-Assessment Consortia Add Resources to Plans: Extra Federal Funds Will Go Toward Curricula, Teacher Training," *Education Week*, Feb. 23, 2011.
3. U.S. Constitution, Art. I, sec. 8; Amendment X.
4. See section 438 of the General Education Provisions Act (20 U.S.C. § 1232a) (rule of construction that no education programs of the Department of Education be construed to authorize any federal department, agency, officer or employee to direct, supervise, or control curriculum or any program of instruction); section 103 of the Department of Education Organization Act (20 U.S.C. § 3403) (establishes relationship between federal, state, and local governments as well as public and private institutions, and provides a rule of construction prohibiting the Secretary of Education or any officer from exercising direction, supervision, or control over curriculum or programs of instruction as well as proscribes the direction, supervision, or control over the selection of textbooks and instructional materials); section 9527(a) of the Elementary and Secondary Education Act (ESEA) (20 U.S.C. § 7907(a)) (rule of construction prohibiting the federal government from mandating, directing, or controlling curriculum or programs of instruction); section 9527(b) of the ESEA (20 U.S.C. § 7907(b)) (prohibits funds under the ESEA from being used to endorse, approve, or sanction curriculum); *see also* S. Rep. No. 91-634 (1970) *reprinted in* 1970 U.S.C.C.A.N. 2768, 2826 and 2901 (discussion of prohibition against federal control of education); H.R. Rep. No. 91-937 (1970) (Conf. Rep.) *reprinted in* 1970 U.S.C.C.A.N. 2939, 2954 (statement of

the managers on prohibiting federal control of education); S. Rep. No 94-882, at 109 (1976) *reprinted in* 1976 U.S.C.C.A.N. 4713, 4821 (discussion of all programs remaining free of federal control in lieu of specific list); S. Rep. No. 96-49, at 6, 31-33 (1979) *reprinted in* 1979 U.S.C.C.A.N. 1514, 1545-1547 (discussion of state and local responsibilities for education); S. Rep. No. 96-49 at 65, U.S.C.C.A.N. at 1579 (discussion of limitation upon authority of federal government over education); S. Rep. No. 96-49 at 95–97, U.S.C.C.A.N. at 1607–1609 (Additional Views of Mr. Durenberger); S. Rep. No. 96-49 at 97–99, U.S.C.C.A.N. at 1609-1612 (Minority Views of Mr. Cohen); H.R. Rep. No. 95-1531, at 13 (1978) (discussion of prohibition of federal interference with curriculum, programs of instruction, textbooks, and other educational materials); *id.* at 41–42 (Dissenting Views of Hon. Leo J. Ryan); *id.* at 43–44 (Dissenting Views of Hon. Peter H. Kostmayer); *id.* at 45–47 (Dissenting Views of Hon. John N. Erlenborn, Hon. John. W. Wydler, Hon. Clarence J. Brown, Hon. Paul N. McCloskey, Jr., Hon. Dan Quayle, Hon. Robert S. Walker, Hon Arlan Stangeland, Hon. Jack Cunningham); *id.* at 48–49 (Dissenting Views of Hon. Paul N. McCloskey, Jr.); H.R. Rep. No. 96-459, at 36 (1979) (Conf. Rep.), reprinted in 1979 U.S.C.C.A.N. 1612, 1615–1616 (discussion of limitations upon federal authority over education).

5. Grover Whitehurst, *Don't Forget Curriculum,* Brookings Institution, 2009; Neal McCluskey, *Behind the Curtain: Assessing the Case for National Curriculum Standards,* Cato Institute, 2010.
6. U.S. Census Bureau, table A-1.
7. U.S. Census Bureau, table C07001. Geographical Mobility in the Past Year by Age for Current Residence in the United States, 2007–2009 American Community Survey 3-Year Estimates.
8. Jonathan Goodman, *A comparison of proposed US Common Core math standard to standards of selected Asian countries.* July 2010; S. Stotsky & Z. Wurman, *Common Core's Standards Still Don't Make the Grade,* Pioneer Institute, 2010; see the following links also for a critical review of the research base for Common Core's standards, by Diane Ravitch and William Mathis; see also Appendix B, an analysis by R. James Milgram of the problems in the Common Core's mathematics standards.
9. William C. Symonds, Robert B. Schwartz and Ronald Ferguson, *Pathways to Prosperity: Meeting the Challenge of Preparing Young Americans for the 21st Century,* Harvard Graduate School of Education, 2011.

JAY P. GREENE is the twenty-first Century Chair and head of the department, Department of Education Reform, University of Arkansas, and fellow in education policy, George W. Bush Institute.

SANDRA STOTSKY is the twenty-first Century Chair in teacher quality, Department of Education Reform, University of Arkansas, and senior associate commissioner of education, Commonwealth of Massachusetts, 1999–2003. She was also a member of the Validation Committee, Common Core Standards from 2009 to 2010.

BILL EVERS is a research fellow at the Hoover Institution and a member of the Institution's Koret Task Force on K-12 Education, specializes in research on education policy especially as it pertains to curriculum, teaching, testing, accountability, and school finance from kindergarten through high school.

GREG FORSTER is a senior fellow with the Foundation for Educational Choice. He conducts research and writes on school choice policy.

ZE'EV WURMAN was a U.S. Department of Education official under George W. Bush, and is currently an executive with MonolithIC 3D Inc.

EXPLORING THE ISSUE

Do American Schools Need a Common Curriculum?

Critical Thinking and Reflection

1. Is a common core curriculum taking away the individual rights and decisions at the state and local areas?
2. Why is it crucial to establish common, knowledge building content as early as possible in a child's education?
3. Why is it important to develop and design a curriculum prior to developing the assessment tools to be used?
4. Should political pressures be reason to move forward with the need for a common curriculum?
5. Will the proposed single national common curriculum really lead to high academic achievement?

Is There Common Ground?

The "wreckage" brought about by the accelerating standards movement in the last two decades is detailed by Alfie Kohn, in "Debunking the Case for National Standards," *Education Week* (January 14, 2010). According to him, "teachers have abandoned the profession after having been turned into test-prep technicians, low-income teenagers have been forced out of school by do-or-die graduation exams, [and] inventive learning activities have been eliminated in favor of prefabricated lessons pegged to state standards." And he warns that now "a small group of experts will be designing standards, test questions, and curricula for the rest of us."

In a more neutral analysis, Mike Rose, in "Standards, Teaching, and Learning," *Phi Delta Kappan* (December 2009/January 2010), recognizes that the current drive to enact and enforce standards dominates schooling, but questions what effects these measures have on instruction. How good are we at explaining our standards to students? How can we use the standards as guides to improving performance? Is there a level of agreement between secondary and postsecondary institutions about what constitutes competence in a given discipline? How reflective are we about the attitudes and assumptions that underlie our standards? Similarly, in the essay cited in the introduction to this issue, Elliot W. Eisner identified four dimensions of schooling that must accompany the delivery of any curriculum, national or local, namely the intentional dimension examining what really matters in schools, the structural dimension covering how roles are defined and time is allocated, the pedagogical dimension, and the evaluative dimension. With attention to this wider context, Eisner contended, "school improvement might become a reality rather than just another golden lever that brings cynical smiles to the lips of those who teach."

For a further understanding of the focal arguments and the larger context of the issue here are a number of additional sources for consideration: Robert Rothman, *Something in Common: The Common Core Standards and the Next Chapter in American Education* (2011); Cheryl Scott Williams, "Just the Facts: Common Core State Standards," *Educational Horizons* (April–May 2012); Douglas B. Reeves, "The Myths of Common Core," *American School Board Journal* (March 2012); and Tom Loveless, "Does the Common Core Matter?" *Education Week* (April 18, 2012).

The March 2012 American School Board Journal has two other interesting articles, Lawrence Hardy's "Common Core Technology" and Nora Carr's "Common Core Communications." The Winter 2010/2011 *American Educator* has a "Common Core Curriculum" theme featuring "The Spark of Specifics" by Diana Senechal, in which she calls for a curriculum detailing what to teach but not how to teach; "Beyond Comprehension" by E. D. Hirsch, Jr.; and "Soaring Systems" by Linda Darling-Hammond, who praises high-performing countries that have created coherent education systems in which all students have equally resourced schools and learn the same core content.

Create Central

www.mhhe.com/createcentral

Additional Resources

J. Matthews, "Why Common Core standards Will Fail," *Education Week* (2012).

National Association for the Education of Young Children, *The Common Core State Standards: Caution and Opportunity for Early Childhood Education* (National Association for the Education of Young Children, 2012).

A. Porter, J. McMakin, J. Hwang, & R. Yang, "Common Core Standards: The New U.S. Intended Curriculum," *Educational Researcher* (2011)

Science and Mathematics Teacher Imperative (SMTI)/The Leadership Collaborative (TLC) Working Group on Common Core State Standards,

The Common Core State Standards and Teacher Preparation: The Role of Higher Education (The Association of Public and Land-grant Universities, 2011).

W. Sloan, "Coming to Terms with Common Core Standards," *ASCD Info Brief* (2010).

Internet References. . .

The Albert Shanker Institute

www.shankerinstitute.org/

Smarter Balanced Assessment Consortium

www.smarterbalanced.org/

The Biggest Weakness of the Common Core Standards

www.washingtonpost.com/blogs/answer-sheet/
wp/2013/11/07/the-biggest-weakness-of-the-common-
core-standards/

Three-Minute Video Explaining the Common Core State Standards

www.youtube.com/watch?v=5s0rRk9sER0

Florida Curbs Role in Consortium Developing Common Core Exams

http://common-core-educational-standards.rsspump.
com/?key=2013092323311c.florida-curbs-role-
consortium-developing

Selected, Edited, and with Issue Framing Material by:
Glenn L. Koonce, *Regent University*

ISSUE

Can the Common Core State Standards Be Successful?

YES: William H. Schmidt and Nathan A. Burroughs, from "How the Common Core Boosts Quality and Equality," *Educational Leadership* (December 2012/January 2013)

NO: Tom Loveless, from "The Common Core Initiative: What Are the Chances of Success?" *Educational Leadership* (December 2012/January 2013)

Learning Outcomes

After reading this issue, you will be able to:

- Identify two insistent problems in U.S. education and how the Common Core State Standards (CCSS) may be related to the problem.
- Distinguish between what the new CCSS standards can and cannot do to improve our overall national education system.
- Critique the downfalls of moving forward in support of the CCSS.
- Differentiate between standards and curriculum.
- Outline the CCSS movement in the United States.

ISSUE SUMMARY

YES: With a focus on the new math standards, Michigan State University researchers William Schmidt and Nathan Burroughs indicate the Common Core State Standards will address two tenacious problems in U.S. education: the mediocrity quality of mathematics learning and unequal opportunity in U.S. schools.

NO: Tom Loveless, a senior fellow at the Brookings Institute, takes the position that chances for the Common Core Standards to be successful are "slim at best" when compared to the claims on how well similar policies have worked in the past.

Expectations for all students to perform at a high level and be prepared for college and career readiness was reset this past fall with the arrival of the new Common Core State Standards (CCSS) to the 2013–2014 academic school year. Some feel it is the biggest challenge that teachers will face during the year. The CCSS is a voluntary state led effort to raise standards in which the U.S. Department of Education has provided some support. Five states have not yet adopted the CCSS: Alaska, Nebraska, Minnesota (English standards only), Texas, and Virginia. For the remaining 45 states, District of Columbia, four territories, and the Department of Defense Education Activity, students Kindergarten through 12th grade in English, language arts and mathematics, are being taught the skills and knowledge necessary to collaborate and compete with their peers around the world. Social studies and science standards are currently being considered as part of the Common Core.

Educators and researchers worked together framing the Common Core standards, linking them with what colleges and employers want young people to know. With a better understanding from fewer, clearer, and higher standards, students and their families can track progress better. Parents could identify earlier, with their children, when and where problems may exist, such as in elementary school rather than in middle or even high school. This would allow for more timely intervention allowing the child to perform better. The same logic applies to the child's teacher as each child/student matriculate from grade to grade and school to school.

Prior to the CCSS each state had its own standards. Now CCSS enable collaboration between states on a range of tools and policies. According to corestandards.org (2013) these tools and policies include:

the development of textbooks, digital media, and other teaching materials aligned to the standards;

the development and implementation of common comprehensive assessment systems to measure student performance annually that will replace existing state testing systems; and

changes needed to help support educators and schools in teaching to the new standards.

Although the CCSS have many proponents, there are certainly those who disagree, even some naysayers. The naysayers say standards haven't worked in the past; they won't work in the future. They also indicate that having lofty standards is much easier than making them actually work. Two of the greatest needs for CCSS to be successful are resources that are the least available: high quality training and teacher time to receive training (Ripley, 2013). Even within the ranks of those states that have already adopted CCSS, there are potential push backs. Politics have been part of the controversy ensuring some resistance. A few states (Kentucky and Hawaii) adopted the standards before they were finalized causing issues. There was heated debate in Massachusetts considered by many as having the highest standards in the country. States that have refused to adopt the CCSS are relying on their own standards resulting in political debates in some of these states.

According to two national polls (Maxwell, 2013) designed to capture the view of K-12 education by the American public, the Common Core is a puzzle and the majority of those surveyed are clueless concerning the CCSS. An even murkier issue in the polls was standardized testing. There is opinion, depending on how the question was posed, that trounces testing and indicates people are fed up with it because testing has not led to better schools. Other opinions show testing is essential for knowing how well students are progressing. The poll's final tally reveals that there are issues that need attention. The Common Core is certainly one of them.

As previously indicated, the other side of standards is assessment (testing). The administration of tests, based on CCSS, will begin implementation in the 2014–2015 academic school year. The debate escalates again where there is discussion in some states regarding the use of student assessment outcomes that are linked to teacher evaluation and in some cases salary (Merit pay). If parents are clueless to CCSS, how would they be able to reflect on this issue? The same would be true of untrained school leaders and for the teachers themselves.

The Association for Supervision and Curriculum Development (ASCD) (Association for Curriculum and Development, 2013) explored myths and fact about the CCSS. One big myth is that the CCSS were developed by the federal government when in fact they were spearheaded by the nation's governors and state education commissioners collaborating with educators, subject matter experts, and researchers. Neither did the federal government require states to adopt the CCSS because adoption is voluntary. The federal government does become involved by requiring states to adopt college- and career-ready standards in order to receive waivers from No Child Left Behind requirements. Additionally, the federal government's Race to the Top grant competition allows applicants (states) additional points for adopting college- and career-ready standards.

The fact that the CCSS is not a curriculum that dictates what and how every educator must teach eliminates another myth. The standards are to be used as a basis for districts and schools to develop their own curricula including course content, instructional strategies, and learning activities.

A final myth explored by ASCD was that the student test scores will sharply decrease on the CCSS test as opposed to current state assessments. The fact is that students will be taking newly designed tests based on the new standards. These assessments are currently designed and will require a new benchmark for student success.

State standards are not new, having been driven by textbook publishers used in series dispersed throughout all of the states for decades. We look to the new CCSS to transform education but at what financial price for design and assessment and at what price for implementation? These standards have polarized policy makers, educators, and scholars alike. Will we embrace them one year and dump them the next?

In the selections that follow Schmidt and Burroughs focus mainly on math standards, but their larger picture addresses how CCSS will tackle the mediocrity quality and unequal opportunity in our schools. Tom Loveless takes the position that chances for the CCSS to be successful are "slim at best."

References

Association for Curriculum and Development, ASCD Policy Points: Common Core State Standards (2013). Retrieved from: www.ascd.org/common-core/core-connection/10-10-13-debunking-common-core-myths.aspx

Common Core Standards Initiative. (2013) Retrieved from: www.corestandards.org/

L. Maxwell, "Common Core: A Puzzle to Public." *Education Week* (vol. 33, no. 2, 2013).

A. Ripley, "The Smart Set: What happens when millions of kids are asked to master fewer things more deeply?" *Time* (vol. 182, no.14, 2013).

YES ↵

William H. Schmidt and Nathan A. Burroughs

How the Common Core Boosts Quality and Equality

The Common Core State Standards Address Two Tenacious Problems in U.S. Education.

The adoption of the Common Core State Standards by 46 states and the District of Columbia represents a dramatic departure in U.S. education. In the past, national efforts to improve education have been directed by the federal government and have emphasized resources or organizational structure. In contrast, the Common Core State Standards in math and language arts were developed under the leadership of state governments to improve the *content* of instruction.

A tremendous commitment of time, money, and human resources has gone into creating the new standards—and even more will go into implementing them. If the ambitions of the Common Core initiative are realized, for the first time almost every public school student in the United States will be exposed to roughly the same content, especially in grades 1–8.

All of which raises the question, Is all this effort worth it? In the case of mathematics, we think the answer is *yes* because the new math standards will address two long-standing problems in U.S. education: the mediocre quality of mathematics learning and unequal opportunity in U.S. schools. In short, the Common Core State Standards have the potential to improve both quality and equality in mathematics education.

The Quality Issue

Extensive evidence points to the inadequacy of mathematics education in the United States. Only 26 percent of U.S. 12th graders reach the threshold of proficiency in math on the National Assessment of Educational Progress (National Center for Education Statistics, 2010). Moreover, U.S. 8th graders posted a mediocre performance on the 2007 Trends in International Mathematics and Science Study (Gonzales et al., 2008) and scored below average on the 2009 Programme for International Assessment (Fleischman, Hopstock, Pelczar, & Shelley, 2010). The need to improve mathematics learning in the United States has been a primary driver of education reform efforts, including the Common Core initiative.

What New Research Shows

Although one can't say for certain what the effects of any policy will be, empirical research suggests reasons for optimism regarding the Common Core standards. A recent study examined the likelihood that the new mathematics standards would improve student achievement (Schmidt & Houang, 2012). This study involved (1) comparing the Common Core State Standards in mathematics with the mathematics standards of the countries with the highest mathematics achievement on international assessments, (2) estimating how close each state's previous math standards were to the Common Core standards, and (3) exploring whether states with standards more like the Common Core standards did better on the 2009 National Assessment of Educational Progress (NAEP) in 8th grade mathematics.

The Trends in International Mathematics and Science Study (TIMSS) demonstrated that the mathematics standards of the world's highest-achieving nations have three key characteristics: rigor, focus, and coherence. A *rigorous* curriculum covers topics at the appropriate grade level; a *focused* curriculum concentrates on a few key topics at a time; and a *coherent* curriculum adheres to the underlying logic of mathematics, moving from simple to more complex topics.

After identifying the common characteristics of the standards of those countries that did best on the TIMSS, the study compared the duration and sequence of topic coverage across grades in these "A+" standards with the Common Core State Standards for mathematics. This comparison revealed an overlap of about 90 percent. If the standards of the world's top-achieving nations are any guide, the new math standards are of high quality.

As we might expect, comparing preexisting state mathematics standards with the Common Core standards revealed wide variation in the quality of state standards. Many states will have to undertake major changes in how they're implementing their curriculums if they're to faithfully execute the vision of the Common Core standards. More important, statistical analysis of the relationship between the proximity of a state's standards to the Common Core standards and that state's average performance on the NAEP uncovered a positive relationship between the quality of a state's curriculum standards and that state's 8th grade mathematics performance.

However, some states with high standards that look very similar on paper to the Common Core standards register middling or even low NAEP scores; in contrast, other states with only average standards post higher mathematics scores on NAEP. At first glance, this might suggest that the Common Core State Standards will have little effect on student achievement—that high standards don't ensure high achievement. But such a simplistic comparison of standards to test scores neglects the crucial role of implementation (Schmidt & Houang, in press).

For example, each state has its own standards—but also its own assessments and cut scores. States with low cut scores devalue the worth of what could otherwise be strong standards, implicitly telling schools not to take the standards seriously. Once proficiency cut scores are accounted for, there's a statistically significant and positive relationship between the similarity of state standards to the Common Core State Standards and average student achievement.[1] One of the aims of the common assessments currently under development is to establish a common proficiency cut point across states, which should reduce the likelihood that states will devalue the new standards as many did their previous standards.

The Equality Issue

Much of the debate about the Common Core State Standards has focused on their potential to improve the overall quality of U.S. education. However, we have not paid enough attention to their capacity to ensure greater *equality* in content coverage among students.

We most often equate education inequality with inequality in the resources available to poorer school districts, unequal education outcomes on student assessments, the fact that underprivileged students are most likely to have inexperienced or underqualified teachers, and the fact that children from impoverished or otherwise difficult home lives are much less likely to have the same kind of supports or enrichment opportunities that their luckier peers do. All these facets of inequality are crucial for policymakers to address.

A Focus on Instructional Equality

However, what's lacking in all these discussions is any concern for inequality in *instructional content*. The U.S. education system is rife with curricular inequalities, by which we mean inequalities in the opportunity to learn challenging content (Schmidt & McKnight, 2012). If a student is never exposed to a topic, he or she can hardly be expected to learn it—a problem that's especially acute in mathematics. The mathematical content that students have an opportunity to learn varies wildly across schools, districts, and states.

The continuing variation within states effectively rebuts a common criticism that asserts that because existing state standards have had no discernible effect on student achievement, we shouldn't expect the Common Core standards to have an effect either. This claim seems to assume that the content taught at a particular grade in any given year is essentially the same in any classroom in the state.

But that's not what we find. Rather, what students have a chance to learn will be based in large measure on what community they happen to live in and what school they happen to attend. In fact, the mathematics content offered in low-income districts is more similar to that of low-income districts in other states than to middle- and high-income districts in the same state. Whether the Common Core standards will mitigate these within-state inequalities remains an open question. The seriousness of purpose accompanying the advent of the Common Core movement—with its new assessments, new textbooks, and the sheer national scope of the enterprise—is a hopeful sign. However, success will depend on effective implementation.

A Widespread Problem

When education inequality becomes a subject for public discussion, there's a strong inclination to suppose that inequality is restricted to minority and low-income children. However, data from the Promoting Rigorous Outcomes in Math and Science Education (PROM/SE) project (Schmidt & McKnight, 2012) revealed that the greatest variation in opportunity to learn mathematics content was among *middle-income districts*. There was greater variability in what topics were covered at what grade level among districts that had neither high nor low socioeconomic status (SES) than among the much more homogenous high- and low-SES districts. Inequality of opportunity to learn is a problem for every student, and for the United States as a whole.

The problem of curricular inequality goes much deeper than differences among schools or districts. The greatest source of variation in opportunity to learn mathematics is actually between classrooms (Schmidt & McKnight, 2012). Students living in the same district, attending the same school, and enrolled in the same grade can have very different classroom experiences.

This problem manifests itself in several ways. Often, classes with identical course titles and textbooks have different instructional content. The level of teacher preparation as well as teacher expectations for the student will vary (Cogan, Schmidt, & Wiley, 2001).

There's also the widespread use of tracking, a process by which students are assigned to classrooms on the basis of perceived ability. Once students are assigned to lower tracks, they almost never move up to higher ones (Schiller, Schmidt, Muller, & Houang, 2010).

Despite the fact that tracking has been roundly criticized by many scholars, policymakers, and activists, the practice remains quite common. Surveys of school administrators and teachers conducted as part of the 2011 NAEP (National Center for Education Statistics, 2011) suggest that three-quarters of 8th graders are assigned to mathematics classrooms on the basis of ability. Even more shocking, nearly a third of 4th graders are assigned in this way. Thus, many students have their long-term academic futures determined for them when they are only 9 or 10 years old.

What the New Standards Can Do

The Common Core State Standards for mathematics represent an opportunity to broaden access to rigorous educational content. Having a common set of standards certainly promotes higher-quality textbooks and assessments and makes it easier for students moving between states to fit into their new schools. However, the greater effect of the standards may be that they alter our approach to teaching mathematics.

The new math standards offer the possibility of a common curriculum within states, districts, and schools. The vision of the Common Core initiative is that teachers will cooperate across classrooms and grades in determining how they'll teach math so that there's a clear, logical progression as a student moves through school. If effectively implemented, the new standards could reduce within-state inequalities in content instruction.

The new math standards enable teachers to deepen their teaching. The new focus should shift the teaching of mathematics from a "spiraled curriculum" approach, in which too many topics are shallowly covered year after year, to one in which a few important topics are mastered at each grade level. For example, the Common Core standards call for focused instruction on fractions in grades 3–5 and on linear equations in grade 8. Because teachers will have more time to teach each topic, they should be more able to ensure that their students understand the material instead of having to cling to the vain hope that struggling students will figure things out in later years.

The new math standards discourage tracking. By insisting on common content for all students at each grade level and in every community, the Common Core mathematics standards are also in direct conflict with the concept of tracking. If the new standards were to do no more than sharply reduce this practice, the policy would be well worth the effort.

What the New Standards Don't Do

Support for the new standards cuts across ideological lines, but so does opposition. In evaluating potential benefits, it's useful to clarify what the standards don't do.

The new math standards don't hold teachers responsible for students' poor math performance. The fact that the greatest source of variation in opportunity to learn is in the classroom doesn't mean that teachers are to blame for curricular inequality. Currently, teachers are deluged with competing signals about what content to teach. State standards, state assessments, and textbooks provide conflicting guidance; and teachers receive neither the preparation nor the support they require to make effective curricular decisions. Easing this situation is one of the key objectives of the Common Core movement.

The new math standards don't end the autonomy of local schools or teachers. Curriculum is only one component of schooling, defining *what* schools should teach, not *how*. Under the present system, teachers and school districts are expected to decide both the content of instruction and the best means for helping students learn that content (along with many administrative and community responsibilities). Instead of teachers having to spend time inventing which content to teach and in what sequence, the new standards help schools and teachers focus their efforts on their core competencies and devise the best means for helping students achieve the standards.

The new math standards are not part of "market-based" education reform. Some advocates of the Common Core standards also support a range of other education reform policies, such as No Child Left Behind, merit pay, and the use of value-added models to assess teacher performance. Although there's no real inconsistency between such reforms and the Common Core State Standards, it would be a mistake to lump them together. The aim of the Common Core initiative is not to introduce market mechanisms in education but to institute high-quality standards that promote equality of opportunity to learn for all students.

The Road Ahead

A recent survey conducted on behalf of the Center for the Study of Curriculum at Michigan State University reveals both positive signs and potential pitfalls in efforts to realize the new standards.

Positive Signs

In our representative sample of more than 12,000 mathematics teachers in the 40 states that had adopted the new math standards as of January 2011, more than 90 percent said they liked the idea of having Common Core State Standards for mathematics because they provide "a consistent, clear understanding of what students are expected to learn" and "a high-quality education to our children." After reading a sample of the standards for the grades they teach, virtually 100 percent of the teachers said they would teach the new math standards. The challenges teachers identified differed little from those that educators so often express with any curriculum—lack of supporting curriculum materials and lack of parental support.

Luckily, parental support may not be an obstacle to implementing the Common Core standards. In our representative sample of more than 6,000 parents of K–8 students, most viewed math as the most important subject for their children, and nearly 70 percent thought that the Common Core State Standards for mathematics were a good idea. More than 90 percent endorsed the idea that math is important for their children's success and that their children should take math every school year, including all four years in high school.

Potential Pitfalls

The survey also suggested areas of concern. Teachers may not have a clear grasp of what's in the new math standards or how the standards differ from the status quo. Most teachers (80 percent) thought that the new standards were "pretty much the same" as previous standards, a belief that research (Schmidt & Houang, in press) shows to be grossly mistaken. Also, many teachers believe that the new standards may require them to add new topics to their current math curriculum. Rather, the Common Core standards call for greater focus on fewer topics at each grade level.

To effectively implement the Common Core State Standards for Mathematics, teachers are going to have to be much better prepared. Fewer than half of elementary teachers we surveyed felt well prepared to teach Common Core math topics at their grade level, compared with 60 percent of middle school teachers and 70 percent of high school mathematics teachers. As for parents, those we asked still knew very little about the Common Core standards (even whether their state has adopted the standards). Moreover, a distressingly large percentage of parents (36–38 percent) believed that some children just can't "get" mathematics.

Cautious Optimism

Inadequate teacher preparation, lack of parent involvement, and insufficient resources and planning could all derail implementation efforts. Realizing the vision of the standards represents a tremendous challenge, but the potential benefits—higher mathematics achievement and greater equality of education opportunity—make it well worth the effort.

References

Cogan, L. S., Schmidt, W. H., & Wiley, D. E. (2001). Who takes what mathematics and in which track? Using TIMSS to characterize U.S. students' eighth grade mathematics learning opportunities. *Educational Evaluation and Policy Analysis, 23*(4), 323–341.

Fleischman, H. L., Hopstock, P. J., Pelczar, M. P., & Shelley, B. E. (2010). *Highlights from PISA 2009: Performance of U.S. 15-year-old students in reading, mathematics, and science literacy in an international context* (NCES 2011-004). Washington, DC: U.S. Department of Education.

Gonzales, P., Williams, T., Jocelyn, L., Roey, S., Kastberg, D., & Brenwald, S. (2008). *Highlights from TIMSS 2007: Mathematics and science achievement of U.S. fourth- and eighth-grade students in an international context* (NCES 2009–001Revised). Washington, DC: U.S. Department of Education.

National Center for Education Statistics. (2010). *The nation's report card: Grade 12 reading and mathematics 2009 national and pilot state results* (NCES 2011-455). Washington, DC: Institute of Education Sciences, U.S. Department of Education.

National Center for Education Statistics. (2011). *Percentages for mathematics, grade 8, by 8th grade assigned to math by ability [C0728011], year and jurisdiction: 2011; Percentages for mathematics, grade 4, by 4th grade assigned to math by ability [C052001], year and jurisdiction: 2011.* Data retrieved from the NAEP Data Explorer at http://nces.ed.gov/nationsreportcard/naepdata/dataset.aspx

Schiller, K. S., Schmidt, W. H., Muller, C., & Houang, R. T. (2010). Hidden disparities: How courses and curricula shape opportunities in mathematics during high school. *Equity and Excellence in Education, 43*(4), 414–433.

Schmidt, W. H., & Houang, R. T. (in press). Curricular coherence and the Common Core State Standards for Mathematics. *Educational Researcher.*

Schmidt, W. H., & McKnight, C. (2012). *Inequality for all: The challenge of unequal opportunity in American schools.* New York: Teachers College Press.

WILLIAM H. SCHMIDT is a distinguished professor at Michigan State University.

NATHAN A. BURROUGHS is research associate at the Center for the Study of Curriculum at Michigan State University.

Tom Loveless

 **NO**

The Common Core Initiative: What Are the Chances of Success?

The Chances are Slim at Best—and Here's Why.

Advocates of the Common Core State Standards are hopeful. They believe the standards offer a historic opportunity to boost the overall quality of U.S. education.

Hope is important in policy debates, but there's also a role for skepticism. The Common Core State Standards are not the first national education initiative to be launched with the anticipation of success. Nor is it the first time policymakers have called on education standards to guide us toward better schools.

Looking into the Claims

In a recent study (Loveless, 2012), I tried to estimate the probability that the Common Core standards will produce more learning. The study started with the assumption that a good way to predict the future effects of any policy is to examine how well similar policies have worked in the past—in this case, by examining the past effects of state education standards. The study conducted three statistical investigations using state data from the reading and math portions of the National Assessment of Educational Progress (NAEP) at both 4th and 8th grades.

The first investigation looked at whether the quality of state standards is related to past gains in student achievement. It turns out it isn't. States with poor standards have made NAEP gains comparable to states with excellent standards.

A second investigation looked at whether the levels at which states set past proficiency standards made a difference in achievement. They don't. States with low bars for student proficiency posted similar NAEP scores as those with high bars.[1]

Finally, the third analysis looked at variation in achievement. A key objective of the new standards is to reduce glaring inequalities. This doesn't mean to perfectly equalize all learning, of course. However, striving to ensure that all students possess the knowledge and skills necessary for college or careers means, statistically speaking, that a reduction in achievement variation should occur.

So how much reduction can we expect? The Common Core standards will surely not affect variation inside each individual state. Schools and districts in every state have been operating under common standards for years. The real opportunity that the initiative presents is harmonizing differences in standards among states.

How much variation on NAEP achievement is there among states? Not much. In fact, within-state variation on NAEP is four to five times greater than variation among states. Put another way, the NAEP score gap between Massachusetts and Mississippi, one of the widest between any two states, exists among different schools and districts in *every* state. Unless the Common Core standards possess some unknown power that previous standards didn't possess, that variation will go untouched.

On the basis of these findings, the most reasonable prediction is that the Common Core initiative will have little to no effect on student achievement.

How might it defy this prediction and prove successful? Advocates of the initiative are counting on two mechanisms—high-quality professional development and improvements in curriculum—to overcome the many obstacles that lie ahead.

The Problem with Professional Development

So what does high-quality professional development look like? The research on the topic is limited, producing suggestive characteristics rather than definitive prescriptions.

Limited Potential for Strong Effects

A white paper on teacher quality from the National Academy of Education (Wilson, 2009) notes that several studies have identified promising features of effective professional development. These features include a focus on subject-matter knowledge; ample time (more than 40 hours per program) with a year or more of follow-up; clear linkages to teachers' existing knowledge and skills; training that actively engages teachers; and training teams of teachers from the same school. A meta-analysis by the Council of Chief State School Officers (Blank & de las Alas, 2009) endorses a similar set of characteristics, although the best programs in this study were longer, delivering 100 hours or more of training.

Both reports note the limitations of professional development research. None of the studies that meet commonly recognized criteria for good evaluations involve middle or high school teachers, only elementary teachers. Also, the list of promising features comes from studies of disparate programs. Their effectiveness when combined into a large-scale, comprehensive program is unknown.

The only randomized field trial—the gold standard of program evaluation—of a professional development program embodying many of the recommended features produced disappointing results (Garet et al., 2008). Participants received training on early reading instruction in content-focused summer institutes, with extensive follow-up during the school year. Teachers' knowledge increased and their pedagogy changed, but there was no improvement in student achievement. The National Academy of Education report (Wilson, 2009) observes that professional development programs with strong effects have been associated with small projects, concluding that "the average teacher has a minimal chance of experiencing high-quality professional development targeted to the subjects, grades, and students he or she teaches" (p. 6).

A Word About External Assessments

To evaluate whether professional development programs had an effect on student achievement, the Council of Chief State School Officers' meta-analysis includes some studies that look at assessments specifically designed by the programs themselves as well as studies that use national, state, and local assessments to judge program effectiveness. The latter group is more relevant to the Common Core standards because the success or failure of the programs depended on how much students learned on external assessments, the type of assessments the Common Core initiative will use.

These evaluations detected educationally insignificant, even trivial, effect sizes: .17 for national norm-referenced tests, .01 for statewide assessments, and .05 for studies that used local achievement tests (Blank & de las Alas, 2009). If professional development typically yields such small effects, then expectations that it will have a significant impact in the context of the new standards are probably unwarranted.

There's an important lesson here for educators who, in coming years, will be bombarded with tales of wonderful professional development tied to the Common Core standards. Be on guard. In an extensive Institute for Education Sciences review of 1,300 studies of professional development (Yoon, Duncan, Lee, Scarloss, & Shapley, 2007), the reviewers cautioned,

The limited number of studies and the variability in their professional development approaches preclude any conclusions about the effectiveness of specific professional development programs or about the effectiveness of professional development by form, content, and intensity (p. 14).

A "Better" Curriculum—But Which One?

The Common Core website makes a point of differentiating between standards and curriculum. The page "Myths vs. Facts" declares, The Standards are not a curriculum. They are a clear set of shared goals and expectations for what knowledge and skills will help our students succeed. Local teachers, principals, superintendents, and others will decide *how* the standards are to be met. Teachers will continue to devise lesson plans and tailor instruction to the individual needs of the students in their classrooms. (National Governors Association Center for Best Practices & Council of Chief State School Officers, 2012)

The curriculum that fleshes out the new standards will, in the end, determine how teachers, parents, and students actually experience the standards. What will that curriculum contain? Given that curricular content is subject to local discretion, how broad are the boundaries for those choices?

Core Knowledge Vs. Partnership for 21st Century Skills

Consider two dramatically different views of curriculum, one supported by the Core Knowledge Foundation and the other by the Partnership for 21st Century Skills. Their philosophies are diametrically opposed, yet both organizations are convinced that the Common Core State Standards embrace their point of view.

Core Knowledge, the brainchild of E. D. Hirsch, holds that content knowledge is king. The author of the Core Knowledge blog, Robert Pondiscio (2012), lauds the Common Core initiative for reminding us "to engage children not just with rote literacy skills work and process writing, but also, and especially, with real content—rich, deep, broad knowledge about the world in which they live." For example, on the Core Knowledge website, model lessons for 8th grade language arts include the study of Greek and Latin root words; William Shakespeare's *Twelfth Night*; Pearl S. Buck's *The Good Earth* (supplemented by a research paper on Chinese culture); and Maya Angelou's *I Know Why the Caged Bird Sings*. The key to becoming a good reader is content knowledge, Pondiscio argues, and he asks, "Yet how many times have we heard it said that we need to deemphasize teaching 'mere facts' and focus on skills like critical thinking, creativity, and problem solving?"

The Partnership for 21st Century Skills promotes exactly what Pondiscio deplores. The partnership has developed a framework of skills it believes are essential to good schooling, including life and career skills; information, media, and technology skills; and what it calls the 4Cs (critical thinking, communication, collaboration, and creativity). The partnership has also published a P21 Common Core Toolkit (Magner, Soulé, & Wesolowski, 2011), which shows how the Common Core initiative and the partnership's framework are aligned. The toolkit also offers vignettes ("lesson starters") to illustrate how the Common Core standards integrate with the partnership's framework.

For example, in contrast with Core Knowledge's 8th grade lesson, an 8th grade English language arts lesson aligned to the partnership's framework proceeds as follows:

After completing a literature circle unit of teen problem novels, students brainstorm a list of significant social, emotional, or health issues that teens face today. Working in groups, students research one issue and create a public service announcement on a closed YouTube channel (viewable only by students in the class) to persuade their peers about one action they should take regarding the issue. Students will select and use references from literary readings (e.g., citing how a particular novel presents the issue) as well as research from nonfiction sources to illustrate major points (Partnership for 21st Century Skills, 2008, p. 8).

This lesson would never occur in a Core Knowledge classroom. The point here is not to settle the argument between Core Knowledge and the Partnership for 21st Century Skills. Rather, it's to illustrate the elasticity of the educational philosophy underpinning the Common Core State Standards. Philosophical ambiguity may be smart politically because it allows for a wide range of supporters—a "big tent" strategy. But if two organizations with such starkly contrasting points of view both see the standards as compatible with their definition of an ideal curriculum, then any guidance about what to teach in local schools is broad indeed.

The Curriculum Conundrum

How will educators make curricular decisions? Hopefully, the effectiveness of curricular materials and programs will factor prominently.

Unfortunately, the research on effective curriculum is as thin as the research on effective professional development. As my Brookings colleagues document in a recent report, educators are "choosing blindly" when making curriculum decisions. Instructional programs can differ dramatically in their effectiveness (Chingos & Whitehurst, 2012).

Mathematica Policy Research conducted a randomized field trial of four primary-grade math textbooks and found huge differences between the most and least effective (Agodini, Harris, Thomas, Murphy, & Gallagher, 2010). Such high-quality studies are rare, and more important, even the most robust studies cannot do the impossible—provide advice on how to choose effective materials from a sea of candidates that have never been rigorously evaluated in the first place.

So what kind of information will inform the selection of local curriculum? Note that the publishers of the four math textbooks just mentioned—both effective and ineffective alike—all advertise that their texts are now aligned with the Common Core standards. As Chingos and Whitehurst (2012) observe,

Publishers of instructional materials are lining up to declare the alignment of their materials with the Common Core standards using the most superficial of definitions. The Common Core standards will only have a chance of raising student achievement if they are implemented with high-quality materials, but there is currently no basis to measure the quality of materials. (p. 1)

Back to Where We Started?

The Common Core State Standards have been adopted by 46 states and the District of Columbia. They enjoy a huge following of well-wishers and supporters who are optimistic that the standards will boost achievement in U.S. schools. Setting aside the cheerleading and fond hopes, what are the real chances of success?

The most reasonable prediction is that the Common Core initiative will have little to no effect on student achievement. Moreover, on the basis of current research, high-quality professional development and "excellent" curricular materials are also unlikely to boost the Common Core standards' slim chances of success.

References

Agodini, R., Harris, B., Thomas, M., Murphy, R., & Gallagher, L. (2010). *Achievement effects of four early elementary school math curricula: Findings for first and second graders.* Princeton, NJ: Mathematica Policy Research.

Blank, R. K., & de las Alas, N. (2009). *Effects of teacher professional development on gains in student achievement.* Washington, DC: Council of Chief State School Officers.

Chingos, M. M., & Whitehurst, G. J. (2012). *Choosing blindly: Instructional materials, teacher effectiveness, and the Common Core.* Washington, DC: Brookings Institution. Retrieved from www.brookings.edu/research/reports/2012/04/10-curriculum-chingos-whitehurst

Garet, M. S., Cronen, S., Eaton, M., Kurki, A., Ledwig, M., Jones, W., et al. (2008). *The impact of two professional development interventions on early reading instruction and achievement.* Washington, DC: Institute of Education Sciences.

Loveless, T. (2012). *The 2012 Brown Center report on American education: How well are American students learning?* Washington, DC: Brookings Institution. Retrieved from www.brookings.edu/~/media/research/files/reports/2012/2/brown%20center/0216_brown_education_loveless.pdf

Magner, T., Soulé, H., & Wesolowski, K. (2011). *P21 Common Core toolkit: A guide to aligning the Common Core State Standards with the Framework for 21st Century Skills*. Washington, DC: Partnership for 21st Century Skills. Retrieved from www.p21.org/storage/documents/P21CommonCoreToolkit.pdf.

National Governors Association Center for Best Practices & Council of Chief State School Officers. (2012). *Myths vs. Facts*. Washington, DC: Authors. Retrieved from www.corestandards.org/about-the-standards/myths-vs-facts

Partnership for 21st Century Skills. (2008). *21st century skills map*. Tucson, AZ: Author. Retrieved from www.p21.org/storage/documents/21st_century_skills_english_map.pdf

Pondiscio, R. (2012, June 14). Nobody loves standards (and that's OK) [blog post]. Retrieved from *Common Core Watch* at www.edexcellence.net/commentary/education-gadfly-daily/common-core-watch/2012/nobody-loves-standards-and-thats-ok.html

Wilson, S. (Ed., 2009). *Teacher quality* (Education policy white paper). Washington, DC: National Academy of Education. Retrieved from http://naeducation.org/Teacher_Quality_White_Paper.pdf

Yoon, K., Duncan, T., Lee, S., Scarloss, B., & Shapley, K. (2007). *Reviewing the evidence on how teacher professional development affects student achievement* (Issues & Answers Report, REL 2007–No. 033). Washington, DC: Regional Educational Laboratory Southwest. Retrieved from http://ies.ed.gov/ncee/edlabs/regions/southwest/pdf/REL_2007033.pdf

Note

1. States that raised the bar from 2005 to 2009 did show an increase in 4th grade NAEP scores, but the correlation is weak, it does not appear in 8th grade, and the direction of causality is unclear. Rather than loftier expectations driving achievement gains, states may have raised the bar for proficiency because of rising achievement.

Tom Loveless is a senior fellow in governance studies at the Brookings Institution, Washington, D.C.

EXPLORING THE ISSUE

Can the Common Core State Standards Be Successful?

Critical Thinking and Reflection

1. Because the Common Sore State Standards (CCSS) are the same for each state participating, should each state also have common proficiency cut scores and common assessments (common assessments are projected in the 2014–2015 school term)?
2. Will states decide that where a student lives along with their socioeconomic factors make a difference in what is being taught?
3. Is there enough quantitative and qualitative research to support the common core initiative?
4. Will the CCSS be the answer to improving the overall quality of U.S. Education.?
5. What is your state's current policy and regulations regarding the CCSS?

Is There Common Ground?

It is a turbulent time for education and both proponents and skeptics are flexing their muscles in the Common Core State Standards (CCSS) debate. The push for these standards is not new. Policy makers, educators, parents, and the public have discussed their existence since President Eisenhower's vision of creating national goals where American students would be more competitive against other nations. The 1983 report, *A Nation at Risk*, raised a red flag noting how far American students had fallen behind other nations and the need to raise standards.

Collaboration on the assessments that allow for state by state comparison of student achievement, the National Assessment of Educational Progress (NAEP) was undertaken by President Reagan and Senator Edward Kennedy in 1988. In 1989, President H.W. Bush was involved in organizations representing the core subjects beginning to develop their own voluntary standards (i.e., The National Council of Teachers of Mathematics). The NAEP was expanded under the Clinton Administration to voluntary national testing in grades four and eight in reading and math. With mixed support and mixed results the No Child Left Behind Act (NCLB) was signed into law by President G. W. Bush in 2001 making assessment mandatory (Sloan, 2012).

Policymakers, educators, and researchers working together have shown there has been much common ground in the past regarding the development of standards in the United States. The "unevenness" of NCLB standards and failure to reauthorize them has provided impetus for the Common Core movement. The fact that the nation had 50 different standards in 50 different states had lowered the bar in student achievement in their view of many individuals. Many asked themselves the question,

"What Now?" The "What Now?" has moved the focus to the Common Core National Standards.

Reference

Sloan, W. "Coming to Terms with Common Core Standards." *ASCD Info Brief* (2012). Retrieved from: www.ascd.org/publications/newsletters/policy-priorities/vol16/issue4/toc.aspx

Create Central

www.mhhe.com/createcentral

Additional Resources

L. Calkins, M. Ehrenworth & C. Lehman, *Pathways to the Common Core: Accelerating Achievement* (Heinemann, 2012).

J. Kendall, *Understanding Common Core State Standards* (Mid-Continental Research Laboratory, 2011).

R. Marzano, D. Yanoski, J. Hoegh & J. Simms, *Using Common Core Standards to Enhance Classroom Instruction & Assessment* (Mazano Research Laboratory, 2013).

D. Reeves, *Navigating Implementation of the Common Core State Standards* (National Book Network, 2012).

H. Silver, R. Dewing & M. Perini, *The Core Six: Essential Strategies for Achieving Excellence with the Common Core* (Association for Curriculum and Development, 2013).

Internet References . . .

Florida School Board Ditches Common Core Reading Suggestions

http://blogs.edweek.org/edweek/state_
edwatch/2013/10/florida_school_board_ditches_
common-core_reading_suggestions.html

Resources for Understanding the Common Core State Standards

www.edutopia.org/common-core-state-standards-
resources

Achieve the Core

www.achievethecore.org/

Experts Speaks Against the Common Core at Wisconsin hearing

http://watchdog.org/111254/wr-common-core-expert-
speaks-out/

Implementing the Common Core State Standards: The Role of the School Counselor

www.achieve.org/publications/implementing-
common-core-state-standards-role-school-
counselor-action-brief

Selected, Edited, and with Issue Framing Material by:
Glenn L. Koonce, *Regent University*

ISSUE

Can Failing Schools Be Turned Around?

YES: Karin Chenoweth, from "It Can Be Done, It's Being Done, and Here's How," *Phi Delta Kappan* (September 2009)

NO: Andy Smarick, from "The Turnaround Fallacy," *Education Next* (Winter 2010)

Learning Outcomes
After reading this issue, you will be able to:
• Compare and contrast failing schools that struggle with failing schools that "turn around."
• Connect the No Child Left Behind (NCLB) mandates with failing schools.
• Analyze schools that have been "turned around."
• Explore the reasons for schools that are not able to be successful.
• Understand why the "fixation" with "fix it" efforts for struggling schools has been misguided.

ISSUE SUMMARY

YES: Karin Chenoweth, a senior writer with the Education Trust and author of *How It's Being Done*, describes strategies employed to bring about dramatic improvements in low-performing schools.

NO: Andy Smarick, a visiting fellow at the Thomas B. Fordham Institute, advocates the closing of failing schools to make room for replacements through chartering.

The question of how to best serve children of poverty has been wrestled with for decades and has become even more crucial during the recent economic downturn. The No Child Left Behind law, with its focus on test-performance improvement, has met with a good deal of negative reaction from frontline educators and academic theorists alike. Richard A. Gibboney, in his article "Why an Undemocratic Capitalism Has Brought Public Education to Its Knees: A Manifesto," *Phi Delta Kappan* (September 2008), puts it this way: "Rather than support policies designed to reduce poverty and its toxic effects on the ability of children to succeed in school, our lawmakers are pursuing the misbegotten path of penalizing schools in poverty-stricken cities and rural areas for their failure to work educational miracles." Richard Rothstein poses the question "Whose Problem Is Poverty?" in *Educational Leadership* (April 2008), offering an inventory of deficits experienced by the poor, including a lack of health care, more lead-poisoning, iron-deficiency anemia, family instability, more exposure to crime and drugs, fewer positive role models, and less exposure to culturally uplifting experiences.

Katherine Bradley, president of the CityBridge Foundation in Washington, DC, has stated that turning around chronically low-performing, high-poverty schools is the grittiest task that educators face. While

the search is on to find a successful turnaround formula, Bradley, in *The Washington Post* (August 7, 2011) piece, expresses concern over a growing sentiment in favor of the "highly disruptive strategy of school closure and restart." Under No Child Left Behind policies, failing schools face the possibilities of "restructuring" whereby half or more of the teachers may be fired or a complete school shutdown after which the state may assume management or a replacement charter school may be authorized. In a June 29, 2010, opinion expressed on AOL News .com, Diane Ravitch pleaded "Don't Close Schools, Fix Them." She suggested that "every state should enlist a team of evaluators to visit every struggling school, document its problems, make recommendations, and stay involved to make sure that the school gets the resources it needs to improve." Ravitch has concluded that "it may take courage to close schools, but it takes experience, wisdom, and persistence—as well as courage—to improve them and to strengthen families and communities." An elaboration of these views can be found in her Summer 2010 *American Educator* article entitled "In Need of a Renaissance: Real Reform Will Renew, Not Abandon, Our Neighborhood Schools."

Andy Smarick, former COO of the National Alliance for Public Charter Schools, has been among the leaders of the movement to develop a new type of system for urban public education, a system of charter schools. In "Wave of the Future," *Education Next* (Winter 2008), he admits that charter supporters, a "motley crew of civil rights activists, free market economists, career public-school educators, and voucher proponents," have yet to fashion a consistent vision. Some states have imposed caps on charter expansion and in some districts funding has been unequal. Often school boards, teachers unions, and school administrators have been antagonistic, but in some quarters collaborative relationships have emerged.

Advocates of internally turning around troubled schools, Deborah Meier, Laura Pappano, Karin Chenoweth, Katherine Bradley, Ruby Payne, and Pamela Cantor, among others, seem to agree on many of the guidelines for resuscitating failing schools, namely staff self-assessment, teacher collaboration replacing isolation, community-building, and serious in-service training. Karin Chenoweth's books, *It's Being Done: Academic Success in Unexpected Schools* (2007) and *How It's Being Done* (2009), provided a wealth of examples of regular neighborhood schools that did whatever it took to dramatically elevate student morale and achievement levels without resorting to magnet programs, charters, or outside management. Chenoweth's profiles revealed a pattern of high expectations for both teachers and students, wise use of time (with extra time devoted to low-performing students), and continual reexamination of practices, all occurring in an atmosphere of respect.

The YES and NO selections pit turnaround advocate Karin Chenoweth against charter proponent Andy Smarick in the search for the best way to deal with failing schools in high-poverty areas.

YES ←

Karin Chenoweth

It Can Be Done, It's Being Done, and Here's How

For decades, a sense of powerlessness has permeated many schools and many educators. "There's not much we can do" has been the mantra of many teachers faced with students who arrive behind and seem to slip backward through their school years.

Maureen Downey of the *Atlanta Journal-Constitution* recently wrote about this phenomenon: "I am always taken aback when teachers tell me that their students are essentially unteachable, that there's little they can do to educate children who arrive at school unfed, unprepared, and unmotivated" (July 15, 2009).

Educators' sense of powerlessness has been bolstered by what seem like endless data demonstrating the correlation of achievement with poverty and race. Poor, black, and Hispanic students achieve at lower levels, on average, than middle-class white and Asian students in study after study, assessment after assessment, giving failure a sense of inevitability.

So what can we make of schools where those patterns are broken—schools where poor students read as well as middle-class students; where black and Hispanic students do math as well as or even better than white students in their states?

Take, for example, George Hall Elementary. Just a few years ago, the school was one of the lowest performing schools in Mobile, Alabama, and suffered mightily from disciplinary problems. With a student population almost entirely low-income and black, in an area of Mobile notorious for high crime rates and intergenerational poverty, its low performance and chaotic atmosphere weren't considered all that surprising. What was surprising was the attitude of its new principal, Agnes "Terri" Tomlinson, and her team after the school was reconstituted in 2004. (Reconstitution meant, in this case, that the entire staff reapplied for their jobs.)

"I knew achievement wouldn't be a problem," Tomlinson said.

Tomlinson, a veteran educator, was right: Once the school was doing what it should have been doing, students' academic achievement rose to a level more often associated with white, middle-class students. In fact, most George Hall students score above the national norm on the SAT 10 test.

George Hall isn't the only school that demonstrates the power that schools have to change the educational trajectory of their students. Graham Road Elementary in Falls Church, Virginia, is another. Once one of the lowest performing schools in Fairfax County, Graham Road is now one of the top schools in the state, outperforming many much wealthier schools. This, even though 80% of the students speak a language other than English at home because they mostly come from low-income families who recently immigrated to this country.

Yet another is P.S./M.S. 124 Osmond A. Church School in Queens, New York, where more than 80% of the students qualify for the federal free lunch program but perform at levels associated with much wealthier students. Still another is Capitol View Elementary in a low-income neighborhood of southwestern Atlanta, where the students—almost all black—post student achievement that rivals the wealthiest schools in Georgia.

What's Different?

So the question is: What's done differently at George Hall, Graham Road, P.S./M.S.124 Queens, Capitol View, and other schools where low-income children and children of color learn at high levels?

After spending the last few years visiting such schools and writing about what they do, I've come to the conclusion that they succeed where other schools fail because they ruthlessly organize themselves around one thing: helping students learn a great deal.

This seems too simple an explanation, really. But, by focusing on student learning and then creating structures that support learning, these schools have drastically departed from the traditional organizational patterns of American schools.

I sometimes think about what Wendy Wachtel, a math teacher at high-achieving Lockhart Junior High School where most students are low-income and Hispanic, told me: "It's not rocket science. You figure out what you need to teach, and then you teach it."

In contrast, consider a recent quotation in the *New York Times* from a teacher who teaches recent immigrants: "American students come to school with a lot of cultural knowledge," she said, "teachers assume they don't have to explain because their kids get it from growing up in this country, watching television or surfing the Internet."

Schools that successfully teach students of poverty and students of color do not begin with the assumption that there are things they don't have to explain. They begin by figuring out what children need to know and be able to do; they assess what their students already know and are able to do; they figure out how to move students from where they are to where they need to be; and then they analyze what students have learned and whether they need further instruction. They do this systematically grade by grade, class by class, student by student, month by month, and day by day, carefully and relentlessly. They know, as Marie Parker, an instructional coach at Graham Road, told me, "If we're not going to do it, who is?"

At Graham Road, for example, teachers go over every test with each student to discuss their wrong answers so that any misunderstandings can be addressed immediately and don't compound. When teachers met to discuss test results, they realized that their students needed to radically improve their vocabularies and their background knowledge. This, of course, is a common need among low-income students around the country.

To help build vocabulary and background knowledge, Graham Road teachers use the thousands of documentary videos that many schools can access. If teachers want children to read a particular book but know they won't understand the book's references to earthquakes and volcanoes, they have students visit the classroom's "background knowledge center"—otherwise known as the computer—to watch short documentaries on earthquakes and volcanoes. They do this because, as Molly Bensinger-Lacy, principal of Graham Road Elementary, said, "We have almost no kids who, if you haven't taught something, will get it."

George Hall uses field trips in the same deliberate, thoughtful way. Classes take field trips about once a month, and teachers think deeply about what vocabulary words and background knowledge students need to understand to get the most out of the trip to the state capital, the local zoo, the theater, or wherever they're going. Then, after the field trip is over, students post on the Internet the photos and videos that they have taken, together with written commentary. Teachers know many of their students have rarely left their neighborhoods and, in order to be educated, need exposure to the wide world. "They live 10 minutes from the bayou," one teacher told me. "But they've never even seen it—or been on a boat. We take them on a boat."

Provide Time for Teacher Learning

My point is not that every school should use videos or field trips or any other particular teaching method (though I do think both are kind of nifty). The point is that every school should engage in the kinds of deep discussion that

Graham Road and George Hall faculties have when they meet together to study their state's standards (and, sometimes, other states' standards), think about what their students already know and are able to do, and decide what more they need to learn. During these discussions, they look at student achievement data, build curriculum maps, and develop benchmark assessments, grading rubrics, and lesson plans. Even more profoundly, they discuss why one teacher is having success teaching fractions while another is not, and what the more successful teacher can teach the less successful teacher.

Such discussions take time, which means that successful high-poverty and high-minority schools must build their schedules carefully in order to ensure that teachers have the necessary time to meet together.

Many of the successful high-poverty and high-minority elementary schools I've visited schedule "specials" in a way that enables grade-level teams to meet together during those times. That means all 1st graders go at the same time to art, music, computer, gym, or whatever other "specials" the school has. At Atlanta's Capitol View, students have, in addition to the specials every day, "back-to-back specials" once a week, permitting grade-level teachers to meet with the principal and assistant principal for almost two straight hours to discuss curriculum, instruction, achievement data, and all the other things that they need to discuss to ensure that their students learn to high levels. At secondary schools, teachers' "prep" periods are scheduled so teams or departments can meet together.

These scheduling practices are so simple and mundane that they hardly seem worth mentioning. But they're one of the many building blocks that help develop the kind of deep teacher collaboration that allows teachers to focus on student learning. This means these successful schools have directly addressed something that too often is overlooked in many discussions of student achievement—the American tradition of teacher isolation.

I should say the topic of teacher isolation is not overlooked in the academic literature of school reform. Richard Elmore, Michael Fullan, Mike Schmoker, and many more have written at length about the role teacher isolation has played in retarding student achievement. Robert Marzano, Rick and Becky DuFour, and many others have long preached the gospel of collaboration as a way to improve student achievement. And yet its importance has yet to permeate the national education discussion.

For the most part, schools are still organized on the principle that teachers close their doors and teach by themselves. But no teacher can be an expert in all aspects of the curriculum, all the possible ways to teach it, and every child who sits in his or her class. Although every teacher should have expertise that can be tapped by other teachers to improve their knowledge of their subject, pedagogy, and students, the traditional organization of schools doesn't allow teachers to pool their knowledge in a systematic, structured way.

Teacher Collaboration

Because they focus so closely on what students need to learn, successful high-poverty and high-minority schools operate as schools, not as a collection of isolated classrooms. That means, among other things, that they tackle such questions as discipline and teacher quality—problems that plague many low-performing schools—with schoolwide responses.

This is what I mean. I recently spent a day in a dysfunctional urban high school in which the staff had voted to prohibit students from wearing hats, hoods, or earphones. A common enough rule, but only a few administrators enforced it. Teachers who cared about the rule enforced it in their classrooms; teachers who didn't care or felt overwhelmed didn't bother. As a result, the rule was openly flouted, and teachers who valiantly tried to enforce the rule felt undermined and lonely. The school had an unlawful feel; the week before my visit, there had been three fires at the school.

The successful high-poverty and high-minority schools I've visited have very different atmospheres. If the school has a rule, every grownup in the school (and that includes nonteaching staff) enforces it because everyone has a stake in providing a safe, respectful, and comfortable environment in which students can learn.

Similarly, teachers who are working collaboratively help guard the quality of the teaching force in ways that are impossible when teachers work in isolation. Once teaching is public and collaborative—meaning that teachers work together to figure out what children need to learn and how to teach it—teachers who don't contribute or openly sabotage such efforts begin to stand out.

Von Sheppard—who as principal took Dayton's Bluff Achievement Plus Elementary from what was widely acknowledged in 2001 to be the worst school in St. Paul, Minnesota, to a well-organized, more-or-less average-achieving school in 2005—calls sabotaging teachers "toxic teachers" because they poison the atmosphere. As Dayton's Bluff developed a collaborative culture, he says, "the [other] teachers in the building began holding these teachers accountable. No one wanted to be associated with a toxic teacher." As a result, the toxic teachers left of their own accord—a fairly common experience in high-achieving high-poverty and high-minority schools.

By acting as a team, all the energy and expertise of the faculty and staff are concentrated, rather than dispersed, and can have a much bigger effect than is possible with the tradition of teacher isolation. That concentrated effect allows students—even students burdened by poverty and discrimination—to learn at much higher levels than has traditionally been expected.

Isolation Hurts Students

There is an interesting argument that has been waged in the education world that I suspect is well known to readers of the *Kappan*, and it goes along these lines: All the talk of a crisis in American education is overblown. There may be problems in some schools, but the problems are mostly concentrated in urban and rural schools and other schools where most of the children are low-income or minority. Most schools, the argument goes on to say, are just fine and serve students well. Besides, schools can affect student achievement only on the margins because so much depends on the social capital that students bring with them. The fact that high-minority and high-poverty schools have low achievement has more to do with the characteristics that students bring to school than with anything the schools do; thus anyone who cares about education should focus their attention not on school practices but on building the social capital of impoverished families.

I would make a different argument: The traditional organization of schools, which relies on isolated teachers doing their jobs with little interference and less support, means individual students are totally reliant on the knowledge and skills of their individual teachers. They (and their teachers) have little access to the broader expertise of a school's faculty or the accrued wisdom of the education field as a whole. Because middle-class students bring more social capital than students of poverty, this tradition of isolation, on average, hurts them less. That doesn't mean it doesn't hurt them, but their parents are more likely to notice a problem in decoding or in mastery of basic math facts and either demand more help or provide it at home, either themselves or with the help of outside tutoring. Their parents are also more likely to fill in the background knowledge that too often teachers assume their children have.

Poor students, on the other hand, are often terribly harmed by that isolation, in large part because their parents are less likely to notice deficits and less able to compensate for them. For the most part, parents living in poverty leave education to the schools—not because they don't care about their children's education but because they often don't feel competent to challenge the knowledge of teachers and because they're more likely to be overwhelmed with the daily logistics of life. This means low-income children are often completely reliant on their schools for their education.

When schools understand that and step up to the challenge—as George Hall, Graham Road, and many others have done—and set up the structures and systems that allow teachers to work together, even students burdened by poverty and discrimination can achieve remarkable success. That does not relieve us as a nation of the obligation to try to ensure that poverty becomes less common and less desperate. Nor does it relieve us of the obligation to provide low-income families with the social and health services that better allow children to learn. But it does require that we think deeply about how we organize schools.

But that raises something that George Hall's principal said to me. She and I were talking about how her students—most of whom live in isolated poverty—are now achieving at levels that in some ways exceed that of well-off, white students in wealthy parts of Mobile and elsewhere in Alabama. "It makes me wonder what they are doing in those schools," Tomlinson said. With students who have many more advantages than students at George Hall, few schools are outperforming George Hall. "I think they're coasting," she said.

I suspect a lot of schools are coasting on the advantages of their students. If they learned the lessons that high-performing schools that are also high-poverty and high-minority schools can teach us, our nation's academic achievement would soar.

Reference

Downey, Maureen. "Are They Unteachable?" *Atlanta Journal-Constitution*, June 15, 2009. www.ajc.com/opinion/content/opinion/stories/2009/06/15/learned_0615_2DOT.html

---

Karin Chenoweth is senior writer at *The Education Trust* and former education columnist at *The Washington Post*. She is author of *How It's Being Done: Urgent Lessons in Unexpected Schools* (2009).

Andy Smarick

 **NO**

The Turnaround Fallacy

For as long as there have been struggling schools in America's cities, there have been efforts to turn them around. The lure of dramatic improvement runs through Morgan Freeman's big-screen portrayal of bat-wielding principal Joe Clark, philanthropic initiatives like the Gates Foundation's "small schools" project, and No Child Left Behind (NCLB)'s restructuring mandate. The Obama administration hopes to extend this thread even further, making school turnarounds a top priority.

But overall, school turnaround efforts have consistently fallen far short of hopes and expectations. Quite simply, turnarounds are not a scalable strategy for fixing America's troubled urban school systems.

Fortunately, findings from two generations of school improvement efforts, lessons from similar work in other industries, and a budding practice among reform-minded superintendents are pointing to a promising alternative. When conscientiously applied strategies fail to drastically improve America's lowest-performing schools, we need to close them.

Done right, not only will this strategy help the students assigned to these failing schools, it will also have a cascading effect on other policies and practices, ultimately helping to bring about healthy systems of urban public schools.

A Body at Rest Stays at Rest

Looking back on the history of school turnaround efforts, the first and most important lesson is the "Law of Incessant Inertia." Once persistently low performing, the majority of schools will remain low performing despite being acted upon in innumerable ways.

Examples abound: In the first year of California's Academic Performance Index, the state targeted its lowest-performing 20 percent of schools for intervention. After three years, only 11 percent of the elementary schools in this category (109 of 968) were able to make "exemplary progress." Only 1 of the 394 middle and high schools in this category reached this mark. Just one-quarter of the schools were even able to accomplish a lesser goal: meeting schoolwide and subgroup growth targets each year.

In 2008, 52 Ohio schools were forced to restructure because of persistent failure. Even after several years of significant attention, fewer than one in three had been able to reach established academic goals, and less than half

showed any student performance gains. The *Columbus Dispatch* concluded, "Few of them have improved significantly even after years of effort and millions in tax dollars."

These state anecdotes align with national data on schools undergoing NCLB-mandated restructuring, the law's most serious intervention, which follows five or more years of failing to meet minimum achievement targets. Of the schools required to restructure in 2004–05, only 19 percent were able to exit improvement status two years later.

A 2008 Center on Education Policy (CEP) study investigated the results of restructuring in five states. In California, Maryland, and Ohio, only 14, 12, and 9 percent of schools in restructuring, respectively, made adequate yearly progress (AYP) as defined by NCLB the following year. And we must consider carefully whether merely making AYP should constitute success at all: in California, for example, a school can meet its performance target if slightly more than one-third of its students reach proficiency in English language arts and math. Though the CEP study found that improvement rates in Michigan and Georgia were considerably higher, Michigan changed its accountability system during this period, and both states set their AYP bars especially low.

Though alarming, the poor record for school turnarounds in recent years should come as no surprise. A study published in 2005 by the Education Commission of the States (ECS) on state takeovers of schools and districts noted that the takeovers "have yet to produce dramatic consistent increases in student performance," and that the impact on learning "falls short of expectations."

Reflecting on the wide array of efforts to improve failing schools, one set of analysts concluded, "Turnaround efforts have for the most part resulted in only marginal improvements. . . . Promising practices have failed to work at scale when imported to troubled schools."

Like Finding the Cure for Cancer

The second important lesson is the "Law of Ongoing Ignorance." Despite years of experience and great expenditures of time, money, and energy, we still lack basic information about which tactics will make a struggling school excellent. A review published in January 2003 by the Thomas B. Fordham Foundation of more than 100 books, articles, and briefs on turnaround efforts concluded, "There is, at present, no strong evidence that any particular intervention type works most of the time or in most places."

An EdSource study that sought to compare California's low-performing schools that failed to make progress to its low-performing schools that did improve came to a confounding conclusion: clear differences avoided detection. Comparing the two groups, the authors noted, "These were schools in the same cities and districts, often serving children from the same backgrounds. Some of them also adopted the same curriculum programs, had teachers with similar backgrounds, and had similar opportunities for professional development."

Maryland's veteran state superintendent of schools, Nancy Grasmick, agrees: "Very little research exists on how to bring about real sea change in schools. . . . Clearly, there's no infallible strategy or even sequence of them." Responding to the growing number of failing Baltimore schools requiring state-approved improvement plans, she said, "No one has the answer. It's like finding the cure for cancer."

Researchers have openly lamented the lack of reliable information pointing to or explaining successful improvement efforts, describing the literature as "sparse" and "scarce." Those attempting to help others fix broken schools have typically resorted to identifying activities in improved schools, such as bolstering leadership and collecting data.

However, this case-study style of analysis is deeply flawed. As the U.S. Department of Education's Institute of Education Sciences (IES) has noted, studies "that look back at factors that may have contributed to [a] school's success" are "particularly weak in determining causal validity for several reasons, including the fact that there is no way to be confident that the features common to successful turnaround schools are not also common to schools that fail."

Researchers have noted that the Department of Education has signaled its own ignorance about what to do about the nation's very worst schools. One study reported, "The NCLB law does not specify any additional actions for schools that remain in the implementation phase of restructuring for more than one year, and [the Department] has offered little guidance on what to do about persistently struggling schools." Indeed, the IES publication, "Turning Around Chronically Low-Performing Schools" practice guide, purportedly a resource for states and districts, concedes, "All recommendations had to rely on low levels of evidence," because it could not identify any rigorous studies finding that "specific turnaround practices produce significantly better academic outcomes."

Still in Its Infancy?

The prevailing view is that we must keep looking for turnaround solutions. Observers have written, "Turnaround at scale is still in its infancy," and "In education, turnarounds have been tried rarely" (see "The Big U-Turn," *features*, Winter 2009). But, in fact, the number and scope of fix-it efforts have been extensive to say the least.

Long before NCLB required interventions in the lowest-performing schools, states had undertaken significant activity. In 1989 New Jersey took over Jersey City Public Schools; in 1995 it took over Newark Public Schools. In 1993 California took control of the Compton Unified School District. In 1995 Ohio took over the Cleveland Metropolitan School District. Between 1993 and 1997 states required the reconstitution of failing schools in Denver, Chicago, New York City, and Houston. In 2000 Alabama took over a number of schools across the state, and Maryland seized control of three schools in Baltimore.

Since NCLB, interventions in struggling schools have only grown in number and intensity. In the 2006–07 school year, more than 750 schools in "corrective action," the NCLB phase preceding restructuring, implemented a new research-based curriculum, more than 700 used an outside expert to advise the school, nearly 400 restructured the internal organization of the school, and more than 200 extended the school day or year. Importantly, more than 300 replaced staff members or the principal, among the toughest traditional interventions possible.

Occasionally a program will report encouraging success rates. The University of Virginia School Turnaround Specialist Program asserts that about half of its targeted schools have either made AYP or reduced math and reading failure rates by at least 5 percent. Though this might be better than would otherwise be expected, the threshold for success is remarkably low. It is also unknown whether such progress can be sustained. This matter is particularly important, given that some point to charter management organizations Green Dot and Mastery as turnaround success stories even though each has a very short turnaround résumé, in both numbers of schools and years of experience.

Many schools that reach NCLB's restructuring phase, rather than implementing one of the law's stated interventions (close and reopen as a charter school, replace staff, turn the school over to the state, or contract with an outside entity), choose the "other" option, under which they have considerable flexibility to design an improvement strategy of their own (see "Easy Way Out," *forum*, Winter 2007). Some call this a "loophole" for avoiding tough action.

Yet even under the maligned "other" option, states and districts have tried an astonishing array of improvement strategies, including different types of school-level needs assessments, surveys of school staff, conferences, professional development, turnaround specialists, school improvement committees, training sessions, principal mentors, teacher coaches, leadership facilitators, instructional trainers, subject-matter experts, audits, summer residential academies, student tutoring, research-based reform models, reconfigured grade spans, alternative governance models, new curricula, improved use of data, and turning over operation of some schools to outside organizations.

It's simply impossible to make the case that turnaround efforts haven't been tried or given a chance to work.

A Better Mousetrap?

Despite this evidence, some continue to advocate for improved turnaround efforts. Nancy Grasmick supports recognizing turnarounds as a unique discipline. Frederick Hess and Thomas Gift have argued for developing school restructuring leaders; Bryan Hassel and Emily Ayscue Hassel have recommended that states and districts "fuel the pipeline" of untraditional turnaround specialists. NewSchools Venture Fund, the Education Commission of the States, and the research firm Mass Insight have offered related turnaround strategies.

And the Obama administration too has bought into the notion that turnarounds are the key to improving urban districts. Education secretary Arne Duncan has said that if the nation could turn around 1,000 schools annually for five years, "We could really move the needle, lift the bottom and change the lives of tens of millions of underserved children." In the administration's 2009 stimulus legislation, $3 billion in new funds were appropriated for School Improvement Grants, which aid schools in NCLB improvement status. The administration requested an additional $1.5 billion for this program in the 2010 budget. This is all on top of the numerous streams of existing federal funds that can be—and have been—used to turn around failing schools.

The dissonance is deafening. The history of urban education tells us emphatically that turnarounds are not a reliable strategy for improving our very worst schools. So why does there remain a stubborn insistence on preserving fix-it efforts?

The most common, but also the most deeply flawed, justification is that there are high-performing schools in American cities. That is, some fix-it proponents point to unarguably successful urban schools and then infer that scalable turnaround strategies are within reach. In fact, it has become fashionable among turnaround advocates to repeat philosopher Immanuel Kant's adage that "the actual proves the possible."

But as a Thomas B. Fordham Foundation study noted, "Much is known about how effective schools work, but it is far less clear how to move an ineffective school from failure to success. . . . Being a high-performing school and becoming a high-performing school are very different challenges."

In fact, America's most-famous superior urban schools are virtually always new starts rather than schools that were previously underperforming. Probably the most convincing argument for the fundamental difference between start-ups and turnarounds comes from those actually running high-performing high-poverty urban schools. Groups like KIPP (Knowledge Is Power Program) and Achievement First open new schools; as a rule they don't reform failing schools. KIPP's lone foray into turnarounds closed after only two years, and the organization abandoned further turnaround initiatives. Said KIPP's spokesman, "Our core competency is starting and running new schools."

A 2006 NewSchools Venture Fund study confirmed a widespread aversion to takeover-and-turnaround strategies among successful school operators. Only 4 of 36 organizations interviewed expressed interest in restructuring existing schools. Remarkably, rather than trusting successful school operators' track records and informed opinion that start-ups are the way to go, Secretary Duncan urged them to get into the turnaround business during a speech at the 2009 National Charter Schools Conference.

The findings above deserve repeating: Fix-it efforts at the worst schools have consistently failed to generate significant improvement. Our knowledge base about improving failing schools is still staggeringly small. And exceptional urban schools are nearly always start-ups or consistently excellent schools, not drastically improved once-failing schools.

So when considering turnaround efforts we should stop repeating, "The actual proves the possible" and bear in mind a different Kant adage: "Ought implies can."

If we are going to tell states and districts that they must fix all of their failing schools, or if we are to consider it a moral obligation to radically improve such schools, we should be certain that this endeavor is possible. But there is no reason to believe it is.

Turnarounds Elsewhere

Education leaders seem to believe that, outside of the world of schools, persistent failures are easily fixed. Far from it. The limited success of turnarounds is a common theme in other fields. Writing in *Public Money & Management*, researchers familiar with the true private-sector track record offered a word of caution: "There is a risk that politicians, government officials, and others, newly enamored of the language of failure and turnaround and inadequately informed of the empirical evidence and practical experience in the for-profit sector . . . will have unrealistic expectations of the transformative power of the turnaround process."

Hess and Gift reviewed the success rates of Total Quality Management (TQM) and Business Process Reengineering (BPR), the two most common approaches to organizational reform in the private sector. The literature suggests that both have failed to generate the desired results two-thirds of the time or more. They concluded, "The hope that we can systematically turn around all troubled schools—or even a majority of them—is at odds with much of what we know from similar efforts in the private sector."

Many have noted that flexibility and dynamism are part of the genetic code of private business, so we should expect these organizations to be more receptive to the massive changes required by a turnaround process than institutions set in what Hess calls the "political, regulatory, and contractual morass of K–12 schooling." Accordingly, school turnarounds should be more difficult to achieve. Indeed, a consultant with the Bridgespan Group reported, "Turnarounds in the public education space are far harder than any turnaround I've ever seen in the for-profit space."

Building a Healthy Education Industry

We shouldn't be surprised then that turnarounds in urban education have largely failed. The surprise and shame is that urban public education, unlike nearly every other industry, profession, and field, has never developed a sensible solution to its continuous failures. After undergoing improvement efforts, a struggling private firm that continues to lose money will close, get taken over, or go bankrupt. Unfit elected officials are voted out of office. The worst lawyers can be disbarred, and the most negligent doctors can lose their licenses. Urban school districts, at long last, need an equivalent.

The beginning of the solution is establishing a clear process for closing schools. The simplest and best way to put this into operation is the charter model. Each school, in conjunction with the state or district, would develop a five-year contract with performance measures. Consistent failure to meet goals in key areas would result in closure. Alternatively, the state could decide that districts only have one option—not five—for schools reaching NCLB-mandated restructuring: closure.

This would have three benefits. First, children would no longer be subjected to schools with long track records of failure and high probabilities of continued failure.

Second, the fear of closure might generate improvement in some low-performing schools. Failure in public education has had fewer consequences (for adults) than in other fields, a fact that might contribute to the persistent struggles of some schools. We should have limited expectations in this regard, however. Even in the private sector, where the consequences for poor performance are significant, some low-performing entities never become successful.

Third, and by far the most important and least appreciated factor, closures make room for replacements, which have a transformative positive impact on the health of a field. When a firm folds due to poor performance, the slack is taken up by the expansion of successful existing firms—meaning that those excelling have the opportunity to do more—or by new firms. New entrants not only fill gaps, they have a tendency to better reflect current market conditions. They are also far likelier to introduce innovations: Google, Facebook, and Twitter were not products of long-standing firms. Certainly not all new starts will excel, not in education, not in any field. But when provided the right characteristics and environment, their potential is vast.

The churn caused by closures isn't something to be feared; on the contrary, it's a familiar prerequisite for industry health. Richard Foster and Sarah Kaplan's brilliant 2001 book *Creative Destruction* catalogued the ubiquity of turnover in thriving industries, including the eventual loss of once-dominant players. Churn generates new ideas, ensures responsiveness, facilitates needed change, and empowers the best to do more.

These principles can be translated easily into urban public education via tools already at our fingertips thanks to chartering: start-ups, replications, and expansions. Chartering has enabled new school starts for nearly 20 years and school replications and expansions for a decade. Chartering has demonstrated clearly that the ingredients of healthy, orderly churn can be brought to bear on public education.

A small number of progressive leaders of major urban school systems are using school closure and replacement to transform their long-broken districts: Under Chancellor Joel Klein, New York City has closed nearly 100 traditional public schools and opened more than 300 new schools. In 2004, Chicago announced the Renaissance 2010 project, which is built around closing chronically failing schools and opening 100 new public schools by the end of the decade.

Numerous other big-city districts are in the process of closing troubled schools, including Detroit, Philadelphia, and Washington, D.C. In Baltimore, under schools CEO Andrés Alonso, reform's guiding principles include "Closing schools that don't work for our kids," "Creating new options that have strong chances of success," and "Expanding some programs that are already proving effective."

Equally encouraging, there are indications that these ideas, which once would have been considered heretical, are being embraced by education's cognoscenti. A group of leading reformers, the Coalition for Student Achievement, published a document in April 2009 that offered ideas for the best use of the federal government's $100 billion in stimulus funding. They recommended that each state develop a mechanism to "close its lowest performing five percent of schools and replace them with higher-performing, new schools including public charter schools."

A generation ago, few would have believed that such a fundamental overhaul of urban districts was on the horizon, much less that perennial underperformers New York City, Chicago, and Baltimore would be at the front of the pack with much of the education establishment and reform community in tow. But, consciously or not, these cities have begun internalizing the lessons of healthy industries and the chartering mechanism, which, if vigorously applied to urban schooling, have extraordinary potential. Best of all, these districts and outstanding charter leaders like KIPP Houston (with 15 schools already and dozens more planned) and Green Dot (which opened 5 new schools surrounding one of Los Angeles's worst high schools) are showing that the formula boils down to four simple but eminently sensible steps: close failing schools, open new schools, replicate great schools, repeat.

Today's fixation with fix-it efforts is misguided. Turnarounds have consistently shown themselves to be ineffective—truly an unscalable strategy for improving urban districts—and our relentless preoccupation with improving the worst schools actually inhibits the development of a healthy urban public-education industry.

Those hesitant about replacing turnarounds with closures should simply remember that a failed business doesn't indict capitalism and an unseated incumbent doesn't indict democracy. Though temporarily painful, both are essential mechanisms for maintaining long-term systemwide quality, responsiveness, and innovation.

Closing America's worst urban schools doesn't indict public education nor does it suggest a lack of commitment to disadvantaged students. On the contrary, it reflects our insistence on finally taking the steps necessary to build city school systems that work for the boys and girls most in need.

ANDY SMARICK is visiting fellow at the Thomas B. Fordham Institute and adjunct fellow at the American Enterprise Institute. He recently became Deputy Commissioner of the New Jersey Department of Education.

EXPLORING THE ISSUE

Can Failing Schools Be Turned Around?

Critical Thinking and Reflection

1. What is the true definition of a school that has been "turned around"?
2. What are turnaround specialists, what do they do and how successful are they?
3. How does research connect with turnaround schools?
4. What is done differently in schools that are successful in "turning around"?
5. What impact will new NCLB legislation have on turnaround schools?

Is There Common Ground?

Public schools in high-poverty areas, especially those in large urban centers, have historically suffered from neglect and underfunding. Recent budget shortfalls and declining enrollments have accelerated school closures in Chicago, Detroit, New Orleans, New York, Cleveland, Milwaukee, St. Louis, Kansas City, and Denver, creating what Monica Martinez characterizes as "Learning Deserts" in her February 2011 *Phi Delta Kappan* article. Those who champion the turnaround strategy believe that closing schools only contributes to the abandonment of urban communities, Martinez states. Others, who embrace charter alternatives, see hope in organizations attracting outside funding "to build portfolios of schools that encompass a variety of educational approaches offered by different vendors in an attempt to address intractable problems in public schools."

An analysis that goes beyond the turnarounds versus charters issue is presented in Jung-ah Choi's "Reading Educational Philosophies in Freedom Writers," *The Clearing House* (May/June 2009). The author extracts four basic philosophical elements that steered the inner-city teacher's success in the film Freedom Writers. They were the following: rewriting the curriculum, treating students as creators of knowledge, classroom community-building, and seeing teaching as self-realization. This entails a refusal to mechanically follow the prescribed curriculum, no longer treating students as mere recipients of knowledge, moving toward a more egalitarian relationship between teachers and students, and elevating the "job" of teaching to a teaching "career."

Another slant on the issue concentrates on the wider social factors impinging upon school quality. This is treated in a Winter 2010 *Education Next* forum titled "Poor Schools or Poor Kids?" The forum features interviews with Joe Williams of the Education Equality Project and Pedro Noguera of "A Broader, Bolder Approach to Education." Among other provocative viewpoints worth considering are the following: "Tackling the Toughest Turnaround—Low-Performing High Schools." *Phi Delta Kappan* (February 2011) by Daniel L. Duke and Martha Jacobson; "Is Education the Cure for Poverty?" *The American Prospect* (May 2007) by Jared Bernstein; "Are Teachers Responsible for Low Achievement by Poor Students?" *Kappa Delta Pi Record* (Fall 2009) by David C. Berliner; and "Hidden Assumptions, Attitudes, and Procedures in Failing Schools," *Educational Horizons* (Winter 2008) by Betsy Gunzelmann.

Create Central

www.mhhe.com/createcentral

Additional Resources

Belinda Williams, *Closing the Achievement Gap: A Vision for Changing Beliefs and Practices*, 2nd ed. (2003).

David Whitman, *Sweating the Small Stuff: Inner-City Schools and the New Paternalism* (2008).

Jamie Vollmer, *Schools Cannot Do It Alone* (2010).

Kathryn M. Neckermann, *Schools Betrayed* (2007).

Laura Pappano, *Inside School Turnarounds* (2010).

Internet References . . .

Turnaround Schools

www.edweek.org/ew/collections/turnaround-schools/

Turning Around Low-Performing Schools in Chicago

http://ccsr.uchicago.edu/sites/default/files/
publications/12CCSRTurnAround-3.pdf

Turnaround Schools (online only)

www.ascd.org/publications/educational-leadership/
summer05/vol62/num09/toc.aspx

School Turnaround Group

www.massinsight.org/stg/

No Excuses University

http://noexcusesu.com/

Selected, Edited, and with Issue Framing Material by:
Glenn L. Koonce, *Regent University*

ISSUE

Are Local School Boards Obsolete?

YES: **Marc Tucker**, from "Changing the System Is the Only Solution," *Phi Delta Kappan* (March 2010)

NO: **Diane Ravitch**, from "Why Public Schools Need Democratic Governance," *Phi Delta Kappan* (March 2010)

Learning Outcomes
After reading this issue, you will be able to: • Distinguish between local school board authority and state authority for school operations. • Explore the decentralized system of public schools found in the United States. • Reflect on the notion of school boards getting out of the business of running schools and focus only on student learning. • Compare schools run by school boards and those run by mayors of a city. • Compile a list of legislative mandates that school boards must follow.

ISSUE SUMMARY

YES: Marc Tucker, president of the National Center on Education and the Economy, calls for shifting the running of public schools to the states, allowing local boards to focus solely on the improvement of learning.

NO: Education historian Diane Ravitch feels that a movement of control to the state level or to the mayor's office will undermine democratic deliberation and move toward a top-down business model.

The American "system" of public schools is one of the most decentralized in the world. Historically, there has been no centralized ministry of education as is the case in many European countries, no national curriculum, no national standards, no national examinations. According to *School: The Story of American Public Education* (2001), edited by Sarah Mondale and Sarah B. Patton (and aired as a PBS special program), by the late nineteenth century local school board membership in the United States was "the largest group of public officials in the world. Education historian Diane Ravitch characterized the developmental years of public schooling as a time when local boards made all of the important decisions about curriculum and personnel, teachers had minimal training, state departments of education had little or no control over local school districts, and federal officials "merely collected and disseminated statistics." Some politically appointed boards were guilty of nepotism and "cronyism" and even those elected by the people (often in low-turnout contests) operated the schools with great frugality and often imposed "provincial ideas and standards." Some boards were taken over by fringe political groups that banned supposedly offensive books (a practice still going on today) and forced teachers to use outdated but "approved" curriculum materials. The

twentieth century saw increasing consolidation of small districts and the assertion of more power by state authorities. By the midpoint of the century political support of federal aid to the nation's public schools grew, culminating in the 1965 Elementary and Secondary Education Act which earmarked poverty-area schools and improvement of math and science instruction, among other things. The current manifestation of this act is No Child Left Behind. With the establishment of the U.S. Department of Education by the Carter administration, the expansion of federal authority over what is legally a state function was set in motion. The fact that some local school boards have not been able to lift student performance levels or close achievement gaps among racial or ethnic groups has opened the door to increased federal and state control. In some large cities, such as Boston, Chicago, Detroit, and New York, mayors have asserted control. This phenomenon is detailed in *When Mayors Take Charge: School Governance in the City* (2009), edited by Joseph P. Viteritti. The shift in power from local school boards to higher levels of government is also treated in Paul E. Peterson's *Saving Schools: From Horace Mann to Virtual Learning* (2010).

The diminishment of local school board power has been welcomed in some quarters. In "First, Kill All the School Boards," *The Atlantic* (January/February 2008),

Matt Miller of the Center for American Progress bemoans the fact that the American obsession with local control still dominates our schools, an artifact of our Colonial past, an iconic symbol of democratic American learning. Miller quotes Mark Twain: "In the first place, God made idiots. This was for practice. Then He made School Boards." He concludes that we should continue the move toward nationalizing our schools even though it goes against every cultural tradition we have. And as this sentiment gains ascendency, school board members, stressed by the weight of federal mandates and regulations, are developing a sense of caution and powerlessness.

A variety of views in support of local school boards were expressed in the March 2010 issue of *Phi Delta Kappan*. In "School Boards: A Neglected Institution in an Era of School Reform" Michael D. Usdan argues that if comprehensive national reforms are to be sustained they will need the support and understanding of local authorities, school boards that are here to stay at least for the immediate future. In "School Boards: Why American Education Needs Them" Michael A. Resnick and Anne L. Bryant see local boards as essential in the task of connecting federal and state laws and strategies with the "real and diverse world of local people in a way that is close to the community and accountable to it."

The YES and NO articles are also from the March 2010 *Phi Delta Kappan*. In the YES article, Marc Tucker wants states to staff the schools and to form partnerships of teachers to run them. In the NO article, Diane Ravitch warns that elimination of local school boards will end budgetary transparency and obliterate a needed forum for parents.

YES ↵

Marc Tucker

Changing the System Is the Only Solution

Long ago, I was a member of the school board in my home town. I've been an observer of school governance in the United States ever since. I come away from these experiences humbled by memories of the countless unpaid hours of hard work put in by people, often good friends, on school boards across the country, people whose contribution to the improvement of the schools is obvious and vital. But I'm also haunted by other observations.

In many suburban and rural districts, board members are made to feel that they have no business involving themselves in educational issues, which, they are told, ought to be the province of the professionals. In districts of all sizes, it is assumed that boards will have a major say in who is hired and who cannot be fired, with all the opportunities for the exchange of favors those relationships imply. Others run for the opportunity to control the letting of contracts by the district, often one of the largest organizations in town, with all the opportunities for the exchange of favors that implies. Although management is often successful at keeping school board members away from strictly educational decisions, school board members almost everywhere have strong incentives to micromanage in other arenas and to serve as advocates for individual parents and staff members in ways that time and again defeat sound management of the schools. For a very long time, superintendents were hired based on considerations other than their record in improving student performance and were fired despite their strong history of improving student performance, and that is still true in all too many districts. To a degree that still might shock many voters, the arguments about school policy are arguments among adults about which adults get what benefits from the school system, not about how to make the most of the district's resources to improve the achievement of students.

Most school board members, superintendents, teachers, and union chiefs are doing the best they can. But they're caught in a system that is dysfunctional.

The problems I just pointed to are not the inevitable consequence of living in a democracy. There are other, better ways to run school districts.

Change Hiring Practices

First, states, not local districts, should hire and employ teachers. That's the only way to break the connection between teacher quality and local taxable wealth. Until that connection is broken, this country will never have an education system that provides a fair chance to all children. Furthermore, if the state employs the teachers, the people who hope to control the patronage system will no longer run for school board.

This also means that bargaining teacher contracts would no longer be a local district responsibility. Instead, bargaining would occur at the state level. This would place both partners in the bargaining on a more even level than is often the case with local bargaining.

Bargaining would focus on pay and working conditions, and those would be narrowly defined. The teacher partnerships that are described below would determine the actual working conditions, just as is the case in other professional partnerships.

Changing teacher employment, of course, changes the role of teacher associations. At the state level, teacher associations would do more than hold on to their union role; they would also assume a new role. Like most other state and national professional associations, the teacher associations would become a principal source for continuing professional development for educators, providing an unending program of courses and seminars for professional teachers across the country. That is what other professional associations do, besides representing their members in Washington and state capitals.

New Role for School Boards

Second, school boards should get out of the business of running schools and focus on improving student learning.

In my scenario, local school districts would no longer own schools. Instead, school boards would contract with third parties to run their schools. These third parties would be partnerships of teachers, organized as companies. These partnerships of teachers would compete with each other to run the schools in the district.

Partnerships that win the right to run a school would receive a performance contract from the district. That contract would specify what and how much students should learn in order to be ready for college when they graduate. The contract would specify how much money the school would receive if students achieve at that level by the end of the year. The contract also would specify a higher level of student achievement that would trigger a bonus payment to the school. Likewise, the contract would spell out the consequences if student performance falls below a specified level after a certain number of years. The consequences should include losing the contract and opening up the competition process anew. The value of the contract doesn't need to depend entirely on student performance as measured by examinations, but that performance would count for a lot.

Partnerships that win these contracts would get a lump sum to run the school. That sum would include the money needed to fund most of the services now provided by the district. The school could buy services from the district, or it could buy services from other providers. The partnership would have an enormous incentive to get the best services for the lowest cost because the personal income of the members of the partnership would depend on it.

The lump sum payment would include an amount for the space needed to run the school. Districts could lease their school buildings to the partnerships, but the partnerships could also lease them from others or create corporations to get mortgage loans to build the buildings and then lease the buildings back from these corporations. The lump sum payments to the partnerships would also include the money required for building maintenance, utilities, and so on.

No Longer a Stepping Stone

In the world I have in mind, people who run for school boards hoping to use the position as a stepping stone to higher office and to gain control of vital community economic functions for their own advancement would no longer do so because the board would no longer control many jobs or services or supply contracts.

Those who run for school board to make a contribution to improving student performance would be more likely to do so because that would be the primary function of the board and they would see that they would have a much improved chance of being joined by other similarly motivated people. Similarly, people who want their schools to reflect the particular needs and character of their community would be more likely to run because formulating the criteria for the school performance contracts would be an important role of the board and a great opportunity to help define what the community wants in its schools, not as a rhetorical exercise, but as the pivot point for contract requirements. School boards would be the sounding board for the community on the strengths and weaknesses of the partnerships providing the school services and would be in the best position to communicate to those providers what they need to do if they want to continue to serve. This emphasis on performance and responsiveness would be the heart of the job. In this system, micromanagement and grandstanding would not be rewarded, but patient service to the community and a genuine contribution to the steady improvement of school performance would.

District staffs would be much leaner, especially in large districts. Much more of the available funds would go to the schools. Teachers would have an incentive to increase class size because the fewer the teachers employed at the school, the more each teacher will be paid, but they would not have an incentive to increase class size to a point where it lowered student performance because their pay would be based on that performance.

The teachers would not put up with work rules that lowered their productivity, because doing so would lower their paycheck. Teachers running the schools would have an incentive to hire the very best teachers and to get rid of teachers who couldn't cut it. They'd also have an incentive to work as hard as they could to get the best results they could for the students. And they'd look for the best value for their money when buying services for the school.

Funding Schools

Principals would no longer have an incentive to spend half their time downtown lobbying the central office for resources, because a formula would determine school funds and those funds would be distributed by the state to the school in one lump sum. The formula would ensure that schools with large proportions of poor, minority, and handicapped children would get substantially more than schools with less challenged populations. The best teachers and principals, instead of fleeing the schools that need them the most, would have an incentive to serve in those well-funded schools.

Districts would be obligated to make sure that there were sufficient places for all the students who needed places. The competitive, data-based market, combined with the performance contracts themselves, would create schools that were constantly seeking to improve their performance year in and year out. The fact that schools serving students from low-income families and other categories of disadvantaged students would get substantially more money than schools with more advantaged student bodies would ensure that these students would be served by high-quality school operators. It would be very hard for low-quality school operators to survive in this environment.

Parents would be seen as customers instead of being viewed as annoying amateurs and persistent rule-breakers where their children's interests are concerned. They would be courted. Teachers would take the time and trouble to help parents learn how to support their children because they would understand the importance of parental encouragement and involvement in learning.

In this system, the district central staff would be responsible for running the performance management system, which anyone with experience with such systems in private industry will tell you is very demanding. It requires clear specification of what is wanted by the community from its schools, with clear measures, the development of high-quality requests for proposals, active recruitment of potential contractors, a careful review of proposals and effective negotiations over the contracts awarded, the constant collection and monitoring of performance data of all kinds, guidance to the contractors intended to help them perform well, and appropriate action when they do not. Many districts will also want to remain active providers of the myriad services that schools need, and they will certainly be able to do so, provided that they can do so effectively and efficiently in the new competitive climate. And the district will still play an important mediating role between the community at large and its schools, on many fronts.

Conclusion

This vision is very different from the current reality. You may not be very comfortable with it. Before you reject it, though, I urge you to stop and think. The American way of governing our schools is almost unique in the industrialized world. So is our high cost and relatively poor performance. Do you really think things are fine just as they are? If you do not like my proposals, what would you do?

MARC TUCKER is president of the National Center on Education and the Economy and was vice chair of the New Commission on the Skills of the American Workforce.

Diane Ravitch   → **NO**

Why Public Schools Need Democratic Governance

Every time some expert, public official, or advocate declares that our public schools are in crisis, stop, listen, and see what he or she is selling. In the history of American education, crisis talk is cheap. Those who talk crisis usually have a cure that they want to promote, and they prefer to keep us focused on the dimensions of the "crisis" without looking too closely at their proposed cure.

The crisis talkers today want to diminish the role of local school boards and increase the privatization of public education. They recite the familiar statistics about mediocre student performance on international tests, and they conclude that bold action is needed and there is no time to delay or ponder. Local school boards insist on deliberation; they give parents and teachers a place to speak out and perhaps oppose whatever bold actions are on the table. So, in the eyes of some of our current crop of school reformers, local school boards are the problem that is blocking the reforms we need. The "reformers" want action, not deliberation.

Local school boards have not been enthusiastic, for example, about privatization of public schools. More often than not, they're skeptical that private entrepreneurs will be more successful running schools than experienced educators. Nor are they eager to open charter schools, which drain away resources and students from the regular schools and have the freedom to remove the students who are most difficult to educate. Local school boards have also been an obstacle to those who want to replace experienced principals and teachers with enthusiastic neophytes.

Local school boards are right to be wary of the latest fad. Our education system tends to embrace "reforms" too quickly, without adequate evidence of their value. Here's just one example from the many I could cite. In 1959, James Conant, the president of Harvard University, led a campaign against small high schools. He said they were inefficient and unable to supply a full curriculum. He called for consolidation of small districts and small high schools, so we could have the advantages of scale. Conant was featured on the cover of *Time*, and suddenly large high schools were the leading edge of reform. In our own time, the Bill & Melinda Gates Foundation poured $2 billion into breaking up large high schools and turning them into small high schools. Now, the Gates Foundation has decided that wasn't such a good idea, and it's off on another tangent, offering rewards to districts that evaluate teachers by their students' test scores.

Today, the public schools once again have a plethora of critics. Some say that public education itself is obsolete. There is a large and growing movement to dismantle public education. Some critics want to get rid of public education and replace it with a completely choice-based system of vouchers and charter schools. Proponents of this view say the market and choice are the only mechanisms that will produce high achievement. Government, they say, has failed. They believe—naively, I think—that in an open market, good schools would thrive and bad ones would die. Personally, I think this is a ludicrous analysis to apply to public education, which is a public good, not a private good or a commodity. As a society, we have a legal, moral, and social responsibility to provide a good public school in every neighborhood and not to leave this vital task to the free-market and not to take unconscionable risks with the lives of vulnerable children.

First Line of Defense

The local school boards are the first line of defense for public education. Critics know this. In 2008, an article in *The Atlantic* was titled "First, Kill All the School Boards." It was written not by a right-wing extremist or a libertarian, but by Matt Miller of the Center for American Progress, whose president, John Podesta, led the Obama transition team. Miller argued that local control and local school boards are the basic cause of poor student performance. He said the federal government should take control of the nation's schools, set national standards, eliminate teacher tenure, and tie teacher pay to student performance. In an ideal world, he wrote, we would scrap local boards and replace them with mayoral control, especially in urban districts. This one act of removing all democratic governance, he claimed, would lead to better education.

This argument lacks logic and evidence. Some localities have high achievement, some have low, and the difference is economics and demography, not democracy. There is not a shred of evidence in Miller's article or in the research literature that schools improve when democratic governance ends.

In a similar vein, *Tough Choices or Tough Times*, a report prepared by the New Commission on the Skills of the American Workforce, proposed turning over all public schools to private managers. The role of school boards would be limited to approving performance contracts with these independent managers, monitoring their performance, and closing schools that didn't meet their goals. Under this proposal, signed by many of our most eminent leaders, local government would get out of the business of running public schools. In effect, every school would be a privately managed school.

Why would schools get better if they're managed by private companies? What secret do private sector organizations have that hasn't been shared with state and local education leaders? What's the logical connection between privatization and quality education? Why are they so certain that any privately managed school will be better than any regular public school?

The recommendation for universal privatization is irresponsible. You don't rip apart a vital part of the nation's social fabric—its public schools—because it sounds like a good idea. You don't destroy democratic governance of public education because of a hunch.

New York Experience

As it happens, New York City has already created a test case of what happens when the local school board is rendered toothless. In 2002, the state legislature turned over control of the school system to the city's newly elected mayor, Michael Bloomberg. The legislation continued a central board, but abolished the city's 32 local school boards. The central board, however, consisted only of appointees who serve at the pleasure of the person who appointed them. Of its 13 members, eight serve at the pleasure of the mayor, and the remaining five serve at the pleasure of the borough presidents who appointed them.

The mayor immediately demonstrated that the new central board was of no importance. He renamed it the Panel for Educational Policy. When he introduced its members at a press conference, he made clear that they would not be speaking out on anything. He said, "They don't have to speak, and they don't have to serve. That's what 'serving at the pleasure' means" (Hernandez 2009). On a rare occasion, when two of his appointees planned to vote against his plan to end social promotion for 3rd graders, he fired them and replaced them on the same day. This central board, which was supposed to provide oversight and a check on the mayor's extraordinary power over the schools, was reduced to a rubber stamp.

Only one borough president appointed a representative who dared to ask questions. Patrick J. Sullivan, a business executive, was appointed to the central board in 2007 as a parent member. Before his term began, he sat in on a meeting and watched the board approve a $17 billion budget, a major labor contract, and a new database costing $80 million, all in less than an hour. He observed that, "The Panel for Educational Policy seemed more a misplaced relic of the Brezhnev-era Soviet Union than a functioning board of directors overseeing the education of 1.1 million children" (2009).

The board exists to do whatever the mayor and chancellor want, not to exercise independent judgment. Sullivan reported that board members seldom had presentation materials in advance. Votes are cast before hearing public comments, not after, as is typical of other public boards. Although the law specified that the board would meet at least once a year in executive session, no such meeting was held in Sullivan's first two years on the board. Time and again, when controversial issues came up, Sullivan was the only dissenting voice on the panel.

When mayoral control of the schools came up for reauthorization before the New York state legislature in 2009, the mayor waged a heavily financed campaign to maintain his complete control of the school system. His advocacy group received millions of dollars from the Bill & Melinda Gates Foundation, the Broad Foundation, and other foundations. On one point, the mayor drew a line: He did not want any board members to serve for a fixed term, even if he appointed them. They must continue to serve at his pleasure. When Citizens Union, a respected civic organization, was considering the possibility of issuing a statement on behalf of fixed terms, it received a personal letter from U.S. Secretary of Education Arne Duncan, opposing fixed terms for any appointees and insisting that the mayor could be effective only if he had complete control.

Because New York City no longer has an independent board of education, it no longer has democratic control of its public education system. There is no forum in which parents and other members of the public can ask questions and get timely answers. Major decisions about the school system are made in private, behind closed doors, with no public review and no public discussion.

Because New York City no longer has an independent board of education, there are no checks or balances, no questioning of executive authority. A contract was awarded for nearly $16 million to the business consulting firm of Alvarez & Marsal to review operations and cut spending. This firm rearranged the city's complex school bus routes and stranded thousands of young children on one of the coldest days of the year without any means of getting to school. Some of the chaos they created might have been averted had there been public review and discussion of their plans. No one was held accountable for their mistakes; they were not chastised, and their contract was not terminated.

Similarly, the Department of Education imposed a grading system on every school in the city. In the name of accountability, each school is given a single letter grade from A to F, not a report card. The grade depends mainly on improvement, not on performance. Some outstanding schools, where more than 90% of the students meet state standards, got an F because they didn't make progress, while some really low-performing schools, even persistently dangerous ones, got an A because they saw a one-year gain in their scores. This approach was imposed without public discussion or review. The result was a very bad policy that stigmatizes some very good schools and helps none. The lesson is, or should be, that public discussion can prevent or mitigate policy errors.

In the absence of an independent board, there is no transparency of budget. There is no public forum in which questions are asked and answered about how the public's money is spent. Consequently, the number and size of no-bid contracts for consultants and vendors have soared into the hundreds of millions of dollars, with no public review or oversight. The education budget has grown from $12 billion annually to nearly $22 billion.

In the absence of a school board to oversee the actions of the executive, there is no accountability. The mayor can do as he wishes in the schools. The chancellor can adopt any policies he wishes; he serves at the pleasure of the mayor and answers to no one else. When a school fails or many schools fail, only the principal is held accountable. Those at headquarters who impose policies and programs are never held accountable.

All this unchecked authority has been used to turn New York City's public schools into a demonstration of choice and free markets in education. Children may choose among 400 or so high schools. They may choose from among 100 charter schools. If the school is successful or popular, students must enter a lottery or go onto a waiting list. In many of the poorest neighborhoods, the number of charter schools has increased, and many have been given space in neighborhood public schools. New York City might be the only district in the nation that places charter schools in public school buildings, taking away space previously allocated to art rooms, music rooms, computer rooms, and other activities. Parents and teachers have protested, but the mayor continues to place charters in public school buildings. By the end of the mayor's third term, there may be neighborhoods that have no public schools, just charters to which students seek entry.

The mayor has promised to open yet another 100 charter schools because he believes that schools should function like a marketplace, with choice and competition. Parents must struggle to get their child into the right high school, the right middle school, or the right charter school. Sustaining and improving regular public schools,

neighborhood public schools, has low priority in the new world of the business model in education.

This business model has impressed the Obama Administration. Secretary Duncan has strongly endorsed mayoral control as a means to improve achievement, even though the results of the National Assessment of Educational Progress suggest caution: Two of the three lowest-performing districts in the nation (Cleveland and Chicago) are controlled by their mayors, while the highest performing districts (Charlotte and Austin) are managed by school boards. The Obama Administration has also required states to remove their caps on charter schools to be eligible for its $4.3 billion "Race to the Top" fund. In this time of budget cutting, every district wants new funding. But the price may be too high if public education is placed in jeopardy.

The business model assumes that democratic governance is a hindrance to effective education. It assumes that competition among schools and teachers produces better results than collaboration. It treats local school boards as a nuisance and an obstacle rather than as the public's representatives in shaping education policy. It assumes that schools can be closed and opened as if they were chain stores rather than vital community institutions.

By endorsing mayoral control and privatization, the Obama Administration is making a risky bet.

References

Hernandez, Javier C. "Schools Panel Is No Threat to the Mayor's Grip." *The New York Times*, April 23, 2009: A1.

Miller, Matt. "First, Kill All the School Boards." *The Atlantic* (Jan–Feb 2008).

Sullivan, Patrick J. "Inside the Panel for Educational Policy." *NYC Schools Under Bloomberg and Klein*, ed. Diane Ravitch. New York: Lulu.com, 2009.

DIANE RAVITCH is research professor of education at New York University and a historian of education. Her most recent book is *The Death and Life of the Great American School System* (2010).

EXPLORING THE ISSUE

Are Local School Boards Obsolete?

Critical Thinking and Reflection

1. Is it likely we will see the demise of local school boards, particularly with more state and federal involvement?
2. What are examples/options for school boards that want to only be involved in student learning and achievement?
3. How far should school board authority extend?
4. Can the high cost and poor performance of schools be directly attributed to school boards?
5. What are the major differences in appointed and elected school boards?

Is There Common Ground?

Assuming that local school boards are destined for either a diminished or altered role in governance in coming years, do the ideas of Marc Tucker and Diane Ravitch hold any promise of mutual accommodation? Would Tucker's relief of school boards' management functions allow them to perform the community tailoring of external demands that Ravitch sees as important? Can current frailties of school board operations be corrected? In "Weighing the Case for School Boards: Today and Tomorrow," *Phi Delta Kappan* (March 2010), Frederick M. Hess points to four indictments: (1) a lack of voter attention makes it difficult to hold board members accountable, (2) electoral apathy allows mobilized constituencies to exert disproportionate influence, (3) elected boards often lack coherence and continuity, and (4) boards operate in isolation from a city's political and civic leaders.

In the near future increased attention will be given to the appropriate roles of the federal government, state and local governments, and representative school boards in the improvement of the nation's schools. Chester E. Finn, Jr., in "How to Run Public Schools in the 21st Century," *Education Next on the web* (June 27, 2011), identifies four major problems that must be recognized and dealt with (1) "local" has gradually become a less accurate way to describe, much less to organize, public education; (2) the dream of keeping education out of politics has turned into a nightmare; (3) keeping K-12 education separate from the rest of the public sector does more harm than good; and (4) our inherited structures presuppose

a quasi-monopoly over K-12 education. These and similar issues are handled in a variety of ways in "Can We Live Without Federal Involvement?" *School Administrator* (June 2010) by Steve Atwater, who sees the federal role as being a support agency concentrating on turning around low-performing schools; in "Federal Involvement in Local School Districts," *Society* (May/June 2005) by Stephen J. Caldas and Carl L. Bankston III; and in "Governance as a Profession," *American School Board Journal* (February 2010) by Rick Maloney, who says that our nation's schools deserve professional leadership at the policy-making level.

Create Central

www.mhhe.com/createcentral

Additional Resources

Chester E. Finn. Jr., "Lost at Sea," *Education Next* (Summer 2004).

Gene I. Maeroff, "School Boards in America: Flawed But Still Significant," *Phi Delta Kappan* (March 2010).

Nancy Walser, *The Essential School Board Book* (2009).

Sarah C. Glover, "Steering a True Course" *Education Next* (Summer 2004).

William G. Howell (ed.), *Besieged: School Boards and the Future of Education Politics* (2005).

Internet References . . .

American School Board Association

http://asba.org

Partnership for Twenty-First-Century Skills

http://p21.org

National Center on Time & Learning

www.timeandlearning.org

Federation for American Immigration Reform (FAIR)

www.fairus.org

National Association for Single-Sex Public Education

http://singlesexschools.org

Unit 3

UNIT

Current Specific Issues

*T*his unit probes specific questions currently being discussed by educators, policy makers, and parents. In most cases these issues are grounded in the more basic questions explored in Units 1 and 2. Views are expressed by a wide variety of writers, including Nirvi Shah, National School Safety and Security Services, David L. Kirp, Douglas J. Besharov, Douglas M. Call, Mara Sapon-Shevin, Wade A. Carpenter, Andrew Coulson, Louis Malfaro, James Cibulka, David Chard, Honorable David Souter, Honorable Clarence Thomas, Chris Gabrieli, Larry Cuban, William Crossman, Erin Dillon, Bill Tucker, Andrew J. Rotherham, Daniel T. Willingham, and Diana Senechal.

Selected, Edited, and with Issue Framing Material by:
Glenn L. Koonce, *Regent University*

ISSUE

Is There Support for Arming Teachers in Schools?

YES: Nirvi Shah, from "Teachers Already Armed in Some Districts," *Education Week* (February 20, 2013)

NO: National School Safety and Security Services, from "Arming Teachers and School Staff with Guns: Implementation Issues Present School Boards and Administrators with Significant Responsibility and Potential Liability" (August 15, 2013), retrieved from: www.schoolsecurity.org/trends/arming_teachers.html

---

Learning Outcomes

After reading this issue, you should be able to:

- Compare and contrast the pros and cons of arming trained school resource officers as opposed to arming teachers and principals in schools.
- Decide on what the criteria will be and how to determine who would be trained and allowed to be armed in a school.
- Assess if ample training and practice will be offered prior to school districts deciding on arming teachers and administrators in schools.
- Distinguish between the challenges of educational professionals teaching and serving children or having them diverted and focused on a mindset to kill an intruder that may enter the classroom.
- Critique the Second Amendment rights to bear arms and how it relates to the school setting and safety concerns?

ISSUE SUMMARY

YES: Nivri Shah examines arming teachers in schools shortly, after the Sandy Hook Elementary tragedy, noting the one Texas district superintendent concluded that "school personnel are the first responders."

NO: Led by President Kenneth Trump, the National School Safety and Security Services assert that teachers want to be armed with "textbooks and computers, not guns."

Armed police resource officers in schools are not new but the notion of arming teachers and principals in schools is new to most. Although very few, there are school systems in the nation where teachers and administrators already are packing firearms in the schools during normal school hours. In the Sandy Hook, Connecticut, school shooting, one of parents greatest fears were brought to reality as 20 elementary school pupils were killed. Five teachers and the principal also died. Thoughts go back to other mass school shootings among them: Columbine High School (12 students and a teacher dead), Red Lake High School (five students and two staff members dead), Amish school house shooting (five dead and five wounded), Chardon, Ohio (three students dead) and most recent Sparks Middle School (one dead and two wounded). These mass killings have left no easy solutions for a fix. Mass shootings are not exclusive to schools; we live in a violent culture. The

Aurora, Colorado, movie theatre shooting where 12 died and 70 were injured and the Washington, D.C., Navy Yard shooting, killing 12 are examples. When the most innocent, elementary school children, are the victims it feels even more tragic.

Guns in schools are not new as students have on occasion brought a gun to school that was confiscated and the student expelled. In the crackdown on school violence in the 1990s not only were students expelled but charged by police with possession of a gun in school; zero tolerance practices regarding possession of a gun on a school campus took effect. The Gun Free-Schools Act of 1994 imposed a federal requirement for mandatory one year expulsion from school for gun possession.

Since guns have been more common in schools, specially trained armed police officers, called School Resource Officers, are assigned to schools across the country particularly in many high schools and middle schools. Some of these programs have been in place for decades such as Chesapeake Public Schools in Chesapeake, VA who began assigning armed and trained police officers in schools during the 1960s. This was part of a partnering police–community effort to have safe schools. Today there is a National Association of School Resource Officers with advanced training courses. Unfortunately, there are not enough School Resource Officers for each school in the nation or even enough for each high school.

Not being able to solve the guns in the schools problem is part of larger societal issues including guns in the wrong hands, frustrations of identifying and treating those suffering with mental health concerns, and protecting Second Amendment rights. Strong individual and organizational support of the right to bear arms has been around since the U.S. Constitution was signed.

As noted, there are already armed teachers and administrators in a few schools in the nation but more important is the stronger call recommending training for school personnel who may or may not want to be armed. Some individuals and groups are expounding that teachers and principals are the real first responders in their schools with the obvious choice to shoot at predators if armed. It makes sense that if an intruder is the only one shooting, devastation does occur and a gun in the possession of school personnel is very powerful. Dave Parker (2013) states, "would we rather trust our children's protection to someone with a gun that is to be used for defense, or would we simply rather hope that the unthinkable doesn't happen to them?" The question that begs answering: Is there support for arming the nation's teachers and principals?

Harold Independent School District in Texas, 150 miles Northwest of Fort Worth and near the Oklahoma border, are carrying concealed guns and have been doing so since unanimously approved by the school board in 2007 (Huff Post Education, 2012). Personnel allowed must have an approved state concealed-weapon permit, undergo training in crisis intervention and hostage situations, carry non-ricocheting bullets, and be individually approved by the school board. After Sandy Hook, a number of other state lawmakers in South Dakota, Oklahoma, Missouri, Oregon, and Minnesota began considering laws similar to Harrold, Texas.

The report of the National School Shield Task Force (Hutchinson, 2013) found that a properly trained armed school officer, such as a School Resource Officer, is crucial to school security and prevention of an active threat on a school campus. The report also found that due to lack of funding, armed security personnel is too expensive, and have resorted to allowing staff to carry firearms to prevent a violent incident on school property. The report goes on to recommend that a model law for all states be adopted for armed school personnel who are designated and trained for the job. A model state law is provided in the report's appendix.

There appears to be substantial majorities that firmly do not want school teachers and principals to be armed. Tom Rebotham (2013) notes that it might be a little absurd to have armed teachers simply because they have a permit to carry a concealed weapon in a school. He notes training for a concealed-weapon consisted of a three-hour class in which the individual goes to the range for 30 minutes to fire a gun at a paper target 15 feet away. The rest of the time is devoted to reviewing laws and gun safety. Certification comes with hitting the paper target with "reasonable accuracy" from the predesignated 15 feet. Robothan explains that it is a tad different pulling a gun on an intruder and determining in a split second whether or not to shoot and then hitting the gunman from the 15-foot paper target range. This is all in retrospect if, indeed, the threat is first read correctly by the teacher with a gun, in a school. It can quickly be conclude that carrying a gun to ensure the safety of school children takes intensive training over a period of months and even years.

There are no known nationwide studies or even local research on arming public school staff. Most want armed school security in the hands of professional and trained security personnel. The growing concern points to the fact that there are no easy answers to the type of violence seen at Sandy Hook or the Washington Navy Yard.

In the selections that follow Nirvi Shah notes that support is present for arming school teachers and principals and is actually happening in a few school districts. Kenneth Trump, President of the National School Safety and Security Services makes the case that teachers do want to be armed; they want to be safe.

References

Huff Post Education, Harrold Texas School Gun Policy Defended After Newtown Shooting (2012). Retrieved from: www.huffingtonpost.com/2012/12/17/harrold-texas-school-guns_n_2316729.html

Hutchinson, A., Report of the National School Shield Task Force (National Rifle Association of America, 2013). Retrieved from: www.nraschoolshield.com/NSS_Final_FULL.pdf

Parker, D. & Robotham, T., "Gun Crazy: Left Side—Right Side." *Hampton Roads Magazine* (June 2013).

YES

Nirvi Shah

Teachers Already Armed in Some Districts

Hiding the Holster

Southland Superintendent Toby Miller said his district considered all of that. School officials kept coming to the same conclusion: "We are the first responders."

Adopting that attitude has dramatically changed the morning routine for one of Southland's employees who brings a weapon to school—at least on the days her clothing will hide it.

"It's actually a lot of looking in the mirror in the morning, asking your other half 'Can you see this?' That's kind of how my morning goes," said the staff member, who spoke with *Education Week* on the condition of anonymity— a necessity for the policy to work, the district says. "You can hide a lot with a long skirt that's kind of flowy."

She has been wearing her weapon in a boot holster— slender legs allow the gun to fit inside easily. But a recent episode of "NCIS: Los Angeles" gave her an inspiration. One of the show's female investigators, dressed in a fitted shirt and tight skirt, was asked by her partner where she was storing her weapon. "She had it inside her shirt," said the Southland employee, who has since ordered her own bra holster.

For another Southland arms bearer, most skirts are off limits now, as are elastic waistbands. Just as for other gun-bearing staff members, her weapon cannot be carried in her purse or locked in her desk but must stay on her person all day. Over time, its presence has become less awkward, but it's not forgotten.

"Whether physically or mentally, you know it's there. You have to conscious of it all the time," she said. The district's training has drilled into her that it is rare or unlikely that she will ever use it. No situation thus far has caused her to contemplate drawing the gun.

"You can resolve most things . . . just by talking with the person," she said.

Southland sits about 15 miles from the nearest law-enforcement agencies, and the response time for any emergency can be 25 minutes, Superintendent Miller said. Tranquilizer guns and Mace, other options the district considered, wouldn't be as disabling or precise as handguns and would require being very close to an attacker, he added. Money for a school resource officer isn't in the budget. And the guns are part of a larger school safety strategy for the district that includes a collection of security cameras.

The armed employees, a small subset of the district's 32-member staff, went through mental-health screenings and trained for their concealed-weapons licenses together. The training will be ongoing, he said, as long as Southland employees carry weapons. And the guns fire so-called frangible ammunition, which breaks into small pieces on contact, preventing ricochet.

"We're not trying to pretend we've got a SWAT team here," said Mr. Miller. "We've done a lot of things that put us in a better position to be able to react directly."

Attitude Shift

Plenty of teachers and national education groups have rejected the idea of arming school employees, although at least some school safety experts say it shouldn't be off the table completely, particularly when limited to a very small number of staff members in highly remote schools without ready access to law enforcement.

But what does worry Michael S. Dorn, who runs the Atlanta-based Safe Havens International, a nonprofit school safety organization, is the new sacrificial and cavalier attitude he has found many school employees adopting since the Newtown shootings, which is, "Now, I'm supposed to die" to defend students, he said.

The disposition is one that may be driving their desire to carry weapons, he said. And it is behind the mishandling of school safety procedures he is seeing when assessing security procedures at schools around the country, said Mr. Dorn, a former school police chief. Too many teachers and administrators have switched to attack mode, in his view.

"We're seeing so many [school employees] saying they would attack" someone, he said, "whether it's two parents coming into the office arguing over a custody issue or people pulling a handgun but not actually shooting anybody."

In drills and hypothetical scenarios, school staff members are "forgetting to protect children while they're doing this. They are failing to clear the room in the process of going after intruders," he said. "The most important thing is [for school employees] to protect themselves so they can protect people in their immediate area and protect the whole school. If they get killed, they can't protect the school."

School safety consultant Ken Trump, the president of the Cleveland-based National School Safety and Security Services, disagrees with arming teachers and staff. He said if anyone is carrying weapons on campus, it should be trained police officers. But he, too, is alarmed by some of his recent consulting experiences. Basic steps to ensure safety from intruders or natural disasters seem to have been forgotten.

"Everything is 'active shooter, active shooter, active shooter, active shooter,'" Mr. Trump said. "I'm still able to walk into school through unlocked doors at schools that are not practicing lockdown drills during normal hours."

Dose of Reality

At the shooting range here, just south of the school district Mr. Johnny Price couldn't emphasize enough the consequences of carrying a weapon.

"We're responsible for everything that comes out of our firearm," he repeated to groups of Clifton district employees who took turns firing.

As acrid gunsmoke drifted over teachers' heads, he stood firm on that point.

"That's why most of y'all aren't ready to carry in the classroom yet, without some additional training, a lot more trigger time, getting familiar with your firearm, . . . without crisis assessment and crisis training, so you don't take it to the next level when you don't have to."

That message hit home for Dianne Bernhardt, who supervises the district's custodial staff. Other than the occasional armadillo she has deflected from her own property with a shotgun, Ms. Bernhardt said she has little experience with guns.

"It's a wake-up call when you're outside the perimeters of where you're supposed to be shooting. Thinking that could be an innocent bystander or a child," she said, her voice breaking, "you know, that you might hurt them in the process . . . Practice is just very important with this type of thing."

The afternoon at the shooting range—a makeshift outdoor setup where the bullets that penetrated the paper targets lodged in a bluff—was both a thrill and a trial for participants. Guns jammed, magazines were loaded backwards, and hands shook. But, eventually, brass casings flew as the mostly novice group of shooters ripped through the required 50 rounds of live ammunition from three-, seven-, and 15-yard distances from the paper targets.

"It was exhilarating," said Stacey Cockrell, a 9th grade special education teacher at Clifton High, at the end of her session. She said she has plans to buy a gun and favors arming teachers.

"I think you need to take each and every measure that you can to make sure you're prepared as you can be and keep those kids as safe as you can possibly keep them safe," said Ms. Cockrell, adding that she'd need a lot more training before taking a weapon to school.

Holding up one of the handguns teachers used to practice their aim, Luke Price, the instructor's son and a trainer himself, summed it up this way: "This is just a rock, unless you know how to use it."

Policies Elsewhere

Some of the staff members believe it's only a matter of time before Clifton joins the other Texas districts that allow employees to carry on campus. They include two that adopted their policies since the Newtown killings, Union Grove and Van.

In the 2,200-student Van school district in East Texas, Superintendent Don Dunn said that although each of the four campuses in his domain are within about a mile of the local police station, the swiftness with which 26 people were killed at the Connecticut school drove his district's decision.

"From the moment we have an armed intruder to the time the police are notified and can actually arrive is a 3- to 5-minute window. During that time period, our kids and our teachers and our staff are completely defenseless," Mr. Dunn said.

Each employee he enlisted will get a one-time stipend to buy a weapon and a monthly check to buy ammunition for practice.

When he recruited staff members, none said no, but he was choosy: "Some teachers don't have any business carrying a gun. I'd never feel good giving them the authority to do it," he said. "It just may be that they don't have the mental makeup to be able to put their life on the line to protect the kids."

Utah school administrators have no say in the matter: "A school administrator cannot ask," said Carol Lear, the director of school law and legislation at the state education department.

The state tweaked its concealed-carry law in 2003, allowing permit holders to bring weapons to schools.

"A school administrator cannot get a list of employees in his building who have permits. Now that I am thinking about it, I guess an administrator could ask teacher to tell him who does not have a concealed permit," she added.

Cori Sorenson, a 4th grade teacher at Highland Elementary in Highland, Utah, recently applied for her permit after years of self-defense and firearm-training courses. Reviewing media accounts of the Sandy Hook shooting, she said she can't help but wonder "if that principal had been carrying, if that teacher had been carrying, what would have been different?"

Mr. Dorn, the Georgia school safety consultant, said basing security decisions on media accounts, however, is a mistake. Until Connecticut State Police release a detailed report of what happened at Sandy Hook, it's impossible to tell what could have been done differently. And schools can't prepare for future incidents based solely on the events of Dec. 14, as they could not previously base all training on what happened at Columbine High School in Jefferson County, Colo., in 1999.

"Sandy Hook didn't look anything like Columbine. Columbine didn't look like Pearl, Miss.," Mr. Dorn said, referring to a 1997 shooting spree in which a student killed two classmates and wounded seven.

But Ms. Sorenson, a 13-year teaching veteran, is among those bolstered by the fact that there haven't been school shootings in Utah since the law changed. Should her license materialize, Ms. Sorenson would not disclose whether she would take a gun to school.

"One person's choice is not the same choice for somebody else," she said. "Along with that choice, comes responsibility."

Nirvi Shah is a reporter for *Education Week* whose beats included school safety, discipline, climate, health, and nutrition. She also covers the states of Kansas, New Hampshire, Vermont, and West Virginia.

National School Safety and Security Services

→ **NO**

Arming Teachers and School Staff with Guns: Implementation Issues Present School Boards and Administrators with Significant Responsibility and Potential Liability

Arming persons at schools should be left to professional school public safety officials: School Resource Officers (SROs) and school police department officers.

"The vast majority of teachers want to be armed with textbooks and computers, not guns," said Kenneth S. Trump, President of National School Safety and Security Services, in response to the national discussion on arming teachers and school staff, and armed volunteers in schools.

Trump advises school districts against allowing teachers and school staff to be armed.

Trump says that while gun control and gun rights advocates typically seize on school proposals to arm teachers to further political agendas, his opposition to arming teachers and school staff focuses solely on implementation issues, not political statements and beliefs about rights to bear arms.

"School districts considering arming teachers and school staff with guns would take on significant responsibility and potential liabilities that I firmly believe are beyond the expertise, knowledge-base, experience, and professional capabilities of most school boards and administrators," Trump said. He added that school board members, superintendents, principals, teachers, school safety experts, and public safety officials he has talked with around the nation consistently do not believe that educators and school support staff should be armed.

Trump said he personally supports the Second Amendment and concealed carry laws, but believes that proposals to arm teachers and other school employees crosses the line of self-protection and protection of one's family into a different level of tasking educators and school support staff to provide public safety, law enforcement functions for hundreds or thousands of individuals in a school.

"Suggesting that by providing teachers, principals, custodians, or other school staff with 8, 16, 40, or even 60 hours of firearms training on firing, handling, and holstering a gun somehow makes a non-law enforcement officer suddenly qualified to provide public safety services is an insult to our highly trained police professionals and a high-risk to the safety of students, teachers, and other school staff," Trump said.

He said it is short-sighted for those supporting the idea to believe that educators who enter a profession to teach and serve a supportive, nurturing role with children could abruptly kick into the mindset to kill someone in a second's notice. Police officers train their entire career and enter each traffic stop and individual encounter with a preparedness and life-safety mindset that is different from the professional training and mindset of educators.

Trump, a 25-year veteran school safety expert who has trained and consulted with school and public safety officials from all 50 states and Canada, noted that school districts setting policy to allow teachers and school staff to be armed with guns would take on an enormous amount of responsibility and potential liability.

He says allowing teachers and school staff to be armed begs a number of questions:

- Does the school board have appropriate and adequate policies and procedures governing the carrying and use of firearms by teachers and school staff?
- What type of "use of force continuum" has the school district created for staff to use firearms? How does that stand up in comparison to such standards held for police officers and others who are armed and deployed in a public safety capacity?
- What types of firearms (types of guns, caliber of weapons, etc.) are staff allowed to carry and not allowed to carry? Will staff carry their own personal firearms or school district-issued firearms? If the school allows staff to carry their personal weapons for the purpose of protecting staff and students, what responsibilities do school boards and administrators thereby assume for making sure the firearms carried are functional? Does the school district have regular "inspections" of staff firearms to make sure they are functional and appropriate to policy, and if so, who on school staff is responsible for that function and what is their level of expertise and training to make such decisions?
- What type of firearms training does the school district provide on a regular, ongoing basis to those staff it authorizes to be armed with guns? Will the school district build and operate its own firearms

range? Who on school staff is qualified to provide such training, operate a firearms range, etc.? Will firearms certification and recertification be added to the school district's professional development training program each year?

- What type of weapons retention training has been provided to staff who are armed and what steps have been taken to reduce risks of a teacher or staff member being intentionally disarmed by a student or other person, or for having a firearm dislodged from a staff member's control when the teacher breaks up a fight in a cafeteria or hallway?

- How is the district prepared to prevent and manage situations where teachers and/or staff members lose, misplace, or have stolen their firearms while on campus?

- How will the school district manage an accidental shooting that could occur?

- What is the impact of this type of board policy and practice on the school district's insurance and potential legal liability posture? If self-insured, is the district able to handle potential lawsuit judgments against them for cases resulting from this practice? If insured by a private carrier, what is the insurance provider's position and concerns, or will they even insure the district for such a practice?

- Most importantly, what other options have we considered as school leaders? For example, if the school district is concerned about first responder response time from the community to the school, has the school district considered employing a school resource officer (SRO) or its own trained, commissioned and certified school police officer who is a school district employee, such as what is allowed in Texas, Florida and other states?

and many other considerations.

Trump recommends that superintendents and school boards get written opinions from their insurance carriers and school district attorneys on the risks and liability of arming non-law enforcement, school employees.

Trump has long supported school districts having school resource officers (SROs) who are city or county law enforcement officers assigned to work in schools. He also supports properly organized and operated school police departments, which are in-house school district police officers that are trained, commissioned, and certified professional peace officers in school districts where state law allows districts to have such departments.

Trump says that the arming of teachers and school staff goes is a significantly different issue that goes beyond simply the issue of an individual's right in a number of states to be licensed to carry a concealed weapon. Unlike an individual being trained and licensed under a state law to carry a firearm for personal protection at their home or on the streets, school districts that permit teachers and school staff to carry firearms on campus are in essence deploying those school employees in a public safety capacity to protect the masses with the expectation and assumption that they can and will provide a firearms-related level of public safety protection services to students and other staff. By tasking those employees with those responsibilities, Trump notes, the school district is also accepting responsibility and potential liability for implementation of such policies.

"There is a huge difference between having trained, certified and commissioned law enforcement officers who are full-time, career public safety professionals that are armed and assigned the duty of protecting students and staff versus having teachers, custodians, cafeteria workers and other non-public safety professionals packing a gun in school with hundreds of children," said Trump.

NATIONAL SCHOOL SAFETY AND SECURITY SERVICES (www. schoolsecurity.org) is an organization dedicated to making schools safer for children, using leading edge strategies that are proven and cost effective. Ken Trump, MPA, is the President.

EXPLORING THE ISSUE

Is There Support for Arming Teachers in Schools?

Critical Thinking and Reflection

1. What impact will having teachers and principals armed in schools have on what the real educational focus should be?
2. What are the liability concerns to consider in arming teachers and principals in school as opposed to trained school resource officers?
3. Will the dialogue continue to be discussed about arming school employees or will another disaster have to occur to keep it in the forefront of people's minds that are making the policy decisions?
4. What should teachers really be focused on each day in their classrooms; educational excellence or being armed for protection and safety of their students?
5. What type of firearm training should a school system provide to the faculty and staff and who will cover the economic cost of training and providing guns and ammunition?

Is There Common Ground?

Most people would agree that policies to reduce any violent act in our schools would be welcome. It is also apparent actions would be stopped at the point where teachers and administrators would be armed. It should be noted that schools are micro-organizations of society and are not immune from the violent acts committed outside the school. With automatic assault rifles becoming more common place in mass shootings and recognizing that mental health care is lacking for many deranged individuals who are capable of committing an unthinkable act, schools and society are vulnerable. In this reflection, it makes sense that if society needs armed police officers, schools do too. The question does not appear to be, arm or not to arm, but who will be armed?

School security has come a long way in the manner in which schools are aware of the potential for extreme violence. On the other hand, schools are designed as learning facilities where teaching takes place and not every thought is for one's safety. School teachers and especially principals are not security experts. They are learning leaders whose expertise is organizing a school for maximum learning, no matter how difficult the instructional task. Security experts are generally defined as peace officers with the mandatory training and certification to be commissioned with arrest powers and the authority to carry a gun. There is a big difference between certification to be a security officer and certification to be a teacher or principal.

The debate on school violence escalates after an incident of mass violence. The rhetoric grows followed by a period where some changes may be made. Then things appear normal and the natural thought of "it won't happen here" pervades in schools across the country once again. This debate should not continue that schools need armed protection; the question is, from whom?

Create Central

www.mhhe.com/createcentral

Additional Resources

Berry, H., *Massacre in Newtown: Adam Lanza's Dark Passage to Madness* (2013).

Giles, D. & Daily, C., *Sandy Hook Massacre: When Seconds Count—Police Are Minutes Away* (White Feather Press, 2013).

Johnson, P. (2012). Sandy Hook school shooting: Few Easy Answers for a violent culture. Christian Science Monitor (December 15, 2012). Retrieved from: www.csmonitor.com/USA/2012/1215/Sandy-Hook-school-shooting-Few-easy-answers-for-a-violent-culture-video

Lysiak, M., *Newtown: An American Tragedy* (Simon & Schuster, 2013).

Trump, K. & Lavarello, C., "Buyer Beware: What to Look for When You Hire a School Security Consultant," *American School Board Journal* (March 2001).

Internet References . . .

In Tiny Texas Town, Teachers Are Armed with Concealed Weapons, a "Better" Solution Than a Security Guard

> www.nydailynews.com/news/national/teachers-armed-guns-texas-school-article-1.1224257

National Association of School Resource Officers

> www.nasro.org/

National School Safety and Security Services

> www.schoolsecurity.org/

Gun-Free Schools Act

> www2.ed.gov/about/offices/list/osdfs/gfsa.html

Guns in School Could Be the Answer—But Just For a While

> www.policymic.com/articles/58439/guns-in-school-could-be-the-answer-but-just-for-a-while

Selected, Edited, and with Issue Framing Material by:
Glenn L. Koonce, *Regent University*

ISSUE

Has the Time Arrived for Universal Preschool?

YES: **David L. Kirp**, from "The Kids-First Agenda," in *Big Ideas for Children: Investing in Our Nation's Future* (First Focus, 2008)

NO: **Douglas J. Besharov and Douglas M. Call**, from "The New Kindergarten," *The Wilson Quarterly* (Autumn 2008)

Learning Outcomes

After reading this issue, you will be able to:

- Create a historical time line pertaining to the progression of preschool programs in America.
- Critique how parenting skills and living conditions can determine a child's educational success.
- Examine the Kids-First Agenda and describe the five powerful ideas that it contains.
- Assess the work of children's advocacy groups in supporting preschool.
- Survey the literature on how little preschool does to solve the problem of the achievement gap that puts low-income, mostly minority children so far behind more fortunate children.

ISSUE SUMMARY

YES: David L. Kirp, a Professor of Public Policy and Author of *The Sandbox Investment,* calls for expansion of federal support for universal preschool and other child care services.

NO: Professor Douglas J. Besharov and Research Associate Douglas M. Call of the University of Maryland School of Public Policy examine the development of child care programs and conclude that the case for universal preschool is not as strong as it seems.

In an article titled "Preschool Education: A Concept Whose Time Has Come," *Principal* (September/October 2005), W. Steven Barnett, Director of the National Institute for Early Education Research, states that "no area in education has grown like preschool in recent decades." Preschool education received a powerful boost when the federal Head Start program was launched in 1964, but major barriers in affordability and accessibility for those not eligible for Head Start have slowed the movement.

Individual states have moved toward providing preschool programs in recent years. Oklahoma and Georgia have led the country in offering voluntary programs for four-year-olds. Florida, New York, North Carolina, and Massachusetts have moved toward universally available programs. However, neither Georgia or Oklahoma has experienced significant improvement in students' academic performance. According to The Heritage Foundation's Backgrounder (May 14, 2009), 80 percent of children in preschool are in programs run by private providers and who would likely be displaced or burdened with heavy regulation if federal support is vastly expanded.

But the Obama administration has pushed for major increases in federal subsidies, with some commentators saying that this effort is second only to universal health care on the liberal policy agenda. In "Protect Our Kids from Preschool," *The Wall Street Journal* (August 22, 2008), Shikha Dalmia and Lisa Snell of the Reason Foundation claim that our understanding of preschool effects is in its infancy, that kids with attentive parents might well be better off spending more time at home during their formative years, and that "the last thing that public policy should do is spend vast new sums of taxpayer dollars to incentivize a premature separation between toddlers and parents." In agreement with this position, Lindsey Burke of the Heritage Foundation states, "While proponents of universal preschool often cite the findings of small, high intervention programs, it is unlikely that any large-scale implementation of universal preschool could mimic their conditions and would thus fail to produce the results promised by proponents."

Among the advocates of universal preschool is the Pew Center of the States with its Pre-K Now campaign. This organization monitors progress in all states and makes recommendations for strengthening the movement. In spite of recent growth, less than 30 percent of three- and four-year-olds are served in publicly funded early education, according to a 2009 report by the Pew Center. The report calls for a new strategy of collaboration with community-based partners (child care centers, Head Start programs, and faith-based organizations, for example) to enhance access and choice. Sara Mead of the New America Foundation is concerned that a major spike in federal funding may get ahead of the capacity to deliver high-quality programs. She calls for expedited alternative routes to Pre-K teaching, creation of research-based Early Education Academies in neighborhoods now served by low-performing schools, and improvement of articulation between Pre-K programs and the elementary school curriculum. Mead, in "A Case for Pre-K," *The American Prospect Online* (July 18, 2007), states that David L. Kirp and other

advocates of universal preschool see it "not as an end in itself but as the groundwork for a more ambitious effort to expand public and social services for children."

In an article in *The Washington Post* (May 15, 2009), "Slow the Preschool Bandwagon," Chester E. Finn, Jr. warns that everybody should pause before embracing universal preschool since "it dumps five-year-olds, ready or not, into public school classrooms that today are unable even to make and sustain their own achievement gains, much less to capitalize on any advances these youngsters bring from preschool. He concludes that "done right, preschool programs can help America address its urgent education challenges, but today's push for universalism gets it almost entirely wrong."

In the following articles Kirp makes a case for both universal preschool and expanded child development action, while Besharov and Call sound cautionary warnings.

YES ⤶

David L. Kirp

The Kids-First Agenda

To say that, when it comes to children's issues, Washington has been asleep at the switch, is much too kind.

Since 2004, as First Focus's 2008 report on the children's budget shows, kids have been losing out to seniors, wealthy taxpayers, and everyone else. A single penny out of every new nondefense dollar is being spent on children's programs; the overall share of federal nondefense spending on kids has dropped by 10 percent; and while other discretionary spending on social initiatives has grown 8 percent, children's programs have been cut by 6 percent. What makes this malign neglect especially infuriating is the impeccable evidence that kids are the best social investment the government can make.

Washington's dereliction is not only a matter of dollars and cents, but the fact that the government has not figured out how to spend its money wisely. The Bush administration's signature initiative, the No Child Left Behind Act, has been a debacle. The promised increased in education funding never materialized, and neither did the predicted improvement in reading and math test scores. What is more, the narrow-gauge, high-stakes testing regimen has distorted educational priorities, giving an entirely new meaning to the practice of teaching to the test.

The lion's share of federal dollars pays for child care, and if that money were well-spent it could make a huge difference. The most famous example, the Abecedarian Program, delivered intensive support to poor children starting a few months after birth. A study done a generation later showed that Abecedarian participants had higher IQs, stayed in school longer and held down better jobs. The annual rate of return over the course of those children's lives is an impressive 7 percent.

Federal policy-makers have ignored such evidence—the rationale for funding child care is not helping kids but expanding the workforce. Child care, as conceived in Washington, is simply a cheap way to park infants and toddlers while their mothers are on the job. There is no Abecedarian—and precious few slots in the considerably less expensive Early Head Start program, despite solid evidence of its success. What is available, whether at child care centers or from the kindly lady down the block, is usually mediocre—and one out of every eight licensed child care centers has been rated "unsafe." Kids do benefit from the sense of self-sufficiency that their parents gain when they are working. But these ill-conceived, on-the-cheap ventures do not help kids. In fact, the worst of them can do harm. Some youngsters who spend long days in impoverished environments become more aggressive.

In the impoverished world into which these children have been dumped, aggression becomes a *Lord of the Flies* survival tactic.

Washington operates too many mini-programs, mostly well-intentioned, but few of them demonstrably effective. The laundry list—everything from educating homeless children to making schools safe and drug-free—has grown haphazardly, with little understanding of what will have the biggest impact. Early Head Start limps along with barely half a billion dollars—essentially a rounding error in the federal budget—and can serve just 2.4 percent of poor children. Meanwhile programs such as teacher quality grants, on which $3 billion is being spent, prosper despite a lack of evidence that, as currently structured, they are worth the investment.

Since the mid-1990s, all the action has taken place outside the Beltway. Forty-one states now support prekindergarten. Public-private partnerships such as Ounce of Prevention have devised exemplary models for infant and toddler care. Foundations have underwritten promising experiments such as the Harlem Children's Zone and the Nurse-Family Partnership. But among Washington lawmakers there is little discussion of which programs need to be overhauled (whether, for instance, Head Start can learn something from the best state-funded preschools), which initiatives should be merged to streamline bureaucracy, and which ought to be dropped. A top-to-bottom rethink of what Washington is doing seems, well, unthinkable.

The public is miles ahead of the politicians. "Overwhelmingly, Americans care about meeting the needs of children," Democratic pollster Geoff Garin has written. And because of their "strong sense of obligation to give children a good start in life" many citizens see the unbenign neglect of children as a "crisis." A new poll commissioned by Every Child Matters, a Washington advocacy group, finds that a sizeable percentage of voters—notably the swing voters—rank increasing the Head Start budget and guaranteeing health care to all children above paying more for homeland security or farm support. The belief that child-rearing ought to be left entirely to parents is being replaced by an ethic of empathy—an acknowledgement that, while parents play a pivotal role, the polity must become a "good steward."

The old saw that children don't matter because they don't vote and don't consume no longer holds true.

Governors from both sides of the political aisle—among them Tim Kaine (Virginia), Bobby Jindal (Louisiana), Phil Bredesen (Tennessee), Richard Riley (Alabama), Ted Strickland (Ohio), and Rod Blagojevich (Illinois)—have made children's needs a priority. Politically, they have done well by doing good. The kids-first agenda is the proverbial $20 bill that economists insist cannot be—but is—lying on the sidewalk, awaiting a politician on the national scene to pick it up. Imagine the impact of a kids-first presidential address, delivered with even a fraction of the eloquence of Barack Obama's meditation on race.

The Kids-First Agenda

- Offer help to families from the start.
- Give families the opportunity for top-quality zero-to-five care and education.
- Promote safe and strong communities, with schools as their hub.
- Provide kids the support of a stable, caring adult.
- Support families that save for their children's future.

What is needed in 2008 is not utopian dreaming but "pragmatopia"—a doable agenda that carries the promise of benefiting all children while narrowing race and class gaps. With a new administration in place, Washington is likely to address the basics—guaranteeing health care to all children (which requires only a modest expansion of the overwhelmingly popular Children's Health Insurance Program); liberalizing the child tax credit to reach the poorest 10 million children whose families pay no taxes and so get nothing, and the 10 million youngsters whose families do not earn enough to benefit from the full credit; rewriting the No Child Left Behind Act to make its testing regimen more attentive to thinking and emotional well-being than to parroting; and improving public education with matching grants for states that couple higher salaries with more rigorous training and greater accountability.

The kids-first agenda builds on these basics. It specifies five powerful ideas that, taken together, confront an array of children's needs from birth through adolescence. These ideas, a few of which show good promise of success, are based on solid research. That is crucial, since at present, a host of untested ideas—as well as a goodly number of demonstrably failed ideas—compete with known successes for scarce dollars and attention. The result is Gresham's Law in action: bad initiatives, usually inexpensive and slickly promoted, drive out the good. The kids-first agenda does not focus on K-12 education, since ideas for revamping—or blowing up—the public schools are already thick on the ground. Instead, it specifies what is needed to pull off what University of Chicago economist James Heckman calls "a policy of equality of opportunity in access to home environments (or their substitutes)."

Modest expectations are in order, since new ideas, however carefully thought through and faithfully put in place, cannot guarantee that lives turn out well. But the kids-first agenda goes a long way toward assuring that all children, whatever their social circumstances, are treated decently. While that may sound like mommy-state-ism run amok, it makes good economic sense. Not only does the kids-first agenda promote the cognitive skills that can lead to decent jobs and effective membership in the society, it also encourages the acquisition of "soft" skills—perseverance, dependability, consistency, and the ability to keep one's emotions in check—that report cards used to call "working and playing well with others." These noncognitive abilities have a powerful effect on which teenagers can find jobs, avoid cigarettes and drugs, keep from becoming pregnant, and stay out of jail.

Anticipating a new political regime, the children's advocacy groups are dusting off their wish lists. The most predictable objection to the Kids-First agenda is that it does not include x or y or z initiative. No short list can hope to cover everything, and there is room for full-throated debate about what should be on it. But the pragmatopia agenda must be short because a flood of competing proposals only assures failure. And it must be based on what is best, not for the politicians, bureaucrats, or professionals, but for the kids.

1. Offer Help to Families from the Start

As every parent appreciates, raising kids is hard work. Its importance in shaping children's lives cannot be exaggerated, because parents are youngsters' first and most influential teachers and their emotional buttress—what sociologist Christopher Lasch memorably called a "haven in a heartless world." This is complicated stuff, and many mothers and fathers will value help that begins during pregnancy and continues through the first years of an infant's life. This used to be the province of mothers and grandmothers, but with so many splintering families and single-family households, as well as a deeper understanding of all that is involved in being a good parent, such support can be invaluable.

First-time, poor mothers, especially teenage moms, are likely to be under the greatest stress and the least equipped to cope. They can benefit particularly from a top-notch program, the best of which is the Nurse-Family Partnership. Beginning with home visits during pregnancy, the intention is to build long-term, trusting relationships between these new young moms and highly-trained nurses. (It is considerably harder to get fathers involved.) Mothers who participate are less likely to need social services such as Medicaid and food stamps, less likely to expose their children to abuse, and less likely to have additional children during their teen years. Their children pick up language more quickly, do better in school and, as teenagers, are less likely to get in trouble with the law. Those positive outcomes translate into $5.70 in benefits for every $1 invested. The Nurse-Family Partnership is a good illustration of why quality, though expensive, is what makes the critical difference: The identical program did not have any impact when carried out by paraprofessionals. What began three decades ago as a three-city experiment now operates in 22 states, and within a decade it will expand to reach 150,000 mothers and their children. While that is impressive, the Nurse-Family Partnership only reaches 3 percent of the target population. There is a political lesson to be gleaned from the success of the pre-K movement: Good ideas need powerful advocates.

Many mothers, not just those who are poor, will fare better if they do not have to go it alone. Second and third children often pose new challenges, and middle class moms can be just as ill-prepared as their poorer sisters. We would do well to follow Vermont's lead and make sure that every new mother receives least one home nurse visit. Promising and widely-used initiatives such as Parents as Teachers, which combines group support with one-on-one relationships, have a broader reach. The effect of such programs is likely to be cumulative: As more parents become actively engaged, more children become better off; as good parenting becomes the norm, a critical mass of knowledgeable parents makes for a better community.

The essential bond between a parent and a child would be stronger if the parent with primary child-rearing responsibility didn't have to return to work soon after giving birth. Even though unpaid leave is guaranteed by federal law, few parents have been able to take advantage of the opportunity, since most cannot do without a salary. Logically, four to eight weeks of paid leave is an idea that should appeal to conservatives as well as liberals because it enables parents to raise their infants. At-home care during the first months significantly lowers the rate of infant mortality, and that adds to its moral and economic appeal. California offers workers up to eight weeks to care for a newborn or a sick relative. The federal government should give incentives to states that do the same.

2. Give Families the Opportunity for Top-Quality, Zero-Five Care and Education

Oceans of ink have been spilled addressing the issue of reforming schools—understandably so, since children spend so many hours of their lives there—but what transpires before kids enter kindergarten makes a bigger difference. By their fourth birthday, children from professional families have heard 30 million more words than youngsters whose mothers are on welfare, while the four year old from a professional family has a bigger vocabulary than the mother who is on welfare.

In a kids-first society, every child would have access to good care and education from birth to the age of five. Infants and toddlers are natural explorers whose brains are developing at a phenomenal rate, and in the right setting they can flourish. And they are social beings who learn from example. Geneticists report that while the genetic potential of well-off children has been maxed out, IQ differences among poor children overwhelmingly depend on

whether they have grown up in a world that is stable or chaotic, nurturing or punishing.

The best-studied early education program, Abecedarian, which began at infancy and extended through the first years of school, cost about $14,000 a year for each child. That amount is not surprising when you consider that the infant-adult ratio was three-to-one. But it is not necessary to spend that much money to make a meaningful difference.

Early Head Start delivers an array of services, including health care, as well as play-centered education and parent outreach. It costs about $9,000, and the research finds a significant impact.

Even if Washington expands Early Head Start so that all eligible children can participate, millions of youngsters who are not living in dire poverty, but whose parents cannot afford decent early education, are still left out. North Carolina's Smart Start has the right idea, one that other states are picking up: Spend public dollars to underwrite higher-quality early education, explain to parents why quality makes a difference, give them options, and let the market do the rest. Instead of building something brand new, that is the approach that Washington should underwrite with incentive grants.

Preschool for three- and especially four-year-olds has lately become popular. No wonder. The landmark studies report returns on investment as unbelievably high at 17:1 for Perry Preschool. While a scaled-up venture of a high-quality pre-K would yield a considerably lower return—RAND Corporation estimated a 2.7:1 return for a statewide preschool initiative in California—that is still impressive, as are new data from Tulsa, Oklahoma's pre-K program. Those returns signify better lives: more children graduating from high school, going to college, getting decent jobs, remaining healthy, and staying out of jail.

Put pre-K together with nurse-family partnerships and care that is as good as Early Head Start and the cumulative effects logically multiply. In Minneapolis, Federal Reserve economist Art Rolnick is testing this approach. High-quality nurse home visiting for poor mothers and scholarships for carefully vetted pre-K programs make a powerful dose of two proven strategies. Give poor kids access to decent elementary schools, with good teachers and a proven curriculum, and there will be still greater gains to report.

As with every kids-first initiative, pre-K will succeed only if it is top-notch. Studies show what "quality" means: engaged parents and small classes so that well-trained teachers can pay attention to each kid. The best teaching uses kids' play as its starting point. It concentrates less on drilling children in the alphabet than on engaging their social and emotional lives: learning to wait in line, to share, to keep their tempers in check, letting them tell their stories. That quality does not come cheap. Perry Preschool cost about $12,000, and despite the benefits such an investment would yield, that is more money than the government is likely to commit. The Chicago Child-Parent Centers, which have been running for 40 years with remarkable success, cost $8,500, about $2,000 more than Head Start, but less than what many public schools spend on elementary school students.

The federal government should not pick a single winner. Instead, it should follow the same approach as in early education: Help states that offer incentives to strengthen pre-K programs and give parents information that makes them informed consumers.

3. Promote Safe and Strong Communities, with Schools as Their Hub

A decade ago, Judith Harris made headlines with her claim in *The Nurture Assumption* that children's peers, not their parents, shape how they grow up. Like so many single-factor explanations, this one proves too simple. But Harris is onto something important. Community characteristics can affect children's health, their readiness for school, and the likelihood that they will commit crimes. What factors other than sheer poverty make the biggest difference is a conundrum with which researchers have long grappled. But when Harvard sociologist Robert Sampson compared the lives of black children growing up in "concentrated disadvantage" with those who lived in more stable neighborhoods, he found the impact of that experience—the cumulative effect of neighborhood conditions on parenting and school quality as well as children's levels of distrust and fear for their own safety—is equal to an entire year of school.

One response that has been tested with mixed success is to take children out of the places that produce bad outcomes and put them and their families in environments that produce better ones. But the moving van is not a solution, since poor neighborhoods are not going to disappear. A kids-first agenda needs to reach kids where they live and to develop place-based solutions.

In most communities, the school makes a natural hub that has the potential to go far beyond teaching the three Rs, as mandated by the No Child Left Behind Act, or even nurturing the growth of the mind. It can bring together parents, kids, and the child-serving agencies and everything from sports clubs to health clinics. That is the strategy of the Schools of the 21st Century, a model devised by Edward Zigler, Head Start's first director. Those schools house child care, health care, after-school and summer programs under one roof. More than 1,000 of these schools are operating across the country. The evidence suggests that they work. Not only do kids do better on standardized tests, they are also physically and emotionally better off.

The Harlem Children's Zone, the brainchild of charismatic educator Geoffrey Canada, has a bolder vision: to build a cocoon for children from birth to age 20 in one of the country's toughest neighborhoods. It has seeded a 97-block area with an array of initiatives that would be the envy of most places. There is something for almost every child and young adult, including pre-K with a 4:1 adult-child ratio, a "Baby College" for young parents, a charter school for elementary and middle school youngsters, an arts program, after-school tutoring and an investment club for high school students, and tech training for young adults.

Canada would like to see similar ventures in other beleaguered cities, and several places, among them Los Angeles and Baltimore, are giving consideration to emulating the model. While the complexity of the enterprise and the character of its force-of-nature founder make replication especially challenging, the reach of its ambition—the commitment to turn a mean-streets neighborhood into one that is truly kids-first—is what makes the Harlem Children's Zone so exciting. Other place-based models deserve a look. Britain's Sure Start, which began a decade ago in the poorest neighborhoods, offering everything from child care to medical check-ups for young children, has gone nationwide because of parent demand. Similarly, Best Start LA, now getting off the ground in Los Angeles, aims to bring together an array of services for parents, infants, and toddlers.

While these community-building ideas are promising, there is no solid evidence of their long-term effects, no Nurse-Family Partnership studies for neighborhood ventures. Still, it is not too early for Washington to become a partner in underwriting and studying promising initiatives—funding 20 "children's zones," perhaps, as Barack Obama has proposed, as well as assisting school districts that operate "Schools of the 21st Century." The dream is powerful and the logic persuasive. Children start forming ties based on love and trust at home. Child care and preschool, and later the school and the neighborhood, build on that foundation. At each of those critical stages, government can help out.

4. Provide Kids the Support of a Stable, Caring Adult

Ask anyone who works with kids what they need most and the answer is almost always the same: a mentor, a stable and caring adult, someone with the know-how to help a youngster navigate the twisting and sometimes treacherous pathway from early childhood to adulthood. As Generations United, a Washington, DC nonprofit, points out, many baby-boomer retirees do not want to spend their retirement on the golf course.

The century-old Big Brother-Big Sister program has shown that it can boost school attendance and achievement and reduce juvenile crime. There are 250,000 adults in the program. It merits public support so that it can expand. The Senior Grandparents Program, a federal enterprise established in 1965, offers services that range from caring for premature infants to mentoring troubled teens. Its current budget, just $68 million, supports 168,000 children, or less than $500 per child, and there is a waiting list of youngsters needing such help.

In San Diego, a more ambitious model is a work in progress. There, bridging the generational divide is not a one or two hour-a-week activity, but is woven into the fabric of government. Kids' impact is the watchword:

Housing for seniors is built on the grounds of an elementary school, Alzheimer's patients are spending time with toddlers in child care centers, and public space is being designed to be child-friendly. The government is looking at the world through kids-first lenses—that is an approach worth replicating with federal support.

5. Support Families that Save for Their Children's Future

The income gap between rich and poor is sizeable and growing. The asset gap, the amount of money that is in the piggybank, is far larger. It also matters more, because it is nearly impossible to spend one's way out of poverty. One way to narrow that gap is for the government to start savings accounts for America's 4.2 million newborns. A kids' saving account plan would give families and children a kick-start in preparing for what is down the road. It is a nest egg built on compound interest that can help to pay for college or job training.

The children's savings account not only puts dollars and cents behind society's commitment to the well-being of the next generation, it also encourages families—especially poor families—to see the payoff from investing in their children's well-being. The best evidence that it works comes from Britain, where 3.2 million accounts have been established since the program was launched in 2001. Three-quarters of these accounts have been invested in stock market funds, and one out of four families has added its own money to the kitty. To encourage parents, as well as neighbors, church, and community groups to chip in, Washington should match additional contributions made by families with limited means.

When Hillary Clinton floated this plan last fall, she was pilloried and quickly backed down. But there is no reason why, as in Britain, the idea's appeal should not transcend party lines. For liberals, it is a step toward equity. Conservatives should find it attractive because it fosters a new generation of capitalists.

From the Kids-First Agenda to Facts on the Ground: Holding Government Accountable

"End child poverty by 2020" was British Prime Minister Tony Blair's bold pledge in 1997, renewed by Gordon Brown this year. Not only did this become the metric that drove policy, it also became a measure of accountability. The press continues to scrutinize the government's success in meeting interim goals, and that oversight by the Fourth Estate has kept the pressure on.

In this country, the Annie E. Casey Foundation's "Kids Count" report highlights differences among the states on a number of measures including child poverty, infant mortality, premature births, teen births, and high school dropouts, while the Education Trust plays a similar role with respect to public education. These foundations are performing a great service, but this is really a job for the government. A national Kids-First Commission would collect information on key indicators, expanding the Casey Foundation's list to include such items as the percentage of children enrolled in prekindergarten, performance on the National Assessment of Educational Progress, and juvenile crime rates. An annual report could spur competition among the states. That is what has happened when states receive grades on "report cards" issued by Pre-K Now, a Washington advocacy group, and are rated by the National Institute for Early Education Research. In Oklahoma, after that state received high marks and flattering national media attention, preschool became a source of state pride, even among conservatives who had strongly opposed it. The same thing happened this year in Alabama, when the state, not usually known as socially progressive, received kudos. A federal seal of approval—or a failing grade—would have an even bigger effect.

The Kids-First Commission would also be charged with seeking out initiatives that have a profound payoff, such as assuring that all children who need them have a pair of glasses; that good dental treatment be made universally available; that pregnant women be screened for HIV (if an expectant mother is treated during the last few weeks of pregnancy with an antiviral drug her child will likely not carry the virus); and that youngsters in the inner cities, where asthma is endemic, receive needed attention.

A "kids' impact" statement also warrants testing. Its purpose is not to add another layer of paperwork, but to encourage agencies to view their programs in a new light. It might encourage HUD to underwrite more cross-generation housing, for instance, or prompt the Health and Human Services Department to join forces with the Education Department in supporting school-based health programs.

For too long, Washington has been an idea-free zone when it comes to children. Thinking "kids first" would change that—and it could change the arc of children's lives as well.

DAVID L. KIRP is Professor at the Goldman School of Public Policy at the University of California at Berkeley. He is the Author of *The Sandbox Investment: The Preschool Movement and Kids-First Politics* (2007).

Douglas J. Besharov and Douglas M. Call   → **NO**

The New Kindergarten

In her Christmas 2007 campaign ad, Hillary Clinton was shown arranging presents labeled "Universal Health Care," "Alternative Energy," "Bring Troops Home," and "Middle-Class Tax Breaks." She then paused, looking somewhat puzzled, before delivering the punch line: "Where did I put universal pre-K?"

"Universal pre-K" has become a politically popular campaign cause. Clinton is no longer a candidate, of course, but Barack Obama has promised an ambitious pre-kindergarten agenda; John McCain's advisers have hinted that he will do the same. And why not? The rhetoric surrounding pre-K programs is quite extraordinary: They close the achievement gap between low-income children and their more affluent peers; they prepare all children, including middle-income children, for school; and they provide financial relief to working mothers who have been paying for child care.

Yet as the Clinton TV spot unwittingly suggested, universal pre-K programs do not have an obvious place in today's crowded child-care world. Sometimes called "the new kindergarten," pre-K is in most cases just what its name implies: a year of publicly funded half-day school before kindergarten—for all children, regardless of whether their mothers work and regardless of family income. Pre-K has hardly enjoyed a universal embrace. Twice in recent history, attempts to create similar national programs foundered on controversy and went down to defeat. In California, voters recently turned their backs on a statewide plan.

In a 2006 referendum, the Golden State's voters rejected universal "free" preschool by a margin of three to two. Proposition 82, "Preschool for All," was backed by the activist actor-director Rob Reiner and the California Teachers Association; it would have given all California four-year-olds "equal access to quality preschool programs" for three hours a day for about eight months a year—to be paid for by a 1.7 percentage-point increase in the tax rate for single individuals making more than $400,000 and couples making more than $800,000 (almost a 20 percent tax increase, by the way). Although attendance was theoretically voluntary, the proposition would have effectively withdrawn government subsidies from other forms of care, so that families needing or wanting a free or subsidized program would have had no choice but to use their local school's pre-K.

The referendum sparked a statewide debate that went beyond the typical mix of platitudes, generaliza-tions, and exaggerations. Yes on 82, the prime sponsor of the referendum, repeated the oddly precise claim of RAND researchers that "every dollar California invests in a qual-ity, universal preschool program will return $2.62 to soci-ety because of savings from reduced remedial education costs, lower high school dropout rates, and the economic benefits of a better-educated work force."

Opponents pointed out, however, that more than 60 percent of California four-year-olds were already in a child-care center, a nursery school, or Head Start, and that the new program would have subsidized the middle-class families now paying for child care while, in the words of a *Los Angeles Times* editorial, establishing "a cumbersome bureaucracy . . . under the state Department of Education, which has done a disappointing job with K–12 schools."

Strangely, the overwhelming rejection of universal pre-K by the voters of our largest state has had no discern-ible impact on the national debate. It's not that California just happened to have more preschool programs than the rest of the country. Nationwide, about 74 percent of four-year-olds now spend time in some form of organized child care.

⟡

To understand what is going on, a little history will help. Beginning in the 1950s, a steadily higher proportion of married women with children took jobs outside the home. Between 1950 and 1970, the proportion of *married* moth-ers in the work force doubled, rising from about 20 percent to about 40 percent. (Single mothers have always had lit-tle choice but to work, or go on welfare.) In 1971, spurred by this change, as well as the emerging women's move-ment, a group of liberal Democrats led by Walter Mondale (D.-Minn.) in the Senate and John Brademas (D.-Ind.) in the House pushed the Child Development Act through Congress. It was an expansive measure, designed to create a federalized system of child development services. Chil-dren were to be enrolled regardless of whether their moth-ers worked and needed child care, on the ground that all children would benefit from a government-supervised child development effort.

Initially, key senior officials in the Nixon administra-tion supported the measure, seeing child care as an impor-tant component of their approach to welfare reform. But after some uncertainty, President Richard M. Nixon vetoed the bill, famously criticizing its "communal approaches to child rearing over [and] against the family-centered approach." His veto—and the specter of "communal" child rearing—not only killed the bill but took the political wind out of the child-care issue for a decade. Mondale himself became alarmed by the backlash even in his politically liberal home state.

Most liberal commentators have seen only conservative politics in the Nixon veto, but even many supporters of a federal child-care program thought the bill was deeply flawed, in ways that its congressional backers may not have understood. The legislation would have jumped past the states to fund hundreds if not thousands of "prime sponsors" (mostly local governments and non-profit organizations)—all to be selected by officials of the U.S. Department of Health, Education, and Welfare. The prime sponsors were, in turn, supposed to establish local "child development councils" composed of parents, children's services specialists, and community activists. These local entities would then fund as many as 40,000 individual providers.

If this web of federally administered, community-based programs sounds like an echo of the War on Poverty, that's because it sprang from the same social agenda—and many of the same activists. They distrusted state and local governments and wanted "community groups" in control. The bill's supporters boasted that this nationwide cadre of well-funded organizations would be a strong political force for their favored causes. Maurien McKinley of the Black Child Development Institute explained: "It is to the advantage of the entire nation to view the provision of day care/child development services within the context of the need for a readjustment of societal power relationships. . . . As day care centers are utilized to catalyze development in black and other communities, the enhanced political and economic power that results can provide effective leverage for the improvement of the overall social and economic condition of the nation."

In the next three-plus decades, child-care advocates struggled to come up with a formula that would be more attractive to voters, but they repeatedly overestimated support for government-provided child care for middle-class children and underestimated the desire of parents for choice and flexibility.

In the years after Nixon's veto, tens of millions of American mothers entered the labor force. By the 1990s, about 70 percent of married mothers had left full-time child rearing for jobs outside the home, and child-care options had proliferated. According to the National Institute for Early Education Research (NIEER), about 74 percent of all four-year-olds are in "formal" child-care centers for at least part of the day, while the remainder are in "informal" arrangements, a category that includes care by anybody from their parents or relatives to the lady down the street.

Married mothers entered the labor force in waves. First came married women with older children, who were in school anyway and often could take care of themselves after school. Then came those with young children, who needed someone else to care for them. In 1975, only 34 percent of mothers with a child under age three worked outside the home; by 1990, 54 percent did. Moreover, new mothers are quick to return to work. About seven percent do so within one month of their child's birth, and about 41 percent within three months.

Some think that American mothers are in the process of completely abandoning their traditional child-rearing role, but the picture is more mixed. The influx of married women with children into the labor force largely came to a halt in the 1990s. About 30 percent of all mothers today still do not work outside the home. Include those who work only part time—most often less than 20 hours a week—and you will find that almost 50 percent of all mothers, and almost 60 percent of those with a child under three, are not in the full-time labor force.

Although some of these women might take full-time jobs if child care were free, most have decided to delay returning to the labor force until their children are older. In fact, even though they do not "need" child care, about half of stay-at-home mothers place their children in a preschool or nursery school (for at least a year) because they want them to be with other children in a structured learning environment. For these mothers, government-funded pre-K might be a welcome financial break, but it would have little or no educational effect.

⁂

Except among women on welfare, the great increase in working mothers had taken place by the late 1980s, when child-care advocates made their second major push for a universal program. In 1987, the Act for Better Child Care Services, or the "ABC bill," as its supporters happily dubbed it, was introduced in Congress. Like the legislation Nixon had vetoed 15 years earlier, the ABC bill sought to create a nationwide system of child development services.

This time, however, there was no Great Society model; the states would administer the program, although they were to be guided by local advisory councils. Each year, the states would distribute $4.6 billion as grants to child-care centers or, in some circumstances, as vouchers to eligible families. Families would be eligible to receive assistance on a sliding scale if their income did "not exceed 115 percent of the State median income for a family of the same size." In high-income states such as Connecticut and New Jersey, that meant a family of four with an income of more than $100,000 would have been eligible. Nationally, the average income cutoff for eligibility for a family of four was about $79,000. (Unless otherwise indicated, all dollar amounts in this essay are in 2007 dollars.)

The ABC bill seemed headed for easy passage until controversy broke out among its liberal backers over a new provision barring the states from expending child-care money for "sectarian purposes or activities." In other words, no money for child care by religiously oriented organizations—even though 28 percent of all center-based programs in 1990 were operated by religious groups—unless they removed all elements of religiosity from their premises.

That provision was a late addition to the bill, apparently at the urging of the National Education Association and the National Parent Teacher Association. These organizations were interested less in the theory of church-state relations than in maximizing the money available for public schools and their employees. And they worried that by using vouchers (thus avoiding strictures against federal aid to religious institutions), the bill would create a precedent for vouchers in K–12 education. Many of the advocacy groups that originally supported the ABC bill—especially those representing religiously based providers, such as the U.S. Catholic Conference and its allies—were incensed.

While the fight over aid to sectarian programs festered for almost two years, another, and ultimately more significant, rift developed among the Democrats who controlled Congress. Key leaders in the House, led by Thomas Downey (D.-N.Y.) and George Miller (D.-Calif.), decided that any new child-care bill should provide greater assistance to low-income families rather than attempt to start a universal child development system, as the ABC bill would. It is unclear whether they opposed a universal federal program in principle—as Marian Wright Edelman of the Children's Defense Fund charged—or were simply being pragmatic. Their own explanation was that a universal system was unlikely to be funded (at least in any meaningful way) and that, in the meantime, low-income families needed help.

Meanwhile, Congress had passed legislation that encouraged mothers to leave welfare for work. Downey, Miller, and their allies wanted to "make work pay" for these mothers—by providing government-funded child care and by supplementing low earnings through an expanded Earned Income Tax Credit (EITC).

In 1990, Congress and President George H. W. Bush finally agreed on a law, much different from the original 1987 ABC bill, that created a $1.3 billion annual program called the Child Care and Development Block Grant and a new half-billion–dollar entitlement for families "at risk" of becoming welfare recipients. It also doubled the EITC, from $11.9 billion in 1990 to $24.6 billion in 1993.

It is difficult to judge what would have happened had the original ABC bill become law, but the narrower Downey-Miller approach was a boon to low-income families. The EITC is now a $45 billion-a-year program, providing financial assistance to more than 23 million families. And the administrative structure it created—especially child-care vouchers—became the basis of the massive expansion of child-care funding six years later under President Bill Clinton's 1996 welfare reform law. That year, the Republican Congress—pushed hard by the Clinton administration—decided that if mothers were expected to work, the government should help pay for child care—the

same argument that had appealed to Republicans as far back as the Nixon administration. In only five years, from 1996 to 2000, federal and related state child-care spending almost doubled, rising from $7 billion to $13.6 billion. Add in funding for Head Start, and the total rose from $11.7 billion to $19.9 billion. Spending has remained relatively flat since then.

The result has been an unprecedented increase in the number of children in government-subsidized child care. But more needs to be done. Only half of all eligible four-year-olds with low-income working mothers (and only 18 percent of those under age two) receive child-care aid.

Both the Child Development Act of 1971 and the ABC bill of 1987 foundered, in part, on the seemingly wide political opposition to a universal child-care program that ignores the immediate needs of low-income families. But rather than learn from this lesson, advocates are pushing yet again for a universal program. This time, the selling point is "school readiness" rather than child development, and the focus is only on placing four-year-olds in public schools. But the result is the same: a middle-class–oriented program that does not meet the needs of low-income families.

Advocates claim that pre-K programs do not have to be in schools, and that they would be happy to see existing child-care centers improved with pre-K funds (though that would leave out sectarian programs). But the "quality" requirements these programs impose, such as college degrees and specialized credentials for teachers, are, in the words of *The Los Angeles Times*, "written in such a way to favor programs at public schools."

In any event, given the strong political support for universal pre-K from teachers' unions and the allied educational establishment, it should not be surprising that most state pre-K money has gone to new programs in public schools. In the 2003–04 school year, about 90 percent of children supported by pre-K funds were enrolled in public schools.

Why add a new, school-based program for four-year-olds when, as we have seen, about 70 percent of all three- and four-year-olds nationwide *already* spend at least some time in some form of center-based child care or Head Start? Wasn't this goal of universality the political and programmatic hurdle that brought down California's Proposition 82? Would it not be sounder policy to expand the programs that already exist?

Perhaps the politicians supporting universal pre-K do not know the extent of existing preschool services. (That seems to have been the case in California.) After all, like the rest of us, they are constantly exposed to a barrage of complaints about the inadequacy of child-care services. And some governors seem to have been persuaded that a pre-K program would raise test scores, thus helping to prevent the financial penalties for failing to meet the standards of the No Child Left Behind Act.

The advocates of universal pre-K, however, know exactly what they are doing. In public, they justify creating a new program by claiming—often with some hyperbole—that existing programs are of such poor quality that displacing them will be a net good. Thus, Nathan James, a spokesman for Rob Reiner, asserted that as few as 25 percent of the four-year-olds in day care were in quality programs. Care for the others "could be baby-sitting or throwing a kid in front of a TV set," he said.

That kind of exaggeration—with its remarkable suggestion that the majority of parents hand their children over to dreadful caregivers—distracts attention from the real question: Would it not make more sense to improve the existing programs than to start up a fresh group of efforts whose quality is far from guaranteed? For example, "Project Upgrade" (funded by the U.S. Department of Health and Human Services) used rigorous evaluation techniques to test a revised curriculum for child-care centers in Florida. It raised test scores on at least some elements of cognitive development as much as the best state pre-K programs—at a much lower cost. (Because pre-K pays teacher-level salaries, on an hourly basis it costs about 50 percent more than center-based care.)

In private, advocates give a more plausible explanation. They say that the phrases "universal preschool" and "universal pre-K" are meant to suggest the extension of public education. The idea is to finesse the major reasons why past efforts to enact a universal child-care program failed. If pre-K is just adding another year to schooling, then it is not taking over child rearing (a prerogative carefully guarded by American parents). And if it is an education program, it might attract the children of stay-at-home mothers and would certainly justify taxpayer spending on middle-class and more affluent families. (After all, schools are free to all, regardless of income.)

Justifying free pre-K is politically important because, contrary to what the news media imply, two-parent families in which the mother works are actually much wealthier than those with stay-at-home mothers. As The *Los Angeles Times* complained, universal pre-K makes a "taxpayer-funded preschool available to middle-class and rich families, which can easily afford it." Although other factors are involved, consider that in 2006 the median income for households with two earners was $76,635, almost 40 percent more than that for married-couple households with only one earner ($55,372).

The key to this "pre-K is just another year of school" argument is the claim that, unlike Head Start, pre-K programs provide educational benefits to all children, not just the disadvantaged. "All children make phenomenal gains" in pre-K, claims Libby Doggett, executive director of the advocacy group Pre-K Now. Rob Reiner told the National Governors' Association that pre-K programs produce a "huger impact" on how all children do "in school and later on in life."

At first glance, the idea that starting school a year earlier would boost the learning of middle-class children might make sense. (Let's pass on the worry that many experts have about the negative impact of starting formal education too soon.) We want our children to do the best they can in school, so, presumably, the earlier they start preparing for school, the better.

Unfortunately, no scientifically rigorous evidence supports the claims of pre-K's impact on middle-class children. James Heckman, a University of Chicago Nobel laureate in economics, is one of the strongest voices in favor of early education for low-income children, but here is what he says about applying the model to the middle class: "Advocates and supporters of universal preschool often use existing research for purely political purposes. But the solid evidence for the effectiveness of early interventions is limited to those conducted on disadvantaged populations." As Bruce Fuller, an education professor at the University of California, Berkeley, and author of *Standardized Childhood* (2007), explains, "For middle-class kids the quality of preschool centers would have to approach a nirvana-like condition to present radically richer environments than the majority of middle-class homes, or home-based caregivers."

It's not that knowledgeable pre-K backers don't know this. Fuller reports on a conversation he had with one of the key foundation funders of the pre-K movement: "When I asked [universal pre-K] benefactor Sue Urahn of the Pew Charitable Trusts why government should subsidize preschools for all families, rich or poor, she acknowledged that 'you probably won't get the degree of benefit for middle-class children that you would for poor kids.' But, she added, universality may bolster the political will to widen children's access to, and to improve the quality of, preschool."

So that's the strategy: promise the middle class a free lunch. Thus far, it seems to be working. Each year sees an increase in the number of children in pre-K programs. In the 2006–07 school year, the NIEER reports, 14 states had 25 percent or more of all four-year-olds in pre-K, and three states had reached 50 percent.

In most places, pre-K programs are simply being added to the mix of preschool programs, with little or no attempt to coordinate them with existing child-care programs or Head Start. The eventual goal, apparently, is to have universal pre-K programs substitute for all programs that now serve four-year-olds.

But is it the right strategy? What about the nearly 500,000 four-year-olds in Head Start? And what about the almost 1.6 million four-year-old children of full-time working women—children who need more than part-time care while their mothers are on the job?

⋅◈⋅

Pre-K is already eating into Head Start enrollments. Last year, Congress responded to what was called "under-enrollment" by allowing Head Start grantees to enroll more infants and toddlers, and to raise income eligibility ceilings. This is, at best, a temporary fix to a long-term problem.

Nonprofit and for-profit child-care centers face a subtler threat. Full-time working mothers who use pre-K (whether because of its presumed quality or because it is free) no longer need their services. And because pre-K fills only a few hours of each day, these mothers tend to patch together some combination of before– and after–pre-K activities for their children. Because they generally cannot use child-care centers for this purpose, children are more likely to wind up in informal care, provided by neighbors, relatives, and others—the very care that pre-K advocates criticize most.

When researchers studying New York State's universal pre-K program raised the possibility that pre-K programs "could negatively impact the enrollment of four-year-olds at nonpublic child-care centers and preschools," a pre-K advocate asked, "Is this necessarily an all-negative outcome?"

Or perhaps advocates would prefer the Oklahoma solution. Using mostly federal funds, the state simply pays child-care centers for a full day for each child, even if the child is only present for four hours. (This practice is documented in government reports, but the folks in Washington either don't know or don't care about it.)

Another troubling aspect of the pre-K movement is that it is a retreat from parental choice in early childhood arrangements, an approach that has been nurtured since the passage of the block grant bill in 1990. Since then, more than $100 billion in child-care subsidies has been distributed through vouchers—with nary a problem—while low-income parents have had the freedom to choose the providers they want, largely without government constraints. (Even unlicensed providers can be used in most states.) But parents in neighborhoods served by pre-K have only one choice: send their children to the public program or dig into their pockets to send them to one of their own choosing.

Vouchers are controversial for K–12 education, but they have been widely accepted in the child-care world—because the context is so different. Remember, the children involved are three-year-olds and four-year-olds. Even some strong critics of vouchers for the schools, such as John Witte, a political scientist at the University of Wisconsin, Madison, have concluded that *for preschool programs* a "voucher system seems to be the best choice to maximize opportunity and equity and educational efficiency."

Besides encouraging responsive programming and service improvement, vouchers provide a high degree of flexibility needed to accommodate the disparate needs of families. Some parents want, or need, only half-day care; some need evening or after-hours care; others need full-day care, perhaps with extended hours. Some parents want their children cared for by other family members; some want to use neighbors; others want a nursery school; still others prefer a care center, perhaps in a church. Some parents may want all their children of different ages in one place; others may not care. Some parents will want their children close

to home; others will want them close to work. The variations are almost infinite. Accommodating such variation is all but impossible in a top-down, pre-K regime.

Perhaps most troubling, universal pre-K does little, if anything, to solve the most vexing educational problem facing America: the achievement gap that puts low-income, mostly minority children so far behind more fortunate children. On a host of important developmental measures, low-income children suffer large and troubling social and cognitive deficits compared with others. This translates into a lifelong achievement gap that curtails the educational attainment, employment opportunities, and earnings potential of large numbers of children—especially among African Americans, Latinos, and other disadvantaged minorities.

⋅⊰⊚⊱⋅

The achievement gap has many causes, from the poverty stemming from a history of discrimination and restricted opportunity to the child-rearing styles of many disadvantaged families. Cause and effect are intermingled in multiple and controversial ways. Early childhood education is a potentially important remedy to some of these problems, but the plain fact is that the family is the primary teacher of young children—and compensatory programs face a much larger challenge than pre-K advocates' rhetoric commonly suggests. What parents do (and do not do) counts much more than any early education program.

Debate rages about how best to close the achievement gap, but all specialists agree that to be successful, programs must be focused on the children's deep needs and be intense enough to make a difference. That means multiple years of educational and support services for the parents as well as the children—and that simply is not something pre-K and its three or four hours of school-based services will provide.

Some observers think that, if pre-K programs really worked for the middle class, they would widen the achievement gap. Bruce Fuller points out, "The well-orchestrated universal preschool campaign at once says their silver bullet will help all kids and close early achievement gaps. That's pretty difficult to pull off. It means that children from middle-class and wealthy families will accelerate in their development, and then poor kids will accelerate even more."

Perhaps sometime in the future all American children will be in free child care, at least by the time they are four years old. But we seem far from that goal. One research group estimates that a universal pre-K system would cost roughly $55 billion a year, more than six times the roughly $9 billion the federal and state governments now spend on four-year-olds. If past estimates for the costs of other social programs are any guide, it would not be unreasonable to double that forecast.

Universal pre-K might be a boon to the middle class—depending on whether, in the end, it is their tax dollars that pay for it—but it would still leave unmet the much more serious needs of low-income children. Half of all eligible low-income working mothers still do not receive child-care subsidies. Would it not be wiser policy to help them purchase better child care than to channel more funding into pre-K programs that serve higher-income children whose parents do not necessarily work?

Twice before, efforts to create a universal program stalled in Washington. But this round's education-based strategy may work. Although it failed with the voters of California, special interests hold much greater sway in the nation's capital. So, to answer Hillary Clinton's question: Universal pre-K is caught in the midst of middle-class and interest-group politics. As usual, the most disadvantaged children may lose out.

DOUGLAS J. BESHAROV is Professor at the University of Maryland's School of Public Policy and a Scholar at the American Enterprise Institute for Public Policy Research.

DOUGLAS M. CALL is a Research Associate at the University of Maryland's School of Public Policy.

EXPLORING THE ISSUE

Has the Time Arrived for Universal Preschool?

Critical Thinking and Reflection

1. Should legislators take a closer look at funding and begin to focus on research-based early childhood education and universal preschool?
2. How has the family unit changed its impact on early preschool programs?
3. Is preschool just another year of school? Explain.
4. Is preschool a strategy to close the achievement gap?
5. What is meant by Kirp's comment, "When it comes to children's issues, Washington has been asleep at the switch"?

Is There Common Ground?

Lisa Snell, in an October 31, 2008 web posting, "Preschool's Failures: Where Are the Long-term Benefits?" cites evidence that the high-quality preschool program in Tennessee produced no statistical achievement difference between those who attended preschool and those who did not. In Oklahoma, where preschool had been in place for 18 years, math and reading scores are still below the national average. In his recently published book, *Reroute the Pre-school Juggernaut* (2009), Chester E. Finn, Jr. attempts to stifle the momentum of the universal preschool campaign spearheaded by secretary of education Arne Duncan, David L. Kirp, Libby Doggett of Pre-K Now, W. Steven Barnett, and others. Precisely as these strategists intend, he claims, "many Americans are coming to believe that pre-kindergarten is a good and necessary thing for government to provide; indeed that not providing it will cruelly deprive our youngest residents of their birthrights, blight their educational futures, and dim their life prospects." The result, he contends, has been strong public support for the movement with little consideration of how it will be paid for.

Further expansion of Douglas Besharov's concerns about the movement can be found in "Preschool Puzzle: As State After State Expands Pre-K Schooling, Questions Remain," *Education Next* (Fall 2008) and in his testimony of June 27, 2007 before the Joint Economic Committee of the U.S. Congress. In these documents Besharov addresses the problem of whether a preschool program can reduce the racial/ethnic achievement gap and the issue of who should receive expanded funding for early care and education.

An even-handed appraisal of the issue can be found in "Invest in Early Childhood Education," *Phi Delta Kappan* (April 2009) by Sharon Lynn Kagan and Jeanne L. Reid and in "Preparing for Change: A Case Study of Successful Alignment Between a Pre-K Program and K-12 Education," *Childhood Education* (Spring 2009) by Christopher Brown and Brian Mowry. The May 2010 issue of *Phi Delta Kappan* offers nine articles on universal preschool.

Create Central

www.mhhe.com/createcentral

Additional Resources

W. Steven Barnett and Ellen Frede, "The Promise of Preschool: Why We Need Early Education for All," *American Educator* (Spring 2010)

Bruce Fuller, *Standardized Childhood* (2007)

Stephen Goldsmith and Nina S. Rees, "Pre-K 101," *Education Next* (Summer 2007)

Susan B. Neuman, "Changing the Odds," *Educational Leadership* (October 2007)

Robert C. Pianta, "Preschool Is School, Sometimes," *Education Next* (Winter 2007)

Internet References . . .

About the Ounce of Prevention Fund

www.ounceofprevention.org/about/index.php

Educational Improvement Tax Credit Program (EITC)

www.newpa.com/find-and-apply-for-funding/funding-and-program-finder/educational-improvement-tax-credit-program-eitc

Smart Start

www.smartstart.org/

Social Programs That Work: Abecedarian Project

http://evidencebasedprograms.org/1366-2/abecedarian-project

The Harlem Children's Zone Project

www.hcz.org/about-us/the-hcz-project

Selected, Edited, and with Issue Framing Material by:
Glenn L. Koonce, *Regent University*

ISSUE

Is the Inclusive Classroom Model Workable?

YES: Mara Sapon-Shevin, from "Learning in an Inclusive Community," *Educational Leadership* (September 2008)

NO: Wade A. Carpenter, from "The Other Side of Inclusion," *Educational Horizons* (Spring 2008)

Learning Outcomes

After reading this issue, you will be able to:

- Interpret the philosophical differences that often occur in inclusive model classroom.
- Distinguish between an inclusion classroom and an inclusive society and how that impacts the structure of a classroom setting.
- Identify the ten strategies for creating a positive inclusive classroom and how they can transfer to a daily inclusive community.
- Examine how socialization can be both positive and negative in a classroom.
- Describe the many lessons inclusive education settings can teach us.

ISSUE SUMMARY

YES: Professor of inclusive education Mara Sapon-Shevin presents a redefinition of the inclusive classroom and offers specific strategies for bringing it about in practice.

NO: Associate professor of education Wade A. Carpenter expresses concerns about the inclusive ideology's uncritical infatuation with socialization.

The Education for All Handicapped Children Act of 1975 (Public Law 94-142), which mandated that schools provide free public education to all students with disabilities, is an excellent example of how federal influence can translate social policy into practical alterations of public school procedures at the local level. With this act, the general social policy of equalizing educational opportunity and the specific social policy of ensuring that young people with various physical, mental, and emotional disabilities are constructively served by tax dollars were brought together in a law designed to provide persons with disabilities the same services and opportunities as nondisabled individuals. Legislation of such delicate matters does not ensure success, however. Although most people applaud the intentions of the act, some people find the expense ill-proportioned and others feel that the federal mandate is unnecessary, heavy-handed, and ill-funded.

Some of the main elements of the 1975 law were that all learners between the ages of 3 and 21 with handicaps—defined as students who are hearing impaired, visually impaired, physically disabled, emotionally disturbed,

mentally retarded, or have special learning disabilities—would be provided a free public education, that each would have an individualized program jointly developed by the school and parents, that each student would be placed in the least restrictive learning environment possible, and that parents would have approval rights in placement decisions.

The 1990 version of the law, the Individuals with Disabilities Education Act (IDEA), has spawned an "inclusive schools" movement whose supporters recommend that no students be assigned to special classrooms or segregated wings of the school. According to advocates of this view, "the inclusion option signifies the end of labeling and separate classes but not the end of necessary supports and services" for all students needing them.

The primary justification for inclusion has traditionally resided in the belief that disabled children have a right to and can benefit from inclusion in a regular educational environment whenever possible. French sociologist Emile Durkheim felt that attachment and belonging were essential to human development. If this is the case, then integration of young people with disabilities into regular classrooms and into other areas of social intercourse would seem to be highly desirable.

According to Richard A. Villa and Jacqueline S. Thousand, in "Making Inclusive Education Work," *Educational Leadership* (October 2003), in some schools inclusion means the mere physical presence or social inclusion in regular classrooms of students with disabilities while in others it means modification of content, instruction, and assessments to enable these students to engage in core academic experiences. Villa and Thousand see inclusion as a general education initiative, not just an add-on unrelated school reform. Karen Agne, in "The Dismantling of the Great American Public School," *Educational Horizons* (Spring 1998), takes a dim view of inclusion and cites examples of classroom disruption, frazzled teachers, and disproportionate expenditures of time and money (citing, for example, a single disabled child being granted over $140,000 per year to meet his special needs). She is especially concerned with disregard of gifted students and the fact that disabled students do not get appropriate academic development in regular classrooms.

In a 2007 book, *Widening the Circle: The Power of Inclusive Classrooms*, Mara Sapon-Shevin puts forth the proposition that the entire classroom, viewed as a learning community, will benefit from a welcoming approach to all students assumed to be full members of the community, perhaps with modifications, adaptations, and extensive support. She frames inclusion in terms of social justice, an excellent idea sometimes badly implemented.

In the articles presented here Mara Sapon-Shevin offers details of her expanded theory of inclusion which develops students who are comfortable with differences, skilled at confronting challenging situations, and aware of human interconnectedness and Wade A. Carpenter offers a pungent, mostly negative, appraisal of the inclusion effort, drawing parallels with another "right-thing-to-do" campaign: desegregation.

YES ↵

Mara Sapon-Shevin

Learning in an Inclusive Community

Schools are increasingly acknowledging the heterogeneity of their student populations and the need to respond thoughtfully and responsibly to differences in the classroom. It's understandable that educators often feel overwhelmed by growing demands for inclusion, multicultural education, multiple intelligences, and differentiated instruction to deal with the growing diversity.

But what if including all students and attending thoughtfully to diversity were part of the solution rather than part of the task overload? What if we put community building and the emotional climate of the classroom back at the center of our organizing values? What if we realized that only inclusive classrooms can fully support the goal of creating thoughtful, engaged citizens for our democratic society?

Redefining the Inclusive Classroom

Alter years of struggle about the politics and practice of inclusion and multicultural education, it's time we understand that inclusive, diverse classrooms are here to stay. But inclusion is not about disability, and it's not only about schools. Inclusion is about creating a society in which all children and their families feel welcomed and valued.

In truly inclusive classrooms, teachers acknowledge the myriad ways in which students differ from one another (class, gender, ethnicity, family background, sexual orientation, language, abilities, size, religion, and so on); value this diversity; and design and implement productive, sensitive responses. Defining inclusion in this way requires us to redefine other classroom practices. For example, *access* can mean, Is there a ramp? But it can also mean, Will letters home to parents be written in a language they can understand?

Differentiated instruction can mean allowing a nonreader to listen to a book on tape. But it can also mean organizing the language arts curriculum using principles of universal design, assuming and planning for diversity from the beginning rather than retrofitting accommodations after the initial design.

Positive behavior management can be a system of providing support to students with diagnosed emotional problems. But it can also mean ongoing community building, classroom meetings, cooperative games, and a culture of appreciation and celebration for all students.

What does it mean to think inclusively, and how can this framework enhance the learning of all children?

There are many lessons that inclusive education settings can teach us. Here are just a few.

Comfort with Diversity

In our increasingly diverse world, all people need to be comfortable with diversity. Inclusion benefits all students by helping them understand and appreciate that the world is big, that people are different, and that we can work together to find solutions that work for everyone.

Inclusion teaches us to think about *we* rather than *I*—not to ask, Will there be anything for me to eat? but rather to wonder, How can we make sure there's a snack for everyone? Not, Will I have friends? but rather, How can I be aware of the children here who don't have anyone to play with? When we are surrounded by people who are different from us, we are forced to ask questions that go beyond the individual and address the community. When we have friends who use wheel-chairs, we notice that there are steep stairs and no ramps. When we have friends who wear hearing aids, we listen differently to comments like "What are you, deaf or something?" When we have friends with different skin colors, we become more alert to racist and exclusionary comments. When we have friends from different religious backgrounds, we are more aware that the decorations in the mall are about only one religion.

In the absence of diversity, it's hard to learn to be comfortable with difference. The white college-age students I teach are often confounded about how to talk about people of color: "Is the right term *African American or black*? What if the person is from Jamaica or Haiti? How do I describe people?" Similarly, many adults are nervous about interacting with people with disabilities, unsure whether they should offer help or refrain, mention the person's disability or not.

The only way to gain fluency, comfort, and ease is through genuine relationships in which we learn how to talk to and about people whom we perceive as different, often learning that many of our initial assumptions or judgments were, in fact, erroneous. The goal is not to make differences invisible ("I don't see color"; "It's such a good inclusive classroom, you can't tell who the kids with disabilities are") but to develop the language and skill to negotiate diversity. Classrooms cannot feel safe to anyone if discussions of difference are avoided, discouraged, or considered inappropriate.

I am always delighted, and a bit stunned, when I see young people easily negotiating conversations about difference that would have been impossible a decade ago and that are still out of reach for many of us. I recently witnessed a discussion of different kinds of families during which children from ages 5 to 8 spoke of adoption, same-sex parents, known and unknown donors, and the many ways they had come to be members of their family. These students, growing up in an inclusive, diverse community, will not need a book that says, "There are many kinds of families." That understanding is already part of their lived experience.

As a teacher, you can successfully facilitate discussions like this by doing the following:

- Familiarize yourself with the current terminology and debates about what people are called: Do Puerto Ricans call themselves *Latino*? Why is the term *hearing impaired* preferred by some but not all "deaf" people? If there are disagreements about terms—for example, some people prefer the term *Native American* and some *Indian*—find out what that conversation is about. Model appropriate language when discussing differences in the classroom.
- Provide multiple opportunities for talking about diversity When a news story is about a hurricane in Haiti, pull down the map: Where is that country? What languages do the people there speak? Do we have anyone at our school from Haiti?
- If you hear teasing or inappropriate language being used to discuss differences, don't respond punitively ("I don't ever want to hear that word again!"), but don't let it go. As soon as possible, engage students in a discussion of the power of their language and their assumptions. Teach students the words *stereotype*, *prejudice*, and *discrimination* and encourage them to identify examples when they see them: "On the commercial on TV last night, I noticed that all the people they identified as 'beautiful' were white."

Inclusion is not a favor we do for students with disabilities, any more than a commitment to multicultural education benefits only students of color. Inclusion is a gift we give ourselves: the gift of understanding, the gift of knowing that we are all members of the human race and that joy comes in building genuine relationships with a wide range of other people.

Honesty About Hard Topics

Inclusion not only makes students better educated about individual differences, but also provides a place to learn about challenging topics. In inclusive classrooms, teachers and students learn to talk about the uncomfortable and the painful.

Often, as adults, we don't know what to do when we are confronted by people and situations that frighten, surprise, or confound us. Children, through their eagerness to engage with the world and seek answers to their questions, can learn important repertoires of communication and interaction in inclusive settings: How can I find out why Michelle wears that scarf on her head without hurting her feelings? How can I play with Jasper if he doesn't talk? Learning how to ask questions respectfully and how to listen well to the answers are skills that will provide a smoother entry into the complexities of adulthood.

In one school, a young boy who required tube feeding provided the opportunity for all the students to learn not only about the digestive system but also about ways to help people while preserving their dignity and autonomy. In another school, a child whose religion kept him from celebrating birthdays and holidays gave other students the opportunity to not only learn about different religions but also brainstorm ways of keeping Jonah a valued and supported member of the classroom. And when a young Muslim child was harassed on the way home from school in the months after the attack on the World Trade Center, the whole class was able to engage in an important discussion of racism and being allies to those experiencing prejudice and oppression.

A student in one classroom was dying of cancer. The teachers, rather than excluding the student and avoiding the subsequent questions, helped all the other students stay informed and involved in his life (and eventually, in his death). With close communication with parents, the teachers talked to students about what was happening to Trevor and how they could support him: "Of course we would miss you if you died." "Yes, it's very, very sad." "No, it's not fair for a 6-year-old to die; it doesn't happen very often." On days when Trevor was in school and feeling weak, the students took turns reading to him. On days when he was not able to come to school, they wrote him notes and made cards. When he died, many of them went to the funeral. Tears were welcomed and tissues were widely used; the teachers were able to show their sadness as well. Teachers had to be thoughtful about discussions of religious beliefs in order to be inclusive: "Yes, some people believe in heaven, and they think that's where Trevor is going."

Although no parents would want their children to have to deal with the death of a classmate, the sensitivity and tenderness of the experience helped bond the class and enabled students to connect to both the fragility and the sacredness of life. When they experience death again later in their lives, they will have some understanding of what it means to offer and receive support and will be able to seek the information and caring they need for their own journeys.

In inclusive classrooms, I have seen students learn to support a classmate with cerebral palsy, become allies in the face of homophobic bullying, and help a peer struggling with academic work. All of these were possible because the teachers were willing and able to talk to the students honestly about what was going on, creating a caring, supportive community for all students rather than marginalizing those who were experiencing difficulty.

TEN STRATEGIES FOR CREATING A POSITIVE, INCLUSIVE CLASSROOM

1. Make time for community building throughout the year. Time spent building community is never wasted.
2. Proactively teach positive social skills: how to make friends, how to give compliments, what to do if someone teases you or hurts your feelings. Don't wait for negative things to happen.
3. Be explicit in explaining to your students why treating one another well and building a community is important. Use key terms: *community, inclusion, friends, support, caring, kindness.* Don't let those words become empty slogans; give lots of examples of positive behaviors.
4. Adopt a zero-indifference policy. Don't ignore bullying in the hope that it will go away. Don't punish the participants, but be clear about what is acceptable. Say, "I don't want that word used in my classroom. It hurts people's feelings and it's not kind."
5. Share your own learning around issues of diversity and inclusion. When students see that you are also learning (and struggling), they can share their own journeys more easily. Tell them, "You know, when I was growing up, there were some words I heard and used that I don't use anymore, and here's why." "You know, sometimes I'm still a little uncomfortable when I see people with significant physical differences, but here's what I've been learning."
6. Think about what messages you're communicating about community and differences in everything you do, including the books you read to your students, the songs you sing, what you put on the walls, and how you talk about different families and world events.
7. Seize teachable moments for social justice. When students say, "That's so gay," talk about the power of words to hurt people and where such oppressive language can lead. When a student makes fun of another student, talk about different cultures, norms, and experiences.
8. Provide lots of opportunities for students to work together, and teach them how to help one another. End activities with appreciation circles: "What's something you did well today?" "How did Carlos help you today?"
9. Don't set students up to compete with one another. Create an atmosphere in which each student knows that he or she is valued for something.
10. Keep in mind that your students will remember only some of what you taught them but everything about how they felt in your classroom.

Mutual Support

Sadly, teasing and exclusion are a typical part of many students' school experience. Bullying is so common that it can become virtually invisible. But inclusive classrooms foster a climate in which individual students know they will not be abandoned when they experience injustice. Inclusion means that we pay careful attention to issues of social justice and inequity, whether they appear at the individual, classroom, or school level or extend into the larger community.

I have used Peggy Moss's wonderful children's book *Say Something* (Tilbury House, 2004) to engage students and teachers in discussions about what we do when we see someone being picked on. In the book, a young girl goes from witnessing and lamenting the mistreatment of her classmates to taking action to change the patterns she observes.

This book and similar materials encourage students to talk about the concept of courage, about opportunities to be brave in both small and large ways, and about how they can make a difference.

Inclusive classrooms give us many opportunities to be our best selves, reaching across our personal borders to ask, Do you want to play? or Can I help you with that? Our lessons about how we treat one another extend beyond the specificity of rules (Don't tease children with disabilities) to broader, more inclusive discussions: How would you like to be treated? What do you think others feel when they're left out? How could we change this activity so more kids could play? How do you want others to deal with your challenges and triumphs, and what would that look like in our classroom?

Teachers in inclusive classrooms consider helping essential. The classroom becomes a more positive place for everyone when multiple forms of peer support—such as peer mentoring and collaborative learning—are ongoing, consistent, and valued. Rather than saying, "I want to know what you can do, not what your neighbor can do," inclusive teachers say, "Molly, why don't you ask Luis to show you how to do that," or "Make sure everyone at your table understands how to color the map code."

Inclusive settings provide multiple opportunities to explore what it means to help one another. By challenging the notion that there are two kinds of people in the world—those who need help and those who give help—we teach all students to see themselves as both givers and receivers. We recognize and honor multiple forms of intelligence and many gifts.

Courage to Change the World

When students develop fluency in addressing differences, are exposed to challenging issues, and view themselves as interconnected, teachers can more easily engage them in discussions about how to improve things.

Having a personal connection profoundly shifts one's perception about who has the problem and who should do something about it. When students have a classmate who comes from Mexico and is undocumented, discussions of immigration rights, border patrols, and fair employment practices become much more real. When students have learned to communicate with a classmate with autism, they understand at a deep level that being unable to talk is not the same as having nothing to say. When a classmate comes from a family with two mothers, reports of gay bashing or debates about marriage rights become more tangible.

A powerful way to combat political apathy is by helping young people make connections between their lives and those of others and giving them opportunities to make a difference in whatever ways they can. Although it's certainly possible to teach a social-justice curriculum in a fairly homogeneous school, inclusive classrooms give us the opportunity to put social-justice principles into action. In inclusive classrooms, students can *live* a social-justice curriculum rather than just study it.

Inclusive classrooms that pay careful attention to issues of fairness and justice bring to the surface questions that have the potential to shift students' consciousness now and in the future: Who gets into the gifted program, and how are they chosen? How can we find a part in the school play for a classmate who doesn't talk? Why do people make fun of Brian because he likes art and doesn't like sports? How can we make sure everyone gets to go on the field trip that costs $20?

Inclusive classrooms put a premium on how people treat one another. Learning to live together in a democratic society is one of the most important goals and outcomes of inclusive classrooms. How could we want anything less for our children?

Mara Sapon-Shevin is professor of inclusive education in the Teaching and Leadership Department in the School of Education at Syracuse University and author of *Widening the Circle: The Power of Inclusive Classrooms* (2007).

Wade A. Carpenter   ➡ **NO**

The Other Side of Inclusion

According to the big shot running the meeting the other day, anyone who questions inclusion is a candidate for commitment. Our special education textbook is almost as supercilious: "Inclusion is a belief system shared by every member of a school as a learning community . . . about the responsibility of educating all students so they reach their potential." It is precisely this kind of simplistic triumphalism that makes it next to impossible to improve practices that are sadly insufficient. So yes, I question it.

Unlike the aforementioned true believer, the textbook goes on to admit that the real world is not quite so tidy and to cite a few sources that show problems:

> In today's schools, what is considered inclusive practice varies widely depending on the clarity of state and local policies related to inclusion, the resources available to foster such practices, teacher and administrative understanding and commitment, and parent and community support.[1]

Ya' think?

If inclusion means on one hand the latest good-willed attempt to solve the problem of what to do for our extreme cases—our privileged, our victims, our victimizers, and our unfortunate—by careful placement and enhanced resources, then I'm for it. But let's acknowledge the reports indicating that this problem is still pretty intractable, and try to do something sensible about it.[2]

If, on the other hand, inclusion means that every kid should be confined for the greater part of the day with students requiring extraordinary attention (much less every psycho, free rider, and drug dealer), then no, I'm not for it, *and the law does not require it.*[3] Our textbook finally acknowledges that inclusion

> does not mean that every student is educated with peers at all times, but it does mean that the responsibility of discovering effective means for all students to learn together is taken very seriously and deviations from this approach are made with reluctance and only after careful deliberation.[4]

With that caveat I have no quarrel. We know that the old special education models did not work adequately, and I'm glad they have been discarded. I believe full inclusion is the right thing to do. Nonetheless, in nearly every conversation I have with practicing teachers, they express

frustration and sadness, usually without prompting of any sort, over students questionably included or included in large classes with inadequate support. In nearly every observation I conduct, I see other kids bored stiff; they could have been challenged and could excel or even come to love learning, except that the teacher is pressured to focus on the "bubble kids" most likely to show substantial improvement on test scores. I also see far too many kids who think they can get by with insubstantial and careless work, and they are probably right. If inclusion for students with disabilities is combined with weak administrative support on behavior problems and modest intellectual goals for everyone, the process is unlikely to work. Making this right-thing-to-do even more problematic is that we are trying to include an extraordinary range of abilities, advantages, disadvantages, and handicaps while also trying to keep the criminals and those who hate school (for no matter how good a reason) in school.

I've seen this situation before, in my generation's struggles with another right-thing-to-do that has, until now, been sacrosanct: desegregation. If by desegregation one meant the morally necessary attempt to resolve three hundred years of racial injustice, to promote domestic tranquility, and to guarantee a decent chance at the American dream to decent people of all races, then I'm for it. In fact, I spent the greater part of my career working awfully hard to make it work, occasionally putting myself at considerable physical risk. By the twentieth century our society had been so morally corrupted and impoverished by generations of racism and discriminatory schooling that we rightly put freedom of association in abeyance, or at least reduced it considerably. But how far can we take that reduction in the twenty-first century and still call ourselves "the land of the free"?

Leveling downward is not compatible with education, either, by any definition of the word to which I care to subscribe. If by desegregation we mean the socially toxic result of miseducating kids of whatever race to the level of the street-corner hustler or the semiliterate Ku Kluxer, then no, I'm not for it at all. I did my high school teaching in Charlotte, North Carolina, the "home" of busing, in the 1970s and '80s, and I witnessed firsthand the results of doing the right thing badly; now I read that just about everything we accomplished for desegregation back then has been undone.[5] For many years I was a good soldier and kept my mouth shut. I'm too old for that stuff now.

From *Educational Leadership*, Spring 2008, pp. 134–138. Copyright © 2008 by Wade A. Carpenter. Reprinted by permission of the author.

Part of the problem, I think, was that we were desegregating without any regard whatsoever for whether or not that particular child belonged in that particular class. I well remember the sweet little old lady from downstairs coming into my classroom at the beginning of every semester with her clipboard, and moving kids—lots of them—to and from advanced and low-level classes *simply to comply with the court order.* You, you, and you are now slow learners. Sorry. You, you, and you are now advanced. Congratulations.

I believe the other problem with desegregation, and now inclusion, lies in an uncritical infatuation with socialization, resulting in a seduction pulled off with an awful cynicism.[6] To quote British philosopher Michael Oakeshott:

> Modern governments are not interested in education: they are concerned only to impose "socialization" of one kind or another upon the surviving fragments of a once considerable educational engagement. . . . [This is] the alternative to education, invented for the poor as something instead of virtually nothing.[7]

While the rationale for both desegregation and inclusion is multi-faceted, nuanced, and intellectually and morally compelling, most of the evidence for their effectiveness has been built around socialization, and socialization done poorly, at that. Discrimination may or may not be an evil, depending on how it's done, but indiscriminate inclusion may bring with it an evil far worse, and I fear it will hurt the kids with disabilities, probably even worse than their nondisabled classmates.

"Socialization" is important, but it is not unproblematic. A facile "They're all equal in God's sight" from developmentally delayed social gospelers just won't do, nor will an equally facile "They all have to learn to get along with all kinds of people" from historically bypassed egalitarians. Most children are perfectly capable of learning about a sewer without having to roll around in one, so it stands to reason that they can also learn about felons without having to sit beside them eight hours per day, one hundred eighty days per year, for twelve (or more) years. Our society has not yet provided enough support or alternatives for exceptional kids, nor has it learned how to discriminate *well.*[8] To make inclusion work beyond the merely "adequate," we need to provide more attractive alternatives for those kids who don't want to be in schools and who detract from the education of those who do. We need to give teachers more support and give the kids more teachers—I would suggest no more than fifteen kids per class in inclusive settings. Blithely asserting that "individualization," "inclusive practices," or a bigger "bag of tricks" will solve the problem of extreme cases applies methodological Band-Aids to political diseases, places undue burdens (including a deeply unfair load of guilt) on conscientious and overloaded teachers, and ultimately hurts far too many kids.[9] As with segregation, this is not a methods problem; it is a policy problem. "Best practices" should never be a bureaucratic placebo for bad policy. A naive notion of equality and socialization is no more helpful than is a bigoted attitude toward diversity and social mobility. Contrary to some egalitarians, a good society rightly honors those who through intelligent good will, artistic talent, athletic prowess, or plain honest hard work make our lives better. Conversely, a good society shelters *all* children from being held down by conservative elitists, held back by liberal egalitarians, or held up by criminals. Benjamin Barber elegantly describes a kinder view of equality:

> When democratic citizenship insists on leveling, it demands that slaves be emancipated, not that masters be enslaved; that suffrage be granted to the dispossessed, not taken from the powerful; that I win the exercise of my rights, not that you lose the exercise of yours.[10]

Contrary to some devotees of socialization, schools are not likely to fix every kid, and not every kid belongs in a school. Unless we figure that out, we will find ourselves increasingly burdened by schools in which nobody belongs, and as usual, the exceptional will be victimized even more savagely, because they are more vulnerable. The thrust of this column is simple: *inclusion is not likely to work if we insist on including the victimizers with the victims.*

Equality and socialization should accompany—not replace—judgment and education. To substitute the former for the latter, or vice versa, is an unsafe practice, pure and simple. No child should be denied the benefits of our education, but many do not deserve the burdens of our schooling—as it is currently practiced.

Notes

1. Marilyn Friend, *Special Education: Contemporary Perspectives for School Professionals.* 2nd ed. (Boston: Pearson/Allyn Bacon, 2008), pp. 20, 21.
2. Start with Friend, then go to the USDOE's site and take up with . . ., and then surf from there. Be forewarned, however: although the research is pretty solid that inclusion seldom hurts and often helps students with disabilities, and may have affective and social benefits for all, the research "suggesting" that it doesn't hurt "the other kids" academically is dated, limited, and unconvincing. Those who even think about it generally finesse the issue. And even its most enthusiastic proponents do not approve of inclusion without adequate support systems—including alternative systems for those who resist schooling and make it difficult for others. And that is my beef. See also Debbie Staub, *Inclusion and the Other Kids* (Newton, Mass.: National Institute for Urban School Improvement, 1999), ERIC ED 439206.
3. "All children have the right to learn together"; "[t]here are no legitimate reasons to separate

children for their education. Children belong together—with advantages and benefits for everyone. They do not need to be protected from each other" (Organization for Inclusion, Acceptance, and Respect, "Questions and Answers about Inclusion" . . .). Such statements are sentimentalist rubbish. Ask any cop, social worker, or even bullying victim whether protection from *some* children is needed. And that kind of bogus "rights talk" just trivializes worthy and weighty matters: one could just as easily invent a "right" to learn separately, a "right" to attend the college or university of one's choice, or even a "right" to live in a smoke-free city. I found it interesting to hear not long ago that Estonia has declared Internet access a "fundamental human right." It may indeed be very desirable, but compared to life, liberty, and the pursuit of happiness . . . c'mon, folks, get a grip.

4. Friend, *Special Education*, 21.
5. My own experience gives me enough lamentable war stories from "back then," and Ann Doss Helms's articles in my hometown *Charlotte Observer* about post-desegregation outcomes are depressing reading. For broader perspectives and some precise figures, see the NAEP reports on the racial gaps at . . .; the Uniform Crime Statistics published yearly by the FBI at . . .; the drug-abuse figures and the teenage-pregnancy figures released by the U.S. Department of Health and Human Services at . . .; and the findings of the Guttmacher Institute at. . . . Maybe I have to confess that although my generation of teachers did a good job with a lot of individual kids, societally we may have been a disaster.
6. Most of us are probably aware that St. Peter left half the statement unsaid: Love may indeed cover a multitude of sins, but infatuation can lead to a lot more. I Peter 4:8.
7. Timothy Fuller, ed. *Michael Oakeshott on Education* (New Haven:Yale, 1989), p. 86.
8. "Enough support or alternatives": my best suggestion at this point is in Wade A. Carpenter (2007): "For Those We Won't Reach: An Alternative" in *Educational Horizons* 85 (3): 146–155.
9. "Methodological Band-Aids . . . political diseases": an intentional mixed metaphor. I'm not disputing the need for better teaching methods for intellectually challenged and behaviorally challenging children; I am asserting that they may be necessary, but they are unlikely to be sufficient.
10. Benjamin R. Barber, *An Aristocracy of Everyone: The Politics of Education and the Future of America* (New York: Oxford University Press, 1992), p. 6. Allow me to add the suggestion that an aristocracy of everyone is the only democracy worth living in.

WADE A. CARPENTER is associate professor of education at Berry College, Mount Berry, Georgia.

EXPLORING THE ISSUE

Is the Inclusive Classroom Model Workable?

Critical Thinking and Reflection

1. Is a full inclusive classroom a feasible model for all classroom settings?
2. What are some of the true "life lessons" that can be learned from observing an inclusive classroom setting?
3. Is inclusion a term used solely for disabled students? If no, who else falls into the inclusive setting?
4. How does diversity play into the inclusion process and what can be learned and transferred to a democratic society?
5. Why should students without physical, emotional, or educational disabilities be in a classroom setting with students not identified?

Is There Common Ground?

One wit has stated that P.L. 94-142 was really a "full employment act for lawyers." Indeed, there has been much litigation regarding the identification, classification, placement, and specialized treatment of disabled children since the introduction of the 1975 act. The 1992 ruling in Greer v. Rome City School District permitted the parents to place their child, who has Down syndrome, in a regular classroom with supplementary services. Also, the decision in Sacramento City Unified School District v. Holland (1994) allowed a girl with an IQ of 44 to be placed in a regular classroom full time, in accordance with her parents' wishes (the school system had wanted the student to split her time equally between regular and special education classes). These cases demonstrate that although the aspect of the law stipulating parental involvement in the development of individual educational programs can invite cooperation, it can also lead to conflict.

Teacher attitude becomes a crucial component in the success or failure of placements of disabled students in regular classrooms. Teacher training institutions have tried to incorporate "special education" material into the preparation of regular classroom teachers, but many of these teachers find themselves at a loss when it comes to dealing with and assisting children with special needs. Some articles dealing with this and related problems are "Disruptive Disabled Kids: Inclusion Confusion," *School Board News* (October 1994) by Diane Brockett and "Discipline Procedures with Students with Disabilities," *The Clearing House* (January/February 2000) by Jean Mueth Dayton.

Of special interest are "The Oppression of Inclusion," *Educational Horizons* (Fall 2000) by David Aloyzy Zera and Roy Maynard Seitsinger; "Americans with Disabilities: Are They Losing Ground?" *The Clearing House* (January/February 2002) by Nathan L. Essex; "More Choices for Disabled Kids," *Policy Review* (April & May 2002) by Lewis M. Andrews; and Lisa Snell's "Special Education Confidential," *Reason* (December 2002).

Create Central

www.mhhe.com/createcentral

Additional Resources

Thomas Hehir, "Confronting Ableism," *Educational Leadership* (February 2007).

Rachel Hughes, "Learning Disabilities and Social Inclusion," *Journal of Intellectual Disability Research* (June 2009).

M. Mastropieri, *The Inclusive Classroom*, 5th ed. (Pearson Publications, 2013).

Joetta Sack-Min, "The Issues of IDEA," *American School Board Journal* (March 2007).

Cynthia G. Simpson, Rebecca McBride, Vicky G. Spencer, John Lowdermilk, and Sharon Lynch, "Assistive Technology: Supporting Learners in Inclusive Classrooms," *Kappa Delta Pi Record* (Summer 2009).

Internet References. . .

Inclusion, Least Restrictive Environment (LRE), Mainstreaming

www.wrightslaw.com/info/lre.index.htm

What is Inclusion

www.kidstogether.org/inclusion.htm

Council for Exceptional Children

www.cec.sped.org/

Maryland Coalition for Inclusive Education

www.mcie.org/index.php

Is the Inclusive Classroom Model Workable?

www.bignerds.com/papers/85490/Is-The-Inclusive-Classroom-Model-Workable/

Selected, Edited, and with Issue Framing Material by:
Glenn L. Koonce, *Regent University*

ISSUE

Do Teachers Unions Stymie School Reform?

YES: Andrew Coulson, from "A Less Perfect Union," *The American Spectator* (June 2011)

NO: Louis Malfaro, from "Lessons on Organizing for Power," *American Educator* (Fall 2010)

Learning Outcomes

After reading this issue, you will be able to:

- Assess the statement that "it now costs more to teach kids less."
- Evaluate what legislative results were driven by the impact of public school employee union contributions to political campaigns.
- Distinguish political positions between the National Education Association (NEA) and the American Federation of Teachers (AFT).
- Analyze how the Bill of Rights supports teacher unions.
- Critique when and how teacher unions moved from better salaries and benefits into other professional issues.

ISSUE SUMMARY

YES: Andrew Coulson, director of the Center for Educational Freedom at the Cato Institute, contends that the NEA and AFT monopolize public school operations, resulting in a collapse of productivity.

NO: Louis Malfaro, an AFT vice president, sees the teachers unions as uniquely able to build productive relationships and exert positive influence on the improvement of teaching and learning.

The vast majority of public school teachers in the United States belong to the National Education Association (NEA) or the American Federation of Teachers (AFT), powerful unions that engage in collective bargaining, lobbying, and political action. While they clearly and effectively represent the interests of educational professionals at all levels, they have come under increasing scrutiny regarding their role in influencing the quality of public schooling and, in particular, the improvement of student academic performance.

The NEA, founded in 1857 as the National Teachers Association, was for many years controlled by school administrators and was disdainful of the younger AFT, a teachers-only group affiliated with the AFL-CIO. The AFT, begun in 1916, negotiated contracts with local school boards and, as it became more powerful, was not reluctant to use the threat of strikes to strengthen its demands. In recent decades the NEA has adopted union tactics and has also built one of the richest political action committees in the nation, wielding considerable power at the federal level.

The initial onslaught against teacher union power was led by William J. Bennett when he was the secre-

tary of education in the Reagan administration. Bennett charged that "almost without fail, wherever a worthwhile school proposal or legislative initiative is under consideration, those with a vested interest in the educational status quo will use political muscle to block reform." Another union critic, Myron Lieberman, stated in 1998 that all public sector unions are adamantly opposed to smaller government, lower taxes, and privatization efforts. The economic downturn that began in 2008 has rekindled antiunion sentiments, with political leaders in many states and localities demanding concessions from public sector unions and, in some cases, seeking to curtail collective bargaining rights.

Public opinion samples taken in 2011 have found that while teachers are held in reasonably high regard but their unions are seen as capable of doing bad as well as good. As reported by Alexandra Rice in *Education Week* (August 24, 2011) a recent poll shows that the public wants to find and retain high-quality teachers who are compensated on the basis of experience, academic degrees, and principal evaluations, with student test scores seen as less important. This would seem to put the public in accord with a basic union position on teacher retention. Education historian Diane Ravitch, in "Why

Teacher Unions Are Good for Teachers—and the Public," *American Educator* (Winter 2006–2007), states that the unions protect teachers' rights, support professionalism, and check administrative power. It is her view that the unions, despite attacks by zealous politicians, "will continue to be important, vital, and needed so long as they speak on behalf of the rights and dignity of teachers and the essentials of good education."

Education columnist Thomas Toch, in "The Teacher Union's Odysseus," *Phi Delta Kappan* (September 2011), reports that both the AFT and NEA have issued position statements that "break sharply with teacher unions' longstanding focus on job protection" by advocating "rigorous teacher evaluations linked to student learning and quicker dismissals of underperformers." AFT president Randi Weingarten, Toch says, has assumed a leading role among teacher unionists in acknowledging that the unions have lost some public support in recent years. Weingarten believes that an emphasis on teacher quality and education reform can outflank those who want to bust up the unions or at least greatly reduce union power.

A number of books have explored the historical development of unionism in the teaching profession, offering divergent perspectives on the current scene. Peter Brimelow's *The Worm in the Apple: How Teacher Unions Are Destroying American Education* (2003) makes the case that union-fashioned agreements have stifled innovation and risk-taking reforms that would raise the level of student performance. Terry Moe's *Special Interest: Teachers Unions and America's Public Schools* (2011) charts the growth of union power and its consequences. Steven Brill's *Class Warfare: Inside the Fight to Fix America's Schools* (2011) advocates expansion of charter schools unfettered by union influence.

In the following selections Andrew Coulson of the Cato Institute specifies the sources of increased union power in recent decades and suggests ways to rein in that power, while union official Louis Malfaro details his personal story of union affiliation in the state of Texas and the positive lessons he has learned along the way.

YES ↵

Andrew Coulson

A Less Perfect Union

Student achievement at the end of high school has stagnated or declined, depending on the subject, since we started keeping track around 1970. Over that period, the cost of sending a child through the K-12 public system tripled, even after adjusting for inflation. Public school employee unions, the National Education Association and American Federation of Teachers, are partly to blame for this, but the attention focused on collective bargaining in particular has been misplaced. The unions' success in driving up costs and protecting even low-performing teachers stems less from their power at the bargaining table than from the monopoly status of their employer. Taxpayers, and most families, have no place else to go.

In his post-apocalyptic film *Sleeper*, Woody Allen explained the apocalypse with the line: "a man named Albert Shanker got hold of a nuclear warhead." This was in 1973, when Shanker headed New York City's muscle-flexing teachers' union. In those days, the goals of school employee unions were widely understood: uniformly better compensation, greater job security, and reduced workloads for their members. That's what labor unions are for. If NEA and AFT leadership failed to pursue those goals, their members would replace them with people who would.

But for a while, during the sustained economic growth of the '80s, '90s, and early '00s, the public ceased to think very much about these unions as unions. The NEA and AFT have often portrayed themselves as selfless champions of children, who sought only to improve the quality of American education. It's hard to say how widely their PR puffery was believed, but certainly it was the dominant framing in the media and was seldom challenged by more realistic appraisals. (Except, ironically, by Shanker himself, who once declared that he would "start representing schoolchildren" when they "start paying union dues.")

Since the late fiscal unpleasantness began in 2008, all that has changed. It has changed because the money has run out. Think of public schooling as a game of Monopoly in which one of the players, the unions, owns 90 percent of the properties (9 out of 10 American students attend public schools). The other players, taxpayers, have some cash and a few properties of their own, but they can't make it around the board without paying ever-increasing union rents—just as, in real life, taxpayers must continue funding public schools no matter how much they cost. They can survive for a while, of course, and while they do

the unions reap handsome rewards. Eventually, though, the taxpayers run out of money. Game over.

In the board game, we'd call the unions the "winners." In reality, their victory is Pyrrhic. They've been so successful in protecting their members' jobs (including those of the mediocre and inept), raising salaries and benefits, and reducing workloads (by inducing more hiring to lower the student/teacher ratio), that they have precipitated budget crises all over the country, derailing their own gravy train.

Consider the numbers. Since 1970, the inflation-adjusted cost of putting a child through the K-12 public school system has risen from $55,000 to $155,000. Over the same period, the *quality* of that education has stagnated in math and reading and declined in science.

Where has all that extra money gone, if not toward improving quality? Some has fueled higher salaries and benefits for teachers, who enjoy total compensation 42 percent higher than their private-sector colleagues. More has gone into expanding the public school workforce. Astonishingly, employment in public schools has grown *10 times* faster than enrollment over the past four decades.

So while every other service or product has gotten better, more affordable, or both, public school productivity has collapsed. It is now costing us more to teach kids less. If our schools had merely maintained the level of productivity they enjoyed in 1970—not improved as other fields have, just held their ground—American taxpayers would be saving roughly $300 billion a year. In California alone, the $26 billion budget deficit would be instantly wiped out and replaced with a $10 billion surplus.

How did this happen? How did unions grow the public school workforce so much faster than enrollment? For those familiar with the overall trend in unionization, their feat at first seems miraculous. Because while the teachers unions were growing extravagantly, unions nationwide were shriveling up. In the private sector, union membership declined from 31 percent to less than 7 percent of the workforce since 1960. Among public school employees, it doubled from 35 percent to 70 percent over the same period.

Upon reflection, it isn't hard to explain this divergence. In the private sector, unionization is self-regulating. In the public sector, it is not. When a business makes excessive concessions to a union and is thereby forced to raise prices above those of its competitors, it loses customers. As

From *The American Spectator*, June 2011, pp. 18–22. Copyright © 2011 by American Spectator, LLC. Reprinted by permission.

it loses customers, it lays off workers, eroding the union's power. If this situation continues, the business fails and the union members who sought above-market compensation lose their jobs. Overly aggressive unions thus price their own workers out of the workforce. Conversely, less aggressive unions have little appeal to workers because they offer costs (in the form of dues) without value (in the form of above-market wages or benefits).

The easier it is for consumers to shop around, the less value unions can add, because consumers can more easily place their orders with competitors. And thanks to advances in technology comparison-shopping has been getting progressively easier for decades. That's made it increasingly difficult for private sector unions to win above-market wages or benefits.

More than that, the heightened competitiveness of modern markets has meant that the interests of workers and management are more closely aligned than ever. A business that tried to raise profits by paying below-market wages would risk losing its best employees to its competitors or to businesses in related fields, injuring its productivity and ultimately its profitability.

None of this has been lost on the workers themselves. As the usefulness of private sector unions has declined, so has their membership.

But what happens in an industry in which one producer is able to give its product away for "free," draws its revenues from compulsory taxation, is able to hide the full cost of its operations from the public, and is legally required to remain in business? Obviously the unions representing workers in that industry can win substantially above-market compensation and pad their membership dramatically without fear of putting themselves out of business in the short or even the medium term. That, of course, is what has happened in our nation's state-run school systems. The self-regulating aspects of union action in competitive markets do not exist in the public sector.

But after nearly half a century, public school employee unions have finally begun to suffer from their own success. State-run schooling has become so profligate under their ministrations that America can no longer afford it. In an effort to moderate the teachers unions' voracious consumption of tax dollars, governors and legislators in several states have sought to curtail their collective bargaining powers. So it's useful to ask: what role have these powers actually played in the unions' ability to drive up spending?

When I reviewed the scholarly evidence on this question for the *Cato Journal* last year, I was surprised to discover that the answer is: not much. Depending on the study, the existence of collective bargaining has little or no impact on school district spending. The real mechanism by which unions have driven up their membership and compensation has been lobbying in state and federal legislatures and packing school boards with their supporters.

The public school employee unions have been the single biggest political contributors at the federal level over the past 20 years. The $56 million they've spent is roughly equal to the combined contributions of Chevron, Exxon Mobil, the NRA, and Lockheed Martin.

But it is at the state level that their lobbying efforts are focused, because that is the level at which the nation's public school monopolies are legally enshrined. So long as they protect that monopoly on roughly $600 billion in tax dollars, they will face no meaningful competition, and so long as they are without competition, they will be able to secure wages, benefits, and staffing levels far above what a competitive market would bear.

In New York State, for example, teachers unions spent $6.6 million on political activities in 2008. The year before, they paid $571,012 to a single luxury hotel, the Desmond, in the state capital of Albany, to facilitate their lobbying efforts. Those efforts have sought to limit competition from charter and private schools and raise public school spending. They've been largely successful. New York is by no means exceptional in this regard: California's teachers unions accounted for half of the state's total initiative campaign expenditures in the first five months of 2009.

At the local school board level, teachers union power can be even greater. Education journalist Joe Williams reported that "United Teachers Los Angeles had such a tight grip on its school board in 2004 that union leaders actually instructed [board members] on important policies and made no attempt to hide their hand signals to school board members during meetings."

Given the fact that political lobbying and the capture of school boards have been the means by which teachers unions have won their above-market concessions, and that collective bargaining *per se* seems to have played a relatively minor role in their success, it seems unlikely that curtailing collective bargaining will return fiscal sanity to American education.

Others have argued that the balance of power can be restored if states stop automatically garnishing teachers' paychecks in the amount of compulsory union dues and sending the money to the unions. If unions are forced to collect the money themselves, they reason, it will make it harder for them to raise the vast sums they've been spending on political action. This view relies on the improbable assumption that public school employees are ignorant of their own interests. Given their huge wage and benefit advantage over the competitive private sector, union dues are the safest and best investment most public school employees could hope to make. At the moment, dues are returning around 2,000 percent annually (public school teachers enjoy a $17,000 annual compensation premium over their private sector counterparts, and dues run only about $800). Where else could they get a return like that without the use of firearms?

If curbs on collective bargaining and mandatory government dues collection won't rein in the unions' budget-busting political action, what will? The answer is to take advantage of the same freedoms and incentives that have prevented unions from going off the rails in the private sector: give parents and taxpayers real choice, and give public schools real competition.

At present, private schools are at a massive disadvantage to state-run schools because the latter have a monopoly on $13,000 per pupil of government spending annually. That makes it hard for parents, and impossible for taxpayers, to seek out private sector alternatives to the state-run schools. And contrary to widespread perception, public schools spend roughly 50 percent more, on average, than do private schools—including all sources of revenue, not just tuition.

The simplest way to simultaneously give taxpayers and parents educational choice is to cut the taxes on families that pay for their own children's education. Such cuts, called "direct" or "personal use" education tax credits, already exist on a small scale in Iowa and Illinois. If adopted in other states and increased in value they would bring the option of independent, privately operated schools within reach of most Americans. And since the credits need not cover the full cost of private school tuition, the migration from public to independent schools would save taxpayers a great deal of money.

Effective as they are, such direct credits have an obvious limitation: they can only help parents with non-negligible state/local tax liabilities. Most lower-income families owe little in taxes and so wouldn't benefit, leaving them stuck in the deficient, inefficient, state schools. Fortunately, there is a simple solution: cut taxes on individuals and businesses who pay tuition for *other* people's children. Seven states already have such programs, including Arizona, Pennsylvania, and Florida. Called "scholarship donation" tax credits, they cut the taxes on those who donate to non-profit Scholarship Granting Organizations (SGOs). The SGOs, in turn, help families pay for K-12 independent schooling.

What makes scholarship tax credits unique among school choice programs serving low-income children is that they offer choice not just to parents but to taxpayers themselves. No one is compelled to donate to an SGO, and if you choose to do so you select the organization that receives your funds. Think that the organization you're currently supporting is no longer helping families as effectively as it should? You can send your money elsewhere. This forces the SGOs to compete with one another in terms of efficiency and service to families, just as other charitable organizations must.

Combining these two types of tax credits and allowing them to expand in response to public demand would end the unions' half-century stranglehold on education funding. As in every other field, the public would finally be able to seek out the best, most cost-effective providers. The result would be the same in education as it has been in other fields: in the presence of efficient markets, salaries and benefits would depend on performance. The

best teachers would easily command much larger salaries than the largest any public school teacher enjoys today. In sectors of the education industry that already operate within the free enterprise system, such as the Asian after-school tutoring market, the top teachers reach tens of thousands of students via web lectures and earn millions of dollars a year (yes, *millions*) thanks to profit sharing with their employers. Schools that charged more than their competitors for a similar or lower-quality education would lose students and fail. With the end of the state school monopoly, unions would no longer be able to bleed taxpayers for above-market compensation.

Educational freedom would thus end the reign of state school employee unions as a powerbroker in American politics. The Democratic Party would be hardest hit. The NEA has given $30 million in federal campaign contributions since 1990, 93 percent of which has gone to Democrats or the Democratic Party. The AFT has contributed $26 million to federal campaigns, of which 99 percent has gone to Democrats.

This perhaps explains why Democratic lawmakers from Indiana and Wisconsin fled their states this spring, in an effort to block legislation that was expected to curb teachers' union power. And it perhaps explains why President Obama, Education Secretary Arne Duncan, and congressional Democrats killed a small private school choice program in Washington, D.C. (which was subsequently reinstated by Republicans in April as part of the budget agreement).

If Democrats continue to cling to the union-dominated state school monopoly as their salvation, they will ride it, like the Titanic, beneath the waves. It is a ship with a yawning gash beneath the waterline. Most elected Democrats, from President Obama on down, want to deal with that catastrophe by shoveling more money into the furnaces. The longer they do this, the less time they'll have to abandon ship when they realize, belatedly, that the system is doomed.

Sooner or later, the public will no longer be able to maintain school employees in the numbers or in the manner to which they have become accustomed. Our state school monopoly is simply not sustainable, and as Herbert Stein observed, "things that can't go on forever . . . don't." When Americans finally discard this system, they will look around to see who fought to preserve it until the last possible moment. If the answer is "Democrats," it will not only be the Democratic Party that is hurt.

Single-party government has not tended to equate to good government. If Republicans enjoy unitary control of Congress and the presidency for some years while Democrats search for a new base of political support, we will not be blessed by a period of cautious, limited government. But Democrats can avert their own irrelevance by acknowledging today the inherent defects of the union-captured monopoly school system, and championing educational freedom in its place. This would give them a platform they could successfully take to voters: educational excellence, educational freedom, fiscal sanity. A platform they could be proud of.

There are indications that such a shift is possible. Florida has the largest private school choice program in the nation—a scholarship donation tax credit serving 33,000 students, which is set to grow by 25 percent annually in the coming years. It received a single Democratic vote when enacted in 2002. Today it enjoys the support of half the state's Democratic caucus. Hopefully, Democrats nationwide will take Florida as a model. The alternative, for themselves and the nation, is bleak.

ANDREW COULSON is director of Center for Educational Freedom at the Cato Institute. He is author of *Market Education: The Unknown History* (1999).

Louis Malfaro   → **NO**

Lessons on Organizing for Power

School systems sometimes make promises they have no intention of keeping. Other times, they can deliver a world of opportunities to our neediest children. They may or may not want to listen to parents or even teachers, but school systems always attend to the demands of the most powerful individuals and institutions in their communities. For the last 20 years, I've been working and organizing to build power through my local union—Education Austin.

Over the summer, as I made the transition from being president of Education Austin to being secretary-treasurer of the Texas AFT, I spent some time reflecting on how union locals—especially locals like mine in states without collective bargaining—build power. Not power for its own sake, but power to work with school districts, policymakers, and institutions on an equal footing, to advance an agenda of issues for members and the children they serve. I don't have a list of lessons learned or a set of simple steps to follow. What I have is a story. It's my story and the story of my union's struggle to give educators a place at the table.

Teaching and Learning the Hard Way

I started teaching in 1987 at Blackshear Elementary School in Austin, Texas, as a second-grade bilingual teacher. Just eight years earlier, Austin had been ordered by the U.S. Supreme Court to bus students; it was one of the last major urban school districts to come under a court-ordered desegregation plan. The district complied, busing students at all levels beginning in 1980. In 1986, a new school board was elected on a let's-get-rid-of-busing platform. By then, the courts had pretty much gotten out of the business of desegregation. The school district was allowed to reinstitute neighborhood elementary schools, as long as it agreed to make certain accommodations for 16 high-poverty "priority" schools—including that they would be staffed by experienced and exceptional principals and teachers.

I arrived on the scene excited to be assigned to Blackshear Elementary, one of the 16 priority schools, where more than 95 percent of the students received free or reduced-price lunch. As a new teacher, I looked forward to being surrounded by veteran colleagues who would mentor and support me as I learned my new craft.

As it turned out, of the five of us assigned to second grade, four had never taught a lick. Our lone veteran colleague had fewer than five years under her belt. I received a quick lesson in how public school systems can work: promises made to communities (and courts) are not always kept.

At about this time, I was solicited through the mail by the Association of Texas Professional Educators, an anti-collective bargaining, anti-union teacher association. Its flier said, "We believe that strikes should be saved for the grand old game of baseball." Over 20 years later, I still recall the steam coming out my ears as I read this paean to passivity. Where I grew up, in Pennsylvania, my teachers were unionized and union workers at Bethlehem Steel forged the beams of the Golden Gate Bridge. I had learned my history too. Reading *The Jungle* in my public high school opened my eyes to an American history rife with abuse of the American worker. I knew that the labor movement played a very significant role in protecting workers' rights and promoting high-quality public schools.

In most states, the right of school employees to union representation is no longer a stirring issue for educators, but in Texas, state law prohibits collective bargaining. Unlike some southern states where the historical practice is to not engage in collective bargaining, in Texas, it is downright illegal, statutorily prohibited not only for teachers but for virtually all public employees (with a few exceptions for public safety workers). When I moved to Texas, I realized that as far as rights on the job are concerned, the lock had been turned back to pre-1960s America.

When I received the anti-union flier, I cursed the ignorance of it, but I didn't sit in the shadows swearing at the darkness. A few weeks later, I was contacted by the AFT affiliate, the Austin Federation of Teachers, Local 2048. I breathed fire into the phone about the flier I'd received. There was an organizer at my school the next day to sign me up as a new member.

The union, for me, was and continues to be a vehicle for forming relationships with people who share my interests and concerns. Within the first year, I signed up to be the building representative—there were only three AFT members at the school! In fact, although there were two AFT affiliates within the school district, a certified teacher local and a PSRP (paraprofessional and school-related personnel) local, the teacher local had fewer than 300 members spread across 80 schools.

Reprinted with permission from the Fall 2010 issue of *American Educator*, the quarterly journal of the American Federation of Teachers, AFL-CIO.

The big group in town was the NEA affiliate. If somebody from there had talked to me first, it's likely that I would have signed up with the NEA. As with the AFT, the NEA's positions on a lot of issues were similar to mine. Over time, I found that our local union was the little-but-loud group—the real union—so I embraced it.

One of my first initiatives as a building representative was to survey the 16 "priority" schools to find out if they had received the promised master teachers or any of the other promised resources. None of the 16 schools had received the experienced teachers. They did get other things, like reduced class sizes and a little extra money to take kids on field trips. So the district hadn't completely failed, but on the critical issue of quality teachers, nothing had been done. There certainly was quality teaching going on in those 16 schools, but there were many, many greenhorns like me with precious little support.

My first year, I literally got a cardboard box full of teacher's editions of textbooks and was turned loose with 15 second-graders. Nobody came into my room for weeks. Weeks turned into months, and I kept thinking to myself, "I can't believe they just put me in here with these kids! I've never taught before, and nobody is coming in here to see how I'm doing!" To make matters worse, I was the only bilingual second-grade teacher in my school, so I was the only person teaching my specific curriculum to kids in Spanish (their primary language) and English. It was an isolating experience.

Desperate, I eavesdropped on the four-year veteran's classroom, which wasn't difficult because our rooms were divided by a folding wall. During my planning period, I parked myself right next to the thin wall and, while grading papers, listened to her teach, to her pace and how she interacted with the kids. Aside from what I had learned from my student teaching, I really didn't know a lot about what I was supposed to be doing.

Nevertheless, I had the same experience many young, energetic teachers have. I fell in love with my students and their families. I poured in many hours and was astounded at how much I learned about children, and at how quickly my children learned. I went into teaching to work with poor, immigrant kids. I knew I would encounter a lot of really bright kids, but I was amazed by the children's capacity and potential. I ran an afterschool Shakespeare club for a couple of years in which we produced elementary school versions of several dramas, including *A Midsummer Night's Dream* and *Romeo and Juliet*.

Despite the lack of mentoring and support, teaching was a great experience for me. It renewed my faith in the importance of public schools, especially for kids whose parents are immigrants or did not go to college. Working in a classroom every day puts one in touch with the unbridled potential that children bring with them to school. Yet, too often, school systems don't invest adequately in teachers, who, like students, fail to reach their potential as a result. They never become as good at teaching as they could be because they haven't been equipped. I think I was an example of how that happens. I was hard working, I was well intentioned—and I'm not saying I didn't have success in the classroom. But I had so much more to learn. My school district did not have a mentoring or induction program, or a well-articulated professional development program, although I did receive some good training here and there. How much more quickly could I have improved with a real expert by my side, and how would that have affected my students?

The union, in contrast, provided a great deal of leadership training. Even though we were a small local, we were part of a bigger network of local AFT affiliates around Texas. I enjoyed meeting other teachers' union leaders from around the state and hearing about their struggles. The Texas AFT had a very strong leadership development program, with summer training that covered how to run a local, the nuts and bolts of what a local should do: advocacy, organizing, grievance handling, internal and external communications, and consultation (which, as I'll explain later, is as close as we have gotten to collective bargaining).

By 1992, I was on the executive board of the Austin Federation of Teachers. We were still the little 300-member, lean, mean fighting machine. Our local president decided abruptly that she didn't want to continue to serve, and the board, which we jokingly renamed "the junta," managed the local for the remainder of that school year.

That was the end of my fifth year in the classroom. I had been accepted into the graduate program at the Lyndon B. Johnson School of Public Affairs at the University of Texas. My plan was to take a leave of absence from school to earn a master's degree in public policy. The board members, thinking that I'd have more free time as a graduate student than they would as classroom teachers, asked me to run for president.

I agreed and was elected president of the local—a job that came with many hours of work and a whopping $50 a week stipend. For two years, I studied state governance, school finance, and other aspects of public policy. Meanwhile, every Monday night I was down at the school board meetings, and all week in the afternoons (when not in class) I was making fliers and visiting schools. Fortunately, it wasn't long before the Texas AFT assigned a staff person to my local.

At the end of graduate school, I had the choice between selling securities or becoming the local president full time, released from teaching. Although I received a very attractive offer from a major investment house, there was never a question in my mind about where I belonged.

Building Power

My time in the classroom taught me there was a need for powerful institutions that could hold the district accountable to its students, staff, and community. But as the new leader of a very small affiliate, I actually felt a little resentment as I listened to Albert Shanker—the iconic president of the national AFT—say that fixing schools and providing professional development are union work. I kept thinking to myself: "In Austin, we don't even have the basic right of recognition. How can we have a meaningful role in any quality-of-education initiative when they don't even recognize us?"

Still, I reflected on the locals doing professional issues work: they were the big locals that had grown enough to negotiate with the district as a peer. They could make demands and back them up with people and money. I began to see a sequence for the union's work. First, we had to build power, and then we could tackle our priorities. So we focused hard on growing the union and talking to teachers about our rights on the job. We also fought for better pay and health care choices.

Unlike my experience as a teacher, in my union work I was anything but isolated. In 1994, my local was awarded an AFT organizing grant, and we hired two organizers. We merged with the local AFT PSRP affiliate, which was called the Allied Education Workers, and Julie Bowman (the then-PSRP local president who now directs leadership development at the Texas AFT) became my copresident.

For five years, we went into schools and work sites, and we organized teachers and school support staff. We built a great local, we elected school board members, we recruited new members, we conducted surveys to find out what motivated our members, and we waged campaigns to improve pay and working conditions.

During this time, my sister began her teaching career in a suburban Philadelphia school district. I used her family as an example when I talked to Austin's school board. My brother-in-law and my nieces and nephews all had health coverage through my sister's teaching job, but in Austin we didn't receive any health coverage for our families. And I would ask: "Why are teachers in some states paid well and treated decently? Why are we so stingy here? Why do you think 18 percent of the staff leaves every year?" We differentiated ourselves from the nonunion teacher groups by explaining that collective bargaining had helped school employees win basic workplace dignity as well as decent pay, pensions, and health benefits. And we kept building a strong organization.

At the heart of that organization were—and still are—the words printed on the original charter the AFT gave us in 1970: "Democracy in Education, Education for Democracy." Our union is an autonomous government of school employees. It is democratic, its leaders are elected, and it is governed by a constitution. What separates democracies in the world from tyrannies of the left and the right is the ability of individuals to associate freely and to speak freely—the basics contained in the Bill of Rights.

Can you imagine employers discouraging their employees from voting? People would be outraged. Yet, that is exactly what employers do when they discourage employees from associating with one another and from forming unions. Protecting our rights, whether at work or in our neighborhoods, is an act of preserving the very underpinnings of democracy. The institutions that make up what we call civil society in this country are fragile and often under attack. Ernesto Cortes Jr. of the Industrial Areas Foundation has pointed out that mobility, technology, and changes in the way we live, work, and associate have transformed human relationships. The neighborhoods where everyone knew one another—went to school together, worked in the same factory, worshipped together—have given way to a more dislocated society. We have to find new ways to build community, and the places we must look to do that are our schools, our workplaces, our neighborhoods, and our places of worship. The ability to associate freely with your coworkers, to organize, and to bring forward common interests and concerns is fundamental to the health and well-being of American democracy.

These notions of building power were in the forefront of my mind as I thought about how to continue growing my local in the late 1990s. At the national level, the AFT and the NEA were talking about merging, but Texas remained one of the few areas of the country where AFT and NEA locals were still fighting each other. San Antonio's representation fight in the mid-'90s was especially bitter. The AFT wrested representation away from the NEA affiliate, but it took a tremendous expenditure of time, money, and energy from both sides.

In Austin, Julie Bowman and I had been paying a lot of attention to the NEA affiliate, partly because we were raiding its members, but partly because we were beginning to question our tactics. If we take all the members from one group and move them into another group, we wondered, have we really made progress in terms of organizing? So we started talking to the NEA affiliate, informally at first, to imagine having one big organization. Soon we had a committee that met quarterly. Eventually we conducted a retreat with both locals' boards.

The negotiations with the NEA local were like a courtship, but in reality we were working on two fronts. Even as we were arguing for the merger, our local worked independently to challenge the NEA's status as the consultation representative with the district. Although collective bargaining is illegal in Texas, school boards are allowed to set up "consultation" mechanisms to take input from their employees. Consultation can't result in a contract, but agreements can be struck and the school board can adopt them as it would any other policy. Austin's school board had a longstanding consultation policy that named the NEA affiliate as the teacher consultation representative. Our AFT affiliate convinced the board to change the policy to require a vote of the employees to elect the representative. We then told the NEA local that we intended to challenge its bid to become the representative—but that we would rather join together and create a new organization instead.

Initially, the NEA local's leaders thought we were trying to take consultation away from them. We told them we didn't want to take it away, we wanted to share it. Since both groups understood that we needed one voice speaking for all employees, we came together to create a single union.

With the date for the election for the consultation representative having been set by the school board, we all felt pressure to bring our courtship to a close. The national AFT and NEA brought in high-powered facilitators from Harvard Law School. With their help, using an accelerated six-month process, we went from rival organizations to allied groups with a merger agreement. Then it took another three months to educate the broader membership and take a vote on both sides.

We started the school year in 1999 with a new superintendent, a new merged union called Education Austin, and a consultation election in which Education Austin was overwhelmingly elected. It was the first time school employees in Austin had ever had the ability to vote on a representative. Our combined membership surged over the next couple of years because people who'd been on the fence about joining were energized by our unity. The funny thing about bringing together two organizations that share a common set of values and goals is that, at the grass-roots level, it inherently makes sense to the members. We surveyed members on both sides, and they overwhelmingly supported unification. They clearly wanted one big, strong organization.

The merger agreement called for a three-year transition in which we had a tripartite presidency of Julie Bowman, who was our PSRP president (the NEA affiliate did not have a PSRP division); Brenda Urps, the NEA local president; and myself. After three years, the tripartite presidency ended and I ran unopposed to be the president of Education Austin.

There were plenty of kinks to work out, but we have thrived as the first merged local affiliate in Texas. Amazingly, San Antonio followed us a couple of years later. Members there realized the only alternative to fighting was to figure out how to follow our path. Other smaller districts around the state also pulled together, although many parts of Texas remain a battleground for the AFT and the NEA.

During our merger talks, we understood that if coming together were just about becoming bigger, then despite what we say in Texas, bigger wouldn't necessarily be better. This new organization needed to actually be better than either of its predecessors. The merger process helped us define what a "better" union should look like. Probably the most important improvement was working to more fully engage our members. We agreed to create structures through which more members would not just pay dues and answer surveys, but would also become actively involved in the union, in politics, in professional issues, in the consulting process with the school district, and in outreach to the community. Today, we have a large group of political action leaders, and myriad standing committees on issues such as early childhood education, special education, assessment, and transportation.

Soon after the merger, Austin Interfaith (a community organization affiliated with the Industrial Areas Foundation and made up of about 30 congregations, schools, and unions) asked our union to join them. The group saw the newly unified Education Austin as a power within the school district and the city. Being a part of Austin Interfaith has helped our union develop and work more broadly to build power. We have borrowed extensively from its organizing style. Education Austin's organizing model asks each individual: What are you interested in? What problems could we work together to solve? Are you willing to form relationships with other teachers and school employees to work on those problems? This approach has defined the union and been very productive. It has also challenged our leaders to take on issues like health care, immigration, housing, and other issues that aren't school issues per se, but that do affect our students and members. Now, our work is expanding again: Education Austin was recently awarded an AFT Innovation Fund grant to work with Austin Interfaith to do community school organizing. Austin Interfaith has a track record of successful school organizing, having worked in the 1990s to organize the parents, teachers, and community at 16 high-needs schools.

Taking Up Shanker's Challenge

Right after the merger and consultation representative election in 1999, Education Austin focused on basic pay and health insurance issues. We negotiated decent pay raises. We persuaded the district to adopt an internal minimum wage for workers, so even the custodial and food service staff start off at a living wage. We also negotiated leave benefits and training for employees. Then we began a long, hard push to include professional issues in our official consultation with the district.

I remember reading a "Where We Stand" column in which Al Shanker bemoaned the fact that when fighting to win collective bargaining, teachers and their unions were accused of only caring about their own pay and benefits—not caring about kids. But, Shanker said, when they won bargaining and tried to negotiate things that would be good for students, like reduced class sizes, they were told that it was not their concern. In city after city, management only wanted to bargain wages, hours, and working conditions. Shanker rightly pointed out the hypocrisy of calling teachers' unions self-interested while restricting what they could negotiate to wages and benefits.

In Austin, the same thing happened when we tried to introduce ideas that would be good for kids and for school quality, such as mentoring programs for new teachers and high-quality professional development for all teachers. We were told those things are management's prerogative. I remember the chief academic officer telling us, "I'll meet with you on the side about that, but we're not going to do that during consultation." It was frustrating.

One of the areas that we really had to fight hard on for many years was assessment, and in particular practice testing. Our district, like many districts over the last 10 years, ratcheted up the amount of time teachers are required to do practice testing with kids. We were told to administer beginning-, middle-, and end-of-year benchmark tests, plus six-week and nine-week tests. Some schools also gave three-week tests, and even weekly tests. None of these were teacher-made assessments. They were all designed to estimate how students would do on the end-of-year state assessment. One of our strongest committees in the last several years has been the over-testing committee. But until very recently, we were rebuffed every year, even though our proposals were reasonable requests, supported by a majority of teachers, to make some of the tests optional.

Recently, with our new superintendent, Meria Carstarphen, we were able to create a labor-management committee to review the district's testing regime. After a full year of work, we arrived at an agreement to significantly reduce the amount of practice testing and to spend another year designing meaningful formative assessments that will take up less class time and better guide instruction. This sort of labor-management partnership would have been unthinkable a decade ago, but with greater power and the political sophistication (on both sides) to engage around tough issues, we have improved the ability to get things done.

Compensation is another example of a difficult issue where labor-management collaboration has had some success. In 2006, we signed a two-year pay agreement, an unprecedented event because normally our pay negotiations are linked to the annual adoption of the budget. Teacher and support staff received raises of 11.5 percent over two years, and an extra $4 million was set aside for development of a new alternative compensation plan that the union and district would design together. The compensation committee was jointly chaired by the human resources director, a business leader, and me. We already knew that we had strong resources from the AFT and the NEA, which both sent staff with experience in developing alternative compensation systems to help us. Many members got involved as the union worked with the district to create a large steering committee plus a smaller design committee. Our teachers helped the district understand that just paying more wasn't going to change anything— teachers needed better support and the right tools to improve.

The result of several years' worth of research, learning together, and work was the Austin Independent School District REACH program, which is now entering its fourth year as a pilot at 15 of our schools. In order to become a pilot site, two-thirds of the teachers had to vote in favor of participating.

REACH provides full-time mentors for teachers in their first three years, support for national board certification, schoolwide performance bonuses based on student growth on the state's reading and math assessments, and individual teacher bonuses based on teacher-developed student-learning objectives. We're comfortable with this approach to alternative compensation because teachers are well supported and the alternative pay is on top of the regular salary schedule. It was important to us to recognize and encourage teacher collaboration, so the state assessment results are only used for school-wide incentives. Instead of looking at current achievement, the district looks at year-over-year growth of the same students and compares it with the growth in 40 similar schools. Bonuses are awarded to schools that rank in the top quartile on growth in reading and/or math. We were also careful in designing the individual incentives: they are teacher selected student-learning objectives, and they are developed by all teachers in every subject and grade, so that the art teacher, French teacher, librarian, gym teacher, band teacher, pre-K teacher, etc., all set goals based on their students and the curriculum they teach.

REACH has started to create a culture of looking at data, setting measurable goals, and assessing personal and group performance. But that's only part of what makes it effective. The other part—probably the more important part—is the mentoring. All of the full-time mentors have completed the AFT's Foundations of Effective Teaching professional development course. The first year, the union paid to send about seven people to the training. The district was so impressed by its quality that it paid the full cost for both the union and the district—around $30,000—in the second year.

When we designed REACH, our plan was to offer all pilot schools the alternative compensation, but to provide full-time mentoring only in the highest-needs schools (i.e., those with the highest concentrations of low-income students and English language learners). We quickly learned that mentoring should be offered to all pilot schools because all new teachers, not just those in our most challenging schools, are really interested in receiving extensive support and feedback. In addition, we found that mentoring new teachers is a huge relief to our senior teachers, who no longer felt pressured to assist their new colleagues. In fact, some senior teachers are seeking out the mentors because they want extra support too, especially in designing their student-learning objectives.

Going forward, all REACH schools will have the same supports, but the highest-needs schools will have added monetary incentives for teachers that include bigger performance bonuses and a retention stipend. For first-through third-year teachers, the retention stipend is $1,000. For those who have been in the school more than three years, it's $3,000. Use of a retention stipend is supported by research conducted by our district that links longevity at the school site with increased student performance.

This is the final year of the REACH pilot. We are still collecting data to determine program effectiveness, but there are some positive early results. We are hoping to expand the program to almost 40 schools, mainly our highest-needs schools.

Interestingly, working on the REACH program has deepened the union's relationship with the entire human capital development wing of the school district. The district now has a chief human capital officer who pays close attention to teacher leadership, professional development, the REACH program, and the development of a new, much more robust teacher induction program for the whole district.

REACH has also built our relationship with the chamber of commerce and the business community. The business community loves performance pay—but our business leaders have also appreciated that the program is a labor-management partnership. They've been real boosters and have supported raising the tax rate to help fund the program.

Developing Leaders

Being a local union leader is transformative because it forces you to be political. You must engage with power wherever it is. One mistake I've seen new local presidents make is not grasping the difference between being political and being partisan. Being political is not just about winning elections. It's about reading the newspaper every day. It's about knowing what's going on in your community. It's about listening to your members. It's about developing other leaders. It's about building webs of relationships within the organization and the community that allow you to reach out and be influential. Even in the absence of collective bargaining, good leaders can still build power.

Linda Bridges, the president of the Texas AFT, is a terrific example of acting politically to build power. When she was still the president of the AFT local in Corpus Christi, she successfully ran the mayor's campaign. She was a pioneer in the field of labor-management collaboration (without the safety or structure of a collective bargaining agreement) and won the prestigious Saturn Award for her local. Among many other responsibilities, she served on the board of the local community college and was president of the Coastal Bend Labor Council. She built relationships that in turn built the union. She understood that she had power because of the people standing behind her, and she used that power to build her strength and the strength of the organization.

As a local leader, I tried to follow Linda's lead, to be political but not partisan. When the new superintendent, Meria Carstarphen, came to town last year, I threw my arms around her, in a manner of speaking. I attended all the forums for staff and the community to get to know her. The school board, with whom we had already built a relationship, brought her to our office her first day on the job. Soon thereafter, she announced plans to hold a big convocation with all 11,000 district employees. I asked to get up on stage with her and talk to the dis-

trict's employees. Although she spoke for an hour and I spoke for 10 minutes, there were only three people on that stage at the event: the president of the school board, the superintendent, and the union president (me). I was there for two reasons. First, my members put me there; they built the power and the strength to enable me to make the demand to be on stage. Second, I asked to be there. I insinuated myself into that situation. Woody Allen said that 80 percent of success is showing up. Sometimes it's awkward and uncomfortable. But if you think and behave politically, if you are able to engage power by offering something and demanding something, and if you are not afraid to show up and not shut up, there are few limits to what you can get done if you have organized people standing with you.

One way to stay focused on the political and on building a broad base of support for the union is to ask a simple question: whom am I developing? It's a question all leaders and organizers should ask themselves constantly. It is not simply a matter of succession, as in "whom am I preparing to someday take my job." Whether you're staying or going, whether you're short term or long term, whether you're a building representative or a local president, you are only as effective as the other leaders you bring with you. I wish I had figured that out much earlier because I would have achieved more and maybe not had to work quite so awfully hard.

In organizations like ours, leadership is everything. But leadership isn't the person sitting at the top. Leadership is the relationships with other people, both inside and outside the union—relationships that bring people along, develop their talents, and tie them to one another through shared interests and a common understanding of what they want to see happen and what they are willing to do to make it happen.

My union includes members who lived in Section 8 housing, who were afraid to go to their children's school because they didn't think they belonged, but who now look mayors and senators and superintendents in the eye and talk to them about their interests and needs, and their community's needs. Some of these leaders have been cultivated by me and by other union organizers. Some of them have come through Austin Interfaith's leadership training. Seeing people grow into strong leaders makes me realize that, although our society is built on the notion of egalitarianism, we don't get social equity unless we teach people how to organize and exercise power. Building power through organizing makes the ideal of egalitarianism a reality.

In our local union, we are instituting a culture among our staff and our leaders to have deliberate conversations with others, to figure out who they are and what makes them angry and what they care about. This is the heart of effective organizing. There is power in knowing other people's stories. It opens up an understanding of what people's needs are, what their interests are, and what's motivating them. A strong organization doesn't just get people to sign up for a march; it knows what brought them to the march, why they chose to march instead of spending time with their family or going fishing. All people are motivated by strong experiences that have shaped them. The union's ability to tap into that, to build relationships and get people to know each other, sets us apart from other kinds of institutions and is our key to building leaders and power.

In turn, our success at cultivating new leaders and building power will be directly proportional to our success at achieving our goals as a union.

Louis Malfaro is vice president of the American Federation of Teachers and secretary-treasurer of the Texas AFT.

EXPLORING THE ISSUE

Do Teachers Unions Stymie School Reform?

Critical Thinking and Reflection

1. What is Al Shanker's challenge and how does it impact what teacher unions do?
2. What are the arguments for and against teacher unions "going to far"?
3. What is the current scene between tearcher unions and the teachers in the field?
4. Are teacher unions a player in school choice?
5. Review the development of teacher unions in this country and why they have such an impact on schooling.

Is There Common Ground?

"Teacher Unions Are Dead! Long Live Teacher Unions!" shouts Thomas Toch in the December 2010/January 2011 issue of *Phi Delta Kappan* in which he concludes that with millions of members and vast political networks the unions are the most powerful force in American education, but they will have to make peace with reform. Long-held positions on merit pay, tenure, seniority, teacher evaluation, and charter schools will have to be modified. While the positions offered in the Coulson and Malfaro articles seem fairly rigidly antithetical, one can discern some evidence of possible convergence when the welfare of students is placed before them. Both would do well to address the "Four Myths About Teachers" described by Ilana Garon in Dissent (Summer 2011). Myth No. 1: The big problem with U.S. education is the teachers. Myth No. 2: Charter schools are better than regular public schools. Myth No. 3: Unions stand in the way of all that is good in education because they keep unfit teachers in their jobs. Myth No. 4: Tenure makes it so that teachers become complacent because it's difficult to fire them since they have no motivation to improve their performance.

An interesting juxtaposition of views is presented in a post by Frederick Hess of *Education Next* on June 13, 2011 titled "Moe v. Meier on Teacher Unions." Hess reports on a panel discussion of Moe's book *Special Interest*. Moe sees "reform unionism" as a pipe dream and contends that school improvement must be driven by incentives to improve student test performance. Panelist Deborah Meier counters that Moe's critique rests on the notion that test scores can usefully measure teacher effectiveness.

Worldwide comparisons of student test performance often show Finland at or near the top. An article in the September 2011 *Smithsonian* by Lynnell Hancock points out that the people in the government agencies overseeing Finnish schools are educators, not politicians and that the teachers union is extremely strong there. A question remains: Does the Finnish union operate differently from ours? If so, what can we learn?

Create Central

www.mhhe.com/createcentral

Additional Resources

"Scenes from the Class Struggle," *The Atlantic* (June 2011).

Mike Antonucci, "The Long Reach of Teachers Unions," *Education Next* (Fall 2010).

Katherine Mangu-Ward, "Education Showdown: The Irresistible Force of School Reform Meets the Immovable Object of Teachers Union," *Reason* (May 2011).

Philip Mattera, "Public Employees and the Public Interest," *Social Policy* (Spring 2011).

Evan Thomas & Pat Wingert, "Why We Can't Get Rid of Failing Teachers," *Newsweek* (March 15, 2010).

Internet References. . .

National Education Association

www.nea.org/

American Federation of Teachers

www.aft.org/

Unions Act in Teachers' Interests—Not Students'

http://articles.courant.com/2012-02-26/news/hc-op-mooney-unions-stymie-school-reform-0226-20120226_1_teachers-unions-teacher-certification-negotiations

How to Stymie the Teachers Unions

http://educationnext.org/how-to-stymie-the-teachers-unions/

School Reform Proposals: The Research Evidence: Teacher Unions and Student Achievement

http://nepc.colorado.edu/files/summary-10.carini.pdf

Selected, Edited, and with Issue Framing Material by:
Glenn L. Koonce, *Regent University*

ISSUE

Should Teacher Preparation and Licensing Be Regulated by the Government?

YES: James Cibulka, from "Strengthen State Oversight of Teacher Preparation," *Education Next* (Fall 2013)

NO: David Chard, from "Training Must Focus on Content and Pedagogy," *Education Next* (Fall 2013)

Learning Outcomes

After reading this issue, you will be able to:

- Assess the need to include courses on the science of reading instruction or on mathematics content in all elementary-educator preparation programs as well as various culture studies due to dramatic shifts in the demographics of our country.
- Evaluate the need to bring public, private, and not-for-profit sectors together to forge a concrete plan for studying and strengthening teacher preparation programs.
- Research the need for a reformed teacher-licensure system in our knowledge-based, globally competitive economy.
- Critique options for ways to improve practices and incentives to help attract high-quality teachers to the educational field of teaching.
- Analyze the difference between increased government licensure regulations and focusing on training in content and pedagogy.

ISSUE SUMMARY

YES: Council for the Accreditation of Educator Preparation President Jim Cibulka states that tightening government licensure regulation is needed to assure candidate and program quality that can result in a more favorable learning environment for Pre-K–12 students.

NO: David Chard indicates that current state control of teacher preparation and licensing does not ensure that teachers will be of high quality.

Licensing of teachers in most states is a function of state boards or state department of education. The common pathways to licensing are through state approved college or university teacher preparation programs. The goal of these preparation programs is to produce teachers who will be successful in attaining higher student academic achievement.

The lack of consistently high student achievement in the United States has been blamed on a variety of groups in almost a sequential order. First, students were blamed for poor work and study habits. Parents followed, being blamed for anything from not helping their children with school work to broken homes and living in poverty. The focus then shifted to blaming schools themselves and the teachers who taught in them. Principals and other school leaders followed. Over the past decade much has been said and written concerning how college and university schools of education are sending ill-prepared teachers into the field. This fact is not the only reason given for poor student achievement but the movement is continuing to grow especially regarding who is accountable for preparation programs success. The government acts with policy and regulation, and colleges and universities respond with their, now, sole accreditor, the Council for the Accreditation of Education Preparation (CAEP). CAEP is actually the blending of the only two accreditors for teacher preparation, the National Council for Accreditation of Teacher Education (NCATE), founded in 1954, and the Teacher Education Accreditation Council (TEAC), founded in 1997. CAEP is viewed in many higher education circles as an opportunity for assisting teacher preparation programs ultimate outcomes which is improved student academic achievement as graduates go into the field.

The downside of teacher preparation is reflected in report after report issuing scathing indictments of schools across the United States who graduates new teachers. The most recent "scathing" report of teacher training programs was issued by the National Council on Teacher Quality (NTCQ) with results published in U.S. News and World Report (June 18, 2013). Though the report's methodologies have been criticized by some educators, it describes teacher preparation as "an industry of mediocrity," accepting students who are generally not high achievers. Upon graduation and assigned to their first students, those students experience a significant loss in learning. Although many schools in the report received higher rankings, Kate Walsh, president of the NTCQ indicated that part of the motivation for the study was to "pressure teacher preparation programs to deliver better teachers" (Adams & Baron, 2013).

Among the most pressing issues in American education is helping teachers get better earlier (Schorr, 2013) and be closer to the real classroom earlier in their studies, especially in places where schools are struggling. Research has shown that a strong teacher makes a huge difference in educational outcomes from students. Much of the current approach to preparing teachers amounts to "weak tea" and supports Art Levine's 2006 study that indicated "more than three in five teachers said their training left them unprepared for the classroom—and principals agreed." (Schorr, 2013).

With half of all new teachers abandoning the profession within five years, how is the crisis in preparation being confronted? Many preparation programs are feeling the pressure. CAEP accreditation is vigorously upgrading and improving their standards, principals, and policies for both teacher and principal preparation programs. CAEP's (caep.org) "mission is to advance excellent educator preparation through evidence-based accreditation that assures quality and supports continuous improvement to strengthen P-12 student learning." People are not ignoring CAEP's critiques.

With the founding of CAEP, tougher standards that emphasize performance were approved in the summer of 2013. For the first time minimum admissions criteria and an emphasis on selecting reliable and valid evidence were addressed. Some programs may close down because they either won't be able to meet the standards, do not have the resources for the cost-intensive and labor intensive requirements, or they simply lack high quality candidates (Sawchuk, 2013).

Accreditation alone is not enough as acknowledged by the organization itself. Standards for teachers such as the Interstate New Teacher Assessment and Support Consortium (INTASC) have been seen as good building preparation programs but have not shown a correlation to a teacher's ability to promote student achievement. To do so, preparation programs for teachers need the following (Education Commission of the States, 2013):

- need for quality students to enter the programs and not drop out
- less focus on "soft" pedagogical knowledge and more on subject matter depth
- not being prepared to teach to student performance standards
- providing more intensive real world practical experience
- be more responsive to the need of nontraditional teacher candidates, especially minorities and mid-career adults
- more rigorous accreditation standards
- greater involvement with the arts and sciences faculty
- emphasize outcomes such as pass rate on state teacher licensure exams
- building solid partnerships between universities and school districts or individual schools
- alternative teacher preparation programs

The basic issue is that not all teacher programs are equal. Not all offer the ten items listed and are ill-equipped to provide a strong faculty, collaboration with other schools and partners, careful oversight of quality student teaching experiences, or the big picture that high achieving applicants be admitted who understand the mission and calling to be a moral and ethical teacher.

In the selections that follow, Jim Cibulka believes that state oversight of teacher preparation can be strengthened and CAEP accreditation is part of the solution. David Chard believes there has been and continues to be a steady decline in the quality of candidates attracted to teaching and that state control does not ensure that teachers will be of high quality.

References

J. Adams & K. Baron, Critical report on teacher preparation programs spark debate. EdSource Today (June 18, 2013). Retrieved from: www.edsource. org/today/2013/critical-report-on-teacher-preparation-programs-sparks-debate/33721#.UnFjAzXD9y0

Education Commission of the States, Teaching Quality Preparation (2013). Retrieved from: www.usnews.com/education/articles/2013/06/18/us-news-releases-nctq-teacher-prep-ratings

S. Sawchuk, S. (2013). "Tougher Requirements Ahead for Teacher Prep." *Education Week* (vol. 32, no. 36), p. 20.

Schorr, J. (2013). A Revolution Begins in Teacher Prep. *Stanford Social Innovation Review* (Winter 2013). Retrieved from: www.ssireview.org/articles/entry/a_revolution_begins_in_teacher_prep

YES ↵

James Cibulka

Strengthen State Oversight of Teacher Preparation

As the president of the sole specialized accreditor for educator preparation, I certainly agree with Dr. Chard's assertion that "[i]mproving educational attainment for all students in today's schools can only happen if we improve the quality of teaching." As Dr. Chard mentions in his essay, the Council for the Accreditation of Educator Preparation (CAEP) is already working toward some of the solutions proposed through development of the next generation of accreditation standards for educator preparation as well as convening a data task force to provide guidance and help determine some of the very research questions for studying and strengthening educator preparation, as Dr. Chard suggests.

While one of the hallmarks of CAEP as a new kind of accreditor is its focus on research and evidence that will further advance the field of educator preparation, this does not negate the need for a reformed teacher-licensure system.

Like many other features of our Pre-K–12 school system, the current design of teacher licensing, or certification as it's often called, has outlived its usefulness. It was suited to a bygone era when the nation's principal concern was to produce teachers that "do no harm" to their students. This concept of *primum non nocere*, originally applied to medical ethics, set a low bar for entrants to teaching. It seems strangely out of place today, when expectations for teachers emphasize their competence to help all learners become successful in a knowledge-based, globally competitive economy. Yet eliminating teacher licensure altogether likely would be to *worsen* the current dysfunctions. I will offer strategies for reforming teacher licensure that I believe have greater potential for success.

The Impact of Teacher Licensing

Some economists argue that the social and economic costs of licensure outweigh its benefits by reducing economic growth and/or the distribution of economic benefits. They argue that by invoking licensure, government improperly values the special interests of the practitioner over other interests. These criticisms date back to Adam Smith, but were given currency by Milton Friedman, who argued that government and professional associations were using licensure to reassert the monopoly of cartels by creating market entry restrictions.

Other economists, however, reject this critique of licensure in favor of a theory of "market failure." According to this perspective, governmental intervention in the market, via such activities as professional licensing, can be justified when the market fails to operate efficiently. Market failure occurs when it is difficult for the consumer to judge the qualifications of a provider or the quality of a provider's work.

The empirical evidence is mixed. With the pathways into teaching growing in number, including training programs offered outside of higher education, it is hard to argue that current licensure policies substantially restrict entry, for example. And even critics acknowledge that licensing may lead to benefits such as higher-quality outcomes for those who obtain services from licensed professionals.

For many critics of teacher licensure, the gold standard is whether it promotes or impedes student learning. Yet research on the impact of licensure on student outcomes is inconclusive, with some studies finding little, if any, difference among traditionally certified and uncertified teachers and others finding substantially higher student test scores among traditionally certified teachers.

The comparisons in a number of such studies are complicated by the fact that teachers self-select into teaching with different skills sets and training, and they are not, of course, randomly assigned to schools, making inferences about their productivity imperfect at best. Moreover, labels can be confusing. Alternative approaches to licensure often are equated with the term "uncertified," yet individuals taking an alternative route are typically intending to become fully licensed while they teach. Alternative paths to certification may produce different outcomes in the field than traditional paths. An analysis by Paul Peterson and Daniel Nadler found that states that encourage alternative licensure have greater diversity in their teacher pools, for example (see "What Happens When States Have Genuine Alternative Certification?" *check the facts*, Winter 2009). Given these complications, the most that can be said is that the research has not shown licensure by itself to have a negative or positive effect on student learning.

Teacher Licensure in the States

Current licensure requirements vary significantly among states, as reported by the testing company Educational Testing Service (ETS):

Praxis: Thirty-six states accept the Praxis exam to establish basic skills proficiency (Praxis I), content knowledge (Praxis II), or both. Thirty-four of these require either the Praxis I or II specifically for at least one level of licensure, generally for the initial level. However, the score required to pass varies considerably: on a 100-point scale, the most demanding states tend to set a cut score 20 to 30 points above those of the least-demanding states, whose cut scores are below what is recommended by ETS.

Bachelor's degrees: All states require some form of bachelor's degree, yet requirements for content-specific degrees are variously defined and inconsistently applied. The standard requirement is a major in the subject, although most states allow substitution of a major with course credits. Due to the inconsistent approaches within higher education, the Praxis examination has, by default, become the threshold for entering the profession.

Master's degrees: Twenty-five states require a master's degree in order to obtain one or more kinds of certification. However, states are moving away from this type of requirement toward outcome-based induction programs.

Alternative routes to licensure outside of higher education: According to a 2010 U.S. Department of Education report, 8 percent of teacher preparation programs were designated as "alternative, not based in institutions of higher education," provided instead by for-profit or non-profit organizations. Combined, the states of Alabama, Florida, Oklahoma, New Jersey, and Texas produce 74 percent of teacher candidates trained outside of institutions of higher education. There is wide variation in the quality of teachers produced both within higher education and via alternative pathways, a signal that the systems of quality control need to be overhauled through regulation and market mechanisms.

Licensing Can Be Improved

Teacher licensure has little impact on teaching quality because it sets too low a bar for entry into teaching. Also, licensure policies have often been relaxed to assure that an adult is in each classroom, but not necessarily a *qualified* adult. In short, educator licensure suffers from weak controls:

- Licensure regulations in some states focus only on courses and degrees for some pathways into teaching. As soon as they enter the classroom, graduates

of preparation programs should show evidence of their ability to teach diverse learners according to rigorous college- and career-ready standards.

- Many licensure tests lack rigor. Worse still, most states use low cut scores that further weaken their rigor. Licensure tests must be redesigned to focus on the more rigorous content required for Pre-K–12 students, general pedagogy, and pedagogy within a discipline (pedagogical content knowledge).
- Current licensure policies make little use of performance-based assessments that capture a candidate's actual preparedness to teach on entering a classroom. Some states are moving away from licensure based on paper-and-pencil tests in favor of assessments that demonstrate competence to teach and to raise Pre-K–12 student learning.

Addressing basic licensure issues could have a considerable impact on teacher quality. More focus on performance assessments such as those noted above would, among other things, lessen unduly burdensome course requirements for nontraditional applicants entering college and university preparation programs. A shift to a focus on measuring outcomes will open the licensure process to high-quality alternative pathways into teaching and encourage innovation among higher education providers who wish to compete on cost and quality rather than on traditional curriculum and seat-time requirements.

Relicensure requirements for practicing teachers should be aligned with improved initial licensure requirements. They should specify a more advanced level of practice with accompanying evidence, including instructional practices, student learning, and other measures. Similarly, advanced master's programs should be redesigned to serve this purpose as well.

More rigorous licensure requirements should focus on meeting the needs of today's diverse learners, whatever the school setting. Also, licensure requirements should complement new, more rigorous teacher-evaluation systems that capture the context within which teachers work, using teacher observation protocols, student learning measures, and student surveys that measure student engagement and related evidence of a teacher's effectiveness. Neither a licensure system nor evaluation alone can accomplish what these quality-control mechanisms can do if they are complementary and rigorous.

Leverage State Authority

If the teacher licensing bar is to be raised, more rigorous state program-approval authority for teacher preparation programs is also needed. The recent report of the Council of Chief State School Officers found that state program-approval policies for preparation programs, both those for "traditional higher education programs and for new pathways, suffer from weak and inconsistent regulation." Weak controls at the front end lead to highly inconsistent quality among entrants to teacher preparation programs and ultimately new hires. This pattern contributes to high retraining costs for school districts and to destabilizing and costly turnover rates. States could use their authority over teacher preparation programs to strengthen the qualifications of beginning teachers and lower costs to districts by focusing on the recruitment and admission of a qualified pool, rigorous clinical preparation, and collecting evidence of program impact (hiring rates, graduate and employer satisfaction, Pre-K–12 student learning, and related measures). States should work closely with CAEP, as the new accrediting body for educator preparation, in aligning program approval and licensure policies with accreditation standards.

Tightening regulation to assure candidate and program quality is likely to lead to a more qualified pool of graduates competing to teach, better hiring decisions, less attrition, and a more favorable learning environment for Pre-K–12 students. Markets have their place as mechanisms for introducing quality. However, the market will work much better if government regulates the providers more effectively and if preparation programs produce graduates whose readiness to teach can be clearly identified by the school districts that hire them.

As Dr. Chard indicated, the efforts of individual groups like CAEP are not enough: we must approach education reform holistically and at a systemic level. In coming years, a record number of new teachers will be hired to replace those retiring. As a nation, we cannot afford to fail. We will have a once-in-a-generation chance to get it right.

James Cibulka, prior to his appointment as President of the Council for the Accreditation of Educator Preparation (CAEP), was president of the National Council for Accreditation of Teacher Education (NCATE), and before that served as dean of the College of Education at the University of Kentucky.

David Chard   ➔ **NO**

Training Must Focus on Content and Pedagogy

What happens inside the classroom is the most critical ingredient in ensuring that all students are able to achieve their career goals. Improving educational attainment for all students in today's schools can only happen if we improve the quality of teaching.

Just over 30 years ago, I decided to become a classroom teacher, specifically a teacher of mathematics and chemistry. I was prepared at a midsize university in the Midwest. Despite the university's great reputation for teacher preparation, faculties in mathematics and chemistry discouraged me from the profession, noting that I was not going to be adequately compensated, would work in difficult conditions, and would be much happier in industry. This should have been a message to me that as a society we had moved down a path that dissuades the best and brightest from seeing teaching as a viable career option.

Nevertheless, I was hired to teach mathematics in California in 1985. At the time, like today, far fewer individuals were being prepared to be mathematics teachers in California than the state needed. Many of us were hired from the Midwest and from eastern states, and given emergency certification in California conditioned on passing a course on California history and the National Teacher Exam in mathematics. I didn't realize then that my experience in California was the beginning of 30 years of slow but steady decline in the quality of candidates we were attracting and preparing to teach in our schools.

Over that period, it has become clear that current state control of teacher preparation and licensing does not ensure that teachers will be of high quality. State regulations that promote a one-size-fits-all approach to teacher preparation have limited our ability to innovate, customize, and study features of preparation programs that may positively affect student achievement. Bold new approaches to teacher preparation that are thoroughly evaluated for effectiveness in the classroom are long overdue.

What's Wrong with the System

Each state sets standards for teacher certification largely through its regulation of the teacher preparation programs that are operated by the institutions of higher education located within its boundaries. With few exceptions, this approach is unsatisfactory. In most states, in order for a program to recommend teachers for certification, it must meet a series of requirements that read like a laundry list. In my home state of Texas, for example, the State Board for Educator Certification (SBEC) requires that in addition to the content standards specified for each grade band, the curriculum for teacher preparation programs must include 17 specific subjects of study. On the surface, there is nothing wrong with any of them. However, given as a list, none appear to have any particular emphasis (i.e., learning theories (#5) seems as important as parent communication (#13) and motivation (#4)); they are not tailored to fit the needs of teachers in any specific context (i.e., urban or rural, turnaround or successful); and they do not consider the developmental stage of the student as it relates to each topic. Perhaps most importantly, this approach assumes a state-held knowledge base on optimal teacher preparation, which simply doesn't exist. The insistence that all preparation programs cover these topics discourages innovation or research on more effective approaches to teacher preparation.

What Makes Teachers Effective?

By all accounts, it is difficult to define precisely what sets good teachers apart from ineffective teachers or even average teachers. We do know that effectiveness in today's classroom is multidimensional.

It is difficult to conceive of an effective teacher who doesn't have a deep understanding of content knowledge. Deep understanding starts with the content itself (e.g., proportional reasoning, Shakespeare, the Krebs cycle), learned through disciplinary study. Content knowledge has to be backed up with experience in designing instruction that conveys content most effectively, enabling students to achieve mastery. In other words, knowing how to solve mathematical problems using proportions falls short of the content knowledge needed for teaching proportional reasoning. An effective teacher must be able to determine where students' understanding has broken down and how to support their cognition.

Unfortunately, it is difficult and time-consuming to master content knowledge and even more so to become an expert teacher. Mastery comes only with adequate experience and professional support. Certainly, in the process of preparation, we can instruct new teachers in how to recognize when students don't understand and how to identify their needs, but the numerous possible variations that underlie students' difficulties reduce the likelihood that new teachers will be experts from the start.

Pedagogical knowledge and skills require an understanding of a child's development involving biology, developmental psychology, cognitive psychology, linguistics, behavioral psychology, and cultural anthropology. That's just to work with one child. When we place students together in groups, we have to consider sociocultural factors, systems dynamics, learning histories, and relationship histories. Then we get down to the engineering of instruction: how to plan and deliver content to groups of students who enter the classroom each day or each period. Teachers must estimate students' level of understanding and take an approach to teaching that will stimulate curiosity and engagement with the content.

I highlight these two components of teaching because they seem to be the most central to the work of teacher preparation programs. In short, they represent the development of a teacher's knowledge of the "what" and "how" of teaching. Recent advancements in education research have brought a new lens to these two areas and suggest that in many cases, teacher preparation programs are not currently designed to provide adequate content knowledge or to teach pedagogical practices that are supported by research evidence. The National Council on Teacher Quality (NCTQ) (see "21st-Century Teacher Education," *features*, Summer 2013) has launched an initiative that will identify those teacher-preparation programs that set high standards with regard to content and pedagogy. As NCTQ found in its analysis, far too few teacher-preparation programs currently provide what is necessary for a new teacher to be successful.

Ideally, our system of teacher preparation would also determine who has the personality and disposition to be a teacher before preparation begins, and ensure that they develop the skills and professionalism needed to be effective within a school. These areas lie on the margin of what is currently in the purview of teacher preparation programs. In addition, there is compelling evidence that the quality of the individuals who are attracted to the field may be more powerful than differences in teacher preparation programs. Recent efforts by the newly formed Council for the Accreditation of Educator Preparation (CAEP) to establish stronger criteria for selecting top-notch candidates are a step in the right direction.

Setting the bar higher is only the first step, however. Over the past several decades, fewer and fewer well-qualified candidates have seen teaching as an acceptable career choice. On average, U.S. teachers earn only about two-thirds of the salaries of other professions with comparable preparation, there is little room for advancement within the profession, and the working conditions in many public schools are challenging at best. Teacher preparation programs alone can't adequately attract a pool of strong new teachers to the field. One of the most

promising outcomes of initiatives such as Teach For America (TFA) is that it helps bring to schools well-educated college graduates who might otherwise not have considered education as a career option. But even TFA falls short of filling the need for new teachers in the next decade. Without powerful new incentives, it seems fewer high-quality teachers will be drawn to the field.

What's the Solution?

In an effort to create immediate and enduring improvements in student outcomes, most states have adopted Common Core State Standards or other content standards that reflect higher expectations for student learning than previous iterations. Efforts to establish similarly comprehensive standards for teacher preparation, such as those being developed by CAEP, should be applauded. We should not simply adopt new teacher competencies, however, without a thoughtful and strategic plan for evaluation and evidence-based revision of our teacher-preparation programs.

I envision the first steps in this process to be a broad and inclusive conversation that brings the public, private, and not-for-profit sectors together to forge a concrete plan for studying and strengthening teacher preparation. While the conversation would be broad, the agenda should be narrow and focus on three immediate needs: 1) radically improving the quality of candidates coming to the field; 2) identifying the specific content of coursework necessary to improve teacher knowledge; and 3) and detailing the practical experiences that new teachers need in order to ensure they are effective in the types of classroom contexts in which they plan to teach. This conversation will require a thoughtful analysis of why our system of teacher preparation has not changed appreciably for decades and what we need to do to make needed changes happen.

In terms of the optimal content of teacher preparation programs, we have only begun to understand what specific amounts of knowledge and skills one needs to possess to be an effective classroom teacher. We also know very little about how those needs change depending on students' developmental stages (e.g., pre-K, middle school) and the teaching context (e.g., urban, suburban, rural). It's easy to see where content is absent, however. Even without empirical evidence, we can make logical decisions about how to improve the quality and quantity of the most important knowledge and skills. For example, it is common in many elementary-educator preparation programs to see few courses on the science of reading instruction or on mathematics content. These limitations should be immediately addressed. Another example involves how little teachers understand about the home language and culture of their students. This is particularly important given the dramatic demographic shifts we are witnessing in most of our country. Efforts to understand the knowledge, skills, and dispositions that are critical to sustained success in the classroom are under way, but further state and federal investment in research is needed to guide the reform of preparation programs.

Finally, we need to encourage experimentation with the practical requirements of teacher preparation. At my institution, we assume that more experience in the classroom than is required by state regulation provides teacher candidates with valuable practice and important information regarding their choices of where to teach. However, the "more is better" approach has not been adequately evaluated. As an example, teacher residency programs have captured interest nationally, but we have only limited evidence of their effectiveness compared to more traditional teacher-preparation programs. Again, logical analyses remain our only short-term tool for making informed decisions, but more evidence is needed to improve our practice.

At a recent dinner for incoming merit scholars to our university, I asked several of them whether they had considered teaching as an option. There was collective nervous laughter. One young lady said that they would never teach because they knew it paid poorly, the working conditions were not good, there was little respect for teachers, and there were no opportunities to advance and lead. Here was a high school senior unwittingly communicating key changes that need to be made to attract high-quality teachers to our field. We will need to set a significantly higher bar for admission to the teaching field and, at the same time, muster financial and professional incentives (e.g., salary, retirement, and career opportunities) to boost interest among our very best candidates for teaching. In addition, attracting top-notch teachers will require more investment in our knowledge of the impact of pay-for-performance models.

Shortly after the turn of the last century, physician preparation in the United States was examined critically for its quality. The results were significant improvements in medical school quality, higher standards for admission, and higher medical costs overall. Similar improvements to teacher preparation could result in better teaching and improved learning outcomes for students. Likewise, these changes will likely require a significant investment in research and development to fuel improved practices and to inform teacher preparation. If we want better teaching, we will have to pay for it.

DAVID CHARD is dean of the Annette Caldwell Simmons School of Education and Human Development at Southern Methodist University and holds a PhD in special education.

EXPLORING THE ISSUE

Should Teacher Preparation and Licensing Be Regulated by the Government?

Critical Thinking and Reflection

1. Will including a design to provide adequate content knowledge and teach pedagogical practices provide what is necessary for a new teacher to be successful?
2. Should the newly formed Council for the Accreditation of Education Preparation (CAEP) be the sole accreditor for teacher preparation and licensing programs?
3. What can be done in the future to convince well educated college graduates to be drawn to the field of teaching?
4. Should the government regulate the Pre-K–12 program providers and tighten regulations to assure candidates and program quality?
5. What is wrong with the current teacher certification standards and what direction should be taken to assure positive change in the future leading to top quality teachers in all classrooms?

Is There Common Ground?

The quality of teaching must improve whether one believes government should play a particular role or not in teacher preparation programs. Teachers must master content knowledge as well as pedagogical knowledge and skills. One solution for common ground is having comprehensive standards for teacher preparation programs, such as those being developed by the Council for the Accreditation of Educator Preparation (CAEP) that are evidence based and offer a strategic plan. The new standards include establishing minimum admissions criteria and the use of "value added" measures. Preparation programs would be assessed on the evidence they produce to meet each standard.

The ultimate outcome for teacher and principal preparation programs is that student's achieve. Using standardized test scores of the students of a university's program are a key measure that is supported by the U.S. Education Department. This is also a measure that CAEP would like to find in their evidence while accrediting preparation programs (The Answer Sheet, 2013). The week of August 16, 2013 the New York City Department of Education released this headline: "New York City becomes the First Major School System in the Country to Comprehensively Collect and Analyze Data on New Teacher Hires from Post-Secondary Schools of Education." The intent is to use the data in the report to support improvement at many levels and as a "first step" to "opening a dialogue" with teacher preparation programs concerning how to improve what they do (The Answer Sheet, 2013). Not many college programs, of any type have indicated they are tracking their graduates into the field to see how they perform.

Since the evidence for significant program improvement is not readily available, there are those who believe innovations and ongoing evaluations need to occur. Perhaps the effort of the New York City Department of Education is the starting point for forming common ground.

Reference

V. Strauss, The big problem with new evaluations of teacher prep programs. *The Answer Sheet* (August 16, 2013). Retrieved from: www.washingtonpost.com/blogs/answer-sheet/wp/2013/08/16/the-big-problem-with-new-evaluations-of-teacher-prep-programs/

Create Central

www.mhhe.com/createcentral

Additional Resources

M. Cockran-Smith & K. Zeichner, *Studying Teacher Education: The Report of the AERA Panel on Research and Teacher Education* (Taylor & Francis e-Library, 2009).

L. Hammond, *Powerful Teacher Education: Lessons from Exemplary Programs* (2013).

L. Hammond & J. Bransford, eds., *Preparing Teachers for a Changing World* (John Wiley & Sons, 2005).

T. Lasley, Why Do Teacher-Education Programs Fear a New Rating System? The Chronicle of High Education (2011). Retrieved from: http://chronicle.com/article/Why-Do-Teacher-Education/129654/

S. Sherman, *Teacher Preparation as an Inspirational Practice: Building Capacities for Responsiveness* (Routledge Taylor & Francis Group, 2013).

Internet References. . .

National Council of Teacher Quality

> www.nctq.org/siteHome.do

Council for the Accreditation of Educator Preparation

> http://caepnet.org/

Educating School Teachers by Art Levine

> www.edschools.org/pdf/Educating_Teachers_Report.pdf

Group Urges Feds to Yank Aid from Poor-Performing Teacher-Prep Programs

> http://blogs.edweek.org/edweek/teacherbeat/2013/09/report_urges.html

Teacher Education Accreditation Council and the National Council for the Accreditation of Teacher Education

> www.teac.org/ and http://www.ncate.org/

ISSUE

Selected, Edited, and with Issue Framing Material by:
Glenn L. Koonce, *Regent University*

Can Zero Tolerance Violate Students Rights?

YES: Hon. **David Souter**, from Majority Opinion in *Safford Unified School District #1 v. Redding* (June 25, 2009)

NO: Hon. **Clarence Thomas**, from Dissenting Opinion in *Safford Unified School District #1 v. Redding* (June 25, 2009)

Learning Outcomes
After reading this issue, you will be able to:
• Critique the term "Reasonableness" as it applies to the law and a student's Fourth Amendment rights.
• Examine the legal principle of qualified immunity.
• Define the legal term "strip search."
• Appraise the future of zero tolerance policies in public schools.
• Analyze the *New Jersey v. T.L.O.* U.S. Supreme Court decision.

ISSUE S UMMARY

YES: Supreme Court justice David Souter, delivering the opinion of the Court, hold that school officials, in carrying out a zero-tolerance policy on drug possession, violated a student's Fourth Amendment right against unreasonable search and seizure when they included a strip search of the girl.

NO: Justice Clarence Thomas, in dissent, states that the majority opinion imposes too vague a standard on school officials and that it grants judges sweeping authority to second-guess measures those officials take to maintain discipline and ensure safety.

Approximately a decade ago, after the tragedy at Columbine, school systems across the nation introduced zero-tolerance policies aimed at the curtailment of harmful student behaviors. The initial focus of these policies was on the elimination of weapons but soon spread to restrictions on any type of drugs or medication, legal or illegal, doctor-prescribed or readily available in stores. By 2006 about 95 percent of schools in the United States had zero-tolerance policies and nearly half of them reported taking serious action against students, including expulsion, suspension, and transfer to an alternative school.

While many of the practices involved in the enforcement of these policies have been welcomed by all members of the school community insofar as they promoted a safer environment for learning, questions have been raised in recent years about the appropriateness of some actions of school officials. Authors exploring this issue include Randall R. Beger, "Expansion of Police Power in Public Schools and the Vanishing Rights of Students," *Social Justice* (Spring/Summer 2002); Mary Ann Manos, *Knowing Where to Draw the Line: Ethical and Legal Standards for Best*

Classroom Practice (2006); Kris Axtman, "Why Tolerance Is Fading for Zero Tolerance in Schools," *The Christian Science Monitor* (March 31, 2005); Bob Herbert, "6-Year-Olds Under Arrest," *The New York Times* (April 9, 2007); and Elizabeth Frost, "Zero Privacy: Schools Are Violating Students' Fourteenth Amendment Right of Privacy Under the Guise of Enforcing Zero-Tolerance Policies," *Washington Law Review* (May 2006).

Media attention to this issue has stirred public concern and parents of students subjected to allegedly unfair treatment by school officials have initiated lawsuits. Lawyers pursuing such cases have often used a precedent established in the 1969 Supreme Court ruling in Tinker v. Des Moines Independent School District that students in school are still "persons" under the Constitution and are therefore possessed of fundamental rights that the state must respect. Subsequent Supreme Court cases involving First and Fourth Amendment rights are reviewed by Nelda Cambron-McCabe in "Balancing Students' Constitutional Rights," *Phi Delta Kappan* (June 2009). She concludes that while the courts have granted school officials considerable latitude in maintaining a school environment conducive to learning they must also honor students' rights in the process. An excellent source on this historical problem of appropriate balance is *From Schoolhouse to Courthouse: The Judiciary's Role in American Education* (2009), edited by Joshua M. Dunn and Martin R. West. The current period of security guards, metal detectors, surveillance cameras, locker raids, and book bag searches has captured the attention of the ACLU and other concerned groups.

The question of how far school authorities can go in fulfilling zero-tolerance policies came to a head in the Supreme Court's recent ruling in Safford Unified School District #1 *v.* Redding, argued April 21, 2009 and decided June 25, 2009. The case involved what is characterized as a strip search of a 13-year-old middle school student, Savana Redding, accused of hiding ibuprofen tablets in violation of the school's no-tolerance policy on drugs that banned

the possession even of nonprescription pain relievers without explicit permission. School officials claimed that they were on high alert because a student had nearly died the year before after taking medication brought to the school by a friend and that they had good reasons to be suspicious of Savana despite her honor roll grades and spotless disciplinary record. After the event, Savana never returned to Safford Middle School. The Supreme Court ruled in her favor.

In the excerpts from the 8-1 ruling presented below, Justice Souter details the bases for the judgment, which included protection of the school officials from further suits, although Justices Stevens and Ginsburg dissented on that point. Justice Thomas, agreeing with the school official immunity point, was the lone dissenter on the central ruling regarding the violation of the student's rights.

YES ↵

Hon. David Souter

Strip Search Violates 14th Amendment

JUSTICE SOUTER delivered the opinion of the Court.

The issue here is whether a 13-year-old student's Fourth Amendment right was violated when she was subjected to a search of her bra and underpants by school officials acting on reasonable suspicion that she had brought forbidden prescription and over-the-counter drugs to school. Because there were no reasons to suspect the drugs presented a danger or were concealed in her underwear, we hold that the search did violate the Constitution, but because there is reason to question the clarity with which the right was established, the official who ordered the unconstitutional search is entitled to qualified immunity from liability.

. . .

The events immediately prior to the search in question began in 13-year-old Savana Redding's math class at Safford Middle School one October day in 2003. The assistant principal of the school, Kerry Wilson, came into the room and asked Savana to go to his office. There, he showed her a day planner, unzipped and open flat on his desk, in which there were several knives, lighters, a permanent marker, and a cigarette. Wilson asked Savana whether the planner was hers; she said it was, but that a few days before she had lent it to her friend, Marissa Glines. Savana stated that none of the items in the planner belonged to her.

Wilson then showed Savana four white prescription-strength ibuprofen 400-mg pills, and one over-the-counter blue naproxen 200-mg pill, all used for pain and inflammation but banned under school rules without advance permission. He asked Savana if she knew anything about the pills. Savana answered that she did not. Wilson then told Savana that he had received a report that she was giving these pills to fellow students; Savana denied it and agreed to let Wilson search her belongings. Helen Romero, an administrative assistant, came into the office, and together with Wilson they searched Savana's backpack, finding nothing.

At that point, Wilson instructed Romero to take Savana to the school nurse's office to search her clothes for pills. Romero and the nurse, Peggy Schwallier, asked Savana to remove her jacket, socks, and shoes, leaving her in stretch pants and a T-shirt (both without pockets), which she was then asked to remove. Finally, Savana was told to pull her bra out and to the side and shake it, and to pull out the elastic on her underpants, thus exposing her breasts and pelvic area to some degree. No pills were found.

Savana's mother filed suit against Safford Unified School District #1, Wilson, Romero, and Schwallier for conducting a strip search in violation of Savana's Fourth Amendment rights. The individuals (hereinafter petitioners) moved for summary judgment, raising a defense of qualified immunity. The District Court for the District of Arizona granted the motion on the ground that there was no Fourth Amendment violation, and a panel of the Ninth Circuit affirmed. . . .

A closely divided Circuit sitting en banc, however, reversed. Following the two-step protocol for evaluating claims of qualified immunity, . . . the Ninth Circuit held that the strip search was unjustified under the Fourth Amendment test for searches of children by school officials set out in *New Jersey* v. *T. L. O.,* . . . (1985). . . . The Circuit then applied the test for qualified immunity, and found that Savana's right was clearly established at the time of the search: " '[t]hese notions of personal privacy are "clearly established" in that they inhere in all of us, particularly middle school teenagers, and are inherent in the privacy component of the Fourth Amendment's proscription against unreasonable searches'" . . . . The upshot was reversal of summary judgment as to Wilson, while affirming the judgments in favor of Schwallier, the school nurse, and Romero, the administrative assistant, since they had not acted as independent decisionmakers. . . .

. . .

The Fourth Amendment "right of the people to be secure in their persons . . . against unreasonable searches and seizures" generally requires a law enforcement officer to have probable cause for conducting a search. "Probable cause exists where 'the facts and circumstances within [an officer's] knowledge and of which [he] had reasonably trustworthy information [are] sufficient in themselves to warrant a man of reasonable caution in the belief that' an offense has been or is being committed," . . . and that evidence bearing on that offense will be found in the place to be searched.

In *T. L. O.,* we recognized that the school setting "requires some modification of the level of suspicion of illicit activity needed to justify a search," . . . and held that for searches by school officials "a careful balancing of governmental and private interests suggests that the public interest is best served by a Fourth Amendment standard of reasonableness that stops short of probable cause" . . . .

From Supreme Court of the United States, June 25, 2009.

We have thus applied a standard of reasonable suspicion to determine the legality of a school administrator's search of a student, . . . and have held that a school search "will be permissible in its scope when the measures adopted are reasonably related to the objectives of the search and not excessively intrusive in light of the age and sex of the student and the nature of the infraction" . . . .

A number of our cases on probable cause have an implicit bearing on the reliable knowledge element of reasonable suspicion, as we have attempted to flesh out the knowledge component by looking to the degree to which known facts imply prohibited conduct, . . . the specificity of the information received, . . . and the reliability of its source. . . . At the end of the day, however, we have realized that these factors cannot rigidly control, . . . and we have come back to saying that the standards are "fluid concepts that take their substantive content from the particular contexts" in which they are being assessed. . . .

Perhaps the best that can be said generally about the required knowledge component of probable cause for a law enforcement officer's evidence search is that it raise a "fair probability" . . . or a "substantial chance" . . . of discovering evidence of criminal activity. The lesser standard for school searches could as readily be described as a moderate chance of finding evidence of wrongdoing.

· · ·

In this case, the school's policies strictly prohibit the nonmedical use, possession, or sale of any drug on school grounds, including "'[a]ny prescription or over-the-counter drug, except those for which permission to use in school has been granted pursuant to Board policy.'" . . . A week before Savana was searched, another student, Jordan Romero (no relation of the school's administrative assistant), told the principal and Assistant Principal Wilson that "certain students were bringing drugs and weapons on campus," and that he had been sick after taking some pills that "he got from a classmate." . . . On the morning of October 8, the same boy handed Wilson a white pill that he said Marissa Glines had given him. He told Wilson that students were planning to take the pills at lunch.

Wilson learned from Peggy Schwallier, the school nurse, that the pill was Ibuprofen 400 mg, available only by prescription. Wilson then called Marissa out of class. Outside the classroom, Marissa's teacher handed Wilson the day planner, found within Marissa's reach, containing various contraband items. Wilson escorted Marissa back to his office.

In the presence of Helen Romero, Wilson requested Marissa to turn out her pockets and open her wallet. Marissa produced a blue pill, several white ones, and a razor blade. Wilson asked where the blue pill came from, and Marissa answered, "'I guess it slipped in when *she* gave me the IBU 400s.'" . . . When Wilson asked whom she meant, Marissa replied, "'Savana Redding.'" . . . Wilson then enquired about the day planner and its contents; Marissa denied knowing anything about them. Wilson

did not ask Marissa any followup questions to determine whether there was any likelihood that Savana presently had pills: neither asking when Marissa received the pills from Savana nor where Savana might be hiding them.

Schwallier did not immediately recognize the blue pill, but information provided through a poison control hotline indicated that the pill was a 200-mg dose of an anti-inflammatory drug, generically called naproxen, available over the counter. At Wilson's direction, Marissa was then subjected to a search of her bra and underpants by Romero and Schwallier, as Savana was later on. The search revealed no additional pills.

It was at this juncture that Wilson called Savana into his office and showed her the day planner. Their conversation established that Savana and Marissa were on friendly terms: while she denied knowledge of the contraband, Savana admitted that the day planner was hers and that she had lent it to Marissa. Wilson had other reports of their friendship from staff members, who had identified Savana and Marissa as part of an unusually rowdy group at the school's opening dance in August, during which alcohol and cigarettes were found in the girls' bathroom. Wilson had reason to connect the girls with this contraband, for Wilson knew that Jordan Romero had told the principal that before the dance, he had been at a party at Savana's house where alcohol was served. Marissa's statement that the pills came from Savana was thus sufficiently plausible to warrant suspicion that Savana was involved in pill distribution.

This suspicion of Wilson's was enough to justify a search of Savana's backpack and outer clothing. If a student is reasonably suspected of giving out contraband pills, she is reasonably suspected of carrying them on her person and in the carryall that has become an item of student uniform in most places today. If Wilson's reasonable suspicion of pill distribution were not understood to support searches of outer clothes and backpack, it would not justify any search worth making. And the look into Savana's bag, in her presence and in the relative privacy of Wilson's office, was not excessively intrusive, any more than Romero's subsequent search of her outer clothing.

· · ·

Here it is that the parties part company, with Savana's claim that extending the search at Wilson's behest to the point of making her pull out her underwear was constitutionally unreasonable. The exact label for this final step in the intrusion is not important, though strip search is a fair way to speak of it. Romero and Schwallier directed Savana to remove her clothes down to her underwear, and then "pull out" her bra and the elastic band on her underpants. . . . Although Romero and Schwallier stated that they did not see anything when Savana followed their instructions, . . . we would not define strip search and its Fourth Amendment consequences in a way that would guarantee litigation about who was looking and how much was seen. The very fact of Savana's pulling her underwear away from her body in the presence of the two officials who were able to see her necessarily exposed her breasts and pelvic area to some degree, and both subjective and reasonable societal expectations of personal privacy support the treatment of such a search as categorically distinct, requiring distinct elements of justification on the part of school authorities for going beyond a search of outer clothing and belongings.

Savana's subjective expectation of privacy against such a search is inherent in her account of it as embarrassing, frightening, and humiliating. The reasonableness of her expectation (required by the Fourth Amendment standard) is indicated by the consistent experiences of other young people similarly searched, whose adolescent vulnerability intensifies the patent intrusiveness of the exposure. . . . The common reaction of these adolescents simply registers the obviously different meaning of a search exposing the body from the experience of nakedness or near undress in other school circumstances. Changing for gym is getting ready for play; exposing for a search is responding to an accusation reserved for suspected wrongdoers and fairly understood as so degrading that a number of communities have decided that strip searches in schools are never reasonable and have banned them no matter what the facts may be. . . .

The indignity of the search does not, of course, outlaw it, but it does implicate the rule of reasonableness as stated in *T. L. O.*, that "the search as actually conducted [be] reasonably related in scope to the circumstances which justified the interference in the first place." . . . The scope will be permissible, that is, when it is "not excessively intrusive in light of the age and sex of the student and the nature of the infraction." . . .

Here, the content of the suspicion failed to match the degree of intrusion. Wilson knew beforehand that the pills were prescription-strength ibuprofen and over-the-counter naproxen, common pain relievers equivalent to two Advil, or one Aleve. He must have been aware of the nature and limited threat of the specific drugs he was searching for, and while just about anything can be taken in quantities that will do real harm, Wilson had no reason to suspect that large amounts of the drugs were being passed around, or that individual students were receiving great numbers of pills.

Nor could Wilson have suspected that Savana was hiding common painkillers in her underwear. Petitioners suggest, as a truth universally acknowledged, that "students . . . hid[e] contraband in or under their clothing," . . . and cite a smattering of cases of students with contraband in their underwear. . . . But when the categorically extreme intrusiveness of a search down to the body of an adolescent requires some justification in suspected facts, general background possibilities fall short; a reasonable

search that extensive calls for suspicion that it will pay off. But nondangerous school contraband does not raise the specter of stashes in intimate places, and there is no evidence in the record of any general practice among Safford Middle School students of hiding that sort of thing in underwear; neither Jordan nor Marissa suggested to Wilson that Savana was doing that, and the preceding search of Marissa that Wilson ordered yielded nothing. Wilson never even determined when Marissa had received the pills from Savana; if it had been a few days before, that would weigh heavily against any reasonable conclusion that Savana presently had the pills on her person, much less in her underwear.

In sum, what was missing from the suspected facts that pointed to Savana was any indication of danger to the students from the power of the drugs or their quantity, and any reason to suppose that Savana was carrying pills in her underwear. We think that the combination of these deficiencies was fatal to finding the search reasonable.

In so holding, we mean to cast no ill reflection on the assistant principal, for the record raises no doubt that his motive throughout was to eliminate drugs from his school and protect students from what Jordan Romero had gone through. Parents are known to overreact to protect their children from danger, and a school official with responsibility for safety may tend to do the same. The difference is that the Fourth Amendment places limits on the official, even with the high degree of deference that courts must pay to the educator's professional judgment.

We do mean, though, to make it clear that the *T. L. O.* concern to limit a school search to reasonable scope requires the support of reasonable suspicion of danger or of resort to underwear for hiding evidence of wrongdoing before a search can reasonably make the quantum leap from outer clothes and backpacks to exposure of intimate parts. The meaning of such a search, and the degradation its subject may reasonably feel, place a search that intrusive in a category of its own demanding its own specific suspicions.

. . .

The strip search of Savana Redding was unreasonable and a violation of the Fourth Amendment, but petitioners Wilson, Romero, and Schwallier are nevertheless protected from liability through qualified immunity. . . .

DAVID SOUTER served on the U.S. Supreme Court as associate justice from 1990, when he was nominated by then–president George H. W. Bush, until his retirement in 2009.

Hon. Clarence Thomas

➜ **NO**

School Officials Deserve Leeway

J<small>USTICE</small> T<small>HOMAS</small>, concurring in the judgment in part and dissenting in part.

I agree with the Court that the judgment against the school officials with respect to qualified immunity should be reversed. . . . Unlike the majority, however, I would hold that the search of Savana Redding did not violate the Fourth Amendment. The majority imposes a vague and amorphous standard on school administrators. It also grants judges sweeping authority to second-guess the measures that these officials take to maintain discipline in their schools and ensure the health and safety of the students in their charge. This deep intrusion into the administration of public schools exemplifies why the Court should return to the common-law doctrine of *in loco parentis* under which "the judiciary was reluctant to interfere in the routine business of school administration, allowing schools and teachers to set and enforce rules and to maintain order." . . . But even under the prevailing Fourth Amendment test established by *New Jersey* v. *T. L. O.,* . . . all petitioners, including the school district, are entitled to judgment as a matter of law in their favor.

. . .

"Although the underlying command of the Fourth Amendment is always that searches and seizures be reasonable, what is reasonable depends on the context within which a search takes place." . . . Thus, although public school students retain Fourth Amendment rights under this Court's precedent, . . . those rights "are different . . . than elsewhere; the 'reasonableness' inquiry cannot disregard the schools' custodial and tutelary responsibility for children." . . . For nearly 25 years this Court has understood that "[m]aintaining order in the classroom has never been easy, but in more recent years, school disorder has often taken particularly ugly forms: drug use and violent crime in the schools have become major social problems." . . . In schools, "[e]vents calling for discipline are frequent occurrences and sometimes require immediate, effective action." . . .

For this reason, school officials retain broad authority to protect students and preserve "order and a proper educational environment" under the Fourth Amendment. . . . This authority requires that school officials be able to engage in the "close supervision of schoolchildren, as well as . . . enforc[e] rules against conduct that would be perfectly permissible if undertaken by an adult." . . .

Seeking to reconcile the Fourth Amendment with this unique public school setting, the Court in *T. L. O.* held that a school search is "reasonable" if it is "'justified at its inception'" and "'reasonably related in scope to the circumstances which justified the interference in the first place.'" . . . The search under review easily meets this standard.

. . .

A "search of a student by a teacher or other school official will be 'justified at its inception' when there are reasonable grounds for suspecting that the search will turn up evidence that the student has violated or is violating either the law or the rules of the school." . . . As the majority rightly concedes, this search was justified at its inception because there were reasonable grounds to suspect that Redding possessed medication that violated school rules. . . . A finding of reasonable suspicion "does not deal with hard certainties, but with probabilities." . . . To satisfy this standard, more than a mere "hunch" of wrongdoing is required, but "considerably" less suspicion is needed than would be required to "satisf[y] a preponderance of the evidence standard." . . .

Furthermore, in evaluating whether there is a reasonable "particularized and objective" basis for conducting a search based on suspected wrongdoing, government officials must consider the "totality of the circumstances." . . . School officials have a specialized understanding of the school environment, the habits of the students, and the concerns of the community, which enables them to "'formulat[e] certain common-sense conclusions about human behavior.'" . . . And like police officers, school officials are "entitled to make an assessment of the situation in light of [this] specialized training and familiarity with the customs of the [school]." . . .

Here, petitioners had reasonable grounds to suspect that Redding was in possession of prescription and non-prescription drugs in violation of the school's prohibition of the "non-medical use, possession, or sale of a drug" on school property or at school events. . . . As an initial matter, school officials were aware that a few years earlier, a student had become "seriously ill" and "spent several days in intensive care" after ingesting prescription medication obtained from a classmate. . . . Fourth Amendment searches do not occur in a vacuum; rather, context must inform the judicial inquiry. . . . In this instance, the suspicion of drug possession arose at a middle school that had

From Supreme Court of the United States, June 25, 2009.

"a history of problems with students using and distributing prohibited and illegal substances on campus." . . .

The school's substance-abuse problems had not abated by the 2003–2004 school year, which is when the challenged search of Redding took place. School officials had found alcohol and cigarettes in the girls' bathroom during the first school dance of the year and noticed that a group of students including Redding and Marissa Glines smelled of alcohol. . . . Several weeks later, another student, Jordan Romero, reported that Redding had hosted a party before the dance where she served whiskey, vodka, and tequila. . . . Romero had provided this report to school officials as a result of a meeting his mother scheduled with the officials after Romero "bec[a]me violent" and "sick to his stomach" one night and admitted that "he had taken some pills that he had got[ten] from a classmate." . . . At that meeting, Romero admitted that "certain students were bringing drugs and weapons on campus." . . . One week later, Romero handed the assistant principal a white pill that he said he had received from Glines. . . . He reported "that a group of students [were] planning on taking the pills at lunch." . . .

School officials justifiably took quick action in light of the lunchtime deadline. The assistant principal took the pill to the school nurse who identified it as prescription-strength 400-mg Ibuprofen. . . . A subsequent search of Glines and her belongings produced a razor blade, a Naproxen 200-mg pill, and several Ibuprofen 400-mg pills. . . . When asked, Glines claimed that she had received the pills from Redding. . . . A search of Redding's planner, which Glines had borrowed, then uncovered "several knives, several lighters, a cigarette, and a permanent marker." . . . Thus, as the majority acknowledges, . . . the totality of relevant circumstances justified a search of Redding for pills.

. . .

The remaining question is whether the search was reasonable in scope. Under *T. L. O.*, "a search will be permissible in its scope when the measures adopted are reasonably related to the objectives of the search and not excessively intrusive in light of the age and sex of the student and the nature of the infraction." . . . The majority concludes that the school officials' search of Redding's underwear was not "'reasonably related in scope to the circumstances which justified the interference in the first place,'" . . . notwithstanding the officials' reasonable suspicion that Redding "was involved in pill distribution," . . . . According to the majority, to be reasonable, this school search required a showing of "danger to the students from the power of the drugs or their quantity" or a "reason to suppose that [Redding] was carrying pills in her underwear." . . . Each of these additional requirements is an unjustifiable departure from bedrock Fourth Amendment law in the school setting, where this Court has heretofore read the Fourth Amendment to grant considerable leeway to school officials. Because the school officials searched in a location where the

pills could have been hidden, the search was reasonable in scope under *T. L. O.*

. . .

The majority finds that "subjective and reasonable societal expectations of personal privacy support . . . treat[ing]" this type of search, which it labels a "strip search," as "categorically distinct, requiring distinct elements of justification on the part of school authorities for going beyond a search of clothing and belongings." . . . Thus, in the majority's view, although the school officials had reasonable suspicion to believe that Redding had the pills on her person, . . . they needed some greater level of particularized suspicion to conduct this "strip search." There is no support for this contortion of the Fourth Amendment.

. . .

⌐⌐⌐

The analysis of whether the scope of the search here was permissible under that standard is straightforward. Indeed, the majority does not dispute that "general background possibilities" establish that students conceal "contraband in their underwear." . . . It acknowledges that school officials had reasonable suspicion to look in Redding's backpack and outer clothing because if "Wilson's reasonable suspicion of pill distribution were not understood to support searches of outer clothes and backpack, it would not justify any search worth making." . . . The majority nevertheless concludes that proceeding any further with the search was unreasonable. . . . But there is no support for this conclusion. The reasonable suspicion that Redding possessed the pills for distribution purposes did not dissipate simply because the search of her backpack turned up nothing. It was eminently reasonable to conclude that the backpack was empty because Redding was secreting the pills in a place she thought no one would look. . . .

Redding would not have been the first person to conceal pills in her undergarments. . . . Nor will she be the last after today's decision, which announces the safest place to secrete contraband in school.

. . .

The majority compounds its error by reading the "nature of the infraction" aspect of the *T. L. O.* test as a license to limit searches based on a judge's assessment of a particular school policy. According to the majority, the scope of the search was impermissible because the school official "must have been aware of the nature and limited threat of the specific drugs he was searching for" and because he "had no reason to suspect that large amounts of the drugs were being passed around, or that individual students were receiving great numbers of pills." . . . Thus, in order to locate a rationale for finding a Fourth Amendment violation in this case, the majority retreats from its observation that the school's firm no-drug policy "makes sense, and there is no basis to claim that the search was unreasonable owing to some defect or shortcoming of the rule it was aimed at enforcing." . . .

Even accepting the majority's assurances that it is not attacking the rule's reasonableness, it certainly is attacking the rule's importance. This approach directly conflicts with *T. L. O.* in which the Court was "unwilling to adopt a standard under which the legality of a search is dependent upon a judge's evaluation of the relative importance of school rules." . . . Indeed, the Court in *T. L. O.* expressly rejected the proposition that the majority seemingly endorses—that "some rules regarding student conduct are by nature too 'trivial' to justify a search based upon reasonable suspicion." . . .

The majority's decision in this regard also departs from another basic principle of the Fourth Amendment: that law enforcement officials can enforce with the same vigor all rules and regulations irrespective of the perceived importance of any of those rules. "In a long line of cases, we have said that when an officer has probable cause to believe a person committed even a minor crime in his presence, the balancing of private and public interests is not in doubt. The arrest is constitutionally reasonable." . . . The Fourth Amendment rule for searches is the same: Police officers are entitled to search regardless of the perceived triviality of the underlying law. As we have explained, requiring police to make "sensitive, case-by-case determinations of government need," . . . for a particular prohibition before conducting a search would "place police in an almost impossible spot" . . . .

The majority has placed school officials in this "impossible spot" by questioning whether possession of Ibuprofen and Naproxen causes a severe enough threat to warrant investigation. Had the suspected infraction involved a street drug, the majority implies that it would have approved the scope of the search. . . . In effect, then, the majority has replaced a school rule that draws no distinction among drugs with a new one that does. As a result, a full search of a student's person for prohibited drugs will be permitted only if the Court agrees that the drug in question was sufficiently dangerous. Such a test is unworkable and unsound. School officials cannot be expected to halt searches based on the possibility that a court might later find that the particular infraction at issue is not severe enough to warrant an intrusive investigation. . . .

⋅◉⋅

In determining whether the search's scope was reasonable under the Fourth Amendment, it is therefore irrelevant whether officials suspected Redding of possessing prescription-strength Ibuprofen, nonprescription-strength Naproxen, or some harder street drug. Safford prohibited its possession on school property. Reasonable suspicion that Redding was in possession of drugs in violation of these policies, therefore, justified a search extending to any area where small pills could be concealed. The search did not violate the Fourth Amendment.

. . .

Clarence Thomas is an associate justice on the U.S. Supreme Court, having been nominated in 1991 by then–president George H. W. Bush.

EXPLORING THE ISSUE

Can Zero Tolerance Violate Students Rights?

Critical Thinking and Reflection

1. What was the major factor in the decision of the court in Stafford Unified School District #1 *v.* Redding?
2. How dot New Jersey *v.* T.L.O. and Stafford Unified School District #1 *v.* Redding compare and where do they contrast?
3. What frequently asked questions (FAQs) should a school principal know about "Zero Tolerance Policies"?
4. Clearly distinguish between a search and a strip search by citing precedent school court cases.
5. Trace the growth of student's rights issues as viewed by the courts.

Is There Common Ground?

While public sentiment and media commentary tended to side with the final ruling in Safford Unified School District #1 *v.* Redding, the conduct of school officials charged with the responsibility of carrying out zero-tolerance policies will most likely come under further legal scrutiny. Does the Fourth Amendment require a stricter standard than "reasonableness" for justifying actions such as student strip searches? Is the zero-tolerance basis for school discipline itself faulty and in need of modification? Does the principle enunciated by Justice Stephen Breyer in an earlier case continue to guide legal opinions, namely that "school officials need a degree of flexible authority to respond to disciplinary challenges and the law has always considered the relationship between teachers and students special"?

These and related questions are explored in depth in "Law and Order in the Classroom" by Richard Arum and Doreet Preiss in *Education Next* (Fall 2009); *Zero-Tolerance Policies in Schools* (2009), edited by Peggy Daniels; and Bryan R. Warnick's "Surveillance Cameras in Schools: An Ethical Analysis," *Harvard Educational Review* (Fall 2007).

Additional perspectives on the privacy issue at hand and important subtopics can be found in these sources: Ross W. Greene, *Lost at School* (2008), which explores the need for changing the culture and practice of discipline in the schools; Joseph A. Lieberman, *School Shootings: What Every Parent and Educator Needs to Know to Protect Our Children* (2008), which identifies characteristics of the antisocial personality; Justin M. Bathon and Martha M. McCarthy, "Student Expression: The Uncertain Future," *Educational Horizons* (Winter 2008); Alfie Kohn, "Safety from the Inside Out: Rethinking Traditional Approaches,"

Educational Horizons (Fall 2004); Pedro A. Noguera, "Rethinking Disciplinary Practices," *Theory Into Practice* (Autumn 2003); Alfie Kohn, *Beyond Discipline: From Compliance to Community* (2006); and Anne Gregory and Dewey Cornell, "'Tolerating' Adolescent Needs: Moving Beyond Zero-Tolerance Policies in High School," *Theory Into Practice* (Spring 2009).

Discipline and classroom management are among the primary concerns of beginning teachers. No foolproof theories of discipline exist, but a wide-ranging exploration of ideas such as those in the sources cited above and those in firsthand anecdotal accounts by first-year teachers can help in the construction of a reasonable approach when coupled with the sage advice of veteran educators.

Create Central

www.mhhe.com/createcentral

Additional Resources

N. Essex, *The 200 Most Frequently Asked Legal Questions for Educators* (2009).

L. Greenhouse, *The U.S. Supreme Court: A Very Short Introduction* (2012).

M. McCarthy, N. Cambran-McCabe, & S. Eckers, *Public School Law: Teachers' and Students' Rights,* 7th ed. (2013).

D. Persico, *New Jersey v. T.L.O.: Drug Searches in Schools* (Landmark Supreme Court Cases, 1998).

J. Raskin, *We the Students: Supreme Court Cases For and About Students*, 3rd ed. (2008).

Internet References...

Cornell University Law School: *Safford Unified School Dist. #1 v. Redding* (No. 08-479)

www.law.cornell.edu/supct/html/08-479.ZS.html

The Ozey Project: *Safford Unified School District v. Redding*

www.oyez.org/cases/2000-2009/2008/2008_08_479

Cato Institute: Legal Briefs, *Safford Unified School District No.1 v. Redding*

www.cato.org/publications/legal-briefs/safford-unified-school-district-no1-v-redding

Bill of Rights Institute: *New Jersey v. T.L.O.* (1985)

http://billofrightsinstitute.org/resources/educator-resources/americapedia/americapedia-landmark-supreme-court-cases/new-jersey-v-tlo/

United States Courts: *New Jersey v. T.L.O.* Podcast

www.uscourts.gov/multimedia/podcasts/Landmarks/NewJerseyvTLO.aspx

Selected, Edited, and with Issue Framing Material by:
Glenn L. Koonce, *Regent University*

ISSUE

Do American Students Need More Time in School?

YES: Chris Gabrieli, from "More Time, More Learning," *Educational Leadership* (April 2010)

NO: Larry Cuban, from "The Perennial Reform: Fixing School Time," *Phi Delta Kappan* (December 2008)

Learning Outcomes

After reading this issue, you will be able to:

- Critique how the current research is showing that more school time correlates with improved learning outcomes.
- Evaluate how budget restraints, local regulation, restrictive state laws, and parental objections affect decisions to extend the school day.
- Examine how charter schools have shown an increase in student achievement and how the amount of school time is a key factor.
- Summarize the three reasons why changing and fixing extended school time is so hard.
- Compare and contrast the reasons for and against extending the school day of American students.

ISSUE SUMMARY

YES: National Center on Time and Learning Chairman Chris Gabrieli claims that current school time schedules are outmoded and calls for expansion of the instructional day and year to close the achievement gap and provide enrichment opportunities.

NO: Stanford University Professor Emeritus Larry Cuban reviews the history of school time expansion and finds scant research to support such demands.

Although wrangling about the quantity and quality of time spent in school has enlivened the discourse of professional educators for decades, the recent performance pressures brought about by the No Child Left Behind legislation and the increase in foreign competition have brought new urgency to addressing the issue. As Naomi Dillon points out, in "More Time for Learning," *American School Board Journal* (March 2010), expectations of student achievement have vastly increased while institutional time has remained stagnant. The efforts to alter the school day and the school year have been curtailed by politics and tradition, she claims. Most school districts adhere to a 6½-hour, 180-day academic calendar. However, on the present scene, the Obama administration clearly has the time-expansion goal on its education agenda and advocacy groups such as the National Center on Time and Learning have gained momentum, particularly as charter schools have multiplied nationwide.

The state of Massachusetts, in the forefront of the extended-time movement, has been joined by many states and local school systems across the nation. The superintendent of schools in Pittsburgh has been quoted as saying, "In 15 years I'd be surprised if the old school calendar still dominated in urban settings." In their book *Time To Learn* (2008), Chris Gabrieli and Warren Goldstein state that we have been mired in a mix of complacency and resignation regarding the expectations we hold for our public school system and our ability to narrow the achievement gap among racial and ethnic groups. The growing acceptance of longer school hours, however, is providing more time on task for students, more opportunities for experiential learning and enrichment activities, and more latitude for teachers to work with diverse skill levels at the same time. Gabrieli and Goldstein see a moral imperative to bring a lengthened school day and year particularly to students in low-income neighborhoods.

Public charter schools, freed from the restraints of the usual calendar, have been quick to embrace the "more time" approach. For example, the Knowledge Is Power Program (KIPP) schools run from 7:30 a.m. to 5 p.m., hold sessions on some Saturdays, and reduce summer vacation to about 7 weeks, thus adding some 600 hours to the school year. Jennifer Davis, president of the National Center on Time and Learning (NCTL), in "A Matter of Time," *Education Next* (Fall 2008), points to research on charter schools in New York City showing that more school time correlates with improved learning outcomes. David A. Farbman, a senior researcher at NCTL, in a December 2009 report, outlines progress at 655 schools in the organization's database in "Tracking an Emerging Movement," *Education Digest* (February 2010). Another report, Extended School Year Fast Facts (March 2009) by the Center for Education Policy, Applied Research and Evaluation at the University of Southern Maine, offers detailed international comparisons on school time showing American students receiving, on average, about 10 percent fewer instructional hours per year than their foreign counterparts. The report cites some cases, notably Sweden and Finland, where students spend fewer hours in school and yet consistently outperform American students on international achievement tests. This raises the question of quantity versus quality, mere allocated time versus academically engaged time. Other research on American public schools has shown large disparities in time allocation among urban areas, with New York City students getting about 8 weeks more than those in Chicago and Houston students getting five more weeks than those in Memphis, for example.

Questions have been raised about the wisdom of the current push for extended time, citing budget realities, restrictive state laws, and local regulations, and in some cases parental objections. Michael Jonas, in "Mixed Messages on Longer School Day?" *CommonWealth Magazine* (May 21, 2010), cites a study of the Massachusetts Expanded Learning Time program showing that an extended day is not making much of a difference—at a cost of an extra $1300 per student. Cristina Corbin, in "Extended School Year Would Have Dire Economic Effects, Critics Say," FOXNews.com (September 29, 2009), cites increased costs to school systems for overtime pay and summer air-conditioning, major cuts in hotel and tourism profits, and serious blows to summer camp operators when the school year is expanded or year-round schedules are adopted.

In the following selections Chris Gabrieli details the justification for the urgent expansion of school time, while Larry Cuban enumerates the many serious barriers to fulfillment of the movement's goals.

YES ↵

Chris Gabrieli

More Time, More Learning

Just a few years ago, Clarence Edwards Middle School in the Boston neighborhood of Charlestown, Massachusetts, typified the achievement gap challenge we face across the United States. The middle school, which serves students in grades 6–8, had low scores on standardized achievement tests, an alarming level of bad behavior, and dwindling enrollment. Now, three years later, the school could be a national poster child for school improvement.

What changed? The school redesigned its education approach around expanded learning time.

Much remains the same there. The students still have the sort of demographics that generally overwhelm schools and tend to be concentrated in the lowest-performing schools—about 90 percent of the students qualify for free or reduced-price lunch, about 90 percent are minority, nearly one-quarter have limited English proficiency, and almost one-third are classified as having special needs. The school is still characterized by a high degree of student mobility.

Yet substantial improvements have taken place. In the past, Edwards students lagged far behind the state averages in their scores on Massachusetts's standardized tests. Bear in mind that Massachusetts is a predominantly suburban state with the highest National Assessment of Educational Progress (NAEP) scores in the United States. Eighth graders at Edwards have now narrowed that gap by two-thirds in science and by more than 80 percent in English language arts; they now score substantially higher than the state averages in math.

Failure rates have plummeted across the board, and the percentage of learners scoring in the highest band of success in math, advanced, has gone from about zero to level with the state average—19 percent. Every traditionally challenged subgroup has shown improvement. Just four years ago, only 15 percent of limited English proficient 8th graders reached proficiency in math; last year, 71 percent of this subgroup reached proficiency, compared with the state average of 12 percent.

The greatest opportunity that expanded learning time offers for improving academic achievement comes from being able to better individualize instruction—putting the right teachers with the right students and focusing on the right skills. The single biggest change in the academic program at Edwards was adding an hour each day during which students receive small-group instruction and tutoring in the subject in which they lag most. Students receive either English or math support in the afternoon, with the students who are strong in both subjects focusing on science during that slot. In addition, more time has enabled the school to offer both science and social studies four days each week—twice the previous level.

The academic gains are matched by growth in opportunities for students to participate in enrichment activities. The school has a performing arts program that sends many students to Boston's audition-based performing arts high school—the Boston Arts Academy, also an expanded learning time school. Edwards is the only Boston middle school fielding teams in a variety of sports, including a football team that plays nearby suburban schools. And every 6th grader participates in the Citizen Schools program, which features elective apprenticeships with such professionals as corporate attorneys and software engineers from Google.

There's now a sense of positive energy, enthusiasm, and optimism in the building. Students have learned that through hard work, they can excel against the odds. But this requires time: Monday through Thursday, students at Edwards start school at 7:20 a.m. and finish at 4:00 p.m.—that's close to a nine-hour day. On Friday, their day finishes at 11:40 a.m.

Given the positive results, every middle school in Boston has now petitioned to become an expanded learning time school. And families are interested, too. Just three years ago, only 17 students picked Edwards as their first choice during Boston's middle school selection process. Last year, 250 chose Edwards—there's now a waiting list to get in.

With President Obama and U.S. Secretary of Education Duncan now challenging educators to move beyond a school schedule and calendar developed for a farm and factory era, expanded learning time is moving to center stage. At a time of diminishing resources, American Recovery and Reinvestment Act (ARRA) stimulus dollars are boosting the model because the Department of Education's regulations identify "increased learning time" as a core innovation that schools should promote. But simply expanding time willy-nilly at schools is not a silver bullet for success. We need to follow the example of Edwards—and use the time well.

The Emerging Field

For a long time, expanding learning time was more a vision than a reality. In 1994, the National Commission on Time and Learning issued a report titled *Prisoners of Time,* which referred to our current schedule as a fundamental "design flaw." The report argued that we needed to go from a system where seat time chiefly determined advancement (that is, time was fixed) regardless of achievement (that is, outcomes varied widely) to one in which we require that all students meet defined learning levels. Struggling students would need more time; advanced students would require additional challenges.

Charter school laws that emerged in the early 1990s gave some education pioneers the chance to create innovative schools. One celebrated example is the KIPP schools. Graduates of KIPP middle schools not only show large academic test score gains, but also carry that momentum forward into higher rates of college completion. One of the program's five core design pillars is an increase in the school schedule by 60 percent: Students attend school Monday through Friday from 7:30 a.m. to 5:00 p.m., a month longer into the summer, and about 18 Saturday mornings each year.

Two other leading charter management organizations—Achievement First (www.achievementfirst.org) and Uncommon Schools (www.uncommonschools.org)—also expand time with good results. Harvard professor Roland Fryer (Dobbie & Fryer, 2009) has recently shown that New York City's Harlem Promise Academies, part of Geoffrey Canada's Harlem Children's Zone, drive large gains for participants. By extending the school day and offering tutoring on Saturdays and in the summer, the academies provide 50 percent more time for all students and 100 percent more time for those who struggle the most.

The most persuasive evidence of the importance of expanding learning time to drive academic gains comes from Caroline Hoxby's major ongoing study of all New York City charter schools. She recently analyzed 30 different design variables at these 42 schools—such as curriculum, approach to discipline, teacher pay structures, and schedules—and found that the feature most convincingly correlated with academic success was increased learning time (Hoxby, Murarka, & Kang, 2009).

Our organization, the National Center on Time and Learning, has just published the first national census of expanded time schools (Farbman, 2009). We identified 655 such schools in 36 U.S. states and the District of Columbia. These schools add, on average, about 25 percent more time each year—or the equivalent of *three extra years of school* for students who attend such schools for their entire school career. Longer days account for most of the time expansion, but 20 percent of the schools have lengthened the school year as well.

These schools serve the neediest students in the United States. Students in expanded time schools are twice as likely to be minorities, and two-thirds are poor. Three-quarters of the schools are charters, but the most rapidly growing group is in-district conversions. We were heartened to see that these expanded time schools show higher academic achievement than the average for their host districts (Farbman, 2009).

For Whom Should the Expanded Day Bell Toll?

The most compelling initial target for expanding learning time [are] middle-grade students in high-poverty schools. The notable success of many expanded learning time schools at this level provides strong encouragement that this approach can succeed.

Children in our highest-poverty middle schools rarely participate in many programs so familiar to their more affluent peers—tutoring, summer institutes, martial arts courses, science camps, sports leagues, and the like—and rarely have strong homework support at home. For these students, schools must be muscular enough to get most of the job done.

Middle school is well documented to be the level at which students seem to diverge into two groups. One group tends to be well socialized to school, proficient academically, and on a strong path to high school graduation; the other group tends to show alienation from school and become at high risk of dropping out.

Through strong core instruction combined with individualized support, expanding learning time can ensure that at-risk students keep up academically; develop attachments to school through such activities as sports, arts, and drama; and develop the beliefs and behaviors consistent with success.

Many elementary schools have benefited from expanding learning time by both raising academic achievement and providing a well-rounded day. More learning time could benefit high schools as well, but to lesser effect in the context of the traditional high school structure. There are a number of impressive high schools across the United States that use expanded learning time, but expanded time did not drive their conversion. Rather, these schools have radically redesigned how they operate, and they happen to need and use more time to get the job done.

A Good Fit

To succeed, expanded learning time has to work for teachers, students, parents, and the education system. In general, teachers agree that they don't have enough time to help all students reach their academic goals, especially when students are already lagging. Teachers usually welcome the improved pace that expanded learning time provides as well as the opportunity to engage students in a wider variety of instructional approaches, including more project-based learning. Teachers' unions want to ensure that established teachers are offered choice and that they receive adequate compensation for more time. Charter schools usually recruit with the longer schedule as part of the plan and sometimes with moderately higher overall pay.

Students are often initially skeptical when they hear about expanded learning time, especially older students. But once they experience it, they typically accommodate to it quickly as their standard schedule. Many students are pleased with the far greater opportunities for enrichment and engagement through art, music, drama, robotics, sports, and the like. They also notice that their teachers have more time to support them and that their achievement typically improves.

Parents often flock to expanded learning time schools when they are available. They usually believe that with more time, schools can help their children do better academically; they also appreciate the better match between their work schedules and their children's school schedules. Affluent parents are more divided in their reaction to potential expansions of school schedules because they have often already invested time and money in placing their children in structured, supervised out-of-school activities to complement the content and schedule of school.

School districts are often eager to identify new levers to drive achievement gains in their lowest-performing schools. Their greatest challenges are finding the necessary funding and accommodating schools working on a different schedule. Charter schools, which have blazed the path, face fewer such challenges, although many raise private funding to help meet the greater costs.

With a Little Help from Uncle Sam

It takes resources and incentives to turn will into reality. In the final Race to the Top guidelines issue in November 2009, the U.S. Department of Education calls for time to be "significantly increased" and points to our research—that a minimum of 300 hours per year is necessary to effect real change. The department indicates that for schools to see the greatest improvements, they need to fully integrate expanded learning time and implement a balanced approach that provides more time for core academics, for enrichment subjects, and for teachers to collaborate and improve their craft. This high-bar definition rules out the possibility of schools adding only modest amounts of time for some students and calling it sufficient.

The Department of Education has laid out the acceptable approaches for state, district, and school use of American Recovery and Reinvestment Act (ARRA) funding to turn around the lowest-performing schools. Of the four alternatives defined, two models, *turnaround* and *transformation,* require the use of increased learning time. These regulations bind the new competitive programs—Race to the Top and Investment in Innovation (i3)—but also cover the longer-term School Improvement Fund. The latter has attracted less fanfare but deserves more attention: ARRA boosts this fund to $3.5 billion, which will flow to all 50 U.S. states, and as an element of Title I it will likely endure well beyond the life of the stimulus package.

Ten Keys to Success

In view of these developments, the increased learning time movement is likely to spread. The following keys are crucial to a successful implementation of expanded learning time for disadvantaged students.

Key 1: Schools must allot a sufficiently large amount of expanded time.
Modest amounts of increased time will not help schools reach their goals. In our experience, schools need a minimum of 300 hours each year—or an additional one hour and 45 minutes each day—to establish a balanced program and drive deep change. Successful expanded learning time schools range from those that offer about 25 percent more time to those that offer as much as 60 percent more time (for example, KIPP schools).

Key 2: Schools must fully integrate expanded time into a redesigned overall schedule.
Visitors to expanded learning time schools often ask, "At what time should I come to see the expanded time?" The additional time, however, is not tacked on to the end of the traditional schedule but rather is deeply integrated into a wholly reenvisioned day. A school could extend a math or English language arts block from 45 minutes to 60 or 90 minutes; add time every day for social studies, science, or physical education; add an elective enrichment class in the middle of the day while core teachers are freed to collaborate in work groups; or expand time for lunch and recess.

Key 3: Schools should allocate expanded time to a balanced program.
Although most schools adopting expanded learning time want to drive academic achievement gains, there should be a healthy balance between the added depth allotted to core academics and the added breadth allotted to restore a well-rounded education. Schools should also strike a balance between expanded time for students to learn and for teachers to collaborate and improve.

Key 4: Schools must prioritize and focus expanded time.
Although expanded learning time is a welcome opportunity for principals and teachers because it holds the promise of benefiting all students, the most common mistake we have seen has been the failure to prioritize and focus. Some schools set out to do too many things and end up doing none of them very well. Including too many electives and enrichment opportunities can take away from

the core mission of improving student achievement. It is important not to substitute a shallow exposure to many fields for a deeper mastery of one or two areas.

Key 5: Schools should change the schedule for all students.

This does not mean that all students have the identical schedule. On the contrary, expanded learning time allows for greater personalization, with students getting the level of intensive support or added challenge their skill levels dictate as well as the variety of education experiences that all children deserve.

Students accept the schedule as a fact of life, a crucial feature for middle and high school students who are unlikely to volunteer to stay longer after school. When all students stay, there is no sense of academic detention for some. The school can redesign the whole schedule; some students will be in music at noon whereas others will be in math at 3:30 [p.m.] Changing the schedule for all students commits the whole school to lasting institutional change.

Key 6: Schools should engage in a schoolwide planning process.

Drawing the faculty and community into the process of considering whether and how to expand learning time is an important opportunity to reinvigorate a school and gain buy-in from the people who will have to make it work. When done well, the process also forces a school to self-examine and use data to define strengths and weaknesses. A good planning process enables a shift to a data-driven, continuous-improvement culture, which is essential to long-term success.

Key 7: Schools should focus on strengthening core instruction and personalizing learning.

Successful expanded learning time schools are deeply committed to raising the quality of core instruction in every classroom through the use of data and collaborative improvement. In addition, these schools use frequent, well-aligned formative assessments to properly assess individual students' strengths and needs and to place students into well-designed interventions aimed at helping them catch up. Many successful expanded learning time schools offer students an extra class each day in the subject in which they struggle the most, with classmates at a similar level and a teacher who has expertise in this area. Some offer small or one-on-one tutoring sessions.

Key 8: Schools should offer engaging enrichment and opportunities for both exposure and mastery.

Enrichment opportunities that are structured as electives, taught by both teachers and outside partners, and interspersed throughout the day and year can engage students who are becoming increasingly alienated from school and who are at risk of dropping out. Students should have the opportunity to experience a wide variety of activities and achieve mastery in at least one of them.

Key 9: Schools should promote effective teacher collaboration and professional development.

Expanded learning time offers the opportunity to embed considerably more time for teachers to work together by grade or department and focus on specific instructional strategies that they can immediately put to use. However, it is easy to squander this time on low-intensity or administrative efforts and miss the chance to improve instructional effectiveness.

Key 10: Schools must change student and teacher beliefs and behaviors.

A growing body of evidence suggests that an optimistic belief that hard work will pay off is crucial to turning around our lowest-performing students and schools (see Blackwell, Trzesniewski, & Dweck, 2007). Struggling students from disadvantaged backgrounds often need help seeing that hard work will be rewarded with success and that delaying gratification and pursuing long-term goals are necessary.

Many teachers believe that with more time, they could succeed with far more struggling students. Expanded learning time enables students to do more of that hard work together and with teacher supervision—as opposed to the solo nature of homework—and allows more intentional efforts to build school community culture and values.

Not Solely Sufficient

If adding time alone were sufficient, every expanded learning time school would be a great success. But not every expanded school succeeds. Experience shows that a cluster of related school reforms needs to happen to enable the sort of performance one sees at Edwards Middle School or a high-performing KIPP school. At least three other drivers are key to success.

First, schools need *high levels of human capital* or, in plainer language, a strong principal and highly effective teachers. The process of planning for and implementing a redesign around more time is an extraordinary leadership opportunity for a principal who is a true instructional leader. Well-led schools can recruit and train excellent teachers and hone the skills of all incumbent teachers by using fair evaluation systems to ensure high standards.

Second, schools need to use *data-driven instructional approaches*. Although most schools in the United States might claim they use such approaches, this has not been our experience. Managing individual students' instruction on the basis of objective measures of their progress while using broader data to drive the discussion of how to improve enables school faculty to use added time most effectively.

Edwards initially used homegrown data to assess students and match instructional supports to their needs. More recently, the school has partnered with the Achievement Network (www.achievementnetwork.org) to implement six interim assessments each year; the resulting data drive professional development. The school credits this practice with a major surge in its third year in instructional effectiveness in English language arts.

Third, schools need to focus on building *high-performance cultures* in which teachers and students expect to succeed. Planning for expanded learning time leads naturally to a healthy discussion about the performance goals a school should pursue. We also encourage policies that require an agreement on goals between the school and the district or state. We favor focusing on exit-year proficiency—shouldn't the school's overall goal be to prepare its graduates for the next level of education?—and on including, in addition to academic goals, measures of student engagement and commitment.

Where We Go from Here

The movement to match learning time to student needs is still in the early stages of development. We need to dig down into the specific classroom practices that expanded time enables and figure out which ones are the most effective and which ones we can most readily scale up. We need to learn how to better use the resources of people, time, and money. For example, to what extent can we use staggered start times for teachers and community-based organizations? Although many of the most successful schools have all teachers at work for all of the expanded schedule, it may be more cost effective and broadly applicable to find ways to vary the approach.

The challenge will be to use the wave of resources from federal ARRA funding to launch thoughtful, well-targeted expanded learning time efforts. We need to understand how to use more learning time well to ensure that the U.S. ideal of equal opportunity for all through excellent public education becomes the norm—and not the celebrated exception.

References

Blackwell, L., Trzesniewski, K., & Dweck, C. S. (2007). Implicit theories of intelligence predict achievement across an adolescent transition: A longitudinal study and an intervention. *Child Development, 78*(1), 246–263.

Dobbie, W., & Fryer, R. G. (2009). *Are high-quality schools enough to close the achievement gap? Evidence from a bold social experiment in Harlem* (Working Paper No. 15473). Cambridge, MA: National Bureau of Economic Research.

Farbman, D. A. (2009). *Tracking an emerging movement: A report on expanded time schools in America.* Boston: National Center on Time and Learning. Available: www.timeandlearning.org/images/12.7.09FinalDatabaseReport.pdf

Hoxby, C. M., Murarka, S., & Kang, J. (2009). *How New York City's charter schools affect achievement.* Cambridge, MA: New York City Charter Schools Evaluation Project.

Chris Gabrieli is chairman of the National Center on Time & Learning and adjunct lecturer at the Harvard School of Education. He is the coauthor, with Warren Goldstein, of *Time to Learn* (2008).

Larry Cuban

→ NO

The Perennial Reform: Fixing School Time

In the past quarter century, reformers have repeatedly urged schools to fix their use of time, even though it is a solution that is least connected to what happens in classrooms or what Americans want from public schools. Since *A Nation at Risk* in 1983, *Prisoners of Time* in 1994, and the latest blue-ribbon recommendations in *Tough Choices, Tough Times* in 2007, both how much time and how well students spend it in school have been criticized to no end.

Business and civil leaders have been critical because they see U.S. students stuck in the middle ranks on international tests. These leaders believe that the longer school year in Asia and Europe is linked to those foreign students scoring far higher than U.S. students on those tests.

Employers criticize the amount of time students spend in school because they wonder whether the limited days and hours spent in classes are sufficient to produce the skills that employees need to work in a globally competitive economy. Employers also wonder whether our comparatively short school year will teach the essential workplace behaviors of punctuality, regular attendance, meeting deadlines, and following rules.

Parents criticize school schedules because they want schools to be open when they go to work in the morning and to remain open until they pick up their children before dinner.

Professors criticize policy makers for allotting so little time for teachers to gain new knowledge and skills during the school day. Other researchers want both policy makers and practitioners to distinguish between requiring more time in school and *academic learning time,* academic jargon for those hours and minutes where teachers engage students in learning content and skills or, in more jargon, time on task.

Finally, cyberschool champions criticize school schedules because they think it's quaint to have students sitting at desks in a building with hundreds of other students for 180 days when a revolution in communication devices allows children to learn the formal curriculum in many places, not just in school buildings. Distance learning advocates, joined by those who see cyberschools as the future, want children and youths to spend hardly any time in K-12 schools.

Time Options

Presidential commissions, parents, academics, and employers have proposed the same solutions, again and again, for fixing the time students spend in school: Add more days to the annual school calendar. Change to year-round schools. Add instructional time to the daily schedule. Extend the school day.

What has happened to each proposal in the past quarter century?

Longer School Year

Recommendations for a longer school year (from 180 to 220 days) came from *A Nation at Risk* (1983) and *Prisoners of Time* (1994) plus scores of other commissions and experts. In 2008, a foundation-funded report, *A Stagnant Nation: Why American Students Are Still at Risk,* found that the 180-day school year was intact across the nation and only Massachusetts had started a pilot program to help districts lengthen the school year. The same report gave a grade of F to states for failing to significantly expand student learning time.

Year-Round Schools

Ending the summer break is another way to maximize student time in school. There is a homespun myth, treated as fact, that the annual school calendar, with three months off for both teachers and students, is based on the rhythm of 19th-century farm life, which dictated when school was in session. Thus, planting and harvesting chores accounted for long summer breaks, an artifact of agrarian America. Not so.

Actually, summer vacations grew out of early 20th-century urban middle-class parents (and later lobbyists for camps and the tourist industry) pressing school boards to release children to be with their families for four to eight weeks or more. By the 1960s, however, policy maker and parent concerns about students losing ground academically during the vacation months—in academic language, "summer loss"—gained support for year-round schooling. Cost savings also attracted those who saw facilities being used 12 months a year rather than being shuttered during the summer.

Nonetheless, although year-round schools were established as early as 1906 in Gary, Indiana, calendar innovations have had a hard time entering most schools. Districts with year-round schools still work within the 180-day year but distribute the time more evenly (e.g., 45 days in session, 15 days off) rather than having a long break between June and September. As of 2006, nearly 3,000 of the nation's 90,000 public schools enrolled more than 2.1 million students on a year-round calendar. That's less than 5% of all students attending public schools, and almost half of the year-round schools are in California. In most cases, school boards adopted year-round schools because increased enrollments led to crowded facilities, most often in minority and poor communities—not concerns over "summer loss."

Adding Instructional Time to the School Day

Many researchers and reformers have pointed out that the 6½-hour school day has so many interruptions, so many distractions that teachers have less than five hours of genuine instruction time. Advocates for more instructional time have tried to stretch the actual amount of instructional time available to teachers to a seven-hour day (or 5½ hours of time for time-on-task learning) or have tried to redistribute the existing secondary school schedule into 90-minute blocks rather than the traditional 50-minute periods. Since *A Nation at Risk*, this recommendation for more instructional time has resulted only in an anemic 10 more minutes per day when elementary school students study core academic subjects.

Block scheduling in public secondary schools (60- to 90-minute periods for a subject that meets different days of the week) was started in the 1960s to promote instructional innovations. Various modified schedules have spread slowly, except in a few states where block schedules multiplied rapidly. In the past decade, an explosion of interest in small high schools has led many traditional urban comprehensive high schools of 1,500 or more students to convert to smaller high schools of 300 to 400 students, sometimes with all of those smaller schools housed within the original large building, sometimes as separate schools located elsewhere in the district. In many of these small high schools, modified schedules with instructional periods of an hour or more have found a friendly home. Block schedules rearrange existing allotted time for instruction; they do not add instructional time to the school day.

Extended School Day

In the past half century, as the economy has changed and families increasingly have both (or single) parents working, schools have been pressed to take on childcare responsibilities, such as tutoring and homework supervision before and after school. Many elementary schools open at 7 a.m. for parents to drop off children and have after-school programs that close at 6 p.m. PDK/Gallup polls since the early 1980s show increased support for these before- and after-school programs. Instead of the familiar half-day program for 5-year-olds, all-day kindergartens (and prekindergartens for 4-year-olds) have spread swiftly in the past two decades, especially in low-income neighborhoods. Innovative urban schools, such as the for-profit Edison Inc. and KIPP (Knowledge Is Power Program), run longer school days. The latter routinely opens at 7:30 a.m. and closes at 5 p.m. and also schedules biweekly Saturday classes and three weeks of school during the summer.

If reformers want a success story in fixing school time, they can look to extending the school day, although it's arguable how many of those changes occurred because of reformers' arguments and actions and how many from economic and social changes in family structure and the desire to chase a higher standard of living.

Cybereducation

And what about those public school haters and cheerleading technological enthusiasts who see fixing time in school as a wasted effort when online schooling and distance learning can replace formal schooling? In the 1960s and 1970s, Ivan Illich and other school critics called for dismantling public schools and ending formal schooling. They argued that schools squelched natural learning, confused school-based education with learning, and turned children into obedient students and adults rather than curious and independent lifelong learners. Communication and instructional technologies were in their infancy then, and thinkers such as Illich had few alternatives to offer families who opted out.

Much of that ire directed at formal public schooling still exists, but now technology has made it possible for students to learn outside school buildings. Sharing common ground in this debate are deeply religious families who want to avoid secular influences in schools, highly educated parents who fear the stifling effects of school rules and text-bound instruction, and rural parents who simply want their children to have access to knowledge unavailable in their local schools. These advocates seek home schooling, distance learning, and cyber schools.

Slight increases in home schooling may occur—say from 1.1 million in 2003 to 2 to 3 million by the end of the decade, with the slight uptick in numbers due to both the availability of technology and a broader menu of choices for parents. Still, this represents less than 3% of public school students. Even though cheerleaders for distance learning have predicted wholesale changes in conventional site-based schools for decades, such changes will occur at the periphery, not the center, because most parents will continue to send their children to public schools.

Even the most enthusiastic advocates for cyber-schools and distance education recognize that replacing public schools is, at best, unlikely. The foreseeable future will still have 50 million children and youths crossing the schoolhouse door each weekday morning.

3 Reasons

Reformers have spent decades trotting out the same recipes for fixing the time problem in school. For all the hoopla and all of the endorsements from highly influential business and political elites, their mighty efforts have produced minuscule results. Why is that?

Cost is the usual suspect. Covering additional teacher salaries and other expenses runs high. Minnesota provides one example: shifting from 175 to 200 days of instruction cost districts an estimated $750 million a year, a large but not insurmountable price to pay. But costs for extending the school day for instruction and childcare are far less onerous.

Even more attractive than adding days to the calendar, however, is the claim that switching to a year-round school will *save* dollars. So, while there are costs involved in lengthening the school calendar, cost is not the tipping point in explaining why so few proposals to fix school time are successful.

I offer two other reasons why fixing school time is so hard.

Research showing achievement gains due to more time in school are sparse; the few studies most often displayed are contested.

Late 20th-century policy makers seriously underestimated the powerful tug that conservative, noneconomic goals (e.g., citizenship, character formation) have on parents, taxpayers, and voters. When they argued that America needed to add time to the school calendar in order to better prepare workers for global competition, they were out of step with the American public's desires for schools.

Skimpy Research

In the past quarter century of tinkering with the school calendar, cultural changes, political decisions, or strong parental concerns trumped research every time. Moreover, the longitudinal and rigorous research on time in school was—and is—skimpy. The studies that exist are challenged repeatedly for being weakly designed. For example, analysts examining research on year-round schools have reported that most of the studies have serious design flaws and, at best, show slight positive gains in student achievement—except for students from low-income families, for whom gains were sturdier. As one report concluded: "[N]o truly trustworthy studies have been done on modified school calendars that can serve as the basis for sound policy decisions." Policy talk about year-round schools has easily outstripped results.

Proving that time in school is the crucial variable in raising academic achievement is difficult because so many other variables must be considered—the local context itself, available resources, teacher quality, administrative leadership, socioeconomic and cultural background of students and their families, and what is taught. But the lack of careful research has seldom stopped reform-driven decision makers from pursuing their agendas.

Conflicting School Goals

If the evidence suggests that, at best, a longer school year or day or restructured schedules do not seem to make the key difference in student achievement, then I need to ask: What problem are reformers trying to solve by adding more school time?

The short answer is that for the past quarter century—*A Nation at Risk* (1983) is a suitable marker—policy elites have redefined a national economic problem into an educational problem. Since the late 1970s, influential civic, business, and media leaders have sold Americans the story that lousy schools are the reason why inflation surged, unemployment remained high, incomes seldom rose, and cheaper and better foreign products flooded U.S. stores. Public schools have failed to produce a strong, post-industrial labor force, thus leading to a weaker, less competitive U.S. economy. U.S. policy elites have used lagging scores on international tests as telling evidence that schools graduate less knowledgeable, less skilled high school graduates—especially those from minority and poor schools who will be heavily represented in the mid-21st century workforce—than competitor nations with lower-paid workforces who produce high-quality products.

Microsoft founder Bill Gates made the same point about U.S. high schools.

> In district after district across the country, wealthy white kids are taught Algebra II, while low-income minority kids are taught how to balance a checkbook. This is an economic disaster. In the international competition to have the best supply of workers who can communicate clearly, analyze information, and solve complex problems, the United States is falling behind. We have one of the highest high school dropout rates in the industrialized world.

And here, in a nutshell, is the second reason why those highly touted reforms aimed at lengthening the school year and instructional day have disappointed policy makers. By blaming schools, contemporary civic and business elites have reduced the multiple goals Americans expect of their public schools to a single one: prepare youths to work in a globally competitive economy. This has been a mistake because Americans historically have expected more from their public schools. Let me explore the geography of this error.

For nearly three decades, influential groups have called for higher academic standards, accountability for student outcomes, more homework, more testing, and, of course, more time in school. Many of their recommendations have been adopted. By 2008, U.S. schools had a federally driven system of state-designed standards anchored in increased testing, results-driven accountability, and demands for students to spend more time in school. After all, reformers reasoned, the students of foreign competitors were attending school more days in the year and longer hours each day, even on weekends, and their test scores ranked them higher than [their] U.S. [counterparts].

Even though this simplistic causal reasoning has been questioned many times by researchers who examined education and work performance in Japan, Korea, Singapore, Germany, and other nations, "common sense" observations by powerful elites swept away such questions. So the U.S.'s declining global economic competitiveness had been spun into a time-in-school problem.

But convincing evidence drawn from research that more time in school would lead to a stronger economy, less inequalities in family income, and that elusive edge in global competitiveness—much less a higher rank in international tests—remains missing in action.

The Public's Goal for Education

Business and civic elites have succeeded at least twice in the past century in making the growth of a strong economy the primary aim of U.S. schools, but other goals have had an enormous and enduring impact on schooling, both in the past and now. These goals embrace core American values that have been like second-hand Roses, shabby and discarded clothes hidden in the back of the closet and occasionally trotted out for show during graduation. Yet since the origins of tax-supported public schools in the early 19th century, these goals have been built into the very structures of schools so much so that, looking back from 2008, we hardly notice them.

Time-based reforms have had trouble entering schools because other goals have had—and continue to have—clout with parents and taxpayers. Opinion polls, for example, display again and again what parents, voters, and taxpayers want schools to achieve. One recent poll identified the public's goals for public schools. The top five were to

- Prepare people to become responsible citizens;
- Help people become economically sufficient;
- Ensure a basic level of quality among schools;
- Promote cultural unity among all Americans; [and]
- Improve social conditions for people.

Tied for sixth and seventh were goals to

- Enhance people's happiness and enrich their lives; and
- Dispel inequities in education among certain schools and certain groups.

To reach those goals, a democratic society expects schools to produce adults who are engaged in their communities, enlightened employers, and hard-working employees who have acquired and practiced particular values that sustain its way of life. Dominant American social, political, and economic values pervade family, school, workplace, and community: Act independently, accept personal responsibility for actions, work hard and complete a job well, and be fair, that is, willing to be judged by standards applied to others as long as the standards are applied equitably.

These norms show up in school rules and classroom practices in every school. School is the one institutional agent between the family, the workplace, and

voting booth or jury room responsible for instilling those norms in children's behavior. School is the agent for turning 4-year-olds into respectful students engaged in their communities, a goal that the public perceives as more significant than preparing children and youths for college and the labor market. In elite decision makers' eagerness to link schools to a growing economy, they either overlooked the powerful daily practices of schooling or neglected to consider seriously these other goals. In doing so, they erred. The consequences of that error in judgment can be seen in the fleeting attention that policy recommendations for adding more time in school received before being shelved.

Teaching in a Democracy

Public schools were established before industrialization, and they expanded rapidly as factories and mills spread.

Those times appear foreign to readers today. For example, in the late 19th century, calling public schools "factory-like" was not an epithet hurled at educators or supporters of public schools as it has been in the U.S. since the 1960s. In fact, describing a public school as an assembly-line factory or a productive cotton mill was considered a compliment to forward-looking educators who sought to make schools modern through greater efficiency in teaching and learning by copying the successes of wealthy industrialists. Progressive reformers praised schools for being like industrial plants in creating large, efficient, age-graded schools that standardized curriculum while absorbing millions of urban migrants and foreign immigrants. As a leading progressive put it:

> Our schools are, in a sense, factories in which the raw products (children) are to be shaped and fashioned into products to meet the various demands of life. . . . It is the business of the school to build its pupils to the specifications [of manufacturers].

Progressive reformers saw mills, factories, and corporations as models for transforming the inefficient one-room schoolhouse in which students of different ages received fitful, incomplete instruction from one teacher into the far more efficient graded school where each teacher taught students a standardized curriculum each year. First established in Boston in 1848 and spreading swiftly in urban districts, the graded school became the dominant way of organizing a school by 1900. By the 1920s, schools exemplified the height of industrial efficiency because each building had separate classrooms with their own teachers. The principal and teachers expected children of the same age to cover the same content and learn skills by the end of the school year and perform satisfactorily on tests in order to be promoted to the next grade.

Superintendents saw the age-graded school as a modern version of schooling well adapted to an emerging corporate-dominated industrial society where punctuality, dependability, and obedience were prized behaviors. As a St. Louis superintendent said in 1871:

> The first requisite of the school is Order: each pupil must be taught first and foremost to conform his behavior to a general standard. . . . The pupil must have his lessons ready at the appointed time, must rise at the tap of the bell, move to the line, return; in short, go through all of the evolutions with equal precision.

Recognition and fame went to educators who achieved such order in their schools.

But the farm-driven seasonal nature of rural one-room schoolhouses was incompatible with the explosive growth of cities and an emerging industrial society. In the early 20th century, progressive reformers championed compulsory attendance laws while extending the abbreviated rural-driven short hours and days into a longer school day and year. Reformers wanted to increase the school's influence over children's attitudes and behavior, especially in cities where wave after wave of European immigrants settled. Seeking higher productivity in organization, teaching, and learning at the least cost, reformers broadened the school's mission by providing medical, social, recreational, and psychological services at schools. These progressive reformers believed schools should teach society's norms to both children and their families and also educate the whole child so that the entire government, economy, and society would change for the better. So, when reformers spoke about "factory-like schools" a century ago, they wanted educators to copy models of success; they were not scolding them. That changed, however, by the late 20th century.

As the U.S. shifted from a manufacturing-based economy to a post-industrial information-based economy, few policy makers reckoned with this history of schooling. Few influential decision makers view schools as agents of *both* stability and change. Few educational opinion makers recognize that the conservative public still expects schools to instill in children dominant American norms of being independent and being held accountable for one's actions, doing work well and efficiently, and treating others equitably to ensure that when students graduate they will practice these values as adults. And, yes, the public still expects schools to strengthen the economy by ensuring that graduates have the necessary skills to be productive employees in an ever-changing, highly competitive, and increasingly global workplace. But that is just one of many competing expectations for schools.

Thus far, I have focused mostly on how policy makers and reform-minded civic and business elites have not only defined economic problems as educational ones that can be fixed by more time spent in schools but also neglected the powerful hold that socialization goals have on parents' and taxpayers' expectations. Now, I want to switch from the world of reform-driven policy makers and elites to teachers and students because each group views school time differently from their respective perch. Teacher and student perspectives on time in school have little influence in policy makers' decision making. Although the daily actions of teachers and students don't influence policy makers, they do matter in explaining why reformers have had such paltry results in trying to fix school time.

Differing Views of Time in School

For civic and business leaders, media executives, school boards, superintendents, mayors, state legislators, governors, U.S. representatives, and the President (what I call "policy elites"), electoral and budget cycles become the timeframe within which they think and act. Every year, budgets must be prepared and, every two or four years, officials run for office and voters decide who should represent them and whether they should support bond referenda and tax levies. Because appointed and elected policy makers are influential with the media, they need to assure the public during campaigns that slogans and stump speeches were more than talk. Sometimes, words do become action when elected decision makers, for example, convert a comprehensive high school into a cluster of small high schools, initiate 1:1 laptop programs, and extend the school day. This is the world of policy makers.

The primary tools policy makers use to adopt and implement decisions, however, are limited and blunt—closer to a hammer than a scalpel. They use exhortation, press conferences, political bargaining, incentives, and sanctions to formulate and adopt decisions. (Note, however, that policy makers rarely implement decisions; administrators and practitioners put policies into practice.) Policy makers want broad social, political, economic, and organizational goals adopted as policies, and then they want to move educators, through encouragement, incentives, and penalties, to implement those policies in schools and classrooms that they seldom, if ever, enter.

The world of teachers differs from that of policy makers. For teachers, the time-driven budget and electoral cycles that shape policy matter little for their classrooms, except when such policies carry consequences for how and what teachers should teach, such as accountability measures that assume teachers and students are slackers and need to work harder. In these instances, teachers become classroom gatekeepers in deciding how much of a policy they will put into practice and under what conditions.

What matters most to teachers are student responses to daily lessons, weekly tests, monthly units, and the connections they build over time in classrooms, corridors, during lunch, and before and after school. Those personal connections become the compost of learning. Those connections account for former students pointing to particular teachers who made a difference in their lives. Teacher tools, unlike policy maker tools, are unconnected to organizational power or media influence. Teachers use their personalities, knowledge, experience, and skills in building relationships with groups of students and providing individual help. Teachers believe there is never enough time in the daily schedule to finish a lesson, explain a point, or listen to a student. Administrative intrusions gobble up valuable instructional time that could go to students. In class, then, both teachers and students are clock watchers, albeit for different reasons.

Students view time differently as well. For a fraction of students from middle-and low-income families turned off by school requirements and expectations, spending time in classrooms listening to teachers, answering questions, and doing homework is torture; the hands of the clock seldom move fast enough for them. The notion of extending the school day and school year for them—or continuing on to college and four more years of reading texts and sitting in classrooms—is not a reform to be implemented but a punishment to be endured. Such students look for creative shortcuts to skip classes, exit the school as early as they can, and find jobs or enter the military once they graduate.

Most students, however, march from class to class until they hear "Pomp and Circumstance." But a high school diploma, graduates have come to realize, is not enough in the 21st-century labor market.

College for Everyone

In the name of equity and being responsive to employers' needs, most urban districts have converted particular comprehensive high schools into clusters of small college-prep academies where low-income minority students take Advanced Placement courses, write research papers, and compete to get into colleges and universities. Here, then, is the quiet, unheralded, and unforeseen victory of reformers bent on fixing time in school. They have succeeded unintentionally in stretching K-12 into preK-16 public schooling, not just for middle-and upper-middle class students, but for everyone.

As it has been for decades for most suburban middle-and upper-middle class white and minority families, now it has become a fact, an indisputable truth converted into a sacred mission for upwardly mobile poor families: A high school diploma and a bachelor's degree are passports to high-paying jobs and the American Dream.

For families who already expect their sons and daughters to attend competitive colleges, stress begins early. Getting into the best preschools and elementary and secondary schools and investing in an array of activities to build attractive résumés for college admission officers to evaluate become primary tasks. For such families and children, there is never enough time for homework, Advanced Placement courses, music, soccer, drama, dance, and assorted after-school activities. For high-achieving, stressed-out students already expecting at least four more years of school after high school graduation, reform proposals urging a longer school year and an extended day often strike an unpleasant note. Angst and fretfulness become familiar clothes to don every morning as students

grind out 4s and 5s on Advanced Placement exams, play sports, and compile just the right record that will get them into just the right school.

For decades, pressure on students to use every minute of school to prepare for college has been strongest in middle- and upper-middle-class suburbs. What has changed in the past few decades is the spread of the belief that every-one, including low-income minority students, should go to college.

To summarize, for decades, policy elites have disregarded teacher and student perspectives on time in school. Especially now when all students are expected to enter college, children, youths, and teachers experience time in school differently than policy makers who seek a longer school day and school year. Such varied perceptions about time are heavily influenced by the socialization goals of schooling, age-graded structures, socioeconomic status of families, and historical experience. And policy makers often ignore these perceptions and reveal their tone-deafness and myopia in persistently trying to fix time in schools.

Policy elites need to parse fully this variation in perceptions because extended time in school remains a high priority to reform-driven policy makers and civic and business leaders anxious about U.S. performance on international tests and fearful of falling behind in global economic competitiveness. The crude policy solutions of more days in the year and longer school days do not even begin to touch the deeper truth that what has to improve is the quality of "academic learning time." If policy makers could open their ears and eyes to student and teacher perceptions of time, they would learn that the secular Holy Grail is decreasing interruption of instruction, encouraging richer intellectual and personal connections between teachers and students, and increasing classroom time for ambitious teaching and active, engaged learning. So far, no such luck.

Conclusion

These three reasons—cost, lackluster research, and the importance of conservative social goals to U.S. taxpayers and voters—explain why proposals to fix time in U.S. schools have failed to take hold.

Policy elites know research studies proving the worth of year-round schools or lengthened school days are in short supply. Even if an occasional study supported the change, the school year is unlikely to go much beyond 180 days. Policy elites know school goals go far beyond simply preparing graduates for college and for employability in a knowledge-based economy. And policy elites know they must show courage in their pursuit of improving failing U.S. schools by forcing students to go to school just as long as their peers in India, China, Japan, and Korea. That courage shows up symbolically, playing well in the media and in proposals to fix time in schools, but it seldom alters calendars.

While cost is a factor, it is the stability of schooling structures and the importance of socializing the young into the values of the immediate community and larger society that have defeated policy-driven efforts to alter time in school over the past quarter century. Like the larger public, I am unconvinced that requiring students and teachers to spend more time in school each day and every year will be better for them. How that time is spent in learning before, during, and after school is far more important than decision makers counting the minutes, hours, and days students spend each year getting schooled. That being said, I have little doubt that state and federal blue-ribbon commissions will continue to make proposals about lengthening time in school. Those proposals will make headlines, but they will not result in serious, sustained attention to what really matters—improving the quality of the time that teachers and students spend with one another in and out of classrooms.

LARRY CUBAN is professor emeritus of education, Stanford University. He is the author of *As Good As It Gets: What School Reform Brought to Austin* (2010), *Hugging the Middle: How Teachers Teach in an Era of Testing and Accountability* (2008), and *The Blackboard and the Bottom Line: Why Schools Can't Be Businesses* (2007).

EXPLORING THE ISSUE

Do American Students Need More Time in School?

Critical Thinking and Reflection

1. What changes can occur when schools like Charles Edwards Middle School (Gabrieli) redesign their education approach based on student time in school?
2. How can adding additional hours to the school day improve academic gains?
3. Can the 10 key factors to success (Gabrieli) improve overall achievement for disadvantaged students?
4. Is there enough quantitative and qualitative research to support American students needing more time in the school?
5. Will extending the school day for students help prepare our youth to work in a globally competitive society?

Is There Common Ground?

One central aspect of the debate over time expansion in schools is this: to significantly improve student achievement the ways in which time is utilized must change. This is the main point of Douglas Fisher's article "The Use of Instructional Time in the Typical High School Classroom," *The Educational Forum* (Spring 2009). Although Fisher's focus is on secondary schools, his observations are relevant for elementary and middle schools as well. Too much "schooling" involves listening and waiting and too little time is spent closing the gap between what students know and what they need to know, Fisher contends. Similarly, Erika A. Patall, Harris Cooper, and Ashley Batts Allen, in "Extending the School Day or School Year: A Systematic Review of Research," *Review of Educational Research* (September 2010), conclude that extending school time can be an effective way to support student learning, particularly (a) for students most at risk of failure and (b) when considerations are made for how time is used. One important qualitative point is made in a Center for American Progress blog titled "Expanded Learning Time by the Numbers" (April 22, 2010) that explores the extent to which community-based organizations such as arts and cultural institutions take on more collaborative roles within extended-time schools.

Another crucial topic for consideration is the contribution of "summer loss" to the performance gaps among various identifiable groups. In "The Case Against Summer Vacation," *Time* (July 22, 2010), David Von Drehle contends that "larking through is a luxury we can't afford." Especially for children of low-income families "summer is a season of boredom, inactivity, and isolation" and this takes a steep toll on them. "It is among the most pernicious—if least acknowledged—causes of the achievement gap," he claims. By the end of elementary school low-income students have fallen nearly three grade levels behind, and summer is the biggest culprit. The topic is further explored by Donna Celano and Susan B. Neuman in "When Schools Close, the Knowledge Gap Grows," *Phi Delta Kappan* (December 2008).

Other aspects of the time allocation and use problem are treated in these sources: Karin Chenoweth, *How It's Being Done: Urgent Lessons from Unexpected Schools* (2009); *Choosing More Time for Students: The What, Why, and How of Expanded Learning* (2007), a Center for American Progress report by Elena Roche; Marilyn Crawford, "Think Inside the Clock," *Phi Delta Kappan* (December 2008); and Michael B. Horn, who, in "Innovative Approaches to School Time," a presentation to a U.S. Senate committee hearing on August 24, 2010, proposes a cost-effective solution: online learning.

Create Central

www.mhhe.com/createcentral

Additional Resources

Hannah Boyd, What's to Gain with a Longer School Day? (2013). Retrieved from: www.education.com/magazine/article/Kids_Need_More_Time_Learn/

Rans Forohar, Foroohar: To Compete, America Needs 6-Year High Schools (2013). Retrieved from: http://business.time.com/2013/10/25/foroohar-to-compete-america-needs-6-year-high-schools/

Neil Howe & William Strauss, *Millennials Rising: The Next Great Generation* (2006).

Karl Weber, *Waiting for "SUPERMAN": How We Can Save America's Failing Public Schools* (2010).

Internet References. . .

Extended Learning Time: Is More Always
Better?

www.masb.org/LinkClick.aspx?fileticket=EwHQEIsXJ
yQ%3D&tabid=244

National Center on Time & Learning

www.timeandlearning.org/

Center on Education Policy Graduate
School of Education and Human
Development George Washington
University

http://www.gwu.edu/~edpol/

Increased Learning Time Under Stimulus-
Funded School Improvement Grants: High
Hopes, Varied Implementation

http://www.google.com/url?sa=t&rct=j&q=&esrc=
s&frm=1&source=web&cd=1&ved=0CCgQFjAA&url=
http%3A%2F%2Fwww.cep-dc.org%2Fcfcontent_
file.cfm%3FAttachment%3DMcMurrer_Report2_
IncreasedLearningTime_071112.pdf&ei=
i0XZUujjH4S_sQTmn4GYDg&usg=
AFQjCNHdhj9luvgpctlUTZ2F8Vo192yVLQ

Longer School Year: Will It Help or Hurt
U.S. Students?

www.huffingtonpost.com/2013/01/13/longer-school-
year-will-i_n_2468329.html

Edwards Middle School

www.bostonpublicschools.org/school/edwards-
middle-school

Selected, Edited, and with Issue Framing Material by:
Glenn L. Koonce, *Regent University*

ISSUE

Is the Road to Virtual Schooling Smoothly Paved?

YES: William Crossman, from "From the Three *R*s to the Four *C*s," *The Futurist* (March–April 2012)

NO: Erin Dillon and Bill Tucker, from "Lessons for Online Learning," *Education Next* (Spring 2011)

Learning Outcomes

After reading this issue, you will be able to:

- Evaluate the Three Rs and the Four Cs.
- Examine virtual public education and identify a variety of providers.
- Critique the research on K-12 virtual education.
- Identify the barriers that constrain virtual education.
- Distinguish between "place-based charter schools and virtual learning that allows choice to be "unbound by geographic constraints."

ISSUE SUMMARY

YES: Futurist Philosopher William Crossman depicts the inevitable movement from brick-and-mortar schools to a flexible learning environment dominated by digital multi-sensory media.

NO: Erin Dillon and Bill Tucker of Education Sector wave caution flags because of the current lack of data on the efficacy of K-12 online learning and the need for independent quality control.

These days "toddlers start consuming digital information not long after they've started consuming food," so tells us Katherine Mangu-Ward in a July 20, 2010 Reason.com blog. She contends, in "Teachers Unions vs. Online Education," that during the past 30 years the per-student cost of K-12 education has more than doubled with no academic improvement to show for it. Meanwhile online education has begun to gain momentum in the state-sponsored Florida Virtual School and such virtual charter school companies as K12 Inc. "If online learning keeps growing, when [today's] 3-year-old with an iPhone graduates from high school in 2025, education will be virtually unrecognizable, and thank goodness for that," she concludes. The seminal book on online learning, *Disrupting Class: How Disruptive Innovation Will Change the Way the World Learns* (2008) by Clayton Christensen, Michael B. Horn, and Curtis W. Johnson, estimated that about half of all American high school courses will be handled over the Internet by 2019.

Not everyone has been as enthusiastic. Paul E. Peterson, in *Saving Schools: From Horace Mann to Virtual Learning* (2010), states that "virtual schooling today is certainly better than nothing, but it is hardly transformative."

However, he adds that we should not underestimate the pace at which things can change when technology takes hold. The National Education Association has taken a hard line on online charter schools, particularly those operated on a for-profit basis. The union expresses concern about the disregard of the important socialization aspect of public education and the lack of the promotion of a sense of community. Michael B. Horn, in "Game Changer," *Education Next* (Fall 2012), counters the NEA's concern by pointing out that education entrepreneurs are increasingly weaving social components into their online learning innovations. He sees this as an opportunity "to increase student engagement and enable students to learn from other students, teachers from other teachers, and students from teachers around the world." The goal, Horn claims, is for every online learner to have access to personalized, tutorial-like experiences on demand. A concrete example of this goal is being reached by the "Teach to One" system of mathematics instruction originated in New York and now expanding across the nation in various forms of "blended learning."

Two other organizations having an impact on the movement are Digital Learning Now! headed by former governors Jeb Bush and Bob Wise and the nonprofit Khan Academy that reaches millions of students through free online instruction and assessments. In addition to Florida, over a dozen states have expanded virtual school programs or have added online course requirements for graduation. According to Lee Fang, in "Selling Schools Out: The Scam of Virtual Education Reform," *The Nation* (December 5, 2011), "this legislative juggernaut has coincided with a gold rush of investors clamoring to get a piece of the K-12 education market." He claims that recession-induced cuts in state spending on public schools and increased attacks on teachers unions have set the stage for an unprecedented expansion of efforts toward privatization. Opposition has also come from teachers unions that have filed mostly unsuccessful lawsuits in Pennsylvania, Minnesota, and Wisconsin and from the Home School Legal Defense Association that sees the movement as a governmental attempt to create small public schools in people's homes. In "Potholes in the Road to Virtual Schooling," *The School Administrator* (April 2010), Gene V. Glass counsels that "the road to the future of education in America is likely to lead to a hybridization of face-to-face and online teaching and learning," but it should be traversed slowly and cautiously.

Such blendings of the old and the new are explored by Jonathan Schorr and Deborah McGriff in "Future Schools," *Education Next* (Summer 2011). Using examples such as Rocketship Education in San Jose charter schools, the Denver School of Science and Technology charter schools, Carpe Diem Collegiate High School in Yuma, and High Tech High in San Diego, the authors see blended schooling emerging at a time when more and more people are open to online learning and school districts are facing new fiscal realities. "In the past," they claim, "technology actually made schooling more expensive, as computers were layered onto an existing model without adding any efficiency." Further examples are presented by Liz Pape in "Blended Teaching & Learning," *The School Administrator* (April 2010).

In the following selections, futurist William Crossman offers his positive vision of a radically redesigned K-12 education and education policy experts Erin Dillon and Bill Tucker identify qualitative factors that must be considered.

YES ↵

William Crossman

From the Three *R*s to the Four *C*s

From the moment that Jessica Everyperson was born, her brain, central nervous system, and all of her senses shifted into high gear to access and to try to understand the incredible new informational environment that surrounded her. She had to make sense of new sights, sounds, tastes, smells, tactile experiences, and even new body positions.

Jessica approached her new world with all of her senses operating together at peak performance as she tried to make sense of it all. Her new reality was dynamic, constantly changing from millisecond to millisecond, and she immediately and instinctively began to interact with the new information that poured through her senses.

Jessica's cognitive ability to access new information interactively, and to use all of her senses at once to optimize her perception of that ever-changing information, is all about her hardwiring. Jessica, like all "everypersons" everywhere, was innately, biogenetically hardwired to access information in this way.

For Jessica's first four or five years, her all-sensory, interactive cognitive skills blossomed with amazing rapidity. Every moment provided her with new integrated-sensory learning experiences that helped to consolidate her "unity of consciousness," as the ancient Greek philosophers called it. Because each learning experience was all-sensory, Jessica's perception of reality was truly holistic. This meant that the ways she processed, interpreted, and understood her perceptions were also holistic. Jessica was therefore developing the ability to both perceive and understand the many sides of a situation—the cognitive skills that form the basis of critical thinking and lead to a broad and compassionate worldview.

During those preschool years, she also became proficient in using the variety of information technologies (ITs) that continued to be introduced into her environment: radio, TV, movies, computers, video games, cell phones, iPods, etc. Early on, she stopped watching TV, which engaged only her eyes and ears, and switched to video games, which engaged her eyes, ears, and touch/tactility. Before she could even read a word, Jessica had become a multimodal multitasker, talking on her cell phone while listening to her iPod and playing a video game.

At this point in her young life, Jessica was feeling very good about her ability to swim in the vast sea of information using the assortment of emerging ITs. Not surprisingly, she was also feeling very good about herself.

Then, Jessica started school!

The Brightness Dims: Hello K-12, Hello Three *R*s (Reading, 'Riting, 'Rithmetic)

On Jessica's first day in kindergarten, her teacher was really nice, but the message that the school system communicated to Jessica and her schoolmates was harsh. Although none of the teachers or administrators ever stated it in such blatant terms, the message, as expressed via Jessica's school's mandated course curriculum and defined student learning outcomes (SLOs), was this: Reading/writing is the only acceptable way to access information. This is the way we do it in "modern" society. Text literacy is the foundation of all coherent and logical thinking, of all real learning and knowledge, and even of morality and personal responsibility. It is, in fact, the cornerstone of civilization itself.

And the message continued: Since you don't know how to read or write yet, Jessica, you really don't know anything of value, you have no useful cognitive skills, and you have no real ways to process the experiences and/or the data that enter your brain through your senses. So, Jessica, from now on, through all of your years of schooling—through your entire K-12 education—you and we, your teachers, must focus all of our attention on your acquiring those reading and writing skills.

The U.S. Department of Education holds every school system in the United States accountable for instilling reading skills, as well as math skills, in every one of its students, and it requires students to take a battery of standardized tests every year to see if both their reading scores and math scores are going up.

If the test scores trend upward, the schools are rewarded. If they stay level or decline, the schools are punished with funding cuts and threatened with forced closure. Schools literally pin their long-term survival on just two variables: First, do the tests show that students can read and write, and second, do the tests show that students can do math?

From that moment on, Jessica's learning experience took a radical downward turn. Instead of accessing a dynamic, ever-changing reality, she was going to have to focus almost entirely on a static reality that just sat there on the page or computer screen: text. Instead of accessing information using all of her integrated senses simultaneously, she was going to have to use only her eyes. And instead of experiencing information interactively—as a two-way street that she could change by using her interactive technologies—she was going to have to experience information as a one-way street: by absorbing the text in front of her without being able to change it.

Welcome, Jessica, to the three *R*s, the essence of K-12 education. Of course, Jessica and her schoolmates, particularly in middle and high school, will take other courses: history, chemistry, political science, and so on. However, these other courses count for almost nothing when students go on to college, where they have to take these subjects all over again (history 101, chemistry 101, political science 101), or when they enter the vocational, business, and professional world, where they have to receive specialized training for their new jobs. College admissions directors and workplace employers really expect only one narrow set of SLOs from students who graduate with a high school diploma: that the students should have acquired a basic level of text literacy.

Jessica, like almost all of her kindergarten schoolmates, struggled to adjust to this major cognitive shift. Actually, for the first year or so, Jessica was excited and motivated to learn to read and write by the special allure of written language itself. The alphabet, and putting the letters together to make words, was like a secret code that grown-ups used to store and retrieve information. The prospect of learning to read and write made Jessica feel that she was taking a step into the grown-up world.

However, this initial novelty and excitement of decoding text soon wore off, and most of the children in Jessica's first, second, and third-grade classes, including Jessica herself, had a hard time keeping up. By the fourth grade, numbers of students were falling further and further behind the stated text-literacy SLOs for their grade level. Their self-confidence was getting severely damaged, and they were feeling more and more alienated from school and education itself. Not surprisingly, Jessica was no longer feeling very good about herself.

Young People's Rebellion Against the Three *R*s and Text Literacy

What's going on here with Jessica and young people in general? Our children are actually very intelligent. From the earliest age, their brains are like sponges soaking up and interpreting experiences and information that floods their senses. Almost all young children love to learn about everything, including about the learning process itself. They're continually asking "why?" in an effort to understand the world around them. It's a survival mechanism that we humans have evolved over millennia, much like

the newborn deer kids that can stand and run minutes after they're born.

Young people's failure to excel, or to even reach proficiency, in reading and writing in K-12 is reflected in the school literacy rates that continue to fall or, at best, remain stagnant decade after decade. Look no further than the National Assessment of Educational Progress, an annual test that most experts consider a fairly accurate gauge of reading scores throughout the United States. The scores for 12th-graders declined from 292 in 1992 to 188 in 2009, while the scores of students in other grades only negligibly improved during that same time period—this despite gargantuan amounts of time, resources, and hundreds of billions of dollars that school systems burned through in an attempt to bring them up.

Yet another reflection of young people's dissatisfaction with reading is the tragic rising dropout rates of middle-school and high-school students, particularly African American and Latino students. The question that parents and educators need to ask themselves is: Do children become less intelligent as they pass through the K-12 years?

The answer is No! Studies consistently show that, although young people's text-literacy rates are falling, their IQs (intelligence quotients) are rising at an average of three points every 10 years. Researchers have been noting this trend for decades and call it the "Flynn Effect," after James Flynn, a New Zealand political science professor who first documented it.

What's going on here is that young people today are rebelling against reading, writing, and written language itself. They are actively rejecting text as their IT of choice for accessing information. They feel that it's no longer necessary to become text literate—that it is no longer relevant to or for their lives.

Instead, young people are choosing to access information using the full range of emerging ITs available to them, the ITs that utilize the fullness of their all-sensory, interactive cognitive powers. Because their K-12 education is all about learning to gather information via text, young people are rejecting the three *R*s–based educational system, as well. Why, Jessica is asking, do I need to spend years learning to read Shakespeare's *Hamlet* when I can download it and listen to it, or listen to it via audio book CD, or watch a movie or DVD of it, or interact with it via an educational video game of the play?

We may be tempted to point out to Jessica and her fellow text rejecters that, when they're text messaging, they are in fact writing and reading. But it's not really the writing and reading of any actual written language—and Jessica knows it. Texting uses a system of symbols that more closely resembles a pictographic or hieroglyphic written language than an alphabetic one. "♥2u" may be understandable as three symbols combined into a pictogram, but it's not written English.

In my opinion, "♥2u" exemplifies not a flourishing commitment to text literacy among young people, but rather the rejection of actual text literacy and a further step in the devolution of text/written language as a useful IT in electronically developed societies.

Replacing Text in Schools—and Everywhere Else

What is text/written language, anyway? It's an ancient technology for storing and retrieving information. We store information by writing it, and we retrieve it by reading it. Between 6,000 and 10,000 years ago, many of our ancestors' hunter-gatherer societies settled on the land and began what's known as the "agricultural revolution." That new land settlement led to private property and increased production and trade of goods, which generated a huge new influx of information. Unable to keep all this information in their memories, our ancestors created systems of written records that evolved over millennia into today's written languages.

But this ancient IT is already becoming obsolete. Text has run its historic course and is now rapidly getting replaced in every area of our lives by the ever-increasing array of emerging ITs driven by voice, video, and body movement/gesture/touch rather than the written word. In my view, this is a positive step forward in the evolution of human technology, and it carries great potential for a total positive redesign of K-12 education. Four "engines" are driving this shift away from text:

> First, evolutionarily and genetically, we humans are innately hardwired to access information and communicate by speaking, listening, and using all of our other senses. At age one, Jessica just started speaking, while other one-year-olds who were unable to speak and/or hear just began signing. It came naturally to them, unlike reading and writing, which no one just starts doing naturally and which require schooling.
>
> Second, technologically, we humans are driven to develop technologies that allow us to access information and communicate using all of our cognitive hardwiring and all of our senses. Also, we tend to replace older technologies with newer technologies that do the same job more quickly, efficiently, and universally. Taken together, this "engine" helps to explain why, since the late 1800s, we have been on an urgent mission to develop nontext-driven ITs—from Thomas Edison's wax-cylinder phonograph to Nintendo's Wii—whose purpose is to replace text-driven ITs.
>
> Third, as noted above, young people in the electronically developed countries are, by the millions, rejecting old text-driven ITs in favor of all-sensory, nontext ITs. This helps to explain why Jessica and her friends can't wait until school is over so they can close their school books, hurry home, fire up their video-game consoles, talk on their cell phones, and text each other using their creative symbols and abbreviations.

Fourth, based on my study and research, I've concluded that the great majority of the world's people, from the youth to the elderly and everyone in between, are either nonliterate—unable to read or write at all—or functionally nonliterate. By "functionally nonliterate," I mean that a person can perhaps recognize the letters of their alphabet, can perhaps write and read their name and a few other words, but cannot really use the written word to store, retrieve, and communicate information in their daily lives.

Since the world's storehouse of information is almost entirely in the form of written language, these billions of people have been left out of the information loop and the so-called "computer revolution." If we gave a laptop computer to everyone in the world and said, "Here, fly into the world of information, access the Internet and the Worldwide Web," they would reply, "I'm sorry, but I can't use this thing because I can't read text off the screen and I can't write words on the keyboard."

Because access to the information of our society and our world is necessary for survival, it is therefore a human right. So the billions of people who are being denied access to information because they can't read or write are being denied their human rights. They are now demanding to be included in the "global conversation" without having to learn to read and write.

Three great potential opportunities for K-12 education in the coming decades arise out of this shift away from text.

- Using nontext-driven ITs will finally enable the billions of nonliterate and functionally nonliterate people around the world to claim and exercise their right to enter, access, add to, and learn from the world's storehouse of information via the Internet and World Wide Web.
- Voice-recognition technology's instantaneous language-translation function will allow everyone to speak to everyone else using their own native languages, and so language barriers will melt away. Consider the rate of improvement in voice-recognition technology over the last decade. As David Pogue points out in a 2010 *Scientific American* article, "In the beginning, you had to train these programs by reading a 45-minute script into your microphone so that the program could learn your voice. As the technology improved over the years, that training session fell to 20 minutes, to 10, to five—and now you don't have to train the software at all. You just start dictating, and you get (by my testing) 99.9 percent accuracy. That's still one word wrong every couple of pages, but it's impressive."
- People whose disabilities prevent them from reading, writing, and/or signing will be able to select specific functions of their all-sensory ITs that enable them to access all information.

The Brightness Returns: Goodbye, Three *R*s; Hello, Four *C*s

Every minute that Jessica and her friends spend getting information and communicating using video games, iPods, cell phones, and other nontext ITs, they're developing new cognitive skills. Their new listening, speaking, visual, tactile, memory, interactive, multitasking, multimodal skills allow them to access information and communicate faster and more efficiently than ever before. I believe that Jessica and her friends are developing the very skills that will be required for successful K-12 learning as we move into the coming age of postliterate K-12 education.

Something good is also happening to Jessica's brain and consciousness as she uses her all-sensory, interactive ITs. Jessica is retraining her brain, central nervous system, and senses. She is reconfiguring her consciousness so that it more closely resembles its original, unified, integrated, pre–three *R*s state. Jessica's worldview is broadening because she's perceiving and understanding the world more holistically. And she's feeling good about herself again.

Jessica's story—and there are millions of Jessicas struggling to succeed in our three *R*s–based classrooms today—points the way to a new strategy for K-12 education in the twenty-first century. Basing K-12 education on the three *R*s is a strategy for failure. We have the emerging ITs on which we can build a new K-12 strategy, one that has the potential to eliminate young people's academic nonsuccess and sense of failure and replace it with academic success and self-confidence.

Instead of the three *R*s, we need to move on to the four *C*s: critical thinking, creative thinking, compspeak (the skills needed to access information using all-sensory talking computers), and calculators (for basic applied math).

As text/written language falls more and more out of use as society's IT of choice for accessing information, so will the text-based three *R*s. It's a trend that's already starting to happen. Videos as teaching–learning tools are surpassing textbooks in innumerable K-12 classrooms. Instructional interactive videos (we won't be calling them video "games" anymore) are already entering our classrooms as the next big IIT—instructional information technology—because students want to be interactive with information.

As the three *R*s exit the K-12 scene, they'll leave a huge gap to be filled. What better way to fill that gap than by helping young people to become better critical and creative thinkers—the most crucial cognitive skills they'll need to help them build a more sustainable, peaceful, equitable, and just world? In order to store and retrieve the information they'll need to develop and practice these thinking skills, they'll also need to systematically acquire the all-sensory, interactive skills to access that information: the compspeak skills.

These compspeak skills are the very same skills that Jessica and her classmates have been developing unsystematically by using their all-sensory ITs, but systematic training in listening, speaking, visuality, memory, and the other compspeak skills should be a central component of their post–three *R*s education. It's ironic, and definitely shortsighted, that, in a difficult economic and budget-cutting climate, classes that support these compspeak skills are the first to be cut: music (listening, visual, body movement, memory), art (visual, body movement), physical education and dance (body movement, memory), speech (speaking, listening, memory), and theater arts (all of the above).

Over the next decades, we will continue to replace text-driven ITs with all-sensory-driven ITs and, by 2050, we will have recreated an oral culture in our electronically developed countries and K-12 classrooms. Our great-great-grandchildren won't know how to read or write—and it won't matter. They'll be as competent accessing information using their nontext ITs as we highly text-literates are today using the written word.

WILLIAM CROSSMAN is a philosopher, futurist, and professor involved with issues of education, media and technology, language and culture, and human rights.

Erin Dillon and Bill Tucker

➜ **NO**

Lessons for Online Learning

Advocates for virtual education say that it has the power to transform an archaic K–12 system of schooling. Instead of blackboards, schoolhouses, and a six-hour school day, interactive technology will personalize learning to meet each student's needs, ensure all students have access to quality teaching, extend learning opportunities to all hours of the day and all days of the week, and innovate and improve over time. Indeed, virtual education has the potential not only to help solve many of the most pressing issues in K–12 education, but to do so in a cost-effective manner. More than 1 million public-education students now take online courses, and as more districts and states initiate and expand online offerings, the numbers continue to grow. But to date, there's little research or publicly available data on the outcomes from K–12 online learning. And even when data are publicly available, as is the case with virtual charter schools, analysts and education officials have paid scant attention to—and have few tools for analyzing—performance. Until policymakers, educators, and advocates pay as much attention to quality as they do to expansion, virtual education will not be ready for a lead role in education reform.

Virtual education is in a period of rapid growth, as school districts, for-profit providers, and nonprofit start-ups all move into the online learning world. But without rigorous oversight, a thousand flowers blooming will also yield a lot of weeds. Real accountability, including the means to identify and end ineffective practices and programs, must be constantly balanced with the time required to refine new, immature technologies and approaches to learning. Both virtual education advocates and education policymakers should learn from nearly two decades of experience with charter schooling, another reform movement predicated on innovation and change within public education. After nearly 20 years of practice, the charter school movement provides important lessons on how to ensure that improved student outcomes remain the top priority.

Focus on Outcomes

At present, virtual education lacks a firm understanding of what high performance looks like. The situation is not unlike that faced by the charter school movement just a few years ago. In 2005, after a decade of rapid growth

in the charter school sector, the National Alliance for Public Charter Schools (NAPCS) was formed to increase the availability of high-quality charter schools. NAPCS soon published "Renewing the Compact," a statement by its Task Force on Charter School Quality and Accountability. "Renewing the Compact" came on the heels of an August 17, 2004, lead story in the *New York Times,* which highlighted findings from a simplistic, and controversial, study of charter school achievement sponsored by the American Federation of Teachers, "Charter School Achievement on the 2003 National Assessment of Educational Progress (NAEP)." According to the *Times,* in "virtually every instance, the charter students did worse than their counterparts in regular public schools." The NAPCS task force did not mince words about the need for a sharper focus on quality within the charter school movement. The report challenged the charter community to "fully 'own' the issue of how well its schools perform" and also challenged charter advocates "to embrace rigorous measures of quality and accountability for our own schools' success."

But the wide range of education options within charter schooling makes "owning" quality difficult, and the variety is even greater for virtual education. Virtual public education can be delivered by all types of providers, including charter schools, for-profit companies, universities, state entities, and school districts. Types of online schools and programs range from state-run programs like Florida Virtual School, where each year 100,000 students take one or two courses online as a supplement to traditional schools, to "blended" models, which allow schools to combine online and classroom-based instruction. The most controversial virtual schools are so-called "cyber" charter schools—fully online public schools that students "attend" on a full-time basis. Funded with public dollars but independently run, many of these cyber schools are managed by private, for-profit companies such as K12 and Connections Academy. John Watson, author of the annual "Keeping Pace" report on the status of K–12 virtual learning, notes that virtual education is "several times more complex than charter schooling."

Such diversity brings challenges. While the International Association for K–12 Online Learning (iNACOL) has published program quality standards, virtual education lacks a commonly accepted set of quality outcome measures. Quality can't be defined by the design of a school or by inputs alone; instead, it must focus primarily on outcomes. Traditional measures, such as attendance and instructional contact hours, do not fit the virtual model. And while federal and state accountability systems, which focus on school-level accountability, provide data on and oversight of the performance of full-time cyber schools, there's little data and few mechanisms for evaluating supplemental and blended programs, in which students take only a portion of their schooling online. Moreover, it's the supplemental and blended courses, increasingly offered by school districts, where growth is likely to be fastest.

Still, complexity can't be an excuse for inaction. Unless providers rise to this task, outside groups, whether supporters or opponents, will define success and the lack of it for them. Once again, the charter experience is worth noting. Less than two years after publishing "Renewing the Compact," the NAPCS, in partnership with the National Association of Charter School Authorizers, which was established in 2004 to push for more professionalism and higher standards among authorizers across the country, convened a working panel on charter school quality with the goal of establishing a "common set of basic quality expectations and performance measures" to assess charter school success. Without these measures, the panel noted, "it is no wonder that judgments about the performance of charter schools are so frequently ill-informed." The result of the working panel was "A Framework for Academic Quality," which provides a list of indicators, such as student achievement levels and growth measures, to which schools should be held accountable, metrics that can be used to assess school performance.

Take Charge of the Data

Even with outcome measures established, it's unwise to assume that providers, be they districts, charter schools, or private companies, will collect data and conduct research on their own. States and districts, through their rapidly evolving data systems, must gather information about virtual course enrollments, demographics, and performance, and encourage further research into determining successful programs and practices.

Paul Hill, director of the Center on Reinventing Public Education at the University of Washington and leader of the National Charter School Research Project, notes that the 2004 *Times* article caught charter school supporters "flat-footed." Before the article, Hill says, "the movement was not thinking about what a bad study would look like." The *Times* story spurred investments in high-quality research on charter school performance—research that goes beyond snapshot comparisons of average charter-school and average traditional public-school performance to examine variation in performance among charter schools, incorporate measures of growth in student outcomes, and employ appropriate controls for student background.

In comparison, research on K–12 virtual education has been limited. A 2010 meta-analysis of virtual education conducted by the U.S. Department of Education, drawn mostly from studies focused on higher education, concluded that "students in online learning conditions performed modestly better than those receiving face-to-face instruction." But the report also found an "unexpected . . . small number of rigorous studies." Studies that only compare virtual learning with traditional instruction, though, like those that compare charter schools with traditional public schools, mask many of the most interesting questions about virtual education. To be useful, research needs to be specific as to "what works for whom, what implementation practices matter, and why," says Marianne Bakia, senior education researcher at SRI International and one of the authors of the Department of Education study.

"Keeping Pace" author Watson agrees. He fears that with districts everywhere experimenting with multiple forms of virtual learning, from online credit recovery to blended learning classes, three years from now we'll still have little to no information as to what actually works in a systemic way. And even if we know that a program is successful, we may not know why.

Watson cautions, however, that reliance on a few time-consuming megastudies would be a mistake. Not only are there a limited number of questions that can be answered in this manner, but perhaps more importantly, the field is moving so quickly that the practices studied may already be outdated before the results are known. Instead, he notes, it's much more important to develop systems to track quality and collect existing information, such as course participation, grades, and assessment results, in a manner that can help monitor student outcomes and practices at the course level. And better data on the impact of curriculum, instructional materials, and teaching practices would benefit all of education, not just virtual learning. But current data, Bakia says, are extremely scarce: "in most places you can't even tell if a course is online."

Paul Hill adds that ongoing data collection and research is especially important for at-risk students and in areas like credit recovery, dropout prevention, and juvenile justice: "Almost every party involved with a poor kid who is about to drop out of school doesn't want to turn that rock over." Without outside pressure, programs for these students could be the most vulnerable to quality concerns.

Secure Independent Oversight

Once providers develop quality measures and relevant data exist, one or more independent entities must be charged with deciding which providers can enter the marketplace and holding them accountable for student outcomes. An independent entity, whether it's an authorizer, district, or state, needs to ensure that competition rewards high quality, not just low cost or easy access.

Markets can offer new choices to parents and students. And unlike place-based charter schools, virtual learning allows these choices to be unbound by geographic constraints. A student in rural Alabama can now look online for better instructional models, make up credits for missed or failed classes, or even access Mandarin Chinese courses.

But policymakers cannot rely solely on parent and student choice to ensure quality. Sixteen-year-olds do not always make the best decisions, and parents have many different motives for choosing a virtual provider. Some may want an accelerated curriculum for a gifted student, others may be looking for more scheduling flexibility, and still others may just be interested in getting course credit quickly, regardless of quality or rigor.

The parallel to the charter experience is striking. "Parent accountability as the only driver of accountability hasn't always worked out for charter schools, "notes Todd Ziebarth of the NAPCS, "Parents sometimes keep sending their kids to schools that aren't academically successful."

The first system of grading charter laws rewarded states for easy access to charters but put little emphasis on quality control over new and existing schools. Since then, things have changed dramatically. A report released in 2010 by the NAPCS graded states not just on the opportunities for charter schooling to expand in the state, but also on the quality of charter school authorizing supported by the state law.

But current charter-school authorizing methods, which focus on an entire school, are not adequate for supplemental or blended virtual-learning providers. Nor is accreditation (until the NCAA halted the practice, fully accredited BYU Independent Study was known to college sports fans as the place where football player Michael Oher, profiled in the movie *The Blind Side,* and others went to quickly raise grades to become eligible for college athletics). And even in the case of virtual charter schools, authorizers are just now beginning to understand the unique qualities of virtual schools that change the nature of oversight, including these schools' capacity to serve tens of thousands of students across wide geographic areas.

Virtual education has the potential to operate in a more nimble and responsive market than charter schools. Without the large up-front costs associated with brick-and-mortar schools and the long lag time for determining school success, the virtual education market may not need as many limits on new entrants. But for the market to yield innovation and high performance, providers need to be rewarded for successful student outcomes, not just enrollments, and an independent agency, whether it's a charter-like authorizer, the school district, or the state, needs to be responsible for quickly shutting down low performers.

Negotiate a Fair Deal

State policies, such as whether the choice to attend a virtual class (and receive access to the funding for that class) resides with the student or the district, can have a tremendous impact on access to virtual learning. It is essential that state laws be clearly thought through from the beginning, something that never happened in the pell-mell rush to enact charter school legislation. In order to get started in many states, charter supporters had to make compromises. These bad bargains underfunded schools, limited their ability to be autonomous and innovative, and allowed districts to create "charters-in-name-only." The same pattern is emerging in virtual education, where legislation that purports to spur virtual education, such as that in Massachusetts, creates unnecessary geographic restrictions or enrollment caps, or sets funding levels well below what traditional schools receive.

The large differences in growth among state-run supplemental virtual school programs illustrate the importance of policies related to funding and access. The states with the most enrollments, Florida and North Carolina, both have funding tied to the state's public-education funding formula.

Most state-run virtual schools are not included in state funding formulas and are instead funded by an annual legislative appropriation. While start-up appropriations make sense—especially when they help to ease fears of competition for funds with traditional schools—eventually, these static funding sources, which bear no relation to the demand or quality of the virtual school offerings, artificially limit access to and therefore demand for online courses. And since access and funding are scarce, there's little capacity or incentive to develop new offerings.

The largest of the state-run schools is Florida Virtual School (FLVS). Its funding model, in which funds follow the student, taken together with the state's strong choice policies (a student's full-time school may not deny access to courses offered by FLVS), enable the school to grow. There are no barriers to enrollment and funding is not capped at a preset amount, providing FLVS with an incentive to be responsive to demand, rapidly increase course offerings, and even experiment with new game-like learning experiences. In contrast, Kentucky's state virtual school, despite its more than 10 years in operation, struggles to grow. The school charges course fees, requires students to get district permission prior to enrollment, and is funded on a small annual appropriation rather than based on demand.

Another challenge to the development of fair and workable funding systems for virtual schooling is one that is endemic to public education in general: the inability to accurately measure cost-effectiveness. Since virtual schooling operates on a very different cost model—few facilities costs, higher technology costs, greater scale—states are struggling to determine the proper per-student funding level for both virtual courses and schools. Without a means to determine value—how additional dollars spent affect student outcomes—states default to either the standard per-pupil funding, or increasingly, decide that virtual schools should cost less and choose an arbitrary funding level. More spurious are the attempts to audit providers and pay only for the "true costs" of virtual education, eliminating any incentive for productivity gains. None of these funding methods are sensitive to the quality of student outcomes. They lead districts to favor the lowest-cost provider. And more importantly, they provide few incentives for providers to fund the research and development necessary to perfect new technologies, student support systems, and innovative methods to effectively serve more costly, at-risk student populations.

Former Florida governor Jeb Bush and former West Virginia governor Bob Wise are leading a new advocacy effort known as the Digital Learning Council. The council recently published a set of state policy recommendations as part of an initiative to spur further growth not only in virtual learning, but also in the use of digital and multimedia content.

The Digital Learning Council recommends that states eliminate restrictions on student access to virtual education, allow students to choose among multiple learning providers, call for removal of seat-time requirements, and judge schools on results rather than inputs such as class size. Taken together, the recommendations would enable all students to access virtual education and end many of the regulatory restraints that stifle the development of innovative options.

But while the recommendations accurately identify the barriers that constrain virtual education, they are light on details for ensuring that innovation actually leads to more high-quality educational options. They suggest, for example, that states evaluate "the quality of content and courses predominately based on student learning data," yet provide few details on how to accomplish this difficult task. Likewise, recommendations for "Quality Providers" focus heavily on the removal of barriers to competition, but offer little discussion of how to enact the recommendation for "a strong system of oversight and quality control." Too often, the recommendations assume that quality will naturally result from regulatory relief.

Overall, as guiding principles, the recommendations make sense. But, as the nation's charter schooling experience demonstrates, policymakers must confront the difficult issue of quality at the same time as they seek new and innovative approaches to schooling.

Same Old Thing, But Online?

Finally, there is nothing magical that ensures either charter schools or virtual education will be innovative and different. Each provides the opportunity for something new

and potentially powerful: charters through a new governance model, virtual learning through a new instructional model.

One big difference between charter schools and virtual education is that by definition, charter schools sit outside of the traditional district system. While many of the first wave of virtual education providers—charter schools, state virtual schools, consortia of schools—incorporated both a different instructional and a different governance model, increasingly, districts are creating and managing their own virtual learning programs. The integration of virtual education into traditional school districts allows for the instructional model change to be incorporated into a system without a change in the district governance model.

The danger is that despite the dramatically different delivery model, virtual education will end up much the same—with no better outcomes than our current system. In an effort to ease concerns about online education from districts, teachers, and parents, providers will be tempted to minimize disruptions to the traditional schoolhouse model, promising that "you won't need to change a thing." But simply putting the same curriculum online is unlikely to result in higher-quality learning. And this approach undercuts the potential of online education to do many of the things it promises: to provide a more personalized and responsive education than the traditional lecture format, to allow students to proceed at their own pace, and to give teachers a new way to teach.

Much like the achievements of an older sibling, the charter school movement's successes and mistakes have a lot to teach virtual schooling about bringing change to public education. Invest in good data and research, avoid bad bargains, and give students choices but don't rely on markets alone to monitor quality are all important lessons from nearly 20 years of charter schooling. If the virtual education movement heeds these lessons, it has the potential to see even more rapid growth across the country than charter schools and—more importantly—to enhance how students learn.

ERIN DILLON has been a research associate with the Beginning with Children Foundation in New York. At the foundation, she managed a research project examining the academic achievement of charter school students and assisted with a college preparatory program for high school students.

BILL TUCKER has helped to lead Bill & Melinda Gates Foundation's Education Sector since its inception in 2005. In his policy work for education sector, he focused on technology and innovation—specifically virtual schooling, assessments, and data systems.

EXPLORING THE ISSUE

Is the Road to Virtual Schooling Smoothly Paved?

Critical Thinking and Reflection

1. Are the Four Cs appealing or non-appealing to educators?
2. Why does Crossman believe that "text" is "already becoming obsolete"?
3. What is the strategy for rebuilding the Three Rs?
4. What are some quality measures of virtual schooling?
5. How are states becoming more involved with virtual education?

Is There Common Ground?

As Larry D. Rosen, in "Teaching the iGeneration," *Educational Leadership* (February 2011), states, "the point is not to 'teach with technology' but to use technology to convey content more powerfully and efficiently. . . . Technology is all about engagement." In agreement, Yong Zhao, in "Technology and the Virtual World Are the New Reality," *Principal* (January/February 2010), calls on educators to provide more opportunities for students to experience and reflect on the outcomes of technology use, to be creative in art and music, to develop social skills in virtual worlds, and to stay engaged with school. In an article aptly titled "Preparing Students to Learn Without Us" in *Educational Leadership* (February 2012), Will Richardson goes beyond a focus on engagement to helping students find their own passions, fostering personal learning and giving students more agency in the process of education, a "deeper degree of autonomy." This is a theme that has trailed through a number of articles presented in this book, starting with John Dewey.

There was a time when some educators said that the radio, and later television, and then video recordings would revolutionize the way students learn and schools operate. It didn't happen. So the question remains: Will the current bombardment of digitalized media bring about a radical alteration of the function of schools in our society? And if that occurs, what will be the dominant effect on the concept of "teacher" and "student"? Nicholas Carr, in his provocative book *The Shallows: What the Internet Is Doing to Our Brains* (2010), puts forth the idea that while the Internet gives us easy access to unprecedented amounts of information, its constant distractions and interruptions are turning us into scattered and superficial thinkers—it is

rewiring our brains. (A summary of his argument can be found in "The Juggler's Brain" in *Phi Delta Kappan* (December 2010/January 2011).)

In addition to this basic concern a number of other critics of so-called cyberschools have warned of lax accountability, oversight issues, and unlicensed teachers. Another concern, the quality and reliability of information found on the Net, is explored by Debbie Abilock in "True—or Not," *Educational Leadership* (March 2012).

Create Central

www.mhhe.com/createcentral

Additional Resources

Tom Vander Ark, *Getting Smart: How Digital Learning Is Changing the World* (2012).

Kevin P. Brady, Regina R. Umpstead, & Suzanne E. Eckes, "Uncharted Territory: The Current Legal Landscape of Public Cyber Charter Schools," *Brigham Young University Education & Law Journal* (no. 2, 2010)

DVD titled "Digital Media: New Learners of the 21st Century" (2010).

Kavita Rao, Michelle Eady, & Patricia Edelen-Smith, "Creating Virtual Classrooms for Rural and Remote Communities," *Phi Delta Kappan* (March 2011).

Bill Tucker, "The Flipped Classroom," *Education Next* (Winter 2012).

Internet References . . .

Q&A: Pros and Cons of Virtual School

www.middlewaymom.com/2013/06/qa-pros-and-cons-
of-virtual-school/

The Pros and Cons of Virtual Schools

www.angelfire.com/in4/virtualschools/pros_cons
.html

Online Learning: The Pros and Cons of
K-12 Computer Courses

www.huffingtonpost.com/2011/04/12/online-learning-
pros-and-cons_n_848362.html

Virtual Schools in the U.S. 2013: Politics,
Performance, Policy, and Research
Evidence

http://nepc.colorado.edu/publication/virtual-schools-
annual-2013

National High School: Online High School

www.nationalhighschool.com/landingPage
.asp?gclid=CLeGru_B07oCFcU5QgodW1cAeg

Selected, Edited, and with Issue Framing Material by:
Glenn L. Koonce, *Regent University*

ISSUE

Is the "21st Century Skills" Movement Viable?

YES: Andrew J. Rotherham and Daniel T. Willingham, from "21st Century Skills: The Challenges Ahead," *Educational Leadership* (September 2009)

NO: Diana Senechal, from "The Most Daring Education Reform of All," *American Educator* (Spring 2010)

Learning Outcomes

After reading this issue, you will be able to:

- Evaluate the 21st Century Skills model for school improvement.
- Assess the statement, "The frenzy over the 21st Century Skills movement will pass like so many before."
- Identify the struggle between "wins" and "losses" in the 21st Century Skills movement.
- Define the implications of the words "national" and "standards" in the context of 21st Century Skills.
- Examine the three elements that must work in concert for the 21st Century Skills effort to be effective.

ISSUE SUMMARY

YES: Education Policy Expert Rotherham and psychology professor Willingham see great promise in the movement to bring needed skills to all students if the delivery system works satisfactorily.

NO: Education Writer and Former Teacher Diana Senechal expresses deep concern about the movement's focus on current societal needs to the detriment of core academic studies.

Calls for adoption of national standards, national tests, and even a national curriculum are on the increase. As Walter Isaacson of the Aspen Institute states, in "How to Raise the Standard in America's Schools," *Time* (April 15, 2009), "Without national standards for what our students should learn, it will be hard for the U.S. to succeed in the 21st century economy." But the prospect of such a development is politically explosive. Isaacson characterizes it this way: "The right chokes on the word national, with its implication that the feds will trample on the states' traditional authority over public schools, and the left chokes on the word standards, with the intimations of assessments and testing that accompany it." The present-day reality is that two-thirds of American students attend school in states with mediocre standards or worse, according to research by the Thomas B. Fordham Institute.

A number of movements are afoot to define what is most needed in the realm of school improvement. The National Governors Association and the Council of Chief State School Officers, with financial support from private foundations and federal support from the "Race to the Top" fund, have begun to develop a Common Core State Standards Initiative (CCSSI) to cover tests, curriculum,

and teacher training. To date 40 states and the District of Columbia have joined the effort. The Thomas B. Fordham Institute recently produced a document compiled by Chester E. Finn, Jr. and Michael J. Petrilli titled "Now What? Imperatives & Options for 'Common Core' Implementation & Governance" (October 2010). The report calls for a Common Core Coordinating Council as a starting point, with the purpose of preserving independence from Washington. The Center for Public Education in Alexandria, Virginia, has issued a report, Defining a 21st Century Education (July 2009) by Craig D. Jerald that analyzes the major forces reshaping skill demands (automation, globalization, corporate changes, demographics, and personal risk and responsibility).

Perhaps most visible is the Partnership for 21st Century Skills in Tucson, Arizona, which has broad support from the business and technology communities and the Association for Career and Technical Education. In its Framework for 21st Century Learning, the Partnership has identified the skills essential for success in today's world, such as creativity, critical thinking, problem solving, communication, and collaboration. The Framework delineates core subjects and twenty-first-century themes (such as global awareness) and life and career skills (such as adaptability, self-direction, productivity, and cross-cultural understanding). Paige Johnson, in "The 21st Century Skills Movement," *Educational Leadership* (September 2009), states that "to successfully face rigorous higher-education courses and a globally competitive work environment, schools must align classroom environments and core subjects with 21st century skills." Or, as Richard H. Hersh, in "A Well-Rounded Education for a Flat World," *Educational Leadership* (September 2009) puts it, we need "a pervasive school culture that refuses to define education as the passive reception of knowledge and instead celebrates demanding, profoundly engaging, and authentic educational experiences." More specifically, Bernie Trilling, global director of the Oracle Education Foundation, in "Leading Learning in Our Time," *Principal* (January/February 2010), espouses "inquiry- and design-based projects rooted in driving questions and real-world problems" that would engage students in a deeper understanding and effective use of knowledge.

Those who have reservations about the 21st Century Skills model are concerned that it may just become another pedagogical fad, that it demands too much change too fast, that it is too oriented to economic forces, that the skills emphasis downplays subject matter content, and that the recommended skills are in need of more specific definition. Education columnist Jay Mathews, initially very doubtful about the model for some of the reasons cited above, was moved toward a level of acceptance by the Craig Jerald report (see above) and educator Tony Wagner's *The Global Achievement Gap* (2008). In his article "Class Struggle," *The Washington Post* (December 4, 2009), Mathews finds that Jerald is especially clear about what the skills movement really means for schools, namely the artful blending of factual knowledge and the types of thinking required to apply that knowledge in meaningful and useful ways.

In the first of the following selections, Andrew J. Rotherham and Daniel T. Willingham offer their version of the "21st Century Skills" approach to the improvement of American schooling. In the second selection, Diana Senechal details her specific objections and calls for maintenance of the true purposes of education.

YES ↵

Andrew J. Rotherham and Daniel T. Willingham

21st Century Skills: The Challenges Ahead

A growing number of business leaders, politicians, and educators are united around the idea that students need "21st century skills" to be successful today. It's exciting to believe that we live in times that are so revolutionary that they demand new and different abilities. But in fact, the skills students need in the 21st century are not new.

Critical thinking and problem solving, for example, have been components of human progress throughout history, from the development of early tools, to agricultural advancements, to the invention of vaccines, to land and sea exploration. Such skills as information literacy and global awareness are not new, at least not among the elites in different societies. The need for mastery of different kinds of knowledge, ranging from facts to complex analysis? Not new either. In *The Republic,* Plato wrote about four distinct levels of intellect. Perhaps at the time, these were considered "3rd century BCE skills"?

What's actually new is the extent to which changes in our economy and the world mean that collective and individual success depends on having such skills. Many U.S. students are taught these skills—those who are fortunate enough to attend highly effective schools or at least encounter great teachers—but it's a matter of chance rather than the deliberate design of our school system. Today we cannot afford a system in which receiving a high-quality education is akin to a game of bingo. If we are to have a more equitable and effective public education system, skills that have been the province of the few must become universal.

This distinction between "skills that are novel" and "skills that must be taught more intentionally and effectively" ought to lead policymakers to different education reforms than those they are now considering. If these skills were indeed new, then perhaps we would need a radical overhaul of how we think about content and curriculum. But if the issue is, instead, that schools must be more deliberate about teaching critical thinking, collaboration, and problem solving to all students, then the remedies are more obvious, although still intensely challenging.

What Will It Take?

The history of U.S. education reform should greatly concern everyone who wants schools to do a better job of teaching students to think. Many reform efforts, from reducing class size to improving reading instruction, have devolved into fads or been implemented with weak fidelity to their core intent. The 21st century skills movement faces the same risk.

To complicate the challenge, some of the rhetoric we have heard surrounding this movement suggests that with so much new knowledge being created, content no longer matters; that ways of knowing information are now much more important than information itself. Such notions contradict what we know about teaching and learning and raise concerns that the 21st century skills movement will end up being a weak intervention for the very students— low-income students and students of color—who most need powerful schools as a matter of social equity.

The debate is not about content versus skills. There is no responsible constituency arguing against ensuring that students learn how to think in school. Rather, the issue is how to meet the challenges of delivering content and skills in a rich way that genuinely improves outcomes for students.

What will it take to ensure that the idea of "21st century skills"—or more precisely, the effort to ensure that all students, rather than just a privileged few, have access to a rich education that intentionally helps them learn these skills—is successful in improving schools? That effort requires three primary components. First, educators and policymakers must ensure that the instructional program is complete and that content is not shortchanged for an ephemeral pursuit of skills. Second, states, school districts, and schools need to revamp how they think about human capital in education—in particular how teachers are trained. Finally, we need new assessments that can accurately measure richer learning and more complex tasks.

For the 21st century skills effort to be effective, these three elements must be implemented in concert. Otherwise, the reform will be superficial and counterproductive.

Better Curriculum

People on all sides of this debate often speak of skills and knowledge as separate. They describe skills as akin to a function on a calculator: If your calculator can compute square roots, it can do so for any number; similarly, if a student has developed the ability to "think scientifically," he or she can do so with any content. In this formulation, domain knowledge is mainly important as grist for the mill—you need something to think *about*.

Skills and knowledge are not separate, however, but intertwined. In some cases, knowledge helps us recognize the underlying structure of a problem. For example, even young children understand the logical implications of a rule like "If you finish your vegetables, you will get a cookie after dinner." They can draw the logical conclusion that a child who is denied a cookie after dinner must not have finished her vegetables. Without this familiar context, however, the same child will probably find it difficult to understand the logical form *modus tollens,* of which the cookie rule is an example. (*If P, then Q. Q is false. Therefore, P is false.*) Thus, it's inaccurate to conceive of logical thinking as a separate skill that can be applied across a variety of situations. Sometimes we fail to recognize that we have a particular thinking skill (such as applying *modus tollens*) unless it comes in the form of known content.

At other times, we know that we have a particular thinking skill, but domain knowledge is necessary if we are to use it. For example, a student might have learned that "thinking scientifically" requires understanding the importance of anomalous results in an experiment. If you're surprised by the results of an experiment, that suggests that your hypothesis was wrong and the data are telling you something interesting. But to be surprised, you must make a prediction in the first place—and you can only generate a prediction if you understand the domain in which you are working. Thus, without content knowledge we often cannot use thinking skills properly and effectively.

Why would misunderstanding the relationship of skills and knowledge lead to trouble? If you believe that skills and knowledge are separate, you are likely to draw two incorrect conclusions. First, because content is readily available in many locations but thinking skills reside in the learner's brain, it would seem clear that if we must choose between them, skills are essential, whereas content is merely desirable. Second, if skills are independent of content, we could reasonably conclude that we can develop these skills through the use of *any* content. For example, if students can learn how to think critically about science in the context of any scientific material, a teacher should select content that will engage students (for instance, the chemistry of candy), even if that content is not central to the field. But all content is not equally important to mathematics, or to science, or to literature. To think critically, students need the knowledge that is central to the domain.

The importance of content in the development of thinking creates several challenges for the 21st century skills movement. The first is the temptation to emphasize advanced, conceptual thinking too early in training—an approach that has proven ineffective in numerous past reforms, such as the "New Math" of the 1960s (Loveless, 2002). Learning tends to follow a predictable path. When students first encounter new ideas, their knowledge is shallow and their understanding is bound to specific examples. They need exposure to varied examples before their understanding of a concept becomes more abstract and they can successfully apply that understanding to novel situations.

Another curricular challenge is that we don't yet know how to teach self-direction, collaboration, creativity, and innovation the way we know how to teach long division. The plan of 21st century skills proponents seems to be to give students more experiences that will presumably develop these skills—for example, having them work in groups. But experience is not the same thing as practice. Experience means only that you use a skill; practice means that you try to improve by noticing what you are doing wrong and formulating strategies to do better. Practice also requires feedback, usually from someone more skilled than you are.

Because of these challenges, devising a 21st century skills curriculum requires more than paying lip service to content knowledge. Outlining the skills in detail and merely urging that content be taught, too, is a recipe for failure. We must plan to teach skills in the context of particular content knowledge and to treat both as equally important.

In addition, education leaders must be realistic about which skills are teachable. If we deem that such skills as collaboration and self-direction are essential, we should launch a concerted effort to study how they can be taught effectively rather than blithely assume that mandating their teaching will result in students learning them.

Better Teaching

Greater emphasis on skills also has important implications for teacher training. Our resolve to teach these skills to all students will not be enough. We must have a plan by which teachers can succeed where previous generations have failed.

Advocates of 21st century skills favor student-centered methods—for example, problem-based learning and project-based learning—that allow students to collaborate, work on authentic problems, and engage with the community. These approaches are widely acclaimed and can be found in any pedagogical methods textbook; teachers know about them and believe they're effective. And yet, teachers don't use them. Recent data show that most instructional time is composed of seatwork and whole-class instruction led by the teacher (National Institute of Child Health and Human Development Early Child Care Research Network, 2005). Even when class sizes are reduced, teachers do not change their teaching strategies or use these student-centered methods (Shapson, Wright, Eason, & Fitzgerald, 1980). Again, these are not new issues. John Goodlad (1984) reported the same finding in his landmark study published more than 20 years ago.

Why don't teachers use the methods that they believe are most effective? Even advocates of student-centered methods acknowledge that these methods pose classroom management problems for teachers. When students collaborate, one expects a certain amount of hubbub in the room, which could devolve into chaos in less-than-expert hands. These methods also demand that teachers be knowledgeable about a broad range of topics and are prepared to make in-the-moment decisions as the lesson plan progresses. Anyone who has watched a highly effective teacher lead a class by simultaneously engaging with content, classroom management, and the ongoing monitoring of student progress knows how intense and demanding this work is. It's a constant juggling act that involves keeping many balls in the air.

Part of the 21st century skills movement's plan is the call for greater collaboration among teachers. Indeed, this is one of the plan's greatest strengths; we waste a valuable resource when we don't give teachers time to share their expertise. But where will schools find the release time for such collaboration? Will they hire more teachers or increase class size? How will they provide the technology infrastructure that will enable teachers to collaborate with more than just the teacher down the hall? Who will build and maintain and edit the Web sites, wikis, and so forth? These challenges raise thorny questions about whether the design of today's schools is compatible with the goals of the 21st century skills movement.

For change to move beyond administrators' offices and penetrate classrooms, we must understand that professional development is a massive undertaking. Most teachers don't need to be persuaded that project-based learning is a good idea—they already believe that. What teachers need is much more robust training and support than they receive today, including specific lesson plans that deal with the high cognitive demands and potential classroom management problems of using student-centered methods.

Unfortunately, there is a widespread belief that teachers already know how to do this if only we could unleash them from today's stifling standards and accountability metrics. This notion romanticizes student-centered methods, underestimates the challenge of implementing such methods, and ignores the lack of capacity in the field today.

Instead, staff development planners would do well to engage the best teachers available in an iterative process of planning, execution, feedback, and continued planning. This process, along with additional teacher training, will require significant time. And of course none of this will be successful without broader reforms in how teachers are recruited, selected, and deselected in an effort to address the whole picture of education's human capital challenge.

Better Tests

There is little point in investing heavily in curriculum and human capital without also investing in assessments to evaluate what is or is not being accomplished in the classroom. Fortunately, as Elena Silva (2008) noted in a recent report for Education Sector, the potential exists today to produce assessments that measure thinking skills and are also reliable and comparable between students and schools—elements integral to efforts to ensure accountability and equity. But efforts to assess these skills are still in their infancy; education faces enormous challenges in developing the ability to deliver these assessments at scale.

The first challenge is the cost. Although higher-level skills like critical thinking and analysis can be assessed with well-designed multiple-choice tests, a truly rich assessment system would go beyond multiple-choice testing and include measures that encourage greater creativity, show how students arrived at answers, and even allow for collaboration. Such measures, however, cost more money than policymakers have traditionally been willing to commit to assessment. And, at a time when complaining about testing is a national pastime and cynicism about assessment, albeit often uninformed, is on the rise, getting policymakers to commit substantially more resources to it is a difficult political challenge.

Producing enough high-quality assessments to meet the needs of a system as large and diverse as U.S. public schools would stretch the capacity of the assessment industry and incentives do not exist today for many new entrants to become major players in that field. We would need a coordinated public, private, and philanthropic strategy—including an intensive research and development effort—to foster genuine change.

Substantial delivery challenges also remain. Delivering these assessments in a few settings, as is the case today, is hardly the same as delivering them at scale across a state—especially the larger states. Because most of these assessments will be technology-based, most schools' information technology systems will require a substantial upgrade.

None of these assessment challenges are insurmountable, but addressing them will require deliberate attention from policymakers and 21st century skills proponents, as well as a deviation from the path that policymaking is on today. Such an effort is essential. Why mount a national effort to change education if you have no way of knowing whether the change has been effective?

A Better, But Harder, Way

The point of our argument is not to say that teaching students how to think, work together better, or use new information more rigorously is not a worthy and attainable goal. Rather, we seek to call attention to the magnitude of the challenge and to sound a note of caution amidst the sirens calling our political leaders once again to the rocky shoals of past education reform failures. Without better curriculum, better teaching, and better tests, the emphasis on "21st century skills" will be a superficial one that will sacrifice long-term gains for the appearance of short-term progress.

Curriculum, teacher expertise, and assessment have all been weak links in past education reform efforts—a fact that should sober today's skills proponents as they survey the task of dramatically improving all three. Efforts to create more formalized common standards would help address some of the challenges by focusing efforts in a common direction. But common standards will not, by themselves, be enough.

The past few decades have seen great progress in education reform in the United States—progress that has especially benefited less-advantaged students. Today's reformers can build on that progress only if they pay keen attention to the challenges associated with genuinely improving teaching and learning. If we ignore these challenges, the 21st century skills movement risks becoming another fad that ultimately changes little—or even worse, sets back the cause of creating dramatically more powerful schools for U.S. students, especially those who are underserved today.

References

Goodlad, J. I. (1984). *A place called school.* New York: McGraw-Hill.

Loveless, T. (2002). A tale of two math reforms: The politics of the new math and NCTM standards. In T. Loveless (Ed.), *The great curriculum debate* (pp. 184–209). Washington, DC: Brookings.

National Institute of Child Health and Human Development Early Child Care Research Network. (2005). A day in the third grade: A large-scale study of classroom quality and teacher and student behavior. *Elementary School Journal, 105,* 305–323.

Shapson, S. M., Wright, E. N., Eason, G., & Fitzgerald, J. (1980). An experimental study of the effects of class size. *American Educational Research Journal, 17,* 141–152.

Silva, E. (2008). *Measuring skills for the 21st century.* Washington, DC: Education Sector. Available: www.educationsector.org/usr_doc/MeasuringSkills.pdf

---

ANDREW J. ROTHERHAM is cofounder of Bellwether Education Partners, an organization working to improve outcomes for low-income students. He was also a founder of Education Sector, a reform group, and served in the Clinton White House advising on domestic policy.

DANIEL T. WILLINGHAM is professor of cognitive psychology at the University of Virginia. He is the author of *Why Don't Students Like School?* (2009).

Diana Senechal

The Most Daring Education Reform of All

It is an old story, a worn deck of words: reformers insist that traditional schooling has failed and that only a new approach can save us. John Dewey wrote in 1899 that "it is radical conditions which have changed, and only an equally radical change in education suffices." He characterized the traditional classroom as "rows of ugly desks placed in geometrical order," all made for listening, which meant "the dependency of one mind upon another," or "passivity, absorption." Over the past century, many reformers have disparaged whatever preceded their proposals, be it the public school system as a whole, a literature curriculum, the teacher standing at the front of the room, or the use of the blackboard. The old ways have to go, they say; to keep them is to cling to failure. In demanding an overhaul, these reformers echo an old American theme: a longing for a new country, a new life, a new structure, a new faith, a new solution, a new invention, a new technology, a new self. They partake in an American tradition without heeding history or tradition; they glorify the new because it is new, while disparaging the old because it is old. Often their "new" reform is not new at all, nor are the "old" practices obsolete. Nonetheless, they brandish jargon, break apart schools, toss out curricula, and proclaim the superiority of their plans, chaining education to passing fashions without considering what should endure.

In recent years, some particularly vocal reformers have demanded that we infuse all learning with "21st-century" skills; like their predecessors, they clamor for newness. The 21st-century-skills movement consists of a loose association of educators, policymakers, government leaders, business and technology firms, and others. Citing changes in the global economy and national job market, they call for an emphasis on 21st-century skills in all of education, from elementary school through college. These skills (all of which existed long before the 21st century) include broad concepts such as creativity, innovation, problem solving, communication, collaboration, teamwork, and critical thinking, as well as media and technology literacy, financial literacy, health literacy, and global literacy. Leading the charge has been a coalition called the Partnership for 21st Century Skills (P21), whose membership organizations include Adobe Systems, Apple, Dell, Hewlett-Packard, Microsoft, and Verizon. P21 argues that "every aspect of our education system . . . must be aligned to prepare citizens with the 21st century skills they need to compete." Accordingly, it offers schools, districts, and states "tools and resources to help facilitate and drive change."

Technology figures large in the 21st-century-skills movement, but technology itself is not the problem. It is a reality of life, and in one form or another it has always surrounded us. Having worked as a computer programmer and electronic publisher, having developed an interactive database for my former school, having recorded and mixed songs on my computer, having stayed up many a night to get a program right, I know how intriguing and promising technology can be. But having wasted many hours on the Internet, I also know how it can distract. Technology should be a tool at our disposal; it should serve rather than hinder us. When states and districts heed reformers' calls for technology in all grades and subjects, this leads to situations where teachers must use technology in class, whether or not it serves the lesson well. The problem lies in the reformers' haste and dogmatism.

Far too often, the 21st-century-skills argument carries a tone of urgency, even emergency: We no longer live in a world of books, paper, and pen. Children grow up surrounded by digital media. They can communicate with peers around the world; they can find obscure information in seconds. Yet they are unprepared for the jobs of today. We still treat them as passive recipients of knowledge; we still drill them on facts that they could just as easily Google. If we do not act now, we will lose our global competitiveness—so everyone who cares about our future should jump on board. Employers need people who can create, solve problems, work together, use technology, and think critically. We must make our students critics, innovators, and team players; we should teach them to communicate in the broad sense of the word by infusing their coursework with blogging, recording, filming, texting, collaborating, and tweeting.

Proponents of 21st-century skills often assume that the schools' primary objective is to meet the demands of the day—including the demands of the workplace and transient fashions. Even the movement's most reasonable and thoughtful proponents sometimes share this assumption. In his report *Defining a 21st Century Education*, Craig D. Jerald acknowledges the importance of a traditional core curriculum yet places overwhelming emphasis on employers' demands. In *The Global Achievement Gap,* Tony Wagner seems at times oblivious to the deficiencies of the schools he praises (and their notable similarities at times to the very schools he chides). Yet both authors deserve credit for steering clear of the movement's excesses. Too often, the champions of the movement laud the liberal arts in the abstract, but make practical suggestions that trivialize subject matter. P21 suggests that students engage in projects such as making an audio commercial for a favorite short story, devising a business plan for selling snacks, or creating an online game to expand younger students' global awareness. P21 claims to support "mastery of core academic subjects" but disregards the structured study, discipline, and concentration that such mastery entails.

As Diane Ravitch has shown, there is nothing new about the proposals of the 21st-century-skills movement. They echo progressive ideas of the past 100 years. Since the late 19th century, progressives have demanded that education be more immediate, useful, and relevant, with more attention to hands-on activities and less emphasis on formal academic study and explicit instruction. While some of these ideas, taken in moderation, have the potential to enhance a curriculum, reformers have often carried them to extremes, forsaking intellectual study in the name of "real life." In 1898, Dewey wrote that systematic reading and writing instruction was rendered unnecessary by "the advent of quick and cheap mails, of easy and continuous travel and transportation, of the telegraph and telephone, the establishment of libraries," and other changes. The schools' "fetich" [*sic*] for reading and writing instruction was a hindrance, he said; "the claims of the present should be controlling." The mantra of the "claims of the present" has been repeated so often that we must ask: Is it perhaps in the nature of a good education to be slightly out of step with the present? Could it be that in order to endure, an education must be unfettered by the times? Is it possible that the claims of the present—which we often cannot accurately identify—should *not* be controlling?

Perhaps so. Efforts over the decades to bring schools up-to-date have not worked as intended. They have met with resistance or obstacles; they have caused losses; they have missed the mark. Of course schools should teach critical thinking, problem solving, and other skills; they should help students master new technologies that can further their intellectual development. But they cannot do any of this without a foundation. When hyperbole goes unchecked, the reform loses sight of the complements it needs. Reformers forget, for instance, that knowledge enhances the very learning process in a number of ways, as Daniel T. Willingham and other cognitive scientists have found. They forget that fluency in the fundamentals allows students to engage in inquiry. They forget that content is not simply dry matter; it has shape and meaning; it is the result of centuries of critical thought and the basis for future critical thought. To neglect to teach our intellectual and cultural traditions is

to limit the kind of thinking that students will be able to do throughout their lives.

What would our schools gain by embracing 21st-century skills, and what would they lose? It is the loss that deserves special attention, as the 21st-century reformers, in their euphoria, have seen only gain in their plans. The gain is possible, but only if we put the skills in proper perspective, recognizing their long legacy and their dependence on subject matter knowledge.

The classroom that 21st-century-skills proponents envision—a place where students are collaborating, creating, and critiquing—may not be as promising as it seems. A video by the George Lucas Educational Foundation shows middle school students comparing two magazine photos in light of gender roles; other students filming a poetry project; third-graders watching a nature film and learning how the film was made; fourth-graders making animated short videos; seventh-graders analyzing newspaper photos of the war in Iraq; and other lessons and activities. These examples are supposed to show what students *should* be doing in class: discussing important issues, analyzing the information around them, and creating things. Near the end of the video, the narrator comments: "As courses and projects featuring elements of media literacy find their way into more and more classrooms, writing English might become just one of several forms of expression, along with graphics, cinema, and music, to be taught in a basic course called communication." This is where the losses begin.

First of all, with such a diffuse curriculum, students lose the opportunity to master the fundamentals of any subject. Students are supposed to jump into "big issues" (for which they may have no preparation) and to express themselves through numerous media before they are fluent in any. How can students learn the basics, not to mention the more complex ideas, when they are spread so thin? There have been similar efforts over the past century to generalize and expand subjects beyond their disciplinary base— for instance, by replacing history with social studies—and the drawbacks have been similar: students end up writing about their own communities, reading charts and graphs in a superficial way, learning disconnected tidbits about cultures around the world, and knowing little history. To learn something well, we need focused study and practice. Survey courses are essential, but their topics should not be as broad and vague as "communication." Filming a poetry project and analyzing war photos may be fruitful activities, but a communications course consisting of disjointed projects is unlikely to teach students how to communicate well. Such a course may offer, in the words of Robert Frost, "A little bit of everything, / A great deal of none."

Second, in their efforts to make schools current, reformers neglect to offer the very stability that students need in order to make sense of the choices, clamor, and confusion of the present—that is, to exercise critical thinking. If teachers must ceaselessly change their curriculum to match what is happening in society (or, more narrowly, the workplace), neither they nor their students will have the opportunity to step back and reflect. It is difficult to think about the workings of a roller coaster while on a roller coaster ride; it is difficult to analyze weather patterns while driving through a blizzard. Critical thinking requires perspective and a certain distance from one's personal experiences. Schools need to offer a degree of stability and quiet—precisely so that students may grapple with important questions and teachers may carry out their responsibilities with integrity.

If we always must be up-to-date, then we are continually distracted and diverted. As soon as a school has caught up with the newest pedagogy and the technology that supports it, something newer comes along, making the newly acquired methods and machines seem dated once again. In the scramble to keep up, schools reflect the incoherence of the larger culture. They become susceptible to suggestions that what they are doing is not good enough, not current enough, not cutting-edge enough. Once, at a school where I taught, I heard a visiting administrator speak to science teachers about ways to boost student performance at the science fair. He told them never to have students use PowerPoint for the presentations. "PowerPoint sends up a red flag," he said. "It's telling everyone that your school is still in the '90s." He recommended using Flash instead. He wasn't concerned with the deficiencies (or strengths) of PowerPoint per se, but rather with its appearance and connotations. It would be unthinkable, presumably, for a student to submit a brilliant science report on paper. Substance defers to fashion in such a world view.

If we keep on chasing the newest thing, we will not only distract ourselves but repeat old mistakes. Educator, historian, and philosopher Isaac Leon Kandel criticized this tendency in 1943, noting in *The Cult of Uncertainty* that too many educators and education reformers "seek novelty rather than perfection and call this process 'adapting education to changing needs.'" Reformers often chastise those who resist change, as though change were always correct. Thus reformers have ignored a great resource; the resisters may have something important to say. By no means should we be complacent—we have a lot of work to do—but we should never sacrifice our best judgment. That would be the worst form of complacency and of change. If we jump on the 21st-century-skills bandwagon (or any bandwagon) just because others say we should, we give up critical thought.

The 21st-century-skills movement brings a third loss, greater than all the rest. When schools rush to adopt whatever is supposedly modern, they lose sight of the true purposes of education. According to E. D. Hirsch, Jr., the central purpose used to be to create virtuous citizens with enough shared knowledge for all to participate in the public sphere. A complementary purpose of education is to prepare us for solitude, which is part of every life; if we know how to be alone, then we may be less prone to distraction, escapism, and boredom. Education also exists for its own sake: an endless adventure, a

struggle, a delight. At its fullest and best, education prepares us to be with others and apart, to enjoy the life of the mind, to survive and prosper, to bring up new generations, to act with integrity and conscience, to pursue useful and interesting work, and to participate in civic and cultural action and thought. If schools try to be up to date all the time, then they are reduced to chasing fads and obeying the whims of the market. Part of the schools' work is to help prepare students for their future occupations, but they do not achieve this by scurrying to meet employers' demands.

Employers may know what kinds of skills they need, but they do not necessarily know how this translates into instruction. Their perceptions are bound to the workplace and should not control curricula. The Conference Board, an organization that disseminates business and economics information, prepared a survey in collaboration with three organizations: P21, Corporate Voices for Working Families, and the Society for Human Resource Management. They asked employers to rank various subjects and skills according to their importance. Only a small percentage of employers assigned a high rank to humanities, arts, history, and geography, while the vast majority assigned a high rank to teamwork, collaboration, professionalism, and work ethic. But does this mean that students do not need humanities, arts, history, and geography? Certainly not—it is hard to imagine how one could be a good journalist or global business analyst without a background in history and geography, a good trade publisher or human rights advocate without a background in humanities, or a good architect or graphic designer without a background in arts. As citizens, all employees need a strong foundation in the arts and sciences. Such education contributes to our quality of life in myriad ways—by enhancing our reasoning, vocabulary, and perspective, by creating common understandings, and by allowing for a varied life outside of work. If schools were to take employers' priorities literally, they would emphasize group projects no matter what they contained. This would not be good academic *or* vocational education.

It is time to stop the waste. Instead of rushing to incorporate 21st-century skills in all aspects of school, instead of embracing any change for its own sake, we should pursue perfection in curriculum and pedagogy. Pursuing perfection is not the same as attaining it; it is unlikely that we will ever have anything close to perfect schools or a perfect society. Yet that is the generosity of perfection. It is unattainable, yet to strive for it is within our reach, and it always gives us more to strive for. It is striving that has led to great accomplishments in letters, sciences, arts, athletics, and manual trades; it is striving that has enabled humans to live and treat each other with dignity; it is striving that has sharpened our senses and our wits. It involves soul searching, as we must examine our performance daily, not in relation to test scores alone, but in relation to our ideals. Today the word "idealist" seems to connote fanciful or wishful thinking, but idealism need not be naive or flimsy. Musicians must be able to imagine how a piece should sound, and they must know how to come closer to that imagined version. The discrepancy does not break them, nor does it break a school. Perhaps that is a form of happiness: having something worth laboring for and having an inkling of how to go about it.

To pursue perfection, we must first establish the meaning and purposes of education, then refine the methods for fulfilling those purposes. We should dare to specify what we will teach: the disciplines, works, ideas, and historical periods; the things to be mastered, grasped, and pondered. Once we have established our core—our understanding of education's meaning, purpose, and content—and once we have a curriculum rich in literature, history, science, mathematics, and arts, we can consider how to make necessary changes to our schools without falling prey to fads, without losing our equilibrium, without letting anyone convince us that things of lasting beauty are passé. In an interview with John Merrow of Learning Matters, Diane Ravitch summed up the problem: "American education doesn't need innovation. American education needs purpose; it needs definition; it needs a vision of what good education is; and it needs to focus on what's important, which is good teachers, involved parents, willing students, adequate community resources, community support for education, and a solid, rigorous, coherent curriculum. Lacking all of those things, . . . innovation is just another distraction, and it has been for many years."

In seeking perfection, we must cherish and strengthen what has worked. Forms of instruction deemed "traditional" have much to offer us still. Moreover, most practices require a union of opposing principles. For students to engage in inquiry, they must have a strong foundation of knowledge. To participate well in class or group discussions, students need to learn to listen. Student collaboration is important, but it requires that students also work alone, so that they may bring something to each other. And students become active learners not only by talking and doing, but by sitting still with their thoughts. Conversely, the student who cannot listen to others is trapped in his or her own limited perspective.

Reformers of different stripes often malign the "traditional" style of teaching, claiming that it has failed our children. Perhaps it worked in the past, they say, but it no longer works; perhaps it worked for an elite but not for the poor; perhaps it never worked to begin with. But what is this traditional teaching? Critics often say that in the old days, the teacher stood at the front of the room and lectured, and students took notes silently. Children, they say, were treated as "empty vessels" to be filled, not as thinking human beings. But this description fails to account for the variety in our tradition, which has included discussions, debates, projects, participatory lectures, seminars, laboratories, tutorials, and different ways of handling all of these. Moreover, it is not true that students who listen to the teacher are empty vessels. To the contrary, listening requires the exercise of knowledge and reasoning. William Torrey Harris wrote in 1897 that the recitation was an excellent way for students to learn from each other: "The pupil can, through the properly conducted recitation, seize the subject of his lesson through many minds. He learns to add to his power of insight the various insights of his fellow pupils." Listening is by no means passive: a student who can silently ponder another person's words will be able to enjoy lectures, plays, speeches, readings, and thoughtful conversations.

Those calling for 21st-century skills often point to the need for greater student engagement. But true engagement is not entertainment; it is involvement, which may be invisible at times. The traditional classroom encourages such involvement when the teachers teach subjects they know and love, the school has a true curriculum, and the students live up to the demands of the course. In these cases, the teachers give stimulating and substantial lessons; students absorb the material, think about it on their own, bring their questions and observations to class discussion, and strive for precision and thoughtfulness in their work. In contrast, when teacher preparation programs emphasize process over subject matter, when schools have weak curricula, and when many students fail to do homework, or are distracted and disruptive during class, the best aspects of this kind of classroom fall apart. The teacher's effort goes into maintaining discipline, and students learn little.

Far too many reformers perceive a lack of student "engagement" but misdiagnose it. They assume that if only the students were more visibly active, the learning would flow from there. Everything, then, is directed toward keeping students busy and stimulated: visuals, group work, individualized instruction, use of social networking tools such as Facebook, the building of self-esteem, and so forth. But this emphasis on activity and good feeling comes at a great cost and leads to complications. Students do not develop the ability to listen, to absorb material, or to think on their own. They become accustomed to rapid chatter, constant visual displays, and frequent celebrations of their accomplishments, which may not be substantial. Students reach the point where they cannot tolerate stillness, where they need to be facing their peers, doing something with their hands, and talking. Or they reach a point where they cannot take their peers any more and break into fights. For teachers, the main challenge in these settings is to make everyone "accountable"—that is, responsible for a concrete task that they must do to complete the group activity. Deeper engagement is sacrificed for a more trivial kind, and quiet, independent thought has little place.

At my former school, I led lunchtime literature clubs for fourth- and fifth-graders. The fifth-grade group read *The Adventures of Huckleberry Finn.* One day, close to the end of the school year, we read the passage where Huck decides not to betray Jim. We discussed Huck's confusion, which was still present even as he made the decision he knew was right. The discussion was slow, with pauses. At one point, the room fell into a long silence. One student said, "Ms. Senechal, you're quiet today!" Another student responded, "She's thinking. There's a lot to think about here." I see her comment as a tribute to the book, not to my teaching, but I am proud that the students were able to appreciate the quiet in the room.

Teachers should not have to give up intellectual authority in the classroom; they should bring their knowledge, insight, and expertise to students. Socrates, lauded by 21st-century-skills proponents for teaching through inquiry, led such inquiry every step of the way. Peter W. Cookson, Jr., speculates that were Socrates alive today, he "would embrace the new learning era with all the energy he had"; yet it seems more likely that he would regard it with deep skepticism. In Plato's *Crito*, Socrates asks, "Should a man professionally engaged in physical training pay attention to the praise and blame and opinion of any man, or to those of one man only, namely a doctor or trainer?" To Socrates, not all opinions were equal, and they should not all be equal in the classroom today. The teacher should encourage students to think for themselves but should also prepare them to do so—through instruction, challenge, and correction. Students should have opportunities to discuss and test their ideas, but they should not be called experts before they actually are. They should be regarded as apprentices. One of the benefits of apprenticeship is that it allows for a long period of learning.

As an undergraduate at Yale, I had the good fortune of taking John Hollander's advanced poetry writing seminar. On the first day of the seminar, he established the guidelines for the course: First, this was not a free-for-all workshop where we would be commenting on each other's work. Second, he was not going to tell any of us whether we had the makings of a poet; it was far too soon to know. Third, class would revolve around the discussion of specific problems, dilemmas, or principles in poetry. I remember how happy I was to hear all of this, to know that I was there to learn from him, not to impress. His lectures were great intellectual romps; I wish I could be in that classroom again. When asked to describe a favorite teacher, I often describe Hollander. He had a gift for going on seeming tangents, then bringing them back to his original point by surprise. As a student listening to him lecture, I was anything but passive. I was enthralled, full of thoughts and questions, and I would stay that way for days as I turned his words over in my mind.

Just as we should preserve the best of traditional teaching, we should preserve the best of traditional content. We may argue about what should be included in a curriculum, but we should not avoid curriculum. We should make sure that young people leave school informed of the past so that they do not get swept up in the rages of the present. We should keep our lives and culture resonant by studying excellent literature, philosophy, historical thought, science, mathematics, and art—by reading poetry aloud, singing, and returning to books we read long ago. We should expect students to memorize poems, monologues, and parts of speeches; to read classic novels and essays; to discuss and analyze what they have read; and to write with clarity and verve. Much of this activity is solitary and requires quiet. In mathematics, they should learn to calculate nimbly so that the more advanced topics do not daunt them, and each topic should be taught in as much depth and with as much precision as possible. Students should read primary and secondary texts in history; they should learn enough facts to describe and explain historical events, discuss historical questions, and conduct research fruitfully. And there should be electives, including rigorous vocational training, in addition to the core studies.

But how are we to accomplish this? The first step is to combat the excessive careerism and pragmatism in educational discussion—to remind ourselves and each other that schools are here not only to serve immediate practical purposes, but to teach things that last a lifetime and merit passing on to future generations. The second is to insist on a superb curriculum, with the best of the old and the best of the new, from the earliest grades on up. The curriculum should be the soul of a school; it should abound with works and topics that fill the mind and deepen one's outlook on life. It should be both fixed and changing: stable enough that teachers need not rewrite it from scratch every year, yet flexible enough that they may supplement it daily, revise it over time, and teach it in the way that they judge best. We must also call for greater emphasis on liberal arts in teacher preparation, so that teachers entering the classroom are fully prepared to teach their subject, and so that the field of education may be enriched by intellectual knowledge and traditions. Many questions remain unresolved, and new ones will arise, but this is a strong beginning.

Certainly, schools should use some projects (as most already do) and some technology (as most already do). When they do, it should suit the situation, and teachers should use their discretion. A Shakespeare course, for instance, need not be infused with 21st-century anything whatsoever. Some teachers teach mesmerizing Shakespeare courses with nothing but the book. Others might supplement readings and discussions with pictures and recordings; circumstances permitting, they might take students to see a Shakespeare play or have them act out selected scenes in the classroom. But whatever they decide to add, it must further students' understanding of Shakespeare. Twitter, Facebook, and texting add nothing to Shakespeare; they are only distractions. On the other hand, technology as a subject is not a distraction; some high schools have developed terrific computer programming, robotics, and sound engineering courses and afterschool clubs. In such cases, students learn how to make technology do what they want, and they learn the science and logic behind it. They learn much more about technology this way than they would by blogging and texting—activities they likely pursue on their own.

If teachers can focus on teaching their subjects, then they can go deeper. Creativity, problem solving, communication, and critical thinking make sense only in the context of specific studies.

Creativity and innovation, for example, require much knowledge and practice. When we take them too lightly, we encourage and even celebrate shoddiness. Mediocre creation abounds, as does false innovation, and it is not clear that this helps either the creator or the audience. Once, I attended a professional development session where we were told about the power of the Internet as a motivator for students. The speaker cited the example of a student who, as a result of a blogging project, had become excited about poetry and started posting her own poems on the school blog. I took a look at the poems that evening, Googled a few lines, and saw that all but one were plagiarized—not from first-rate poets, but from websites that featured sentimental and inspirational verse. Why was this not caught earlier? Anyone paying close attention to the poems themselves would likely have suspected that they weren't hers (the language was an adult's, and hackneyed at that). The presenters were genuinely excited that the Internet had motivated a student to write; perhaps they chose not to judge the poems lest they interfere with her creative process. This is the danger: when we value creativity (and technology) above the actual quality of the things created, we lose sight of what we are doing and why.

Proponents of 21st-century skills often treat innovation as though it can be taught on its own—yet our most celebrated innovators did not make discoveries in a void. Benjamin Franklin studied the writing of Joseph Addison in order to arrive at his own style. Albert Einstein read Euclid's *Elements* at age 12 and called it the "holy little geometry book." Aaron Copland praised his composition teacher, Rubin Goldmark, for bringing forth a generation of composers through rigorous traditional instruction. Even our democratic system of government was influenced by ancient democracies and by the British parliamentary system; its founders were well versed in history and philosophy. This is not to say that the study of the past guarantees innovation, only that innovation cannot do without it. To say we should teach innovation is really to say we need a strong liberal arts curriculum, which will supply the foundation for innovation.

Problem solving, when taken out of context, means just as little as creativity or innovation. To solve problems well, students must understand the problem to be solved, have the necessary information for solving it, and know solutions to similar problems. To translate a literary work, one needs not only knowledge of the source and target languages, but a keen sense of the nuances of words, the rhythms of phrases, the author's tone, and much more. In mathematics, one problem leads to the next; someone familiar with the Pythagorean theorem will grasp its corollaries with much more ease than one who has never seen it. Even listening to music is a kind of problem solving; we need musical knowledge in order to find our way through the sounds, to recognize allusions, and to grasp how the composer plays with forms.

Communication is likewise dependent on knowledge and practice. To communicate well, students must have something to say and models for saying it well. We do nothing to elevate the level of communication by having them read and write blogs, watch and make videos, and send text messages and tweets during English and history classes. Students know how to use the equipment, but their writing ability remains deplorably weak, forcing colleges to offer remedial writing courses and to assist students with basic writing throughout their undergraduate years. To write well, students must read excellent writing, and they must study subjects in depth and detail. Students learn much more about communication through the study of logic, philosophy, history, and literature than through immersion in social networks, online chatter, and other media already familiar to them. To learn the basics of argument and fallacy, students might read Corbett and Connors' *Classical Rhetoric for the Modern Student,* Strunk and White's *Elements of Style,* and George Orwell's "Politics and the English Language." As they read Shakespeare, they might consider how words can be twisted by listener and speaker alike—by Macbeth and the witches, by Lear and the Fool. In works with a political allegory, such as Orwell's *Animal Farm* and *1984,* they might look at how language is used to control people and distort the truth. They may also observe the nobler uses of language—for instance, to bring about good, preserve cultural memory, and promote understanding—as well as the playful, fantastical, and musical aspects of language. Any history or literature course should involve close study of the meanings, origins, pitfalls, power, and delight of words.

Through such study, students not only come to a deeper understanding of language, but begin to see their problems and needs in perspective. They learn that humans can communicate not only in "real time" but across cultures and centuries. If they read the *Iliad,* they will see Hector's tenderness toward his wife and son when he explains why he must go to war; they will see Achilles' ambivalence about entering battle, his knowledge of his "two fates"; they will see complex humans in a strange and brutal war. Students learn to appreciate both the familiar and unfamiliar; literature does much more than illuminate their lives, though it does this amply. Students learn that people throughout the ages have experienced joys, losses, jealousies, and triumphs. Young teens flummoxed by fleeting attractions may enjoy the vicissitudes of *A Midsummer Night's Dream* or Gogol's short stories. Those feeling sadness may find company in a Tennyson poem; those experiencing tumult may revel in Baudelaire; those critical of social trends may delight in the essays of Chesterton; those thirsting for justice may be inspired by the writings of Martin Luther King, Jr. But such literature does not stop at meeting our needs; it takes us beyond what we have felt and known. Education philosopher Michael John Demiashkevich wrote, "Now, would it not be good if instead of a whirl to the next town which may leave one as empty if not more so than he was before taking it, people developed liking for recreational excursion into literature which, in the words of Sir Walter Raleigh, 'is the record of man's adventures on the edge of things.'"

Perhaps critical thinking—thinking on the edge of things—is the trickiest of all the 21st-century skills. If we want to encourage and teach critical thinking, we should practice it ourselves. This means that we should beware of comprehensive solutions, sweeping reforms, catch phrases, and fads. Instead, we should closely study curricula and instructional approaches of the past, to find the best in them, learn from them, and build on them where possible. We could look at 19th-century textbooks (such as John S. Hart's grammar books or the McGuffey Readers) to see what insights they hold. We could seek ways to combine disciplined practice with inspiring lessons, projects, and discussions. We could seek out the best textbooks—not necessarily those that dominate the market—and supplement them with an array of primary and secondary sources, especially since so many important primary sources—many dating back centuries—are now online. We could hold professional development sessions on academic topics themselves. We could look at inspiring examples of other teachers and schools; we could take our own education to new levels, whether through formal coursework or independent study. The point is to act with full mind and conscience, to make the learning rich and thorough, and to keep an eye out for substance, beauty, and meaning.

When the frenzy over 21st-century skills passes—and it will—students will see that their opportunities depend largely on their knowledge. Many will graduate with blogging experience, but those who can write a strong essay on a Supreme Court case will be better prepared to enter the fields of history, law, or journalism. Many will have online science portfolios, but those who have studied calculus, have read parts of Newton's *Principia,* and can prove Kepler's second law (for example) will be much better prepared to study physics at an advanced level. Many will have written acrostic poems, but those who have studied sonnets closely will be familiar with a kind of poetic logic that they can carry into their life, work, and writing. Many will have communicated with peers around the world in English, but those who study a modern or ancient language will gain deeper insight into other cultures as well as their own. The ability to make a YouTube video or podcast will mean little in the long run if the other things are absent. Moreover, those technologies may be obsolete in another few years, but literature, science, languages, mathematics, history, music, art, and drama will stay.

Our schools are in need of repair—but we will not improve them by scorning tradition or succumbing to the "claims of the present." We will never reach perfection, but the more we strive for it, learning from history as well as experience, the closer we will come. We must be willing to seek out excellence, nurture it, defend it, and live up to it. We must be willing to lift the levels of the subjects we teach, the books we include, the assignments and corrections we give, and the way we conduct ourselves daily. Lifting the levels does not mean racing to catch up with a movement's demands; it means standing back from the race, focusing on what it means to educate in the full sense, and honoring this understanding in all of our work. To make changes thoughtfully—to keep the layers of past and present in everything we do—may be the most daring education reform of all.

Diana Senechal taught English and theater in the New York City public schools and has worked as an editor and counselor. Her recently released book is *Republic of Noise: The Loss of Solitude in Schools and Culture* (R&L Education, 2011).

EXPLORING THE ISSUE

Is the "21st Century Skills" Movement Viable?

Critical Thinking and Reflection

1. Are 21st Century Skills model actually global in outcomes?
2. What are the risks in moving to a 21st Century Skills model?
3. How would 21st Century Skills impact the Common Core State Standards?
4. Is the main focus in the 21st Century Skills model based on advancing technological expertise?
5. Is the 21st Century Skills movement just a fad?

Is There Common Ground?

The focus of this issue has been on the 21st Century Skills model for school improvement and the concerns about its appropriateness at this time and its potential effect on traditional elements of the curriculum. The larger context is the growing desire in many quarters for a nationwide consensus on what needs to be taught and how it should be taught.

The larger context also has political ramifications. The locus of control has been shifting away from the American tradition of local financing and decision making as both Republican and Democratic administrations have fashioned national policy agendas. This trend is detailed in the Alliance for Excellent Education's 2009 policy brief titled Reinventing the Federal Role in Education: Supporting the Goal of College and Career Readiness for All Students. Some other commentary on the political dimension can be found in "E Pluribus Unum?" *Education Next* (Spring 2009), a forum by Chester E. Finn, Jr. and Deborah Meier; "National Education Standards: To Be or Not To Be?" *Educational Leadership* (April 2010) by Paul E. Barton; "The Race to Centralize Education," *The New American* (October 25, 2010) by William P. Hoar; "Standards, Teaching, and Learning," *Phi Delta Kappan* (December 2009/January 2010) by Mike Rose; "Why Public Schools Need Democratic Governance," *Phi Delta Kappan* (March 2010) by Diane Ravitch; "School Boards in America: Flawed But Still Significant," *Phi Delta Kappan* (March 2010) by Gene I. Maeroff; and "Debunking the Case for National Standards," *Education Week* (January 14, 2010) by Alfie Kohn.

The Winter 2010/2011 issue of *American Educator* features the theme "Common Core Curriculum: An Idea Whose Time Has Come," with provocative articles by Diana Senechal, Linda Darling-Hammond, and E. D. Hirsch, Jr. Of special interest are Diane Ravitch's "In Need of a Renaissance," *American Educator* (Summer 2010) and "In the Future, Diverse Approaches to Schooling," *Phi Delta Kappan* (November 2010) by Paul Hill and Mike Johnston who contend that schooling alternatives are now emerging and that new approaches to government funding and oversight are also likely to emerge.

Create Central

www.mhhe.com/createcentral

Additional Resources

J. Bellanca & R. Brandt, eds., 21st *Century Skills: Rethinking How Students Learn* (2012).

L. Darling-Hammond. & J. Bransford, Eds., *Preparing Teachers for a Changing World: What Teachers Should Learn and Be Able to Do* (2007).

K. Kay and V. Greenhill, *The Leader's Guide to 21st Century Education: 7 Steps for Schools and Districts* (2012).

B. Trilling & C. Faddell, *21st Century Skills: Learning for Life in Our Times* (2012).

T. Wagner, The Global Achievement Gap: Why Even Our Best Schools Don't Teach the New Survival Skills Our Children Need—and What We Can Do About It (2008).

Internet References . . .

Partnership for 21st Century Skills

www.p21.org/

What Are 21st-Century Skills?

http://atc21s.org/index.php/about/what-are-21st-century-skills/

Center for 21st Century Skills

www.skills21.org/

ASCD: 21st Century Skills

www.ascd.org/research-a-topic/21st-century-skills-resources.aspx

Musems, Libraries, & 21st Century Skills

www.imls.gov/about/21st_century_skills_list.aspx

Selected, Edited, and with Issue Framing Material by:
Glenn L. Koonce, *Regent University*

ISSUE

Does the Four-Day School Week Deserve Another Look?

YES: Marissa Skogen, from "Four-Day School Week: A Viable Option for Small Public Schools," University of Great Falls, MT (2012)

NO: Jonathan A. Plucker, Katherine Cierniak, and Molly Chamberline, from "The Four-Day School Week: Nine Years Later," Center for Evaluation and Education Policy (2012)

Learning Outcomes

After reading this issue, you will be able to:

- Evaluate the benefits of implementing a four-day school week along with its disadvantages.
- Analyze the positive aspects of the four-day school week despite some of the inconclusive research available.
- Critique if the four-day school week is educationally sound for all students and for all groups of students, including young children, those with special needs, and at-risk students.
- Appraise instructional time requirements between a four-day and a five-day school week.
- Summarize the argument that the four-day school week saves school districts money in operating costs.

ISSUE SUMMARY

YES: Researcher Marissa Skogen contends that there are not enough overriding negative consequences of the four-day school week to inhibit schools from making the change.

NO: Educators Jonathan A. Plucker, Katherine Cierniak, and Molly Chamberline have some positive comments, but conclude their review of the four-day school week with concerns that include: no conclusive evidence of the impact on student achievement; districts not having experienced originally anticipated savings to the operating budget; potential negative impact for at-risk students; arranging childcare on the fifth day; and lack of peer-reviewed research.

The four-day school week is still present, but many school districts implement it and then sometimes later end it. In some cases a district returns to the five-day school week, while another district implements a four-day week for the first time. In 2013 (Education Northwest), 21 states had districts that operated on a four-day schedule. Others, like Alaska, are considering implementing it. Many of the districts where four-day schedules can be found are smaller and

more rural. For example, four-day schedules currently occur in Idaho, Montana, Oregon, and Wyoming. In Colorado over a third of the school districts are on a four-day schedule. Typically, a four-day schedule means shortening the school week by eliminating Monday or Friday and adding more time to each day. This is accomplished in order to meet state mandated instructional hours that would be found in a traditional five-day week. However, not all is well with a four-day school week, thus the debate. Hewitt and Denny

(2011) report that the four-day school week originated in 1936. For the most part, wide implementation did not occur until the early to mid-1970s when there was a need to conserve energy and reduce operating costs. As recently as May 23, 2014 (Bonham), eight of the eleven school districts in Minnesota currently are on a four-day week but will be switching back to five-day weeks over the next two years. The Minnesota State Department of Education has determined "test scores have not improved enough to continue with the schedule" (p. 1). Test scores were also the focus of a study in 2011 (Hewitt and Denny) who investigated how standardized test scores of schools in Colorado with a four-day school week compared with a traditional five-day school week. Student performance on the Colorado Student Assessment Program in reading, writing, and mathematics for grades 3 through 10 were studied. Results in mean scores in 11 of the 12 test comparisons were slightly higher in five-day a week schools. In one area, higher elementary writing scores, a statistically significant difference was found. The researchers concluded that "it does not appear that concern over student academic performance should be used as a reason not to implement a four-day school week" (p. 2).

An editorial from the *Grand Forks Herald* (2014) stated, "there are benefits beyond the academic and as long as students aren't being hurt academically by a four-day week, state officials should consider that the schedules may be helping in other ways"(p. 2). Other ways include: possible budgetary savings in a number of areas (i.e., parent, student, and teacher support, and various operating costs).

The most positive impact of the four-day school week derives from happier students, parents, and teachers. Although not true from the onset of moving to a four-day school week, having a Friday or Monday with no school normally gains high acceptance and is seen as beneficial. Parents, students, and teachers can make appointments, run errands, spend time together, or allow older students to work on those days.

Shortening the week to four days originally was perceived to impact the reduction of operating costs by one day or 20 percent. This assumption is far from reality even though school districts have reported their savings through the years. As reported by the Education Commission of the States (ECS) (Griffin, 2011), "districts that moved to a four-day week have experienced actual savings of only between 0.4% and 2.5%"(p. 1). ESC also reports that there is literally no savings in teacher salaries and benefits by moving to a four-day week. The largest expense in public education is the cost of personnel (educator pay) and benefits (health care, retirement, vacation pay, etc.). It has not been the case that these costs are reduced even though the school week is reduced 20 percent. The largest savings is produced by reducing operations and maintenance, school administration, student support, transportation, and food service costs. Calculating the 2.5 percent as a savings to the district budget, a small rural district like Bisbee Unified School District in Arizona could save around $154,000 a year and a very large district like Duval County Public Schools in Florida could save $7 million a year (Griffith, 2011). If one subscribes to a savings then it is easy to see why some districts make the move to a four-day school week. It is important to note that school budgets are complex systems affected by many factors.

An additional issue arising from a four-day school week is the actual and perceived negative impact on at-risk students served by the schools. These populations include those students participating in special education, alternative education, professional-technical education and even gifted/talented programs. No matter the issues, both pro and con, nothing of a highly definitive nature, including student achievement or operating costs, makes the decision to move to a four-day school schedule easy. Even pro and con articles are not persuasive, thus much debate exists on the question, "Does the four-day school week deserve another look?" Marissa Skogen's research implies that the four-day school week is very viable for rural communities. Jonathan Plucker, Katherine Cierniak, and Molly Chamberlin conclude in their structured policy brief that there are a few advantages to a four-day school week but note disadvantages such as: the negative impact for at-risk students; decreased wages for non-teaching staff; arrangements for child care on the fifth day; districts not experiencing the savings originally anticipated; inconclusive evidence regarding the impact on student achievement; and the lack of scholarly research regarding the whole topic relying on antidotal resources and recommendations from the districts themselves.

References

1. Bonham, K. (May 23, 2014). "Minnesota education officials roll back 4-day school week." *Grand Forks Herald,* Grand Forks, North Dakota. Retrieved from http://0-eds.a.ebscohost.com.library. regent.edu/eds/detail?vid=10&sid=f440ffac-29d4-40ea-afa0-114542e005b0%40sessionmgr4003&hid=4202&bdata=JnNpdGU9ZWRzLWxpdmU%3d#db=n5h&AN=2W6317451506

2. Education Northwest (May, 2013). "Four-day school week—Evidence blast." Retrieved from

http://educationnorthwest.org/resource/evidence
-blast-four-day-school-week

3. *Grand Forks Herald* (May 2, 2014). "Four-day school week deserves another look." Grand Forks, North Dakota. Retrieved from http://0-eds.a.ebscohost.com .library.regent.edu/eds/detail?sid=140dc8f6-3f26-4c27-b0bdf4942c200b38%40sessionmgr4003&vid=3&hid=4202&bdata=JnNpdGU9ZWRzLWxpdmU%3d#db=n5h&AN=2W61102336506

4. Griffith, M. (May, 2011). "What savings are produced by moving to a four-day school week?" Financed Scheduling / School Calendars, Education Commission of the States. Retrieved from http://www.ecs.org/clearinghouse/93/69/9369.pdf

5. Hewitt, P. & Denny, G. (2011). "The four-day school week: Impact on student academic performance." *Rural Education,* Winter, 2011. Retrieved from http://files.eric.ed.gov/fulltext/EJ987605.pdf

YES ↵

Marissa Skogen

Four-Day School Week: A Viable Option for Small Public Schools

Literature Review

The four-day school week gives faculty and students opportunities to learn in a structured and consistent environment. Research has shown that the four-day school week has demonstrated an improvement in attendance, for both the faculty and the students, increased student academic achievement, and an increase in instructional hours. "A school survey conducted in Custer School District in rural South Dakota which adopted the four-day week in 1995, found that the switch boosted morale, reduced absenteeism, decreased the need for substitute teachers, and led to a boom in participation in extracurricular activities" (Keller and Silvernail, 2009, p. 9). There have been numerous studies done on the four-day school week, but a conclusion has not been agreed on because there are so many factors affecting student success in schools. The issues and concerns of those impacted by the four-day school week are addressed in this review. There are a growing number of schools that are changing to a four-day school week. In Wilmoth's study (as cited in Hewitt and Denny, 2010), 84 school districts are on a four-day week, and all but 13 are recognized as rural (p. 3). Similarly, Chamberlain and Plucker (as cited in Keller and Silvernail, 2009) found "the majority of districts utilizing a four-day week are small and rural and serve on average less than 1,000 students" (p. 2). Initially, many based their decision on financial purposes; however, they are finding increased benefits in other areas as well once they've made the change. The four areas generally looked at when deciding whether to implement the four day week are as follows: financial savings, student achievement, other student and teacher outcomes, and stakeholder satisfaction (Keller and Silvernail, 2009, p. 5). Those who are skeptical of the change are not basing their judgments on solid research, mostly because there isn't a lot available on the four-day school week; nevertheless, positive aspects continue to be cited by those doing research on the four-day school week.

According to Kordosky (2011), "the recent recession of 2008 has accelerated this shift in priorities as public school systems have had to make decisions about what educational priorities for schools should be" (p. 2). This facet demonstrates the initial reason that many schools began looking at the four-day school week, especially the smaller rural schools. Instead of cutting educational programs to save money, school districts are exploring the possibility of a four-day school week and then applying the money they will save to invest into the academic programs. As stated by Goodwin (2012) on *McRel News Room*, "districts can save up to 20% of their transportation, food service, and janitorial costs, as long as they 'severely restrict or eliminate . . . activities . . . not conducted on regular school days" (p. 1). Along those same lines, Johnson (as cited in Hewitt and Denny, 2010) reports "that by switching to a four-day week, schools could save 20% on energy costs from savings in transportation and utilities" (p. 5). "Anticipated savings are typically in transportation, food and food service staff, hourly staff, as well as facilities energy costs and substitute teacher pay" (Keller and Silvernail, 2009, p. 5). More than $200,000 was saved last semester by Peach County, Ga., school officials and is on target to saving 39 teaching positions and $400,000 by the end of the school year (Herring, 2010). Kordosky (2011) cites that "utilities cost savings for electricity, heating oil, propane, water and sewer runs about 12%–14%; overall, you can look to a savings . . . of up to 18% of your annual classified employee costs; if a sub costs you $200 a day a decrease in teacher absences by 15%–25% is a substantial savings; your buses will be driven 20% less, and will have 20% less wear on the tires, brakes, etc." (p. 86–87).

Improved reading and math skills in elementary students were found in Colorado districts that have switched to a four-day school week (Downey, 2012). Mary Beth Walker and D. Mark Anderson co-authored *"Does Shortening the School Week Impact Student Performance? Evidence from the*

Four-Day School Week." In this study, they found that "the four-day school week is associated with an increase of over 7 percentage points in the percentage of students scoring proficient or advanced on math achievement test" (Downey, 2012). Schools in New Mexico on the four-day school week were studied and McCoy (as cited in Keller and Silvernail, 2009) showed that "not only did students' achievement not suffer as a result of the change in calendar, in some districts it actually improved" (p. 8). Some possibilities as to why this could be are student attendance rates have increased, teacher morale has increased—leading to more efficient instruction, or teacher absences have decreased.

A significantly greater amount of research is needed in order to infer the effect that the four-day school week has on students' education. Although studies have been conducted, there is still minimal information about the four-day school week. It's not accurate to make a complete conclusion based on the information out there because it should be applied to each case to see if it would be a positive addition to the school district. Many of the articles accessed stated more personal opinions than research. The following table is one that illustrates the side-by-side comparison of the positive and negative aspects of the four-day school week vs. the five-day school week. [See Table below.]

Hewitt and Denny (2010) report that the four-day school week results in less absences for both the faculty and students because they are able to make business or medical appointments on the extra day, which regularly would've caused them to miss school (p. 7). Blankenship, Koki, Grau and Shaughnessy, Sagness and Salzman (as cited in Keller and Silvernail, 2009) regularly found that the four-day school week increases attendance in teachers and students

(p. 8). "Eliminating Friday from the school week allows extra-curricular activities to take place without students missing school for distant athletic events" (Hewitt and Denny, 2010, p. 9). Along with fewer absences, Chmelynski found (as cited in Hewitt and Denny, 2010) there were less disciplinary actions reported due to the four-day school week (p. 7). Additionally, Koki reported (as cited in Keller and Silvernail, 2009) there is a decline in student disciplinary actions (p. 8). Even once a four-day school week has been decided to be put into play, a common argument is whether the Friday is eliminated or the Monday eliminated. The argument for eliminating Monday is gymnasiums still need to have light and heat to hold athletic events or extra-curricular activities on Friday, whereas on Monday, fewer events take place (Keller and Silvernail, 2009, p. 4).

One of the common viewpoints regarding the four-day school week that make it unpopular is shared among many who oppose it. York, a critic of the four-day school week, states (as cited in Hewitt and Denny, 2010):

> Because a four-day week means that at least one more hour, possibly one and a half, would be added to each of the four days school is in session, it's almost a given that this extra time will be wasted on "brain-dead" students and teachers. That is not an efficient.

Although this is generally a common perspective at the beginning, it is reported that parents and staff come to appreciate the four-day school week (Hewitt and Denny, 2010, p. 8). Hewitt and Denny (2010) share that teachers reported there was a lot of wasted time on the

Negative Aspects	Positive Aspects
• Worries about child care on 5th day	• Student attendance rates increase
• Perception that long days for elementary students will cause fatigue	• Student discipline rates decrease
• Dec. in work hours for some classified staff	• Teacher absence rates decrease (less substitutes in the building)
• Students who are absent a day will miss more instruction	• Half days eliminated: consistency (4 days every week)
• Difficulty in parent/community reaction to plan	• Custodial use of Fridays for tasks typically put off until summer
• Perceived lessening of instructional hours	• Dec. maintenance/transportation costs
• Concerns that "canned" 5 day school week instruction will not fit 4 day	• Employee morale boosted/Turnover decrease
• Concerns that students will not be cared for or fed on days that they aren't in school	• Teachers use class time more effectively
• Bus routes may need adjusting	• Student engagement increase
• Bus driver "recovery time" needs to be addressed	• Student academic achievement improves or remains the same
• Requires many meetings to review & evaluate	• 90% of communities that adopt are very happy & don't return to 5 day
• Requires effort to schedule more contests on non-instructional days	• Increased teacher vitality & vigor due to 3 day weekends
	• Students miss less class time due to athletics
	• Decreased cost of running schools & districts
	• Increased instructional hours
	• Instead of sending students home so teachers can do non-instructional work you bring teachers in on Fridays when students are not in school
	• Eliminate half days

five-day school week and the four-day school week forces a more focused instruction (p. 10). In order to combat the wasted time of the five-day school week, MSAD 3 in Maine enacted the four-day school week to "bring about a shift in teaching practice toward a more individualized learning program in order to increase teachers' effectiveness with students" (Keller and Silvernail, 2009, p. 4). Durr shares (as cited in Keller and Silvernail, 2009) a survey given to teachers in Custer School District in South Dakota which is on the four day week illustrated that teachers felt they covered more academic material during class than they had under the five-day calendar (pp. 9–10).

Despite the common benefits found, researchers have yet to find a strong connection to academic achievement. Hewitt and Denny (2010) explain an example where students were first "taught on a five-day week for the first two years and then switched to a four-day week for the next two years. They found that the switch to the four-day week had no effect on student achievement" (p. 11). Although this was reported, Chmelynski reported (as cited in Hewitt and Denny, 2010) that Merryville High School in Merryville, Louisiana, shared that their "ACT scores rose from an average of 18.7 the four years before implementing the four-day week to an average of 20 since the implementation of the schedule" (p. 12). One school district in South Dakota found changing to a four day boosted morale, reduced absenteeism, decreased the need for substitute teachers, and led to an extreme increase in extracurricular activities (Keller and Silvernail, 2009, p. 9).

In summary, researchers have found both positive and negative aspects of implementing the four-day school week; however, there are not enough overriding negative consequences of the four day week that should inhibit schools from making the change. The review of literature illustrates the positive impact on rural school districts, showing the viability of the implementation of the four-day school week. Many studies reveal that the four day impacts both students and teachers positively resulting in positive school morale. Almost all of the studies are done on small, rural school districts, but no reasoning is given as to why these are the chosen subjects for the studies. The results of the given studies provide overwhelming evidence of the potential of the four-day school week and the positive impact on schools, families, and communities.

Statement of Problem

This is a fairly new concept in Montana; therefore, I only know of one school that has changed to a four-day school week. This one school may not give me enough information to work with from an observation standpoint.

Research Questions

Throughout my research, I was most interested in the opinions of the students and teachers and how they felt about the four-day school week. The following research questions were the focus of my investigation.

1. How has the four-day school week changed the planning from the administration standpoint? Teacher standpoint? Student standpoint?
2. Does each group feel it is a positive change or negative change?
3. Has the change impacted the level of retention of information for students?
4. What do the students do with their extra day?
5. Do the students feel it affects their extracurricular activities that fall on Friday, specifically sports?
6. How does this affect the school system financially?

Methods

The present investigation was a study aimed at determining the impact of the four-day school week at a rural school district. To gain information about the school and subjects' viewpoints, many methods of analysis were used including student and faculty interviews, classroom observations, and field notes. Informed consent was obtained from the superintendent and principal prior to the commencement of the study.

Participants

Research consisted mainly of the perspectives of the high school students and teachers, rather than the financial aspects. Preceding the study, I explained the point of my study to the superintendent and asked him for permission to observe in the classroom and interview staff and students. Upon my request, he sent out an e-mail that informed the faculty of this information.

The participants were one superintendent, one high school principal, one secretary, three high school teachers, one middle school teacher, forty-four high school students, and thirteen middle school students.

Students met four times a week for fifty-nine minutes for each class period. During the fifty-nine minutes, I sat in the classroom and observed students being taught by their teacher and looking at the dynamics of the classroom. For student interviews, I was able to pull them aside during class and gather information. For faculty interviews, I set up an appointment during their prep periods.

Data Sources

Evidence for the four-day school week research came from several sources:

1. *Interviews:* Towards the end of my observations, I met with participants one-on-one for an interview. I explained my purpose in observing and interviewing prior to the start of the interview. Interview responses to the questions were recorded and transcribed at a later date. Interview questions were intended to gain the perspectives of the individuals and their feelings about the four-day school week. The interviews looked at reasons for changing, student perceptions of the effects, teachers' instructional methods, and teacher perspectives. Interviews ranged in length from 3 to 12 minutes.

2. *Observations and Field Notes:* I observed in the classrooms at Centerville Public Schools and main office during my observation period of the study. My field notes logged observations of the way the classroom was set up, the behavior of the participants, and the way the teacher taught his or her lesson. I included questions and concerns in the field notes.

3. *School Records:* The school records I used regarded the attendance levels from last year to this year. Financial records were not available at the time because they won't know how the change affected them until the end of the school year.

Data Analysis

I began the study with investigative questions to help focus my direction of research. As I advanced in the study, my questions were changed to narrow the topic. I typed up my field notes as soon as possible in order to retain accuracy. The interviews were recorded and transcribed at a later date. I first looked through the data looking for any sort of patterns or common topics addressed; therefore, applying open coding. Once I established these categories, I applied axial coding and looked at each category on its own in order to see its relationship to the other categories found. This was continued until I organized all of the information gathered.

Results

The interviews that were conducted with administration, teachers, and students revealed that they felt it was a positive change both personally and academically. For example, Mr. Bell, a high school science teacher at Centerville Public Schools says "number one, it's really nice to have that Friday off, and I say that because I can do 80 to 90% of my medical appointments on Friday and I don't have to prepare for a sub." Senior Derek Pearsall agrees with this viewpoint stating "Especially during basketball, you get the whole day to prepare for your games." Rhonda, a secretary in the office, shares their enthusiasm for the four-day school week explaining "Often we get more work done on Friday in the four hours that we're here, than all week long."

At the time of my study, Centerville Public Schools was waiting until the end of the year to gather financial records so it was too soon to tell if the change has made a difference financially; however, they have looked at attendance records and have noticed a significant decrease in both student and teacher absences. Administration believes the four-day school week is one of the main reasons for increased attendance. The academic disciplinary list, also known as those being ineligible, has also gone down. There were only two on the list first semester, down from the ten last year.

Teachers feel the extended class periods, due to the four-day school week, allow for more teaching to occur during class. Bell reiterates "I can teach one chapter in a continuous flow. I can cover all of the main topics in one day. I can come back on day two and fill in some minor details that help tie the bigger concepts together. On day three and day four, I can kind of work these in together and discuss it or if I have a lab, then I can work that in, too." Supporting Bell's argument, Mike Taylor, a middle school teacher shares the change to the four-day school week brought benefits such as "more time in the classroom, less interruptions. I kind of feel like I get more done. I don't have the worry of 'am I going to have to push it to tomorrow?'"

Implications

The research has shown that the four-day school week is a very viable option for rural communities. This can be contributed to the perception that there is no evidence of a negative effect on academics or schools. In some studies, there were even improvements in student's grades. I believe the other schools in the 8C district should consider changing to a four-day school week in order to align with Centerville Public Schools and receive the benefits that Centerville is. Prior to implementing the four-day school week, schools should do their research and discover how the four-day school week would affect their students' learning. The four-day school week would most likely benefit the smaller or rural school districts versus the larger city schools.

Research proposes that the four-day school week assists teachers in creating a lesson that flows and allows them to teach in a consistent pattern. It also implies that students gain more time in guided instruction. Teacher morale is increased due to the extra day and this often positively affects how the students react to their teachers.

References

Downey, M. (2012, March 1). New study: Four-day school schedule improves math and reading performance. Retrieved from http://blogs.ajc.com/get-schooled-blog/2012/03/01/.

Goodwin, B. (2012). McRel news room: Education hot topics. Retrieved from http://www.mcrel.org/newsroom/hottopicfourdayweek.asp

Herring, C. (2010, Mar. 8). Schools' new math: The four-day week. In *The Wall Street Journal*. Retrieved from http://online.wsj.com

Hewitt, P.M., & Denny, G.S. (2010). The four-day school week: Impact on student academic performance. *NCPEA*, Retrieved from http://edle.uark.edu/Four-Day_School_Week_NCPEA_2010_2ndEd.pdf.

Donis-Keller, C., & Silvernail, D.L. Center for Education Policy, Applied Research and Evaluation, University of Southern Maine (2009). A review of the evidence on the four-day school week.

MARISSA SKOGEN just completed her Master's in Education with endorsements in English and Business Education at the University of Great Falls, MT.

Jonathan A. Plucker, Katherine Cierniak,
and Molly Chamberlin

The Four-Day School Week:
Nine Years Later

Introduction

As school districts face increasing budget cuts, district leaders must make decisions on how to best adjust expenditures to handle decreased funding. Some districts have chosen to move to a four-day school week as a means of balancing their budget by cutting transportation and operation costs. For many districts, the move to a four-day week provided an alternative to more drastic budget-balancing measures such as closing schools or cutting extracurricular programs.

A small number of districts across the country have adopted a modified school week, with approximately 120 districts across 21 states operating on a four-day week (Donnis-Keller & Silvernail, 2009). Over the last 10 years, this number has not changed dramatically, likely due to a balance of new districts adopting a four-day schedule and other districts choosing to return to a five-day school week. To date, this schedule has predominantly been implemented in rural school districts and mostly in Western states such as Colorado, Montana, and Wyoming (Dam, 2006; Donnis-Keller & Silvernail, 2009; Reeves, 1999; Ryan, 2009). Transportation costs tend to be considerably higher in rural districts, as they often serve a student population that is scattered over a large geographic area, with buses traveling long distances in order to transport students to and from school (Griffith, 2011). Though discussions about moving to a four-day week have also begun to occur in urban areas like Milwaukee, no large metropolitan areas have yet adopted the modified school week (Richards, 2011; Turim, 2011).

Existing literature on the topic indicates that there are a number of advantages and disadvantages to the shortened week. For example, while the four-day week allows for an additional free day for students and teachers each week, it means longer days at school, which can be a challenge for some students (Donnis-Keller & Silvernail, 2009; Fager, 1997). Additionally, though districts tend to

experience savings by going to a four-day week, it is often less than originally anticipated (Beesley & Anderson, 2007; Donnis-Keller & Silvernail, 2009; Gaines, 2008; Hewitt & Denny, 2010; Juneau, 2009). Finally, there is no strong evidence that the four-day week has either a positive or negative effect on student achievement. Rather, the majority of evidence suggests that the schedule does not strongly impact student achievement (Beesley & Anderson, 2007; Donnis-Keller & Silvernail, 2009; Hewitt & Denny, 2010; Ryan, 2009).

As Indiana schools continue to face budget cuts and explore ways to reduce expenditures, some may consider the four-day week as an option. In 2003, the Indiana Education Policy Center (now CEEP) released an Education Policy Brief, The Four Day School Week (Chamberlin & Plucker, 2003). In the current brief, the discussion of the four-day week continues, including advantages and disadvantages of the modified schedule, the steps a school might take to make the switch, and recommendations for districts considering the change. Examples of districts that have made the switch are also included. This brief intends to provide information and guidance for school districts and policymakers considering the possibility of a four-day school week.

Logistics

Districts moving to a four-day week must take a number of factors into account, including revised school hours, state requirements for instructional time, teachers' collective bargaining agreements, and schedules and wages for classified and support staff. Many districts also choose to actively seek out input from the community as they consider moving to a four-day week. Given the complexity of such a change, districts often invest months in making the decision to adopt a modified schedule.

Schools adjust the length of each school day most often by adding between 60 to 90 minutes each day, in order to provide the same number of instructional hours as a traditional, five-day schedule (Beesley & Anderson, 2007; Dam, 2006; Reeves, 1999; Ryan, 2009). Some districts make other adaptations as well, such as shortening a long lunch period. At the secondary level, individual class periods are extended during each school day. For elementary students, blocks of instructional time are increased. The adjustment in the school schedule also impacts extracurricular schedules. With the school day ending later, after-school activities also end later in the evenings. For example, in Minnesota's MACCRAY school district, extracurricular activities end at 6:15 PM most nights of the week (Schmidt, 2011).

Districts typically choose Monday or Friday as the day off from school, with school in session for four consecutive days. Each district makes the decision about which day to take off by considering several factors. For example, in Webster County, Kentucky, schools are closed on Mondays, minimizing the need to further adjust the schedule for federal holidays which primarily fall on Mondays (Yarbrough & Gilman, 2006). However, in other districts, students do not attend school on Fridays, in order to more closely align with the school's athletic schedule and extra-curricular calendar (Dam, 2006; Reeves, 1999).

With an additional day off each week, the four-day schedule offers flexibility for professional development and teacher collaboration days. Webster County delegates 12 Mondays each year for mandatory teacher planning days, in addition to the 4 professional development days the district requires. With Mondays off of school, teachers have found that they rarely need to meet after school, and that they can use these days for grade-level meetings, research teams, committees, and group planning (Yarbrough & Gilman, 2006).

In addition to schedule adjustments, considerations for school personnel and support staff must be made. While teachers, principals, and secretaries may work the same or an increased number of hours, support staff may see a decrease in work time with a shortened week. On the modified schedule, bus drivers and lunch room workers lose a number of working hours each week and potentially face a cut in wages (Chmelynski, 2002; Gaines, 2008). Some districts have adopted measures to protect the salaries of these employees. Webster County in Kentucky, for example, increased wages for classified staff to compensate for the loss of salary from shortened work weeks (Weldon, 2008). As a means of keeping up morale, Shelly School District in Idaho chose to keep the salaries of support staff and hourly employees the same after the schedule change, instead of cutting their wages (Beesley & Anderson, 2007; Sagness & Salzman, 1993).

While a large number of districts adopt the four-day week for the entirety of the school year, some choose to implement the modified schedule during parts of the year. In some districts, schools operate on a four-day week only during the winter months, due to higher energy costs in the winter (Donnis-Keller & Silvernail, 2009). In Webster County, Kentucky, schools were in session nine Mondays during the 2008–09 school year, primarily in April and May, to allow students extra time to prepare for standardized achievement tests (Weldon, 2008). Even in districts that follow the four-day week for the entire school year, a fifth day may be added to some weeks to make up for snow days or other school cancellations (Schmidt, 2011).

When making the change to a four-day week, districts must also consider state requirements for instructional time and whether they will need to get permission from their state's department of education to make the change (Beesley & Anderson, 2007; Dam, 2006; Gaines, 2008). Some states allow a degree of flexibility with the school schedule that does not require additional approval. In other states, however, districts must get permission from the department of education. For example, districts in Colorado wanting to hold less than 160 days of school in the school year must get such approval (Dam, 2006). Some states, such as Montana and Idaho, require a minimum number of instructional hours, rather than a required number of instructional days. This gives districts room to adjust their schedules and adopt a four-day week, without needing to seek additional special permission. Other states, like Oklahoma and Kentucky, have provisions for both a minimum of instructional days and hours (Bush, Ryan, & Rose, 2011). In both cases, states often outline minimum instructional hours for different grade levels. For example, in Idaho, grades 1–3 must have a total of 810 hours, grades 4–8 must have 900 instructional hours, and grades 9–12 are required to have a total of 990 instructional hours within a school year. Montana requires students in full-day kindergarten through grade 3 to have a total of 720 instructional hours per year and grades 4–12 to have 1,080 hours total (Bush, Ryan, & Rose, 2011). Because teachers' schedules also change when a four-day week is adopted, districts are often required to work with teachers unions to make appropriate adjustments to collective bargaining agreements (Beesley & Anderson, 2007; Gaines, 2008; Juneau, 2009).

Schools implementing a four-day week utilize the fifth day in a variety of ways (Dam, 2006; Donnis-Keller & Silvernail, 2009; Gaines, 2008; Yarbrough & Gilman, 2006). Given that childcare is one of the most frequently voiced concerns among parents, some schools have chosen to offer programming on the fifth day or to provide childcare training for older students, who are potential babysitters. Beesley and Anderson (2007) recommend districts strive to find ways to implement programs to address the need for childcare. For example, Webster County's Child Care Program provides babysitting and first aid training for secondary students. Other districts offer supplemental academic programming on the fifth day for students. Midland High School in Louisiana, for example, offers three hours of remediation on Fridays for students with failing grades (Chmelynski, 2002). Beauregard Parish in Louisiana offered "Fabulous Fridays," a voluntary program in which students can work with tutors or practice for standardized tests (Johnston, 1997). Some districts have enlisted the help of local community organizations to implement and fund programming on the fifth day, which helps to keep costs down for school districts that may not otherwise be able to afford to provide programming on the fifth day (Donnis-Keller & Silvernail, 2009; Herring, 2010; Yarbrough & Gilman, 2006). While some districts utilize the fifth day for extracurricular activities, others keep buildings open to allow for maintenance or teacher planning (Callahan, 2011; Dam, 2006). Districts must balance the need to provide childcare with the need to cut operating costs.

Advantages and Disadvantages

With a change in the schedule to a four-day week, districts have noted a number of advantages and disadvantages (see Table 1). Having one weekday off of school each week allows more flexibility for teachers and families, as they are able to schedule appointments during the fifth day rather than during the school week. It has been noted that this is especially advantageous in rural areas, where doctors' or dentists' offices may be a considerable distance from the community (Dam, 2006; Reeves, 1999). Many districts have experienced increased student and teacher attendance with this schedule because appointments and other personal matters can be attended to on the fifth day rather than during school hours (Donnis-Keller & Silvernail, 2009; Johnston, 1997; Juneau, 2009, 2011; Sagness & Salzman, 1993; Yarbrough & Gilman, 2006). As a result of increased teacher attendance, school districts have found they are able to save on expenditures for substitute teachers (Beesley & Anderson, 2007; Juneau, 2011; Sagness & Salzman, 1993; Yarbrough & Gilman, 2006). Additionally, a number of districts have reported increased morale among teachers and students as a result of the shortened week (Donnis-Keller & Silvernail, 2009; Juneau, 2011). Perhaps related to this increased morale, a number of districts have also noted fewer behavior problems and experienced a drop in discipline referrals (Beesley & Anderson, 2007; Chamberlin & Plucker, 2003; Chmelynski, 2002; Dam, 2006; Koki, 1992).

Some districts have also noticed positive impacts on instruction and the use of classroom time, as teachers find they must teach material more efficiently with the compressed schedule (Beesley & Anderson, 2007; Donnis-Keller & Silvernail, 2009; Sagness & Salzman, 1993; Yarbrough & Gilman, 2006). In the Custer school district in South Dakota, teachers reported that they felt they were able to provide 20% more instruction on the adjusted schedule,

Table 1

Potential Benefits	Potential Drawbacks	Unknowns
• Increased attendance rates for teachers and students	• Difficulty finding childcare on fifth day	• Impact on student achievement
• Boosts morale among teachers and students	• Actual savings often less than anticipated savings	• Effectiveness and appropriateness in large school districts and urban school districts.
• Additional time available for professional development and teacher planning	• May have negative impact on at-risk students, students with special needs	
• Savings on transportation, heating and cooling costs	• Longer day may be difficult for younger students	
• Decreased need for substitute teachers; savings in substitute teacher wages	• Wages decrease for cafeteria workers, bus drivers, who lose one day of work per week	
• More efficient use of classroom time		
• Fewer discipline problems		

given the longer class times and drop in absences (Kingsbury, 2008). With fewer opportunities for interruptions in addition to extended instructional periods, some teachers and administrators report increased on-task time in classrooms with a four-day schedule. To prepare for the change, some districts have provided professional development and training for teachers, enabling them to adjust instruction to fit the needs of the new schedule (Donnis-Keller & Silvernail, 2009; Juneau, 2009). Although the effect of the four-day schedule on student achievement has not been comprehensively addressed, one preliminary study provides evidence of achievement gains (Anderson & Walker, 2012), which may be partially explained by the factors listed above.

In addition to the benefits of the four-day week, there are also a number of potential drawbacks. One of the main concerns regarding the four-day week is childcare during the fifth day when students are not in school (Dam, 2006; Donnis-Keller & Silvernail, 2009; Yarbrough & Gilman, 2006). Despite this concern, many districts have found that parents are able to arrange childcare for that fifth day, sometimes looking to high school students in the community to provide childcare services. However, childcare may be more of a challenge in urban districts, where more parents are working outside the home. Childcare is also a concern, as some students may be home alone and unsupervised on the fifth day (Chamberlin & Plucker, 2003; Chmelynski, 2002; Post, 2008; Turim, 2011). Additionally, there is some concern that the four-day week is not appropriate for at-risk students and for students with special needs, who may struggle more to retain academic information with one less day of reinforcement in school (Dam, 2006; Fager, 1997; Gaines, 2008; Juneau, 2009; Reeves, 1999).

Despite the overwhelming number of districts that cite budgetary concerns as the primary reason for changing to a four-day week, most districts do not see the savings that they had originally anticipated. The Montana Department of Education noted this point in the 2009 evaluation of their experience with the four-day week. Data from the Education Commission of the States (ECS) also supports this claim. The ECS notes that the maximum potential savings for any district is 5.45%, with most districts experiencing a savings of .4% to 2.5% (Griffith, 2011). Despite this small percentage of savings, ECS notes a number of districts have found it to be significant enough to continue with a modified schedule. For example, Peach County, Georgia reports that they were able to save 39 teaching positions as a result of switching to a four-day week (Dixon, 2011). MACCRAY superintendent Schmidt noted in 2008 that though they were only saving $85,000

in an annual budget of $7 million, it was a significant savings (Post, 2008).

ECS reports that the largest savings can be seen in transportation, operations, and maintenance; student support services, food services; and school administration (Griffith, 2011). Schools that offer programming such as academic or childcare services on the fifth day, consequently, do not experience the same kind of savings as districts that entirely close their schools on the fifth day (Beesley & Anderson, 2007; Dam, 2006; Gaines, 2008; Griffith, 2011).

Examples

Jackson County and Webster County, Kentucky

Between 2003 and 2006, a handful of districts in Kentucky made the move to a four-day school week. Two of these districts included Jackson County and Webster County. Despite the similar characteristics of the two districts— both rural districts with a high percentage of low-income residents—they had very different experiences implementing the four-day week. Both Jackson and Webster Counties adopted the modified schedule after budget shortfalls in their district. Jackson County abandoned the four-day week after roughly three months (Weldon, 2008). Webster County, on the other hand, is in its eighth year of implementation (Dixon, 2011; Yarbrough & Gilman, 2006).

The differences between the experiences of the two districts can be attributed to a few factors. In Jackson County, local media reports from 2005 point to community concerns over the district's move to a four-day week and its communication with parents and community members about the change. According to the media reports, families in Jackson County felt that the district had failed to adequately communicate with them as stakeholders, and residents felt they were not informed of the decision prior to the school board's vote on it. Community members also felt the district had not indicated how the four-day week would work or what it would look like in their district. Many also felt that the district had reached the decision to make the change much too swiftly (Matthews, 2005; Niemi, 2005).

Additionally, the majority of the school's students received free and reduced lunch at the school. Cutting back one day that the students would receive school lunch was a concern for the district (Callahan, 2011; Weldon, 2008). While there is no explicit indication from the district of the specific reasons behind their switch back to a five-day week, it appears that community concerns over the district's communication, the speed of change to a four-day schedule, and providing meals for low-SES students contributed to Jackson County's return to a five-day week (Callahan, 2011; Matthews, 2005; Niemi, 2005; Weldon, 2008).

Webster County began using the four-day school week in 2003. The district spent nearly a year researching the four-day week prior to implementation (Yarbrough & Gilman, 2006). They report that teachers have been satisfied with the change and that teachers feel more focused and able to teach material more efficiently (Yarbrough & Gilman, 2006). To address some of the community concerns over childcare on the fifth week day, the district initiated a program to train high school students in child care. The Child Watch Program provided training in babysitting, CPR, and first aid for high school students, as they were potential babysitters for younger students. In addition to the school district, a community family resource service center, 4-H extension staff, and local community emergency responders contributed to the program (Yarbrough & Gilman, 2006). Webster County continues to follow a four-day schedule.

Saratoga, Arkansas

Of the districts that have adopted the four-day week, some have seen diminishing returns over the course of time. Saratoga School District in Arkansas implemented a four-day week in 1995 and returned to the traditional five-day week in 2002 (Delisio, 2004). Despite reported initial success with the four-day week, they found that the long days took a toll on students, and that they were not as productive in the afternoons (Delisio, 2004; Guigon, 1998). Like many districts, Saratoga pursued the four-day week because of a budget shortfall. After making the switch, they experienced a savings of $30,000 to $40,000 per year in transportation; utility and fuel costs; and substitute teacher fees. Once the district's financial situation improved, they chose to return to a five-day week. Saratoga went to the four-day week under superintendent Lewis Diggs, who strongly supported the implementation of the four-day week in Saratoga, and changed back to the five-day week under superintendent Kenneth Muldrew, who served as superintendent from 1999-2002 (Delisio, 2004).

MACCRAY School District, Minnesota

The MACCRAY school district in Minnesota served as the state's leader in the change to a four-day week. In 2007–08, the district, which covers a total of 320 square miles and includes the communities of Maynard, Clara City, and Raymond, faced yet another round of budget

cuts (Schmidt, 2009). Prior to making the change, district officials explored a number of options for accounting for the shortfall, such as reducing staff, closing an elementary school building, offering early retirement or leave of absence incentives for veteran teachers, and switching to a four-day week. When it came to the four-day week, the team invested nearly two months researching the potential schedule change by speaking with districts implementing the four-day week, visiting schools, and examining the existing literature. As part of the planning process, the school board and administrative team also held meetings in each of the three communities to get feedback from the constituents. After getting feedback from community members and the district's transportation provider, MACCRAY applied to the Minnesota Department of Education to get approval for a "flexible school year," and received approval in July 2008 (Schmidt, 2009).

Upon implementing the change, the district adjusted the schedule of its schools, adding 65 minutes per day to the schedule. They found the change added a total of 17.28 instructional hours per year. To align with the change in the school schedule, the district also adapted its after-school schedule. Extra-curriculars ran until 6:15, except on Wednesdays, which was community night, when they ended at 5:45 (Schmidt, 2011). MACCRAY chose Mondays as the "off day." In 2008–09, they had four five-day weeks and in 2009–10, they had three five-day weeks. While no five-day weeks were scheduled in 2010–11, two were added due to snow days (Schmidt, 2011). The district found that students reported using the Mondays for doing homework, working a part-time job, or completing the district's 20 hours of required service learning. When events were held at the school on Mondays, the thermostats were not turned up (Schmidt, 2011).

MACCRAY found that one of the main concerns, childcare, worked itself out as they made the switch to the four-day week. Families in the MACCRAY communities pitched in to help one another. Local community education organizations as well as the local 4-H partnered together and began to train students as babysitters. The YMCA also offered Fun Day Mondays and a number of community education classes and special events were held on the "off day" (Schmidt, 2011).

The district has found that while the days are longer for students, they return home from school at nearly the same time as their parents Tuesday through Friday. On the other hand, given the distance that buses need to travel to pick up students, some students are picked up as early as 6:44 AM, and some elementary students return home around 5:00 PM. While the schedule means later evenings for students and teachers on school days, the district reports that the overwhelming majority are happy with the change and enjoy having Mondays off. Additionally, both teachers and students at the secondary level indicated that they enjoy having longer class periods. Of the drawbacks of the four-day schedule, elementary students reported there was not enough recess time and that they were hungrier during the day. Parents also noted that the new schedule meant later evenings for students, which made it challenging to complete homework (Schmidt, 2011). MACCRAY continues to follow the four-day schedule and additional districts in Minnesota have explored or implemented this modified schedule.

Conclusions and Recommendations

Though over 100 districts across the country operate on a four-day week, there is a lack of peer-reviewed research on the topic and on the outcomes associated with changing to a four-day school week (Donnis-Keller & Silvernail, 2009; Gaines, 2008). Most of the existing research is anecdotal and has been conducted by districts themselves or by state departments of education. Consequently, recommendations come from districts themselves rather than from scholarly research.

Existing data on the effect of the four-day week on student achievement have been inconclusive. Some districts report student academic gains after moving to a four-day schedule, while others report only slight increases or no change at all. Webster County, Kentucky, experienced a continued improvement in standardized test scores after switching to a four-day week, reflecting the trend they had seen in prior years. Yarbrough and Gilman (2006) state that the trend suggests that the four-day schedule did not have a negative effect on student achievement and that it probably contributed to continued improvement. Slight gains in student achievement have also been noted in Merryville, Louisiana (Chmelynski, 2002). While there has been some evidence of improvement in certain districts; there is stronger evidence that the four-day week simply does not negatively impact student learning (Dam, 2006; Donnis-Keller & Silvernail, 2009; Gaines, 2008; Hewitt & Denny, 2010). A study conducted by the Colorado Department of Education found little difference in student achievement between districts on a four- or five-day school calendar (Lefly & Penn, 2009). The superintendent of Custer School District in South Dakota, which has been operating on the four-day schedule since 1995, also reports that test scores have not changed significantly (Kingsbury, 2008).The majority of studies and literature about the four-day week suggest that there is no direct link between student achievement and the implementation of a four-day calendar. "The broadest

conclusion that may be drawn from the limited research on the impact of the four-day week on student achievement is that it has no negative impact," Donnis-Keller and Silvernail (2009) at the University of Southern Maine report.

For districts considering implementing a four-day week, different studies and reports on the topic offer a number of recommendations. First, communication with stakeholders is consistently recommended for districts considering moving to a four-day schedule (Beesley & Anderson, 2007; Juneau, 2009, 2011; Sagness & Salzman, 1993). "Devise a collaborative plan for gathering teacher, staff, student, parent, and community input. At all costs, avoid the appearance of unilateral decision-making, and leave plenty of time for the entire decision process so that no one feels rushed" (Beesley & Anderson, 2007). Montana recommends holding open-forum meetings with all constituents, and states simply, "communicate, communicate, communicate" (Juneau, 2009, 2011). Montana's Department of Education encourages districts to make the process as transparent as possible.

According to Dr. Michael Kaplan, director of the alternative education unit in the New Mexico Department of Education, the Department of Education recommends that districts spend one year planning the change and discussing it with community members. When a district has 75–80% community support, the Department of Education is in favor of the district making the shift. In other words, the New Mexico Department of Education strongly feels that the move to a four-day week requires the input and support of the community (Delisio, 2004).

Careful decision-making is also recommended for those districts considering the switch to a modified schedule (Beesley & Anderson, 2007; Donnis-Keller & Silvernail, 2009; Sagness & Salzman, 1993). Taking time to research the four-day week and considering ways to tailor it to the district's specific needs appear to be keys to its success (Dam, 2006; Juneau, 2009, 2011; Yarbrough & Gilman, 2006). The majority of Montana's districts invested between one and six months in researching and planning for the change, while others took over six months or even over a year to research and plan (Juneau, 2011). Many Colorado districts visit four-day districts as part of the decision-making process, and the research team in MACCRAY visited schools operating on the four-day week as they considered the change for their district (Dam, 2006; Schmidt, 2010).

Recommendations

- Gather information about the four-day week, including other districts' experiences with the modified schedule; conduct adequate research.

- Communicate with parents, teachers, and community members about the potential change. Gather input and feedback before moving forward.
- Consider district-specific characteristics and needs when deciding on a calendar.
- Carefully consider costs and benefits of offering programming on the fifth day.

Conclusion

Districts adopting a four-day week have noted a number of advantages to the schedule, including increased attendance for both students and teachers, a boost in morale, and more efficient use of instructional and planning time. Concerns related to switching to a four-day schedule include arranging childcare on the fifth day, potential negative impact for at-risk students, and decreased wages for cafeteria workers and bus drivers. Additionally, many districts have not experienced the savings originally anticipated. Rather, districts have saved between .4 to 2.5% of their budget by switching to a four-day week. There is no conclusive evidence regarding the impact of the four-day week on student achievement, other than that it appears to have no detrimental effects (Donnis-Keller & Silvernail, 2009).

Districts considering switching to a four-day week should be sure to gather a great deal of information regarding the potential schedule change and dedicate time to planning the change. Additionally, they should plan for sharing this information with the community and actively seek input. Adequate research and communication with stakeholders is key in making the decision to adopt a modified school week. In preparing for the change, districts should provide professional development for teachers, so that they may incorporate instructional strategies that address the demands of the new schedule. A four-day week may not be appropriate for all school districts, though a number of districts have found it to be a viable option when facing budget cuts.

References

Anderson, D.M., & Walker, M.B. (2012). *Does shortening the school week impact student performance? Evidence from the four-day school week.* Atlanta, GA: Georgia State University, Andrew Young School of Policy Studies.

Beesley, A.D., & Anderson, C. (2007). The four day school week: Information and recommendations. *The Rural Educator, 29*(1), 48-54.

Bush, M., Ryan, M., & Rose, S. (2011). *Number of instructional days/hours in the school year.* Retrieved from http://www.ecs.org/clearinghouse/95/05/9505.pdf

Callahan, J. (2011). *How does the four-day school week work elsewhere?* Ocala.com. Retrieved from http://www.ocala.com/article/20110618/ARTICLES/110619694

Chamberlin, M., & Plucker, J. (2003). *The four-day school week.* Bloomington, IN: Center for Evaluation & Education Policy.

Chmelynski, C. (2002, October 20). *Small schools save money by switching to a four-day week.* Alexandria, VA: National School Boards Association. Retrieved from http://www.nsba.org/site/doc.asp?TRACKID=&VID=2&CID=313&DID=8209

Dam, A. (2006). *The four day school week.* Denver, CO: Colorado State Department of Education.

Delisio, E.R. (2004). Could four-day weeks work for you? *Education World.* Retrieved from http://www.educationworld.com/a_admin/admin/admin279.shtml

Dixon, A. (2011). *Focus on the alternative school calendar: Year-round school programs an update on the four-day school week.* Atlanta, GA: Southern Regional Education Board. (www.sreb.org)

Donnis-Keller, C., & Silvernail, D.L. (2009). *Research brief: A review of the evidence on the four-day school week.* Portland, ME: University of Southern Maine, Center for Education Policy, Applied Research and Evaluation.

Fager, J. (1997). *Scheduling alternatives: Options for student success.* Portland, OR: Northwest Regional Educational Laboratory. Retrieved from www.nwrel.org/request/feb97/article4.html

Gaines, G.F. (2008). *Focus on the school calendar: The four-day school week.* Atlanta, GA: Southern Regional Education Board. Retrieved from http://www.buenabands.org/4-day/articles/gaines-08S06_Focus_sch_calendar.pdf

Griffith, M. (2011). *What savings are produced by moving to a four-day school week?* ECS Finance: Scheduling/School Calendars. Retrieved from http://www.ecs.org/clearinghouse/93/69/9369.pdf

Guigon, A. (1998). Is the four-day school week coming your way? *Education World.* Retrieved from http://www.educationworld.com/a_admin/admin/admin073.shtml

Herring, C. (2010, March). Schools' new math: The four-day week. *Wall Street Journal.* Retrieved from http://online.wsj.com/article/SB20001424052748704869304575104124088312524.html

Hewitt, P., & Denny, G. (2010). *The four-day school week:* Impact on student performance. Paper presented at the National Council of Professors of Educational Administration Annual Summer Conference, Washington, D.C., August 4, 2010. Retrieved from http://edle.uark.edu/Four-Day_School_Week_NCPEA_2010_2ndEd.pdf

Johnston, J.C. (1997). A matter of time: Schools try four-day week. *Education Week.* Published online November 19, 1997.

Juneau, D. (2009). *Four-day school week report in Montana Public Schools: October 2009.* Helena, MT: Montana Office of Public Instruction.

Kingsbury, K. (2008, August). Four-day school weeks. *Time Magazine.* Retrieved from http://www.time.com/time/magazine/article/0,9171,1832864,00.html

Koki, S. (1992). *Modified school schedules: A look at the research and the Pacific.* Honolulu, HI: Pacific Regional Educational Laboratory.

Lefly, D.L., & Penn, J. (2009). *A comparison of Colorado school districts operating on a four-day calendar.* Retrieved from http://www.cde.state.co.us/cdeassess/documents/res_eval/2009_Colorado_districts_4day_school_week.pdf

Matthews, P. (2005, October 20). Jackson's 4-day school week survives challenge. *The Lexington-Herald.* Retrieved from http://www.redorbit.com/news/education/277955/jacksons_4day_school_week_survives_challenge/

Niemi, L. (2005, September 24). Jackson County, KY, school week cut to 4 days. *The Lexington-Herald.* Retrieved from http://www.redorbit.com/news/education/249970/jackson_county_ky_school_week_cut_to_4_days/

Post, T. (2008, May 13). Maccray school district plans for 4-day week to save money. Saint Paul, MN: Minnesota Public Radio. Retrieved from http://minnesota.publicradio.org/display/web/2008/05/13/maccray/

Reeves, K. (1999, March). The 4-day school week: Originally intended for cost savings, the shorter week struggles now to find academic benefits, too. *The School Administrator.* Retrieved from http://www.aasa.org/SchoolAdministratorArticle.aspx?id=14858

Richards, E. (2011, March). MPS considering a 4-day school week? *Journal Sentinel Online.* Milwaukee, WI. Retrieved from http://m.jsonline.com/118101864.htm

Ryan, M. (2009). *Four day school week.* ECS State Notes: Scheduling/School Calendar – Week. Retrieved from www.ecs.com

Sagness, R.L., & Salzman, S.A. (1993, October). *Evaluation of the four-day school week in Idaho suburban schools.* Paper presented at Annual Meeting of the Northern Rocky Mountain Educational Research Association, Jackson, Wyoming.

Schmidt, G. (2009). MSBA 4-day week presentation 2009 [PowerPoint presentation]. Retrieved from MACCRAY School District website: http://www.maccray.k12.mn.us

Schmidt, G. (2010). MSBA 4-day week presentation 2010 [PowerPoint presentation]. Retrieved from MACCRAY School District website: http://www.maccray.k12.mn.us

Schmidt, G. (2011). MSBA 4-day week presentation 2011 [PowerPoint presentation]. Retrieved from MACCRAY School District website: http://www.maccray.k12.mn.us

Turim, A. (2011, April). Year-round vs. 4-day-week schooling. *Journal Sentinel Online.* Milwaukee, WI. Retrieved from http://www.jsonline.com/news/opinion/119285319.html

Weldon, T. (2008). Dark days at school: Some states allow school districts to shorten week to cut costs. *State News, 50*(10), 30–33.

Yarbrough, R., & Gilman, D. (2006). From five days to four. *Educational Leadership, 64*(2), 80–85.

JONATHAN PLUCKER is director of the Center for Evaluation and Education Policy and professor of Educational Policy and Cognitive Science at Indiana University.

KATHERINE CIERNIAK is a Graduate Research Assistant at the Center for Evaluation and Education Policy.

MOLLY CHAMBERLIN is the Associate Commissioner for Information and Research at the Indiana Commission for Higher Education

EXPLORING THE ISSUE

Does the Four-Day School Week Deserve Another Look?

Critical Thinking and Reflection

1. Is there enough research to support urban school districts switching to a four-day school week?
2. What are the advantages and disadvantages when considering issues such as child care or length of school day?
3. Can a four-day school week provide any real cost savings?
4. How does the four-day school week impact student achievement?
5. Is a four-day school week educationally sound for all students and for all groups of students, including young children, those with special needs, and those who are at-risk?

Is There Common Ground?

The literature surrounding the four-day school week is mostly in agreement regarding common ground. Although there are citings where slight increases in student achievement have been noted, overwhelmingly there is no conclusive data that indicates the four-day school week increases student achievement. The good news is that in most cases there is no negative impact either. It would appear that scholars should design studies that produce outcomes that address the student achievement question.

Researchers report that school districts implementing a four-day school week have found savings in operating costs that includes transportation, food services, utilities, and support staff. Although some districts have attained higher financial gains most are around 2.5 percent. Teacher and administrators usually receive the same pay whether it is a four- or five-day week schedule.

A final area for focus on common ground is that in most studies, surveys, and articles regarding the four-day school week parents, students, and teachers support the schedule. There appears to be initial pushback on the change but once implemented, stakeholders are generally satisfied. It does not benefit all school districts. Rural districts adapt much easier than larger districts. Child care for many communities is a concern. Debating the issue will, no doubt, bring more common ground that may likely keep districts and communities from seriously considering a four-day school week.

Create Central

www.mhhe.com/createcentral

Additional Resources

http://www.stormlakepilottribune.com/story/2043431.html

http://crosscut.com/2012/01/12/education/21791/ Parents-bus-drivers-cringe-as-Eatonville-eyes-four/

http://www.idahostatesman.com/2013/09/02/2738621/ schools-test-4-day-weeks.html

http://www.perdaily.com/2010/03/the-four-day-school -week-or-when-thursday-becomes-the-new-friday.html

http://www.idahopress.com/members/cossa-could-move -to-four-day-week/article_fbc8291e-ed30-11e3-82f3 -0019bb2963f4.html

Internet References . . .

Does Shortening the School Week Impact Student Performance? Evidence from the Four-Day School Week

http://papers.ssrn.com/sol3/papers.cfm?abstract_
id=2008999

Shorter School Week Negative in Multiple Ways

http://www.ocala.com/article/20120115/
OPINION/120119784

Most Read of 2013: #9, the Four-Day School Week

http://crosscut.com/2013/12/24/education/118042/9-
most-read-2013-four-day-school-week-why-less-rea/

Could a Four-Day School Week Mean Better Students?

http://news.msn.com/us/could-a-four-day-school-
week-mean-better-students

School Calendar, Four-Day School Week Overview

http://www.ncsl.org/research/education/school-
calendar-four-day-school-week-overview.aspx

Selected, Edited, and with Issue Framing Material by:
Glenn L. Koonce, *Regent University*

ISSUE

Should Educators Be Cautious Regarding Flipped Classrooms?

YES: Allison Mousel and Leah P. McCoy, from "Flipping the High School Mathematics Classroom," *Studies in Teaching 2013 Research Digest*, Wake Forest University (2013)

NO: Amy Roehl, Shweta Linga Reddy, and Gayla Jett Shannon, from "The Flipped Classroom: An Opportunity to Engage Millennial Students Through Active Learning Strategies," *Journal of Family and Consumer Sciences* (2013)

Learning Outcomes
After reading this issue, you will be able to:
• Compare and contrast the pros and cons of a flipped classroom.
• Explore the criticisms and downsides to flipped learning.
• Construct elements of a flipped classroom for a course being taught.
• Analyze how technology has been infused into the classroom.
• Assess if the flipped model of learning has the potential to transform student learning.

ISSUE SUMMARY

YES: Allison Mousel and Leah McCoy are not against flipped learning but caution it cannot conclusively suggest that the flipped instructional method has an effect on students' belief of competency, compared to traditional instruction.

NO: Amy Roehl, Shweta Linga Reddy, and Gayla Jett Shannon affirm the benefits, even transformational effect, of a flipped classroom that includes a current level of urgency for alternative methods of instruction.

Note: The Flipped Learning Network (2014) indicates flipped classroom and flipped learning are not interchangeable because "Flipping a class can, but does not necessarily, lead to flipped learning. To engage in flipped learning, teachers must incorporate four pillars into their practice: (1) Flexible Environment; (2) Learning Culture; (3) Intentional Content; and (4) Professional Education". In this issue, flipped classrooms are considered a major element of flipped learning.

The New York Times (Rosenberg, 2013) uses the phrase "Turning Education Upside Down" (p. 1) as the title for its article that describes the flipped classroom. Reported as being in its early stages and not rigorously studied, the new pedagogical concept has an impressive track record in schools. Most were identified from short anecdotal online blogs and academic-oriented newspaper articles. In addition, there are numerous websites being created that are dedicated to promoting the flipped classroom ideology. The Flipped Learning Network reports that in 2011 there were 2,500 teacher members on its social media site. The number rose to 9,000 teachers in 2012 (Goodwin & Miller, 2013). The popularity and "buzz" surrounding flipped classrooms also includes a number of marketing materials designed to assist teachers who want to implement the flipped model in their classrooms. Bishop and Verleger (2013) state that the main focus of these materials are resources for making "screencasts and Khan Academy-style instructional videos" (p. 3). One company awards a certificate for "certified" flipped classroom instructors (p. 3).

The term "flipped classroom" or "flipped learning" has just recently "popped" up in educational settings across the country. Bermann (2014) indicates that the term(s) are relatively new. Although a vast majority of its growth has occurred over the past few years, flipped classrooms or inverted learning can be found as early as 2000 and is connected with the online learning movement. In addition, technology growth has had a major impact on the opportunity to flip learning. In 2001, Massachusetts Institute of Technology (MIT) announced its OpenCourseWare (OCW) initiative allowing open access to information that had previously only been available to tuition paying MIT students. The trend continued when in 2006, MIT graduate Salman Khan founded the Khan Academy which released over 3,200 videos and 350 practice exercises. Khan's work and others that followed have led to the conclusion that for conveying basic information, video lectures are as effective as in-person lectures. This concept has been key to the thinking behind flipped classrooms: "pre-recorded lectures can be assigned to students as homework, leaving class time open for interactive-activities that cannot be automated or computerized" (Bishop & Verleger, 2013).

Often referred to as the pioneers in flipped learning, two Colorado chemistry teachers, Jonathan Bergman and Aron Sams, were instrumental in the coming of age for flipped classrooms. Being classroom teachers in a very rural area they frequently had students who missed class, end-of-day activities, competitions, games, or other events at their home school or other school sites. Beginning in 2007 they began using live video recordings and Screencasting software, among other technology tools to record lectures and activities for their students. The reported results were very favorable with student interaction rising in classrooms with more flexible time being available for individual attention (Hamdan, McKnight, P., McKnight, K., & Arfstrom, 2013).

The literature does not indicate a consensus definition for flipped (or inverted) classrooms mainly due to the limited amount of scholarly research on its effectiveness (Bishop & Verleger, 2013). Basically, flipped classes work as they sound: "Students work on homework in class and watch their teacher's lectures videotaped and uploaded online-at home" (Hutchins, 2013). Bishop and Verleger state that in the flipped class "events that have traditionally taken place inside the classroom now take place outside the classroom and vice versa". In a white paper written by Hamden, McKnight, McKnight, and Arfstrom (2013) a more elaborate definition for flipped learning was noted:

"In a Flipped Learning setting, teachers make lessons available to students to be accessed whenever and wherever it is convenient for the student, at home, in class, during study hall, on the bus to a game, or even from a hospital bed. Teachers can deliver this instruction by recording and narrating screencasts of work they do on their computers, creating videos of themselves teaching, or curating video lessons from trusted internet sites. Students can watch the videos or screencasts as many times as they need to, enabling them to be more productive learners in the classroom. Since direct instruction is delivered outside the group learning space, teachers can then use in-class items to actively engage students in the learning process and provide them with individualized support" (p. 4).

Two major players in the "Flipped" model are Aaron Sams and Jonathan Bergmann who coauthored "Flip Your Classroom," a how-to-manual for flipped learning. They indicate that students become inquisitive and in charge of their own learning through a "Flipped" model. Sams and Bergman also note that lectures are out of the classroom and more individualized instruction, labs, and/or projects take their place. Terms found in the "Flipped" learning model include active learning, student engagement, hybrid course design, and both individual inquiry teamed with collaborative effort. Sams and Bergmann have new careers based on their success working and consulting in the field in workshops and conferences (Lafee, 2013).

On the other hand, there are skeptics who question whether significant numbers of students possess or have access to the technology in their homes to be active and successful independent learners. In addition, do students possess the necessary motivation, understanding, and training to make it work? The same is true for teachers who would have different preparation and in-class instruction modalities to master in moving to a flipped model. Preliminary research at Harvey Mudd College "suggests that the benefits of flipping a classroom are dubious" (Atteberry, 2013) noting flipped classrooms might not make any difference at all in student learning.

In May 2014, Bormann released his study: "Affordances of Flipped Learning and Its Effects on Student Engagement and Achievement" finding both positive support for flipped learning and areas that still remain unclear thus creating fertile grounds for continuing debate. In the selections that follow, Chris Aviles indicates his major criticisms to implementing the flipped classroom method. Amy Roehl, Shweta Linga Reddy, and Gayla Jett Shannon provide high praise for this blended method of learning.

References

Atteberry, E. (December 5, 2013). "Flipped classrooms" may not have any impact on learning. *USA Today*. Retrieved from http://www.usatoday.com/story/news/nation/2013/10/22/flipped-classrooms-effectiveness/3148447/

Borman, J. (2014). Affordances of flipped learning and its effect on student engagement and achievement (Master's thesis: University of Northern Iowa). Retrieved from http://www.flippedlearning.org/cms/lib07/VA01923112/Centricity/Domain/41/bormann_lit_review.pdf

Bishop, J. & Verleger, M. (June, 2013). The flipped classroom: A survey of the research. Paper presented at the American Society for Engineering Education Annual Conference & Exposition, Atlanta, GA

LaFee, S. (March, 2013). Flipped learning. *School Administrator* (3/70). American Association of School Administrators

Flipped Learning Network (2014). What is flipped learning? Retrieved from http://flippedlearning.org/cms/lib07/VA01923112/Centricity/Domain/46/FLIP_handout_FNL_Web.pdf

Goodman, B. & Miller, K. (2013). Evidence on flipped classrooms is still coming in. *Educational Leadership*, 70/6

Hamden, H., McKnight, P., Mcknight, K., & Arfstrom, K. (2013). A White paper based on the literature review titled: A review of flipped learning flipped learning network. Retrieved from http://www.flippedlearning.org/cms/lib07/VA01923112/Centricity/Domain/41/WhitePaper_FlippedLearning.pdf

Hutchins, S. (November 25, 2013). More teachers switch to flipped classroom techniques. *The Virginian-Pilot*. Retrieved from http://hamptonroads.com/print/698071

Rosenberg, T. (October 9, 2013). Turning education upside down. *The New York Times*. Retrieved from http://opinionator.blogs.nytimes.com/2013/10/09/turning-education-upside-down/?_php=true&_type=blogs&_r=1&

YES ↵

Allison Mousel and Leah P. McCoy

Flipping the High School Mathematics Classroom

Mathematics is often still taught in a historically traditional manner. That is, teachers often require students to read the textbook on their own time and they lecture in class to synthesize and extend that material. According to Deslauriers, Schelew, and Wieman (2011), lecturing remains the prevailing pedagogy for teaching math, even though an increasing number of studies suggest there are alternative methods that are more effective. Many educators are trying to evolve the current system to be more relevant and responsive to the current generation's needs. While some are focusing on technological innovations, others have delved into reformatting instruction to veer away from the teacher-centered atmosphere (Cubukcu, 2008).

Educators refer to one of the emerging formats of instruction as the flipped classroom. In the flipped classroom, the instructor reverses the roles of class work and homework. Lectures, slideshows, and formal instruction occur on the students' own time. Subsequent investigation, problems, and projects occur in the classroom under the teacher's supervision. The flipped methodology encompasses various elements from other forms of instruction. Specifically, online education, student centered education, and hybrid or blended education are three of the foundational pedagogies of the flipped classroom. This study investigated the effects of the flipped classroom model of instruction on student perceptions, attitudes, and beliefs of competency in high school mathematics.

Literature Review

Online Instruction

Through online instruction, an instructor can reach a much wider population. The expansion of technology and related resources has enabled this form of education to grow worldwide. Researchers have found that student attitudes are inconsistent towards online instruction.

George-Palilonis and Filak (2009) found that students often believed video lectures were boring. They also point out that in some cases students have a negative attitude towards this style due to the lack of personal contact. On the contrary, Cubukcu's (2008) findings reveal that university students tend to have positive attitudes and view the Internet and technology in general as helpful educational tools. Online lessons can diminish feelings of embarrassment because students have the ability to review the lecture as needed and need not feel publicly ashamed for their trouble understanding (Flipping the Classroom, 2011).

Generally, researchers agree that online instruction and traditional instruction create similar belief levels. Frederickson et al. (2005) did not find a difference in students' perceptions of competency when taught through online instruction versus traditional instruction. However, researchers did find that online instruction increases student achievement. Students have a greater level of control over the pace of the instruction in web-based learning, leading to this increase in achievement (Frederickson et al., 2005).

Student-Centered Instruction

Minogue (2010) explains student-centered learning as teachers collaborating with students and taking on a supporting role in the learning process. Wang, Myers, and Yanes (2010) believe that the improvements in technology have helped the transition from teacher-centered to student-centered classrooms. Taking a student-centered approach to classroom instruction can result in more positive student attitudes, shown through increased engagement and interest. Depaepe, De Corte, and Verschaffel (2007) stress that this shift in education deemphasizes the teacher and the focus on algorithms and procedures, and instead emphasizes the importance of reasoning, problem solving, and application. Deslauriers, Schelew, and Wieman (2011) found that student engagement nearly doubled with student-centered learning, and attendance increased 20% (Deslauriers et al., 2011).

Researchers hold contrasting opinions on the effect of student-centered instruction on achievement. In one study, Wentland (2004) found that a collaborative instructional approach failed to result in significant achievement gains for the majority of students. Wu and Huang (2007) provide evidence that ultimately student-centered instruction led to no significant increases in student achievement. However, researchers also note some positive aspects of the student-centered approach. For instance, engagement positively correlated with academic achievement on standardized tests (Wu & Huang, 2007). Similarly, Choi and Yang (2010) found that student-centered learners had better long-term retention than those in teacher-centered classes.

According to Wu and Huang (2007), student-centered classes resulted in increased confidence, decreased anxiety, and overall increased positive attitudes towards the material. They further suggest that students may need more support if they are not accustomed to student-centered learning because they may lack confidence in their creative self-efficacy, affecting their discovery and inquiry skills.

Blended Instruction

George-Palilonis and Filak (2009) explain blended, or hybrid, learning as a combination of traditional and digital content delivery. Doerr and English (2003) stated their belief that the textbook limited students and their learning experiences. George-Palilonis and Filak (2009) supported this idea, realizing that traditional models often fall short of addressing all students learning styles. If used properly technology can address this issue in a blended classroom, reaching more students through various methods of instruction.

Researchers have found that blended learning significantly improved student attitudes. Choi and Yang (2010), George-Palilonis and Filak (2009), and Oliver (2008) all found in their respective studies that blended learning instruction reduced students' negative emotions towards the subjects. Another important finding is that blended learning increased students' beliefs of competency in the subject. Cascaval et al. (2008) concluded that the blended classroom structure added significant value to education with notable improvements in perceived performance and overall experience. Likewise, George-Palilonis and Filak (2009) agreed that students felt a greater sense of pride in their own work as a result of blended learning instruction. Students also saw the application of the material more realistically and could then connect with it on a more meaningful level (Choi & Yang, 2010; Doerr, 2003; George-Palilonis & Filak, 2009).

Additionally, researchers agreed that blended learning led to significantly higher achievement. As Wentland (2004) explains, incorporating technology may be the key to increasing achievement in the current generation of students. Cascaval et al. (2008) discovered that archived lectures helped students grasp the challenging concepts taught in this class by giving them the opportunity to rewind and replay lectures (Cascaval et al., 2008). Hwang (2011) found that pre-class reading or videos and electronic discussions had a significantly positive impact on achievement.

Methods

The participants in this study were 22 high school juniors enrolled in an International Baccalaureate Standard Level math class. Students received instruction under the flipped classroom model for lessons in a unit on trigonometry. Table 1 shows a brief description of the lessons. Upon conclusion of the unit, students completed a ten-item survey questionnaire consisting of both Likert-scale and open-ended questions regarding student perceptions, attitudes, and beliefs of competency.

Results

In the first question, participants were asked to weigh each of four aspects of the flipped classroom based on the amount each helped them learn. Results can be found in Figure 1.

Figure 1

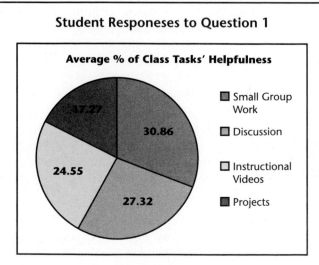

Student Responeses to Question 1

Average % of Class Tasks' Helpfulness

- Small Group Work
- Discussion
- Instructional Videos
- Projects

Table 1

Flipped Classroom Trigonometry Unit Outline

Topic	Essential Question	Homework: Prior to Class	In Class Activities
Unit Circle	How can I use the unit circle to evaluate trigonometric functions?	Two Khan Academy instructional videos online posted to class website	• Hands on creation of individual unit circles through use of special triangles • Exploration activity: How trigonometric functions relate to the unit circle
Trigonometric Graphs	What do the graphs of the trigonometric functions look like?	Two Khan Academy instructional videos online posted to class website	• Discovery activity using spaghetti and the unit circle for students to develop the graphs of trigonometric functions
Trigonometric Graphs – Continued	How do I interpret [changes in] trigonometric functions?	Two Khan Academy instructional videos online posted to class website	• Explore parts of trigonometric graphs and equations. Discover amplitude, period, and shifts and their effects
Applications of Trigonometric Graphs	How do I represent data using trigonometric functions?	Two Khan Academy instructional videos posted to class website	• Use real data to develop equations and interpret equations
Applications	How do I use trigonometry in the real world?	Two Khan Academy instructional videos posted to class website	• Application activities for graphs, data, triangles, etc. • Student development of applications that use trigonometric functions

Questions 2–6 were Likert scale questions addressing student attitudes, perceptions, and beliefs of competency. In summary, a clear majority of students felt more motivated in math due to the flipped classroom and felt as though the flipped style helped them learn math. However, the sample was relatively split on the enjoyment of the videos for homework, the relative learning of material, and confidence going into the test.

The remainder of the questionnaire was open-ended for student feedback. With regards to the most challenging aspects of the flipped classroom, most students did not note any element as being challenging. Some students mentioned difficulties with the hands-on approach due to learning styles, distractions from group work, boring videos, and general difficulty adjusting to a new style of learning. Contrarily, 13 students mentioned group work, hands-on activities, and/or classroom projects as the most enjoyable aspect. Students explained that this time allowed for more freedom, experience, and fun. When asked whether they would prefer to learn in the traditional manner or the flipped style of instruction, 13 students chose the traditional, while seven chose the flipped, and two students had no preference. Of those that would prefer traditional means of instruction, the majority indicated this was their preference because it was what they were accustomed to. Of those that would prefer the flipped style of instruction, the main draw was the exploratory nature and integration of more applications.

Discussion

George-Palilonis and Likak (2009) found that video lectures were often described as boring or too static, which was reflected in the results of this study as well. Many students did not like watching the videos for homework because they found them redundant and difficult to pay attention to. For this study, previously developed instructional videos from outside sources were used, which may have affected the students' opinions of and attention to the videos.

Further, this study found a near even split between students who felt they understood the material better learning in a flipped classroom as opposed to those who did not, as well as a split between students who felt confident going into the test after learning in a flipped classroom and those who did not. Some of this can surely be attributed to the delivery of direct instruction through video lectures and is supported by the answers to the questionnaire, as mentioned.

The findings of this study support Wang et al. (2010) who claimed that the improvements in technology have helped to transition from teacher-centered to student-centered classrooms. This study found that students generally like working in groups and valued this time in class when learning under a flipped style of instruction. Some students mentioned that the increased group work helped improve their motivation, understanding, and interest in the topic. Further, one student mentioned that they liked the class activities because it allowed them access to the teacher when they had questions with applications, a benefit of the flipped style over traditional. Overall, the shift towards a more blended and student-centered classroom environment was found to increase positive student attitudes, which aligns with previous research. However, this study found that students might need more time to adjust to the different style of the flipped classroom.

This study found the flipped classroom model of instruction to have a generally positive effect on student attitudes and perceptions, specifically relating to the classwork aspect aligned with that of student-centered and blended classrooms. However, it cannot conclusively suggest that the flipped instructional method has an effect on students' beliefs of competency, compared to traditional instruction. Further research is needed in the area of the flipped classroom to address these and other educational questions. Other areas that could yield potentially significant insights are how the flipped classroom model affects long term retention of material and the development of higher-order thinking skills.

References

Cascaval, R. C., Fogler, K. A., Abrams, G. D., & Durham, R. L. (2008). Evaluating the benefits of providing archived online lectures to in-class math students. *Journal of Asynchronous Learning Networks, 12*(3–4), 61–70.

Choi, H. J., & Yang, M. (2010). The effect of problem-based video instruction on student satisfaction, empathy, and learning achievement in the Korean teacher education context. *Higher Education, 62*(5), 551–561.

Cubukcu, Z. (2008). Preferences on internet based learning environments in student-centered education. *Turkish Online Journal of Education, 9*(4), 154–174.

Depaepe, F., De Corte, E., & Verschaffel, L. (2007). Unraveling the culture of the mathematics classroom: A video-based study in sixth grade. *International Journal of Educational Research, 46*(5), 266–279.

Deslauriers, L., Schelew, E., & Wieman, C. (2011). Improved learning in a large-enrollment physics class. *Science, 332*, 862–864.

Doerr, H. M., & English, L. D. (2003). A modeling perspective on students' mathematical reasoning about data. *Journal for Research in Mathematics Education, 34*(2), 110–136.

Flipping the classroom. (2011). *The Economist.* Retrieved from http://www.economist.com/node/21529062

Frederickson, N., Reed, P., & Clifford, V. (2005). Evaluating web-supported learning versus lecture-based teaching: Quantitative and qualitative perspectives. *Higher Education, 50*(4), 645–664.

George-Palilonis, J., & Filak, V. (2009). Blended learning in the visual communications classroom: Student reflections on a multimedia course. *Electronic Journal of e-Learning, 7*(3), 247–256.

Hwang, W. (2011). The effects of pre-reading and sharing mechanisms on learning with the use of annotations. *Turkish Online Journal of Educational Technology, 10*(2), 234–249.

Minogue, J. (2010). What is the teacher doing? What are the students doing? An application of the draw-a-science-teacher-test. *Journal of Science Teacher Education, 21*(7), 767–781.

Oliver, R. (2008). Engaging first year students using a web-supported inquiry-based learning setting. *Higher Education, 55*(3), 285–301.

Wang, L., Myers, D. L., & Yanes, M. J. (2010). Creating student-centered learning experience through the assistance of high-end technology in physical education: A case study. *Journal of Instructional Psychology, 37*(4), 352–357.

Wentland, D. (2004). A guide for determining which teaching methodology to utilize in economic education: Trying to improve how economic information is communicated to students. *Education, 124*(4), 640–648.

Wu, H., & Huang, Y.-L. (2007). Ninth-grade student engagement in teacher-centered and technology enhanced learning environments. *Science Education, 91*(5), 727–749.

ALLISON MOUSEL is a mathematics teacher at Millbrook High School, Raleigh, NC.

DR. LEAH MCCOY is a professor in the Department of Education at Wake Forest University, NC.

Amy Roehl, Shweta Linga Reddy, and Gayla Jett Shannon   ➔ **NO**

The Flipped Classroom: An Opportunity to Engage Millennial Students Through Active Learning Strategies

*"**F**lipping" the classroom employs easy-to-use, readily accessible technology in order to free class time from lecture. This allows for an expanded range of learning activities during class time. Using class time for active learning versus lecture provides opportunities for greater teacher-to-student mentoring, peer-to-peer collaboration and cross-disciplinary engagement. This review of literature addresses the challenges of engaging today's students in lecture-based classrooms and presents an argument for application of the "flipped classroom" model by educators in the disciplines of family and consumer sciences.*

A sense of urgency to adapt to Millennial learning preferences is heightened as educators increasingly struggle to capture the attention of today's students. Unlike previous generations, Millennials reared on rapidly evolving technologies demonstrate decreased tolerance for lecture-style dissemination of course information (Prensky, 2001). Incorporation of active learning strategies into the classroom is critical in order to reach Millennial students. This review of the literature investigates the "flipped" or "inverted" classroom model (Bergmann & Sams, 2012; Lage, Platt, & Treglia, 2000) in order to address challenges of student engagement in lecture-based classrooms. The authors present an argument for the possible application of this model by educators in the disciplines of family and consumer sciences.

The Millennial Student

Millennials are individuals born between 1982 and 2002 (Wilson & Gerber, 2008). Millennial students, referred to as "digital natives" (Prensky, 2001), have been exposed to information technology from a very young age. Millennials' access to technology, information, and digital media is greater than that of any prior generation. According to McMahon and Pospisil (2005), characteristics of Millennial students include 24/7 information connectedness, a preference for environments that support multitasking, and gravitation toward group activity and appreciation of the social aspects of learning. This generation is distinguished by their access to technological and collaborative experiences.

Millennial students drive change in learning environments around the world. The technology, with which digital natives matured, has induced today's students to "think and process information fundamentally differently from their predecessors" (Prensky, 2001, p. 1). Although educators bemoan this generations' inability to focus, Millennial expert Marc Prensky (2010) pointed out that "it is not our students' attention capabilities that have changed, but rather their tolerance and needs" (p. 2). This characteristic actually validates the urgency to adopt alternative methods of instruction, and many teachers are incorporating active learning strategies as a better way to engage these students.

Active Learning

For decades, educators and educational researchers have questioned the effectiveness of teaching methods that are entirely lecture-based (Barr & Tagg, 1995). Despite innovations in technology enabling alternative techniques for pedagogy, lecture formats continue to be the primary method for teaching adult learners (Bligh, 2000). Educators and researchers have come to recognize the "complexities of teaching and learning for understanding as opposed to just knowledge retention" (Ritchhart, Church, & Morrison, 2011, p. 7). If the goal of teaching is to engender understanding, educators must move from rote memorization of knowledge and facts, known as "surface learning," toward "deep learning," where understanding is developed through "active and constructive processes" (Ritchhart et al., 2011, p. 7). To achieve this objective, educators must shift from a teaching-centered paradigm toward a learner-centered paradigm.

Chickering and Gamson (1987) suggested seven principles as ideal best practices in active learning. Active learning is an umbrella term for pedagogies focusing on student activity and student engagement in the learning process (Prince, 2004). Teaching methods promoting active learning are those "instructional activities involving students in doing things and thinking about what they are doing" (Bonwell & Eison, 1991, p. 1). Activities should be designed to emphasize important learning outcomes requiring thoughtful participation on the part of the student (Prince, 2004).

Four broad categories of instructional approaches for use in an active learning classroom have been identified: (a) individual activities, (b) paired activities, (c) informal small groups, and (d) cooperative student projects (Zayapragassarazan & Kumar, 2012). These methods encompass many activities such as conceptual mapping, brainstorming, collaborative writing, case-based instruction, cooperative learning, role-playing, simulation, project-based learning, and peer teaching (Zayapragassarazan & Kumar, 2012). Active learning methods require students to utilize higher-order thinking skills such as analysis, synthesis, and evaluation (Bonwell & Eison, 1991). This more holistic approach to instruction engages students with varied learning styles and appeals to the typical Millennial learner who thrives in an environment of variety and change (Prensky, 2010).

The Flipped Classroom

Active learning pedagogies continue to evolve, and new methods of delivering course material are being developed. Assimilating active learning can be as simple as integrating in-class activities alongside traditional lecture. Yet educators in elementary through post-secondary education are finding innovative ways to restructure the classroom (Strayer, 2007) in order to focus attention on the learner (Bergmann & Sams, 2012). Instructors adopting the flipped classroom model assign the class lecture or instructional content as homework. In preparation for class, students are required to view the lecture. According to Tucker (2012), students utilize the time in class to work through problems, advance concepts, and engage in collaborative learning.

Lage et al. (2000) performed a study using the flipped classroom for an economics course. They found easy-to-use, readily accessible technology to develop course materials for the flipped model. These instructors reported

spending about 2 hours per topic to create videotaped lectures and digital slide presentations with voiceovers. Although contact hours remained the same, they found preparation time was significantly reduced after the initial groundwork was completed. They reported that question and answer sessions at the beginning of each class took about 10 minutes of class time followed by students working and learning together on "an economic experiment or lab that corresponded to the topic being covered" (p. 4). As anticipated by Blair (2012), the use of flipped classrooms could result in less effort creating lecture presentations. This increase in available time might be redirected to create in-class activities that deepen concepts and increase student's knowledge retention.

With internet access widely available on most college and university campuses, students may view web-based instruction on their own time, at their own pace. This provides opportunities to utilize the classroom for the application of information addressed in the online lecture. Because students have viewed the lecture prior to class, contact hours can be devoted to problem solving, skill development, and gaining a deeper understanding of the subject matter (Bergmann & Sams, 2012). The teacher is able to provide students with a wide range of learner-centered opportunities in class for greater teacher-to-student mentoring and peer-to-peer collaboration, increasing the possibility to engage Millennial students (Prensky, 2010).

Learning Using Non-Lecture Based Strategies

A flipped, or inverted, classroom model could be adapted easily to multiple disciplines such as textile design, apparel design and construction, interior design, and nutrition. Of particular relevance are courses in which a lecture is primarily based on disseminating information and learning occurs when students apply these instructions to complete a task or an assignment. The flipped classroom model suggests the use of a variety of technologies in preparing and posting lessons for students' access prior to class. The implementation of computer-aided instruction (CAI) can be used to assess the likelihood of success in a flipped classroom within different disciplines.

Slocum and Beard (2005) provided a list of topics for which CAI has been developed. Among the topics are textiles, flat pattern design concepts, concepts in clothing construction, and visualizing three-dimensional designs from two-dimensional patterns. Slocum and Beard (2005) argued that the development of additional CAI modules could allow instructors to use limited class time to guide students through unique learning paths appropriate to individual skill level or project needs. Therefore, we can safely deduce that the flipped classroom could be beneficial for topics where class lecture is predominantly utilized to provide instruction. For example, implementing the flipped classroom in clothing construction would allow students and instructors to focus class time on skill development, problem solving, and active learning of construction concepts while executing assignments.

Similarly, Byrd-Bredbenner and Bauer (1991) conducted an experimental study to compare the effectiveness of the CAI modules with traditional lectures for a college nutrition course. Their findings indicated that students enjoyed using CAI and that nutrition knowledge was improved. The benefit of a mixed method technique (Carew, Chamberlain & Alster, 1997; Zubas, Heiss, & Pedersen, 2006) was evident in studies conducted in the discipline of nutrition; students who accessed lecture material posted online or completed self-paced online tutorials in addition to attending the traditional classroom lecture demonstrated improved test scores in the respective nutrition courses. All of the above findings support Wishart and Bleases' (1999) claim that environments in which technology is used innovatively can lead to both improved learning outcomes and teaching. Technology provides opportunities for teachers to meet the needs of students with various learning styles through the use of multiple media (Bryant & Hunton, 2000).

Benefits of Using a Flipped Classroom Model

Instructors implementing a flipped classroom use various methods for preparing the online content. Strayer (2007) made useful observations and suggestions for instructors who consider using the flipped classroom model. When the focus of the flipped classroom is on giving students the freedom to interact with the content according to their own learning style, the flip seems to be more successful. Due to the structural differences of the flipped classroom model, students become more aware of their own learning process than do students in more traditional settings. Students will therefore need more space to reflect on their learning activities in order to make necessary connections to course content. The teacher must plan for a component in the course structure allowing for reflection to take place. It is important for the teacher to be able to see and comment on specific aspects of student reflection. This feedback cycle will be crucial in assessing student learning.

Flipping the classroom allows for a range of teaching methodologies to be employed such as videotaping the instructor while lecturing, creating videos with voiceover

and screen-capture software, instructions accompanied by visual aids, utilizing videos found online from sources such as YouTube and TeacherTube, and integrating discipline-specific websites of videos available through professional organizations and companies (Roehl, 2013). This allows instructors to improve communication and connection with students possessing a broad range of abilities.

With a traditional lecture format, teachers might not be aware of student progress until after testing (Chickering & Gamson, 1987). A flipped classroom allows teachers greater insight into students' grasp of information and learning as a result of increased student/teacher interaction. The time gained by removing the lecture portion from class allows for more one-on-one personal engagement between the teacher and students. Furthermore, a flipped classroom allows students who may be hesitant to ask questions in the middle of a lecture to seek assistance from the teacher during their individual feedback sessions. Students also have the opportunity to "replay" the lectures several times before formulating their questions.

Additional benefits of the flipped classroom model include the ability for the class to move forward despite both teacher and student absences. Flipped classroom pedagogy has the potential to address situations in which students miss lectures due to illness and for students who are engaged in university-supported activities such as athletics. It allows absent students to stay on track without lengthy interaction with the instructor. Similarly, it is beneficial for teachers as it allows students to move forward with course material even when the teacher is absent. This feature enables the course to proceed as scheduled without unnecessary delays.

Limitations of Using a Flipped Classroom Model

The flipped classroom may not be applicable to all subjects. For instance, Strayer (2007, 2012) performed a comparative study between a flipped classroom and the traditional classroom for an introductory statistics course. The findings of this study demonstrated that students participating in the flipped classroom were less satisfied with the teaching format than students in the traditional classroom were. Students participating in the flipped classroom did not adjust swiftly to their new learning environment. Some students were uncomfortable participating in group learning activities because they preferred working alone. Others were accustomed to the old method of doing assignments on their own, in the setting of their choice. The radical change was not well received. However, students in the flipped model experienced more innovation and cooperation in their learning when compared to the traditional classroom students.

Challenges with the flipped classroom model include adapting traditional lectures to alternative media in order to post content online. Other challenges teachers face include making changes to the online lectures. The flexibility required to make adjustments to course content may be dependent on the technology originally used to create the lecture. Complexity of making changes could vary between re-recording an entire video lecture or could be as simple as adding an additional slide to a PowerPoint presentation. As technology used for presenting information gets smarter, faster, better, and cheaper, educators will be forced to learn and access more of these tools (Prensky, 2010).

The flipped classrooms, as well as active learning, require students to assume more responsibility for their individual learning experience. Teachers must include clear expectations of self-direction and motivation within their syllabus or framework of the course. For this reason, verification, through application of information in a project-based scenario, may be one indication that students have performed the task of viewing the lecture prior to entering the classroom. For example, Woodland Park High School chemistry teachers Jonathan Bergmann and Aaron Sams used the flipped classroom model whereby they posted their lectures online. Bergmann said he checks students' notes during class. He requires each student to come to class with a question as verification of watching the lecture. However, as Bergmann pointed out, it takes a while for students to get accustomed to a new system of learning. He observed the benefits of the new system when students were asking better questions and thinking more deeply about the content as the year progressed (Tucker, 2012).

When discussing the use of the flipped classroom model, it is important to recognize the financial limitations of public schools, teachers, and students who may have limited financial resources. The success of this model relies on the availability of computers and access to the internet outside of the classroom. Therefore, educators must be cautious in implementing this system if they are unclear as to whether all learners will be able to easily and consistently access the online content.

Conclusion

The introduction of any new strategy requires a shift in the minds of both educators and students. Teachers must be willing to experiment with alternative strategies in the classroom. For those instructors who are willing to apply these new methods, it is important that they periodically reflect on their teaching effectiveness. At the same time, students may require more than a semester to adapt to the new method of instruction and to recognize its value. Through active learning and technology-enabled flipped classroom strategies, students may develop higher order thinking skills and creativity.

The effective application of vital competencies such as critical thinking, creativity, communication, and collaboration (Blair, 2012) at one's workplace is more likely if these skills are acquired in college. In addition, one's adaptability to new technologies is crucial for graduating students to succeed in the workplace. This underlines the need for the provision of technology-infused learning environments at educational institutions. Training must be provided for educators in the application of existing and emerging technologies.

At a time when educational institutions face increasing demands to improve learning experiences and capture the attention of Millennial students, the flipped classroom strategy provides an opportunity to address both these concerns. These pathways toward more powerful learning outcomes, retention of knowledge, and increased depth of knowledge suggest an optimistic future for education.

References

Barr, R. B., & Tagg, J. (1995). From teaching to learning: A new paradigm for undergraduate education. *Change, 27*(6), 12–25.

Bergmann, J., & Sams, A. (2012). *Flip your classroom: Reach every student in every class every day.* Eugene, OR: International Society for Technology in Education.

Blair, N. (2012). Technology integration for the new 21st century learner. *Principal, (January/February)* 8–13.

Bligh, D. A. (2000). *What's the use of lectures?* San Francisco, CA: Jossey-Bass.

Bon well, C. C., & Eison, J. A. (1991). *Active learning: Creating excitement in the classroom.* Washington, DC: School of Education and Human Development, George Washington University.

Bryant, S. M., & Hunton, J. E. (2000). The use of technology in the delivery of instruction: Implications for accounting educators and education researchers. *Issues in Accounting Education, 15*(1), 129–163.

Byrd-Bredbenner, C., & Bauer, K. (1991). The development and evaluation of computer assisted instruction modules for an introductory, college-level nutrition course. *Journal of Nutrition Education, 23*(6), 275–283.

Carew, L. B., Chamberlain, V. M., & Alster, F. A. (1997). The evaluation of a computer-assisted instructional component in a college-level nutrition course, *Journal of Nutrition Education, 29*(6), 327–334.

Chickering, A. W., & Gamson, Z. F. (1987). Seven principles for good practice in undergraduate education. *American Association for Higher Education Bulletin.* Retrieved from http://www.eric.ed.gov/ERICWebPortal/detail?accno = ED282491

Lage, M. J., Platt, G. J., & Treglia, M. (2000). Inverting the classroom: A gateway to creating an inclusive learning environment. *The Journal of Economic Education, 31*(1), 30–43.

McMahon, M., & Pospisil, R. (2005). Laptops for a digital lifestyle: Millennial students and wireless mobile technologies. *Proceedings of the Australasian Society for Computers in Learning in Tertiary Education,* 421–431.

Prensky, M. (2001). Digital natives, digital immigrants. *On the Horizon, 9*(5), 1–6.

Prensky, M. R. (2010). *Teaching digital natives: Partnering for real learning.* Newbury Park, CA: Corwin.

Prince, M. (2004). Does active learning work? A review of the research. *Journal of Engineering Education, 93*(3), 223–231.

Ritchhart, R., Church, M., & Morrison, K. (2011). *Making thinking visible: How to promote engagement, understanding, and independence for all learners.* San Francisco, CA: Jossey-Bass.

Roehl, A. (2013). Bridging the field trip gap: Integrating web-based video as teaching and learning partner in interior design education. *Journal of Family & Consumer Sciences, 105*(1), 42–46.

Slocum, A., & Beard, C. (2005). Development of a CAI module and comparison of its effectiveness with traditional classroom instruction. *Clothing & Textiles Research Journal, 23*(4), 298–306.

Strayer, J. F. (2007). *The effects of the classroom flip on the learning environment: A comparison of learning activity in a traditional classroom and a flip classroom that used an intelligent tutoring system.* Doctoral dissertation, The Ohio State University. Retrieved from http://search.pro quest. com/do cview/3 0483 4174

Strayer, J. F. (2012). How learning in an inverted classroom influences cooperation, innovation and task orientation. *Learning Environments Research, 15,* 171–193.

Tucker, B. (2012). The flipped classroom. *Education Next, 12*(1), 82–83.

Wilson, M., & Gerber, L. E. (2008). How generational theory can improve teaching: Strategies for working with the "millennials." *Currents in Teaching and Learning, 1*(1), 29–44.

Wishart, J., & Blease, D. (1999). Theories underlying perceived changes in teaching and learning after installing a computer network in a secondary school. *British Journal of Educational Technology, 30*(1), 25–42.

Zayapragassarazan, Z., & Kumar, S. (2012). Active learning methods. *NTTC Bulletin, 19*(1), 3–5.

Zubas, P., Heiss, C., & Pedersen, M. (2006). Comparing the effectiveness of a supplemental online tutorial to traditional instruction with nutritional science students. *Journal of Interactive Online Learning, 5*(1), 75–81.

AMY ROEHL is assistant professor of Interior Design, Ahewta Linga Reddy is assistant professor of Fashion Merchandising, and Gayla Jett Shannon is assistant professor of Professional Practice in Interior Design, all from the Department of Interior Design & Merchandising at Texas Christian University, Fort Worth, TX.

EXPLORING THE ISSUE

Should Educators Be Cautious Regarding Flipped Classrooms?

Critical Thinking and Reflection

1. Is the flipped classroom a fad that may soon go away or is it a transformational teaching method that is here to stay?
2. Is it crucial to establish a teaching model that is grounded in technology?
3. Is there enough quantitative and qualitative research to support the flipped classroom model?
4. Who will ultimately decide if flipped classroom are used in the nation's public schools?
5. Does "flipping" a classroom actually free class time for learning?

Is There Common Ground?

Focusing more of the responsibility for learning and achievement onto the student certainly is a worthy goal and outcome for education. Much can be said for the state of current technology that supports a flipped pedagogical approach to teaching and learning. Research during the past decade consistently shows teaching as the first and most important among school-related influences on learning. Does the flipped learning and/or flipped classrooms models change this fact? Whether or not a change is made in pedagogy it appears that traditional classrooms and flipped classrooms point to the teacher for successful student outcomes.

Student responsibility for learning, instructional use of technology, and teacher pedagogy are areas educators can gravitate to, but student achievement is the accountability measure to which all teachers are held. The question for consideration is "are flipped methods effective?" The common ground for responding to this question is further study. Controlled studies should be employed comparing traditional pedagogy versus flipped pedagogy. Quantitative, qualitative, and mixed methods should be designed and both theory and practice be examined. From this, best practices will emerge revealing any common ground for the issue question.

Comparing the love affair growing in the use of flipped learning to the cries announcing "Don't flip," there is little data affirming one or the other is the only way to go in schools across the nation. Even so, flipping is rapidly moving into the mainstream, at the same time it is being viewed as a fad.

Create Central

www.mhhe.com/createcentral

Additional Resources

Bergmann, J. (2012). "Flip your classroom: Reach every student in every class, every day." International Society for Technology in Education. ISBN-10: 1564843157

Gerstein, J. (2012). *The flipped classroom: The full picture* [Kindle Edition]

Honeycutt, B. (2014). *101 ways to FLIP* [Kindle Edition]

Bergmann, J. (2014). *Flipped learning; Gateway to student engagement.* ISBN-10: 1564843440

Walsh, K. (2014). *Flipped classroom workshop in a book (Learn how to implement flipped instruction in your classroom)* [Kindle Edition]

Bretzmann, J. (2013). "Flipping 2.0: Practical Strategies for Flipping Your Class." The Bretzmann Group. ISBN: 0615824072

Internet References . . .

The Flipped Classroom, Putting Learning Back into the Hands of Students

http://search.proquest.com/docview/1439941102

Flipped Classrooms Turn Everything Around

http://www.sophia.org/flipped-classroom

Flipped Learning Model Dramatically Improves Course Pass Rate for At-Risk Students

http://assets.pearsonschool.com/asset_mgr
/current/201317/Clintondale_casestudy.pdf

Flipped Classroom: A New Method of Teaching Is Turning the Traditional Classroom on Its Head

http://www.knewton.com/flipped-classroom/

How "Flipping" the Classroom Can Improve the Traditional Lecture

http://chronicle.com/article/How-Flipping-the-Classroom/130857/